Worldwide
Laws of Life

❖

Worldwide Laws of Life

John Marks Templeton

TEMPLETON FOUNDATION PRESS

Philadelphia & London

The following publishers have generously given permission for the use of quotations from copyrighted works: From *You'll Believe It When You See It,* by Dr. Wayne Dyer. Copyright 1989 by Wayne Dyer. Reprinted by permission of William Morrow and Company, Inc. From *Religion Guided My Career,* by Cecil de Mille. Copyright 1946 by Guideposts, Carmel, NY 10512. Reprinted by permission of *Guideposts Magazine.* From *Tough Times Never Last But Tough People Do,* by Dr. Robert Schuller. Reprinted by permission of Crystal Cathedral Ministries, all rights reserved. From the Unity Booklet, *Triumphant Living.* Reprinted by permission of Dr. Donald Curtis. From the Unity Booklet, *Take the Wings of the Morning.* From *Dear Abby* column, reprinted by permission of Universal Press Syndicate.

TEMPLETON FOUNDATION PRESS
Two Radnor Corporate Center, Suite 320
100 Matsonford Road
Radnor, Pennsylvania 19087

Printed in the United States of America

Library of Congress Cataloging-in-Publication Data

Templeton, John, 1912–
    Worldwide laws of life : two hundred eternal spiritual principles
/ John Marks Templeton.
      p.   cm.
    Includes index.
    ISBN 0-8264-1018-9
    1. Spiritual life.   I. Title.
BL624.T44   1997
248.4–dc21   96-51495
                                     CIP

Contents

CONTENTS

CONTENTS

viii

CONTENTS

x

WEEK THIRTY-NINE

WEEK FORTY

Introduction

What is to become of me? What does the future hold? How can I set out on my own into a world that seems filled with conflict and strife? How do I cope with day-to-day pressures? How do I find peace in the midst of turmoil? What will allow me to be in *the world, but not* of *the world? How can my life be useful and happy?*

These are questions asked by many people today. Fortunately, there are positive responses and definite guidance that can enrich the life of every individual who sincerely seeks to learn. To be a happy and useful person, it is important to understand and practice the *Laws of Life*. These laws are simply the "set of rules" by which we should live. They come from a vast array of sources—the major sacred Scriptures of the world; various schools of philosophical thought, both ancient and modern; storytellers, such as Aesop; scientists, such as Isaac Newton; and from various artists and historians—to name a few. There seem to be literally hundreds of such laws, and most families and religions seek to teach the laws they were taught. Some laws are so clear that most people can agree they are true. For example, honesty and truthfulness rank high as values in cultures and societies around the world.

Our stay on this small planet called Earth is a brief one, and we have an excellent opportunity to leave the world a better place than we found it through our choice of how we live our lives. One way to accomplish lasting improvement is to master the *Laws of Life*. The poet Henry Wadsworth Longfellow wrote, *"Lives of great men oft remind us that we can make our lives sublime and departing leave behind us footprints in the sands of time."* The truth of this statement can be demonstrated if we look to the lives of the famous as well as those of the unsung heroes of the past and present. Here we find many models for useful, happy living. And, when we examine their words and deeds, we often discover the principles that inspired and sustained their benefits to present and future generations.

The world operates on spiritual principles just as it operates on the laws of physics and gravity. It is up to us to learn what these principles are and then choose to live by them. Let's look at this idea. You might ask, "What is spiritual law?" We may answer that it is an invisible law and, being of spirit, is not dictated by the laws of our physical world. Spiritual law isn't shaped by current opinion or whim. It is not determined by people. Spiritual laws are impartial because they apply equally to everyone throughout our world. They work without prejudice or bias at all times and in all places. These laws are self-enforcing and are not dependent on human authority or commandments.

Followers of the ancient Chinese sage Lao Tzu understood spiritual law as the *Tao*. The simplest interpretation of *Tao*, or spiritual law, is *"This is how things work."* One way to comprehend this law is to realize the relationship between the mind and its thoughts, feelings, and ideas and the physical activities that give those thoughts, feelings, and ideas expression. There is a relationship between the invisible thoughts and feelings of our minds and the visible actions we take as a result of them.

Worldwide Laws of Life is aimed at assisting people of all ages to learn more about the universal truths of life that transcend modern times or particular cultures in the hope that it may help people in all parts of the world to make their lives not only happier but more useful. The two hundred laws of life that were chosen for this book are important and possible to apply in one's life. Each law is presented in an essay format, with applications, opinions, stories, examples, and quotations offered to emphasize the validity of the law. Each quotation that serves as the title of an essay points to a particular law that holds true for most people under most circumstances. The material is designed to inspire as well as encourage you; to help you consider more deeply the laws you personally live by; and to reap the rewards of their practical application.

Although *Worldwide Laws of Life* may be read like any other inspirational book, its organization follows that of an academic study program. The laws are arranged into the forty weeks of a typical school year. Alongside each essay, you will find wisdom quotes pertaining to the topic; and at the end of each week, you will find highlights from the material presented and guideline exercises for "living the laws." At the conclusion of the recommended study process, you will have read and become familiar with the meanings of the two hundred laws of life contained in this book. The book's format can provide useful guidance and a meaningful study program for individuals, families, study groups, organizations, colleges, and schools.

The laws described herein may be used as *effective, practical,* and *workable* tools. When you apply them consistently, you can draw forth the power to transform your life into a more deeply useful and joyful experience. Even if your life is already working well, it's possible that it can work even better as you incorporate more of the wisdom contained in these pages. If I had found a book of two hundred basic laws of life during my college years, I could have been far more productive then and in the years that have followed. Possibly one of the laws in this book may encourage you to try something that, until now, you may have only dreamed of attempting!

Let's look for a moment at some possible ways you may benefit from the laws by applying them to various activities in your life:

* An informal discussion group could be formed with your friends, or with a school, church, or social group. People often benefit by coming together with others to study topics of mutual interest. In addition to exploring a variety of points of view on the importance and meaning of the laws of life, support and encouragement for individual members of the group may be provided as they begin to make changes in their lives. If you choose this approach, you might select a single essay; read it aloud as a group; then spend an hour or so discussing the key ideas. This kind of sharing often develops trust and allows the group members to deepen their relationship to the concepts and to each other by sharing personal experiences as you apply the laws to your life.

* Another approach is to work with this material privately. Set aside a block of time when you are unlikely to be disturbed. As you relax and allow your thoughts and feelings to become peaceful and settled, think about something that may be paramount at the present moment in your life. This could be a

decision of some kind that you may be making, a situation or circumstance that could be troubling you, or you may simply be open and receptive for guidance. Choose your focus and formulate a relative question. Open *Worldwide Laws of Life* to the table of contents. Allow your eyes to scan the listing of essays until a particular one catches your attention. Then, open the book to that particular essay, and listen with inner perception to the message that may help to bring insight into your life.

* Individually, or in the group context, you might select all of the essays relative to a particular law. For example, you may choose "Giving" and then concentrate intensively on that particular subject. Brainstorm possibilities of ways of demonstrating this law. One idea could be to create a "circulation day" in your hometown. Those of you with things to give away could take these items to a central location where homeless people and others are invited to take what they need. Great satisfaction might be experienced in seeing unwanted things put to good use by those who need them. Of course, an activity of this kind creates a vacuum in the lives of the givers into which more good can flow! From this direct experience in working with a spiritual law, those involved may learn firsthand the truth of the statement *"It is more blessed to give than to receive."*

* If you don't have access to a group, you may enjoy keeping a spiritual journal in which you record your responses to what you've read and to what is happening in your life. In fact, keeping a journal is *highly recommended* because activities will be offered in the "Spotlights" and "Living the Laws" sections that can serve as a bridge to take you from the teachings of the essays to their adventures in your everyday life. Writing encourages you to focus your thoughts and, more precisely, to identify your feelings. They—your thoughts and feelings—are the most vitally important part of your life. The more clarity and understanding you have in these areas, the richer can be your experiences.

I'm confident that you can probably find other ways to use this wisdom of the ages; and, indeed, I would welcome and encourage the submission of ideas and evidence for verification of any law by your sending in essays that either illustrate, support, or disprove any of the two hundred laws of life in this book. I am especially interested in scientific experiments or studies of any laws of life. Can you, dear readers from around the world, also help me discover other spiritual laws in different countries that are not in conflict with any Scripture or prophet? It would also be helpful to know how you use this book and what results you may experience.

Rewards can be given for your assistance in discovering laws that may be different from, or more clear and workable than, the information expressed in this edition of *Worldwide Laws of Life*. Write an essay of 1,000 to 1,500 words about any law you have discovered. Your law may be derived from any tradition—Jewish, Muslim, Hindu, Buddhist, Christian, or others. I encourage scientists in any field to contribute. If I decide to use your material in a later edition, I will pay you $1,000. Your ideas and reflections can be mailed to John Templeton Foundation, P.O. Box 8322, Radnor, Pennsylvania 19087-8322, U.S.A.

The John Templeton Foundation also welcomes proposals from anyone with a doctorate degree in any science for financing statistical or other scientific tests to verify or falsify any one or more of these two hundred proposed eternal principles, or others not included in this book. The purpose is to continually improve these studies in a way readily acceptable worldwide!

A few years ago, I began offering support for a "Laws of Life" essay contest in my boyhood home of Franklin County, Tennessee, in the United States. Mr. and Mrs. Handly Templeton assist in operating the program. Prizes for the essays—which can run from one hundred to two thousand words in length—are awarded semi-annually, with a first prize of $2,000; a second prize of $800; and a number of runner-up prizes. The response has been gratifying. The number of entrants for each six-month period has risen to its present size of six hundred students. It would give me great pleasure to learn that your locality wants to embark on its own version of the Franklin County program.

You might even be inspired to create a "Laws of Life" contest in your hometown. It would indeed be wonderful progress if the youth of the world were to concentrate their efforts on the subjects of love, justice, kindness, friendliness, helpfulness, forgiveness, self-respect, charity, and loyalty. If *Worldwide Laws of Life* can push that goal a few inches forward, it will have proven worthwhile.

We presently live in a period of unprecedented discovery and opportunity—a blossoming time for humanity. We also live in a world of dramatic changes—political, economical, cultural, scientifical, and spiritual. Many people are searching for guidance, comforting words, inspirational thought, and practical and workable ways effectively to meet and handle the day-to-day circumstances and situations. This book is intended to assist the reader in looking forward with expectancy and hope. The subject matter of *Worldwide Laws of Life* and the sensitivity and arrangement of these materials allow the possibility for this book to be used in many nations as an inspirational textbook for courses in religion or ethics in many schools and colleges. Because I know the value of *learning* the laws of life and *applying* them to everyday living, I would like to offer a prize of $5,000 to the school or college, and $5,000 to the teacher, for the best five courses taught at a school or college through June 30, 1999. To make this submission, the teacher should provide us with an essay describing how they used *Worldwide Laws of Life* as a textbook! To apply, please write to Worldwide Laws of Life Course Program, John Templeton Foundation, P.O. Box 8322, Radnor, Pennsylvania 19087-8322. To qualify, these essays of two to ten thousand words should contain an outline of how the material in the book was presented, a general profile of the students in the class, responses of the teacher and students to the material, and a summary of insights, perceptions, and actual results of working with the book.

In my teenage years, I was inspired by the courage and vision of Rudyard Kipling's poem "If." This poem taught me to dream but also to be master of my dreams! I learned from the great English poet that the earth belongs to us all and that, with courage and enthusiasm, progress is likely to follow. The final stanza of "If" still rings in my ears:

> *If you can fill the unforgiving minutes*
> *With sixty seconds of distance run,*
> *Yours is the Earth and everything that's in it,*
> *And—which is more—you'll be a Man, my son!*

Behind this book is my belief that the basic principles for leading "a sublime life," to paraphrase Longfellow, can be examined and tested just as science examines and tests natural laws of the universe. By learning the laws of life and applying them to everyday situations, more and more people may find themselves leading joyful and useful lives. It has been well said that *"Life is a tough school because the exams come first and the learning afterwards."* This book is a sincere attempt to provide some opportunities for learning before the exams arrive!

Acknowledgments

Without the help of many individuals who shared their ideas and wisdom with me, this book would not have been possible. Over the years I have employed most of these people for their help in providing ideas, writings, explanations, examples, and editing for this collection of laws. Some of these contributors were ministers and lay people associated with religious groups; others were private individuals who share a similar hopeful outlook on life and a fundamental belief in the principle that *"Life works better when you play by the rules."*

For their contributions to *Worldwide Laws of Life* in the form of ideas, writings, and editing, I would like to express my gratitude especially to the following persons: Rebekah Alexander, Clare Austen, Robert Brumet, Douglas Bottorff, Amy Butler, Janet Carney, Edward Conrad, Judy Covell, Matt Dioguardi, James Ellison, Sharon Frisby, Mari Gabrielson, Pauline Garcia, Jean Grissom, Ellie Harold, David Hayward, Marie Juneau, William Juneau, Mary Ann Keen, Mary Louise Kitsen, Charles and Betty Lelly, Kathy Long, Matthew Long, Tricia McCannon, Doris Maxwell, Kim Neafoy, Marty Newman, Marshall Norman, Cheryl Ramos, Nancy Reed, Paul Roach, Frances Schapperle, Joanne Starzec, Sylvia Taylor, Becky Templeton, Tom Thorpe, Patricia Trentacoste, Duke Tufty, Lois Webb, Crystal Yarlott, my colleagues in business and charities, and my family.

JOHN MARKS TEMPLETON

Worldwide
Laws of Life

❖

Week One

LAW 1

When you rule your mind, you rule your world
—Bill Provost

Great teachers down through the ages have described the importance of our mind and of being master over our thoughts. Buddha said, *"The mind is everything; what you think, you become."* Ramakrishna, the beloved Indian mystic put it this way: *"By the mind one is bound, by the mind one is freed. . . . He who asserts with strong conviction, 'I am not bound, I am free,' becomes free."* William James wrote, *"The greatest discovery of my generation is that a human being can alter his life by altering his attitudes of mind."* And Charles Fillmore, American cofounder of Unity School of Christianity, describes our mind in the following manner in *The Revealing Word*: *"The mind is the seat of perception of the things we see, hear, and feel. It is through the mind that we see the beauties of the earth and sky, or music, of art, in fact, of everything. That silent shuttle of thought working in and out through cell and nerve weaves into one harmonious whole the myriad moods of mind, and we call it life."*

> *"The greatest of all laws is the law of progressive development. Under it, in the wide sweep of things, men grow wiser as they grow older, and societies better."*
> —Christian Bovee

If you desire to understand the reason behind the statement *"when you rule your mind, you rule your world,"* it is important to take a look at what some religious teachers and spiritual philosophers call "Infinite Mind," and "The Law of Mind Action." Some say there is in reality one Mind, sometimes called "Spirit," "God Mind," etc. This Mind is the life, intelligence, power, and creativity in the entire universe. Yet, they say the Law of Mind Action includes a very important manifestation in which we are individual and yet remain a part of the whole. We have free will and are not puppets and can exercise the use of our free will. Here is the starting point of our actions, our spoken words, our thoughts, and even our feelings. It makes a great deal of difference in your daily life what you think about God, yourself, your family, your neighbors, your acquaintances, your work associates, in fact, about everything! And as Joseph Addison said, *"One of the most difficult things for a powerful mind is to be its own master!"*

A positive attitude toward life can be difficult for some people to accept for it may seem unrealistic. These skeptics may find it hard to believe that positive thinkers can accomplish most anything they choose. But, with a positive attitude, your chance for success in any situation can be greater if you look for workable solutions rather than allowing negative thinking to limit your decision-making. Zig Zigler, a sales motivation expert, says, *"Your business is never really good or bad out there. It's either good or bad right between your two ears!"* He describes the most essential component of successful selling as the ability to understand and meet the other person's needs, saying, *"You can get everything in life you want if you will just help enough people get what they want."* The ability to listen to others and appropriately interpret their needs depends to a great extent on a receptive mental attitude. Ralph Waldo Emerson emphasized the importance of the spiritual perspective in our life as well as the power of the mind when he said, *"great men are they who see that the spiritual is stronger than any material force, that thoughts rule the world."*

Mary Kay Ash, founder of Mary Kay Cosmetics, is probably one of the most remarkable success stories of our time. Since 1963, her company has grown from a modest store front beginning in Dallas, Texas, U.S.A., to an international multimillion dollar operation with a sales force numbering over two hundred thousand. Her approach to management is based on meeting the needs of others. With well-grounded Christian values contributing significantly to her business philosophy, she also asks everyone in her organization to focus on meeting the needs of others as their top priority.

It is essential to control the impulse to ask, "What's in it for me?" before taking action. Selfishness overlooks a key principle to success—that of helping others. By observing and analyzing what makes successful people successful, a clear pattern emerges. First of all, they meet the needs of others because they feel good about themselves. Then, by subordinating their possibly selfish motives to the greater motive of being of service, they are able to negotiate successfully the programs in life they choose. As with successful men and women throughout the world, our success can also be proportionate to the number of people we have helped to grow and prosper.

Our thoughts are, most assuredly, things. They are conceived in the mind and travel through time and space like ripples in a pond affecting all that they touch. Thoughts are the building blocks of our experience. The world we see is the one we have created with our thoughts for "mind is the builder."

LAW 2

Where there is no vision, the people perish
—Proverbs 29:18

An ancient proverb states, *"Where there is no vision, the people perish."* It is a way of saying that everyone needs dreams and a goal in order to live life fully and satisfactorily. If we don't have a specific goal in mind or we don't know where we want to go, we may be likely to end up in places not of our choosing. Establishing goals, along with guidelines on how to achieve them, helps to keep us focused and energized and often makes our lives more interesting, useful, and successful.

"No wind favors him who has no destined port." —Michael de Montaigne

The story of Florence Chadwick provides a clear illustration of the importance of keeping our goals in sight. She swam the Catalina Channel in southern California and established national and international records. Chadwick then attempted to break the record for swimming the English Channel. On the day set for the Channel swim, Chadwick encountered heavy seas. However, because she had trained in the Atlantic Ocean, she was in peak condition and prepared to do battle with the large waves. Along with the rough weather, Chadwick encountered chilling cold. That was a problem, but, again, her training made a big difference. She was accustomed to cold water and her trainers had greased her body to help provide insulation from the elements. In addition, Chadwick's trainers, rowing alongside her, were able to sustain her with hot soup from a thermos and comforting words of encouragement as she fought the cold, rough sea.

Yet, with all the planning and superior training, the one thing Chadwick and her trainers had not anticipated was fog. As a fog bank descended, visibility closed to only a few feet, obscuring the horizon and distant shore. Chadwick started to flounder. With the loss of visibility, the ice-cold, heavy seas seemed to grow waves of towering proportions. Chadwick began to suffer cramps in her arms, legs, feet, and hands from the effects of the severe cold. Her muscles screamed in pain as she battled the huge waves. Finally, she asked her trainers to bring her on board and take her ashore.

Later, when she was warm and dry, newspaper reporters asked her if she knew that she'd been only a very short distance from the shore when she gave up her valiant effort for the record. She responded that even though her trainers told her the same thing, it simply hadn't made a difference to her. "You see," she said, "I lost sight of my goal. I'm not sure I ever had it firmly in mind."

When we have no goal, or when our vision of the goal is obscured, we may lose our sense of purpose. Even when we've prepared ourselves well and have an aptitude for a given activity, poorly directed efforts can rob us of vital energy. We can spend a great deal of our time, money, and other resources running around in circles. Unless we create specific goals that match our purpose in life and unless we keep a clear vision of these goals, we may eventually falter and fail.

In his book *How to Succeed*, Brian Adams described how Henry Ford used the art of visualization to commence what became the second largest automobile company. Ford pictured in his mind's eye the type of automobile he wanted to build at a price most people could afford. He created a mental blueprint of his dream car long before it was ever put to paper. Then he pictured great numbers of people buying and driving it. The idea of a low-priced car (below U. S. $500) was reasoned by his conscious mind as feasible. It was then accepted by his subconscious as an undertaking to be accomplished. It became only a matter of time before Ford's vision became a reality.

Classic advice for golfers has been, "Keep your eye on the ball." The professional knows it is virtually impossible to hit a golf ball if you're not looking at it! If you want to be "on the ball," it is important to decide how you want to make a difference in the world. Once you have your purpose clearly in mind, explore the various ways you can make it happen, and visualize the process you believe can work best. Set goals, do what it takes to accomplish them, and enjoy your process.

❖

LAW 3

Love has the patience to endure the fault we cannot cure
—J. Jelinek

Because the word "love" is often loosely used to describe a variety of feelings and relationships, it can be easy to become confused about love's real meaning. Society today tends to define love as a romantic expression for someone of the opposite sex. But it's possible to think of love in much broader terms: the basic feeling of goodwill for another, care for their health and well-being, and the desire to have only good come to them. This includes our parents, siblings, friends, and everyone!

Love is the ideal and the dream, in some manner of expression, of every person who lives, for in the Creator's Love were our souls conceived and in Love lies our destiny to express. We are fulfilled when we are in the state of love, and somehow emptied without it. Love becomes the purpose of our being alive when we sprang from the celestial womb. Although there have been billions of words written about love in its many expressions, not one—or all—of them can fully capture the essence of love.

Sometimes when we think we love someone, we're actually loving what we think the other person may be able to give us. This can be an aspect of "conditional" love. Love at its highest level demands nothing in return. It loves for the sake of loving. It is not concerned with *what* or *who* it loves, nor is it concerned with whether or not love is returned. Like the sun, its joy is in the shining forth of its nature.

Love is an inner quality that sees good everywhere and in everybody. It insists that all is good, and by refusing to see anything but good, it tends to cause that quality to appear uppermost in itself and in other things. Love takes no notice of faults, imagined or otherwise. Love is considered the great harmonizer and healer in life.

Several years ago, a businessman pointed out the tremendous success power of unconditional love. Harry's work involved constant contact with a variety of shapes, sizes, and

"A coward is incapable of exhibiting love; it is the prerogative of the brave."
—Mohandas K. Gandhi

"Love is more than justice." —Henry Ward Beecher

"What I cannot love, I overlook. Is that real friendship?"
—Anaïs Nin

"Every time we hold our tongue instead of returning the sharp retort, show patience for another's faults, show a little more love and kindness; we are helping to stockpile more of these peace-bringing qualities in the world."
—Constance Foster

"Love, which is the essence of God, is not for levity, but for the total worth of man."
—Ralph Waldo Emerson, *Friendship Essays,* First Series

"He drew a circle that shut me out—
"Heretic, rebel, a thing to flaunt.
"But love and I had the wit to win;
"We drew a circle and took him in."
—Edward Markham, "Outwitted," in *The Shoes of Happiness and Other Poems*

nationalities of people. A key to successful communication with this kaleidoscope of associates was needed. He described his own private success formula for communication, especially with sometimes troublesome people.

When an important appointment was upcoming, he retired to his office, closed the door, and became still and quiet. He filled his mind with a mental picture of the person, or persons, he was to interview and blessed everyone with an affirmation of love. Here is his affirmation:

I am a radiating center of universal love, mighty to attract
my good, and with the ability to radiate good to others,
especially, (here he spoke the name of the client).

This action on his part generated a powerful energy force to which both he and the client became attuned. He remarked that it wasn't enough merely to verbalize the words. It was important to *feel* what you were saying; to feel the power of universal, unconditional love pulsing through you and your words with your heart, mind, soul, and strength. Acknowledge this glorious divinity within, and your "higher self" responds like an unfolding flower to your interests, your desire, your attention, your appreciation, and your love. Love expressed in this manner can overcome many barriers. Every single atom in the universe responds and yields its deepest secrets to unconditional love. George Washington Carver, in the United States, loved the lowly peanut into a multi-million dollar industry!

From an early Christian manuscript comes a beautiful admonition:

Nor can that endure which has not its foundation upon love,
For love alone diminishes not, but shines with its own light;
Makes an end of discord, softens the fires of hate, restores
   peace in the world, and brings together the sundered,
Redresses wrong, aids all and injures none;
And who so invokes its aid will have no fear of future ill,
But shall find safety and have everlasting peace.

In human relationships we sometimes forget that true love is given freely with no strings attached. Love is our personal "GO!" light, while anything less than a loving nature is a definite "STOP!" light! Love is real. It works! Love is gentle, yet undoubtedly one of the strongest tools you have to work with. Let love bring the patience to handle every situation.

Law 4

There are more possibilities in the universe than one can imagine
—Anonymous

From the time of our birth, we have been taught to think in terms of limits, boundaries, and restrictions. Fences surround our property, speed limits slow us down, and, some say there are even "limits to our endurance!" It has been proven, however, that all limits change as humanity progresses. The edge of the world was pushed back and finally eliminated by Columbus and other explorers. Astronomers pushed back the earlier belief in a dome-shaped firmament covering the earth and gave us knowledge of galaxies millions of light years away. Gerontologists assure us that a life span of one hundred years is conceivable in the near future. In fact, one-hundredth-birthday celebrations are becoming more common! Athletic records are being surpassed so rapidly that one wonders if there are any limits left! So much is happening that pushes back boundaries of heretofore seeming limitation.

It may be difficult for persons born in this century to imagine the small amount of knowledge and the limited concept of the cosmos that was prevalent when the Scriptures of the major religions were written. This thought brings about a question: Do Scriptures need reinterpreting to accommodate an expanded notion of the universe?

Teilhard de Chardin called for a new theology that would incorporate the modern scientific discoveries of the "*immensity of space, which imbues our accustomed way of looking at things with a strain of Universalism,*" and the progressive "*duration of time which . . . introduces . . . the idea of a possible unlimited Progress Futurism.*" Because of these two concepts, universalism and futurism, Teilhard believed we now possess a higher and more organic understanding of the cosmos, which could serve as a basis for new spiritual information.

Dr. Richard Maurice Bucke wrote in his book *Cosmic Consciousness*, "*The immediate future of our race is indescribably hopeful. In contact with the flux of cosmic consciousness all religions known and named today will be melted down. The human soul will be revolutionized. Religion will absolutely dominate the race. . . . The*

"The most beautiful and most profound emotion we can experience is the sensation of the mystical. It is the sower of all true science. He to whom this emotion is a stranger, who can no longer wonder and stand rapt in awe, is as good as dead. To know that what is impenetrable to us really exists, manifesting itself as the highest wisdom and the most radiant beauty which our dull faculties can comprehend only in their most primitive forms—this knowledge, this feeling, is at the center of true religiousness."
—Albert Einstein

"We live in a world of change, and nowhere is that more profound than in the sciences. Indeed, a textbook unrevised for several years is practically useless in some fields, and a laboratory with ten-year-old equipment is like a museum. But most scientists are quick to point out that some things in science are far more secure—the periodic table, the laws of thermodynamics, relativity, the genetic code, biological evolution—and that we are steadily building a foundation of unchanging fact from which a more complete picture of physical reality is emerging. . . . It has become apparent that we can no longer talk about scientific concepts and even mechanisms as though they were literal descriptions of objective reality."
—John M. Templeton and Robert Herrmann, *Is God the Only Reality?*

evidence of immortality will live in every heart as sight in every eye. Doubt of God and of eternal life will be as impossible as is now doubt of existence; the evidence of each will be the same. . . . Each soul will feel and know itself to be immortal, will feel and know that the entire universe with all its good and with all its beauty is for it and belongs to it forever."

Life is consciousness! If we are conscious of limitations in our life, then so it will be for us. If we believe with the poet, *"No pent-up Utica contracts our powers but the whole boundless universe is ours,"* then our lives may be boundless. There is no place in the world that is truly empty, without substance or energy. Wherever we look, we see some form of life, of growth, or vitality. All around us is the matter from which we build and create. George Santayana offers an interesting perspective: *"The universe, as far as we can observe it, is a wonderful and immense engine. . . . If we dramatize its life and conceive its spirit, we are filled with wonder, terror and amusement, so magnificent is that spirit."*

If we turn from the physical world and look within our minds for an empty space, we may quickly realize that the mind is constantly active—filled with ideas and thoughts. Even the great mystics of the ages taught that to still the mind is to simply realize an unseen power and activity far greater than ourselves.

This speaks of a great truth of another law of life: *There is no limit in the universe.* Look around at the many objects that have been made by humans. Now, look beyond those things and see before you the vastness of the resources from which objects are created—and the greatest of these resources is the mind. Our minds are filled with ideas and thoughts that show us how to build or create the things our imagination can conceive.

❖

LAW 5

As you give,
so shall you receive.
The Golden Rule
—Matthew 7:12 and Luke 6:31

If you knew of one specific thing you could do that would bring you happiness, poise, courage, success, and contentment, would you do it? Do I hear an enthusiastic "Yes!" Such a tool is available right now. The Golden Rule can help you achieve these things if you will practice what it says.

Jesus gave his own wording to the Golden Rule, and it is expressed in various forms in every major religion. Similar ideas of conduct are found in the literature of Hinduism, Buddhism, Islam, and in the writings of Aristotle, Plato, and Seneca. In Jewish literature the negative expression of the Golden Rule appears in various places as *"What you hate, do not do to anyone."* The words used by Jesus for the Golden Rule are found in Matthew 7:12 and in Luke 6:31. In five different translations of the New Testament, the Golden Rule is stated in the following words:

1. *King James Version:* And as ye would that men should do to you, do ye also to them likewise. Therefore all things whatsoever ye would that men should do to you, do ye even so to them; for this is the law and the prophets.

2. *Revised Standard Version:* And as you wish that men would do to you, do so to them. So whatever you wish that men would do to you, do so to them, for this is the law and the prophets.

3. *New English Bible:* Treat others as you would like them to treat you. Always treat others as you would like them to treat you: that is the Law and the Prophets.

4. *Phillips Modern English:* Treat men exactly as you would like them to treat you. Treat other people exactly as you would like to be treated by them—this is the meaning of the Law and the Prophets.

5. *Jerusalem Bible:* Treat others as you would like them to treat you. So always treat others as you would like them to treat you: that is the meaning of the Law and the Prophets.

Think for a moment about the person, Jesus, to whom these words are accredited. Jesus started his career as a carpenter. He knew the importance of good tools. Later on, when he began to teach principles of living, he used words as tools to communicate his ideas. He "hammered home" the idea that it is just plain, good common sense to treat others the way you wish to be treated yourself. If you don't want to be cheated, don't cheat! If you don't want to be lied to, don't lie to others! When you treat others fairly, you will feel good; they will feel good, and a lot of deceit and skullduggery can be avoided.

To build a fine structure, you need good building materials. You certainly would not use a rotten piece of wood to build your house. If you used lumber that had been warped by the weather, the foundation might not be secure and the walls in

"Getters generally don't get happiness; givers get it. You simply give to others a bit of your-self–a thoughtful act, a helpful idea, a word of appreciation, a lift over a rough spot, a sense of understand-ing, a timely sugges-tion. You take some-thing out of your mind, garnished in kindness out of your heart and put it into the other fellow's mind and heart."
—Charles H. Burr

your house might not hang straight. The building would be said to lack structural integrity. Likewise, as a builder of your own life, you need good attitudes to create your house of living. If you act in ways that are abusive to others, you may find yourself abused. Your life may not work well, and others may not trust your integrity.

Kindness, caring, and consideration have often been described as "love in action." Each day offers many opportuni-ties for anyone to do some little kindness for another and to be caring and considerate, understanding and supportive. Yet, many people are busy, harried, and sometimes worried about situations in their own life and fail to see the blessed opportu-nity to be love in action. Do you rush so fast from one thing to another, perhaps from one appointment or meeting to another, that you fail to notice how others are feeling or what may be happening in their lives? Begin to bring about a positive change for good by shifting your awareness outside of yourself to oth-ers. Surely, someone whose life you touch today can use your gift of kindness. Surely, your sincere caring would be appreciat-ed by some person in your world. And the whole world needs our consideration and support. The Golden Rule offers a pat-tern, or a plan, that we can read and follow and build upon to bring all kinds of good things into our lives to share with others. We can move in the direction of attaining our desires and often enriching the lives of those around us. To treat others as you wish to be treated is a plan that works wonderfully from all angles, on all sides, and for all concerned.

There must be something powerfully effective in the Gol-den Rule because its guidance, perhaps with slightly different phrasing, is found in every major religion and regarded as one of the basic spiritual principles of life. Let's look for a moment at the Golden Rule from various translations or paraphrases:

Brahmanism: This is the sum of duty: do naught unto others which would cause you pain if done unto you.

Buddhism: Hurt not others in ways that you yourself would find hurtful.

Christianity: Treat others as you would want them to treat you (Phillips).

Confucianism: Do not unto others what you would not have them do unto you.

Hindu: The true role of life is to guard and do by the things of others as they do on their own.

Islam: No one of you is a believer until he desires for his brother that which he desires for himself.

Judaism: Whatever is hurtful to yourself, do not to your fellowman. That is the whole of the law, the rest is merely commentary.

Persian: Do as you would be done by.

Taoism: Regard your neighbor's gain as your own gain and your neighbor's loss as your own loss.

Spotlights!

1. There are universal Principles, or Laws of Life, that lead to usefulness and happiness. *"Progress consists largely of learning to apply laws and truths that have always existed."* –Jim Allen May

2. The Laws of Life work for the highest good of all.

3. A Law of how things work is: as within, so without!

4. Establishing goals, and guidelines to achieve them, can help you live an interesting, useful and more successful life.

5. Every effort we make in a positive manner can move us to the completion of great undertakings.

6. Small attempts can lead to big accomplishments.

7. Life is a growing process similar to the one we experience in school.

8. Life is consciousness! We have the ability to exercise free will in our choices.

9. Everything is available to meet our needs and, in reality, there is no limit in the universe.

10. The Golden Rule is a pattern, or a plan, that you can read, study, and follow to build a sound "house of living."

Living the Law!

The best way to change your life is to make daily changes in the way you think, feel, speak, and act. An enthusiastic commitment to bring out the best within you and your world can bring about results. Reflect on the five laws you've studied this week. This can be a time to start thinking of your life—thinking about the people and activities that fill your days, thinking about the direction your life is going. Are you happy with where you're headed? Or would you like to establish a different road map?

Begin to observe how every person and situation you encounter can contribute to your journey toward transformation. The people in your life are the soil in which you're rooted. Take a moment and think about those individuals who are closest to you. Write their names in your journal and about each one note a quality that provides guidance to you and your goals.

Speaking of goals, what are some of the things you would

like to accomplish? Remember how we talked about the importance of setting goals and guidelines to help you achieve your
desired result? Make a list of specific goals you would like to
achieve within the next month. Take some time to think about
this before you begin to write. Each day's essay in this book can
provide assistance through ideas and practical applications
toward achieving your goals.

Week Two

LAW 1

Your life becomes what you think
—Marcus Aurelius

Thought—the act or process of thinking—is one of the greatest powers we possess, and like most powers it can be used positively or negatively, as we choose. A great majority of people have never been taught how to use thought, the master power of the mind. It is just as essential to know how to think correctly as it is to know how to speak or act correctly. Ernest Holmes, founder of Science of Mind, offers why he believes this is so; he said, *"Life is a mirror and will reflect back to the thinker what he thinks into it."*

With modern scanning equipment, we can see the brain, but we cannot see the brain working. We see only the results of the brain activity. The mind, which is invisible, directs the thinking process. It tells the brain how to sort experience and fact, and how to give shape and form to new ideas. The indirect action of thought is easy to understand, for obviously a person must think before he can do anything. Thought is the motivating power behind an action, just as electricity is the motivating power behind lighting our home. Thought also has a direct action on matter. Regardless of whether or not we translate our thought into actual performance, the thought itself has already produced some kind of effect.

Have you ever had an original idea and wondered where it came from? It's as if your mind planted a seed of the idea in the brain. Your brain recalled your experience and knowledge and developed the idea in a way that could finally be expressed by you coherently and persuasively. The idea probably improved as you tested it under various conditions.

In the same way, the mind can tell the brain what to think about. It's tempting to believe that we have no control over what comes into our heads but, in reality, we do. If a thought comes to you that is not in your best interest, you can, with very alert

"People are afraid to think, or they don't know how. They fail to realize that, while emotions can't be suppressed, the mind can be strengthened. All over the world people are seeking peace of mind, but there can be no peace of mind without strength of mind."
—Eric B. Gutkind

"My clearest recollection of a long ago interview with Thomas A. Edison is of a single sentence that was painted and hung on a wall in his room. In effect, the sentence was: 'It is remarkable to what lengths people will go to avoid thought.' That is tragically true. Some of us think, more of us think we think, and most of us don't even think of thinking. The result is a somewhat cockeyed world." —Pollack

practice, begin thinking something else, so that the undesirable thought will go away.

Sound difficult? Try the following experiment. If someone says to you, "Don't think about bananas!" you immediately have a picture of a banana right in the middle of your consciousness. To tell yourself to stop thinking about something doesn't do a great deal of good then, does it? The undesirable thought must be replaced with a desirable thought. If you don't want to think about bananas, try thinking about Valentine hearts. Once these two words are planted in your mind, you can picture the Valentine heart, in all its beauty, and the bananas are gone.

This is called the "crowding-out technique." (See *The Templeton Plan*, Harper Paperbacks, p. 113). If you fill your mind to capacity with thoughts that you think are good and productive, you won't have room for the bad ones. The thoughts you can "crowd out" are those of envy, hatred, covetousness, self-centeredness, damaging criticism, revenge, and any time-wasting thoughts that are unproductive for your ultimate goals in life. Another method for crowding out negative thoughts is to quietly release them. You might affirm, "I lovingly release you to the vast nothingness from whence you came." Then let them go.

When you face an unpleasant task, such as mowing the lawn, it can be tempting to complain about it. However, when it's in your best interest to finish the job, why not make it more fun now that you know you can? How? Use a "mind talk" with yourself. For example, do you like the color of your lawn mower? If so, every time you catch yourself thinking, "I don't like mowing the lawn," think instead, "I like my red lawn mower." Ask your family and friends to help you. If you say something negative about mowing the lawn, they can wink and smile and say, "Oh? What color is your lawn mower?"

It is important for you to find something that is true for you, however insignificant it may seem, with which to replace the negative thought. It could be that you enjoy the fresh air, the sunshine, being outside, the smell of newly mown grass, or that you may get to visit with a friend over the back fence. If you allow yourself to think in a particular manner today, it can be easier to think in that same manner tomorrow. Anything to change your negative thought to a positive one will change your attitude and, as a result, your experience around it. Your grass may not only get mowed, but you will feel better about yourself.

Be kind to yourself in this process. If you've worked at changing your thoughts and the negative ones seem to keep roosting in your mind, laugh at yourself. Accept that you're doing your best, and return to thinking your replacement thought. As you become more adept at controlling your thoughts, your positive, good thoughts will change your life for the better.

LAW 2

Love given is love received
–John M. Templeton

There's a strange thing you can observe about love. People search, run after, try to earn, get, grasp, and hold onto something that is as naturally theirs as the air they breathe! And what mental and emotional rigors we put ourselves through in order to get it. Many of us think it all depends on having the right person see us in just the right way, so that person will feel the right way and love us. That raises the pressure of trying to be just what the person wants, trying to please, trying to be good enough to deserve their love. Having to look just right, say the right things, do the right things. Otherwise, we may not "get" the love we want or, if we have it, we might lose it. Nothing makes people more emotionally crippled, dependent, self-pitying, bitter, and cynical than thinking they don't have love unless someone gives it to them.

Of course, whether we admit it or not, each of us instinctively wants to experience love. The reason it's considered the treasure of life is that love is the true nature of every soul. It's the nature of your soul to live and create experiences of love, because love originates in the essence of your being. The power, force, and energy of love reside self-existent within us as our very life's blood. And it is so important to express that love! The world-renowned opera singer Luciano Pavarotti said, *"You never know what little bundle of encouragements artists carry around with them, what little pats on the back from what hands, what newspaper clipping, what word of hope from what teacher. I suppose that the so-called faith in ourselves is the foundation of our talent, but I am sure these encouragements are the mortar that hold it together."*

An ancient story describes how the greatest gift of life was hidden. When the gods were creating the human race, they

"Love all God's creation, the whole and every grain of sand in it. Love every leaf, every ray of God's light. Love the animals, love the plants, love everything. If you love everything, you will perceive the mystery in things. Once you perceive it, you begin to comprehend it better every day. And you will come at last to love the whole world with an all embracing love." —Fedor M. Dostoevsky

wondered where to hide this most precious and powerful treasure so it would not be misused or mistreated by the universe. "Shall we hide it atop the highest mountain? Shall we bury it deep within the earth? Shall we entomb it at the bottom of the deepest ocean? Or, shall we conceal it in the heart of the thickest, darkest forest?" After great pondering, they finally decided on the answer. They would implant the gift within the human beings themselves, for surely they would not think to look there! And just to make certain, the gods designed human eyes to look only outward, not inward.

Now the secret is yours. You can look within to find the treasure and experience it in every area of your life. A *sure* way to experience love is to give love. Giving love demonstrates to yourself that you have it, because you cannot give something you don't have, can you! There is no one without love to give. You need not search for the right people who will recognize and understand love the way you do. Neither expect love to be given back to you by those to whom you gave it. If someone does return your love, it may not be in the same way you gave it forth.

Love holds mind and body together. It is an attractive force that draws our good to us according to the depth and strength of our realization and understanding of love. When we live in love, with a conscious choice to express and to experience love, we participate in a most powerful force that is active in our lives and world. Dr. George Washington Carver was aware of the power of love when he said, *"Anything will give up its secrets if you love it enough."*

Start with whoever is around you: men, women, girls, boys, old people, young people, yourself. Giving love doesn't mean contrived sentimentality or flattery. It is a natural attitude and demeanor of good will, kindliness, support, caring, and benevolence. It is also a willingness to do what you can to be helpful, and make things a little better for someone. Giving love consciously through thoughts, words, and deeds can help you to become your own force field of love.

Because you can feel the power and beauty of love within you so strongly, you may cease to differentiate between love given and love received. You may eventually take little notice of whether it's attracted back to you. The gift, the giving, and the receiving can be one harmonious flow of the most powerful force in the universe.

LAW 3

To be forgiven, one must first forgive
—John M. Templeton

Roy Masters, in his book *How Your Mind Can Keep You Well,* says that we ought to be grateful when someone offends us. They are doing us a favor, he suggests, because when we forgive those who have offended us, it erases some of the self-destructive effects of offenses we may have caused others. In this way, we learn a valuable lesson: *"To be forgiven, we must first forgive."*

The person who cannot forgive may become physically, mentally, emotionally, or spiritually ill, as the story of Kathy so convincingly demonstrates. Kathy had hated her father all her life and felt justified in her extreme feelings. He reportedly abandoned Kathy, her mother, and six other children. Each time the mother became pregnant, the father disappeared until the new baby arrived. When he returned, the sad process would repeat itself. While the father was home, he physically abused everyone, even occasionally beating the mother with a horse whip. She and the children were terrified of him. None of them knew when he would lose his temper and turn violent. Kathy sometimes hid under the table or bed in fear, and many people agreed that she was justified in hating her father.

However, Kathy's chronic state of anger violently affected her own life and affairs more than anyone else's. Like her father, Kathy would lash out at those nearby with only the slightest provocation. Her actions cost Kathy job after job and many strained and unhappy relationships.

Hatred and bitterness finally ate away at her health. She suffered from headaches, stomach problems, and eventually developed arthritis. She fell victim to every germ that came along in spite of what doctors and medicines could do. By her twenty-fifth birthday, Kathy looked middle-aged.

She knew she would be better off if only she could learn to forgive her father, but she just couldn't do it, nor did she want anyone else to forgive him. "He's just a terrible person," she would cry as she relived the miseries of the past. "Look at what he's done." But Kathy's inner guidance kept reminding her that "to be forgiven, you must forgive." We have all done things for which we need forgiveness, and Kathy was no exception. She

"He that cannot forgive others breaks the bridge over which he must pass himself; for every man has need to be forgiven."
—Lord Herbert

wanted to be relieved of things she had said and done. She wanted to be forgiven. So, she started the forgiveness process with a statement that went something like this, "I forgive you, you sorry so-and-so."

At first it was difficult, and Kathy felt dishonest because she didn't feel at all forgiving. But as she persisted, the statement became softer. Soon she was able to drop the "you sorry so-and-so." As she came to understand how her father could have acted so violently, she began to feel pity for him, then compassion, and finally real love.

When Kathy learned to forgive her father, she began to forgive and actually love herself. Eventually, her physical problems cleared up, and her life became transformed for the better. Through experience, she discovered that forgiveness benefits both the forgiven and the forgiver.

A person can move forward with a renewed sense of peace when there is no longer the burden of withheld forgiveness. The mind is a wonderful tool, for it can store information to be reexamined at a later time. If a negative thought about some slight—actual or perceived—exists, the ability to transform that mental image also exists. The negative memory can be changed through the activity of forgiving the other person and forgiving yourself for holding on to the image of hurt.

"They who forgive most shall be most forgiven."
—Josiah W. Bailey

However, just knowing the importance of forgiveness does not make a situation easier when we feel we have been wronged. Circumstances of the situation cannot be changed, but it is possible to change the patterns of our thoughts. A positive lesson in this area is offered in the little book *The Nibble Theory*. The author explains in simple terms that, like a snowflake or fingerprint, each person is a unique individual with special contributions to offer. The book also suggests that appearances along our pathway may manifest as "nibblers," (thought energies that continue to take little "bites" out of our positive attitude and self-esteem) which can, over an extended period of time, diminish our uniqueness. A few of these "nibblers" could be finding fault with yourself or others, losing patience with yourself or others, and harboring any kind of negative or unforgiving thought.

Pause to examine your thought patterns from time to time. As Henry H. Buckley said, *"Keep your thoughts right—for as you think, so you are. Thoughts are things, therefore, think only the things that will make the world better and you unashamed."* Look for little indicators of "nibblers" that may arise in your actions, your conversations, your emotions, as well as your thoughts. For some, it may be necessary to *learn* how to forgive. Theodore Cuyler Speers emphasized this idea when he said, *"How to forgive is something we have to learn, not as a duty or an obligation, but as an experience akin to the experience of love; it must come into being spontaneously."*

❖

LAW 4

An attitude of gratitude creates blessings
—John M. Templeton

Do you awaken every morning with a song of praise on your lips? Do you feel full of appreciation for life as you live it every day? Or, do you have to think long and hard before finding something to be grateful for?

Consider your response to these questions carefully, for they could be crucial to a life of usefulness and joy. It is a law of life, and an inexorable principle, that if we develop an *attitude of gratitude* our happiness will increase. The very reasons for being thankful can begin to multiply. And it may be necessary to educate ourself to begin thinking in a different manner, as exemplified in the words of Albert Schweitzer: *"To educate yourself for the feeling of gratitude means to take nothing for granted, whatever it may be, but always to seek out and value the kind will that stands behind the action. Constrain yourself to measure everything good that is done for you as a matter of course. Everything originates in a will for the good which is directed at you. If you try seriously and continuously to educate yourself for the feeling of gratitude, your stubborn human nature will cause you or no one trouble."*

"But how does this positive approach really work?" you may ask. The only way to prove it to yourself is to give it a good try and see what happens. Otto Friedrich Bollnow wrote: *"The virtue of gratitude . . . directly touches the ultimate foundations of human existence, for there is hardly another quality of man that is so suited to reveal the state of his inner spiritual and moral health as his capacity to be grateful."* Whether you know it or not, you have multitudes of reasons to break out in wonderful song of praise at this very moment!

In Russell Criddle's story *Love Is Not Blind*, he describes

"No one can be grateful to himself, for gratitude goes from one person to another."
—Thomas Aquinas

what it means to be blind and then to recover one's sight through an operation. *"Everything looked beautiful. Nothing looked ugly. The wad of paper discarded in the gutter, just the words convey an image of filth, but I saw white and black and colors, straight lines and symmetry, unbelievably different from any other wad of paper in any other gutter. . . . I felt no great thrill that I was no longer blind, only the awful sense of beauty thrilled me to the limit of my endurance. I hurried into the house and up to my room and buried my head in the pillow. Not because I was no longer blind, not because I could see, but because I just didn't have the capacity to digest so much grandeur. I wept."* Surely, this was gratitude that could not be measured!

Whatever you give your attention and belief to becomes your experience. So, focus your attention on the way you would like to see yourself. Give thanks for the realization that you are right now becoming that person. Give thanks for all of the abundance you're presently enjoying, and give thanks for the abundance of every good thing that's on its way to you. As you count your blessings and become increasingly aware of how truly blessed you are, you can begin to build an attitude of gratitude. Your life will be blessed in ways you never thought were possible. Practice waking up each day with an inherent expectation of good and with a wonderful feeling of thanksgiving for life itself. Your days will be filled with exciting adventures.

True, you can choose to focus solely on what you perceive as lacking in your life. You can bemoan the fact that you don't have your share of earthly possessions. You can go around complaining about fate, your parents, your pocketbook, and the faults and frailties of others. These are choices that many people have made before you and continue to make.

Or, you can change yourself. You can become wise to wonderful ways of playing the game of life. You may already realize the wisdom of an attitude of gratitude. If so, it could be only a small step for you to begin to open yourself to greater appreciation and greater abundance. As you become a good steward of the abundance that is yours right now, an increasing attitude of gratitude will bring greater blessings to you and, then through you, to our world. The attitude of gratitude—it can work for you!

"Gratitude is a fruit of great cultivation; you do not find it among gross people."
—Samuel Johnson

LAW 5

You fear what you do not understand
—Anonymous

There was recently a replay of what had been a live simultane-
ous broadcast between San Francisco and Leningrad. Audiences
in both cities were able to see the programs presented. One of
the most dramatic moments came near the end of the broadcast
when the reality of the situation dawned on both audiences and
they began to wave to each other. Tears of joy were shed in both
cities. People who were on opposite sides of a Cold War for
more than a generation suddenly became aware that people on
the other side were just like them. This new level of understanding increases the potential for peace in the world.

 During World War II, Allied soldiers referred to the
Germans as "Jerrys," During the Korean and Vietnam conflicts,
the Red Chinese, North Korean, and Vietnamese were called
"Gooks." These names served to dehumanize the enemy and
create a sense of superiority and loathing (which is a form of
fear) in the troops that had to fight them. If the name callers
had understood that the troops on the other side were also
fighting for what they believed in, killing them would have
become an infinitely more difficult task. An old Moorish
proverb brings to mind a great truth: *"He who is afraid of a thing
gives it power over him."*

 We all have fears of different sizes and shapes, and it is
important to learn what they are and face them directly.
Courage overcomes the feeling of helplessness and encourages
us to think clearly and take action in any given situation. When
we increase our understanding of ourself and others, fear and
hatred are much less likely to take root. When the audience in
San Francisco understood that the people in Leningrad also
had hopes and aspirations, fear and misunderstanding began to
evaporate. When the audience in Leningrad understood that
the people in San Francisco looked like them, laughed like
them, and had a similar vision of the future, the world took a
giant step closer toward realizing peace and brotherhood.

 We tend to fear the unknown. When early hunters sought
out man-eating animals for food, there was always a sense of
fear and anxiety inherent in the hunt—not because the hunter

*"The way of a superior
man is threefold.
Virtuous, he is free
from anxieties; wise, he
is free from perplexi-
ties; bold, he is free
from fear."*
—Confucius

"Your fears can be overcome if you deal with them properly. Fear is an emotion. Emotions come wholly from within, and have only the strength we allow them. As human beings, we enjoy the possession of an intellect, and it is the intellect, not the emotions, that must be the supreme guiding force of our lives if we are to know any measure of happiness here.

"Emotions are the color of life; we would be drab creatures indeed without them. But we must control those emotions or they will control us. This is particularly true of the emotion of fear, which if allowed free rein, would reduce all of us to trembling shadows of men, for whom only death could bring release."
–John M. Wilson

didn't know what he would find, but because he didn't know *when*. Today, it is rare to encounter a man-eating animal in our normal pursuits, so there is little reason for us to fear for our lives from this danger. Yet, we continue to experience fear and anxiety for the future. We believe there may be the potential for terrible things to happen to us and we don't know when. However, the truth is that, by approaching life without fear, things tend to work out for the best.

If we choose to remain in fear, then one fear leads to another fear, which can only lead to additional fears. If we live in a fearful state, there can always be something to be afraid of. Most fears are educated into us and can be educated out! Fear may be a lack of the awareness of the presence of God as a real force in our lives. With the realization of God's active presence in our lives, many aspects of fear may disappear into the mists of the unreal. Like a snowball dropped into a pail of hot water, fear dissolves, and its energy is transmuted into positive faith.

Take the example of recovering alcoholics. During the course of the disease, these people increasingly come to deny they have a problem with alcohol. Most of them have to hit bottom—some literally have to wake up in the gutter—before they can look up and see that the solution lies in recovery. The fear and anxieties that were the cause of their drinking had to come to light so they could face and defeat them.

But you don't have to hit bottom to look up. You can begin right now to understand that life without fear works out for the best. You can begin now to understand that people on "the other side" of the world are just like you and me—they only want to be free to be happy and useful. You don't have to be afraid to reach out for new experiences or take new risks to acquire an increased expectation of good. You can go forth without fear in the direction of success, harmony, health, prosperity, and usefulness.

Spotlights!

1. Thought—the act or process of thinking—is one of the greatest powers you possess and, like almost all powers, it can be used positively or negatively.
2. Should a negative thought arise, replace it immediately with a positive one.
3. Love is the "spiritual glue" that holds everything together.
4. Look within yourself to find the treasure of love.
5. The first step in being forgiven is to forgive!
6. Remember that one of your best teachers is daily experience.

7. Look around you. In appreciation, find beauty and joy, and invite them to be permanent guests in your home.
8. As you begin to realize that God is lovingly in charge of your life, you may also understand that there is really nothing to fear.

Living the Law!

A strong reaction is produced upon the thinker by the thoughts one generates. If your thought is directed toward someone else, it flies like a well-directed missile toward that person. If your thought is connected mostly with yourself, it remains close, just waiting for an opportunity to react upon you and reproduce itself.

The following is a deeply meaningful quote on our thoughts. Read it and think about the many levels of awareness it may stimulate, and write down your own perceptions. Be aware this week of how the wisdom contained in this quote may be applicable to your personal life.

> *All that we are is the result of what we have thought; it is founded on our thoughts and made up of our thoughts. If a man speak or act with an evil thought, suffering follows him as a wheel follows the hoof of the beast that draws the cart* (*Dhamapada*, Collection of ancient Buddhist poems).

Work with this exercise several times this week, and apply the ideas from each essay to your thinking process. Make notes in your journal of any special thoughts, awarenesses, or ideas that come.

Week Three

❖

LAW 1

Nothing can bring you peace but yourself
—Ralph Waldo Emerson

"If you are yourself at peace, then there is at least some peace in the world. Then share your peace with everyone, and everyone will be at peace."
—Thomas Merton

A man who was weary of the frantic pace of city life gave up his job, sold his apartment, and moved into a small cabin in the woods. He wanted to find the peace of mind that eluded him in the city. For a few weeks, he thought he had found contentment, but soon he began to miss his friends and the conveniences of the city. When his restlessness grew acute, he felt the urge to move again.

This time he decided to try a small town. There would be people with whom to talk, and he could enjoy the conveniences of the city without the pressure of the noise, the size, and the constant "hurry, hurry" atmosphere. Surely, in this best of both worlds, he would find peace. Life in the small town, however, brought unanticipated problems. People were slow to accept an outsider, yet they seemed quick and aggressive when it came to prying into his personal affairs. Soon he discovered, to his annoyance, that strange rumors about him were circulating. Again the man grew restless and discontented and concluded that it was not possible to find peace anywhere. He moved back to the city, resigned to a life of inner turmoil.

This unfortunate man could have profited from an important truth realized by Ralph Waldo Emerson, who wrote, *"Nothing can bring you peace but yourself."* Emerson understood that inner peace does not depend on where you live or even whom you're with. True peace is a quality you carry within yourself regardless of external circumstances.

The Bible Scripture John 14:27 states: *"Peace I leave with you, my peace I give unto you. Not as the world giveth, give I unto you. Let not your heart be troubled, neither let it be afraid."* These comforting words, attributed to Jesus, seem to indicate that the world can give us a certain kind of peace. It can offer us a lovely country place, away from the hustle and bustle of the city; a quiet and beautiful park tucked amid the city's activities; a peaceful, scenic beach upon which to stroll; or a distant mountaintop where all is serene and still. Although people may travel to far-away places, the journey is made in the company of one's own consciousness, and we return home with ourselves. We cannot get away from our own inner being. If we have a problem, we take it with us wherever we may go. On the other hand, if our consciousness is imbued with gentle serenity, then it can also be imbued with power. *Quiet, inner power.*

One way to be successful in the world is to go forth to do what is ours to do with peace in our consciousness. This peacefulness is a state of receptivity that can allow us to be more open to other people. How can we get in touch with this inner peace? A simple exercise can help. Reserve some time each day—even a few minutes can be beneficial—in which you can be alone and undisturbed. Sit in a comfortable chair, close your eyes, breathe deeply and slowly, and let your mind and body relax. Repeat slowly to yourself, "I am now letting go. I am now letting go." Mentally release the events of the day, one by one, until you feel yourself moving into a realm of stillness and peace.

This place of inner stillness and quiet is termed "the Silence." A minister friend described it in this manner: "In the Silence, we enter an elevated state of awareness, of heightened receptivity, a time of being fully alive to the moment. It may sound strange, but when we are in the Silence, we do absolutely nothing. We are content just to *be*, and we luxuriate in the ecstasy of being consciously with God. The Silence is a time of stillness when we think neither of the past nor of the future. It is a state when we are detached from the ordinary world. If we are thinking about business, troubled relationships, or any other problem, we are not in the silence. And yet, although we are not thinking about ideas, concepts, or perceptions, we remain alert. Our receptivity and sensitivity are increased. It is truly an ineffable experience; words are inadequate to describe it."

Anwar Sadat, Egyptian military and political leader, understood the power of peace when he said, *"Peace is much more precious than a piece of land."* He spoke of the peace that cannot be bought, but that is available to us all, if we so choose. As new buildings and structures may be created from new plans and materials, so, too, can new thought structures be built. Through our peaceful thoughts, prayers, and activities we can build a consciousness of peace.

There may be times in the life of every person when he feels

"Peace comes to us through love, understanding of our fellow men, faith. Peace does not include selfishness nor indifference. Peace is never wrapped at a counter for a price. It is earned by giving of ourselves. Our own earned peace will ignite peace in our family, in our community, city, state, country, and flow over the entire world. If we have not peace within ourselves, it is in vain to seek it from outward sources."
—François La Rochefoucauld

the Presence of the Creator and becomes aware, in one way or another, of an actual transcendental Presence, Power, and Peace. With this awareness often come a liberation and a freedom from negative thoughts and things of this world: its fears, doubts, cares, and problems. The degree of transformation may be immediately apparent in the visible realm, but, bit by bit, it becomes evident in the outer world.

Jesus acknowledged this truth and taught about the existence of an inner peace that "passes all understanding," a peace that is not dependent on outer circumstances. As you discover this inner realm for yourself, you eventually realize it is the only real peace you can ever have. You don't have to travel far to find it; you need only look deeply within yourself. External events can change at a moment's notice and what you thought was peace may suddenly evaporate. But once it's yours, true peace will remain with you—even in the midst of a rapidly changing world.

Try not to make the same futile mistake as the man who sought external peace by moving to various locations. That route leads to disappointment. Instead, spend some time each day in your quiet place. Release your cares until you make contact with your inner realm of peace. Today can be a day of transformation. The depth of increasing inner peace can continue to bring forth greater spiritual light, wisdom, and guidance, so that every day can be a day of deeper discernment.

Law 2

Listen to learn
—Alcoholics Anonymous

There's an old saying that God gave us two ears and one mouth so we may hear more and talk less. How well we use our ears can play an important part in determining what we learn as we go through life. It is true that the good listener adds immeasurably to the art of true conversation—and to the enjoyment of those around him.

A story is told about a reporter who was visiting the monkey house in New York's Bronx Zoo, in the United States. As he stood there in front of the monkey house, listening to the ceaseless yapping of the monkeys, a strange feeling of déjà vu swept over him. He recalled a cocktail party he had attended the previous week. He saw in his mind's eye the crowded room and the full-speed, full-volume chatter with nobody really saying anything, and nobody really listening. "We miss so much," he thought as he walked away from the monkey house.

Conversational give-and-take can be among the most enjoyable and rewarding of mental activities. Like serious study, it informs. Like travel, it broadens. Like friendship, it nourishes the soul. However, it calls for a willingness to alternate the role of speaker with that of listener, and it calls for "digestive pauses" by both!

A major reason why some relationships break down could be that one or more of the parties involved hasn't learned to listen! Listening is a *learned* skill, and when we develop it to the fullest, we increase not only our capacity to learn but also our ability to maintain healthy relationships. A true conversation is an opportunity to learn something *about* one another *from* one another.

There are two kinds of listening—*active* and *passive*. Most of us are good at passive listening. We appear to be listening when, in fact, our minds may have wandered off to the movie we saw last night or what we are going to wear tomorrow. Our attention can drift from a speaker during a lecture, or a sermon, or while watching a television show, and even when we're with close friends and family members.

Active listening can be difficult because it requires staying focused on what the speaker is saying. It depends on using our ears the way a photographer uses a camera. To get the best pictures, the photographer must adjust the lens until the settings are correct. As active listeners, we must adjust the focus of our attention to remain aware of what the speaker is telling us. The more we listen and learn, the better able we are to develop the potential we possess.

A presentation by the Sperry Corporation in the United States on effective listening quotes studies showing that students spend sixty to seventy percent of classroom time listening. In business, listening is cited as one of the most important skills a manager can possess. Sadly, most of us are ineffective listeners. We allow our minds hardly any opportunity for the essential process of assimilating what has come in and organizing what is to go out in response. In many of today's ping-pong conversations, you rarely find an interval between the cessation of one person's talking and the clamor of a "listener" to get *his* paddle in!

"All wise men share one trait in common: the ability to listen."
—Frank Tyger

"Hearing is one of the body's five senses. But listening is an art."
—Frank Tyger

"A good listener is not only popular, but after a while he knows something."
–Wilson Mizner

Have you ever played the childhood game "Gossip," in which people sit in a circle and someone whispers a story into the ear of the person next to him? That person turns and whispers the story to the next person, and so on until everyone in the circle has heard and retold the story. When the last person tells the story, it is usually so far removed from the original that it bears no resemblance to it. This is the result of poor listening.

The value of listening has been emphasized through the ages. Amen-em-Opet, an Egyptian scribe (ca. 1200 B.C.E.) said, *"Give your ears, hear what is said. At a time when there is a whirlwind of words, they will be a mooring-stake for your tongue."* And Ben Sira, a Hebrew scholar of the second century B.C.E., commented, *"If you love to hear, you will receive, and if you listen, you will be wise."*

It takes practice and concentration, but we *can* become better listeners, and better listeners are better learners. God gave us not only two ears and one mouth, but also the potential to learn. The more we listen and learn, the better we may be able to realize the God-given potential that each of us possesses.

LAW 3

Wisdom is born of mistakes; confront error and learn
–J. Jelinek

Norman Cousins made the statement, *"Fortunately or otherwise, we live at a time when the average individual has to know several times as much in order to keep informed as he did only thirty or forty years ago. Being 'educated' today requires not only more than a superficial knowledge of the arts and sciences, but a sense of inter-relationship such as is taught in few schools. Finally, being 'educated' today, in terms of the larger needs, means preparation for world citizenship; in short, education for survival."*

"Wisdom, thoroughly learned, will never be forgotten."
–Pythagoras

There is a difference between *acquiring* knowledge and information and *possessing* wisdom. You may acquire knowledge from a university, your travels, your relationships, the books you read, and other activities in which you participate. But are you also gaining wisdom?

Webster's Dictionary defines "wisdom" as *"the quality of being wise . . . implies the ability to judge and deal with persons, situations, etc. rightly, based on a broad range of knowledge, experience and understanding."* In other words, a wise person is one who has the ability to look for the deeper meaning of things. But in order to acquire wisdom, it seems logical that one must have lived enough to have developed a certain depth of philosophical reflection in order to be in a position to evaluate our experiences and learn from them. Epictetus may have held similar thoughts in mind when he wrote, *"On the occasion of every accident that befalls you, remember to turn to yourself and inquire what power you have for turning it to use."*

Some of our mistakes—or as Maria Montessori called them, *"learning opportunities"*—are clearer than others! Sometimes it seems as if the world is filled with people who gladly inform us of our mistakes. The person who is willing to hear another's point of view and admit there may be other approaches that could be taken is the one who will grow in wisdom as the reservoir of knowledge is expanded.

The Talmud asks, *"Who is a wise man?"* and answers, *"He who learns of all men."* To become wise, we must be willing to suspend our personal beliefs about something, set aside prejudices, and think with an open mind. It is important to branch out eagerly and learn in many different areas, even at the risk of being embarrassed or looking foolish. Are we able to admit that we don't yet know everything and are willing to learn? Learning is a desirable process that may include making mistakes along the road to knowledge. Can we allow the learning process to be important? True wisdom acknowledges that the more we learn about a subject, the more interesting it becomes and the more there is to learn!

Many of us have heard someone say, "I learned my lesson! I'll never do that again!" But all too rarely do we hear, "That was a wonderful lesson. I'm glad it happened just the way it did, even though I was uncomfortable going through it. I now understand why I experienced the pain. With this new awareness, I can change my behavior so I won't make the same mistake in the future." This person is bravely acknowledging his responsibility for creating the situation. He recognizes he has choices, and that he *can* choose differently as long as he stays alert to each challenge, whether the situation seems to be positive or negative.

The wise person is also a courageous person. We often think of courage in terms of outer forms of bravery—physical prowess and fearlessness in battle or in sports. Yet there are many inner

"You cannot run away from a weakness. You must sometimes fight it out or perish; and if that be so, why not now, and where you stand?"
—Robert Louis Stevenson

forms of bravery that are not recognized by anyone but ourselves as we struggle to overcome shortcomings. By fearlessly confronting the role you play in the experiences you may have judged as mistakes in your life, you can make future experiences fruitful and increase your wisdom. This sincere willingness to look at ourselves honestly and courageously can be the first, and perhaps most important step we can take on the road to wisdom.

"There is no purifier in this world equal to wisdom."
—Bhagavat Gita

LAW 4

Humility leads to prayer as well as progress and brings you in tune with the infinite
—John M. Templeton

At this present moment, the human race, even after thousands of years of historical development, is poised at the dawn of a new creation. When you recognize the wonder of all that is around you—whether it be a morning glory or a galaxy—a state of awe and humility can be experienced.

In fact, *humility is the key to progress*. Without it we may become too self-satisfied with past glories to launch boldly into the challenges ahead. Without humility we may not be wide-eyed and open-minded enough to discover new areas for research. If we are not as humble as children, we may be unable to admit mistakes, to seek advice, and try again. The humble approach is for all of us who are concerned about the future of our civilization and the role we are to play in it. It is an approach for those of us who are not satisfied to allow things to drift and who want to channel our creative restlessness toward helping build the kingdom of God on planet Earth. I use the word "humility" here to mean understanding that God infinitely exceeds anything anyone has ever said of Him, and that He is infinitely beyond human comprehension and understanding. As we realize this and become more humble, we thereby reduce the stumbling blocks placed in our paths by our own egos.

In his book *The Beautiful Way of Life*, Charles Lelly wrote,

"There is something in humility which strangely exalts the heart."
—St. Augustine

"Even though our starting point may be the consideration of ordinary things, our objective is to go beyond the physical—to penetrate the object and find the source of its beauty, its form, its very existence! We point to something greater than the sum of its parts. The implication is that a mysterious wonder is embedded in every particle of the universe and that our purpose in living is constantly to increase our awareness of the Source of our being."

Think, for a moment, on an analogy. As a furnace purifies gold, so may life purify souls. When a man is born into the world, he is like a piece of charcoal. It is soft and amorphous, so when rays of sunlight fall upon it, it reflects nothing. Then, in the crucible it is subjected to such intense pressure and heat that the charcoal is transformed into a diamond. The natural diamond is appraised by the master craftsman; its inner design is determined, and the stone is then cut with many facets to become the precious and radiant jewel. Now, when the sun's rays fall upon it, the colors of the rainbow are reflected, creating a magnificent symphony of beauty and radiance. So it is with a man between the time he is born into the material world, where he is "cut and chipped" by life's experiences and the choices he makes, and then born again into heaven where the humility his soul has achieved begins to reflect the divine light of God. Maybe this was God's purpose for creating the crucible called earth.

One of the major lessons to learn while on earth is that building our heaven is up to us. Emanuel Swedenborg wrote that we will not be in heaven until heaven is in us. So, how may we begin to build that heaven within? True humility can lead us into a prayerful attitude, and prayer can bring us in tune with the infinite. There is a real mystical power in prayer, and it works! Through your prayer times and your attunement with God, you are increasing your own spiritual light. You are building a better expression of life in every way and you are attracting exactly what you are building—more light! There is a larger power you are touching. There is a larger life you are building. Prayer can make difficult tasks easier, can consecrate every effort to a more noble use, and produce successful results. The prayer life is a life of humility and gratitude and is made sacred by the intimacy of the soul with its Creator.

Have you observed that there are persons who seem to have modified their egos, those who desire to give rather than to get? In a sense, they have become "unselfed"! Becoming "unselfed" opens the door to communication with God. The person who relies on wisdom, or beauty, or skill, or money tends to shut

"There is no holiness without humility."
—Thomas Fuller

God out. But the person who is humble and grateful for these God-given blessings opens the door to a kind of heaven on earth here and now. It is important to free ourselves of self-will and surrender to God's will. Can you see how letting go of ego-centeredness can help one become a clear channel for God's love and wisdom to flow through, just as sunlight pours through an open window? Ralph Waldo Trine writes: *"Within yourself lies the cause of whatever enters into your life. To come into the full realization of your own awakened interior powers, is to be able to condition your life in exact accord with what you would have it."*

In humility we have an opportunity to learn from one another, for it enables us to open to each other and see things from the other person's point of view. We may also share our views with the other person freely. It is by humility that we avoid the sins of pride and intolerance and avoid religious strife. Muhammad, the Prophet of Islam, stated, *"Whoever has in his heart even so much as a rice grain of pride cannot enter into paradise."* Humility opens the door to the realms of the spirit, and to research and progress in religion. Humility is the gateway to knowledge.

LAW 5

Failing to plan is planning to fail
—Benjamin Franklin

If you decide to drive from Maine to California, one of the first things you will probably do is study a road map. You will see that there's a choice of routes you may take to reach your destination. If you're in a hurry, you may choose the route that will get you there the quickest. You can then estimate how long the trip will take and plan a more accurate arrival time.

What holds true for a trip holds equally true for the accomplishment of any goal. Without a road map, your mind can wander aimlessly and be ineffective in reaching out for solutions. Through formulating a plan to achieve your goals, in much the same way as you would use a road map, and by being systematic and studying the various alternatives, you focus the direction of your thoughts and find yourself capable of reaching almost any reasonable goal you please.

In *How to Succeed*, Brian Adams wrote, *"Plans are guideposts to success. Success arrives by design; failure by the lack of it. Plans are the guide posts along life's road to success; without them the road is an unsure and rocky one. Poorly devised plans will never harvest riches. Achievements can be no greater than the undertakings. If your plans are sketchy and your aims low, you can never hope to achieve high rewards. When you pursue goals in a scientific way you succeed more times than fail."*

Shakespeare wrote, *"There is a destiny that will shape our end, rough hew it how we will."* This statement seems to mean that there may be an ultimate goal, or a divine plan, established for each person who comes into this world. Now, the big question is, How can I discern the personal path that will bring me the fulfillment of my divine plan? That's a good question! The answer to it is another intriguing question: What is the best thing I can do for myself and for all concerned in the particular circumstances of my life with respect to the spiritual ideal?

The spiritual ideal refers to purpose, intent, desire, motivation, incentive, and the "spirit in which you do anything." You may realize already that life isn't totally made up of big things. It is also made up of seconds, pennies, ounces, atoms, grains of sand, blades of grass, strands of hair, etc. We, as human beings, are also made up of many things; the most effective things in our daily living are our thoughts and feelings. And every single thought and feeling contributes toward bringing you closer to your heartfelt desire, or builds a roadblock in your path! Can you see why planning is so important in your life? The American president Abraham Lincoln said, *"I will study and get ready and some day my chance will come."* Excellent awareness!

An old stonemason was laying a rock wall, which, because it looked natural, was a thing of great beauty. The owner of the estate, while walking in his fields, noticed that the stonemason took as much care in placing the small stones as he did in placing the large ones. So, the estate owner walked over to the worker and asked, "Old man, wouldn't that wall go up faster if you used more of the larger stones?"

"Aye, most certainly, Sir," the old man replied. "But you see, I'm building for lasting beauty and strength, not for speed." The stonemason thought for a moment and then added, "Sir, these stones are like events in the lives of men. Many small ones are needed to support the fewer big ones and hold them in place. If

"Four steps to achievement: plan purposefully, prepare prayerfully, proceed positively, pursue persistently."
—William A. Word

you leave out the small stones, the big ones will have no support and they may fall."

Many people know what they want out of life, but few turn their dreams into a carefully planned successful journey. They often depend on lucky breaks or the help of others. When they fail, they may often say of those more successful, "They just happen to know the right people," or "They get all the lucky breaks." They fail to realize that planning for success has no more to do with luck or knowing the right people than does planning carefully for a cross-country trip. It's true that when you start moving toward your goal, you'll meet people who can help you advance. But you'll know that you earned those breaks because you had a goal and a plan in place to help you achieve that goal.

To develop a workable plan of action, mentally visualize the things you want to accomplish. Jot them down across a sheet of paper, then list the steps necessary to accomplish your plan. Long-term objectives, of course, may involve more steps and more elaborate planning, but the principle remains the same. When you know what you want to achieve, create a plan for getting there. Once you have a basic plan, devote some time often to adjusting it as you gather new information. Then follow through with the plan until you achieve your objectives.

Stephen Covey, author of *The Seven Habits of Highly Effective People*, recommends that you "begin (planning) with the end in mind." The best planning encompasses what you want to accomplish and where you want to end up. Whether it is a special project or a simple daily routine, begin by setting a goal that takes into account the steps needed to reach it. If your goal is composed of many levels, you might want to prioritize them. Make a list, giving them a rating of A, B, or C. Then tackle the A's first. Professional planners have shown that tasks written down are much more likely to be completed.

The following guidelines may help you to achieve your goal:

1. Think of your goal not as some vague and nebulous idea but in clear and specific terms.
2. Outline your goal in writing in detail.
3. Keep your goal in the forefront of your mind by reviewing it almost every day.
4. Learn everything you can that relates to your goal.
5. Be willing to work as hard as you can toward achieving your goal when the opportunity comes along.
6. Give the universe an opportunity to assist in achieving your goal by affirming, "This or something better!"
7. Stay open to receive all possibilities for achieving your goal.

Remember, *"failing to plan is planning to fail."* Just as a road map is an indispensable tool for a trip, a plan is an indispensable tool when you travel the journey of life toward your goals. Follow your plan to a more successful life!

Spotlights!

1. Use daily prayer and meditation to create the inner harmony and peace that can free you from stress and frustration.
2. True peace is a quality you carry within yourself, regardless of external circumstances.
3. Surprising and interesting things happen to those who keep their ears and their minds open and alert!
4. Be willing to look at yourself honestly and courageously. Every day!
5. There is no such thing as a problem without a gift for you in its hands!
6. *"Wisdom is not to be obtained from textbooks, but must be coined out of human experience in the flame of life."* —Morris Raphael Cohen
7. To become wise, we must be willing to suspend our personal beliefs about something, set aside prejudices, and think with an open mind.
8. Humility helps us be open to one another and provides an opportunity to see things from the other person's point of view.
9. No one can say in advance just what discoveries may be made by proper research in the science of the soul.
10. Clarify what you want. Create a plan of action that delineates your path to the goal. Avoid irrelevant side tracks!

Living the Law!

Rules for Being Human

You will learn lessons.
  We're all enrolled in a full-time school called "life on planet Earth."
  Every person and incident is your teacher.
There are no mistakes—only lessons.
  "Failures" are the stepping stones to "success."
A lesson is repeated until learned.
  It is presented in various forms until you learn it—then you go to the next lesson.

If you don't learn easy lessons, they get harder.

Pain is one way the universe gets your attention.

You'll know you've learned a lesson when your actions change.

Only action turns knowledge to wisdom.

"There" is no better than "here."

When "there" becomes "here," you'll find another "there" that again looks better than "here."

Others are only mirrors.

You can only love or hate something in another that reflects something you love or hate in yourself.

Your life is up to you.

Life provides the canvas; you do the painting.

Your answers lie inside you.

All you need to do is look, listen, and trust.

You'll tend to forget all this.

You can remember anytime you wish.

—author unknown

Week Four

LAW 1

Beautiful thoughts build a beautiful soul
—John M. Templeton

Have you ever thought of beauty as a necessity in your life? Beauty isn't only pleasant to the eye, but it is an essence that helps us to live more productive and happy lives. When we are receptive to seeing and feeling the beauty around us, we become more attuned to the creative Presence of God within.

How would you describe beauty? Some people say beauty is the quality that pleases and gratifies us because of its harmony, excellence, and truth. When we look at an object, it appears beautiful to us if it is in balance and proportion and exhibits order and continuity. These qualities stimulate the same qualities that abide deep within our being—within our soul—and we recognize the common truth of beauty within and without.

Beauty is inherent within the soul of each person, and this beauty can be made more apparent as we affirm it within our life and world and focus our minds to comprehend more clearly. It has been said that *"beautiful thoughts build a beautiful soul."* This is a great truth that we can actually observe in our daily life. For a moment, pause and ask yourself these questions:

What is it that makes the difference between a tiny ant and the small grains of sand the ant uses to build the little mound of dirt around its hole in the earth? It isn't merely cell construction, but something in the cells themselves. It is the beauty of the inner life in majestic expression.

What is it that enables an animal of microscopic dimensions, after having been frozen in Antarctic ice for years, to resume activity as soon as the ice melts? It is the beautiful marvel called life.

What is it that makes the tiny mustard seed sprout and grow into a mature plant? It is that same mystery and marvel called life. And just what is this life? It is said to be the expression of

"The famous Cambridge astronomer Sir Arthur Eddington tried to unite quantum physics and relativity with what he called his own "mysticism," his conviction that the universe worth studying is the one within us. He suggested that a person should use 'the higher faculties of his nature, so that they are no longer blind alleys but open into a spiritual world—a world partly of illusion, no doubt, but in which he lives no less than in the world of illusion, revealed by the senses.'"
—John M. Templeton, *The Humble Approach*

*"Such as are thy habit-
ual thoughts, such also
will be the character of
thy soul–for the soul is
dyed by thy thoughts."*
—Marcus Aurelius

*"Every year of my life I
grow more convinced
that it is wisest and
best to fix our attention
on the beautiful and
the good, and dwell as
little as possible on the
evil and the false."*
—Richard Cecil

*"A man's inner nature
is revealed by what he
praises–a man is
self-judged by what he
says to others. Thus a
man is judged by his
standards, by what he
considers the best. And
you can't find a more
crucial test. It reveals
the soul."*
–Hugh Black

God that manifests itself as animation, activity, vigor, and beauty in all of the varieties of life. A poppy sprouts, buds, blooms, and returns to the soil a poppy still. Yet, a person can be born in seeming poverty and unenlightenment, but by mastering and controlling his destiny through his thoughts, feelings, actions, and choices, he can rise as the master over limitations; and at the end of his incarnation, he may make the transition as a more spiritually evolved soul. Isn't this beautiful potential worth the effort to use rightly the tremendous gift and power of your mind?

There are certain good ideas, or *laws of life*, that we need to learn, practice, and cooperate with to lead a happy and successful life. Seeing the good in everyone and everything is one such idea. Recognizing and appreciating the beauty that is all around us is another. These ideas, when believed in, begin to work a kind of magical transformation in our lives. For example, if we look at ourselves and find that we could be more loving individuals, we may entertain in our minds the idea of love. We may give our minds and hearts to this idea. We may let it have its way with us as if it were some kind of living entity. We give ourselves to the good idea of love.

It is a law of life that whatever we give our attention to, and believe in, tends to become our experience. A West African Yoruba oracle poem states, *"Anyone who sees beauty and does not look at it will soon be poor."* And the Vietnamese poet The Lu sang, *"I am but passionately in love with beauty, in its myriad shapes and guises."* The law of good ideas instructs us to begin to practice the art of giving our attention and belief to such good ideas. As we practice abiding by the ideas of abundance, wisdom, strength, love, faith, imagination, life, and health, we begin to see positive and distinct changes for the better transforming our lives.

Is your life beautiful? Do you live in surroundings that you have made beautiful through your own unique, creative ideas? To expect and lovingly require beauty to be apparent in all areas of your life is to be deeply loving to yourself, your soul, your world, and shows reverence to God and all of life.

There is always something beautiful to be found, right where you are, if you will look for it. Concentrate your thoughts on the good, the beautiful, and the true things of life. This positive, loving attitude of mind can help you perceive the presence of God active in your life and put into operation the divine magic that can open doors to greater usefulness and joy.

LAW 2

Progress depends on diligence and perseverance
—John M. Templeton

Do you realize that one of the most precious resources we have is our time? According to the *Wall Street Journal*'s book *On Management: The Best of the Manager's Journal*, the most important aspect of being a role model and leader is how we handle our own personal time. The book described the importance of gathering information and its influence on decision-making, and states that we must consider seriously the impact of our own work habits on those around us.

In order to manage time effectively, we must be able to prioritize our activities on a daily basis. One of the keys to time management is the quality of endurance. In most athletic competition, it is not always the most talented player who wins, but the one who's the best at the finish line. As expressed in the book of *Ecclesiastes*, chapter 9, *"The race is not to the swift, nor the battle to the strong."* And the well-known American actress Helen Hayes once said, *"Nothing is any good without endurance."*

These statements seem to emphasize diligence and perseverance. The ability to endure is an important ingredient in realizing personal success, in business as well as in other areas of our lives. Often, we resolve to exercise regularly, lose weight, spend more time with our family, or eat more nutritiously. The commitment, however, is often forgotten because, over the long haul, we may fail to demonstrate the endurance needed to reach our goal.

There are so many avenues of opportunity where we can develop our own unique talents and abilities. Whether it's a career in the arts, sports, business, or the professions, the way to perfect our skills is through diligent practice and study on a consistent basis. This means making the commitment to develop our self-discipline and to persist and endure until the goal is met. This commitment to "finish the race" may not always be easy. There are often occasions when we may be tempted to spend valuable time pursuing those interests that give pleasure while neglecting our long-range priorities.

The ancient Chinese sage Lao Tzu set down laws of effective

"No man is able to make progress when he is wavering between opposite things."
—Epictetus

"Diligence is to be particularly cultivated by us, it is to be constantly exerted; it is capable of effecting almost everything."
—Cicero

living that he discovered after years of meditation and careful
observation of the evidences of life around him. He called his
invaluable teaching the *Tao Te Ching*, or *How Things Work*. Many
of his teachings reflected the effects of diligence and perseverance. One meaningful example is described in "The Ripple
Effect" from the *Tao*:

*"Do you want to be a positive influence in the world? First, get your
own life in order. Ground yourself in the single principle so that your
behavior is wholesome and effective. If you do that, you will earn
respect and be a powerful influence.*

*"Your behavior influences others through a ripple effect. A ripple
effect works because everyone influences everyone else. Powerful people
are powerful influences. If your life works, you influence your family.
If your family works, your family influences the community. If your
community works, your community influences the nation. If your
nation works, your nation influences the world. If your world works,
the ripple effect spreads throughout the cosmos. Remember that your
influence begins with you and ripples outward. So be sure that your
influence is both potent and wholesome. How do I know that this
works? All growth spreads outward from a fertile and potent nucleus.
You are a nucleus."*

Doesn't this "bigger picture" offer inspiration for diligence
and perseverance! In order to realize the wonderful feeling of
accomplishment that comes with meeting our goals, the ability
to endure hardship is essential. The statement *"No one ever said
it would be easy"* is no less true for being a familiar saying. So,
hang in there! Don't give up easily! You have the ability to make
striking progress in the pursuit of your goals. If we truly want to
be all we are capable of being, we must be committed, and we
must prepare ourselves to endure—to be a strong finisher in the
race of life.

LAW 3

Love thy neighbor as thyself
—Matthew 19:19

The actor-humorist Groucho Marx once joked that he would
never belong to any club that would accept him as a member.
For people, though, the inability to appreciate themselves is no

laughing matter. People who suffer from low self-esteem often resign themselves to a life of painful alienation.

The belief that you are less worthy, less attractive, less intelligent, or less good than another in any way sets you apart from those who would love you and would accept your love in return. Feelings of inadequacy, shame, and self-pity can consume your energies in an emotional tornado that drives destructively through all of your relationships. The devastation that often occurs as you live out your self-doubts serves only to reinforce the beliefs that you hold. A vicious cycle is then perpetuated—a self-fulfilling prophecy. It's a law of life that says, *what you send forth, you get back.*" Some people grow up believing so many limitations about themselves that, after a while, their lives actually begin to manifest those limitations. We may hear ourselves saying things that we accept as truth when, in fact, they are misbeliefs that have turned into our truths. How many times have you heard someone, a friend perhaps, say, "I can't help the way I am; I've always been this way"; or "It's my nature and in my genes and can't be changed"; or "My family background is responsible for my personality"; or "Well, I'm the result of my culture and times"? All of these statements are untruths about the person speaking them.

If you believe you must always be the way you have always been, you are arguing against growth. If you are convinced that your family is responsible for the kind of person you are today, you are trapped in that cycle. The belief that society is shaping your life is a part of the illusion that you are formed by a "bigger and better" social force. If you so choose, you have the power to reject behaviors, attitudes, and beliefs coming at you that you find objectionable. Although you can't eliminate the negative influences that were a part of your childhood, you can decide whether or not you will allow them to persist.

The human mind often breaks reality down into simple forms. Black or white, good or bad, me or you. This either/or way of thinking may confuse some into believing that it's not possible to treat another with care, while at the same time giving care to ourselves. With cultural traditions that value love and thoughtfulness to other people, many are convinced it is selfish to be considerate of their own feelings and needs. While you may have been taught that you should *love thy neighbor as thyself,*" in truth, to love others, it is helpful to love yourself also.

It is important for the scales of loving human relations to be balanced. This can happen when each individual is honored as being of value. If you're in the habit of putting yourself down,

"What is love in the spiritual sense? . . . We can see that this love is not something far-off, nor is it anything that can come to us. It is already a part of our being, already established within us; and more than that, it is universal and impersonal. As this universal and impersonal love flows out from us, we begin to love our neighbor, because it is impossible to feel this love for God within us and not love our fellow man."—Joel S. Goldsmith

"The love of thy neighbor hath its bounds in each man's love of himself."
—St. Augustine

"The transcendent importance of love and goodwill in all human relations is shown by their mighty beneficent effect upon the individual and society."
—George D. Birkoff

"Just remember the world is not a play-ground but a school-room. Life is not a hol-iday but an education. One eternal lesson for us all: to teach us how better we should love."
—Barbara Jordan

you may make it difficult for others to accept you. Holding your-self in healthy self-respect is different from being narcissistic. Narcissus, the figure in Greek mythology who spent his days pining after his own reflection in a pool, neglected everyone else in his life because he was so preoccupied with himself. He was like those who spend hours trying to get their hair perfect or their makeup flawless so that others will think them beauti-ful. The underlying assumption is that they're not good enough as they are, that they must alter and improve themselves in order to be acceptable in other's eyes.

True self-esteem belongs to the one who looks in the mirror, not to criticize or admire, but to see past physical appearance into the essential child of God reflected there. The one who moves past fear and discomfort to look deeply and lovingly into his or her own eyes should be able to share that look of love fully with another. Accept the person you are, risk sharing your-self with others, and then watch how you grow.

LAW 4

To be wronged is nothing unless you continue to remember it
—Confucius

"A kind speech and for-giveness is better than alms followed by injury."
—Qur'an

"Codependency" and "dysfunction" are two important words in today's psychological vocabulary. Support groups are every-where for every problem—Sexaholics Anonymous, Workaholics Anonymous, Neurotics Anonymous, Victims Anonymous, Overeaters Anonymous, and Alcoholics Anonymous—to name a few. It isn't unusual for one person to be in several recovery programs at the same time.

Individually, most of these groups are indeed worthwhile. It is vital that people stop annihilating themselves with alcohol, drugs, gluttony, or promiscuity. It is also important to get drug addicts off the streets and into programs that can offer cures and rehabilitation. It is critical for people to come to terms with themselves and release the anguish of having been sexually molested, physically abused, or psychologically tormented. The Unity School of Christianity in Unity Village, Missouri, U.S.A., offers this maxim, *"If you can feel it, you can heal it."* And awareness certainly plays a major role in healing a situation.

At the same time, it is vital to address the common-sense approach expressed by Confucius, *"To be wronged is nothing unless you continue to remember it."* This advice may be more important than the recovery craze. If we can let our past remain in the past, we are not compelled to endlessly re-enact it.

Yes, it hurts to be wronged. It can be maddening, infuriating, and unfair. But repeatedly reliving what happened a day, week, month, or even years ago is not healing but "rehearsing." It becomes a process of practicing old routines, rather than learning new responses or thinking in fresh channels. When we continue to pick at emotional scars, we are indulging in useless, unnecessary suffering instead of getting on with our life.

On occasion, it can be a healing experience to recall and face traumatic experiences. This type of remembering can enable us to see past events for what they were and release them, instead of dreading some future time when there may be hurting or embarrassing revelations.

Forgiveness can be a powerful healing agent. Forgiveness is a process of giving up the false for the true, erasing error from mind and body and life. Forgive yourself. Forgive others. Forgive everything! Forgiveness sometimes involves a flight of imagination—being able to understand the influences that may have shaped your oppressor's behavior. If we seek to understand, to the best of our ability, where another person may be coming from, observe what situations may be prevalent in his life, and put forth the effort to "walk a mile in his shoes." We may be less quick to take offense at what may be directed toward us. Once you can comprehend the dynamics behind the abuse, you may be more ready to forgive. An old African proverb says, *"he who forgives ends the quarrel."* Are you willing to be the instigator of such a positive action?

Understand that forgiving does not mean excusing. But dwelling on past slights or offenses contracts us rather than expands us. If we want to become a fully functional person, whole and free in every way, we must release the pain from the past, reframe the experience, and renew our allegiance to life. This thought, feeling and action can take you back to your true purpose of living, and you can walk through the gateway to freedom from past miseries. Are you prepared and willing to get on with the purpose of your life and "let go and let God" handle everything else? Can you learn to love every person on earth without exception?

"Nobody will be able to forgive me but myself."
—Ding Ling, Chinese writer

"Let us forget and forgive injuries."—Miguel de Cervantes

"Only the brave know how to forgive. . . . A coward never forgave; it is not his nature."
—Laurence Sterne

❖

LAW 5

Enthusiasm facilitates achievement
–John M. Templeton

George Joe was a high school student in a town in northwest central Texas (U.S.A.), an area famous for its love of high school football. In small schools, there often aren't enough players to field separate teams for defense, offense, and special teams so each person must do double duty or even triple duty. George Joe did quadruple duty. He was the quarterback on offense, running and passing the ball expertly; a cornerback on defense; kick returner on receiving teams; and punter on kicking teams. Even more remarkable was the fact that he was usually the *smallest* man on the field, standing barely five feet, six inches tall, and weighing no more than one hundred forty pounds. He didn't possess great speed, although he was quick and agile.

How did a small boy hold so many jobs on a team that had a history of winning year after year? He had a great love for the game and competition and exhibited boundless enthusiasm. He poured every ounce of his energy and ability into each play, and he did it joyfully. George Joe was fifty percent inspiration and fifty percent perspiration and a thrill to watch!

A story is told of another young boy who wanted to become a radio announcer and entertainer, but he stuttered so badly it was painful to listen to his attempts to carry on a conversation, let alone hear him perform in public or in a broadcast. A career in radio seemed impossible, and no one gave him much hope. However, he was not to be deterred by the lack of confidence of others. He read that a very famous person in Greek history with a similar problem had gone to the beach, filled his mouth with pebbles, and shouted into the surf until he overcame his disability. Although this young man had no beach or pebbles near at hand, he filled his mouth with marbles and worked day after day until he, too, overcame his problem. Dedication and enthusiasm eliminated the difficulty this man faced and today he is a successful television entertainer.

One of the most respected and famous former American presidents, Theodore Roosevelt, had a vision of American ships being able to go from the Pacific to the Atlantic ocean and back without having to make the arduous trip around the tip of the

"Are you in earnest? Seize this very minute . . . what you can do, or dream you can, begin it; boldness has genius, power and magic in it. Only engage, and then the mind grows heated. Begin it, and the work will be completed."
–J. W. von Goethe

South American continent. There were many difficulties to overcome. First was the opposition of his own countrymen who lacked the vision to foresee what a great boon to shipping the proposed canal would be. There was also the opposition of other world leaders who didn't wish to see the United States in control of such a project and the South American leaders who opposed the intrusion of the United States in their domain. Teddy Roosevelt was not deterred by any of these problems. He was enthusiastic about his vision and through negotiation with the governments of Columbia and Panama gained the right to build a canal across the Isthmus of Panama from Colon on the Atlantic coast to Panama City on the Pacific coast.

The problems did not end there, and the whole effort was almost brought down by mosquitoes carrying yellow fever. President Roosevelt licked the problem in his typical fashion. Medicine was found to fight the disease and insecticides to fight the insects. He wanted the canal to be a showplace to attract tourists as well as shipping, and he realized that people will not visit places where their health is at risk. When it was completed, the Panama Canal was a model of sanitation, a tribute to the enthusiasm and determination of Theodore Roosevelt.

It has been said that "to enthuse" means "to fill with spirit," and that spirit of enthusiasm is awaiting release or manifestation. Enthusiasm can be harnessed and activated. It can be transferred from one person to another. The energy of enthusiasm is similar to a radio signal that carries around the world. It can be transmitted and received; and when enthusiasm is shared by a group of people, it can be potentiated to a higher degree of power.

The boy who loved football, the boy who dreamed of becoming a radio announcer, and a president of the United States understood, and profited from, an important law of life: that *enthusiasm facilitates achievement.*

Spotlights!

1. Think about ways you can develop a loving, empowering attitude toward yourself.
2. Know that you are a beautiful and valuable human resource and deserving of love and respect.
3. Spend some time each day in total, complete *awe* at the beauty within and around you!
4. Make a personal choice to release past angers, hurts, and bitterness.

"From the glow of enthusiasm I let the melody escape. I pursue it. Breathless I catch up with it. It flies again, it disappears, it plunges into a chaos of diverse emotions. I catch it again, I seize it, I embrace it with delight. . . . I multiply it by modulations and at the last, I triumph in the first theme. There is the whole symphony."
—Ludwig van Beethoven

"Talent for talent's sake is a bauble and a show. Talent working with joy in a cause of universal truth lifts the possessor to a new power as a benefactor."
—Ralph Waldo Emerson

5. Remember that emotional pain is an experience through which you can learn and grow—it will not destroy you. You have the power to overcome!

6. Love should and can be unconditional. Affirm, "I can be loved for myself!"

7. Are you able to distinguish your feelings from your thoughts?

8. Think about some ways that you can reach out to a loved one and build a bridge over past hurts instead of a wall?

9. Enthusiasm can be created, harnessed, and activated; and it can be transferred from one person to another!

10. To develop a plan of action, begin to visualize mentally what you desire to accomplish.

Living the Law!

We know of the rich rewards that come through giving and receiving love; through being diligent and persevering in our heartfelt goals; through releasing old ideas and emotions that may have held us in bondage; through the cleansing power of forgiveness; and through the forward thrust of enthusiasm!

The capacity to feel and experience these things exists within us. Few of us choose to live our lives in a private room, closing out the rest of the world. It is the open-hearted, open-minded person who sees life as a real adventure. The person who is open to new experiences and sees them as part of the growing process can face life with anticipation rather than fear. When we are open to life, we see the potentiality for good in others and in ourself.

This week, would you pause for a moment before you leave the house each day, take several deep breaths and close your eyes? Remember a place of serene beauty that you may feel especially close to. Breathe in the beauty of that place. Allow yourself to feel the essence of that beauty in your thoughts and your emotions. Feel yourself becoming free with the freedom of Spirit and savor the joy in life and in your personal relations with others.

Envision yourself rising above any troubled state, letting go of preconceived ideas and releasing any perceived unhappiness that may have been caused by the words or actions of other persons. Decide and declare that you are not bound in personal consciousness. Lift your thoughts to God and feel the freedom of Spirit. Complete this time of communion with this affirmation:

I give the Creative Source of all there is the gift of my attention to the activities of this day. I do this by looking for, and dwelling upon, the good in my world. I know when I look for the beautiful and the good–in everything and everyone–this is what I find. I give God full attention as I perform my daily tasks and serve in whatever way I am called upon to serve. As I give the gift of my attention, I become more aware of my oneness with Spirit and I go forward confidently.

Week Five

❖

LAW 1

By giving you grow
—John M. Templeton

After serving for more than eighteen years in the U. S. Army, Sam was dishonorably discharged for drinking and fighting. Depressed and unable even to imagine himself holding a steady job, he soon exhausted the little money he had managed to save during his Army career and became a "street person."

"Living on the streets was worse than Vietnam," Sam recalls. "At least in Vietnam you usually knew who your enemy was. On the streets, you never knew who might knock you out and steal your shoes right off your feet!"

Early one afternoon, while waiting for lunch to be served at a church-run center, Sam answered a call for volunteers to help move some furniture and roll up a rug that needed replacing. It was the first time he had done anything for anyone but himself in quite some time. It really felt good.

As he was leaving the building after lunch, Sam noticed a heavy growth of moss on the roof that threatened to damage the shingles. He volunteered to remove it. "You're welcome to help, but you know we can't pay you," the supervisor said. Sam went ahead with the work anyway, again experiencing an unexpected good feeling.

Sam developed the habit of offering his services whenever he heard of a job he thought he could do. It wasn't long before the center needed a volunteer typist. Sam learned to type in the Army and offered his services if someone would help him purchase a pair of reading glasses. Money was found to pay for the glasses, and Sam became an enthusiastic office volunteer.

Soon after he began working in the office, Sam moved from the streets to a spare bedroom in the home of one of his co-workers. Then, without his asking for it, the manager of the center offered Sam a small salary and increased his responsibil-

"Giving of yourself, learning to be tolerant, giving recognition and approval to others, remaining flexible enough to mature and learn—yields happiness, harmony, contentment and productivity. These are the qualities of a rich life."
—Jack C. Yewell

ities in the office. Another co-worker offered Sam a good used automobile for a reasonable price, with payments he could easily afford.

Today, Sam manages a community food closet operated by the same organization to which he first volunteered his services. He rents his own apartment and is planning to marry. Sam believes that the positive changes in his life started when the people at the center began to believe in him. Others believed in Sam, it's true, but it seems clear that Sam was the one who took the first step. With his first gift of willing service, Sam began to establish himself in the creative, prospering flow of abundant life. He began to *see himself in a new light.*

We can all experience a similar reward as Sam, almost regardless of our circumstances. No matter how well or how poorly our lives seem to be going, we can become part of a greater flow of good and increase our awareness by doing something more than we have to do—by giving of ourselves. One of the keys to prosperity is realizing that true prosperity doesn't come by *getting* more—it comes by *giving* more! We can prosper by emphasizing what we are giving rather than by concentrating on what we are getting.

The parable of the talents is a good analogy of what happens when we give. When we merely try to hold on to what is given or entrusted to us, life may seem to take away even that. But when we choose to *use* what life has given us, the return of abundance can include friendship, companionship, financial blessings, homes, transportation, and security in wonderful ways. The universe holds nothing back from the one who lovingly and sincerely gives.

As we become aware of our potential for giving, there is no limit to the good we can receive. Giving can naturally lead to actions that are positive experiences for all concerned. Think of some ways you can use your mind, your energy, and your time. Are you using the hours of the day in the best and most creative ways? Is there something constructive that you would like to do that could add to the good of the world? Remember, "little things can mean a lot." Plant one seed and it can yield many fruits. This is how nature operates, and we are a part of nature. Look around you from the perspective of determining opportunities to express your talents and abilities. Find some way in which you may give, and then do it with a loving heart.

Stabilize your faith in true prosperity by frequently affirming a declaration of your faith: "I accept the abundant supply that God is unfailingly providing. I give thanks for this abundant

"I don't know what your destiny will be, but one thing I know: the only ones among you who will be really happy are those who have sought and found how to serve."
—Albert Schweitzer

"So far as the human mind can shake off selfishness and act from a sacred regard to truth, justice and duty, so far will men not only be virtuous, but fearless in virtue."
—Sarah Joseph Hale, *Sketches of American Character*

good by giving generously of all that I have to give—my time, talents, and treasure."

❖

LAW 2

Lost time is never found again
—Benjamin Franklin

When the moments that make up our lives go unappreciated, we may find our capacity to experience and enjoy diminished. It is *our* own life that is passing away as slippery and elusive as mercury.

"No person will occasion to complain of the want of time who never loses any."
—Thomas Jefferson

To understand time is to be aware of how it operates in our lives, for time is a subjective experience, different for everyone. We've all experienced how each minute seems to stretch interminably when we're unhappy or when the task at hand is unpleasant; yet we're also aware how fast time races by when we're engaged in a creative and useful project. Many people have also had those moments of total absorption when the clock's minute and hour hands seem frozen—with reality compressed into the experience of *now*.

"Have a time and place for everything, and do everything in its time and place, and you will accomplish more, but have far more leisure than those who are always hurrying, as if vainly attempting to overtake time that has been lost."
—Tyron Edwards

Recently, there was a magazine article on making good use of time. *"If you had a bank that credited your account each morning with U.S. currency in the amount of $86,400, and every evening cancelled whatever part of the amount you failed to use, what would you do? Of course, you would draw out every cent of the deposit!*

"Well, time is just such a bank. Every morning it credits you with 86,400 seconds. Every night it writes off as lost whatever of those seconds you have failed to invest to good purpose. It carries no balance forward to the next day. It allows no overdrafts. Each day it opens a new account with you. Each night it burns the record for the day.

"If you fail to use the day's deposit, the loss is yours. There is no going back. There is no drawing against tomorrow. You must live in the present—on today's deposit. Invest it so as to get the most in health, happiness and service."

While it's true that we all have the same twenty-four hours available to us in each day, we can manipulate our perception of time in order to alter our relationship to it. Dead and boring time can be revived by the creation of a deadline; and the pressure of an unyielding deadline is often relieved by the promise of a vacation.

Time, like money, can be valuable precisely because it *is* limited—we are all allotted a finite amount. Even if our time on earth were unlimited, we would still need to use it well in order for it to retain its value. Only by putting the amount of time we have to good use can we find success and satisfaction in our lives.

Time is like the cement that turns over and over in a concrete mixer. The cement exists only as a potential until the operator opens the chute and lets the mixture pour into a form where it can harden into something useful. Time wasted is the concrete that never gets poured, or that gets poured from the chute but finds no form to contain it. We can prosper if we learn to shape our lives within increments of time. Through efficient use of time, we are more able to take stock of ourselves and express the inner genius in tangible ways that can help others and bring joy and satisfaction to our lives. In learning time-management skills, we discover strategies for developing new responses that give us more hours in every day.

One of the best strategies for giving form to our time is to establish long-term and short-term goals for ourselves. What do we hope to accomplish? What steps need to be taken today to fulfill tomorrow's goal? Each day, make a list. Use every minute because if you don't, you'll lose it! And the time lost today is gone forever!

"An inch of time is an inch of gold. But an inch of gold cannot buy an inch of time."
—Chinese proverb

"I must govern the clock, not be governed by it."
—Golda Meir

L AW 3

The family that prays together, stays together
—Common Saying

"The family that prays together, stays together" is a common saying most of us have heard so many times that the words may have become meaningless. Yet, there must be some truth to this statement because it has helped so many.

What images come to your mind as you think of a family praying together? It might be a family of pilgrims giving thanks that their table is full, or a modern family in the face of a crisis. How can the average family apply this principle to their lives and why would they want to?

"Ziyad, the slave of Aiyash, Son of Abu Rabi'a said, 'I am more afraid of being hindered from prayer than of being denied an answer to my prayer.'"—al-Jahiz, Arab philosopher

"My lot is low, my purpose high; but I am confident of one thing, that God will be gratified to hear me, though fools may laugh."
—Tulsidas, Indian poet

"We (Allah) are nearer to him [man] than his jugular vein."
—Qur'an

"He prayeth best who loveth best. All things great and small; For the dear God who loveth us, He made and loveth all."
—Samuel Taylor Coleridge, "The Ancient Mariner"

"I pray to heaven to bestow the best of all blessings on this house and all that hereafter shall inhabit it. May none but honest and wise men rule under this roof."
—John Adams, inscription in the United States White House

Let's take a look at this old adage and begin by examining prayer. What is prayer? *Webster's Dictionary* gives one definition of prayer as to "entreat or petition." This implies communication, knowing what we want and need and learning to ask for it. Prayer plays an important role in most of the religions of the world and is expressed in a variety of ways. Charles Fillmore, cofounder of Unity School of Christianity in the United States, speaks of prayer as *"entering the silence."* He says, *"There is a quiet place within us all and by silently saying over and over, 'peace be still,' we shall enter that quiet place and a great stillness will pervade our whole being."* So to pray could mean to go into the silent place within ourselves and commune with something wise within us, the result of which can bring peace.

The silent communion can look different to each of us. It isn't so important how we enter the silence as it is that we do. In his booklet *The Golden Key*, Emmet Fox described prayer as *"the golden key to harmony and happiness. Scientific prayer will enable you to get yourself, or anyone else, out of any difficulty. . . . The ability to draw on this power is not the special prerogative of the mystic or the saint, as is so often supposed, or even of the highly trained practitioner. Everyone has this ability. . . . This is because in scientific prayer it is God who works, and not you, and so your particular limitations or weaknesses are of no account in the process. . . . As for the actual method of working, like all fundamental things, it is simplicity itself. All you have to do is this: Stop thinking about the difficulty, whatever it is, and think about God instead."*

When we pray with our families, whether they consist of our parents, brothers and sisters, or a family of our closest friends, we may be going together to a silent place of wisdom and peace. It is an experience that can mend hurt feelings, calm anger, encourage love and forgiveness, and help us to remember how important we are to one another.

For a family, prayer can happen when there are no longer words to speak. If you've ever come home from school feeling hurt or afraid and someone has quietly held your hand, you have entered into the silent place together. Maybe, when you were a child, you sat with your brothers and sisters on a special holiday, feeling warm and safe together or, when you were older, took a quiet walk through the woods with a favorite friend. These are some ways of communing together in prayer. As a family begins consciously to make the choice to pray together in their own way, conflict begins to resolve itself and love increases.

What are some ways your family has "prayed" together in the past?

Law 4

If at first you don't succeed, try, try again
—William Edward Hickson

When Thomas A. Edison, working in America, and J. W. Swan, working in England, invented the electric light bulb, the end seemed to have been reached in that kind of experimentation. A safe means of lighting streets and buildings now existed. What further uses could there be for the electric light bulb?

After a time, however, researchers developed new types of light bulbs that made use of ultraviolet rays and infrared heat rays. Still others were developed that killed bacteria in the air, and, before long, these were produced in numerous styles and sizes for use in hospitals, schools, homes, and even in chicken coops! Then came the blessings of halogen and fluorescent bulbs.

"God helps those who persevere."
—Qur'an

These are only a few of the uses discovered for what, at first, seemed to be a simple and self-contained invention. To this day, researchers continue to search for new and better ways to make use of the electric light bulb. There is a lesson here that can be applied to our own lives. Often, when we reach a high level of performance, or achieve a breakthrough in our profession, we're so proud of ourselves that we rest on our laurels. We stop trying to do better.

"Never, never, never, never give up."
—Winston Churchill

Success can be defined in many ways, and it is important to realize that your individual definition needs to be clear in your mind. Once you have established your personal vision of success, you can begin the process of achieving your goal. Many successful people can attest to the multitude of difficulties that were overcome on the journey to their destination. Sometimes the obstacles seem insurmountable, but when that happens, clearly bring forward your original vision to your conscious mind. Re-picture your dream repeatedly until you have the courage and patience to await the next development. Often patience and anticipation are precisely what is required for new breakthroughs.

Beau, who has always suffered from minor learning disabilities, is making a C average in college. "That's okay," he says. "I'm just average and I've never had an easy time in school. I'll just settle for that ole' C."

"Victory is not won in
miles, but in inches.
Win a little now, hold
your ground, and later
win a little more."
—Louis L'Amour

"Character cannot be
developed in ease and
quiet. Only through
experience of trial and
suffering can the soul
be strengthened, vision
cleared, ambitions
inspired, and success
achieved."
—Helen Keller

Ashley is making As. "I worked pretty hard to pull my grades up, and now I can relax," she says.

"I just got a big raise for selling the most advertising pages in our magazine," says Gregg. "I can afford to coast now and take a few extra days off." And so on.

It's true, Beau, Ashley, Gregg, and others like them have achieved something and have made some progress. But have they accomplished all they're capable of doing? Have they made full use of their abilities?

If Beau's a C student, chances are that, even with his problems, he could go beyond a C if he became willing to try a little harder. Or, at least, he could strengthen that C so it would mean more to him later on.

Ashley's A average shouldn't be an end in itself. If she doesn't continue doing good work, those A's could take a quick tumble. She may need to find new outlets for her considerable intellectual endowments. For example, she could develop a personal reading program, learn a new language, or make a contribution to the community in some special way. Gregg needs to realize that he succeeded by working harder than most others, and that continued success will demand the same level of hard, conscientious work.

Success is often based on a high level of striving, day after day, in everything we do. It's important to understand that we never actually "arrive." Success isn't a destination, but rather a journey. It's a journey of seeking and learning in each situation, trying to better ourselves as human beings. Like the researchers who continue to find new ways to use electricity, we must struggle to perform at maximum capacity, even though we may sometimes fail and make mistakes.

Ask yourself what areas of you life could stand improvement. Are you being sensitive enough in your friendships? Are you spending enough quality time with your family? Are you putting enough honest effort into your job? Or whatever requires your attention?

It is always helpful to remember that, "If at first you don't succeed, try, try again."

LAW 5

It is better to light a single candle than to curse the darkness
—Motto of the Christophers

Darkness is one of the first things most people fear. Darkness holds the unknown and the undefinable. When we wake in the middle of the night from a nightmare, we are in the darkness. We may stay there, paralyzed by fear, and do nothing but curse our situation. Or, we may reach for a nearby lamp and switch it on, thus freeing us from the terror. Problems affect us much like the darkness does. When we are faced with tough situations, we may become too scared to make a move and curse our situation, rather than make the effort to do something about it.

Is there anything to be gained by cursing the darkness? Or the situation? Not really. Nothing has changed. The darkness or the fear remains, totally unaffected by our outburst. But when our perception of the darkness changes, or we acknowledge that a problem exists, then we can begin to make some headway. We have been told that a problem cannot be solved at the level it began. It is necessary to move to a higher level of consciousness. Isn't this like turning on the light? We move the focus of our thoughts from the difficulties of the situation and begin to look for a solution. We become *pro*-active instead of *re*-active!

Any scientist can tell you that the proper definition of any problem is the biggest single step toward its solution. Understanding is a strong foundation of progress, and a little old-fashioned introspection is good for what ails you! A lot of people are living in the abject depressive atmosphere of the darkness of fear. In the early stages of the evolution of humanity, fear was positive and productive. It was needed to guide the instinctive intelligence of the lower forms of nature into the correct use of themselves and their environment so they could preserve themselves as long as possible. For the people of that time, fear played a positive role.

In the present day, however, fear—which is in our lower physical consciousness and is a part of the instinctive nature—*is the basis for many of the mistakes we make*. One who is riddled by fear finds it difficult to concentrate his mind in order to think. In a state of fear, which is also the result of the emotional nature try-

"We do not see things as they are, we see things as we are."
—Talmud

*"The appearance of
things changes accord-
ing to the emotions
and thus we see magic
and beauty in them,
while the magic and
beauty are really in
ourselves."*
—Kahlil Gibran

*"Through this dark
and stormy night
"Faith beholds a feeble
light.
"Up the blackness
streaking;
"Knowing God's own
time is best,
"In patient hope I rest
"For the full day
breaking!"*
—John Greenleaf
Whittier, "Barclay of
Ury"

ing to rid itself of some threat, we can become almost helpless—until we decide to *"turn on the light and dispel the darkness!"*

The divine nature of our soul is the very opposite of anxiety or fear of anything. It is creative; it is positive, and it shows us certain kinds of knowledge and wisdom and power or inspiration without which we may sink back into the depths of darkness and fear.

There can be times when we may need others' help. Certainly, if we curse the darkness, others will realize that we are faced with a problem. Yet, unless they see us trying to solve the problem, they may be unaware that we could use their support and assistance.

Until we make an active effort to solve our problems, they may not go away. Even the smallest effort can bring us closer to solving the problem and overcoming a difficult situation. In attempting one possible solution, we may realize different and better solutions.

Thus, cursing the darkness is to no avail. It does nothing but magnify the problem. It pushes others away from us who may have the power to help. Only by putting forth the effort to do something about a problem can we expect to solve it. To curse the darkness may be a first reaction, but hopefully it will not be our last.

Spotlights!

1. Choose to be part of the solution rather than part of the problem.
2. Begin to establish yourself in greater expressions of living by *seeing yourself in a new light.*
3. See yourself in the light of being prosperous or productive in *every* area of your life—mentally, emotionally, physically, and spiritually.
4. Learn time-management skills and develop the ability to utilize the hours of your day more comprehensively.
5. No one can create anger or stress within you, only you can do that by virtue of how you process your world.
6. *"When you squeeze an orange you get orange juice because that's what's inside. The very same principle is true about you. When someone squeezes you—puts pressure on you—what comes out is what's inside. And if you don't like what's inside you can change it by changing your thoughts."*—Wayne Dyer
7. Fear is overcome by knowledge, familiarity, and by facing it with the awareness that fear has no power over you other than the power you allow it to exert.

8. Shine the light of understanding in every situation and there will be no need to curse the darkness.

Living the Law!

Let's prepare a "launch pad" this week to blast off from anxieties, worries, and fears. An excellent launch pad is a detailed list of everything that disturbs, worries, or concerns you. Carry a small pocket notebook, or three-by-five cards, wherever you go for a while. Promise yourself that you will be especially sensitive to every feeling of worry, anxiety, or fear that tries to sneak up on you, and *jot it down in your notebook*. Be certain to make note of even the seemingly small things that make you feel uncomfortable. And do your recording on the spot! It's too easy to forget if you "wait 'til later." Don't be embarrassed at the thought of admitting a few fears. Every man, woman, and child who has walked on this earth has most likely experienced fear in some manner. So, you're not alone! Let's look at some possible categories where fears could lurk:

1. *Fear of the unknown,* resulting in
   fear of death
   fear of "punishment" by God
   fear of impending negative events
   fear of lack of control in my life
2. *Fear of bodily harm,* resulting in
   fear of automobile, plane, or other carrier accidents
   fear of pain
   fear of germs and illness
   strong squeamishnesses about heights or enclosed spaces
3. *Fear of failure,* resulting in
   worry about effectiveness on the job
   thinking and acting defensively
   being unnecessarily critical of others
   hesitancy to undertake new projects
4. *Fear of being unloved,* resulting in
   jealousy and possessiveness
   feelings of rejection
   inferiority complex and insecurity
   feelings of not being needed
5. *Fear of being ridiculed,* resulting in
   tendency to be shy and overly quiet
   hesitancy to express new personal ideas
   fear of speaking before a group of people
   being easily embarrassed

6. *Special personal fears,* like:
　　fear of being misunderstood
　　fear of being overriden by a specific person
　　fear of crawling insects
　　fear of being emotionally hurt
　　fear of being inadequate sexually

　　Give yourself about a week to add to your personal list as a respectable time to gather a representative sampling of your haunting fears. Next, arrange your fears in patterns or groups, as demonstrated above. Now, start examining these fears, one by one. Ask each one, *"O.K., WHO is your mother and father?"* Where did the fear originate? Question each fear in the silence of your own quiet place, and then pause and wait to receive an answer. You can receive an impression, or feeling, from the deep recesses of your mind. Write it down, regardless of how seemingly insignificant.

　　Work with your list daily to build an increasing understanding. Knowledge and experience are great positive antidotes to fear, worry, and anxiety. Combine your efforts with a good, strong dose of a positive mental attitude, love, and prayer and you can free yourself forever.

Week Six

Law 1

It is better to love than be loved
—St. Francis

When we travel around the world or in our home country and see the streams of consciousness that go into making up a nation or a group of people, we can't help but wonder at the incredible variety and the amazing capacity within each individual, and each group of individuals, to express their inner qualities. As we choose to "open our eyes" to everything around us, we begin to recognize that in our uniqueness and diversity there is a deep unifying, underlying unity that moves in and through all people. Many things are taking place around our world, and every individual on the planet can help this action because we are coming into an area in human experience that seems unlike anything we've ever experienced before!

There's a sweet, sweet spirit moving through people—the sweet spirit of love and compassion. The poet Carl Sandberg described what's happening in these words: *"Not always shall you be what you are now. You are going toward something great. I am on the way with you and, therefore, I love you."* The Sacred Scriptures of the Holy Bible, in Paul's letter to the Corinthians, portrays this sweet spirit in another way; he said, *"Faith, hope, and love, these three abide, but the greatest of these is love."* Love! The great potential that is within you!

Consider the sun for a moment. It is a self-sustaining unit that receives energy from internal thermonuclear reactions. The energy released in these reactions is so great that the sun could shine for millions of years with little change in its size or brightness.

Love is like the sun. It sustains itself. It needs neither thanks nor reward for it to give out its powerful and healing energy. Love is always present, although at times it may seem to be

"Love is above the laws, above the opinion of men; it is the truth, the flame, the pure element, the primary idea of the moral world."
—Madam de Stael

"Love is the vital essence that pervades and permeates, from the center to the circumference, the graduating circles of all thought and action. Love is the talisman of human weal and woe—the open sesame to every human soul."
—Elizabeth Cady Stanton, speech at tenth National Woman's Rights Convention

*"I believe that love is
the greatest thing in
the world; that it alone
can overcome hate;
that right can and will
triumph over might."*
–John D.
Rockefeller, Jr.

*"Love doesn't have to
be perfect. Even imper-
fect it is still the best
thing there is for the
simple reason that it is
the most common and
constant truth of all, of
life, all law and order,
the very thing which
holds everything
together, which permits
everything to move
along in time and be
its wonderful or ordi-
nary self."*
–William Saroyan

invisible. Even when the clouds of human emotions hide it, love
is as present as the sun is present when clouds hide it from the
earth. Our lives thrive on the energy of love. Because love is
self-sustaining and creates its own energy, we need not search
outside ourselves. It lies deep at the center of our being.

As we release the energy of our love, a chain reaction takes
place similar to the thermonuclear reactions within the sun that
change hydrogen into helium. The energy of love flows within
us, changing and enlarging us. Love can open hearts that may
have once been closed by bitterness, and love has the power to
replace that bitterness with acceptance and joy. Hate no longer
erodes our soul, and caring and compassion replace apathy.
Changes are evidenced in our lives as we begin to love ourselves
and see ourselves as love.

Love's energy is a healing balm. Like the sun, it has no perception of good or evil. Love simply *IS*. It doesn't say, *"I'll love
this person because it's the right thing to do,"* or *"I'll love this person
because I may gain position and wealth in return."* When we allow
love to express itself through us as our basic nature, it automatically radiates out to every aspect of our environment. Just as
photosynthesis is the process by which the sun and plants
together make food, a similar process takes place within us as
we allow the energy of love to transform our lives. Love
becomes food for ourselves and others. As we allow the energy
of love to *fill* us, it is equally important to allow that energy to
flow *from* us.

Once the spark is kindled within and begins to burn brightly,
we can't stop it from flowing from us to others. Some may not
come close enough to feel the warmth of our love. Others may
bask in the glow of our energy. Because we *are* love, it doesn't
matter if we receive thanks or recognition. Like the durability of
the sun, love gives and gives with no diminution of its supply.
As Iris Murdoch, the Irish writer stated, *"We can only learn to
love by loving."* It's true! Our lives become brighter the more we
express love. We can shine like the sun and we can radiate love
for all persons—without exceptions!

Law 2

Thanksgiving leads to having more to give thanks for
—John M. Templeton

Thanksgiving normally centers on things to give thanks *for*. This is good and helpful for, as someone once said, *"A grateful mind is a great mind which eventually attracts to itself great things."* The grateful mind is more than simply a response to the condition of things in life; it is a celebration of an ever-present spiritual reality. This "attitude of gratitude" can open the door to the increased flow of abundance in one's life. However, a deeper and seldom considered interpretation of thanksgiving can focus on what you have to give thanks *from*. This insight deals with the level of consciousness that enables you to see things from a higher perspective.

Thanksgiving is a creative force that, if lived on a continuous basis and not just for one day each year, can create more good in your life. Perhaps we could call this way of life *thanksliving*. Thanksliving is based on the premise that living a life of appreciation and gratefulness leads to having more to be thankful for. We have the ability to create blessings in our life through the power of mind action and the choices we make. Let's look at some ways we can choose to practice thanksliving.

First, let's take a look at our life and find the good that is already expressing and praise this good. An old adage states that *"where your attention goes, your energy flows."* This means we tend to attract that to which we give our attention. A good idea can get even better as its possibilities for greater good are explored. The more good you can see and praise, the more you direct creative energy to positive results. Even in situations that at first appear difficult or unpleasant, see all the good you can and bless the good you can see! Praise the good and watch it multiply.

A second way to experience thanksliving is to give thanks ahead of time for whatever good you desire in your life. Feel as if you have *already* received this good. One law of life can be stated in these words: *"Thoughts held in mind will reproduce in the outer world after their own kind."* In other words, you help create your outer life according to the way you have created your inner

"When we learn to give thanks, we are learning to concentrate, not on the bad things, but on the good things in our lives."
—Amy Vanderbilt

"I can no other answer make but thanks, and thanks, and ever thanks."
—William Shakespeare, *Twelfth Night*

*"Thanksgiving comes
to us out of the pre-
historic dimness, uni-
versal to all ages and
all faiths. At whatever
straws we must grasp,
there is always a time
for gratitude and new
beginnings."*
–J. Robert Moskin,
*The Heritage of
Judaism*

life—with thoughts, beliefs, and attitudes. Thanksliving can help
us to create what we want. Instead of postponing uplifting, satisfied feelings until after the fact, practice experiencing those
good feelings now. If what you desire is a more prosperous
lifestyle, start feeling and acting like a grateful and prosperous
person today. Your attitude tends to draw prosperity to you like
a magnet.

A third way to experience thanksliving—perhaps the most difficult, yet the most powerful of all—is to give thanks for your
problems and challenges. As you face your situations and overcome them, you grow in strength, wisdom, and compassion.
One of the best ways to learn mathematics is to be given a problem to solve. One of the best ways to prepare for an athletic
event is to practice with a strong, competitive opponent. An
ancient proverb says, *"A donkey may carry a heavy load of sandal-
wood on its back and never know its preciousness—only its weight."*
Sometimes people feel the weight of circumstances and lose
sight of the precious nature of the many and various gifts of life.
Adversity, when overcome, strengthens you. So you are giving
thanks, not for the problem itself, but for the strength and
knowledge that result from the experience. Giving thanks for
this growth ahead of time helps you to *grow* through—not just *go*
through—any challenges that arise.

LAW 3

You cannot be lonely if you help the lonely
–John M. Templeton

*"There are those who
have little and give it
all. These are the
believers in life and the
bounty of life and their
coffers are never
empty."*
–Kahlil Gibran,
The Prophet

"Alone, alone, all, all alone; Alone on a wide, wide sea." Have you
ever felt the kind of loneliness expressed by the poet Coleridge?
Have you ever looked at a picture of a deserted beach in winter
or caught a glimpse of the bleak emptiness of a city street at
five o'clock in the morning and shivered as a feeling of isolation
identified you with the scene? What is this thing called loneliness? Is it simply being alone? No. As one writer observed,
"Cannot the heart in the midst of crowds feel alone?" On the other
hand, cannot a person be alone and still feel a sense of closeness with loved ones?

The feeling of loneliness is not the same as being alone. Loneliness is described as a state of mind, a deficiency of the spirit; and it can be corrected by overcoming that sense of deficiency. Loneliness cannot be overcome by getting something; it must be remedied by giving something!

Few people remember the days when special services were paid for by sharing what you had with the one who provided the service. A farmer could offer sacks of grain to the town doctor for setting a broken arm. Chickens might be given to the blacksmith and his family or potatoes to the village midwife for assistance in the delivery of a child.

An old friend often reminisced of his childhood days when his mother, Sarah, became very skillful at making tantalizingly delicious dishes from frequent gifts of cabbage, rutabagas, and yams. His father was a minister, and the family of the town parson was held in high regard in southern Mississippi, in the United States. A visit to the Reverend and his wife in their modest, frame cottage was a rare treat indeed. The moment a knock was heard at the door, Sarah bustled with a flourish to greet her guests with hugs, kisses, and warm words of welcome. Always dressed in the traditional black clerical suit with starched white collar, the Reverend followed Sarah to extend a warm hand and twinkling smile, saying, "The Lord blesses you, come in." Their gentle manner was the same, whether their visitor was a cherished relative, a pauper needing a meal, or the town's mayor.

As time laid to rest Sarah's best friend, she elected to move to a port city in another state to be closer to her son and daughter. As was her custom for over fifty years, she arose daily before dawn, dressed meticulously with cloak and a tiny veil, and walked to the church. She polished and prepared all the vessels and linens necessary for the priest to offer the sacrament. She tended to every menial task needed by the church personnel. Upon finishing, she went out, walking to the hospital to visit and cheer those who were ill. Afterwards, one by one, she visited the homes of the shut-ins, sharing her joy and kindness and what might be needed of her slender pension.

When news came that Sarah had left this life, a touching story was told. That day she had made her service offering at the church, as usual. Returning home, she gathered a few items of hand-washed laundry from the clothes line and laid her wrap over the back of the sofa. When she was found, she was resting with eyes closed, in her favorite lounge chair and with a gentle, sweet smile on her lips. The tiny net veil was still in place. Spending a few hours in the presence of this special lady con-

"When people are made to feel secure and important and appreciated, it will no longer be necessary for them to whittle down others in order to seem bigger by comparison."
–Virginia Arcastle

"Live and let live is not enough; live and help live is not too much."
–Orion E. Madison

veyed the essence of more gratitude and joy than any sermon or lecture. To Sarah, loneliness was an ill to be tended to and abolished. She used every waking moment to instill, or perpetuate, a bit of happiness in someone's life.

Mother Teresa reported in some of her television interviews that she finds the greatest poverty and desolation among the wealthy of the world today. She noted that there is a stark need for missions to offer love and nurturing to the barren of heart.

Opportunities are limitless when one seeks to fill a need in humanity. Surprisingly, within three blocks of your own home, you might find desperation and helplessness. Often those most pained are unable to discern for themselves the source of their anguish. Hunger, shelter, and the need for gainful productivity are easily recognized. Emotional pain and inner desolation, however, may require more gentle effort and sensitivity. Looking within yourself, you may find valuable assets, special resources, and talents that can be shared. When thoughts are turned outward in search of usefulness, loneliness often melts and disappears.

Beginning with one effort, such as spending an unselfish hour with someone less fortunate, can produce a miracle for the giver and the receiver. If these two should remember another friend in need and go together to help that friend, three or more agents of caring are now in action. This positive force multiplies in energy, which moves joy, love, and sustenance into the world to dispel sorrow and lack. Sharing these priceless gifts of caring, encouragement, appreciation, and praise fills our day with rich purpose.

LAW 4

You are sought after if you reflect love, joy, peace, patience, kindness, goodness, faithfulness, gentleness, and self-control
—John M. Templeton

If you look into a mirror, what do you see reflected? Is the light in your eyes joyous? Does your facial expression reflect peace and kindness? Is your smile patient and understanding? Do you like the "self" you see? To be liked and appreciated is a natural and deep-seated human desire. That is why toothpaste and deodorants are sold by the millions from advertising that promises popularity for the cost of the advertised product! In poll after poll, the personal wish that appears most often is the desire to be well liked.

So, the experience of getting along well with others is no small matter! It is an important skill that must be mastered if we are to be effective and happy. How is this done? The answer may appear simple, but it is extremely vital: *to sincerely like people*. Successful people advise us to work diligently, think positively, but, first of all, like people. Like them *sincerely* and not for ego fulfillment.

A Sufi story tells a tale about a man, whose head was full of imagined knowledge and arrogance as a result, who traveled a great distance to visit Koshyar, a wise teacher. Koshyar looked intently into the man's heart and taught him nothing, saying, *"You may think yourself wise, but nothing more can be put into a full pot. If you are full of pretense, you are, in fact, empty. Become empty to fruitless ideas so that you may come and fill yourself with higher perceptions and understand the real meaning of life."*

Living is a process of learning and growing in wisdom from the lessons we learn. One of my favorite quotations states, *"Life is real. Life is earnest. And the grave is not its goal. Dust thou art, to dust returneth was not spoken of the soul!"* One lesson worth learning early is that life reflects back to us what we give to it. Among the greatest gifts we may offer to our world are love, joy, peace, patience, kindness, goodness, faithfulness, gentleness, and self-control. These are the gifts of a humble and sincere individual and come directly from the heart. *"The intellect by itself moves nothing,"* said Aristotle, and modern psychology has affirmed this statement. We encounter those circumstances in life that reflect the quality of our deeper consciousness: thought and feeling, mind and heart—blended into our actions. When we exhibit those attributes in our lives, others benefit because those qualities have the effect of rubbing off on them.

Others may realize that we are trustworthy. When we deal with people honestly, and with kindness, faithfulness, and gentleness, we send the message that we care. In return, we are treated the same way, because what we give to others often comes back to us. The man who moves in accord with his inner self moves in accord with a force that no outside power in the world can alter, and he moves joyously. An internal discipline

"Today the most useful person in the world is the man or woman who knows how to get along with other people. Human relations is the most important science in the broad curriculum of living."
—Stanley C. Allyn

"The life given us by nature is short, but the memory of a well-spent life is eternal."
–Cicero

can set each individual "house" in order, allowing the self to be mastered and ruled by a power greater than the individual ego. This self-discipline breeds the stuff of which heroes are made. Tenacity and determination are results of an ingrown faith and confidence in the great and good ends of life and the worthiness of human destiny.

When we develop self-control, we gain a balance in our lives that enables us to live the other qualities more fully and completely. Without self-control we lack the ability to be patient with ourselves and with others and the ability to love unconditionally. Self-control gives us the ability to put the ego in the correct perspective so that we bring no harm to ourselves or others. When we are able to do this, we realize the true value of the ego as the vehicle for our expression and not as a tyrant that has to have its way. The ego that insists on having its own way is a destructive ego and can lead to destructive habits. Learning self-control is a key to gaining mastery over our lives.

LAW 5

A smile breeds a smile
–Ted Engstrom

"Wear a smile and have friends; wear a scowl and have wrinkles. What do we live for if not to make the world less difficult for each other."
–George Eliot

"Smile and the world smiles with you; cry and you cry alone." Everyone likes to be around someone who smiles easily. Strangers can pass in the street, and, if one of them smiles, the other is likely to smile in return. Most everyone appreciates the person who can generate a smile from us. A smile, no matter how brief, can uplift us from the mundane task before of us. A smile reaches down inside of us and pulls to the surface reasons for rejoicing in our lives. This is a gift we can pass on to everyone we meet—a gift we can give to ourselves, a gift that costs us only the effort of giving. Living life with a smile is like throwing yeast into a bowl of flour, adding warm water and waiting for the flour to rise. It multiplies many times over.

A smile can be triggered by a thought, an idea, or remembrances of happy times past. We can allow the effect of that smile to permeate our being, warming us and reminding us to be happy and relaxed. A smile from another can shake us loose from our perception of life's severity, and connect us with another person. In a brief passage of time, we may gain a friend. Or, if we choose to ignore the smile, we may miss out on a gift of friendship.

Most of us tend to be drawn to those who have a positive outlook on life. An optimist has a reason to smile, and his smile reveals his faith in life. The pessimist, on the other hand, thinks he has no reason to smile and lives his life without smiles, without faith, and often alone. The ability to smile in the face of life's adversities has escaped the pessimist. He has unconsciously chosen to ignore the many blessings life has given him.

When we learn to smile in the face of life's adversities, we can overcome our problems more effortlessly. Ella Wheeler Wilcox wrote,

> 'Tis easy enough to be pleasant,
> When life flows along like a song;
> But the man worthwhile is the one who will smile
> When everything goes dead wrong.

There are three simple words that almost seem to have magical properties for developing a positive attitude in our life. *Feel supremely happy!* When you let yourself feel supremely happy—regardless of outer appearances—your whole body changes. Your thoughts, your facial expressions, your health, your attitudes, in fact, everything about you changes for the better. It is possible to achieve a similar state of mind as does the mystic when he contacts universal power. If you persist with this feeling and attitude until it becomes a vital part of your life, you can be in harmonious communion with the universe—and all because you are thinking and believing the power of thought energy behind these three little words: *feel supremely happy!* Living life with a smile enables us to see the joy of life, no matter what is going on around us. We can spread that joy with a simple smile.

A smile is contagious! There may not be any visible sign of acknowledgment of a smile, but something within us will tell us we've been given a gift. In choosing to return a smile, we say "yes!" to life. We express the truth that even in the face of adversity, we have faith in the process of life. We can allow our smile to spread that faith and joy to all we meet.

Although there may be times when it is inappropriate to giggle or laugh aloud, a genuine smile is never out of place. Can you think of a time or place when the world could not use a little more light and love? Although not all of us smile in the

"No matter how much madder it may make you, get out of bed forcing a smile. You may not smile because you are cheerful; but if you will force yourself to smile, you'll end up laughing. You will be cheerful because you smile. Repeated experiments prove that when man assumes the facial expression of a given mental mood—any given mood—then that mental mood itself will follow."
–Kenneth Goode

same situations or in the same way, we can bring a little more warmth into a sometimes cold world with a smile that brings forth our best part. The smile you bring to a difficult life situation infuses the challenge with the light of understanding and love, which attracts harmonious solutions. It also inspires those around you to respond in a similar manner. Your smile makes a difference!

When the bullet that began the American Revolution was fired at Concord, it was called "the shot heard 'round the world.'" Your smile, aimed in the direction of any hostile emotions, could be the smile felt around the world. "Brighten the corner where you are." The world needs your smile.

Spotlights!

1. As we allow the energy of love to *infill* us, it is equally important to allow that energy to flow *from* us.
2. Love's healing energy is a balm for one's spirit, soul, body, and affairs.
3. We tend to attract that to which we give our attention.
4. See all the good you can and bless the good you can see!
5. The art of listening is one of the great secrets of being well liked!
6. Loneliness cannot be overcome by *getting* something; it must be overcome by *giving* something.
7. Opportunities are limitless when one seeks to fill a need in humanity. What are some of your resources, inner and outer, that you may share with others?
8. A smile is contagious!
9. When you *feel supremely happy*, everything about and around you changes for the better!

Living the Law!

A story is told that in the spiritual community led by G. I. Gurdjieff in France, there lived an old man who was the personification of difficulty—irritable, messy, fighting with everyone, and unwilling to clean up or help in any manner. No one was able to get along with him. Finally, after many frustrating months of trying to stay with the group, the old man left for Paris. Gurdjieff followed him and tried to convince him to return, but it had been too hard, and the man said, *"No."* Finally Gurdjieff offered the man a very big monthly stipend if he would return to the community. How could the man refuse? When the old man returned everyone was aghast. Upon hearing that he was also being paid (while they were being charged a fair sum to be there), the community was up in arms. Gurdjieff called everyone together for a meeting and after hearing their complaints, he laughed and explained: *"This old man is like yeast for bread. Without him here you would never really learn about anger, irritability, patience and compassion. That is why you pay me and I hire him!"*

Life's challenges are the "yeast" for our psycho-spiritual growth. Like Gurdjieff's students we often do not see them as such because we are focusing on the discomfort or disruption these situations create in our lives. Nevertheless, each experience of this nature provides valuable lessons for us to learn and opens doors to our higher self. This week, you are invited to spend some quiet time thinking about the following questions. Again, it is recommended that you write the questions in your journal along with whatever insights you may receive.

1. What are some specific challenges the universe may have provided for you to learn from in your life? Look at various areas: home, school, friends, work, relationships, activities.

2. What challenges are you currently facing? Can you see possible valuable lessons being provided through the situation that may enhance your growth?

3. Can you embrace the lesson and give thanks for the grand opportunity to learn? Write down some specifics for which you are grateful in the situation.

4. Can you feel the love that is a healing balm flow through you and into the situation? Are you able to say, *"I forgive, release, and allow divine inspiration to provide guidance, right here and now."* And then do it?

5. Where will you direct your focus so your attention doesn't remain on the challenge?

6. What are some things you might do to eliminate any feelings of "aloneness"?

7. As you move beyond the challenge in your mind, what can you visualize on the other side of the problem? For example, new insights? Greater ability to express love? A deeper feeling of peace, etc.?

Week Seven

❖

LAW 1

Great heroes are humble
—St. Francis

Humility is vastly undervalued in our modern Western culture. It is a prevalent belief that humility is fine for the pious or holy, but in the "real" world it won't get you very far. Many people consider pride and aggressiveness as virtues and humility as a weakness. This may be because they don't understand the meaning of humility. They may equate humility with self-debasement and a sense of inferiority when, in fact, this is not true humility.

"Those who are greedy of praise prove that they are poor in merit."
—Plutarch

Actually, the opposite is true. Most really great people are quite humble. Those among the most respected who have ever lived acknowledge that their greatness came, not from their personal self, but from a higher power working through them. The true meaning of humility is knowing that the personal self is a vehicle of a higher power. Jesus of Nazareth said, *"It is not I but the Father within that does the works"* (John 14:10). Other great spiritual leaders have recognized this; true genius has a deep sense of personal humility. First Imam of the Sh'ia branch of Islam, fourth caliph, said, *"Hide the good you do, and make known the good done to you";* and Ben Sira, the great Hebrew scholar commented, *"The greater you are, the more you must practice humility."*

Sir Isaac Newton, one of the world's greatest scientific explorers, made the following statement near the end of his life: "*I feel like a little child playing by the seashore while the great ocean of truth lies undiscovered before me.*" Another great scientist, Albert Einstein, was also known for his childlike simplicity. With all of his achievements in the world, he maintained a strong sense of humility. Dr. Walter Russell, a genius in many fields, echoed Jesus' teaching when he said, *"Until one learns to lose oneself, he cannot find himself. The personal ego must be dissolved and replaced by the universal ego."*

What is this universal ego and what's the difference between it and the personal ego? To begin with, the personal ego is what most of us identify as our "self." It's who we believe ourself to be. It contains the modes of expression we give to our current opinions of ourself. The personal ego identifies with our appearance, our achievements, and our possessions. It is this self that can be inclined to compete with others and may feel hurt or angry if it doesn't get what it wants. The human ego-self wants to feel important, to be right, and in control. The human ego also causes people to try to solve problems by human effort alone without turning to seek assistance in God's wisdom. Sound familiar?

Some people would say, "You've just described the human nature." Perhaps this may be a description of the most familiar part of human nature. Yet, there is another part, a "higher self," that exists in each of us as a spark of the divine. Unfortunately, most of the time this higher self remains hidden by the personal ego just described. We often can't see this universal or "higher" self because we are blinded by our identification with the personal. It may be likened to trying to see the stars during the day. They are present in the universe but obscured by the light of the sun. Only when the sun goes down do we see these heavenly lights.

The true, universal self within us is an individualized center of God consciousness. As we become more willing to release the personal ego, we open the door to greater communication with God. The one who relies on his own wisdom, beauty, skill, or money seldom relies on God. But the one who is humble and grateful for all such God-given blessings opens the door to heaven on earth here and now. Although God's principles are spirit and cannot be seen, they are more real than tangible things. Who today does not have faith in cosmic rays and radio waves, even though they are invisible? For each of us to grow in spirituality, it is important to free ourselves of self-will and seek God's will. When we avoid the ego-centeredness, we may become clear channels for God's love and wisdom to flow through us.

To express greatness in our lives, we should learn to be humble. In becoming humble, we can discover that humility rewards itself. To acknowledge humbly that we know only a little of God's truth does not make us agnostic. If a medical doctor can admit with an open mind that he does not understand all diseases, symptoms, and cures, surely we can be humble by admitting we each have more to learn about God.

"A humble man can do great things with an uncommon perfection because he is no longer concerned about accidentals, like his own interests and his own reputation, and therefore, he is no longer needing to waste his efforts in defending them."
—Thomas Merton

"To live, mankind must recover its essential humanness and its innate divinity; men must recover their capacity for humility, sanity and integrity; soldiers and civilians must see their hope in some other world than one completely dominated by the physical and chemical sciences."
—George F. G. Stanley

LAW 2

Agape *given grows;* agape *hoarded dwindles*
—John M. Templeton

Probably no other word in our language has been given so many definitions or been written about in such depth in poetry, theater, novels, and philosophical and theological texts as "love." Regardless of how it is defined or what is written about it, surely the most important thing about love is what we do with it.

The Greeks developed several definitions of love. *Eros* is romantic love, the kind that puts butterflies in your stomach. *Storge* is the type of love that we feel for members of our family; it is the love of security. *Phileo*, or comradeship, is the type of love we feel for our friends. The most important love, however, is *agape*.

Agape is the unselfish love that gives of itself and expects nothing in return. It is the love that grows as you give it to others. Miraculously, the more *Agape* you give, the more you have to give. It is the love that great spiritual teachers such as Jesus, Buddha, Muhammad, Lao Tzu, Confucius, and others taught us to practice.

The writer C. S. Lewis likened *agape* to the tools it takes to grow an abundant garden. We always have a choice. We can let the garden of our life grow wild and unattended until it fills with weeds, or we can take up the proper tools and tend to our garden until we create a place of unimaginable loveliness—full of flowers and all the vegetables we need. One of the most important tools can be our willingness to extend our love to others.

It is said that there is no power in the universe greater than love, and no act more important than loving. Meher Baba commented to his followers once, *"Love has to spring spontaneously from within. It is in no way amenable to any form of inner or outer force. Love and coercion can never go together; but though Love cannot be forced on anyone, It can be awakened in him through Love itself. Love is essentially self-communicative. Those who do not have It catch It from those who have It. True Love is unconquerable and irresistible; and It goes on gathering power and spreading Itself, until eventually It transforms everyone whom It touches."*

"The measure of a man is not determined by his show of outward strength, or the volume of his voice, or the thunder of his action. It is to be seen rather in terms of the strength of his inner self, in terms of the nature and depth of his commitments, the sincerity of his purpose, and his willingness to continue "growing up."
–Grade E. Poulard

Can we truly give without love? Sai Baba says, *"All acts of service are meaningless unless they are given with Love."* When we discover the miracle of love, we cannot stop ourselves from giving—nor do we want to stop. It is obvious to the lover that love only increases when it is given and dwindles when we attempt to conserve it.

Agape is the unconditional love God gives us regardless of what we look like, how much money we have, how smart we are, and even regardless of how unloving our actions may sometimes be. God loves us unconditionally, and that is what we should try to do as well. When we practice *agape*, it becomes easier to love our enemies, to tolerate those who annoy us, and to find something to appreciate in every person we meet.

Consistent training isn't only for musicians, athletes, and others who must apply themselves constantly to develop their skills. To develop *agape* we, too, should practice expressing sincere love until it becomes second nature—as natural to us as breathing. When it does, love may flow out of us and into us as easily as air flows in and out of our lungs when we inhale and exhale.

Agape is a deliberate choice, one you can make right now. It does not depend on how you feel, but on loving *regardless* of how you feel. It resembles an exercise program. When you start a program like walking, running, or lifting weights, you don't immediately sign up for a marathon or reach for the heaviest weight. You exercise every day, and, as you do, you are able to walk farther, run faster, or lift heavier weights.

The rewards of consistent exercise include feeling good about your accomplishments and improving your ability. The rewards of practicing *agape* include feeling good about others as well as about yourself—two components to living a happy life.

"A man is a little thing while he works by and for himself, but when he gives voice to the rules of love and justice, he is godlike."
—Ralph Waldo Emerson

LAW 3

A measure of mental health is the disposition to find good everywhere
—John M. Templeton

Have you ever noticed how some people seem to be happy no matter what is taking place in their lives? There is a buoyancy to

"Five- and six-year-old children can be taught to have optimistic attitudes. Parents can talk about past positive experiences. They can help their children develop a sense of control, and display optimistic attitudes themselves."
–Julius and Zelda Segal, "Raising an Optimist," *Parents Magazine*

their spirit and a sparkle to their personalities. A kind of glowing field of energy seems to radiate from their faces, their words, even the way they walk. There are others who seem to be predisposed to gloomy, negative thoughts. They seem to live in a perpetual shower of unhappiness. What can make the difference between a healthy, happy person and a miserable, gloomy person? *Choices!* One person is an *optimist* and the other is a *pessimist*. The optimist sees the good in all things, builds upon the most hopeful and cheerful view of matters, and expects the best possible outcome in a situation. The pessimist sees only the darker side of life. Both of these are subjective realities. They are attitudes, not events.

Every great endeavor usually has an optimist at its helm. Without optimism, Magellan would never have circumnavigated the globe. Without optimism, Charles Lindbergh would not have made his way across the Atlantic Ocean on the first solo flight, thus opening the way for intercontinental travel. And, without a belief that things could change for the better, there would not have been social or political reform in various countries.

I've been impressed a number of times by the effect of positive thinking on one's health and also how dark, negative thoughts tend to induce illness. Holding negative thoughts can be dangerous. In the Bible, Job declared, *"The thing I greatly feared is come upon me"* (Job 3:35). And Job wasn't the last person to find that you can bring catastrophe upon yourself by unhealthy thinking!

Occasionally, one comes across some dramatically clear-cut example of this fact. Several years ago, the *London Daily Mail* carried a story describing the curious death of Gem Gilbert, a British tennis star. She died as a dentist was about to extract a tooth.

Years before, when Gem Gilbert was a small girl, she had gone to the dentist where her mother was to have a tooth extracted. And a most unusual and tragic thing happened. The little girl, terrified, watched her mother die in the dentist's chair. What happened? Her mind painted an indelible picture of herself dying in the same way. The picture became a mental reality. Gem Gilbert carried it in her mind for thirty years. This fear became so real that she would never go to a dentist, no matter how badly she needed treatment.

Finally, there came a time when she was suffering such acute pain that she finally agreed to have a dentist come to her home at a seacoast place in Sussex to extract a tooth. Her medical doctor and her minister with her, Gem sat in the chair. The dentist put a bib around her. He took out his instruments, and at the sight of them—she died!

The writer in the *Daily Mail* remarked that Gem Gilbert had been killed by "thirty years of thought." This is an extreme case, of course, but people throughout the world are doing great damage to themselves by holding sickness-producing attitudes compounded with defeat, fear, guilt, and hatred. Obviously a most important technique of good health, especially mental health, is to rid the mind of unhealthy thoughts. Bernard Baruch said, *"Two things are bad for the heart: running up stairs and running down people."* This is true not only of the heart but of the entire physical being.

One definite step that some people have found helpful in applying positive attitudes to physical well-being is that of *affirmation*, or the use of definite positive statements. Words are dynamite! The words we habitually use are reflections of strongly held thoughts, and thoughts can affect us in every aspect of our being. Forces favorable to one's well-being may be stimulated by the constant use of positive words or affirmations. And, it is a fact that positive thinking is usually stronger than negative thinking just as faith is stronger than fear.

Properly employed, affirmations may improve your health, lengthen your life, rejuvenate your body, increase your happiness, bring you success, and the most important gift of all—peace of mind. Here are some examples of affirmations that have been used successfully by others:

1. *My entire being is filled with radiant health. I think health. I practice health. I feel health.*
2. *I am a child of God. In him I live and move and have my being. I am strong, vital, and joyous. The kingdom of God is within me and I am grateful.*
3. *I feel wonderful today. This is going to be a happy day of my life!*

L AW 4

What the mind can conceive, it may achieve
—Anonymous

It has been wisely said that each one of us is the ruler of the greatest nation on earth: our *imagi-"nation!"* We constantly create images in our minds. Many of us; however, don't realize that we

"When you look at the world in a narrow way, how narrow it seems! When you look at it in a mean way, how mean it is! When you look at it selfishly, how selfish it is! But when you look at it in a broad, generous, friendly spirit, what wonderful people you find in it!"
–Horace Rutledge

"Your morning thought may determine your conduct for the day. Optimistic thoughts will make your day bright and productive, while pessimistic thinking will make it dull and wasteful. Face each day cheerfully, smilingly and courageously, and it will naturally flow that your work will be a real pleasure and progress will be a delightful accomplishment."
–William M. Peck

have a choice about how we use our innate capacity to imagine. Imagination is more than a matter of wishful thinking. It is the faculty of mind that images and forms. In other words, our imagination has the power to shape and form thought. With our imagination, we can lay hold of ideas and clothe them with substance. If we consistently connect our imagination with belief and determination, we can actually manifest what we want to achieve.

Our imagination has been called *"the cutting scissors of the mind"* that shapes our heart's desires—the picturing power of the mind. Picture power carries an incredible impact! If you hold a picture in your mind daily of what you desire or "see" for yourself, you are offering your mind a super-fantastic opportunity to be productive! This wonderful picturing power of the mind has been discovered by psychologists who say that imagination is one of the strongest powers of the mind.

You may recall seeing pictures of carvings on the walls of caves done by prehistoric humans of the food he hoped to obtain. They may have believed that if they looked at these pictures often, some great unseen power would bring the food near them in the form of game, fish, or fowl. The Egyptians also used the picturing power of the mind with artwork in the tombs of their pharaohs. When a royal child was born, in some cases, his tomb was immediately started. In this tomb, pictures were painted showing all the experiences the child would have throughout his life . . . a happy life, filled with victorious achievements. And some Egyptians believed these pictured events would come about in the life of the royal child. Some Greeks surrounded their prospective mothers with elegant statues, beautiful pictures, and lush scenery so that the unborn children would receive the benefits of health and beauty from the mind-pictures of the mother!

Keep in mind that your pictured good may come into manifestation if your subconscious mind can accept it! If you have been a "negative thinker," or an "I can't have," type of person, your pictured good may seem so vastly different from what your mind is accustomed to experiencing that it may take a little time for the subconscious to absorb this new way of thinking and decide that you really mean business. That's where persistence pays off. Hang in there! Go that "extra mile" in holding on to your desires and your faith in favorable imaginings. Remember the old saying, *"What your mind can conceive, it may also achieve."* Some people think they live on earth. But the reality is that you can live only in your mind. God has given you the freedom to train your mind to be either a "hell-hole," or a beautiful garden, regardless of your surroundings. How do you direct your imagination to work for you? The French philosopher Simone Weil wrote, *"Imagination and fiction make up more than three-quarters of our real life."* And Muhammad Ali, an American athlete, said, *"A man who has no imagination has no wings!"*

Be aware of the importance of being clear and concise in your picturing. If your pictured good may seem slow in coming, it could be because you've cluttered your mind with too many abstracts, or too many pictures, or you may be trying to produce too much too fast. A one-person craft shop cannot produce the same quantities as an assembly-line factory. Take one step at a time. Do your *thinking* clearly. Do your *contemplating* wisely. Do your *deciding* definitely. Do your *picturing* positively and power-fully—step by step. Clarify your desires and then begin to picture progressive steps toward what you most want. This may open up the way for picture power to guide you to fruitful endeavors.

"To accomplish great things, we must not only act, but also dream; not only plan, but also believe."
—Anatole France

The human mind is a creative tool. Usually we are either creating negative, limiting patterns that repeat themselves with deadening regularity, or we are creating new possibilities for positive expansion in our lives. Imagination and positive thinking have been responsible for many a successful battle against failure by turning attention from our weakness to our strengths and talents. As you conceive of being the person you desire to be and visualize greater good flowing into your life—*to be used for greater good—* spiritual power can begin to help you.

"Your imagination has much to do with your life. It pictures beauty, success, desired results. On the one hand, it brings into focus ugli-ness, distress and fail-ure. It is for you to decide how you want your imagination to serve you!"
—Philip Conley

Refuse to say that you've had a hard time in life (even if you have). Stop talking about unhappy experiences. As long as these are the pictures that you hold in your mind, you are still emo-tionally attached to those particular difficult experiences. You continue to feel depressed emotionally and visually. You are keeping limits on yourself, and you leave less room in your imagination for a better experience!

CONCEIVE IT! BELIEVE IT! ACHIEVE IT!

❖

LAW 5

By prayer you receive spiritual energy
—John M. Templeton

Most men and women are convinced that there is a divine power of some sort; but many are not sure what it is, nor do they know how to bring this divine presence and power into

"The minds of people are so cluttered up with everyday living these days that they don't, or won't, take time out for a little prayer–for mental cleansing, just as they take a bath for physical, outer cleansing. Both are necessary."
–Jo Ann Carlson

"When we pray, we link ourselves with an inexhaustible mature power."
–Alexis Carrel

their daily experience. Throughout the world, and throughout the ages, there have been spiritually endowed men and women who have described conscious union with God. Everybody in the world knows *God*, but not everyone *knows* God. For many, God has remained a word, a term, a power outside the self. However, as humanity moves forward in evolution, more and more people are becoming aware of the Creator in an intimate and personal manner through prayer.

Prayer has been described as being a concerted effort for the physical consciousness to become attuned to the consciousness of the Creator, either collectively or individually. Since the beginning of time, prayer, in some form, has been observed in almost every culture recorded and studied. The desire to attune one's self toward a higher point of view is an innate part of the human soul. As we grow from childhood to adulthood and our lives become more complex and our concerns more encompassing, prayer often becomes the last resort for many people. We forget the Scripture guideline to "pray without ceasing."

I attribute a large part of my own formula for success to the power of prayer in my daily life. In fact, I begin all my shareholders' and directors' meetings with prayer. Whatever you do in life, whether you get married, bring a case to a court of law, perform surgery on a child, or buy a stock, it is wise to begin with prayer. That prayer should be that God may use you as a clear channel for his wisdom and love.

The four words, *"thy will be done,"* are probably the most difficult and yet the most important part of any prayer. Perhaps some of us stopped praying, either because we didn't feel our prayers were being answered, or we didn't like the answers we received from God. Sometimes we have a tendency to ask God to do things for us, hoping he will agree that our requests make sense and will grant them. This relationship with God playing the part of a divine fairy godfather may not always work out to our liking, but it doesn't mean God isn't listening. It may mean that God is wiser than we, or we're not fully understanding the meaning of the words, *"thy will be done."*

In C. S. Lewis's book *Letter to Malcolm: Chiefly on Prayer*, he notes that *"thy will be done"* doesn't necessarily mean we must submit to disagreeable things that God has in store for us, but rather that there is a great deal of God's will to be done by his creatures. The petition, then, is not merely that we may patiently suffer God's will, but also that we may vigorously *do it*. Lewis also notes the tendency to overlook the good that God offers us because, at that moment, we may have expected something else. But that doesn't necessarily mean some prayers aren't answered, only that God is wiser than we.

By communicating with God on a regular basis, we may receive guidance and the power to understand as well as receiving an increase of energy to do his will. The more we talk with God, the more he reveals himself to us. Chester Tolson and Clarence Lieb, in their book *Peace and Power through Prayer,* suggest that by understanding the implication of God's will being done, *"Man receives a new wave of spiritual energy."*

In his book *My Favorite Quotations,* Dr. Norman Vincent Peale wrote the following about prayer: *"If you want to utilize the matchless power of prayer, begin praying immediately and continue at every opportunity. I have observed from a number of enquiries that the average person probably spends about five minutes a day in prayer. That is one-half of 1 percent of one's waking hours. Back in the days of Prohibition in the United States, half of 1 percent alcohol was declared by act of Congress to be non-intoxicating. That percentage is also non-intoxicating in religion! If you want to experience the heady energy of prayer, practice it more often. The physician, Alexis Carrel, a spiritual pioneer, advised praying everywhere: in the street, the office, the shop, the school. You can transform spare moments by praying for your need, for everyone and everything you can think of. Then believe that your prayers will be answered. They will be. And prayer is always answered in one of three ways: no, yes, or wait awhile."*

"Pray without ceasing" (1 Thessalonians 5:17), and allow it to work in your life daily in tune with God's will, and you may fully benefit from what some have described as one of the most powerful weapons on earth—Prayer.

> *"Man is a spiritual being. What advocates that spirit is good. What deprecates that spirit is evil."*
> –Winston Churchill

Spotlights!

1. Consider this: the majority of truly great people are humble.
2. *"It is not I, but the Creator/Father within who does the works."*
3. The true universal, "higher" self within us is an individualized center of God-consciousness.
4. One of the most important things about love is what we do with it.
5. Practice expressing sincere love until it becomes second nature—as natural as breathing.
6. A most important technique of good mental health is to rid the mind of unhealthy thoughts.
7. The words we habitually use are reflections of strongly held thoughts, and thoughts can affect every aspect of our being.
8. Imagination is the picturing power of the mind.

9. Try never to be *too busy* to pause to pray.
10. Consider the importance of the prayer-thought, *"thy will be done."* What are some ways you can see yourself aligning your will with God's will?

Living the Law!

For this week's exercise, you are invited to work with the idea of sacred prayer. For many people prayer is a natural and comfortable association with God. For some, the activity of prayer may be less comfortable. Have you ever heard someone say, "I don't know how to pray"? There are many, many kinds of prayers—probably as many as there is a variety of people on this earth. One thing I have become aware of is that God already knows a great deal more about the contents of our hearts than we do. Our real purpose of prayer is to keep the contact lines open, well lubricated, and unbroken with him and the cosmic universe. The words of a prayer are not as important as some people may think. What is important is the motivating factor behind the words—our sincerity and our desire to become in tune with the Infinite. Some guidelines that you may find helpful toward effective prayer are offered now.

1. Desire the love, peace, joy, and harmony of the kingdom of God and God's will for everyone above all else.
2. Recognize God as Father and Creator of everything and much more.
3. Acknowledge your oneness with God, and see yourself as his beloved child.
4. Let your prayer come from the depths of love for everyone within your heart.
5. Close the door on thoughts and interests of the outer world so your focus may be "within."
6. Believe that your prayer is already answered and is coming into manifestation.
7. Free your mind of unforgiving thoughts. Let go and let God take over.

Week Eight

LAW 1

What appears to us as the impossible may be simply the untried
—Seyyed Hossein Nasr

"It's simply impossible! It cannot be done!" How many times have you heard that expression? In some instances people grow up believing in so many limitations that, after a while, their lives may actually begin to manifest those limitations. You are living on this earth right now. You are housed for this lifetime in a physical body, which may seem to cause some limitations. That body may be host to a shy and retiring personality; it may have grown up in a dysfunctional home; it may have a speech impediment; or it may play host to various phobias and fears. But that body also may house a great mind, which may be capable of creating many kinds of miracles. Sometimes, people can become so caught up in the nagging doubts of the moment when faced with a challenge or problem, they may find it more convenient to fall back on one of the most popular words in the English language—*impossible*.

If you align yourself with a belief in limitations, then "impossible" may seem appropriate conjecture. Clearly not everything is possible in this life. Al Kali, the Arab philosopher and philologist, said, *"If you cannot accomplish a thing, leave it and pass to another which you can accomplish."* But frequently we throw in the towel because it may seem expedient to do so. Is it *really* easier to assume that a stubborn problem cannot be solved than to put time and energy into finding a solution? Is it ultimately more rewarding to give up on a quarrelsome colleague than to seek a common meeting ground with him? "Impossible" may indeed be a convenient word, but can it facilitate the achievement you desire?

In fact, *the impossible is merely the untried.* What about the per-

"Nothing is impossible; there are ways that lead to everything, and if we had sufficient will, we should always have sufficient means. It is often merely for an excuse that we say things are impossible."
—François La Rochefoucauld

"Few things are impossible in themselves; application to make them succeed fails us more often than the means."
–François La Rochefoucauld

"Few things are impossible to diligence and skill."
–Samuel Johnson

son who uses the power of the mind to overcome a stuttering problem; to graduate from college with *two* engineering degrees in spite of being told he was dyslexic; to lift himself or herself out of a dysfunctional family, or relationship, and proceed to enjoy balanced and successful living? These people proved the possibility of the seemingly "impossible!"

Earlier in this century, many people may have agreed it was impossible to safely jump from an airplane in flight. However, if the overall consensus had decided to file that dream away as an impossibility, then today there might be neither parachutes nor parachutists! Yet, at least one person believed in the possible and worked to find a solution to the problem of the rapid acceleration of falling objects as related to earth's field of gravity.

In the early phases of development, parachutes sometimes failed, but the inventors refused to cry, "Impossible!" They continued their research until workable solutions were found. This same progression toward resolutions may be possible in our individual situations. We must often search for answers to our money needs, our friendship and spiritual needs, and our needs at school and work. It is certainly more important to make efficient use of our time rather than to complain that there aren't enough hours in the day. How can we find a solution to our time crunch unless we say to ourselves, *"Yes, it's possible. It can be done!"*

Rebecca was born without a left arm from above the elbow. Fortunately, her parents were supportive as well as loving, and they believed that the *impossible is the untried*. As a result, Rebecca learned to swim, to ride a bike, to shuffle a pack of playing cards, and to tie her shoes. She grew up with a sense of pride, with a belief in her abilities, and with a desire to be useful to others.

What would happen if we choose to look, with fresh vision, at the word *"Impossible"* and changed it to *"I'm possible!"* The alphabetical letters are the same, but the difference is reflected in the punctuation, pronunciation, or emphasis. How can you know something is impossible if little attempt has been made to achieve a desired result? The understanding distills down to personal responsibility and a willingness to exert effort in a particular manner toward a particular goal. Nothing "out there" should control what is within you. *As you think, so shall you be.* Your thinking is yours, originating within you. *"The impossible is the untried,"* as a law of life, can help you attain the apparently unattainable and believe that the inconceivable may, in fact, be conceived and then expressed.

LAW 2

*I shall allow no man to belittle my soul
by making me hate him*
—Booker T. Washington

Whom does hate change? What conditions does it improve? The answer may be surprising. Hate, like prayer, changes the person involved in the activity, not the person who may be the target of the activity. If you kick a brick wall that's in your way, you're the one who gets hurt, not the wall. Hate doesn't change the person being hated. In this context, it often diminishes the person doing the hating.

We are individually responsible for controlling our outlook on life as well as our attitudes. Hate, as an emotion, can be the alternate of a most powerful kind of feeling. When we seek to understand some of the natural human attitudes, we often find that the most strenuous hatreds are usually based on either a fundamental fear or a strong personal desire. This understanding can go a long way toward helping distinguish and separate in our mind between a person and our disapproval of that person's actions. Isn't it true that sometimes we may feel resentful of someone whose actions seem to deprive us of something we want? The American writer James Baldwin said, *"I imagine one of the reasons people cling to their hates so stubbornly is because they sense, once hate is gone, they will be forced to deal with their pain."*

African-American educator Booker T. Washington was keenly aware of this truth when he vowed, *"I shall allow no man to belittle my soul by making me hate him."* An emancipated slave, Washington lived in poverty so severe that he went to work at the age of nine. He could easily have blamed his situation on circumstances and used these as an excuse for hatred. Instead of permitting this emotion to fester within his soul, he managed to harness his energies and channel them into improving his own condition and that of others.

Washington worked as a janitor to obtain an education—the method that he believed would lead to self-improvement and eventual improvement of conditions for humankind. He took command of his life rather than view himself as a victim of his circumstances. After graduation and some teaching experience, he was eventually asked to head a new school for blacks at Tuskegee, Alabama. He accepted the position.

*"Heads are wisest
when they are cool and
hearts are strongest
when they beat in
response to noble
ideas."*
–Ralph J. Bunche

"Not the state of the body but the state of the soul is the measure of the wellbeing of each of us."
–Winfred Roades

"Let us not throw away any of our days upon useless resentment, or contend who shall hold out longest in stubborn malice."
–Samuel Johnson

The challenges of little money, no equipment, and having only two converted buildings did not make the new administrator envy wealthy schools or hate those who were more fortunate. Instead, Washington began working toward his goal. He permitted no negative interferences. During his administration, Tuskegee Institute grew to have nearly two hundred faculty members and one hundred well-equipped buildings.

When Washington's emphasis on education drew criticism from members of the black community who believed that political activism was the path to genuine progress, Washington calmly followed the direction he believed to be true. Rather than seeing the differences as an excuse to hate and fight, the United States educational leader continued his positive work on the academic front.

A person is in control of what he allows to abide in his conscious awareness. By concentrating on retaining mastery over the inner self, a wise person averts negative emotions and destructive activities. Negativity is not likely to have positive results. Washington realized this truth. Rather than waste valuable energies in unproductive arguments, he followed inspiration to fulfill his vision of education. *He allowed no one to belittle his soul because he remained responsible for his inward self.* Like other great men and women, Washington was aware that only he could control his inner being.

As the writer in the *Dhamapada* stated, *"Hatred does not cease by hatred; hatred ceases only by love. This is the eternal law."* Love, founded on truth and not on someone's mood, knows by its own fires of devotion how to make calamities serve a useful purpose. Obstacles, regardless of the kind, can often lead to success. Great moments ultimately can come out of dark periods.

LAW 3

Real success means not to remain satisfied with any limited goal
—Seyyed Hossein Nasr

The dictionary defines success both as a favorable or satisfactory outcome and as the gaining of wealth, fame, and rank.

Opportunities for success can come in many ways—for example, graduating from college, winning a football game, getting high scores on a test, or going out with someone you like. These are easy and measurable ways of sharing what the outer world terms as "success."

There are far more subtle ways of achieving success that can be equally as spectacular, even if they aren't accompanied by social fanfare. You certainly can feel successful when you help a friend who needs your assistance, maintain a confidence you promised to honor, stay on a diet or exercise program, and refuse to give in to peer pressure because someone whose high opinion you desire may be persuasive. In fact, honoring the personal commitments you've made with yourself may be a higher form of success than all the fanfare because it is an inner personal experience.

The author and speaker Wayne Dyer commented, *"Success is a journey, not a destination, and half the fun is getting there!"* So how do we "get there" and what makes the difference between a life filled with struggle and one that is full of earned pleasure? Two of the most fundamental laws of the universe—the *law of attraction* and the *law of inertia*—may help place that question in a more clear context.

The law of inertia states, *"It is easier for something in motion to stay in motion. Conversely, once an object (or person) is at rest, it is easier to stay at rest."* This can be tantamount to saying that fifty percent of the doing of a task is to begin it! Once the task is begun, the law of inertia can propel you to finish it. In fact, it may often be more difficult *not* to finish the task—to stop in the middle—than to keep on going. On the other hand, when you are at rest—unmotivated or quiet or withdrawn—it can be easier to stay there than to make the effort to move ahead.

Once you overcome your initial inertia to stay at rest, you can use the energy of the inertia of motion to succeed at the goal you commit to beginning. Thus the law, *"success breeds success,"* may be reflected in your continuing to create what you have created in the past, or what you are creating in the present.

The law of attraction, which also breeds success, states that *"like attracts like."* It is a law that deals with the attraction between ourselves and other individuals, places, conditions, and things. We accomplish the manifestation of this law through our thoughts and beliefs. They bring to us, through the law of attraction, the people who are part of our universe—relatives, friends, enemies, work associates, and others with whom we come in contact. Our thoughts and beliefs also bring to us, through the law of attraction, the situations that become an

"All successful men have agreed in one thing—they were causationists. They believed that things went not by luck, but by law; that there was not a weak or a cracked link in the chain that joins the first and last of things."
—Ralph Waldo Emerson, *Power*

"The Law of Attraction—the law that all conditions and circumstances in affairs and body are attracted to us to accord with the thoughts we hold steadily in consciousness."
—Charles Fillmore, *The Revealing Word*

"The common idea that success spoils people by making them vain, egotistic and self-complacent is erroneous; on the contrary, it makes them for the most part, humble, tolerant and kind. Failure makes people cruel and bitter."
–W. Somerset Maugham

"All success consists in this: You are doing something for somebody–benefiting humanity–and the feeling of success comes from the consciousness of this."
–Ethel Jacobson

"I must admit that I personally measure success in terms of the contributions an individual makes to her or his fellow human being."
–Margaret Mead

"Enthusiasm is at the bottom of all progress. With it there is accomplishment. Without it there are only alibis."
–Henry Ford

important part of the creation of our personal world. This law functions like a boomerang, bringing back to us that which we project onto others, either for good or ill.

You have three options, then, of things that may be attracted to you in your universe. Two of these are easy: that which you like and that which is like yourself. By becoming the person you most admire—a person of honesty, integrity, and compassion—you can attract those of similar value. Your "inner success" can create your "outer success." It is important to keep personal commitments, because the loyalty and honesty reflected in such behavior can return to us.

However, from time to time you may also encounter things that you dislike. Obviously, no one wants to attract undesirable qualities, people, situations, or things. Yet, by assuming a non-judgmental and nonresistant attitude, you can neutralize those negative experiences. Whenever we resist something, it persists. By refraining from judgment and resistance, you can dissipate the energy that attracts undesirable qualities to you.

By focusing on the good in yourself and in others, people will enjoy being in your presence. They will treat you as a successful person because you help them feel good about themselves. As you begin to walk along the pathway of life by seeking inner guidance and developing and using your ideals, choices, and purposes for the highest good, your confidence increases as does expressions of truth and faith. These qualities lead to greater understanding that the process of positive thinking works, and you may transform your life into a wonderful journey. Success is indeed a journey and not a destination, for a destination means the journey is over. And life is ongoing!

LAW 4

Enthusiasm is contagious
–John M. Templeton

A small church in a low-income area of Brooklyn, New York, in the United States, asked a businessman if the neighborhood children could play in a vacant lot he owned until another use was made for the property. The man agreed to allow the space to be used as a playground with two specifications. First, the church had to pay for insurance. Second, the church had to take responsibility for cleaning up the lot. The congregation of the church decided they would manage insurance payments somehow, and the entire membership agreed to meet on a certain Saturday to clean the lot.

A few of the families were slightly late in arriving, and among the late arrivals was a couple with a crippled ten-year-old daughter. As the family made its way to the lot, many of the volunteers wondered why the couple had brought the girl. What could she possibly accomplish? After all, she could hardly walk!

But the young girl plunged into the project with gusto. Propping herself up by leaning on her crutches and leaving her hands free, with a huge smile and happy expression, she held the plastic bag open while her father and mother filled it with trash. The family laughed and talked about the many sports and activities they visualized taking place on the lot. Their enthusiasm became contagious! A little crippled girl had inspired the other volunteers with her attitude. Yet, a few found themselves wondering why the girl was so excited. It seemed to them unlikely that the child would be able to use the playground. How could she? When asked how she planned to participate when the playground opened, the little girl was totally enthusiastic, *"I'll keep score and be a referee and stuff like that,"* she grinned.

The individual who takes up any activity as a positive adventure can inspire the same attitude in others. The worker who looks for ways to enjoy his work, to be enthusiastic about it, sets the stage for others to follow his example. Always remember that what a person does, for good or ill, can be contagious. A smile is contagious, but so is a frown. Although no one can be sunny all the time, if we take up our tasks with enthusiasm, it is likely those around us may also catch our spirit. Incidentally, the derivation of the word "enthusiasm" is "filled with spirit!" Enthusiasm really is contagious!

"The energy that makes organizations move, depends upon individual enthusiasm. Leaders with bright ideas and the ability to inspire high thought and action in others are the main generators of energy. Their individual brand of enthusiasm rubs off onto other people and inspires them to greater works."
—Brian Adams, *How To Succeed*

"Study the unusually successful people you know and you will find them imbued with enthusiasm for their work which is contagious. Not only are they themselves excited about what they are doing, but they also get you excited."
–Paul W. Ivey

❖

LAW 5

Small attempts repeated will complete any undertaking
—Og Mandino

When entering the first grade, some children experienced fear. The objectives seemed monumental in comparison to anything up to that point. But with the assistance and support of our parents and teachers, we steadily progressed and accomplished mastery of many basic skills.

"Better to do a little well, than a great deal badly."
–Socrates

For some first graders, learning the strange figures of the alphabet may be initially overwhelming. They have not been required to draw on their memory to such an extent before. However, with practice in writing each letter repeatedly and speaking the sounds aloud, each child learns the ABCs. This accomplished, the young students are next asked to pull out certain letters from the alphabet, mix them up, and place them in special arrangements to form words. When the children learn how to form words, they begin working on making sentences, then paragraphs, and eventually, by the end of the first year, each one is able to write a story. With practice and repetition, undertakings of increasing complexity are completed. What at first seemed an impossible task has now become routine. Every person who learns to read and write takes a giant-sized problem and, through daily practice and persistence, works away at it until he masters it. In school, every grade presents us with new problems. As we learn how to solve these problems, we progress to a higher grade with more difficult situations or opportunities to learn.

"He who waits to do a great deal of good at once will never do anything. Life is made up of little things. It is rarely that an occasion is offered for doing a great deal at once. True greatness consists in being great in little things."
–Samuel Johnson

Life is a process similar to the one we experience in school. As we move through life and attempt to improve ourselves, to become better people, to expand our awareness of who we are and what life is all about, we encounter new problems. Whenever we try something different or attempt to bring about change, it often seems a new challenge arises. Such is the schoolroom of daily living! It may, occasionally, be like learning a new alphabet. There can be new factors, new considerations, and possible adjustments that become necessary to incorporate into our lives. If we do not become overwhelmed by the magnitude of the problem, but proceed steadily and with confidence, we can complete almost any undertaking that comes our way.

We are all free spirits, and we are not bound or restricted unless we think we are. An old adage says, *"Behold the turtle, who makes progress only when he sticks his neck out!"*

Life seldom presents us with challenges we can't meet, with obstacles we can't overcome, or with problems we can't solve. We simply approach each situation with a positive attitude, take one step at a time, and know it's only a matter of persistence and time before we arrive at a solution. Just as in the first grade, "small attempts repeated" help children overcome the problem of learning how to read and write, every effort we make in a positive manner can move us to the completion of any undertaking.

Spotlights!

1. The impossible is the untried.
2. We may need to search for answers to our needs, but he who searches—finds!
3. A person is in control of what he will allow into his conscious awareness.
4. Hatreds cease by the activity of love.
5. The law of inertia: *"It is easier for something in motion to stay in motion. Conversely, once an object (or person) is at rest, it is easier to stay at rest.*
6. The law of attraction: *"Like attracts like."*
7. Success is a journey and not a destination, for a destination means the journey is over.
8. If you take up any activity enthusiastically, you can inspire enthusiasm in others.
9. What a person does, for good or ill, can be contagious.
10. Love is an inner quality that sees good everywhere and in everything.

Living the Law!

You are invited to take a short imaginary journey. Find a time when you can be alone and relaxed. You may wish to read this visualization onto an audio tape so you may play it back and fully focus on the description of the activity. Also, your subconscious mind is very susceptible to the sound of your own voice. If you use the visualization in a group setting, ask a member of the group to be the guide for the visualization. Or, the taped version would be acceptable.

Imagine for a moment that every event, every circumstance in your life at the present time is in a different pot sitting on a giant stove! When you were born into this life, you were given a set of gleaming cookware and a chef's hat. You were told that you were to prepare a gigantic feast of multiple choices, all to be cooked at the same time. Each pot is but an empty vessel and may be filled by you in any manner you choose. Your pots can contain a grand feast, or the burnt leftovers of yesterday's ideas!

There's one pot for family relationships, a pot for your studies, pots for your health, prosperity, relationships, vocation, and others of every size for each area of your life. *Each pot is a container for unlimited potential!*

The smart cook, seeking the gourmet meal, will refer often to the *Cookbook of Life* called *Spiritual Attunement.* In it is a listing of ingredients to make life a fabulous success. There is a diet for the body, for the mind, and for the soul. These recipes can feed you with the nutrients needed in life.

This giant stove and these pots are magical, because whatever is put into the pots begins to cook and multiply of itself! These pots are the vessels for thoughts and ideas from your own mind. They hold quite an aggregation of mind-work—the fresh, the sour, the good-tasting, and the bitter. All ingredients are added by our own free-will choice.

In God's recipe, there is one magical ingredient that can save any meal, even one that has gone sour. This one ingredient dissolves the incorrect ingredients that we may have added in our moments away from the cookbook. Any error ingredients that may poison us are dissolved into nothingness by the magical ingredient of . . . LOVE!

The stove is your mind. No matter what you are cooking, in whatever pot in your life, this one ingredient is the staple for your diet.

If one of your pots contains a meal for an unhappy home life—add love!

If one of your pots contains a failing business or career—add love!

If one of your pots contains past mixes that are making you sick in mind and body—add massive doses of love!

Whatever the pot, whatever the recipe, love saves the meal!

Now, in a time of quiet, pause and look at the pots on your stove. What's in them? How are they cooking? Are you happy with what you see? Is there anything you wish to change? If so, add the magical ingredient. *Love.*

When the visualization is completed, make notes in your journal about your thoughts and feelings as you allowed your visualization to unfold.

Week Nine

LAW 1

Defeat isn't bitter if you don't swallow it
—Ted Engstrom

At one time or another in our lives, we have experienced failure. In fact, the more often we are willing to risk trying a new approach or a fresh concept, the more likely we may be to experience failure, at least in the short run. It isn't easy to succeed when we first try something new and ambitious, and if we're afraid to fail we may be quite hesitant to take risks. Yet, if we never dare to step forward, we can certainly stagnate. Growth requires a willingness to risk failure and defeat. If, as toddlers, we were afraid of failure, few of us would have learned to walk and talk! To learn to walk we had to be willing to fall down at times, scrape our knees, and bruise our shins. Confucius said, *"Our greatest glory is not in never falling, but in rising every time we fall."* To be successful—to become victorious—we must be willing to risk failure. But the important lesson to learn is *failure is not defeat unless you let it be.*

Everyone can improve himself regardless of his situation, place in life, or circumstances. But it is important to prove *to yourself* that by your own thoughts and actions you have the power *to accomplish that which you make up your mind to do.* Fear and hesitancy are paralyzers of mental action and feed the idea of defeat. They can weaken both mind and body, throw dust in your eyes, and attempt to hide the mighty spiritual forces that are always with you.

The spiritual power of the universe does not know defeat or failure! How many times have you been on "rock-bottom," and kind words and thoughts of encouragement spoken by a friend lifted you up and made you feel like a person again? Perhaps you kept going because someone believed in you. Well, that's as good a reason to continue on as any! It seems that the "down

"It is defeat that turns bone to flint, gristle to muscle and makes a man invincible, and form those heroic natures that are now in ascendancy in the world. Do not, then, be afraid of defeat. You are never so near victory as when defeated in a good cause."
–Henry Ward Beecher

"A failure is not always a mistake; it may be simply the best one can do with the circumstances. The real mistake is to stop."
–B. F. Skinner

"Happy is the man who can endure the highest and the lowest fortune. He who has endured such vicissitudes with equanimity has deprived misfortune of its power."
–Seneca

"What is defeat? Nothing but education; nothing but the first step to something better."
–Wendell Phillips

times of defeat" are when we need courage the most and find it most difficult to draw from within ourself. It is your divine birthright to express yourself as a healthy, happy, prosperous, and successful person. Yet it may seem impossible for you to express your true inner self as long as you are fearful and feel defeated instead of courageous. *Real courage* is a spiritual idea stemming from the mind of God! When you desire courage with all the intensity of your heart, believe in it and seek it until it becomes an awakened part of your nature; then you become able to handle difficult situations. You can have the strength to keep on keeping on.

In the process of inventing the electric light bulb, it was said that Thomas Edison tried and failed over a thousand times! It has been reported that someone asked Edison if he didn't grow discouraged by all his failures and consider giving up. He replied, *"Those were steps on the way. In each attempt I was successful in finding a way not to create a light bulb. I was always eager to learn, even from my mistakes."*

In other words, while Edison did not always succeed, he refused to allow defeat to take up residence in his mind. Edison tasted defeat many times, but he did not allow it. To swallow defeat is to believe that because you failed at something, *you* are a failure. There is a critical difference between saying, "I failed," and "*I am* a failure." To swallow defeat is to believe that what you do, or fail to do, makes you the person you are.

When we swallow defeat, our ability to function effectively is impaired from that moment on. Every great leader, athlete, explorer, thinker, inventor, and business person has made mistakes and experienced failure in some manner. These people, however, became great because they did not blame themselves or anyone else for their failures; instead, they used their mistakes as lessons on how to improve their performance. They knew that failure was momentary and did not necessarily mean defeat. They refused to swallow the bitterness of failure and were willing to struggle on to the sweetness of success.

A defeat can be one of the best things that ever happens to us if we choose to learn from the experience. A defeat may be bitter; but after all, bitter is not bad, and some food wouldn't taste nearly as good were it not for the touch of "bitter." Likewise bitter experiences can help us spice up our lives if we choose to learn from them rather than to be afraid of them or become embittered by them.

LAW 2

The unexamined life is not worth living
—Socrates

The study of human behavior is not new to our time. The ancient Greeks were probably the first to ask questions about what motivates people. The origins of psychology are often linked to the Greek philosopher Aristotle, who lived in the fifth century B.C.E. Aristotle built on the groundwork of Plato and Socrates. The phrase *"Know thyself"* is attributed to Socrates, the Greek philosopher who urged his fellow Athenians to live noble lives, to think critically and logically, and to have probing minds. He believed, along with Plato and Aristotle, that evil arises from ignorance and the failure to investigate the reasons why people behave as they do. He is also credited with saying, *"The unexamined life is not worth living."*

Most people sincerely desire to live noble and moral lives. One way to accomplish this can be through understanding the behavior of friends and associates as well as our own. Once we understand why others behave as they do, we can have more compassion and empathy for them. When we recognize our roots in the human family, we no longer feel a need to stand in judgment of others. Judgment only condemns and separates people. It places one person or group against another, whereas compassion and empathy can bring people together and promote clearer communication. *"I care about you and I want to support you"* is the clear message.

Socrates emphasized the Greek ideal of self-control. He believed in a divine principle, expressed through an inner voice that directs our actions along the path of morality. He taught us to explore our thinking and behavior, to reach within, and to expunge those behaviors that are unworthy of us. Honest self-analysis can help us to see if we react to people and events because we may have been socially conditioned in a certain way, or if our behavior is guided by the divine principle and inner voice within us. As important as it is to understand the behavior of others, our own behavior is the only behavior we can change. Learning the reasons behind what we do and why we do it helps us to be honest with ourselves; it builds integrity into our lives. We learn what is *real* to us, what *matters* to us. And we learn to

"Life is meant to be lived, and curiosity must be kept alive. One must never, for whatever reason, turn one's back on life."
—Eleanor Roosevelt

"Life itself is a strange mixture. We have to take it as it is, try to understand it, and then to better it."
—Rabindranath Tagore

"Unless the young man looks around for himself and uses his own powers of observation and proves the assertion to be the falsity that it is, he falls under the spell of the misguidance and succumbs to the life of drudgery."
—Edward K. Bok

"All life is an experiment. The more experiments you make, the better."
–Ralph Waldo Emerson

"Two little words that make the difference–START NOW!"
–Mary C. Crowley

act rather than simply react. We learn to be true to ourselves and to live our lives with dignity.

We take the time to examine our life, to see where we've been, and begin to formulate where we are going. We become centered and focused in the oneness of our beingness with the Creator. God, to the dull self, can be as nebulous as the butterfly may be to the caterpillar. A caterpillar cannot recognize the butterfly when it lands on the leaf beside it. The caterpillar may not even *see* the butterfly, for the butterfly is not in the caterpillar's reality! Yet, there comes one fine morning when the caterpillar becomes transfigured into a butterfly and drinks the nectar of the gods. It then "knows itself" as the magnificent creation it was created to be.

Introspection, with an emphasis on growth and change, can help us achieve a fuller and more fulfilled life. So can taking the time to understand the motives behind the actions of others. Learning to have compassion and empathy for others and for ourselves often leads to a peaceful, successful existence that is truly worth living.

LAW 3

You are only as good as your word
–John M. Templeton

"A man's behavior is the index of the man, and his discourse is the index of his understanding."
–'Ali

Much has been written about the power of the spoken word. In the Holy Bible, we are informed that the creative power of speech had its derivation in the creative power of sound. In the book of Genesis, God literally "speaks" the universe into existence. *"Let there be light. . . . Let there be a firmament."* Each verse of the entire first chapter of Genesis begins with the notable acclamation, *"Let there be. . . ."* And with the same potency begins the Gospel of John—the most mystical of the four Gospels: *"In the beginning was the word."* What may be the significance of such translations? And what impact can they have on our life today? Simply that the "Word" was not necessarily something which God "said" or "did" a long time ago; rather, the WORD of God's creative power may be ensouling, permeating, informing, and conveying God to and through all living things here and now.

You've probably heard the story of the experiment in which the opera singer with a vibrant voice shatters a drinking glass by the tone emitted through her voice. And what about soldiers breaking cadence when they cross a bridge! The principles of prosperity tell us that our words determine whether we "have" or "have not," because our words are *instruments of sound* with which we build our world. We can help to shape our world with the use of our words and how we follow through on what we say!

Let me share an analogy. Sally became so absorbed in the book she was reading that she decided to skip a promised telephone call to her friend Millie. A few days later, an opportunity came for Sally to go into a nearby city with her girlfriend who lived next door, and she decided to do so. She made a last minute call to Becky, another school friend with whom she had made a prior commitment, to explain what had come up. "We can go to the Burger Heaven anytime. I know you'll understand," Sally said.

Two weeks later, Becky and Millie and three other girls made plans for a trip to the local zoo. "Aren't we going to invite Sally?" asked one of the girls. "Let's not," Millie replied. "She isn't good about keeping her word." Sally was heartbroken when she discovered her friends had planned a special day without her. It never occurred to her that good friends keep their word. The old saying, *"You are only as good as your word,"* is very true. And not being as good as your word can lead to unhappiness and a lonely existence.

When it comes to keeping your word, there is no such thing as a "small" situation. Promising you will call someone and then neglecting to do so may seem small to you, but it can loom large in the mind of the person to whom you made the promise. That person may have needed someone to talk with at the moment. Perhaps they may not be very active socially, and a telephone call could mean a great deal to them. They could simply like you as a friend and look forward to the promised chat. By failing to make that call, not only are you risking making someone unhappy, but you may also be hurting yourself. Things might go badly for you in the near future, and you may need friends more than ever. But if you were not good at keeping your word, they may have decided to give up on you. This is the negative view of "being as good as your word."

There is also a strong positive side, as Jim's case shows. Every

"Words are the most powerful agents of mind. Every time we speak, we cause the atoms of the body to tremble and change their place. Not only do we cause the atoms of our own body to change their position, but we raise or lower the rate of vibrations and otherwise affect bodies of others with whom we come in contact."
–Charles Fillmore

"For one word a man is often deemed to be wise, and for one word he is often deemed to be foolish. We should be careful indeed what we say."
–Confucius

"The power of words is immense. A well-chosen word has often sufficed to stop a fleeing army, to change defeat into victory, and to save an empire."
–Emile DeGirardin

time Jim made a promise, no matter how small or seemingly insignificant, he kept his word. If he made plans with someone and then was offered the opportunity to do something more exciting or interesting, he never hesitated. He would say, "Thank you. I would love to do it, but I already have a commitment."

Jim's behavior invariably brought two reactions, both positive. The first friend would be pleased because he and Jim stuck to their plan, and the second friend would be impressed. While sorry that Jim couldn't join him, he appreciated the fact that Jim could be counted on. Jim was not only well liked during his school years, but he was respected and successful as an adult. His word was his bond, and both friends and business associates liked and trusted him. "Jim's as good as his word," a professional friend said of him. Not only were his words pleasant to hear, but they carried the conviction of his integrity. Truly, to be noted as being "as good as your word" is high praise in today's world.

LAW 4

Tithing often brings prosperity and honor
–John M. Templeton

Nearly all civilizations have practiced some form of philanthropy. Many ancient civilizations levied a tithe, or tax, for the poor. The Egyptians and Greeks gave money to establish libraries and universities. By encouraging members to tithe, medieval churches supported hospitals and orphanages.

"One always receiving, never giving, is like a stagnant pool, in which whatever flows remains, whatever remains corrupts."
–John A. James

The word "tithe" is from the Anglo-Saxon word "teotha," which means a tenth part. To tithe means to tax one-tenth of a person's income. In the Bible, to tithe was to support the religious order given in Numbers 18:26–27, *"When you receive from the Israelites the tithe I give you as your inheritance, you must present a tenth of that tithe as the Lord's offering. Your offering will be reckoned to you as grain from the threshing floor or the winepress."*

Many people believe that by tithing they appease their God and secure their place in heaven. Inside of King's College Chapel in Cambridge, England, are these words of William

Wordsworth, *"Give all thou canst; high Heaven rejects the lore of nicely calculated less or more."* The underlying belief is that if we give our bountiful share of this life's abundance, then we will receive all we are due on earth and in heaven.

Benjamin Franklin is remembered not only for his statesmanship but also for his tithing. George Washington wrote as follows to Franklin in 1789: *"If to be venerated for benevolence, if to be admired for talents, if to be esteemed for patriotism, if to be beloved for philanthropy, can gratify the human mind, you must have the pleasing consolation to know that you have not lived in vain."*

In his will, Franklin left five thousand dollars each in trust for two hundred years to Boston and Philadelphia for philanthropic purposes, a sizable amount of money at that time. Franklin also established America's first city hospital, the Pennsylvania Hospital for the Unfortunate.

Andrew Carnegie used a large share of his fortune to establish many cultural, educational, and scientific institutions. He believed that *"surplus wealth is a sacred trust which its possessor is bound to administer in his lifetime for the good of the community."* In 1901, Carnegie's fortune was estimated to be an outstanding $500 million of which he donated $350 million to a variety of causes. His generosity established 2,500 public libraries throughout the world, provided construction for the famed Carnegie Hall in New York City, and created the Carnegie-Mellon University in Pittsburgh and the Carnegie Institution of Washington to encourage research in biological and physical sciences.

Carnegie said, *"Individualism will continue, but the millionaire will be but a trustee of the poor; entrusted for a season with a great part of the increased wealth of the community, but administering it for the community far better than it would have done for itself."* Tithing often brings prosperity and honor because it is an important aspect of the *Law of Giving and Receiving,* which is an integral part of the *Law of Cause and Effect—"As you give forth, so shall you receive."*

A lot of people right now are seeking economic healing. One of the quickest ways to relieve economic stress and effect economic healing is to tithe—or give! Not only is tithing a prospering activity; it is also a healing activity. Upon researching the activity of tithing, it is found that tithing establishes a consistent method of giving and for stewarding the bounty in one's life. This consistency can help the mind to build in awareness toward supply, abundance, and further giving. In my lifetime of observing many hundreds of families, almost without exception, the

"Under the law of compensation there is no such thing as getting something for nothing. We must give full measure for all that we receive at some time. Every day is a day of judgment in which the balance between giving and receiving is struck. Every instant of time, the state of mind, body, and circumstance shows just where we stand, just how well or how poorly we have observed the spirit of the law."
—Georgiana Tree West, *Prosperity's Ten Commandments*

"Tithing is a tacit agreement that man is in partnership with God. . . . It brings into the consciousness a sense of divine order that is manifest in one's outer life and affairs as increased efficiency and greater prosperity. It is the surest way ever found to demonstrate plenty."
—Charles Fillmore, *The Revealing Word*

family that tithes for more than ten years becomes both prosperous and happy. This is the one investment suitable for all persons.

Charles Fillmore, cofounder of Unity School of Christianity in the United States, made a powerful statement regarding our thoughts and money. He said, *"Watch your thoughts when you are handling your money, because your money is attached through your mind to the One Source of all substance and all money. When you think of your money, which is visible, as something directly attached to an invisible source that is giving or withholding, according to your thought, you have the key to all riches and the reason for all lack."*

LAW 5

Self-control wins the race
—Anonymous

Can you imagine what it was like to live in the world when it took a month or more to cross the Atlantic Ocean? When you might have had to wait months in San Francisco for a letter to arrive by Pony Express from New York? When you had to travel long distances over bumpy dirt roads to the nearest town to buy a new pair of shoes? The slow pace of life at the turn of the century may be difficult to comprehend today when the Concorde travels between New York and Paris in three hours, when fax machines transmit letters in seconds, and the local mall is only minutes away by car and super highway. Cutting-edge technology allows us to do almost anything instantly. As accustomed as we are to the high speed of life today, we sometimes fail to realize that, as a wise person once said, *"The faster we go, the behinder we get!"*

The ancient fable about the hare and the tortoise illustrates this peculiar phenomenon. The hare was a long-legged creature capable of leaping and bounding over long distances in a short amount of time. He enjoyed teasing the tortoise, who was, after all, just a sluggish old turtle with short legs, who moved only a little faster than a snail. One day the tortoise had enough of the hare's boasting about how speedy he was and challenged him to a race. The hare was delighted to oblige.

When a forest animal gave a starting whistle and the race began, the hare literally ran circles around the tortoise, laughing and bragging, totally confident that he was going to win the race. The tortoise simply ignored him as he plodded along the race course that ran several miles down a country lane. When the hare couldn't get a rise out of the tortoise, he sped on down the road to see what kind of fun he could have. He chased a squirrel off into a field and explored several rabbit holes. Having grown tired from his chasing around, and confident the tortoise would never catch up, the hare decided to take a nap in a soft bed of grass. Meanwhile, the tortoise continued to put one foot in front of the other. He moved slowly, one step at a time, along the race course. Eventually, he reached the place where the hare was sleeping soundly by the side of the road. Quietly the tortoise passed him and moved on toward the finish line. The sound of the other animals cheering for the victorious tortoise awakened the hare, who skulked off into the woods, embarrassed that in his hurry to be the fastest and the best he had neglected to stay in the race. Although he had been the faster of the two, he failed to finish. The steady tortoise had put him in his place.

The ability to do something quickly can be a useful quality, but, as the tortoise taught the hare, speed isn't everything. In fact, the hare was so beguiled by his natural ability to outrun most other creatures that he made the mistake of thinking no effort was required of him. Because he was so sure he would win, the hare allowed himself to be distracted by other interests and eventually tired himself out. The tortoise, on the other hand, made up for his lack of speed with an abundance of determination and discipline. He realized that natural gifts can take you only so far. In the long run, using what you have to the fullest degree is the way to attain lasting success. I do not mind at all if people take advantage of me in any small way, but I try very hard never to take advantage of anyone. It is good that others are good to me, but the important thing is that I should be good to others.

Do you sometimes envy people who seem to have it made without even trying? They have the money, looks, talent, connections, and they're on the fast track to success; but you may seem to plod along, making progress a small step at a time. It's important to remember that it's not *what* you have, but what you *do* with what you have that counts. Like the hare, the best and brightest often resemble fireworks. They dazzle onlookers with their spectacular display but lack the staying power for real

"In your area of responsibility, if you do not control events, you are at the mercy of the events."
–Harland Svare

"The greatest things ever done on earth have been done little by little."
–Thomas Guthrie

"To win, one must be big enough to see the worth in others, big enough to cheer when others score."
–Lucie Campbell Williams

"Who but the self can be master of the self? With self well controlled, another master is hard to find."
—*Dhamapada,* a collection of Buddhist poems

accomplishment. However, if, like the tortoise, you keep an eye on the goal and your feet on the ground, you can be able to go the distance in any endeavor. You may be tempted by instant success, but history has proven that "slow and steady" translates into lasting progress over the long term. Cheng Yi, a Chinese scholar, said, *"If one concentrates on one thing and does not get away from it . . . he will possess strong, moving power."* If you want to back a winner in today's rapid-paced world, study the wise and steady tortoise. He embodies the law that perseverance and self-control win the race.

Spotlights!

1. We can learn from every situation we are involved in, regardless of how challenging it may first appear.
2. Our inner goals mostly determine our experiences. We are not a mere victim of the world.
3. Failure is not defeat unless you allow it to be.
4. Examine where you are in your life. Contemplate what is real to you and what *really* matters.
5. It is important to start paying attention to your *attention!*
6. Living life is not to have all the answers but to enjoy the quest in finding them!
7. You literally shape your world with your words and how you follow through on what you say.
8. What you *utter* becomes *outer!*
9. Tithing is an investment suitable for all persons.
10. Using what you have to the fullest degree is a way to attain lasting success.

Living the Law!

In his book *Learning How to Learn,* Idries Shah presents a contemplative story. You are invited to read the story, let it rest in your consciousness for a little while, then read it again. Next, contemplate how many of this week's Spotlights! you can see paralleled in the story.

> *Bayazid Bistami, walking through the streets with some of his followers, made an occasion to demonstrate the shortcomings of such superficial assessments, as reported in Attar's Musibat-Nama, "The Book of Calamity."*
>
> *A dog was walking toward them, and Bayazid made way for it. One of the disciples thought to himself that this must be wrong. Bayazid was a great saint, accompanied by students, allotted a high status, and a dog was after all only a dog.*

Bayazid perceived his man's feelings and explained.

The dog had seen them coming and had projected the thought to Bayazid that he must be sinful to have been created a dog, while this great man must be saintly because he was able to appear is such resplendent and honored form.

"It was because of this idea of that dog's," said Bayazid, "That I gave him precedence."

Week Ten

❖

LAW 1

Freedom is a fact of life
—Anonymous

"The free man is not he who defies the rules . . . but he who, recognizing the compulsions inherent in his being, seeks rather to read, mark, learn, and inwardly digest each day's experience."
–Bernard I. Bell

Pause for a moment and take an honest look at your world from your present perspective. Does your life feel open and flowing? or do you sometimes feel restricted and confined in any areas? Do you feel that you have a good grasp on the direction of your life? or are there occasions when you feel tossed by the winds of change and buffeted by other people's opinions and actions? Are you able to pursue your chosen aims without restriction? or do you feel someone or something may be hampering you—that your life is not fully yours to do as you please?

To be fully alive and *living*—not just existing—in today's world, it is important to allow ourselves to be in a harmonious flow with the people and events around us and still be able to continue moving in the direction of our sincere desires for our life. We cannot afford to confine ourselves to any rigid picture of who we are or how we think things should be done. An oriental sage once said that the secret to freedom and happiness is to *"cease to cherish our opinions."* This awareness provides great insight. Often, we stuff ourselves into habitual ways of doing things in a certain manner. Then, if things don't go in the direction we expect, or if someone comes along with a different idea or perspective, we get upset and become a nuisance to ourselves and those around us. One way to be free is to break the molds of old ways of thinking and rigid ways of doing things.

In *Man's Search for Meaning*, Viktor Frankl tells of his own experience in a Nazi concentration camp. He reflects on the irony that he never felt so free as he did during that dreadful period. How could that be true? Even though all obvious freedoms had been taken away from him and he was living in constant threat of sickness, torture, and death, he discovered a depth of freedom inside of himself that he had never before experienced.

We are free spirits, and our minds not bound to anything *unless we think we are*. Several years ago, there was an old Three Stooges comedy routine on American television in which Larry would call out to Moe, "I can't see! I can't see!" Moe would immediately rush to Larry's aid, asking, "Why not?" Larry would then smile and proclaim, "Because I got my eyes closed!" Then, of course, Moe would promptly bop Larry on the head. It is a good idea to pause occasionally to think about what we may not be seeing in our world because we have our eyes closed. (And preferably do this before we get "bopped" on the head by circumstances!) We can consider whether it is life that may be restraining us or if we are confining ourselves with limited thinking. Our happy realization can be that our minds cannot be tied to any experience unless we are bound by our own thoughts.

If we come to understand that freedom is inescapable, that understanding can serve us greatly in living a happy and productive life. In the middle of one of the most restrictive environments imaginable, Viktor Frankl discovered this truth about freedom. He learned that no matter where life might take him, no matter how terrible the external conditions might be, he still had the freedom of his own thoughts and attitudes. He could choose to see with the eyes of a free spirit.

"Freedom which has genuine meaning is more than a timeless abstraction, more than an absence of restraints."
–Helen M. Lynd

We may often give this inalienable freedom away by believing that our parents, teachers, friends, employers, or whoever cause us to feel a certain way. However, when we truly understand that no one can make us think or feel anything unless we give them permission, we begin to understand the vastness of our freedom. No person or circumstance has the power to change that truth. Viktor Frankl has shown us, eloquently and movingly, that, even in the midst of a horrible experience, valuable lessons can be learned. He could have thrown up his hands in despair at the outer circumstances. He could have convinced himself the Nazis made him give up. Instead, he realized that even dictators could not control his thoughts and attitudes and that he had the choice of making his experience whatever he desired.

If your thoughts sometimes flow in a negative attitude toward life, do you feel this is the result of some external force? Do you ever hear yourself saying that you have no future because someone is coercing you in a particular direction? Do you feel you could be happy if only others would change? Or are you choosing to look for the meaning and the good in every situation?

"What other liberty is there worth having, if we have not freedom and peace in our minds—if our inmost and most private man is but a sour and turbid pool?"
–Henry David Thoreau

We cannot escape the truth that we are free to think as we choose, and we *are* responsible for our own thoughts and attitudes. If they're not what we desire, we can change them and, thereby, change our experience of life. So long as we cherish our freedom to *think* and *be*, it can never be taken from us. Routines cannot bind us unless we believe in them. Patterns were given to serve us—not for us to live for them. An old adage says, *"Behold the turtle who makes progress only when he sticks his neck out!"* Do you dare to go boldly and freely forward—positively? True freedom can come to us only by way of self-dominion. When a sincere desire for spiritual help begins to grow in the heart, that help is at hand and freedom is assured. You then may become fully independent!

LAW 2

By asserting our will, many a closed door will open before us
—Seyyed Hossein Nasr

Paul's large family owned and operated a successful cattle ranch in Montana for three generations. Along with his friends and neighbors, he shared a love of the land and the livestock. Paul respected ranching life and assumed, as did others, that he would continue this vocation as an adult. He studied agro–business at the nearby college and worked on the ranch during summers and school breaks.

"Where the willingness is great, the difficulties cannot be great."
–Niccolo Machiavelli

After taking a scuba diving class at the college, Paul began to feel pulled in another direction. His underwater experience was in a swimming pool and a large, silty river, plus a big field trip to the ocean two states away. For Paul, who had never learned to swim, a major challenge was the course requirement to swim one mile. He had to take a swimming class on the side and run daily (not his favorite activity) to develop the necessary physical endurance to pass the test.

Some of Paul's happiest moments as a child were when he watched Jacques Cousteau's television program about the undersea world. The French oceanographer seemed more at home underwater than on land, and his inventions and contributions to undersea exploration intrigued Paul. He began thinking more and more about this fascinating realm. He read everything on it he could find and sent for additional literature to feed his growing interest. He daydreamed about exploring coral reefs and identifying exotic fish. He talked of the sea with wonder, awe, and increasing knowledge. Eager to explore tropical waters, Paul withdrew his savings and flew to the Cayman Islands to dive during a spring break—an adventure that opened up a beautiful new world.

Paul's family thought his attraction to the sea was only a passing interest like others he'd had over the years. When he began investigating dive schools around the country, however, they were concerned. This area of Paul's interest had no relation to their world, and they doubted its practicality. They loved Paul very much, but saw his activity as a flight of fancy and a waste of money. Paul held deep love, respect, and loyalty for his family, and, like most young people, he cared about their approval. He suffered from the conflict between what he felt guided to do and his family's wishes for him. In addition, the schools were far from home, and he knew he would miss his family.

"The will to win is worthless if you do not have the will to prepare."
–Louis Pasteur

Ultimately, he made a decision; he chose the school he thought best and sent in his application. The school was expensive, but Paul worked long and hard at unpleasant jobs; he lived simply and saved his money. Because few people understood or supported his goal, he knew he was regarded as "different." Time passed, full of delays and setbacks. At times his dream seemed far away, and he wondered if circumstances were telling him to give it up and settle for something more "realistic." But Paul knew what he wanted and persevered in his efforts.

Three years passed before Paul finally entered school. He applied himself and graduated at the top of his class, earning the school's first recommendation for a job at a dive resort in the Bahamas. After valuable experience there, he was invited back to join the school's teaching staff. He took more schooling and became qualified to instruct instructors. From the additional education, Paul discovered his love of the scientific aspects of his work, which opened up further avenues of potential.

His success fed on itself and created more success. At age twenty-seven, Paul is respected as one of the top people in his field. Not only is he in demand as a teacher, but he also writes articles for publication; co-owns a dive shop; travels around to trade shows; has his diving equipment provided; and has become an accomplished underwater photographer. He meets people from all over the world. He knows he can go anywhere he likes and enjoy work and friends. Paul's family is very proud of his accomplishments, and he enjoys his trips home to see them. He may be different, but he's the most interesting person they know—and one of the happiest!

Paul's story is a wonderful example of listening to the inner guidance, making a decision of what you want to do and moving toward your goal in the best way you know how at that moment. He exemplified the idea of focusing his mind to a point of power, which is similar to allowing the rays of sunlight to flow through a magnifying glass until the concentration of the rays actually causes combustion—lighting a fire with a piece of glass! When strong desire is concentrated, it becomes a powerful means of manifesting that which you desire or precisely envision. And even difficulties can provide the strength of overcoming. Ask yourself: am I willing to commit to an activity strongly, or is my will fragile or weak? Remember, where there is a will, there is a way!

LAW 3

Count your blessings and you will have an attitude of gratitude
–John M. Templeton

It was only a few days until Christmas, and Jennifer Noble, a British citizen, was feeling low. This was the first holiday season since her divorce, and she was living in the United States, thousands of miles away from her home and family. She had married an American eight years earlier, and for the past two years, they lived in the Midwest while he studied for a new career. Following the divorce, Jennifer made a decision to remain in the United States. But most of her friends had moved on, and, although she made new friends and was successful in rebuilding her life, on this particular day, Jennifer felt sorry for herself.

Not being one to wallow in self-pity for long, Jennifer knew a good way to feel better was to make a "gratitude list." She wrote down all the things in her life she was grateful for, and, as her list expanded, her spirits began to lift. She also knew that gratitude was not simply a feeling but something to be put into action, and Jennifer was determined not to slide back into her "poor me" state of consciousness.

In order to shake off the blues and increase her feeling of well being, Jennifer decided to help others less fortunate than herself. She went to the local Salvation Army shelter and began to assist with their Christmas dinner preparations. She also bought a few inexpensive toys for the children who were there. The light in the children's eyes when they were given the toys touched Jennifer's heart, and the laughter and holiday cheer among those who were preparing the dinner brought a warm feeling of comradeship. Her holiday unfolded with special warmth and sparkle because Jennifer decided to give of herself.

There are many ways one can make choices to fit a variety of needs and temperaments, and Jennifer's choice may not be yours or mine. We can give thanks for our blessings simply by picking up the telephone and calling someone we haven't spoken with for a while, or writing a note of thanks for a gift, or telling our family and friends how much we appreciate their presence in our lives.

Actively acknowledging our good creates more good. When we are grateful for the blessings we already have, our very gratitude attracts extra good to us. Gratitude can be a powerful magnet that draws to us friends, love, peace, health, and material good. Those who are grateful experience the wonderful balance of being both givers and receivers. Gratitude nurtures within us a positive, joy-filled consciousness and unifies us with life's flow, which gives birth to inner fulfillment.

Many of the world's great figures have been faced with problems so large that, at first, they seemed insurmountable. What would have happened if Beethoven had wallowed in self-pity because of his deafness? The world would not have benefited from the legacy of his profoundly beautiful music. What would our transportation system be like today if the Wright brothers had given up after their first test flight? What if Herman Melville had stopped writing because, at the time of publication, *Moby Dick* was ignored by both critics and readers?

Counting our blessings can transform melancholy into cheerfulness. Laughter and joy are expressions of praise and thanksgiving for life's glories. True gratitude is a spiritual quality that is built into the soul with each day's practice, and its reward is rich and infinitely satisfying. Neither conditions nor circumstances nor appearances can make any difference to the heart that is lifted up in thanksgiving. A bird could never leave the

"If one should give me a dish of sand, and tell me there were particles of iron in it, I might look for them with my eyes, and search for them with my clumsy fingers, and be unable to detect them; but let me take a magnet and sweep through it and how would it draw to itself the almost invisible particles by the mere power of attraction. The unthankful heart, like my finger in the sand, discovers no mercies; but let the thankful heart sweep through the day, and as the magnet finds the iron, so it will find, in every hour, some heavenly blessing. Only the iron in God's sand is gold!"
–Henry Ward Beecher

"Ingratitude is sooner or later fatal to its author."
–Twi (West African) proverb

ground on folded wings. Thanksgiving is the power that lifts us on widespread wings of faith and joy into the light and life of God. Try your wings the first thing in the morning and see what they will do for you. Use them if thoughts start slipping into unhappiness and anxiety.

When looking at the glass that symbolizes our life, we can view it as half full or half empty. The choice is ours. The person who sees the glass as half empty may bemoan his lot. But the person who cultivates an attitude of gratitude will more readily see the glass as half full, and this positive outlook is self-perpetuating. The more joyful we are, the more attractive we become. When we feel gratitude for our experiences, it becomes easier to see the good that always exists. When we give a smile to someone else, we are likely to receive one in return, and that smile reflects a happy heart that is open and receptive to what the good life has in store.

LAW 4

We learn more by welcoming criticism than by rendering judgment
–J. Jelinek

"No man ever distinguished himself who could not bear to be laughed at."
–Marie Edgeworth

Like everything else in life, arguments can be managed. When someone is expressing anger toward us or seems to be overly critical, we have two basic choices. We can defend ourselves, or we can learn from the conflict. In a defensive conflict there may be lots of anger, blame, and criticism coupled with a minimum of listening to what the other person is saying. Nothing is learned if no one is listening.

When we opt for the method of argument, we do whatever may be necessary to protect our position, our feeling that we are right and the other person is wrong. Defensive arguers often use the strategy of hurling accusations back at the other person, shouting to prove a point, and walking away in a silent rage. A story is told about the English judge George Jeffreys, pointing with his cane at a man about to be tried. Jeffreys remarked, "There is a rogue at the end of my cane." The accused looked

Jeffreys straight in the eye and asked, "At which end, my lord?" In the heyday of his career as an art critic, John Ruskin maintained that it should in no way affect his friendship with an artist if he panned his work. The artists, of course, saw matters in a rather different light. "Next time I meet you I shall knock you down," one of his victims retorted, "but I trust it will make no difference to our friendship."

Using the learning method to solve conflicts, on the other hand, encourages calmness and patience under pressure. We force ourselves to remain silent long enough to hear other people's points of view and allow the expression of their feelings. If we ask questions to clarify a misunderstanding instead of summoning arguments to protect our position, we might find that what our friend is saying is not what we thought we heard. Or, we might find that the anger being expressed is the residue of an earlier argument or may be aimed at someone else and has nothing to do with us.

But whether or not another's argument or criticism is valid, we will always be better off asking questions and exploring the feelings behind the case being made. In that way we learn about ourselves, and, at the same time, we honor our friend by showing acceptance rather than rejection. Listening to a different point of view shows respect for the friendship and will help it deepen over time. Developing trusted friends and establishing relationships that will last a lifetime depends on our being unafraid of opinions at odds with our own.

Thinking habitually about people, their actions, their human limitations, tends to bond one to personal consciousness. To lift our consciousness above personality and human limitations, it is important to rise to the place where we are able to see the perfect image and likeness of God in all people. Sometimes the worldly press of matters may take our attention away from the spiritual side of life. During these times, we can pause for a moment and reflect on the creative energy that made and sustains the whole universe and every living creature, including ourselves. When our thoughts flow in this manner, there is little room, or desire for criticism or judgment of another human being.

Every moment of our life we are molding character, and it is our character that determines our destiny. We continue to create all of the conditions that now exist until we give birth to a change of thinking through an ever-growing awareness of ourselves and our connectedness with one another. Part of being human is realizing we may not be perfect all the time. We don't

"I claim no superior intellect, but do subscribe to a gut feeling which says, 'I am not afraid to intellectually test any idea contradictory to my own because from that direction, truth will surely come if I do not now possess it.'"
–W.M. Pepper

"There is nothing sacred or untouchable except the freedom to think. Without criticism, that is to say, without rigor and experimentation, there is no science, without criticism there is no art or literature. I would also say that without criticism there is no healthy society."
–Octavio Paz

have to assume an argument is an attack on our worth as a human being. Instead, we can use it to determine if our behavior or thinking might need adjustments. It has been aptly said, *"We learn more by welcoming criticism than by rendering judgment."* Where judgment can destroy friendships, our willingness to listen to another honestly and openly helps to deepen them.

LAW 5

Ask not what you can expect from life; ask what life expects from you
—Viktor Frankl

What are we going to get out of life? This can understandably be a question of fundamental importance to us. We begin with certain basic needs and desires. It is important to have a comfortable home, plenty of food, a meaningful and well-paying job, comfort, companionship, and joy. However, many of us have not fully realized a simple, basic principle: for our receiving to take place, we must first give. Giving and receiving are two aspects of the same law of life.

President John F. Kennedy advised Americans, *"Ask not what your country can do for you; ask what you can do for your country."* This is an expression of the law of giving and receiving, and it applies to everyone in our world. For example, if we seek a certain type of employment and there are no jobs available in that area, we might see if there is some volunteer position to be found in our area of interest. Rather than demanding of life that we receive the job we want, we ask if there is anything we can give. Through volunteering, we gain experience and contacts, and, oftentimes, the job we've been seeking eventually becomes ours.

Lowell Fillmore shared a special thought about giving. He said, *"Those who think they have nothing to give should remember that they can always give themselves, and that they can always render some kind of service even if it be nothing more than a few words of cheer."* The gift of ourself, our time, and energy may often be one of the most important and wonderful things we can give. On a rainy afternoon a kindly old gentleman noticed a newsboy

"It is necessary to give freely if we are to receive freely. The law of receiving includes giving. The knowledge that substance is omnipresent and that man cannot, therefore, impoverish himself by giving (but rather will increase his supply) will enable man to give freely and cheerfully. 'Freely ye received, freely give'" (Matthew 10:8).
–Charles Fillmore, *The Revealing Word*

shivering in a doorway trying to protect his papers from the rain. As he bought a paper, the gentleman said, "My boy, aren't you terribly cold standing here." The boy looked up with a smile and replied, "I was, Sir, before you came."

Every time an opportunity comes your way that allows you to give, welcome that opportunity with open arms! It may be heaven's call to fulfill your highest destiny. And the attitude of the giver may be more important than the gift itself. It has been said, *"The manner of giving is worth more than the gift."* It is often easy to forget about giving when we are constantly encouraged to "go for it" and "get ahead" in life. We may become so busy taking advantage of what life has to offer that we overlook the opportunity to give back something in return. Life's gifts that we continually benefit from are, in themselves, a good reason to develop and maintain an attitude of gratitude. Many of us want love and companionship, but it is a law of life that we must first be loving and friendly if we would attract to us the love and companionship we desire. We give and then we receive. It is often true that we must first release negative attitudes and judgments about other people for our love to be given.

"We are not here to get all we can out of life for ourselves, but to try to make the lives of others happier."
–William Osler

The law of giving and receiving also asks us to be good receivers. As we give of ourselves, our time and resources, our positive attitudes and loving thoughts and actions, it is also important to be able to receive the gifts of others in a graceful way. Everyone truly loves to give, and there are times when we are being of service by graciously receiving what another would give us—when we find a way to say, "Thank you, I accept your thoughtful gift."

"The truly important ingredients of life are still the same as they always have been–true love and real friendship, honesty and faithfulness, sincerity, unselfishness, the concept that it is better to give than to receive, to do unto others as you would have them do unto you. These principles are still around; they haven't gone away."
–Nancy Reagan

The law of giving and receiving is basic to a life of successful and graceful living. If we are feeling a lack in some area, our first thought could increasingly be, "What can I give? What do I have to give?" If we remain open and receptive, we will know how we may give. The more we give, the more we receive.

Spotlights!

1. We are free spirits and we are not bound by anything unless we think we are!
2. One secret to freedom and happiness is to *"cease to cherish our opinions."*
3. Decide what you want to do and persevere. Where there is a will, there is a way.
4. Let no day go by without counting your blessings.
5. If there are difficulties in your path, be thankful for them. They will test your capabilities of resistance, and you will gain strength for life.

"It is a fundamental rule of human life that if the approach is good, the response is good."
–Jawaharlal Nehru

6. *"You can't solve a problem? Well, get down and investigate the present facts and the problem's past history! When you have investigated the problem thoroughly, you will know how to solve it."* –Mao Zedong, People's Republic of China

7. Look around you. Find an avenue where you can offer the gift of yourself.

8. The Law of Giving and Receiving is basic to a life of successful and graceful living.

Living the Law!

In her book *Love,* Lao Russell, wife of Dr. Walter Russell, wrote about the power of love in one's life. Both Lao and her husband dedicated themselves to the transformation of world human relations. Dr. Russell's life was so fabulous that it almost seemed incredible. He was official painter to President Theodore Roosevelt, official sculptor to President Franklin D. Roosevelt, as well as an architect, composer, author, philosopher, and scientist. In her book, Lao presented the code of ethics that governed their lives and provided the foundation for their school, the University of Science and Philosophy. It is shared here for your contemplation.

Code of Ethics

To bring blessings upon yourself, bless your neighbor.
To enrich yourself, enrich your neighbor.
Honor your neighbor and the world will honor you.
To sorely hurt yourself, hurt your neighbor.
He who seeks love will find it by giving it.
The measure of a man's wealth is the measure of the wealth he has given.
To enrich yourself with many friends, enrich your friends with yourself.
That which you take away from any man, the world will take away from you.
When you take the first step to give yourself to that which you want, it will also take its first step to give itself to you.
Peace and happiness do not come to you from your horizon.
They spread from you out to infinity beyond your horizon.
The whole universe is a mirror which reflects back to you that which you reflect into it.
Love is like unto the ascent of a mountain. It comes ever nearer to you as you go ever nearer to it.

Week Eleven

LAW 1

You find what you look for: good or evil, problems or solutions
–John M. Templeton

Reality is often a matter of personal perception, as much as objective fact. The way two people respond to the same incident reveals this almost every time. Imagine the following scene. Two friends are having dinner at a restaurant. They overhear the couple at the next table talking excitedly. Neither speaks of the situation until later. Then one woman says, "Could you believe the nerve of that man! Telling her what to eat? Why, he treated her like a child!"

"Well, the menu was in French and I think he was simply helping her decide what to order," her companion responds.

Here is one event with two entirely different interpretations. Each interpretation is based on the perspective of the individual. The great teacher Seneca said, *"Eyes will not see when the heart wishes them to be blind."* Does not this wisdom request that we open our inner eyes and begin to see with the "eyes of Spirit"? How can this be accomplished? By lifting our vision. By choosing to look for the good in all situations. By deciding to place our attention on workable solutions to problems rather than focusing on what we perceive as wrong.

If the outlook of a situation isn't bright, we may have been looking *out* too much, giving ourselves too much to external appearances. Possibly, we may be discouraged and looking down to earthly things, looking away from the spiritual perspective. The solution lies in looking within, not out; in looking up, not down; in looking for the good, not the so-called evil. In looking up, we direct our vision away from the limited beliefs of the world. We no longer see ourselves or our circumstances according to the limited viewpoint of the world.

"Life is like the movie you see through your own unique eyes,"

"The people who get on in this world are they who get up and look for circumstances they want and, if they can't find them, make them."
–George Bernard Shaw

"The people with whom you work, reflect your own attitude. If you are suspicious, unfriendly, and condescending, you will find these unlovely traits echoed all about you. But if you are on your best behavior, you will bring out the best in the persons with whom you are going to spend most of your waking hours."
–Beatrice Vincent

"We always paid for our suspicion by finding what we suspect."
–Henry David Thoreau

"Attitude is the mind's paint brush. It can color a situation gloomy or gray, or cheerful and gay."
–Mary C. Crowley

Denis Waitley writes in his book *The Winner's Edge*. *"It makes little difference what's happening out there. It's how you take it that counts."* Do you know that many people lack health, happiness, prosperity, joy, and love because their outlook is not what it could be? Can you remember a time when you felt most bound to the power of people and things of the external world, and realize this as being a time when you were the least conscious of your inner strength and power? Do you remember that when you looked away from the outer attractions and focused on the light of truth you increased the power of your own might, which is the might of God within you?

Ask any professional athlete what is the attitude that allows one person to win and another to lose; what separates those who try and fail from those who try and succeed. The answer is likely to be belief. Belief is the vision of what can be accomplished. Belief is the athlete's own internal vision of himself as a winner. Belief is part of our personal perspective!

"Men are disturbed not by things that happen but by their opinion of the things that happen," Epictetus said over two thousand years ago. How many times have we overreacted in a situation because we misinterpreted what we thought was happening? *"I know I'm not seeing things as they are, I'm seeing things as I am,"* said the singer Laurel Lee. And truly, our interpretations of events tell as much about ourselves as about those we are describing. If we find ourself feeling jealous in a relationship, it could be because we haven't learned to trust ourselves. Perspectives! What a difference how we view our world makes in our life. Ken Keyes writes in *Handbook to Higher Consciousness*, *"A loving person lives in a loving world. A hostile person lives in a hostile world."*

Each morning when we awaken, we outline the day's events by our attitude. A speaker once posed the question, "When you get up in the morning, do you greet the day with 'Good morning, God!' or 'Good God, morning!'?" Can you grasp the simple philosophy of the upward vision? Doesn't the very act of looking up fill you with renewed hope and flood your being with the glory and sunshine of possibilities?

"Thoughts are like boomerangs," Eileen Caddy writes in *The Dawn of Change*. They come back to us. If we believe in a positive unfolding good, then that is what we will see in the events around us. We can search for silver linings in the darkest of clouds because we are committed to a way of thinking that involves growth. Negativity and pessimism are blocks to embracing the part of ourselves that already knows the answers. With our eyes centered upon the truth of our inner being, the outside world is unlikely to rise against us or defeat us. We can tap into the inner knowing that we have the ability to turn away from any appearances of disease, defeat, or failure and behold the heavenly vision of radiant health, overcoming strength and success because your perspective is the high vision!

❖

LAW 2

Every ending is a new beginning
—Susan Hayward

Nature demonstrates that almost everything occurs in cycles. The earth rotates on a daily cycle. The moon evolves around the earth on a monthly cycle, and the earth revolves around the sun in an annual cycle. During the year, the four seasons take us from cold to warm and again to cold as plants and animals cycle from a dormant to an active stage and then, as another winter approaches, again become dormant. Tides flow daily toward, and away from, the shore. Each day closes with a sunset, which is followed by a sunrise. Winter ends; spring begins. And so it goes. Every beginning has an ending, and all endings herald a new beginning: life out of death.

Kofi Awoonor, the Ghanaian writer, stated, *"In our beginnings lies our journey's end."* Our lives also have seasons and cycles. Each of us experiences an endless flow of beginnings and endings. Every season of our life has a beginning and an ending that leads to a new beginning. Childhood ends and adolescence begins; adolescence ends and adulthood begins; young adulthood ends and middle age begins; middle age ends and old age begins.

We generally like beginnings—we celebrate the new. On the other hand, many people resist endings and attempt to delay them. Much of our resistance to endings stems from our unawareness, or inability, to realize that we are one with nature. Often we don't feel the joy of an ending, perhaps because we forget that in each ending are the seeds of beginning. Although endings can be painful, they are less so if, instead of resisting them, we look at time as a natural process of nature: as leaves budding in the spring, coming to full leaf in the summer, turn-

"Birth and death are not two different states, but they are different aspects of the same state."
–Mohandas K. Gandhi

ing red and gold in autumn, and dropping from the trees in winter. It can be comforting to comprehend that we are an integral part of the great scheme of nature.

And nature's great scheme involves change. *"The world alters as we walk in it,"* wrote nuclear physicist Robert Oppenheimer, *"so that the years of man's life measure not some small growth or rearrangement or moderation of what he learned in childhood, but a great upheaval."* Today, this great upheaval signals nothing less than the beginning of a new era in the history of the world, for with our recent changes we have reached and begun to transcend the heretofore ultimate limits of nature and the earth itself. In the past, change was isolated, infrequent, and limited. Today it is becoming ubiquitous, continuous, and universal.

In his book *Mastering Change*, Leon Martel described how we now have the capacity of communicating simultaneously with every person on earth. In the summer of 1982, nearly half of the earth's population could watch the World Cup Soccer finals—at the same time. Someone has noted that it took five months to get word back to Queen Isabella about the voyage of Columbus, two weeks for Europe to hear about Lincoln's assassination, and only 1.3 seconds to get the word from Neil Armstrong that a person can walk on the moon! Old eras of communications end and new ones begin.

The more we allow ourselves to trust that every ending is a new beginning, the less likely we are to resist letting go of old ideas and attitudes. The less resistance we have, the less pain we experience in making the journey through the many cycles of our lives. Many people have a fear of change. Yet, our divine self is calling us to grow, to become more, to expand our horizons, and to experience the kingdom of heaven. Life demands change. We can choose to flow gracefully or to resist and become immobilized in fear. We can coast downhill, but mountain climbing is the journey of the Soul. D. H. Lawrence said, *"We are changing, we have got to change, and we can no more help it than leaves can help going yellow and coming loose in autumn."* Wouldn't it seem desirable and exciting to experience all the good that our gracious universe is trying to provide for us?

For a moment, imagine you are a caterpillar. You have this strange urge to spin a cocoon around your body—certain death! How difficult it must be to let go of the only life you have ever known, a life of crawling on the earth in search of food. Yet, if you are willing to trust, as caterpillars seem able to do, the end of your life as an earthbound worm may be the beginning of your life as a beautiful winged creature of the sky.

The powerful potential behind change lies in the possibility that each new beginning will bring us greater joy and freedom than we have ever known. Whether or not that actually happens—whether or not we continue to grow through the cycles of our lives—is largely up to us. We play a part in what happens by choosing how we see our changes, our beginnings, our endings. We can see each ending as a tragedy and lament and resist it, or we can see each ending as a new beginning and a new birth into greater opportunities. What the caterpillar sees as the tragedy of death, the butterfly sees as the miracle of birth.

LAW 3

The only way to have a friend is to be a friend
—Ralph Waldo Emerson

A friend has been described as a gift we give ourselves, another part of ourselves, a mirror reflection. *Webster's Dictionary* describes a friend as *"one who is personally well-known and for whom one has warm regard and affection."* Friendship not only involves us, it begins with us. The attractive force of friendship has its source within the individual's actions. What does a friend do? How does a friend act? What does a friend require of another friend? The answers to all of these questions revolves around the word "love." A friend loves!

"Wherever you are, it is your friends who make your world."
–William James

When Paul defines love in his first letter to the Corinthians, he lists the attributes of a true friend. *"Love is always patient and kind; it is never jealous; love is never boastful or conceited; it is never rude or selfish; it does not take offense, and is not resentful. Love takes no pleasure in other people's shortcomings but delights in the truth; it is always ready to excuse, to trust, to hope, and to endure whatever comes* (1 Corinthians 13:4–7).

"The most I can do for my friend is simply to be his friend."
–Henry David Thoreau

Reaching out to another with love means reaching within to find the love we want reflected back to us. When we love ourself, when we are a friend to ourself, we are in a position to attract a friend to us. As our own best friend, we have that gift to give to another.

When healthy friendship reaches outward to involve another human being, it becomes a two-way street, one that may include an occasional detour when opinions differ. Relationships are seldom consistently smooth. Captain Eddie Rickenbacker, the famous World War II pilot, crashed into the Pacific after leading a special mission. He and his crew were lost at sea for twenty-one days. He later wrote the following of his experience: *"In the beginning many of the men were atheists or agnostics, but at the end of the terrible ordeal each, in his own way, discovered God. Each man found God in the vast empty loneliness of the ocean. Each man found salvation and strength and prayer, and a community of feeling developed which created a liveliness of human fellowship and worship, and a sense of gentle peace."* The community of friends, the crew, that Rickenbacker speaks of was not a group of their own choosing. They were thrown together by the vicissitudes of war. Having come together in such calamitous circumstances, they were forced to support each other not only on the level of physical survival but eventually on the higher level of spiritual growth. They became friends.

What friends have in common is the best interest of each other. Friends seek to coexist, complement, and grow toward greater good with each other. One example of such a friendship is the relationship between Ruth Eisenberg and Margaret Patrick, pianists who have played to audiences in Canada and the United States. Because of the effect of strokes, one woman plays the piano with her right hand and the other with her left. Together they produce the mutually harmonious music they both love because each woman is willing to share the best of herself.

Friendship begins when we learn how to be our own best friend. How can we do this? By identifying our true self and then being that self with all our heart, soul, and body! As we come to know our true self and discover more of our wonderful assets, it becomes easier to love ourself. This has nothing to do with human ego. As the biblical Scripture says, *"As he thinketh within himself, so is he"* (Proverbs 23:7). When we realize our true spiritual identity, we not only believe that we are wise, loving and powerful—we also humbly know that we are these things. Then, it is easy to be a friend to others. Love always has power. Love gives of itself. Once we feel solid in self-friendship, we are in a position to offer the gift of friendship to another. As Emerson put it so well, *"The only way to have a friend is to be a friend."*

LAW 4

Man is what he believes
—Anton Chekhov

There is a story about a woman who dreamed she was being chased by a large, ugly, and terrifying monster. Everywhere the lady ran, the monster would always be right behind her, drooling, making ghastly noises, and breathing down her neck. In an attempt to get away, the woman ran into a canyon that proved to be a cul-de-sac. She was trapped. With her back against the tall mountainous wall, she watched as the monster came closer and closer. When he was within inches of her, she cried out, "What horrible thing are you going to do to me?"

The monster looked at her and said, "That's up to you. It's your dream!"

At that point she could decide to be devoured by the monster, have the monster turn into a handsome prince, or even choose to have the monster disappear. It was her dream, and she had the power to determine how it would play out.

To a certain extent, many of us create monsters out of our self-image. We come to view as wrong those aspects of ourselves that are different and unique and spend most of our lives trying to hide those "bad" qualities from the world around us. We try to run away from who we are because we feel there's something about our natural selves that isn't right.

Our lives are very much like our dreams. We have control over our thoughts and can view our lives anyway we choose. If our thoughts have created a monster out of a certain aspect of ourselves, then our thoughts can take control of the monster and turn it into something that can create a positive self image.

Every person often appears to others as he appears to himself. If you believe a part of you is wrong, is a failure, or is not all that it should be, and those beliefs cause you to dislike any part of yourself, then that's how you'll present yourself to the world, and the world will react in kind. We all desire friendships, harmonious relationships, the comforts of life, and enough of the luxuries to help us feel loved and blessed. What we want within we can have without if we are willing to believe in ourself, in life, and follow through with action. It isn't enough merely to wish that people love us; it is up to us to be kind,

"Those who think nobly are noble."
–Isaac Bickerstaff

"You're always believing ahead of your evidence. What was the evidence I could write a poem. I just believed it. The most creative thing in us is to believe in a thing."
–Robert Frost

"What we think of our-
selves makes a differ-
ence in our lives, and
belief in immortality
gives us the highest
values of ourselves.
When we so believe, we
achieve proportions
greater than mere
matter."
–Jesse William Stitt

helpful, and thoughtful to others. We must do more than long to be successful; it is important to develop the skills, the interest, and the perseverance that goes into the achieving of success.

The truth about every person's life potential is so incredibly rich that Jesus called it the kingdom of God within. This great teacher also pointed out that, while it is our Creator's good pleasure to give us this inner kingdom of good, we must learn to tap its infinite resources and share them with our world. The way to freedom from any limiting condition in the world of mental, emotional, and physical expression is revealed as we accept, experience, and express the resources of our inner being. We have the ability to set aside any sense of burden or apprehension and start rejoicing and giving thanks for the good in our world—if we believe this is possible!

Every tree, every flower, every blade of grass is magnificently and magically different. You, too, are wondrously unique. Instead of thinking negatively about how you may be different from others, accept the challenge, the joy, and the wonder of variation. You can create the kind of self that you will be happy to live with all your life. Make the most of yourself by fanning small sparks of possibility into flames of achievement. Do you dare to be different? Are you willing to set your own pattern. Remember the words of Shakespeare, who was divinely inspired to write, *"To thine own self be true, And it must follow, as the night the day, Thou canst not then be false to any man."* Each of us tends to become what we think we are, and if we present to the world a person whom we honestly believe is "okay," the world will respond to us positively and with acceptance.

LAW 5

Our quantity of spiritual knowledge is smaller than Ptolemy's knowledge of astronomy
—John M. Templeton

Claudius Ptolemaeus, familiarly known as Ptolemy, was a famous astronomer and geographer of the ancient world, whose theories placed the earth at the center of the universe. His two most important works, the *Almagest* and the *Geography*, brought to a culmination ancient scientific investigations in the fields of astronomy and geography. So seemingly perfect were his masterworks that they dominated scientific research for 1,400 years! Although Ptolemy was the most celebrated ancient authority, he was not the most gifted or creative mathematician, astronomer, or geographer. His genius lay rather in his extraordinary ability to assemble the research data of his predecessors, to introduce improvements of his own, and to present the results as a logical and complete system, written in a readily intelligible form. His very mastery of the art of compiling the equivalent of textbooks on scientific subjects helped retain the level of knowledge in these subjects to the limitations of Ptolemy and his times. But Ptolemy never imagined that the earth is only one of many planets around only *one* star from one hundred *billion* in our galaxy, which is only *one* of over one hundred *billion* galaxies in the universe.

The study of the universe leads to a reexamination of humanity in relation to its surroundings. It has been said that humanity as a whole has entered the era of spiritual awakening and pockets within it are stirring in their sleep and are beginning to ask themselves some questions. The winds of change are upon the earth. The human mind is stretching, and many feel the growing pains. Few can deny that there is an evolutionary life process going on in the human picture. That human consciousness is unfolding on a progressive upward spiral may be born out by the fact that years ago, when nations had conflict of interest, they seldom sat down to discuss their problems, but settled them by going to war. Now, nations are trying to solve international problems through methods other than warfare. In business and industry we see more arbitration and mediation, which represents an evolution in consciousness. In many legal disputes, the direction is to settle lawsuits outside of court rather than force every case into court.

One mystic described life as a "parenthesis in eternity." It is obvious that we have come from the past into a parenthesis in time where we can look back at history and, in some respects, determine "how far" we've come. We are part of a grand program, moving forward in accordance with the unfolding of our expanding consciousness. Presumably, the sphere of the spirit may enclose, not only this planet, but the entire universe, and so God as the fullness of nature, is inseparable from it, and yet exceeds it! Could it be possible that nature is a transient wave on the ocean of the work of an infinite Creator?

"Scientists and theologians should see opportunity in a theology of humility to pool their resources and explore together the vast reaches of the universe. We take as our models those careful scientists who are not deluded by intellectual pride and who do not deny the non-physical facts. Only arrogance would lead others to assert that what they cannot comprehend cannot exist. We see the opportunity for cooperation of the disciplines of science and religion. The really paramount questions about our nature and the meaning of our pilgrimage are strongly interdisciplinary. Already science is demonstrating the fruitfulness of interdisciplinary studies in the relatively new field of neural science and the very new field of cognitive science. We forecast tremendous advances in human understanding and development when humble scientists and

theologians meet together in joint inter-disciplinary research, in a kind of experimental theology.

"The future may be open to the scientific exploration of spiritual subjects such as love, prayer, meditation, and thanksgiving. This new exploration may reveal that there are spiritual laws, universal principles that operate in the spiritual domain, just as laws operate in the physical realm.

"Such an experimental theology would be God-centered, recognizing that God also manifests himself through a spiritual dimension we live in. Such an experimental theology may recognize that a new Renaissance in human knowledge is coming, building on the powerful insights of the past with new data from the physical and human sciences. The future religious emphasis can

Ralph Waldo Trine commented in his book *In Tune with the Infinite*, "The great central fact of the universe is that spirit is that infinite life and power that is back of all; that self-existent principle of life from which all has come, and not only from which all has come, but from which all is continually coming. If there is an individual life, there must of necessity be an infinite source of life from which it comes. If there is a quality or force of love, there must be the all-wise source back of it from which it springs. The same is true in regard to peace, the same in regard to power, the same in regard to what we call material things."

From the standpoint of our spiritual development, it might be important for us to realize that we came from an unknown somewhere; we brought with us an attained state of consciousness; and while we are here, we are expanding that consciousness. From some perspectives, it may seem that we are making giant strides, but from the greater overview, our quantity of spiritual knowledge is smaller than Ptolemy's knowledge of astronomy!

The household of spirit is vast. How can "infinity" be defined? The reservoir of truth is limitless. As residents of planet Earth, we are not entirely dependent on our human state of consciousness. We may attract to our livingness a spiritual atmosphere, a spiritual support and guidance because, on the level of spirit, there are no such barriers as heaven and earth. All is one. Attaining the spiritual life does not usually come quickly. It often results from continuous dedication to that which is greater than our human activities and knowledge.

Science is revealing to us an exciting world in dynamic flux, whose mechanisms are ever more baffling and staggering in their beauty and complexity. These same scientists are learning to live and work with quantum uncertainty and major discontinuities in evolution and complexity in cellular differentiation. Yet, scientists have turned these and other discoveries into opportunities, and many of them have expressed a new openness to philosophical and religious questions about life and the universe.

I hold a vision of the establishment of a new branch of science: the science of spiritual information and research. Perhaps research foundations, religious institutions, and people could devote resources and effort to these scientific researches in the spiritual realm, equal to or greater in magnitude than those currently expended on medicine. There could be enormous rewards in terms of increased peace, harmony, happiness, spirituality, information, and productivity. Like Ptolemy, we may also begin by seeking from the known resources and assemble the earlier research.

Spotlights!

1. Reality is often a matter of personal perspective as much as objective fact!
2. Each morning, upon awakening, we have an opportunity to outline the day's events by our attitude.
3. Every season of our life has a beginning and an ending that leads to a new beginning.
4. Our divine self is calling us to grow, to expand our horizons, and to experience the kingdom of heaven within.
5. Friendship not only *involves* us, it *begins* with us.
6. Make the most of yourself by fanning small sparks of possibility into flames of achievement.
7. Being a spiritual being involves the ability to touch your "invisible" self.
8. We are all part of an endless universe.
9. Like Ptolemy, we may seek from the known resources and assemble the earlier research.
10. The activity of spirit can make us a better human being.

Living the Law!

Let's think for a moment of building a house. An important threefold relationship is present in this analogy which may shed some light on our life. We often hear expressed the importance of our *thoughts*, *feelings*, *words,* and *actions*. Let's take a closer look at how these aspects of ourself interact.

1. Our *thoughts* and *feelings* provide the materials from which our house of life, love, and understanding is built.
2. Our *words* are the tools that enable us to join these materials together.
3. Yet, it is our *actions* that will use the tools to construct our house of living.

Be honest with yourself and search the deep corners of your mind to determine the strength and effectiveness of the ingredients and tools that have constructed your present house of living. Are there areas you would like to modify or change? Would you like to add an additional "room" or two? Are there any old resentments, fears, hurts, angers hiding in your mind—even though you thought you had released them? If so, release them again.

We may not know who is listening on the fringes of our world

encourage thinking that is open-minded, and conclusions that are tentative. It can encourage diversity rather than syncretism, even as our universe has proved to be in a constant change and progressive development."
–John M. Templeton and Robert L. Herrmann, *Is God the Only Reality?*

as we communicate with others. Would you be comfortable if anyone heard every word you said? Would you be comfortable talking with God in the exact way you talked with a person you may feel has "done you wrong?" Are your actions in accord with your thoughts, feelings and words, or are there occasions when you think one thing, say another, and do a third? This is a house divided against itself. Do you act, or re-act?

Write down the first thought that comes into your mind as you review this section and ask yourself some pertinent questions. A beautiful thing about life is that there is always an opportunity to change for the better and build a stronger, more workable and more beautiful house of living.

Week Twelve

LAW 1

Helpfulness, not willfulness, brings rewards
—Anonymous

Are you willing or willful? Do you work well with other people's ideas and direction? or do you demand to have your own way? When we exert our will in every situation, we may be forming a logjam that blocks the flow of good in our lives. When we allow others to express their ideas and to share in planning and direction, we open ourselves to different ideas and find new direction in the flow of life.

After trees are felled for processing into wood products, they are often floated downriver to the mill. Occasionally, logs will become stuck on rocks or some other obstruction. More logs become entangled until virtually all of them are caught in a massive logjam. Dynamite is then used to untangle the mess, remove the block and start the logs moving downstream again. Although the dynamite removes the block, it also blows what would have been usable lumber into an unusable scattering of mulch, resulting in a tremendous waste of raw materials.

When we are willful—when we are full of our own will—we may be blocking the flow of good in our lives, just as the logjam blocks the flow of logs. What happens when we become stuck in our own willfulness? Like the lumberjack who uses dynamite to break up the logjam, life will come along with someone or some event that can blow us out of our stuck place. The results are often painful and destructive. The more we resist the flow of life, the greater the potential for an unpleasant occurrence. The more logs that are piled up in the jam, the more dynamite is necessary to get it unstuck.

Science has made us aware of forces in nature that, because they are greater than ourselves, we may never overcome. Some call these forces God, or Mother Nature, or Tao. Whatever they

"To willful men, the injuries they themselves procure must be their schoolmasters."
–William Shakespeare

"The races of mankind
would perish did they
cease to aid each other
. . . we cannot exist
without mutual help."
–Walter Scott

"No man or woman of
the humblest sort can
really be strong, gentle,
and good, without the
world being better for
it, without someone
being helped and com-
forted by the existence
of that goodness."
–Philip Brooks

are called, our lives are much more enjoyable and fulfilling when we learn to work harmoniously with them. Willingness means being willing to work with the mighty forces of nature and with the forces or laws of life.

When we are at variance with someone, the argument we use enables the other person to see quite well that we wish to win out; which may be why he prepares to resist rather than to recognize the truth. A battle of human wills often unfolds. By beginning in this way, instead of making some kind of opening in his mind, we usually close the door of his heart. On the other hand, how quickly we may open the door to cooperation by gentleness, humility, and courtesy.

David and his brother, Michael, were complete opposites. Michael was a successful businessman, while David took seasonal jobs at dude ranches, parks, and resorts. Concerned for David's welfare, Michael tried to entice him with the good life. He would send David photos labeled "my new sound system," "my new computer," or "my. . . ." The campaign ended when Michael received a poster from his brother showing a breathtaking view of Wyoming's Grand Teton National Park in the United States. On the back of the poster was David's message: "My *backyard!*"

Too often we tend to take the facts of our lives for granted. We may learn to work within the self-imposed limitations we've experienced in our development; or, we may have developed the habit of floating from one logjam to another, allowing the forces of life to explode our world and reduce our potential for inner greatness. We have the ability to work with the forces in our lives in various ways to experience greater expression of who we are and what we're capable of being. This requires a willingness to take a new look at our current attitudes; it requires the willingness to change our minds, to think again, to make new choices, to subordinate our willfulness in favor of willingness. We can start anew from where we are right now. We can choose to work with and not against the spiritual forces of life and to experience the good that is present for us.

Willpower, which is understood to be the strength of mind that makes it capable of meeting success or failure with equanimity, is not to be confused with willfulness, which is a demanding of one's personal wishes with no thought or consideration of other possibilities.

LAW 2

Birds of a feather flock together
—Robert Burton

There was once a small boy named Sam who felt lonely and bored after his family moved to a new city. He wished dearly to have some friends. After scouring the neighborhood for several days, he finally found a group of boys who accepted him into their group. At last he felt as if he belonged! Unfortunately, the group that befriended Sam was not one of which his mother approved. One day, Sam overheard her talking with a neighbor. His mother sighed, "Well, I guess my son's just not the boy I thought he was. After all, you know what they say, *'Birds of a feather flock together.'"*

The small boy was devastated. He didn't want to displease his mother, so he immediately stopped playing with his new friends. Fortunately, he found another group of boys of whom his mother did approve. From that incident on, however, the boy interpreted this law of life in the following way: If you hang out with the "bad" crowd, then you are a "bad" person.

Although this could be a wise and useful interpretation, it does leave something to be desired. Who defines the "bad" crowd and the "good" crowd? Were Sam's initial friends really a "bad" crowd because of his mother's disapproval? Or, was she merely reflecting her perspective? Personal interpretations of persons or circumstances may lead to decision-making that is based on opinions rather than facts. Given this possibility, should we throw out the "birds-of-a-feather-flock-together" law of life altogether? Of course not. Often we search for persons and groups that are like ourselves and, by affiliation, fulfill this law of life by showing that, indeed, birds of a feather do flock together. The point here, however, is, How can we use this law to help us grow in life? Perhaps we can interpret it differently by observing and learning from role models.

Often the way we talk, eat, and work arises from observing other people. Thus, if we want good role models, it makes sense to associate with people who display the characteristics we desire. Albert Einstein interpreted this law of life in a similar way. Although many regard Einstein as a peculiar and solitary eccentric, this is not really the case. While Einstein was working

"A true friend never gets in your way unless you happen to be going down."
–Arnold Glasgow

"We inherit our relatives and our features and may not escape them; but we can select our clothing and our friends, and let us be careful that both fit us."
–Volney St. Reamer

on his first theory of relativity, he often invited many friends to his home, where they discussed physics, philosophy, and literature. Einstein wanted to be someone who knew lots about these things, so he managed to center himself in a group of people who knew lots about them. Thus, Einstein never wasted his time deciding whether it was good to be in one group or another. Instead, he formed his own group of people whom he admired and could use as role models.

It is natural to enjoy the companionship of others of like mind. Like attracts like is a master law of life dealing with the attraction between ourselves and other individuals, places, things, and conditions. We accomplish this linking or connection through our thoughts and beliefs. Most of us are familiar with magnets that attract or cling to a piece of steel or other magnets. Physics teaches us that two magnets can be attracted to each other by their magnetic fields. It has been scientifically established that these invisible fields exist within and outside the body of the magnets. Two such magnets, properly oriented and even some distance apart, will draw together because of the attracting force of the fields existing between them.

A second law of life applies in cases in which a search for balance exists: As you seek, you attract and are attracted to that which will fulfill your search. In view of this, it is logical that people who are thinking along similar lines are drawn together. It is also a universal principle that you may attract the possibility and the ability to become that which you innately desire to be. God knows your potential and provided that innate desire for fulfillment through the use of your talents and abilities. As you recognize and accept that desire, the energy of your mind begins to work in various areas to attract and build the possibilities and abilities that you need in order to accomplish your desire.

Can you imagine life as an artist, constructing a picture of us? We are life's canvas, its colors, its brushes. Artists love their colors and enjoy combining them in skillfully contrasted and integrated relationships to increase and vary the forms of beauty. Life loves to paint the picture of God's idea of you on the canvas of your selfhood. Authorities estimate that there may be over five billion human beings on this planet, and life needs every one of us to express itself, for life is infinite. Is it any wonder, then, that some of us will be drawn together by the magnetic pull of similarity and the brush strokes of blending the colors of people, events, and situations into magnificent expressions of God's creativity on life's canvas!

❖

LAW 3

Crime doesn't pay
—Anonymous

We've heard the adage that "crime doesn't pay," and we know this is true. But do we really realize how *much* crime doesn't pay? We know that most people who commit crimes are arrested sooner or later, and we also know that a person who is found guilty can receive a sentence that may forever change his life. However, there are many other ways in which crime doesn't pay.

For example, if you've committed a crime, you may begin to worry that someone saw you. Nothing may happen immediately, but there are many stories about someone being arrested several months after the crime was committed. Fear of getting caught may haunt you and create tension, causing you to jump when the phone rings or the doorbell sounds. You may have to find excuses for avoiding a person or place because of what you did. Sleep can become difficult as you find yourself tossing and turning with guilt. It's a horrible way to live.

There are so many ways you can pay for committing a crime. How will you feel when your family finds out? They will probably continue to love you; and most likely forgive you, but your relationship may never be the same. How will you handle facing your friends when they learn about your crime? What if you are arrested? Do you know that means being questioned repeatedly; being fingerprinted and having your picture taken for police records? Can you imagine what it's like to be locked in a jail cell? Even a holding cell can be a painful experience. The conferences with your lawyer are very different from those depicted on television. What if a trial ensues and what you did makes the newspapers and other media?

Even probation presents problems. You can be checked at any time unannounced, and teachers or employers may be questioned about your progress. There are understanding employers, of course, but there are also those who prefer not to have "someone like you." Teachers, employers, friends, and even family may watch you more closely. Some of those in your life may no longer wish to associate with you. The element of faith has been violated. A new friend may turn cool when informed about your past. The consequences of committing a crime pre-

"All crime is a kind of disease and should be treated as such."
–Mohandas K. Gandhi

"'Honesty is the best policy,' 'A dollar saved is a dollar earned,' 'Look before you leap,' 'The laborer is worthy of his hire,' may be scoffed at by some intellectuals as trite copybook rules, but nonetheless, they sum up the elementary experience of the race in creating and consuming wealth . . . people may change their minds as often as their coats, and new sets of rules of conduct may be written every week, but the fact remains that human nature has not changed and does not change, that inherent human beliefs stay the same; the fundamental rules of human conduct continue to hold."
–Lammot du Pont

"No people is finally
civilized where a dis-
tinction is drawn
between stealing an
office and stealing a
purse."
–Theodore Roosevelt

"Don't tell me there are
crimes
more or less beautiful
because there are no
beautiful crimes.
There are no degrees
in crimes.
Don't attempt to con-
vince me
that every hope
has to be for a time in
the hands of execu-
tioners . . ."
–Hereberto Padilla,
Cuban poet

sent a sad and unhappy situation. Although you may prove yourself as a trustworthy person and overcome the scandal of the
crime, the better way is to simply never commit a crime in the
first place.

When asked what measures could be taken to eliminate
law-breaking and crime within a state, Solon, the Greek legisla-
tor and respected statesman, replied, *Wrongdoing can only be
avoided if those who are not wronged feel the same indignation at it as
those who are.* In other words, he emphasizes the importance of
aligning one's being with honesty and appropriate conduct.

What can you do if you recognize a possible weak area in your
character that could present a problem? Fear? Anger? Hurt feelings? Inferiority? Alcohol or drug problems? Co-dependency?
How can one go about turning a weak point into a strong point?
Many service and support organizations are available to help.
And there are some things you can personally do to turn your
life around.

Dr. Norman Vincent Peale presented the following six-point
formula (which was developed by H. C. Mattern) in his book
The Amazing Results of Positive Thinking.

1. Isolate your weakness; then study and know it thoroughly.
   Plan a real campaign against it.
2. Precisely specify the strength results you wish to attain.
3. Picture or visualize yourself as becoming strongest at your
   weakest point.
4. Immediately start *becoming* the strong person you wish to be.
5. Act as though you are strongest where you have been
   weakest.
6. Ask God to help you and *believe* that He does.

H. C. Mattern was described as a thoroughly negative person,
so much so, that on a balmy night he walked into a lonely meadow on Long Island, New York, and tried to commit suicide. He
felt that life was worthless and there was no hope available. He
lifted a vial of poison to his lips, drank it, and slumped to the
ground. The next thing he knew, he was staring in astonishment
into a moonlit sky. At first, he wondered if he was dead. When
he realized he was still alive, Mattern suddenly wanted very
much to live. He thanked God for sparing his life and dedicated
himself to a life of helping other people. Never be afraid to
acknowledge your deepest feelings. It is by looking deeply and
honestly into one's self and recognizing what possibilities lie
within that we can make the choices that direct us on the path
of self-improvement.

❖

LAW 4

You can make opposition work for you
—Anonymous

Is something or someone bothering you? Is there a troublesome person or difficult situation you would like to eliminate from your life? How about experiences in your past? Or present? Are you facing an imminent and difficult situation that you wish would simply go away?

A story from the life of Abraham Lincoln, American president, affords a wonderful lesson for living. During Lincoln's presidency, an appointee was always finding ways to challenge and disrupt whatever the president tried to do. If Lincoln was in favor of an issue, you could bet that this fellow would be opposed to it. When this had been going on for quite some time, a friend of Lincoln's asked him why he didn't have this person replaced by someone more agreeable. Lincoln answered by telling his friend the following tale.

Lincoln was walking down a country road one day and came upon a farmer plowing his field with a horse-drawn plough. As he drew near and was about to give a greeting, Lincoln noticed a big horsefly on the flank of the horse. As the fly was obviously biting and bothering the horse, Lincoln started to brush it off. As he raised his hand, the farmer stopped him and said, "Don't do that, friend. That horsefly is the only thing keeping this old horse moving."

If you reflect on your life, you may recall times when you couldn't see the value of some person and were tempted to brush him or her off. It takes hindsight to recognize that the very situation you may have seen as an irritating bother turned out to be a blessing in disguise. Wouldn't life be a much more enjoyable and meaningful experience if we decided to look at the difficult people and irritating situations as blessings in disguise? If we look deeply enough, we might see these experiences as situations that motivate us to grow and change for the better. Like the horsefly, they may well be what is keeping us going!

One of the most important truths we can know when facing life's challenges is the following: *this experience came to give me soul-growth and to bless me.* If we seek to avoid the experience, we deprive ourself of the blessing contained therein. We often forget the Laws of Mind-Action and Cause and Effect. If we didn't

"Many of life's noblest enterprises might never have been undertaken if all the difficulties and defects could be foreseen."
—Theodore L. Cuyler

"A certain amount of opposition is a great help to a man; it is what he wants and must have to be good for anything. Hardship and opposition are the native soil of manhood and self-reliance."
—John Neal

"You can surmount the obstacles in your path if you are determined, courageous and hard-working. Never be fainthearted. Be resolute, but never bitter. Bitterness will serve only to warp your personality. Permit no one to dissuade you from pursuing the goals you set for yourself. Do not fear to pioneer, to venture down new paths of endeavor."
–Ralph J. Bunche

need the experience for our growth, it would be unlikely to come to us. Or if it did, we wouldn't be affected or even bothered! We would serenely and confidently move through the situation.

It's important to remember that we have a choice on how we respond to life. A wise person once said that it's not what happens to us in life that's most important, it's how we *respond* to what happens to us. This wonderful law of life can be practiced and perfected. As a start, it's important to realize that there's good in everything and everyone. Before we brush away troublesome people and difficult situations, let's take a closer look. That troublesome person or difficult situation may very well be a blessing in disguise.

As an expression of God, you are always greater than any problem, condition, experience, or situation. When you are tempted to doubt, fear, or resist what is happening, there is a tool you can effectively use. It is the simple truth statement: *This came to bless me!* Sometimes a situation that seems so unnecessary is essential to us and to our spiritual growth and unfolding. The Bible assures us that *"all things work together for good to those who love God."* Think of how the seeming worst-case scenario has often been transformed into the absolute best in the lives of those who believed this truth and accepted it into their life.

In Lewis Carroll's immortal *Alice in Wonderland*, Alice stands trembling before the Queen of Hearts, who proclaims, "Off with her head!" Alice is about to succumb to a fit of terror when she suddenly comes to herself in the realization, "Why, you're nothing but a pack of cards!" And they all fly away! Alice's blessing came through realization and understanding and the return of courage. You have the ability to make opposition work for you.

LAW 5

No one knows what he can do until he tries
—Publilius Syrus

Robert the First, king of Scotland, struggled to protect his kingdom against the invasions of the English. There came a time when he was driven from his castle and forced to flee to keep from being taken prisoner. He took refuge in a cave, where he suffered from great depression and uncertainty about what course to follow. He felt that everything was lost. As King Robert sat dejectedly in the cave and contemplated his next move, he spotted a tiny spider spinning its web. Time and again, the spider attempted to spin its web, paused, and remained still for a few moments before it put forth another effort. Finally, after repeated failures, the spider succeeded, and the web was completed.

In the process of watching the spider, King Robert discovered three outstanding characteristics of the creature: its tremendous patience, its tolerance, and perseverance. The spider never gave up!

King Robert cleared his mind of all anxious thoughts. He became still and quietly waited for the conflict and confusion within him to go away. He began to concentrate more objectively and logically on the current state of affairs that had plagued him for so long. Lastly, he determined to make every effort to regain his people and never stop until the mission was accomplished. He persevered and moved consistently toward his dream. Eventually, King Robert consolidated his position, and his people forced the English to recognize Scottish independence in 1328.

"All human power is a compound of time and patience."
–Honoré de Balzac

Each of us possesses the same three characteristics that King Robert observed in the spider and utilized for himself. Life may seem to wall us in, but we have the wings of spirit. We are transcendent creatures and have power to rise above obstacles. When faced with difficult or challenging situations, we can utilize our strength to become calm, wait patiently for confusing and conflicting thoughts to cease, and then move forward with a well-planned strategy for overcoming obstacles. And where we are right now is the best possible starting point. We can overcome most any limiting situation by being willing to direct our attention in an appropriate manner.

"This is the lesson: Never give in . . . never, never, never, never, . . . in nothing, great or small, large or petty–never give in except to convictions of honor or good taste."
–Winston S. Churchill

Somerset Maugham spent twelve long years as an unknown writer before he got his break. During this period there was much frustration and disappointment and a career that seemingly was doomed to failure. But rather than concentrate on the obstacles, Maugham focused on the lessons he learned about human nature and worked these insights into his plays. He kept growing and writing, even though no one showed an interest in his work.

One day a London producer was looking to replace a play that had failed. Searching through his files, the producer came up with a script that had sat unnoticed for some time. It was Maugham's *Lady Frederick*. The play went into production and

"High, but not the highest intelligence, combined with the greatest degree of persistence will achieve greater eminence than the highest degree of intelligence with somewhat less persistence."
–Catherine M. Cox

opened. The producer was amazed that this "fill-in" play was so enthusiastically accepted by audiences and became an overnight smash hit. Soon, everyone wanted Maugham's plays. And he was ready. Within a year, three of his works were simultaneously playing to packed houses, and critics were acclaiming this new-found genius. Maugham, however, must have felt like Paderewsky: *"Before I was a genius, I was a drudge."*

When times seem troubled and you may feel you are in a "drudge" period, pause for a moment. Think of the predicament of King Robert and the observations he made that allowed him to regroup his people. Remember the patience and persistence of Somerset Maugham. It is a great truth that *"no one knows what he can do until he tries."*

Spotlights!

1. The door to cooperation may be quickly opened by gentleness, humility, and courtesy.
2. You can begin life anew at any time from where you presently are.
3. Personal interpretations of persons or circumstances may lead to decision-making that is based more on opinions than facts. It is important to get the facts.
4. Like attracts like can be considered the master law of attraction.
5. If we desire a good role model, it is logical to associate with people who display the characteristics we desire.
6. The consequences of committing a crime present a sad and unhappy situation.
7. Understand the importance of aligning one's self with honesty and appropriate conduct.
8. Never be afraid to acknowledge your deepest feelings.
9. Every life experience may bring soul-growth to bless us.
10. You can be greater than your problem, condition, experience, or situation.

Living the Law!

Releasing Exercise

The moment we choose to take charge of ourself and our lives, we begin to create a loving, supporting influence in our external world. We have learned that our environment is merely a reflection of our consciousness. The good news is that our circumstances will automatically improve with our every attitude and action of personal responsibility. The first step in restoring our life is the honesty with which we review the situations and experiences that may have caused the murky water that is creating a barrier to our present happiness and fulfillment and preventing us from accomplishing our divine purpose in this life. You are invited to work with this exercise in the sacred space of your soul.

Step One

Reflect back on your life. Are there persons you feel uncomfortable with? Are there situations you would like to change? Make a list of these persons and situations in your journal. Write down key words that come to mind in each situation. For example: My best friend and I had a disagreement and parted in anger. The key words would be "best friend" and "anger."

Step Two

When you finish making your list, return to the first item and tell the truth to yourself about each experience. Be fully honest.

Step Three

If there is something you can do to correct the situation, make note of this and take the action steps. For example: A phone call and an apology. It doesn't matter who's wrong. Are you willing to take the first step back into love and harmony?

Step Four

Make a new commitment to a lifestyle of honesty and integrity with every person, place, condition, or thing in your life by acknowledging the presence and power of God in your life. List some key words you can use as motivators to remain in an open and clean consciousness. For example: sincerity, honesty, integrity, truthful, respectful, etc.

Review

Answer the following questions for each person or situation listed in step one.
  * Do you feel you learned the lessons being presented?
  * Have you grown from the experience?
  * What have you learned about your ability to relate to other people?
  * What insight does this awareness give you about yourself?
  * Is the learning experience completed?
  * Are you able to close the door now on past experiences and move forward, lighthearted and free, into a more illumined life of joy?

May the blessings of love rest upon you as you take charge of your life!

Week Thirteen

❖

LAW 1

'Tis the part of the wise man to keep himself today for tomorrow, and not venture all his eggs in one basket
—Miguel de Cervantes

Helen Keller once said, *"I do not simply want to spend my life, I wish to invest it."* For many people throughout the ages, human life was simply spent in doing what was necessary for survival. The hand-to-mouth existence of our prehistoric ancestors precluded their deep consideration of the future. At that time, to live through a single event may often have been an accomplishment.

"We must make progress slowly so as to preserve the progress we have already made."
–Haile Selassie

As human civilization mastered survival, life became more refined, and the pursuit of a life to be spent in comfort, ease, and physical pleasure preoccupied many people. In the developed state of our world today, many people have the prospect of an extended life-span and the assurance of luxuries undreamed of a hundred years ago. We can spend our life doing a moderate amount of work to obtain a maximum amount of comfort if that is our desire. Yet, those persons who are on the leading edge of human evolution realize, as did Helen Keller, that the greatest happiness in life comes not from the comforts and pleasures that money can buy but from the investment of the days of our lives in a purpose that transcends purely personal interests.

Each of us has a purpose for living beyond our own survival and pleasure. Every individual is like a thread in a beautiful tapestry with a vital contribution to make, not only to the sustenance of life as we know it, but in the creation and development of more beneficial expressions of life. Investing, rather than spending, our lives involves the commitment of our resources—ideas, love, talents, time, energy, money—to those activities that support this larger purpose. We think about how we can contribute to the overall good, focus on our talents, and then invest our energies in our chosen work. The return on a wisely made investment can be happiness and usefulness.

The successful person learns to avoid wasting precious moments. The Greek playwright Antiphanes summed it up when he said, *"Everything yields to diligence."* And the English statesman and man of letters Lord Chesterfield carried the idea of using our time wisely: *"It is an undoubted truth that the less one has to do, the less time one finds to do it in. One yawns, one procrastinates, one can do it when one will, and, therefore, one seldom does it all; whereas, those who have a great deal of business must buckle to it; and then they always find time enough to do it."*

Investment of time, energy, and resources can be exciting. Whether you watch a worldwide organization or a simple project in which you have invested yourself successfully, you can share in the success with the knowledge that in some way it might not have happened without your contribution. When you see your investment joining with others to make a positive difference in a community, in a state, in a country, or in the world, you can get a sense of the power that like-minded individuals have to effect change. The return on a successful investment can be a tremendous motivation to invest again and again.

Although you may be delighted with the success of an initial investment, the advice of the experienced investor is that you concentrate in more than one area and share your resources with many deserving organizations or people. The wise investor follows a simple rule based on the law of life, *"Don't put all your eggs in one basket."* For, as Mark Twain acknowledged, if you put all your eggs in one basket, you'll have to watch that basket!

Dependency on an investment or any kind of human relationship breeds a watchful concern based on a fear of the loss of that in which one may have invested a great deal. If you have one friend to whom you devote most of your energies and affections, then you come to expect a lot from that person. And what if your friend, for some reason unrelated to you, cannot fulfill your expectations from that friendship when you need it? For some people in this situation, disappointment and resentment, which puts a strain on the friendship, may result. In this situation, your investment may not provide a positive return. If, however, you invest yourself in several friendships, when one friend cannot fulfill an expectation, there can be others who may be available to provide nurturing and support. Because you do not depend solely on any one person, you can have the blessings and rewards of many friendships. The author of Ecclesiastes writes, *"Cast your bread upon the waters, for you will*

"If one is moderate in developing one's justifiable inclinations and succeeds in freeing oneself of inhibitions, this will not shorten one's life span, but increase it. All of these things can be compared to fire and water: only their excessive use is harmful."
–Ko Hung

"Stretch the bow to the very full, and you will wish you had stopped in time."
–Lao Tzu

find it after many days. In the morning sow your seed, and at evening withhold not your hand; for you do not know which will prosper, this or that, or whether both alike will be good" (Ecclesiastes 11:1).

You have the ability to formulate an idea, plan ahead carefully, and then invest yourself totally in the work at hand. Investment in those endeavors that fulfill a higher purpose can be vital to achieving happiness in life. The advice of Harlow Herbert Curtice, an automobile manufacturer, was to *"do your job better each time. Do it better than anyone else can do it. Do it better than it needs to be done. Let no one or anything stand between you and the difficult task. I know this sounds old-fashioned. It is, but it has built the world."* You have much to give, so give it to as many as you can.

LAW 2

Thoughts are things
—Charles Fillmore

"The brightest flashes in the world of thought are incomplete until they have been proved to have their counterpoints in the world of fact."
—John Tyndall

Thoughts are things. Thoughts create things. Thoughts shape things. *Thoughts are real!* The invisible process going on inside our heads that we call thinking produces objects as real as the ground we walk on or the food we eat. Consider for a moment your thoughts as a flowing mountain stream. The life-giving stream begins high in the mountain, flows down to the valley below, and then empties out into the fields and orchards of your life. You want to keep that stream as pure and fresh as when it emerged from its source. You wouldn't dream of pouring polluting chemicals or refuse into that lovely stream because you know you would reap the results in terms of an unhealthy and scanty harvest in your fields and orchards.

"Thought means life, since those who do not think do not live in any high or real sense. Thinking makes the man."
—Amos Bronson Alcott

Your personal world depends on your stream of thought for its prosperity, health, beauty, harmony, and well-being in the same way a farmer's field depends on unpolluted water to produce its maximum yield. We can look around our planet and see problems caused by pollution. Consider what might be happening in our minds and bodies as a result of the polluted thoughts and feelings that we allow to reside in our minds! Pollution may sound like a negative word, so perhaps we could think in terms of mental ecology. *Webster's Dictionary* defines the word "ecology" as *"a branch of science concerned with the interrelationship of organisms and their environments."* Mental ecology, then, means the branch of study that deals with the thought relation between human beings and their environment. The Bible hints at the importance of mental ecology when it states the thought relation between human beings and their environment in this manner: *"As a man thinketh in his heart, so is he"* (Proverbs 23:7). And a proverb from the Buddhist *Tripitaka* reminds us, *"All that we are is the result of what we have thought: it is founded on our thoughts and is made up of our thoughts."*

Mental pollution describes thoughts, feelings, and attitudes that are basically negative. As example, emotional responses of anger, hate, envy, jealousy, guilt, fear, resentment, and recrimination are pollutants that disrupt the mental and spiritual ecology of our mind. And the eventual suffering can be as certain as unabated pollution of the atmosphere, land, and waters of our earth can bring serious problems. Think about emotionally charged times when you have been a participant in negative conversations, actively or passively, about hard times, or illnesses; injustices or inequalities. How did you feel? How did your body respond?—perhaps with increased pulse rate, flushed face, or clammy hands? The positive reminder is that you are in charge of your thoughts. It is almost automatic to turn your head aside when someone in close proximity to you coughs or sneezes. You can use the same principle for mental ecology. Turn your thoughts away. You can refuse to accept any unwholesome thoughts that may be trying to attract your attention.

Let's consider thoughts now from a different perspective. Thoughts can shape things. Almost everything that we use and come in contact with each day was originally a thought. For example, the paper this book is printed on and the machines that made the paper were once thoughts, ideas, theories, and dreams. Similarly, the car we drive, its motor, tires, wheel, and mechanical parts came into being as thoughts in someone's mind. The material things we take for granted in life and that make living easier or more pleasant—pencils, ballpoint pens, chewing gum, magazines, textbooks, candy, ice cream, telephones, television, radios and VCRs, houses and apartment buildings, schools, churches, and so much more—started as thoughts, as ideas.

Because thoughts are invisible, we may not be aware of their tangible existence. Also, the material manifestations of thoughts

"One of the axiomatic truths of metaphysics is that 'thoughts are things.' That the mind of man marshals its faculties and literally makes into living entities the thoughts that it entertains is also a foregone conclusion. The word "things" expresses poorly the active and very vital character of the thoughts to which the mind gives life, substance, and intelligence. We see many inanimate "things" around us in the material world. If we compare our creative thoughts with them, we get an inferior conception of the marvelous ability of our mind in its creative capacity. . . . Thought is controlled by the right use of affirmation and denial—by the power of the mind to accept and reject."
–Charles Fillmore, *The Revealing Word*

"Nurture your mind with great thoughts; to believe in the heroic makes heroes."
–Benjamin Disraeli

may come hours, days, months, or even years after their inception as ideas. It would be a mistake to underestimate the power of the mind. Our thoughts mold the kind of people we become and are as important as our behavior. In fact, our thoughts are a form of behavior. If we think negative thoughts, we can become negative, reactive, and uncreative. But if we think positive thoughts and seek to see the good in every situation, our attitude and response to life reflect a sunny and pleasant disposition.

If we fill our mind to capacity with thoughts that we think are good and productive, we won't have room for the negative ones! Learn to discipline and direct your thinking. Focus on thoughts and actions that build up rather than tear down. Think of St. Paul's words to the Philippians (4:8), *"Finally, brethren, whatever is true, whatever is honorable, whatever is pure, whatever is lovely, whatever is gracious, if there is any excellence, if there is anything worthy of praise, think about these things."*

LAW 3

As within, so without
—Hermetic principle

Have you ever thought of yourself as living in two worlds? It's true. We inhabit both an inner and an outer world. We also may develop a preference for one world or the other. Some people turn almost exclusively to the inner world, while others direct their thoughts and interests toward the world of externals. But in order to be happy and well-integrated people, it becomes important to function in *both* worlds with ease and satisfaction— to achieve balance in how we live.

"The fortunate circumstances of our lives are generally found, at last, to be of our own producing."
–Oliver Goldsmith

In his *Essays on Happiness*, Carl Hilty says in behalf of happiness and balanced living, *"The paths by which people journey toward happiness lie in part through the world about them and in part through the experience of their own soul."* This can be another way of saying that our happiness lies in the development of our two worlds, the inner one and the outer one.

What we conceive of as reality may really be appearance. As Jorge Luis Borges, the Argentinean writer, succinctly stated, *"Reality is not always probable, or likely."* Maybe the only reality is the Creator. He and his works are the permanent things. Let's put it this way: the things that are unseen may be reality. Illusions could be the temporary things that we see. To be successful, each of us may seek to build our own soul from our vision of the Creator. We can express our faith in various situations—at work, at home, with friends. The unseen, the beauty that exists as potential in each of us, is what makes us alive.

We may feel that we have built up a busy and successful outer life, so free from problems that we seldom feel the need to fall back on our inner resources. However, regardless of how good life may seem, how filled with multiple interests, events, and congenial people, the outer world is often not enough. Those inevitable times arrive when we are thrown back upon ourselves and our inner resources. Most people want to know how to rise above hurt feelings and injured pride. They want to experience self-realization and the full development of their innate powers and abilities. Nothing the outer world offers can compensate for the satisfaction of the hungers and desires of our souls.

On the other hand, some people have built an inner world that provides more happiness than the outer one. It may be easier to create a thought world of pleasure, harmony, and accomplishment than to build a meaningful life. For some, it is easier to love people and feel harmonious with them if they can avoid intimate contact. It may also be easier to be great doers in the world of thought than to put forth the effort and experience the disappointments that go with outward accomplishment. It is often easier to feel that we are children of God than to prove it. But life does not allow us to escape. There is work to be done and a multitude of things that call us forth from our inner seclusion.

To live successfully in the outer world we need to live successfully in the inner world. Almost everyone desires friendships and the comforts of life. And what we want within, we can have without when we are willing to follow through with action. It isn't enough to wish for people to love us. It is important to be kind, helpful, compassionate, and thoughtful to others. We must do more than long for worldly success. We must develop the skill, the interest, and the perseverance that contribute to achieving the elements of such success. God has given transcendent powers to us and it rests with us, whether we express them or not.

"We are not forced into unpleasant activities. We either allow them to come about or we encourage them to come about."
–William Saroyan

No greater musical fiasco could be imagined than that which seemed to be in the making at Berlin's austere Academy of Song in March of 1829. A rambling work so unwieldy that it called for *two* sets of orchestras and choruses was in rehearsal. A *Passion,* based on the Gospel of St. Matthew, had caused little attention at its first performance one hundred years before. Its composer was as little known as the music: Johann Sebastian Bach had lain in an unmarked grave for eight decades. And conducting this Passion was its equally unknown "discoverer," a twenty year old named Felix Mendelssohn, who would now stand before a combined orchestra and chorus for the first time. As a young boy, Mendelssohn had come across a manuscript of the Passion at his teacher's home and fallen in love with it. The music had almost no other credentials.

Members of the Academy spread such favorable reports of the rehearsals that, for the public performance, every seat was taken! From the first notes, the listeners were swept up in a tide of exultant emotion, for the St. Matthew *Passion* is among the most deeply stirring music ever written. So great was the genius of Bach that he seemed able to merge notes, to paint vivid scenery, and create mood lighting. Bach's inward nobility of spirit received rough packaging, but the fervor of spirit flamed within the man who praised God in his scores. The beauty and power of the inner spirit poured forth into the outer world to entrench a visioned man into our hearts and lives.

Truth teaches us to relate the inner to the outer, to integrate the spiritual with the physical, to unify our thoughts, feelings, and actions into a harmonious oneness. There is an old adage that goes, *"As within, so without."* It means that what appears in our outer world—friends, jobs, opportunities, schools, career—reflects what is happening inside ourselves. Almost every successful person will tell you that he first thought out his moves in the inner consciousness. The door to success opens from within. Combinations of circumstances can arise as the result of conscious union with the inner forces of being.

L AW 4

Thanksgiving, not complaining,
attracts people to you
–John M. Templeton

It was the four-year-old's birthday. Around the room were strewn heaps of wrapping papers and tangles of ribbon. Everyone smiled expectantly when the mother said, "Dear, what do you say now?"

The child answered, "Where are the rest of my presents?"

That may be typical behavior for a four-year old, but how many of us still ask similar questions? "Is this all I get?" There seems to be an expectation of more—of something better, newer, faster, hotter, colder, bigger, grander. We can be grateful for the things we have, or we can focus on things we don't have and make ourselves and others miserable. Our mind has the power to determine if we'll be satisfied or left wanting more. What is it we want so badly? What is this emptiness we may be trying to fill?

Winston Churchill loved to tell the story of a little boy who fell off a pier into deep ocean water. An old sailor, heedless of the great danger to himself, dived into the stormy water, struggled with the boy, and finally, exhausted, brought the lad to safety. Two days later, the boy's mother came with him to the same pier, seeking the sailor who rescued her son. Finding him, she asked, "Are you the one who dived into the water and rescued my son?"

"I did," the sailor replied.

The mother then quickly demanded, "Well, where's his hat?"

One might wonder how a hat could have such importance when a child's life had been at stake, but the story depicts how many people focus on what's wrong rather than what's right. One of the great truth principles is that the feeling of gratitude is a mighty energy that attracts all manner of good things to us. When we make an effort to practice gratitude as a regular activity, it becomes obvious that life can be good, very good, and then expansively good! The universe responds regularly to gratitude by providing more opportunities, friends, activities, and means for one's life to grow and expand. Keep centered in the feeling of thanksgiving. Your thanksgiving is a celebration of

"Then I do not think of all the misery, but of the glory that remains. Here is also the difference between mother and me: She advises, 'Think of all the misery in the world and be thankful that you are not experiencing it.' I say: Go outside into the fields, nature and the sun, go out and seek haziness in yourself and in God. Think of the beauty that again and again discharges itself with and without you and be happy."
–Anne Frank

"Whoever willingly thanks God becomes rich himself."
—Albert Schweitzer

the truth, which can become an assurance of a continuity of blessings, leading toward happiness for you.

With great courage, give thanks also for the challenges in your life, for through them you can grow stronger and more aware. The limitations of the realm of appearances often stands in the way of those who do not know this great law of increase through praise and thanksgiving.

One man who had reached the state of consciousness of being grateful for everything in his life was talking with some friends one day and commented that, if given a nucleus, even though it appeared useless, he could produce something without the use of capital. His friends challenged him to prove his statement. They found a pile of scrap tin which was about to be disposed of, chided him to begin with that worthless pile, and then left the shop laughing.

The man looked at the pile, concentrated his mind on the tin, and said, "I am grateful for this opportunity to open my mind to spirit. This tin can tell me what it can do, what it can shape and form, and what can come out of it." Then he sat quietly for a few minutes, holding a piece of tin in his hand. There came to his mind a picture of a little matchbox. So, he began to cut and bend and pretty soon he had shaped a matchbox. The man called to a boy who was passing by and asked the lad to take the matchbox and sell it for forty percent commission. The boy sold the matchbox for twenty-five cents. The man, from his share of the profit, bought a bit of paint with which to decorate other matchboxes he had made. Several neighborhood boys were then recruited to sell the colorful tin boxes. Over the course of several weeks, the man's friends were shown the results of considerable capital which had been realized from the small and seemingly worthless pile of tin scraps. The man demonstrated the capital of creative ideas coupled with an attitude of gratitude.

We often look for things outside ourselves to satisfy our deepest hungers. We might hope for fame to fill our desire for belonging, or we may believe that money can bring satisfaction to our cravings. Some may turn to drugs to alter their senses so they don't have to be conscious of failure and hopelessness. These things result from the belief that we don't have what we need to be happy and productive.

"I can work better when I'm making more money," someone may say. In truth, better work brings greater rewards, and the best work is done for the joy of working. A great reward is a sense of having been of service to others and doing the job well. "When I'm famous, everyone will love me," we may tell ourselves. But fame doesn't bring true love. One is loved for who one is, and everyone on the face of the globe is worthy of being loved. This sense of being loved and lovable is the thing that attracts people to us. When we know we're lovable, we can be alone without being lonely. Knowing our true worth can be the best defense against the empty feelings that often lead one to mind-altering substances. Being grateful for who we are and what we have puts a smile on our face and gives us a radiance that attracts even greater things to us.

The psalmist in the Bible proclaims, *"Enter into his gates with thanksgiving, and into his courts with praise!"* (Psalms 100:4). The writer is inspiring us to give joyous and full expression to our feelings of thankfulness for the blessings God has given us. And we surely have received many blessings! Here is a heart filled with gratitude and a mind filled with the understanding that God is the source. To "enter into his gates" simply means to have a consciousness that we may be a little part of God's infinity. When we have this quickened consciousness within us, we can become aware of our unity with God's presence, God's life, God's love, and God's divine purpose in the universe and also within every person and every situation.

Praise, not complaining, increases the good and the blessing in whatever it is directed toward. When we speak words of praise as our consistent, joyous response to life, we increase the good and draw out the best in others. Isn't that the energy we want to program into our daily livingness!

LAW 5

Perseverance makes the difference between success and defeat
—Anonymous

A despondent man who had lost his job and completed more than a dozen interviews without finding new employment was given the advice to continue looking forward to his next interview. In amazement, he questioned such advice. Why should he try again? In reply he was told that with every rejection he was

"Perseverance is failing 19 times and succeeding the 20th."
–J. Andrews

moving a step closer to the good job that was waiting for him. He continued to persevere.

Imagine a goal you strongly desire as resting at the summit of a steep and slippery mountain. Next imagine a heavy stone placed on your back just before you begin to climb. How do you feel the higher you climb? Excited? Tired? Frustrated? If you fail to reach your goal the first time or even the second, what keeps you going?

The answer may include many qualities, but at least one of them is perseverance. To persevere is the ability to persist in, or remain constant to, a purpose, an idea or task in the face of obstacles or discouragement. Removing obstacles in the path leading to your goals can be difficult and frustrating, leaving you with a possible desire to abandon the goal and the energy and belief required to achieve it. Perseverance is the voice within, constantly urging you that *"if at first you don't succeed, try, try, again."*

A humorous story is told by Ignace Jan Paderewski about the perseverance of a parrot. "I shall always believe that Cockey Roberts, a parrot who used to come regularly to my room when I was practicing, was really interested in my playing. If I had closed the door, he would knock sharply with his beak. I would keep very quiet, and he would knock again, a little harder. 'Who is there?' I would call out. An angry voice would answer, 'Cockey Roberts.' 'Who?' I would say, pretending not to understand, and that angry, shrill little voice would come again, 'Cockey Roberts! Cockey Roberts!' Of course I had to let him in after that, and he would walk straight to the piano and perch on my foot for hours. The pedaling—and my pedaling is very strenuous—did not seem to disturb him in the least. He would sit on top of my foot, and from time to time he would say in a very loving and scratchy voice, 'Oh, Lord, how beautiful! How beautiful!' Ah, it was touching!"

Reaching a goal may require repeated attempts, each one bringing you closer to achieving the objective, while in the process of reaching other goals as well. Among these may be personal redirection or the achievement of a greater good not initially planned.

George Washington Carver, born about 1864, had a dream of enriching the depleted soil of the southern United States. He persevered in getting an education when to do so was extremely difficult, especially for a black man. Rather than give up, he continued with his efforts, and in 1896 earned an M.S. degree from Iowa State University. Afterwards, he persuaded southern

"The greatest results in life are usually attained by simple means and the exercise of ordinary qualities. These may, for the most part, be summed up in these two—common sense and perseverance."
–Owen Feltham

farmers to plant soil-enriching peanuts and sweet potatoes instead of cotton. After achieving initial success, he went on to discover more than three hundred uses for the peanut, thus encouraging a steady market for the crop.

At the age of twelve, Thomas A. Edison became a railroad newsboy, and at age fifteen he earned his living as a telegraph operator. He studied and performed experiments in his spare time. Although he fathered many useful inventions, it cost him more than $40,000 in unsuccessful experimentation to produce the first incandescent lamp in 1879. In a period of fifty years he filed for 1,033 patents. He continued to try and try again.

With the kind of effort exemplified by George Washington Carver and Thomas Edison, we not only come closer to our goals but, in the process, we also learn about ourselves. Through perseverance we discover virtues we may not be aware of in ourselves. At the same time, we may discover areas in our personalities that need further development before our goal can be reached. We gain satisfaction as we master tasks that lead to success. In the process of persevering, we increase our inner strength. We develop our spiritual muscles when we continue working faithfully toward the desired end that we label success.

Only in the dictionary does "success" come before "work." Though failure seemed to be his constant companion, Abraham Lincoln never stopped reaching for his dreams. Many of his detractors found little in Lincoln's background to suggest that as president he could bring the Civil War to a successful conclusion. Here was a man who had faced a series of failures:
—death of his mother and sister when he was a child
—death of his sweetheart
—suffered a nervous breakdown
—death of three of his young sons
—defeat as a candidate for state legislature in 1832
—failed business partnership in a general store
—large debt to be paid off after a partner died
—defeat as a candidate for Congress in 1843
—defeat as a candidate for Congress in 1844
—lost nomination as commissioner of the general land office
—defeat as a candidate for the Senate in 1855
—defeat as a vice-presidential candidate in 1856
—defeat by Stephen Douglas for Senate seat in 1858.

When asked how he overcame so many personal defeats and failures in his life, Lincoln attributed his success to his undying faith. He said, *"Without the Divine Being, I cannot succeed. With*

"Courage and perseverance have a magical talisman, before which difficulties disappear and obstacles vanish into air."
–John Quincy Adams

that assistance, I cannot fail." Lincoln found solace and comfort from his belief in God and from reading the Bible.

Thomas Edison was not a religious man but believed in a "supreme intelligence." Lincoln had very little schooling and was described as a "wandering, laboring boy," who grew up without an education. Edison had only three months of formal education. One of Edison's teachers called him "addled," so his mother pulled him out of school and taught him at home. Later he said that formal school bored him.

Dedication is another attribute of success. Edison said, *"Genius is one percent inspiration and ninety-nine percent perspiration."* He was never discouraged when he didn't get results even after countless experiments. When a friend consoled Edison after his repeated failures to make a storage battery work, he said, *"I have not failed. I've just found 10,000 ways that don't work."* In his later years, when asked how his developing deafness was affecting him, he said, *"I find it easier to concentrate now."*

When we pursue a goal, we may sometimes encounter setbacks. There are many men and women throughout history who achieved incredible success only after trying, then trying again and again. And we can do the same.

Spotlights!

1. Those who learn the secret of hard work can find success.
2. Don't waste time on the impossible when you can make valuable headway in the area of the possible.
3. An idea is only an idea until you put it to work!
4. Search for ways to turn problems into opportunities.
5. Remember that you are what you think. Your mind creates the environment in which you live and function.
6. Never forget that the only reality may be the Creator. He and his works may be the only permanent things, including the universe.
7. The door to success opens from within!
8. Heartfelt gratitude is one of the most powerful spiritual tools we have.
9. Practice tuning in to the gratitude frequency every day.
10. In the process of persevering, we can increase our inner strength.

Living the Law!

Gratitude is an energy multiplier. Heart-focused gratitude is one of the most powerful tools we have been given. Perhaps you

would like to deepen your own awareness of the power of gratitude and appreciation in your life. Here are some helpful ideas
to assist you in your practice.

1. Practice tuning in to the gratitude frequency. Set aside a
   time when you will be undisturbed. Be sure to have a pencil
   or pen and paper handy.
2. Sit quietly and become still. As you begin to relax, direct
   your attention toward your heart.
3. Send love and genuine appreciation through your heart to
   those people, experiences, and resources that are present in
   your life. Feel your heart begin to respond with warmth and
   love.
4. Now give thanks to and for the areas of your life that may be
   challenging for you. If you cannot send genuine appreciation,
   pause for a moment and write the name of a person or an
   experience on the top of your paper. Move your thoughts to
   your heart and find three things about this person or experience that you can appreciate and write these under the name
   of the person or experience. Send genuine appreciation to
   the situation. Repeat this action until you have covered other
   areas in your life that may be presently challenging. Repeat
   this exercise each day until you feel a release within and genuine gratitude is present.
5. Remind yourself that where you rest your attention and
   invest your energy is the seed and field of your harvest.
6. Whenever you find yourself in a challenging moment during
   your day, pause for a moment, immediately say thank you,
   and go about your work.

Week Fourteen

LAW 1

The secret of a productive life can be sought and found
–John M. Templeton

In his book *A Guide to Confident Living,* Dr. Norman Vincent Peale tells of an experience at a railroad station news stand. His attention was drawn to an extensive display of magazines and books dealing with the common problems of everyday living. Dr. Peale commented to the salesgirl, "I notice you have a great deal of this literature for sale."

"Yeah," she replied, "and I'm telling you that kind of stuff sure does sell."

"More than murder mysteries or movie magazines?" Dr. Peale inquired.

"Yeah, more than all of those and they even out-top the love stories," she declared. "This self-improvement literature is what we count on to pay the profits of this business."

"What is the reason?" Dr. Peale asked.

"The answer's easy," she replied. "The poor things (referring to her customers) are all tangled up. There are so many things they want to get away from, mostly themselves, I suppose. I guess they're looking for someone to release them from all their troubles."

One learns not to be surprised at wisdom that comes from unexpected sources. An observant salesgirl daily serving the public may develop shrewd insights into the ways of human nature and the needs of human beings. In the process of dealing with today's world and its many complexities, some people seem to have developed increased tension, greater nervousness, deeper fears, and more profound anxieties. The profession of personal counseling has expanded extensively over recent years in an effort to assist people in these situations. This work is

"God has given each normal person a capacity to achieve some end. True, some are endowed with more talent than others, but God has left none of us talentless."
–Martin Luther King

largely performed by psychiatrists, psychologists, clergymen, social workers, and physicians. We are learning that the condition of our emotional health can indicate whether or not we shall have peace, serenity, and strength in our daily lives. And mental, emotional, and spiritual health are essential to successful living.

In determining how to handle some of the stresses in life and learn more about ourselves as individuals, we gain fruitful insights from the Plains Indians. Experts say each person had an important part to play in the life of their tribe. At an early age, the young people participated in an activity known as the "vision quest." It emphasized self-denial and spiritual discipline, extending to a lifelong pursuit of wisdom of mind, body, and soul. The Indians believed that through the proper preparation for the vision quest—prayer, fasting, meditation, the ceremony of the sweat lodge, and spending time in solitude—the individuals could receive a special vision of their purpose in life. The personal revelatory experience received during the vision quest then became the fundamental guiding force for the individual. The dogma of tribal rituals and the religious expressions of others became secondary to the guidance for living a productive life that one received from his personal visions. To emphasize the uniqueness of the vision quest as a fundamental guiding force in some Amerindian medicine is to underscore certain universal aspects of the experience and invite comparisons with the *samadhi* of the Yogi, the *satori* of the Zen Buddhist, Dr. Raymond Bucke's *cosmic consciousness*, and the *ecstasy* of the Christian mystic.

In our contemporary world, we begin school at an early age and become educated to varying degrees. This process of education seems to operate on the theory that information *must be added to us,* and, when enough facts are added, we may then be ready to be of service and become more productive in our world. We may ask the question, *"How productive is this process?"* By understanding the philosophy of the Plains Indians, we learn to view the child as a person who has come to us with a special gift to give instead of as a product of the educational system. We use the educational process to discover the special gift, or talents, inherent within each child and then begin to develop those areas.

Are you struggling with a sense of unfulfillment? Do you have a feeling that you're here on earth for reasons that presently elude you? A lot of the world's creative work has been achieved by people who did it under whatever conditions they had to

"If I had influence with the good fairy who is supposed to preside over the christening of all children, I should ask that her gift to each child in the world be a sense of wonder so indestructible that it would last throughout life, as an unfailing antidote against boredom and disenchantments of later years, the sterile preoccupation with things that are artificial, the alienation from our sources of strength."
–Rachel Carson

*"Try not to be a man
of success, but rather
try to become a man of
value."*
–Albert Einstein

work with. Begin to practice the belief that you *do* have a significant part to play in life and take steps to discover what it is.
How? Each time an opportunity comes your way that will allow
you to express your talent, welcome that opportunity with open
arms! Since good things may be attracted to you when you put
what you know and believe into action, it is important to
practice, practice, what you know. Imagine what it might feel like
to live a productive life and then assume that attitude. Go forward to meet life with self-confidence and self-assurance. Do
what you are doing so well that people may be amazed at how
talented you are! Let the joy in your heart give great inspiration
and good cheer to others. Let your caring and consideration for
others be reflected in your thoughts, words, and actions. *"Seek
and you shall find"* is excellent guidance for leading a productive
life!

LAW 2

Happiness is always a by-product
–John M. Templeton

*"Happiness is a
by-product of an effort
to make someone else
happy."*
–Getta Palmer

The Constitution of the United States says that every person is
entitled to life, liberty, and the pursuit of happiness. And
there's an old adage that states, *"we are born to be happy."* For
some people, the primary goal in life seems to be the attainment of happiness. There must be an innate knowing that our
purpose in life is to be happy, because we seek happiness with
all our hearts. The sad fact is that we are often seeking it *outside*
ourselves. It's somewhat like the search for the Holy Grail! Any
person who spends his life running in a race that he is bound to
lose is really "out of it." This can also be true of those who pursue happiness. It never seems to yield to the direct frontal
attack. The happiest people seem to be those who are working
to give happiness to others. *Happiness is not found by seeking it; it
is a by-product of trying to help others.*

Most of us know in our hearts that there is great value in happiness. But we may delude ourselves into believing that happiness can be bought. A lot of money may be spent in being enter-

tained because often, while being entertained, we express joy. But the truth of the matter is that what we gain from others may be temporary; what we do for ourselves can be eternal. The mere fact that we falsely believe that others can bring happiness to us could be part of the reason why we may not have found the real joy within ourselves. Joy isn't achieved by paying another person to bring us happiness. We cannot get happiness from a pill, or from a psychedelic drug, or any kind of drug used internally or externally. We can only attain happiness by trying to give it away.

Hugh Black, who was for thirty years professor of practical theology at the Union Theological Seminary in New York, said, *"It is the paradox of life that the way to miss pleasure is to seek it first. The very first condition of lasting happiness is that a life should be full of purpose, aiming at something outside self. As a matter of experience, we find that true happiness comes in seeking other things, in the manifold activities of life, in the healthful outgoing of all human powers."* One example of this statement is to develop your talents and become excellent in a particular line of work, and happiness and success can follow from the blessings you bring to others.

A young friend of the British philosopher Bertrand Russell once found the philosopher in a state of profound contemplation. "Why so meditative?" asked the young man.

"Because I've made an odd discovery," replied Russell. "Every time I talk to a savant, I feel quite sure that happiness is no longer a possibility. Yet when I talk with my gardner, I'm convinced of the opposite!"

Reflection on Russell's comment can bring an awareness that happiness is not the completion—the *getting*—of something. Happiness comes from the work, the endeavor, the pursuit of a goal—the *giving*. Production, not consumption, is at the core of happiness and success.

A friend described a woman who always bubbled over with joy when she arrived in the office where he worked each morning. Many of the other employees stared into a newspaper, out into space, or over a half-filled cup of coffee. But this woman boosted each person with her joy and enthusiasm. One day, when asked what her secret was, she replied, "I push the 'happy button' before I get up each day."

"The happy button?" someone asked. "What is that?"

"Well," she responded, "before I get up, I remind myself that this is a fresh, new day. God has made it happy and wonderful because he made it out of himself. *I count my blessings.* Then, I

WEEK FOURTEEN

153

"How to gain, how to keep, how to recover happiness is, in fact, for most men at all times the secret motive of all they do, and all they are willing to endure."
–William James

"Human felicity is produced not so much by great pieces of good fortune that seldom happen as by little advantages that occur every day."
–Benjamin Franklin

"Happiness in this world, when it comes, comes incidentally. Make it the object of pursuit, and it leads us a wild goose chase, and is never attained. Follow some other object, and very possibly we may find that we have caught happiness without dreaming of it."
—Nathaniel Hawthorne

"True religion is not mere doctrine, something that can be taught, but is a way of life. A life in a community with God. It must be experienced to be appreciated. A life of service. A living by giving and finding one's own happiness by bringing happiness into the lives of others."
—William J. H. Botecker

laugh for the sheer joy of being alive and get up and start my day! Push the 'happy button' for yourself and see what happens."

My friend did push the happy button. The next day. He remarked that he has been doing it ever since and found it a marvelous way to begin the morning, and especially if the day promised to be a busy one. He was also following the wisdom of the French writer Colette, who said, *"Be happy. It's one way of being wise."*

Perhaps Mother Teresa of Calcutta epitomizes better than anyone the concept that happiness can be achieved by what you do. She believes in showing love to those who are near you and to those who cross your path every day. Spiritual awareness shines through in her comment, *"How can we love God if not through others?"* A powerful reward of loving service is the deep inner knowing that you have given the greatest gift—yourself—and that is a happiness money cannot buy.

A lot of people know in their hearts that there is a great value in happiness.

What do you really like to do? What brings you the greatest fulfillment? If these are the things that take up your time, then you are probably happy! If you can use more happiness in your life, try pushing the "happy button" and you may find a rewarding, useful, and spiritually satisfying experience. Let the joy of God express itself through you. Be as happy as you are intended to be. Seek the heaven within and be joyous!

LAW 3

The way to mend the bad world is to create the right world
—Ralph Waldo Emerson

"Let there be peace on earth and let it begin with me" are the opening words to a famous song. But what do the words really mean? How can being filled with peace inside one's self lead to peace on earth? The brilliant philosopher Teilhard de Chardin refers to the *"unimpeachable wholeness of the universe."* What does this

mean to us? It means that we are a part of the universe; we are a part of the wholeness of creation. We do not walk our path of life alone. The whole universe walks with us, and we, as a human race, are coming to a greater realization that we are all "one" in spirit.

Maybe each one of us is somewhat like a pixel. Just as a hologram is made up of numerous pixels—each one containing all of the information that can be found in the total image—so each person may be a tiny particle of life, containing all the data that is present in the sum total of existence.

Gautama Buddha, whose original name was Prince Siddhartha, grappled with the problems of human existence. Though his words had not been written down, his disciples memorized many of his teachings and passed them to succeeding generations by word of mouth. In the principal teachings of the Buddha called the "Four Noble Truths," it is stated first that human life is intrinsically unhappy; second, that the cause of this unhappiness is human selfishness and desire; third, that individual selfishness and desire can be brought to an end; and fourth, that the method of escape from selfishness involves what is called the "Eightfold Path": right views, right thought, right speech, right action, right livelihood, right effort, right mindfulness, and right meditation. Certainly, this awareness of "rightness" and the letting go of personal negativities can do a tremendous amount to create a loving, caring, and more beautiful world.

A good way to create a better world is for each of us to be better individuals. There are certain laws of life that, when followed, can make life sweeter, more harmonious, prosperous, healthy, and free. When we choose to abide by these laws, we reap the benefits of living in harmony with the universe. When we don't, we risk experiencing sickness, war, economic insecurity, and unemployment. The problems that create turmoil, pain, misery, and suffering in our world can change when each person makes a *conscious* decision to act and think for the good of all. Personal motive is always a good guide. Ask yourself, "Why am I doing the things I do?" and allow the inherent wisdom of spirit to provide the true answer. If your motives are pure, then good should come of them. The positive ideas we believe in today can constantly expand and grow in our consciousness. This could be termed being "on beam" with life. Pilots often fly using a radio beam as a guide. As long as they remain "on beam," they are safe. If they get off the beam, they're in danger.

Each human person, too, has an inborn "beam"—a con-

"Where a man does his best with only moderate powers, he will have the advantage over negligent superiority."
–Jane Austen

"If you have no friends to share or rejoice in your success in life—if you cannot look back to those to whom you owe gratitude, or forward to those to whom you ought to afford protection, still it is no less incumbent on you to move steadily in the path of duty; for your active exertions are due not only to society, but in humble gratitude to the Being who made you a member of it, with powers to serve yourself and others."
–Walter Scott

"I believe that any man's life will be filled with constant and unexpected encouragement if he makes up his mind to do his level best each day, and as nearly as possible reaching the high-water mark of pure and useful living."
–Booker T. Washington

science. While we are in tune with the way things were designed to be, we are "safe." When we are out of tune, we may show it in the form of greed, fear, sickness, addiction, and jealousy. Some people experience a lifetime of having the flu each winter, allergies in the fall, headaches, indigestion, and all the so-called minor ailments that we accept as a part of life. Sometimes it isn't necessary for this to be so. Each of us has the inner power to encourage health, happiness and serenity. We are capable of re-educating our bodies and our thinking.

By thinking and acting always with good in our hearts; by becoming responsible for ourselves, and, as an old Irish saying has it, *"If you see a job that needs doing, that means it's yours to do,"* we can begin to change our wrong world into a right world. It's time to stop saying that "they" need to be changing things around here. When we start saying, "I need to be giving life a helping hand," we then begin to benefit life. It has been said that "a journey of a thousand miles begins with the first step." Let each one of us take that step and make it count!

LAW 4

It is better to praise than to criticize
–John M. Templeton

"I have yet to find a man, whatever his situation in life, who did not do better work and put forth greater effort under a spirit of approval than he ever would under a spirit of criticism."
–Charles M. Schwab

"I feel like saying 'thank you, thank you, thank you,' I feel like saying 'thank you' to this world of mine!" This is a line from the kind of song you might enjoy singing from time to time. It could be the perfect song to sing when you really mean it—when things are going great and you feel on top of the world. It may also be the right song to sing when you *don't* feel the words, when things are not going so well, and you feel it's difficult to see the daylight for the darkness. Sometimes *"acting as if"* tends to bring about the reality one desires. Either way, the song can leave you feeling better about yourself and about life.

The reason is that praise is a powerful tool. Remember that the spoken word is like a seed. It must grow. We can leave the how, when, and where to God. Our job is to say what is good and to give forth blessings, knowing that the moment we have spoken gratitude we may begin to receive. To find contentment in the heart and a sense of fulfillment in the mind, it becomes important that we learn to praise and affirm life and the goodness of living. Living with an affirmative attitude means saying "yes" to the very best that life has to offer. Look to God for results; listen to his direction; then welcome God's fulfillment.

Be thankful. Your attitude of gratitude awakens in you a higher realization of the omnipresence and power of God. Praise can be the mental attitude that stimulates, quickens, whirls into action, and establishes in character the ideals of which it is the vehicle. Through an inherent law of mind action, you increase whatever you praise. You may praise a fearful heart into peace and trust, want into supply, sickness into radiant health, a problem into the perfect solution.

Give thanks always for all things, recognizing that *"in everything God works for good with those who love him."* The sun shines. Birds sing. Flowers bloom. Clouds form and dissolve, and you are blessed by these things. Give praise. Be thankful. You are included in the miracle of life, and all can be harmonious. If you attune your mind to the infinite presence of God each day and acknowledge that presence in your life, you can give forth love instead of malice; you can see good in everything around you; you can count your blessings until they number into the thousands; and you can have the peace knowing that your world is in tune with the infinite.

We may be involved in a situation that is challenging to us and feel we're just not up to the task. But what happens when we begin to praise our own abilities? And this is not focusing on an inflated ego, but on appreciation and praise. What happens when we begin sincerely to give thanks for our wonderful minds and our strong and healthy bodies? It's not at all difficult to believe that our own senses of confidence and self-worth are actually activated and strengthened.

Through the ages, the wise and thoughtful among us have said that there is good in everything and everyone if we just take the time to look for it. A Chinese proverb states, *"In our actions we should accord with the will of Heaven; in our words we should accord with the hearts of men."* We have experienced how wonderful it feels to receive praise and gratitude from others. It is equally wonderful to give praise. Children who are praised and encouraged achieve better results in school and play than those whose accomplishments are ignored. Although some people might argue whether there really is good in everything and everyone, few would doubt that looking for the good leads

"The deepest principle in human nature is the craving to be appreciated."
–William James

"A student never forgets an encouraging private word, when it is given with sincere respect and admiration."
–William Lyon Phelps

"Praise is warming and desirable, what the human race lives on like bread. But praise is an earned thing. It has to be deserved like an honorary degree or a hug from a child."
–Phyllis McGinley

to greater happiness and well-being. To look for the bad seems a waste of time if we're sincerely interested in the happiness of ourselves and others. Let's encounter every situation with the exciting truth that there is something wonderful awaiting us. As we learn to praise ourselves and our world, we begin to blossom in ways that are wonderful to behold.

LAW 5

Laughter is the best medicine
—Norman Cousins

"Mirth is God's medicine; everybody ought to bathe in it. Grim care, moroseness, anxiety—all the rust of life—ought to be scoured off by the oil of mirth."
—Orison Swett Marten

When the United States entered World War II in 1941, patriotism was at a high point, and young men by the thousands rushed to recruiting places, eager to serve their country. Movie stars of Hollywood were no exception, although some who applied were not accepted. Comedian Bob Hope was not accepted as a recruit. The country's leaders felt he could serve a better purpose with the U.S.O., entertaining the troops. He protested vigorously that he didn't want to receive any preferential treatment, but the government stood firm. They could not possibly have known at the time what a wise decision they made.

Hope and his group of entertainers logged millions of miles and gave thousands of performances for the troops in Europe and the Far East. These men and women risked their lives many times by performing in combat zones. They visited the hospitals where the wounded were treated and brought a lot of joy to many people. Always the positive entertainer, Hope didn't dole out sympathy or pity. He would ask a wounded serviceman questions such as, "Did you see our show, or were you already sick?" The therapeutic value of laughter was never questioned by those who received his visits. Laughter can be a doorway from misery to joy.

When a person laughs, many good things happen. Muscles relax, the breathing is deeper, the bloodstream is more fully oxygenated. Pain and gloom are forgotten, or at least put into proper perspective. It's difficult for a person who is shaking with laughter to think negative thoughts. Often the most serious of matters can best be solved by giving the situation "the light touch."

In volume 3 of *The Life and Teachings of the Masters of the Far East*, Baird Spaulding described his meeting with the "laughing disciple." Traveling with a group of pilgrims through extremely treacherous territory in the Himalayan mountains, the author tells how the laughing disciple assisted the group in their journey: *"In all, it was an arduous climb, but at the rough places, the chela (disciple) went ahead with laughter and song. At the more difficult places, his voice would ring out and it seemed as if it lifted us over them without an effort. . . . We thought the trail on its flanks stony and perilous but now we labored over a trail much of the distance on hands and knees. Still, the song and laughter of the chela bore us onward as though on wings. . . . Can you, dear reader, not see why the trail that day was not long and arduous? It all passed in an instant. The vibrations of strength, power, and harmony that are always sent forth from the temples but serve to urge the travelers onward to these peaks."*

We are also travelers over the mountain pathways of life. How tremendously valuable is the power of joy and laughter to enliven our soul as we go forward to meet our goals. Laughter can lift us over the high ridges and lighten up the dark valleys in a way that makes life much easier. A happy heart generates a forcefield of love and joy in which doubt, fear, disaster, and dismay have no power to interrupt the universal flow of good. And in some instances, laughter has been considered to be a high form of prayer! Truly, when you are in the consciousness of the joy of the spirit, you are praying from the very heart of your being.

An interesting story is told about how laughter can be so uplifting in a tense situation. In September of 1862, Abraham Lincoln, president of the United States, called a special session of his closest advisers. When they arrived, he was reading a book. At first he paid little attention to their entrance, then started to read aloud to them a piece by the humorist Artemus Ward entitled *A High-Handed Outrage at Utica*, which Lincoln found very funny and laughed heartily at the end. But no one joined in. The cabinet members sat in stony disapproval of the president's seeming frivolity. Lincoln rebuked them, *"Why don't you laugh? With the fearful strain that is upon me night and day, if I did not laugh I should die, and you need this medicine as much as I do."* Then turning to business, he told them that he had privately prepared "a little paper of much significance." It was the draft of the Emancipation Proclamation!

"There is no greater every-day virtue than cheerfulness. This quality in man among men is like sunshine to the day, or a gentle renewing moisture to parched herbs. The light of a cheerful face diffuses itself, and communicates the happy spirit that inspires it." —Thomas Carlyle

"People who laugh actually live longer than those who don't laugh. Few persons realize that health actually varies according to the amount of laughter." —James D. Walsh, M. D.

"Mirth prolongeth the life, and causeth health."
–Nicholas Udall

Those who bring laughter also seem to be beneficiaries. Although we can't all be professional comedians, opportunities may be available to share our laughter and good humor with everyone we meet. We can visit hospitals, convalescent centers, and homes for the aged and give of the joy of our spirit. The people who live in these homes are often terribly lonely. They may feel forgotten by the ones they love, and visitors are welcome, especially those who bring moments of healing laughter.

For those who may feel unsure of themselves as natural wits or stand-up comedians, books and videos and audio tapes are available which can be shared. The sharing is the important part. It can brighten a lonely person's life; it can improve your relations with those close to you. The reward for bringing laughter is extremely high and it is better than any "spring tonic" for yourself. Laughter is the best medicine!

Spotlights!
1. Recognize that a productive life begins *within* you.
2. Refuse to let yourself feel limited by outer facts, experiences, or circumstances.
3. Listen to your indwelling creative spirit in quietness each day, and be guided by the loving whisperings of inner wisdom.
4. Happiness is an inside job!
5. A journey of a thousand miles begins with the first step. Decide to take that step toward creating a better world.
6. Praise is the mental attitude that stimulates, quickens, whirls into action, and establishes in character the ideals of which it is the vehicle.
7. Laughter, in some instances, has been considered to be a high form of prayer.
8. Those who bring laughter to others are also beneficiaries.

Living the Law!
Earlier this week, thoughts were shared about the Buddha and his efforts to assist mortal humanity out of their misery and into a more enlightened state of being. In the *Mahayana* (the Greater Vehicle of Salvation) the belief is that no person lives alone, and an individual's salvation must therefore be involved with the salvation of others. In the *Hinayana* (the Lesser Vehicle of Salvation) the followers believe that each individual must seek and find his own salvation. The Greater Vehicle teaches that a person's principle guide is the heart, and "the way" is compassion. For the followers of the Lesser Vehicle, the principle guide is the head, and "the way" is wisdom.

For this week's exercise, study *The Eightfold Path* as presented below, and determine how you can see both the heart and the head, compassion and wisdom, being exalted through this beautiful teaching.

The Eightfold Path

Right Belief (Views) — that Truth is the guide of each person

Right Resolve (Thought) — to be calm at all times and not to harm any living creature

Right Speech — never to lie, never to slander anyone, and never to use coarse or harsh language

Right Behavior (Action) — never to steal, never to kill, and never to do anything one may later regret or be ashamed of

Right Occupation (Livelihood)— never to choose an occupation that is considered bad

Right Effort —always to strive for that which is good and avoid that which is evil

Right Contemplation (Mindfulness) — of the Noble Truths, in calmness and detachment

Right Concentration (Meditation) — will then follow and lead to the path of perfect peace.

Week Fifteen

"Pride is a deeply
rooted ailment of the
soul. The penalty is
misery; the remedy lies
in the sincere, life-long
cultivation of humility,
which means true
self-evaluation and a
proper perspective
toward the past, pres-
ent, and future."
—Robert Gordis

"True humility is not
an abject, groveling,
self-despising spirit; it
is but a right estimate
of ourselves as God sees
us."—Tryon Edwards

"Fullness of knowledge
always and necessarily
means some under-
standing of the depths
of our ignorance and
that is always con-
ducive to both humility
and reverence."
—Robert A. Milikan

"Sir Bernard Lovell
wrote that we have
'never obtained scien-
tific answers to the
problem of whether the
universe is finite or
infinite, or how it
began, and how it will
end. Nevertheless, the
perspective of these
questions and the

❖

LAW 1

Humility, like darkness,
reveals the heavenly light
—Henry David Thoreau

If you walk outside on a clear, dark night and look up into the sky you can see thousands of stars. Did you ever consider that if it were not for the darkness of space the starlight would never be revealed to us on earth?

We tend to think of anything dark or black as bad and per-haps not as valuable as white or light. Or, we may perceive black as nothing at all since it has no color. Scientifically, it is the absence of light and could be called an illusion or invisible. Going to a movie can remind you of how important it is for the theater to be dark, for it is the darkness that allows the movie to be seen most clearly.

Perhaps the heavenly light within each one of us—our divine purpose of potential—also has a dark background against which it becomes illumined. This is not a destructive or negative dark-ness, rather a necessary foundation of strength. Could this dark-ness perhaps be what is called *humility:* our ability to admit we may not know everything or be all things to all people?

Humility is not self-deprecation. To believe that you have no worth, or were created somehow flawed or incompetent, can be foolish. Humility represents wisdom. It is knowing you were cre-ated with special talents and abilities to share with the world; but it can also be an understanding that you are one of many souls created by God, and each has an important role to play in life. Humility is knowing you are smart, but not *all-knowing*. It is accepting that you have personal power, but are not omnipo-tent. The unseen—the beauty that exists as potential in each of us—is what makes us alive. If we don't believe we're alive with inner potential, we may not be progressive in our life. But if we are aware of the tremendous potential within and the value of our self-worth, we can understand that the true reality abides in God. When we reach this stage of maturity and moral development, we can become consistently more productive and useful. We may also become more outgoing. We can feel a surge of joy when others experience good fortune. The desire to accomplish something of lasting benefit can reside at the forefront of our thoughts and bring us closer to success.

As a tree requires a strong root system to grow tall, or a sky-scraper must have a deep foundation to hold tension against stress, we need the strength of humility to reach our greatest heights. This strength can serve as our foundation for living and help us step forth in faith and valiantly challenge life, daring to take risks. Wise is the person whose love of work, of family and friends, of colleagues and peers, and of life itself stems from his love of God. We have unlimited potential to create, but it must be rooted in the knowledge of understanding of the perimeters of our personal power.

The humble attitude is a flexible attitude. Just as the tree and the building must sway with the wind, our agility in dealing with whatever life throws our way can become our strength. Inherent in humility resides an open and receptive mind. We don't know all the answers to life, and sometimes not even the right questions have been revealed to us. Humility can be a strength that serves well; it leaves us more open to learn from others and refrains from seeing issues and people only in blacks and whites.

The opposite of humility is arrogance—the belief that we are wiser or better than others. Arrogance promotes separation rather than community. It looms like a brick wall between us and those from whom we could learn. An example could be Virginia Smith, a young woman who was about to graduate from college with honors. She held a high opinion of herself and lofty visions of greatness. As Virginia descended from the podium in her cap and gown, she carried her diploma . . . and an air of intellectual smugness. From out of the crowd of onlookers an old woman stepped to Virginia's side. We can call her Wisdom of the World. She spoke casually to the young graduate, "Well, who have we here?"

"You evidently don't know me," said the young woman in an arrogant tone. "I am Virginia Cordelia Smith, A.B."

"Well, my young friend," said Wisdom of the World with a chuckle, "Come with me and I will teach you the rest of your alphabet!"

This young woman undoubtedly contained a bright light to

nature of the possible scientific answers have constantly changed since ancient times.' This should be enough to cause all men and women to pause humbly before the majesty and infinity of what Jefferson called, 'nature and nature's God.' Discovery and invention have not stopped or even slowed down. Who can imagine what can be discovered if this acceleration continues? Now, even the acceleration of discovery seems to be accelerating! The more we learn about the universe, the more humble we should be, realizing how ignorant we have been in the past and how much more there is still to discover."—John Templeton, *The Humble Approach*

"Humility leads to strength and not to weakness. It is the highest form of self-respect to admit mistakes and to make amends for them."
—John J. McCloy

"Not what we have, but what we use; not what we see, but what we choose, these are the things that mar or bless the sum of human happiness." —Joseph Fort Newton

"The measure of choosing well is whether a man likes and finds good in what he has chosen."
—Charles Lamb

"Life is the acceptance of responsibilities or their evasion; it is a business of meeting obligation or avoiding them. To every man the choice is continually being offered, and by the manner of his choosing, you may fairly measure him."
—Ben Ames Williams

shine on the world. She had great potential for doing good, but she had yet to understand how much of life would be a mystery to her. Teresa of Avila made the comment, *"Humility must always be doing its work like a bee making honey in the hive: without humility all will be lost."* If the young graduate could only gain humility, her "heavenly light" could surely shine and her life would be much sweeter.

LAW 2

Use wisely your power of choice
—Og Mandino

A man watching a squirrel jump from one tree to another saw the squirrel miss the first limb but land safely on the limb below. He remarked, "Well, I guess they gotta jump unless they want to stay in the same tree all of their lives!" We, too, may see a worthwhile goal and use our faculty of choice to "make the jump." Making a choice to take the initiative may involve a certain risk as we pull ourselves out of the usual flow of activities. How do we know unless we make the effort? Of all the powers that you possess as a human being, the greatest power is the power to *choose*. What you are right now is the sum total of the choices you have made in your life. The power to choose is also a power, or ability, to create *who you are*!

Every choice that you make forms a building block of your life. Every act, every word, every decision becomes a part of you. The way that you see and respond to the world in which you live results from the choices you have made. So, in a sense, not only do your choices make you who you are, they, in effect, make your world because the world that you "see" is the world in which you live. We are given the opportunity to shape and mold our world through the use of our consciousness. We have the power of free will to determine what we want in life, and we have the authority to call forth our good through the powers of decree, imagination, enthusiasm, joy, and faith.

Some choices are obvious. We choose the clothes we wear, the food we eat, the work we do, the friends we have, etc. Pause for a moment and look at your life. Are you experiencing any kind of lack or limitation? Are you happy with your diet? Are you suffering from any type of physical ailment? Do you find your work boring or unfulfilling? Do you *like* your friends? Whether your answer to these questions is "yes" or "no" isn't the point. The point to consider is that you are experiencing results from that which you have already chosen! You cannot experience anything in life—positive or negative—unless you *accept* it as such. You cannot accept anything unless you make up your mind to do so. And when you make up your mind about anything, that is the action of *choosing*! Some decisions may be easy and some may be difficult; but you do have the choice. True, we may be encouraged or sometimes even pressured to make certain decisions. Yet, ultimately, it is we who make the choice. Whenever we believe that we have no choice and that we are powerless over our life experiences, we are denying one of our most important powers—the power to choose.

If it seems necessary to do something you don't like, ask yourself, "Is there another way to accomplish this task that might work better for me? What is the time element consideration? What alternatives do I have now or in the future?" When you really become conscious of your power of choice it may amaze you as to the variety of choices that are available. You have much more power over your life than you may realize. You have the power to change your life and indeed even to change who you are through your power of choice. Use it wisely!

A story is told about John Muir, a United States naturalist who was born in Scotland. Muir was largely responsible for the establishment of Yosemite National Park and was active in the shaping of national conservation policy. It seems financial consideration played only a small part in the satisfaction John Muir chose to derive from life. On one occasion he declared that he was richer than magnate E. H. Harriman. *"I have all the money I want and he hasn't!"* Muir chose to be happy with the abundance that was his.

If it is obvious to you that you are constantly making choices every moment of every day, isn't it time to start choosing rightly? You can make a decision right now to do what you want to do, to be what you want to be, and to do what you have to do. As a friend has so aptly put it, *"We are the master of our own destiny only in the measure of our ability to choose wisely and constructively."*

"Where previously you may have been using the action of the Law of Mind erratically, with the result you felt you had to wage a solitary battle against the universe, you will find that the proper use of the creative power of your thought, and its immutable action through Law, will align your life in harmony with the beneficial nature of God. When you properly understand this, you will find that Life is for you; then you can avail yourself of all Its good in your life. You can use the Law for your benefit. It is futile to battle against Its action; you direct Its action in the manner you desire.
Your ability to direct this action resides in the nature of the God-given creative power of your own thought."—Willis Kinnear, *Riches of the Mind and Spirit*

"Temptation is a part
of life. No one is
immune–at any age.
For temptation is pres-
ent wherever there is a
choice to be made, not
only between good and
evil, but also between
higher and lower
good."–Ernest T.
Thompson

"If we have not
achieved our early
dreams, we must either
find new ones or see
what we can salvage
from the old. If we
have accomplished
what we set out to do
in our youth, then we
need not weep like
Alexander the Great,
that we have no more
worlds to conquer.
There is clearly much
left to be done, and
whatever else we are
going to do, we had
better get on with it."
—Rosalyn Carter,
Something to Gain

"Go for the moon. If
you don't get it, you'll
still be heading for a
star."
—Willis Reed

LAW 3

If you do not know what you want to achieve with your life, you may not achieve much
—John M. Templeton

Those who set no goals in their lives drift aimlessly through the average three score and ten years, often complaining that "life's not fair." They also may say, to paraphrase the Rolling Stones, "I can't always get what I want." On the contrary, however, in keeping with an important law of life, they are receiving in proportion to what they are prepared to give. Many of us are quite clear about what we *don't* want in our lives, but how many of us are prepared to do the inner work that can lead us to what we *do* want? If we were asked to give someone directions on how to get from point A to point B, we would tell them in which direction to drive and the correct turns to make. Our lives can be run on the same principle, yet many people insist on working from the premise of what they don't want rather than what they do want. Once we know what we want, we can move into a position to establish goals and work toward achieving them.

You may have experienced this situation yourself with your friends when discussing which movie to attend. "Well, I don't want to see *Benji Goes to the Seaside*, and I've already seen *Rambo 9*, so I don't want to see that again." It's only when you start talking about what you do want to see that you end up in the theater with a tub of popcorn in your hands!

By setting goals, you give yourself the opportunity to develop greater potential. Hold a vision of your goal in minds, and the more you work toward this goal, the closer it can come to reality or manifestation. It can also be quite helpful to write your goals in a journal so you have a nearby daily reminder

As a quiet young man, publisher Robert Bernstein had a job at New York's radio station WNEW. Albert Leventhal, head of sales of the publishing house of Simon and Schuster, liked the looks of the tall, red-headed, engaging Bernstein and enticed him into publishing. Bernstein turned out to be a phenomenon of energy. Once Leventhal happened to enter the office at the early hour of 7:30 A.M. and found his protégé already busy at work. Bernstein looked up at his employer, saw his questioning look, and said, *"I'm ambitious. What's your excuse for being here at this unearthly hour?"*

Julius Caesar, Roman general and statesman, decisively defeated the king of Pontus, Pharnaces II, at Zela in Asia Minor. He announced his victory in Rome with the immortal, *"Veni, vidi, vici"* ("I came, I saw, I conquered"). Caesar had a goal, went for it, and achieved it! By setting goals and being ambitious toward realizing them, we give ourselves the opportunity to develop our full potential. We have a vision in our minds of an ideal, and the more we focus upon it and work toward it, the closer the ideal comes to reality. Some people find it helpful to put their goals and dreams in writing so they have them in black and white as a reminder. Making a "treasure map" by cutting out pictures from magazines and making a collage of the things you would like to see successfully fulfilled is a manner of establishing goals. And this goes beyond the material to such areas of life as emotions, family, and relationships.

Most of us know the story of the little red engine, climbing the hill, who kept saying to himself, *"I think I can; I think I can."* As a result of this, he accomplished the seemingly impossible climb. He had a goal and a vision of himself doing it, and he achieved what he pictured in his mind.

Napoleon Hill said, *"Whatever the mind of man can conceive and believe, it can achieve."* Locked within the human superconsciousness are the answers to our questions and the secret to the mysteries we may encounter. But in order to tap into and activate this reservoir, it is necessary to decide the avenue we wish to follow. Making a decision of what we want to achieve can be like putting a bit in a horse's mouth. The bit is probably the smallest part of the harness of a horse, but it is the most important. With this bit, we can control the movements of the horse. With a mere tug on the bit we can get the horse to move his whole body in any direction we wish it to go. Without the guidance of a goal, we may flounder without direction and not achieve very much.

"What our deepest self craves is not mere enjoyment, but some supreme purpose that will enlist all our powers and will give unity and direction to our life. We can never know the profoundest joy without conviction that our life is significant–not a meaningless episode. The loftiest aim of human life is the ethical perfecting of mankind–the transfiguration of humanity."
–Henry J. Golding

"Destiny is not a matter of chance, it is a matter of choice; it is not a thing to be waited for, it is a thing to be achieved."–William Jennings Bryan

"Concentrate on finding your goal, then concentrate on reaching it."–Col. Michael Friedsam

LAW 4

More is wrought by prayer than this world dreams of
—Alfred Lord Tennyson

Prayer is communion between God and a person. Prayer can be a *way of life* rather than a series of isolated acts. It is an attitude of the soul that, at times, expresses itself in words. But prayer can often be most effective when offered silently from within. Prayer is the recognition by your soul of God in everything it does and says. It is the home-life of the soul; it is the work of the soul, the deepest reality and creator of everything, It is the source, the center, and the goal. Prayer's eloquence can be expressed in deeds, and its breath rises in aspiration.

Nothing in your life should be foreign to prayer. Everything, both great and small, may be swept within its sacred circle. The circumference of the circle includes the most remote province of your individual life. The heart and mind that recognizes and touches God through prayer can tap a limitless reservoir of universal substance that spirit brings forth into powerful demonstrations or manifestations in one's life. In truth, you cannot afford not to pray! When you pray, you move away from outer human personality into the great individuality within, which is the real you.

Your times of prayer are *"food for the soul"* and can work wonders in your life. Through the action of meditation and prayer, you can learn to *"practice the presence of God,"* or begin to see God as everything in the universe. Closer to home, you become aware that your daily life is contained within God. The sincere desire that goes forth from your heart does not return to you void. One important thing to remember is that prayer may not change God, but it certainly can change *your attitude* about God.

Just as the sunlight floods into a darkened room when the curtains and doors are opened, so does the light of Truth pour into your heart when you become open and receptive to the circumstance of life through prayer. Prayer is like dialing a number on your telephone. It can be the *conscious connection* you make with God. You call; God answers!

A prayer is your brain-child, your heartfelt desire. Prayer may not accomplish what you wish because you are intellectually wise. It may not do your bidding because you have absorbed the contents of a book. However, when you have established authority over your thoughts, prayer can work for you—not because you command it but because the very nature of the universe has placed you in the driver's seat! Through positive thoughts and feelings, you have aligned yourself in harmony with life. Prayer is a constructive direction, and it adds to your creative and redemptive power of light and love. When prayer is released with understanding and sincerity, it may invoke healing streams of the life force of God.

Some real blocks to success are feelings of insecurity, inferiority, and unworthiness. *Prayer can assist in removing these blocks!* Look around you. Look at the glorious sunshine; this is God's light. Look at the fragrant flowers in your garden and home; these are God's beauty. Look at your loved ones; you are seeing individual expressions of God. Think of the mountains, the seashore, the rolling plains; this is God's diversity. Recognize God as unlimited. *There is no place separate from God!* Prayer may be your process of affirming this truth. Situations may be healed, overcome, or accomplished! Dreams and visions may manifest and become realities in your life.

Whatever pathway your life may take, you never can leave the presence of God. What a comforting thought! What an assist this awareness can bring to every need and desire! Approach your time of prayer with the intention of experiencing this presence of God for yourself. Know what it feels like. Truth is individually sought, individually prepared for, and individually received. No effort you put forth is lost or wasted. The supreme laws of life measure your efforts, expose your human self, point out errors, show you the simple truth, uplift your spirit, and enfold your mind, body, and soul with the universal embrace of love.

It is a grand truth that *"more is wrought by prayer than this world dreams of."* The call to prayer is heard in all languages. Every culture in the world, every civilization—regardless of how primitive—has some kind of spiritual activity that may be referred to as a "prayer process." Prayer is a natural function, and prayer is indigenous to human beings. The beloved philosopher Kahlil Gibran caught this theme when he said, *"For what is prayer but the expansion of one's self into the living ethers."*

We can compare ourselves to a wave in the ocean. A wave is simply a part of the ocean expressing itself as a wave. It has no identity outside the ocean. If you look at this idea objectively, you realize it would be rather ridiculous for a wave to go look-

"For me, happiness came from prayer to a kindly God. Faith in a kindly God, love for my fellow man and doing the very best I could every day of my life. I had looked for happiness in fast living, but it was not there. I tried to find it in money, but it was not there. But when I placed myself in tune with what I believe to be fundamental truth of life, when I began to develop my limited ability, to rid my mind of all kinds of tangled thought, and fill it with zeal and courage and love, when I gave myself a chance by treating myself decently and sensibly, I began to feel the stimulating, warm glow of happiness and life for me began like a stream between smooth banks."
—Edward Young

"We should not be discouraged if our prayers go unanswered; if some were, we most certainly would have grave reservations about the sanity of God."
–J. K. Stuart

ing for the ocean. The one thing the wave cannot find is the ocean for the two are part of the whole. The human being, like the wave, may be a movement in God, an activity of the infinite universal flow. So, when we look, search, and reach for God, or worry about "finding" God, maybe we have, through our thinking, moved out of the flow. We may be looking outside ourselves for that which can be found within. When, through prayer, we become still, release our thought of the outer world, and look within, we may renew our conscious connection with life, creation, and abundance. And the accomplishments may be wondrous to behold!

LAW 5

Everything and everyone around you is your teacher
—Ken Keyes

"We live very close together. So our prime purpose in this life is to help others. And if you can't help them, at least don't hurt them."
– Dalai Lama

"You must look into people, as well as at them."
– Lord Chesterfield

Would you like to find the greatest teacher in the world? The one who could teach you what you most need to learn at this moment? You can, and it's easier than you may think. Just look around you. Your teachers are everywhere. Your life is set up to teach you what you need to learn. Whether you recognize it or not, you possess an inner wisdom that is capable of showing you who your teachers are and what they have to teach you.

To find those teachers, look at those closest to you—your family, your friends, your co-workers. The people you spend the most time with can tell you much about yourself. How? One way is that, quite often, what we see in others is, in some way, a reflection of something within ourselves. What we most admire in another may be a quality we possess but have failed to recognize.

Conversely, what we dislike most in another may also reflect some trait within ourselves that we weren't aware was there. This can be especially true when we have very strong feelings, positive or negative, about someone. Other people can be our teachers, not necessarily because of what they themselves know or do, but rather because of the way we react to them. In other words, other people can serve as mirrors to teach you about yourself. President James Garfield stated in his address to Williams College alumni in New York on December 28th, 1871, *"I am not willing that this discussion should close without mention of the value of a true teacher. Give me a log hut, with only a simple bench, Mark Hopkins on one end and I on the other, and you may have all the buildings, apparatus and libraries without him"* (Mark Hopkins was president of Williams College and president of the American Board of Commissioners for Foreign Missions at that time).

The way people respond to us can add to our self-knowledge as well. This doesn't mean that if we aren't popular we're "bad," or that if a lot of people like us we're necessarily "good." How people respond to us is certainly their choice; yet we can use their reactions to learn something about ourselves. This is especially true when we see several people responding to us in a similar manner.

Another way we can learn from others is simply to look at the characteristics of the people we choose to associate with. We may need to allow ourself to be sufficiently imaginative and sympathetic to see through a crust of self-consciousness or fear to the inner person. There can be goodness waiting to be released. We may be in a position to teach as well as be taught! Again, this becomes not a matter of judging anyone as good or bad but rather recognizing there could be something within ourselves that may be attracting us to these persons, and them to us.

It can also be helpful to look at those activities you spend the greater part of your time pursuing. What do your time priorities tell you about yourself? Also examine yourself in other areas: How do you spend your leisure time? On what do you spend most of your money? What thoughts do you most often hold in your mind? What feelings do you experience most often? These things—indeed, everything in your life around you and within you—can teach you a great deal. We may have difficulties, sometimes a crisis, and once in a while we may have to go through some experience that seems like a tragedy. But the point to remember is that we can meet what we have to meet and go through it if we use our will power to keep on keeping on. Sometimes what seems to be a most difficult experience can become one of our greatest teachers as we gain the wisdom and understanding contained in the situation. Socrates wrote, *"The Delphic oracle said I was the wisest of all the Greeks. It is because that I alone, of all the Greeks, know that I know nothing."* Surely, these

"A teacher who can arouse a feeling for one single good action, for one single good poem, accomplishes more than he who fills our memory with rows on rows of natural objects, classified with name and form."
–J.W. von Goethe

"He who hath compassion upon others receives compassion from Heaven."
–Talmud

are the words of a teachable man. The truth is, you are teaching yourself, and as you use your life and the world around you as your textbook and your classroom, you can become your own greatest teacher.

Spotlights!

1. Develop the ability to admit that you may not know everything, or be all things to all people.
2. Wise is the person whose love of work, of family and friends, of colleagues and peers, and life itself stems from his love of God.
3. The power to *choose* is a power to create.
4. What you are right now is mostly the sum total of all the choices that you have made in your life.
5. By setting goals and being ambitious toward realizing them, we give ourselves the opportunity to develop our full potential.
6. The more we focus upon our ideal and work toward it, the closer the ideal comes to manifestation.
7. Prayer is communion between God and man.
8. Prayer should be a way of life rather than a series of isolated acts.
9. If you seek progress, remain open-minded, read widely, travel extensively, continually ask questions, be alert to new methods in your work—and remain teachable!
10. Be willing to pit yourself against your past performances!

Living the Law!

Because prayer is so important to one's life, let's direct this week's focus toward becoming aware of ways to make prayer a more conscious aspect of everyday situations. Remember that nothing in life is foreign to prayer and prayer is creative.

For this exercise, you are invited to think about the light that can become manifest as the result of a prayer experience. Healing. Peace. Prosperity. Guidance. Wisdom. Friendship. Prayer is not a way to turn on the light in God, but it is a way to turn on the light in yourself . . . and God is that light! When you decide you want light in your living room, you don't call the electric company and say, "Please give me light in my living room." It would be rather confusing if everyone did that! Instead, you enter the room, turn on the switch, and immediately the room becomes filled with light. Prayer is a way of telling yourself to let go, relax, and turn on the light!

God meets you on whatever level of consciousness you may be

experiencing at the time. Perhaps another way of saying the same thing is the following: "Your world reflects how you think and feel." That's the way the laws of life work. The power of prayer can work with you, and for you, as it works *as* you. This connecting link with God can appear as the dedication required to achieve the goal, the stamina to stay with it, the medicine to ease emotional pain, and the attracting force to bring people into your life with a similar vibration in consciousness. A fervent, heart-felt prayer spoken from a consciousness of oneness with God may be answered, with the fullness of the deliverance dependent upon the measure of faith set in motion. *"According to your faith be it done to you"* (Matthew 9:29).

Week Sixteen

LAW 1

Hitch your wagon to a star!
–Ralph Waldo Emerson

*"Greatly begin!
Though thou have
time
But for a line, be that
sublime–
Not failure, but low
aim is crime."*
–James Russell
Lowell

A young woman who had recently graduated with honors from a good college aspired to write novels, but her ideas kept ending up as short stories. The thought of such an ambitious project as a novel seemed overwhelming. One day she confessed to a friend how discouraged she was, and he suggested that she needed a larger vision for her work. He advised outlining a series of novels that would include and develop the powerful stories and characters that were already living in her imagination. He recommended the outline incorporate a plan that would unfold over several years, or possibly over her lifetime!

Following his advice, the writer built scenarios around the characters and projected how the various stories would mesh together and expanded that idea to include how the novels would emerge, one after another. Her outline became a design for an exciting and successful career. When the plan was completed, she could easily see her work expressed in a larger context and realized where she needed to begin. Her first book was mentally clear. The young woman began to write and, by the time the first novel was published, she was well into the second.

*"Success often comes to
those who dare and
act; it seldom goes to
the timid who are ever
afraid of the conse-
quences."*
–Jawaharlal Nehru

A wise friend helped her realize that the problem was not with her writing ability but stemmed from a limited vision of who she was and what she could accomplish. Her expanded vision assisted in fulfilling a heart desire, which resulted in a productive and joyful career. Ralph Waldo Emerson understood the importance of looking at life from the highest possible vantage point when he said, *"Hitch your wagon to a star."*

In her book *The Longevity Factor*, Lydia Bronte, Ph.D., describes how Millicent Fenwick held the high vision. Millicent Fenwick's most important career peak began shortly before her sixty-fifth birthday, when she was elected to the U. S. House of Representatives. Born and raised in the state of New Jersey, Fenwick married in 1929 at the age of nineteen and began a family. She undoubtedly thought her life would be spent comfortably as a housewife, much as her mother's had been. But the marriage did not work out. Divorced in her early thirties, she found herself with no professional or career training (she hadn't even finished high school), two young children, and a huge burden of debt run up by her former husband.

Spurred on by desperation and her sense of responsibility, she spoke with another friend, who put her in touch with someone at *Vogue* magazine, and she found a position on their staff. There she wrote the *Vogue Book of Etiquette*, which became quite popular and widely used. Meanwhile, she was gradually repaying the financial obligations left over from her marriage and putting her children through school.

During the years when she was at *Vogue*, Fenwick gradually became active in public service. When she moved back to New Jersey after her children left home, she was asked to join a local recreation commission, which became highly successful under her chairmanship. It was then suggested that she run for local council. At first she was doubtful. "They had never had a woman elected," she said. But to her surprise she won! This initial success encouraged her to run for higher office, and it led eventually to a seat in the House of Representatives in 1974. Fenwick served four terms in the House, with distinction, before launching a bid for a Senate seat in 1982. Although this campaign proved unsuccessful, she was appointed the following year as U.S. Ambassador to the UN Food and Agriculture Commission in Rome.

The German philosopher Goethe explained that *"the greatest thing in the world is not so much where we stand as in what direction we are moving."* Fenwick was definitely moving forward! We, too, need to think big and aim high when planning our goals. Ambition can sustain us—with our thoughts and hopes up in the stars—while traveling along the path toward success. And the journey may take some time to accomplish. Many famous and successful entertainment stars, whose names and faces we see everywhere, spent years in clerical or restaurant jobs while waiting for an opportunity to express the talent they were convinced lay within. People who became successful in business may have tried many ideas and faltered before they discovered the idea that worked. Many of the innovations that change our lives were once the dreams of inventors who, at first, came up

"Find a purpose in life so big it will challenge every capacity to be at your best."
–David O. McKay

"Have a purpose in life, and having it, throw into your work such strength of mind and muscle as God has given you."
–Thomas Carlyle

"You must have long range goals to keep you from being frustrated by short range failures."
–George H. Bender

against seeming dead ends and sometimes the skepticism of family and friends.

What happens to us in life is important; the real question can be whether or not we use it to grow. To grow can mean to develop, to learn, to increase our ability, to improve our methods, and a growing person is often a happy person. To stop growing can be deadly to the mind, the emotions, to successful achievement, and even to our world.

These successful entertainers, business people, and inventors had one quality in common. To realize their dreams, ambitions, and individual growth, they managed to see the bigger picture of their lives. They believed in themselves and aimed for the best.

LAW 2

The price of greatness is responsibility
–Winston Churchill

Winston Churchill's comment that *"the price of greatness is responsibility"* has been proven to be true again and again by the actions of people who have helped shape the world for the better. The climb to greatness, as well as the time spent there, often requires taking on large responsibilities and handling them with diligence and skill.

"We are not put here on earth to fool around. There is work to be done. There are responsibilities to be met. Humanity needs the abilities of every man and woman."
–Alden Palmer

If you hope to accomplish great things, begin by accepting responsibility for the smaller things facing you today. The student who fails to do homework assignments or to take on extra research in school subjects may not develop the ability and the knowledge needed to be successful as an adult. The young person who fails to act caringly and responsibly at home and with friends may often fail in crucial relationships, professional and personal, later in life because compassion and understanding were too long left to others. A business may fail because the record keeping and other areas of exacting work have been neglected.

The words of Winston Churchill need not refer only to future greatness. They can apply to what you accomplish today. Tom, a senior in high school, was interested in working in a summer program as a crossing guard for an elementary school. He felt that it would be a worthwhile activity as well as one that would be a credit to him. However, after a few days, Tom became careless. He would talk to a friend who dropped by to see him and pay little attention to the traffic. Tom was removed from the program at once. When the article was published that year about the school program, it noted that the record was marred by one student's lack of responsibility. Embarrassed and hurt, Tom learned a very important lesson, albeit one for which he paid a high price in humiliation.

Sarah wanted to be a nurse. She greatly admired a neighbor who was a head night nurse at the local hospital. This nurse had been honored many times for her service, always above and beyond simply doing her job. Sarah aspired to be like her. She decided a good first step would be to sign up as a candy-striper at the hospital. Sarah became even more convinced that nursing was for her because being a candy-striper was such fun. She chatted with her girl friends, enjoyed breaks at the commissary, and was often slow in performing her responsibilities. When patients complained about long waits for fresh water because Sarah was watching something interesting on the patient's TV, she was first warned and then dropped from the program. Her performance record at the hospital made acceptance into a school of nursing more difficult, and, to a greater extent than her classmates, she had to prove herself capable of handling responsibility.

How capable do you feel at this moment in your life? I would be less than honest with you if I didn't tell you that although you do have amazing power to attract abundant good into your life, *there are certain steps that are important to take in order to accomplish your goal.* First, it is important to know what may be keeping you from making the progress you desire. Let's take a short personal X-ray ! Ask yourself the following questions; respond honestly from the depth of your being; and write your response in your journal for further consideration:

* Do you habitually feel sorry for yourself?
* Do you hesitate overly long when making changes in your life?
* Do you lack the faith in yourself (in any way) to accomplish great things?
* Do you fear what people may say if you move out of the rut you may have made for yourself?

These statements represent some success-crippling habits that

"The greatest man is he who chooses the right with invincible resolution, who resists the sorest temptations from within and without, who bears the heaviest burdens cheerfully, who is calmest in storms and most fearless under menace and frowns, whose reliance on truth, on virtue, on God, is most unfaltering."
–William Ellery Channing, *Self-Culture*

"We sometimes speak of winning reputation as though that were the final goal. The truth is contrary to this. Reputation is a reward, to be sure, but it is really the beginning, not the end of the endeavor. It should not be the signal for a let down, but rather, a reminder that the standards which won recognition can never be lowered. From him who gives much–much is forever after expected."
–Alvan McCauley

*"Responsibility walks
hand in hand with
capacity and power."*
–J.G. Holland

can cause roadblocks to the inflow of your abundance. A great antidote for any of the above success-cripplers can be to *take responsibility for your life and begin to count your blessings daily!* Counting your blessings is important because you cannot be aware and grateful for the abundance you have already received and feel deprived at the same time! Free yourself from any self-imposed bondage by taking full responsibility for your life. An old adage says, "If you don't believe in yourself, no one else will!" You can do most jobs you make up your mind to do. Remember, you attract to yourself what you think and believe.

Taking responsibility nurtures self-confidence, and self-confidence can help you be a more interesting and attractive person. And best of all, the more you believe in yourself, the more power you possess to attract your good. Dr. Viktor Frankl said that on the west coast of the United States we should erect a "statue of responsibility" to balance the Statue of Liberty on the east coast. It might be even better to erect statues of both standing hand in hand, on both coasts. Those who speak constantly of their right to freedom must understand that an irresponsible act does not bring greater freedom but only greater bondage to the action. One law of life says, *"If we are to enjoy freedom, we must accept responsibility."* A great awareness is expressed in this statement.

LAW 3

Good words are worth much and cost little
–George Herbert

*"The way a man
speaks lays bare the tex-
ture of his mind, the
goodness in his heart,
the inner pain, or the
sweet serenity that are
his companions in soli-
tude."*
–Harriet Van Horne

Have you ever felt that there seems to be a grouch in every crowd? This is the person who never seems to have a good word for anyone. He recounts his tales of woe to anyone who listens, telling about what's currently wrong in his own life, or about the latest tragedy he saw on television, or overheard on the street. For the grouch, the world seems a place of doom and gloom, filled with bad guys ready to pounce on him and rob him of his rightful due. He arms himself with a sharp tongue and a bitter temper in order to keep everyone at a distance, even those who might care about him. He paints himself into a corner of anger and contempt, where he stands alone, often wondering why it seems to difficult to get out.

The grouch is often unemployed, in debt and emotionally bankrupt—and needs help. When most people are plagued with pessimism, words of understanding and hope can be as rare as gold bullion. Good words are like money in the bank—the more of them you can accumulate and put to work in your life, the richer you become. Nasir-i-Khusraw, the Persian writer, made this comment: *"Your words are the seed, your soul is the farmer, the world is your field; / Let the farmer look to the sowing, that the soil may abundance yield."* Invested liberally in your conversations, good words of joy, encouragement, compassion, and support can earn you interest from the vast treasury of good will, and *that* is always at your disposal and tax-free. While no one wants to spend time with a grouch, everyone enjoys being with the person who expresses enthusiasm, care, and concern.

Constructive and uplifting words pay big dividends. In times past, when one person looked another directly in the eye, shook hands firmly, and gave his word, a matter was settled as securely as if a dozen lawyers had drawn up a fifty-page contract. A person's word was his promise to bring the best of his capabilities to bear in fulfilling the agreement between the two parties. Sensitive words of love and understanding are like promises: they help to create new ways of being in the world. Good words bear the promise of a more enriching life for both the giver and receiver. The power of our words is appropriately described by Gabriel Okara, the Nigerian writer, *"What of spoken words? Spoken words are living things like cocoa-beans packed with life. And like cocoa-beans they grow and give life. . . . They will enter some insides, remain there and grow like the corn blooming on the alluvial soil at the riverside."*

Use positive words and positive thoughts in everything you do. Plant within your soul the seed idea of rising above any seeming limitation. Ask to manifest only the outworkings of this seed idea—to have health, to express harmony, and to realize abundance. Fill the seeming blank spaces around you and your words with thoughts of God, Infinite Good. Then remember the Word of God as a seed. It must grow. Leave the how, when, and where to the divine intelligence of the universe. Your route is to speak your caring word and give forth blessings.

Perhaps the grouch became a grouch by being deeply hurt as

"A word is not a crystal, transparent and unchanging, it is the skin of a living thought and may vary in color and content according to the circumstances and time in which it is used."
–Oliver Wendell Holmes, Jr., *Towne v Eisner,* Supreme Court decision, Jan. 7, 1918

"One kind word can warm three winter months."
–Japanese proverb

"Speech is the mirror of the soul; as a man speaks, so is he."
–Publilius Syrus

"Honesty of thought and speech and written word is a jewel, and they who curb prejudice and seek honorably to know and speak the truth are the builders of a better life."
–John Galsworthy

"Speak fitly, or be silent wisely."
–George Herbert

a child because only a few good words were spoken to him. Or, he may have been wounded by an intimate friend who broke a sacred trust. Acceptance and forgiveness of past events can free him to open a trust fund account of good words in his own name. This gift to himself and to the world can be compounded daily. It is important to remember that: *"Good words are worth much and cost little."*

LAW 4

You can never solve a problem on the same level as the problem
—Emmet Fox

The prophets of Old Testament times, esteemed in leadership positions, assumed two major roles in their society: as advisors they had an aptitude for solving the problems that confronted the ancient Hebrews; as seers they had the ability to anticipate the outcomes of various plans the "chosen people" considered as their culture developed. Today, seers are sometimes called *research analysts* because they seek to anticipate outcomes. Advisors are known as doctors, lawyers, merchants, business executives, and others who also try to anticipate outcomes and solve problems in their area of expertise.

"No matter how big and tough a problem may be, get rid of confusion by taking one little step towards solution."
–George F. Nordenhold

Emmet Fox, a twentieth-century author and problem-solver, wrote that the only way to solve a problem is to *"lift your consciousness above the level where you met the problem."* A problem appears as an obstacle unlikely to be seen accurately because it dominates our mental landscape. From the meadow, the forest may appear ominous and troubling; the trees may seem to block our journey to a desired destination. A lifted consciousness, however, functions like a hot air balloon—when it gets up high enough, the forest can be revealed in is entirety, and shown in proper relationship to its surroundings. Distance, height, and growing awareness can provide an encompassing perspective that may be helpful in showing us how to cope with challenging circumstances.

Often a successful problem-solver is one who creates a new

context in which to view the problem. This can often be done by directing one's attention away from the distracting details of the difficulty. From a detached perspective, we may examine the situation in a new or different light and, after exploring information and options, choose an appropriate course of action.

King Solomon was noted for his wisdom. As an aid in solving the problems that were presented to him, he examined the inner motivation of the participants in order to gain perspective. His decision in the case of two women who claimed the same child has become legend and illustrates how he used wisdom and imagination to get inside of people's true feelings. Solomon examined the motivation of the woman by suggesting that the infant be divided in half so that each woman could have an equal share of the child. The true mother begged him not to do so, preferring that her child should live, even if with the other woman, rather than be destroyed so that she could have her "fair share." Solomon easily determined the rightful parent by her concern for the child.

Prophets are perhaps most widely acclaimed for their ability as seers. But prophets are not the only ones endowed with some capacity to anticipate outcomes. Each one of us possesses the ability to discern, that is, to make choices. Each one of us can examine the appearance of a situation, look at motives, and then make an informed decision.

Some judgments or choices must be made based on information from the five senses—touch, taste, smell, sight, and hearing. Other judgments yield more beneficial results when made at the level beyond what may be readily available as fact. This kind of discernment may be recognized through a hunch (sometimes called intuition), and sometimes it may be deemed truly wise.

Dr. Ralph E. Coleman, a neuropathologist, has for many years made a study of psychophysics—the science of relations between mental and physical processes and phenomena. Today this science is closely connected with such other new sciences as biophysics, cybernetics, biomedical engineering, and medical sciences of a neural or behavioral type. Dr. Coleman made a speciality of the relationship of the seen and the unseen, the physical and the nonphysical, the body and the mind in our human existence—a speciality that was waiting for ages to have persons of high quality devote their attention to it. In a paper entitled "The Enigmas of Psychophysics," Dr. Coleman writes, *"Man is innately curious about life and its significance. His curiosity has caused him to search (and research) in hope of escaping the dissatisfactions of the present and of obtaining a future knowledge and free-*

"I have found that the greatest help in meeting any problem with decency and self-respect and whatever courage is demanded is to know where you yourself stand. That is to have in words what you believe and are acting from."
–William Faulkner

"Obstacles are those frightful things you see when you take your eyes off the goal."
—Hannah More

dom from discontent. . . . Modern medical science considers the mind and the living physical body inseparable parts of the whole person."

This wonderful "mind" within each person may be the catapult to lift us above the present level of any problem. Remember, you may not be able to change or control the people or circumstances around you, but you can determine the level of consciousness on which you meet them and react to any situation. This is one of the most significant discoveries we can make. You do not have to be fearful, and you really do not have to worry or be anxious. You can determine your reaction and then your course of action, and you can choose a higher level of wisdom.

The Old Testament prophets understood higher wisdom and judgment. They used it; they sought to anticipate results as a way to solve problems. They were the leaders of their day. Often the ability exists today in you, as it did in the ancient prophets, to rise above the problem, examine motives, look at options, and make choices.

LAW 5

Happy relationships depend not on finding the right person, but on being the right person.
—Eric Butterworth

In the fairy tale *The Sleeping Beauty*, the heroine is saved from her seeming endless sleep by a kiss from the handsome prince, who whisks her away to his palace where they live happily ever after. This same idea is portrayed in *Snow White* and in countless other stories. Even in the 90s, many films and novels continue to follow a similar plot concept. Many people grow up believing the false information given to us by television, radio, film, and the printed word that something or someone can rescue us from our mundane lives and turn us into all that we want to be. Even our parents may inadvertently give us the impression that the right person can make everything just fine. Young women dress up like fairy princesses in white lacy dresses on their wedding day, propagating this myth even further.

Why, then, do so many people seem discontented in their marriages and relationships? Why do people divorce and then often remarry someone who may resemble their previous partner? Is one reason because they remain the same within? And like attracts like? So they continue on and on, attracting the same painful and unsatisfactory relationships for as long as they continue to live with the same old attitudes.

When a person begins to work on changing himself from within, he begins to attract different types of people and experiences into his life. The junkie who is using drugs is likely to associate with other drug users. When he reforms himself and starts to change his attitudes, he may start associating with a different sort of person. This is because *he* is changing from within.

Most people think of love as some sort of power outside of themselves that will "take them away from all of this." Sadly, that is not the case. Love exists only within our own hearts, and to have happy relationships we must first become truly loving people. And as we fill our hearts with love by expressing love toward others in thought, word, and deed ("acting as if" until we make it happen if necessary), that love can heal our own lives, help to solve our problems, and enable us to feel good about ourselves.

The Biblical Scripture 1 John 4:16 states, *"So we know and believe the love God has for us. God is love and he who abides in love abides in God and God abides in him."* It is easy and natural to love family and friends. But how about the people who hurt us and make us angry? How about those who do not live up to our own standards of appearance and conduct? Do we love them, or do we simply tolerate them? The fact is that the harder someone is to love, the more he needs to be loved! There is nothing that indicates the degree of our maturity so well as our ability to love well. One of the great challenges of the human experience is to love the so-called unlovable. On a television program entitled *The Word from Unity*, Ernest Borgnine commented, *"A few times in my life, I've gotten a glimpse of the real self of a person. It was only because I looked with eyes of love. I cannot say what I saw, but I knew it was something that was inexpressibly beautiful. I believe that's what I'd see if I saw the real self in you, but I have to look with the eyes of love! Love raises vision to a higher power than eye charts can measure."* Isn't that beautiful! And this can be what happens when we look with the eyes of love, or see ourselves and others with

"The person of tomorrow must have ability to live with himself. This assures inner strength to do what is right in material and human relationships. Its fruits are peace of mind and serenity of being."
—Roger M. Keyes

*"Any life, no matter
how long and complex
it may be, is made up
of a single moment—the
moment when man
finds out, once and for
all, who he is."*
–Jorge Luis Borges

the love with which God sees us. Can we believe the love that God has for us? And then allow ourselves to be a channel through which this love may flow?

In Alan Cohen's book *The Healing of the Planet Earth*, the following passage pours a beautiful light on how love is the real key to success in all of our endeavors, whether it be work, relationships, family, achievements, or harmony among the nations and peoples of the world. *"The real secret of success is love. We must love ourselves enough to know that we are worthy to succeed. We must believe that those around us want us to win at life, and that our winning can only support their winning. We must know that God wants us to be happy in all the arenas of our life. We must understand that there is no need to struggle, strain, or live in pain or a state of lack. These hellish conditions are but signals that we must try another way. We must never settle for less than whole and holy abundance in our health, relationships, and livelihood. We are not born to scratch the dirt with chickens—we were born to soar with the eagles!"*

Being the right person can be the real story of our life. When we live centered and focused in the light of truth, we become a shining beacon, drawing to us our own. And we are not alone—ever! When we walk holding the hand of Spirit, the very heavens open to pour forth abundant blessings. In his famous prayer, St. Francis asks that he may seek rather to *"love than to be loved. For it is by self-forgetting that one finds. It is by forgiving that one is forgiven."* So, too, it can be our experience that it is by loving that we are loved; it is by being the right person that we find the right person.

Spotlights!

1. We need to think bigger and aim higher when planning our goals!
2. What happens to us in life is less important; the real question can be whether or not we use the experience to grow.
3. Accomplishing great things in life often has its foundation in accepting responsibility for smaller things today.
4. Free yourself from self-imposed bondage by taking full responsibility for your life.
5. *"Your words are the seeds of your soul, your soul is the farmer, the world is your field"* (Nasir-i-Khusraw).
6. Use positive words and positive thoughts in everything you do.
7. A problem appears as an obstacle that cannot be seen accurately because it dominates our mental landscape.

8. To solve a problem, lift your consciousness above the level where you met the problem.
9. *"God is love and he who abides in love abides in God and God abides in him"* (John 4:16).
10. *Being* the right person is the real story of our life—and we can draw to us our own.

Living the Law!

Several years ago, the newspaper column "Dear Abby" offered a powerful Thanksgiving message. Since every day is a Thanksgiving and thanks*living* day, and since the article is so apropos with our focus this week, it is reproduced here for your personal inspection. Write your response, after sincere contemplation of these powerful words, in your journal.

Dear Readers:

Today is Thanksgiving, so take a few minutes to think about what you have to be thankful for.

How's your *health*? Not so good? Well, thank God you've *lived* this long. A lot of people *haven't*. You're hurting? Thousands— maybe millions—are hurting *more*. (Have you ever visited a Veterans' Hospital? Or a rehabilitation clinic for crippled children?)

If you awakened this morning and were able to hear the birds sing, and use your vocal cords to utter human sounds, and walk to the breakfast table on two good legs, and read the newspaper with two good eyes—*Praise the Lord!* A lot of people *couldn't*.

How's your *pocketbook*? Thin? Well, most of the living world is a lot poorer. No pensions. No welfare. No food stamps. No Social Security. In fact, one-third of the people in the world will go to bed *hungry* tonight.

Are you *lonely*? The way to *have* a friend is to *be* one. If nobody calls *you*, call *them!* Go out of your way to do something *nice* for somebody. It's a sure cure for the blues.

Are you concerned about your *country's* future? Hooray! Our system has been *saved* by such concern. Concern for *honesty* in government, concern for *peace*, and concern for *fair play* under the law. Your country may not be a rose garden, but it also is not a patch of weeds.

Freedom rings! Look and listen. You can still worship at the church of your choice, cast a secret ballot, and even criticize your government without fearing a knock on the head or a knock at the door at midnight. And if you want to live under a different system, you are free to go. There are no walls or fences—nothing to keep you here.

As a final thought, I'll repeat my Thanksgiving prayer:

O, heavenly Father: We thank Thee for food, and remember the *hungry*.

We thank Thee for health, and remember the *sick*.

We thank Thee for friends, and remember the *friendless*.

We thank Thee for freedom, and remember the *enslaved*.

May these remembrances stir us to *service*;

that Thy gifts to us may be used for *others*. Amen."

—Abby

Week Seventeen

LAW 1

We receive freely when we give freely
—Anonymous

Each year thousands of people hang a "Gone Fishin'" sign on
their doors and trek to mountain streams and deep, placid lakes
to pursue a great outdoor sport. Armed with the most sophisticated rod, reel, and fancy tied flies, or with a simple bamboo
pole, string, and a worm, the aficionado casts his bait upon the
waters. Employing a curious mixture of intuition, skill, and perseverance, the fisherman lands his catch and soon is savoring
his success as it sizzles to golden, delicious perfection.

Chris Hartley is in the fishing business. He is a young man
with his own boat who lives in some of the best fishing territory
in the world. The clear, turquoise-green waters of the Bahamas
teem with many varieties of fish, and charter boats abound that
will take visitors on fishing trips out of Nassau. However, Chris
doesn't fish from his boat, and neither does he allow others to
fish from it. Furthermore, he will not eat fish that anyone else
has caught. You might think such a fisherman would have a
hard time running a successful business, but Chris is thriving in
his endeavor. He has a different kind of tourist fishing business,
based on the universal principle that as you give freely, you also
receive freely, and his enterprise profits by using this principle.

Chris loves to be underwater and seems to be in his element
there. Capitalizing on his affinity for the sea, he procured a
boat and some equipment, which allowed him to establish
"Hartley's Underwater Wonderland," a business that takes
tourists on boat excursions to a nearby coral reef. There, wearing diving helmets, the tourists can walk along the sea floor
fifteen feet below the surface, while Chris introduces them to
the magnificent flora and fauna of the sea world.

Halfway through the tour, on perfect cue, a big black-and-

*"A really great man is
known by three
signs—generosity in the
design, humanity in
the execution, modera-
tion in success."*
–Otto Edward
Bismarck

white-striped fish swims up to Chris, who pets "Harry, the Grouper" as he would a cat or dog. Harry then swims to each of the underwater guests, allows himself to be touched by them, and poses for photographs that Chris later sells to the tourists. One year Chris dressed Harry up with a Santa Claus hat, snapped his picture, and made a unique Christmas card souvenir.

If you're wondering why Harry performs so well for Chris, it's because of Chris's practice of giving and receiving—one of the laws of life that he lives by. When Chris began his business, he realized that a tame fish around the coral reef could offer a great attraction for tourists, but most fish were afraid of people, and a basic instinct for survival caused them to stay away. Chris realized he would have to give the fish an assurance that they wouldn't be killed and that he was coming to them as a friend. Chris began to bring food to the fish—food for them to eat, not bait on the end of a hooked line. Although Chris had no guarantee the fish would respond, they did by flocking around the coral reef every time his boat appeared. Given freely of Chris's loving attention and food, the fish responded with their friendship, and Chris has benefited tremendously by sharing that friendship with his customers.

"He gives not best who gives most; but he gives most who gives best. If I cannot give bountifully, yet I will give freely, and what I want in my hand, I will supply by my heart."
—Arthur Warwick

In 2 Corinthians 9:6 we read, *"He who sows sparingly shall reap also sparingly; and he who sows generously shall reap also generously."* Throughout the sacred Scriptures of the world, we are reminded often of the importance of the great law of giving and receiving. In fact, one of the basic laws of prosperity states: *Give and you will receive.* Sow and you will reap. Like attracts like.

Once we plant the seeds for spiritual growth and prosperity, the reaping may take place right away. How can this happen? By seeing beyond appearances of lack! A special something often happens that may not be explained by human or physical logic when we make the choice to work with things of Spirit—for it seems that Spirit often supersedes all else.

"Our true acquisitions lie only in our charities, we get only as we give."
—William Simms

There is an important aspect to remember. The fact that prosperity stands on our doorstep may not necessarily assure it in our life! Why? Because there may be something for us to do. We should claim it; we should accept it with thanksgiving; and then we use this prosperity in the highest and best manner to help others. A good example of why a person may not achieve an objective of prosperity comes from a magazine cartoon some years ago. Here's the scenario: A man is imploring God, "Please let me win the lottery!" From the clouds above comes a booming voice, presumably God, declaring, "At least buy a ticket!"

Therein lies the problem. Too often people may desire prosperity but may not be willing to pay the price. What is the price? It is sharing, giving, loving, and caring. Prosperity needs an inflow and an outflow, just as any body of water does if it is to remain fresh and clean. Otherwise, stagnation often results. The Dead Sea falls into this category. It does not have an outflow; it only receives, and so the water becomes stagnant. Almost nothing grows there.

Perhaps you've been led to believe that in order to have profit and gain in an enterprise, someone must lose—that for you to win this game we call life there must be a loser. What Chris Hartley demonstrates is that you rarely lose by giving, whether it's food for fish or love for friends. For in giving freely without guarantee of return, you may set into motion a great momentum of goodness. When we give, everyone is a winner.

"We are rich only through what we give; and poor only through what we refuse and keep."
–Anne Swetchine

LAW 2

The truth will make you free
—John 8:32

"You will know the truth and the truth will make you free." How can "knowing the truth" make anyone free? It may seem as if your freedom comes through a change in external circumstances. This certainly could be an avenue for freedom. It may appear that your boss or your bank account might have more to do with your freedom than anything you know or believe. These could certainly be influences.

We often tend to see freedom, or lack of freedom, as the result of something outside ourself, and so it may appear. Once, a volunteer from a nightclub audience was hypnotized and told that he was chained to his chair. He was then instructed to try to get up and walk around. Regardless of how hard he tried to pull away from the chair, he could not break the invisible chain that bound him.

Was the chain real? It would not be real to you and me, yet it was absolutely real to the man who was hypnotized. Anyone in the audience could get up and leave if they wanted to, but this man could not because of his *belief*, a belief that kept him in

"Truth, Life, and Love are a law of annihilation to everything unlike themselves, because they declare nothing but God."
—Mary Baker Eddy, *Science and Health with Key to the Scriptures*

bondage. Because the observers knew the truth, they were free to move about as they pleased. The man in the chair could not become free until he, too, knew the truth.

A person in a hypnotic state may be highly suggestible to the commands of the hypnotist. What he says goes unchallenged, accepted by the subject's subconscious mind as the absolute truth—sometimes accepted so deeply, in fact, that what the hypnotist tells the subject is what he or she will see and believe. Convinced that "seeing is believing," the subject's eyes will confirm what he or she is already certain is true.

Everyone may be suggestible to a certain extent, which can be why advertising is so effective, and why it is important to examine your beliefs from time to time to see where they originate. How much of what you believe is the result of what others told you? How much of what you believe about yourself comes from what others believe about you?

What if someone grew up believing that he was very bright but not very attractive? The chances are that this person would accept these statements as true and act accordingly. This person could be like the man who was chained to the chair because someone told him this was true. This person could be in bondage because of something he believes, and whether it is true or not wouldn't make the slightest difference.

What is a great truth that can make you free? Possibly this. No matter what your condition, your environment, or your situation may be; no matter how unhappy or miserable you might think you are; no matter what you may be facing in the way of problems; the answer and the remedy may be right within yourself. Those who have chosen to believe this truth and practice the principles involved in it can become the people of peace and joy and happiness and abundant living. These ones know that within them is an unconquerable spirit. They have been touched by its power, and they have felt its presence. They live by this truth constantly.

The Indian spiritual and political leader Mohandas K. Gandhi spoke thus of truth: *"In the dictionary of the seeker of truth there is no such thing as being 'not successful.' He is or should be an irrepressible optimist because of his immovable faith in the ultimate victory of Truth, which is God."* And the Arab philosopher Rasa'il al-Kindi expressed in this way: *"We should never be ashamed to approve truth or acquire it, no matter what its source might be, even if it might have come from foreign peoples and alien nations far removed from us. To him who seeks truth, no other object is higher in value. Neither shall truth be under-rated, nor its exponent belittled. For indeed, truth abases none and ennobles all."*

The secret of a physical world of peace can possibly lie in the transformation of individual lives. Lives are transformed by the renewing of the individual mind and the awareness of the indwelling and loving Spirit of God within every person.

"This sounds fine," you may say, "but how do I make contact with this Spirit and become acquainted with it? How can I realize its values and advantages?"

There may not be one simple answer to these questions, as there are various pathways toward contacting the Spirit within. However, whatever method you use involves self-discipline. Just as the concert pianist spends month after month at the piano in determined effort to master the repertoire; as the champion athlete practices for many hours of every day; as the professional person dedicates years of study and the application of that study to his chosen career, so is it important for the person seeking God's presence in his life and affairs to practice living in that presence. It is also important to bring our thoughts, feelings, words, and actions into alignment with our understanding of God's will. Through these applications one may invite the presence of Spirit and victorious living into one's life. The truth really can make us free once we realize that much of what we believe, especially about ourselves, is not necessarily the truth but is instead a "hypnotic suggestion" we have accepted from others. Seek to become aware of what you believe about yourself, about others, and regarding the world around you. Ask yourself, "Is this really true or could it be an illusion?" If your beliefs seem to be limiting your options in life by keeping you in bondage, they probably do not represent the truth. When you know the truth about who you really are, you may indeed be free!

"It is heaven upon earth to have man's mind move in charity, rest in providence, and turn upon the poles of truth."
—Francis Bacon

LAW 3

If you would find gold, you must search where gold is
—William Juneau

In the 1930s television had not been invented and radios were scarce because so many people were poor. Movie theaters were

*"When you have cho-
sen a great purpose,
and are certain you
have chosen well and
wisely, concentrate
upon it. Bend your
best energies to it.
Guard yourself against
subtle and innumer-
able influences that
tend to divert you from
it. Make that single
great purpose the defi-
nite aim of your daily
life. Your thought and
time will be solicited by
many influences, and
you will do well to take
special means to pro-
tect yourself against
them. Make your reso-
lutions so clear and
firm that nothing can
lure you from your cho-
sen path of purpose
and duty. Substitute
doing for dreaming,
and achievement for
wishing. The great
things of the world are
done by men who spe-
cialize and concen-
trate."*–Glenville
Kleiser, *Riches for the
Mind and Spirit*

available, but again, many were unable to pay the twenty-five-cent price of admission. People entertained themselves most of the time by singing songs, telling stories, and playing games.

Occasionally, a circus or carnival would come to town, and the people who had a bit of money to spare would attend these activities. During this era, another kind of entertainment came to town two or three times a year. It was called a "Medicine Show" because the carnival owners put on a vaudeville type of entertainment—admission free—and made money by selling patent medicines, soap, and candy. Their main product was a tonic they claimed would cure any known disease, including dropsy and the vapors, neither of which is heard of nowadays. That was their internal medicine, composed to a great extent of grain alcohol flavored with licorice, cinnamon, or cloves. They also had an external medicine. It was a fiery liniment guaranteed to cure arthritis, gout, and a variety of skin conditions.

The entertainment was not high quality, but it was free, so medicine shows were popular. In one of the skits, an actor would come out on the stage and conduct a thorough search of the area. A second actor would enter and ask, "What are you looking for?"

"I dropped a dime a few minutes ago," the first actor would reply.

"Did you drop it at the front of the stage or at the side?" the second man asked.

"Neither place. I dropped it around behind the wagon," the first man replied.

"Then why don't you look for it back there?"

"Because there ain't no lights back there," was the punch line.

We can appreciate the ridiculous humor of the comedian's logic. Yet, we often see people every day searching in the wrong places for the things they desire. Too many of our fellow humans try to find peace and happiness in drugs, alcohol, and sensual excitement. And it doesn't work. If we desire peace, the first place to look is within ourself. Peace isn't an external condition so much as an internal context. We can progress in consciousness by going on to the next larger context of thought and realization. Becoming aware of the next larger context of life, we may be, by the nature of our being, impelled onward. A higher plateau of consciousness beckons. The desire for a deeper reality to experience the golden truth of reality—not the "fool's gold" of illusion—whispers in our soul that "there is more."

Often true growth requires that we "unlearn" some things in

order to reach the higher point of view. It may take a dose of humility and cleansing disillusionment to prompt us to release the old habits and ways of life that bring pain and suffering. Facts can have a fleeting reality of dimension, condition, and circumstances. Transitional growth experiences sometimes pose contradictions to the past. The psyche can learn to reorganize and adapt itself in preparation for entering the next larger context. This could be a new stage in life, a new state of consciousness, or even a radical move in our personal affairs and environment.

It is said that Walt Whitman, who many felt had a cosmic appreciation of life, was criticized for changing his mind and sharply replied, "Do I contradict myself? Very well, then, I contradict myself!" The American philosopher Charles Fillmore made it clear on a number of occasions that he reserved the right to change his mind. If a student quoted to him something he had written some years earlier, he was likely to ask that person, "But what do you think?" Then he would explain that he did not wish to be bound to what he had understood or expressed in the past, affirming that he was continually in a stage of spiritual unfoldment. And so are we!

"The thing that counts is not what we could do but what we actually do."
–Leo L. Spears

To find the pure gold of truth often means getting a more universal viewpoint of life, of yourself, and of everything that comprises your world. The greatness and power of many souls of the past resulted in their seeing in a higher context than perhaps the average person. They knew where to look to find the golden nuggets of truth. Time does not prevent us from knowing these higher truths; our stage of consciousness makes the difference.

Each day, as we look a little farther in our quest for truth, explore a little deeper in the great wisdoms that abound, and search for the golden threads of light and love, we can be led in the path of righteousness

Those in search of an easier, softer way to obtain the important things of life often find cheap imitations or nothing at all. The miner who searches for gold on the beach because the digging is easy may certainly find lots of sand, but it's unlikely he will find gold. Sometimes we must dig among stones and hard clay to find the treasure we seek. And when we do, we may learn our efforts have not been wasted.

"It is more important to know where you are going than to get there quickly. Do not mistake activity for achievement."
–Mabel Newcomber

LAW 4

Habit is the best of servants,
the worst of masters
–J. Jelinek

Everyone has habits. Getting up in the morning, doing the things that create order in your environment, eating nutritious meals, exercising your body, practicing good hygiene, getting enough sleep are habits. These habits enable you to function at full strength both at work and play. Good study habits enable you to organize your thinking and use your time for effective learning. Habits of courtesy create natural good manners that make others comfortable in your presence. Consistent practice habits enable you to develop a skill or talent like music, sports, painting, crafts, or writing.

A habit is a pattern of behavior we have acquired that has become so automatic it may be difficult to modify or eliminate. Many habits can become unconscious, and we no longer have to think about where, when, how, or whether to do things. It almost seems as though they're done outside of our conscious will. The Hungarian-American mathematician George Polya likes to tell stories about David Hilbert, the great German mathematician. At a party at Hilbert's house, his wife noticed that her husband had neglected to put on a clean shirt. She asked him to go upstairs and do so. He went upstairs. Ten minutes passed, and Hilbert did not return to the party. Mrs. Hilbert went up to the bedroom to find her husband lying peacefully in bed. As Polya puts it, *"You see, it was the natural sequence of things. He took off his coat, then his tie, then his shirt, and so on, and went to sleep!"*

Habitual behaviors can certainly be helpful. We rarely need to think about the way we use our bodies to walk, run, and climb stairs. We can be robotic about the way we hold a pencil, fork, or a cup. Drivers may get into the habit of operating the accelerator, brake, and turn signal of a car efficiently, never giving the process a thought. Agatha Christie wrote of habits in *Witness for the Prosecution*, *"Curious things, habits. People themselves never knew they had them."*

Habits of politeness, such as saying "hello," "please," "thank you," "you're welcome," and "excuse me," promote harmony as

"Excellence is an art won by training and habituation. We do not act rightly because we have virtue or excellence, but we rather have those because we have acted rightly. We are what we repeatedly do. Excellence, then, is not an act, but a habit."
–Aristotle

we communicate with each other in our daily routines. Hygiene habits also aid us in our journey through life. Bathing our bodies, brushing our teeth, and eating nutritious foods in the proper amounts contribute to healthy bodies. Keeping our clothing and living quarters clean and neat are habits that can promote self-esteem and success. Once learned, these good habits often become beneficial, although perhaps unconscious, ways of life.

The habits of doing routine things in a certain order can sometimes assure completion of a project. For instance, putting everything you need for work in the same place near the door before you go to bed at night can help you get a smooth start the next morning. If, before you leave the house each day, you form the habit of taking a few seconds to visually scan the room and think about what you need to take with you, time and possible embarrassment could be eliminated. Thinking about what needs to be turned off (like stoves), or unplugged (like curling irons), can help keep your home safe.

Still, not all habits are helpful, and bad habits can become cruel masters that are detrimental to our well-being. Smoking, drinking, and taking drugs can rapidly develop into habits sabotaging our health and our relationships with others. While the dangers of addictive drugs are becoming more obvious each day, sometimes habits that are much more subtle can be just as detrimental to our development into successful individuals.

The habit of thinking negatively about ourselves and our opportunities is self-destructive, as can be the habit of day-dreaming instead of concentrating on our work. Procrastination is an insidious and self-defeating habit that has ruined many lives. Blaming other people or circumstances for our failures can become a habit that may prevent us from moving forward toward the completion of our goals.

By the time a behavior pattern becomes a habit, it can feel so familiar that it seems to be a natural part of us, but, in fact, *habits are learned and practiced.* Just as we have learned them over time, we can "unlearn" these practiced behaviors. By observing yourself, you can become aware of the habitual ways you think and act that could be harmful. When you're conscious of a habit you want to change, you can unlearn it by replacing the automatic behavior with a different, more thoughtful response. You may make mistakes or slip back into old ways, but it's important not to give up. Simply correct your behavior as soon as you're aware that you've slipped back into the old habit. Determine how to be the master of your habits, so that your habits can be useful servants to you.

"The nature of men is always the same; it is their habits that separate them."
—Confucius

"The habit of being uniformly considerate toward others will bring increased happiness to you. As you put into practice the qualities of patience, punctuality, sincerity, and solicitude, you will have a better opinion of the world around you."
—Grenville Kleiser

"Life is never a habit with me. It is always a marvel."
–Katherine Mansfield

"No habit has any real hold on you other than the hold you have on it."
–Gardner Hunting

LAW 5

You cannot discover new oceans until you have the courage to lose sight of the shore
—Anonymous

The eagles that live in the canyons of the state of Colorado in the United States use a special kind of stick with which to build their nests. A female eagle can sometimes fly as many as two hundred miles in a single day in order to find a branch from an ironwood tree. Not only are the ironwood sticks as strong as their name suggests, but they also have thorns that allow them to lock together so the nest can set securely on a ledge high up in the canyon. After building the nest, the eagle pads it with layer upon layer of leaves, feathers and grass to protect future offspring from the sharp thorns of the ironwood.

In her preparations, the female eagle goes to great lengths to promote the survival of the birds she will hatch. This interest in their survival extends well beyond their birth, although the expression of that interest changes. As the young eagles grow, they begin to fight for space in the nest. The chicks' demands for food eventually become such that the mother eagle is unable to fulfill their needs. She instinctively knows that in order to survive, her brood is going to have to leave its nest.

To encourage the young eagles to fend for themselves, the mother pulls the padding out of the nest so the thorns of the ironwood branches prick the young birds. As their living conditions become more painful, they are forced to climb up on the edge of the nest. The mother eagle then coaxes the young eagles off the edge. As they begin to plummet to the bottom of the canyon, they wildly flap their wings to brake their fall, and end up doing what is the most natural thing in the world for an eagle—they fly!

As human beings, we may often find ourselves in a similar situation. When our lives can no longer provide us with the growth we desire and change must take place, we may need to leave safety and familiarity behind and journey into unknown territory. Just as the baby eagles are reluctant to leave the nest, we may also resist change. Even though conditions may not be

"I find the great thing in this world is not so much where we stand, as in what direction we are moving. To reach heaven, we must sail sometimes with the wind and sometimes against it—but we must sail, and not drift, nor lie at anchor."
–Oliver Wendell Holmes, Sr.

pleasant, we sometimes make an effort to tolerate the increasing discomfort because we're afraid of the unknown. But if your ship is tied up at the dock, it doesn't matter how you turn the rudder—that ship isn't going anywhere!

Many times unpleasant conditions in our lives tell us that we are ready to move on and experience new areas of our potential. While our fear of the unknown might temporarily increase our tolerance of an uncomfortable situation, life's circumstances may likely get thorny enough that, like the growing eagles, we'll be coaxed into moving on. We can trust life and move ahead into new experiences with confidence because, in a wonderful way, we live in a friendly universe—a universe designed to support us and our activities. Dr. Irving Oyle recognized this when he commented, *"The universe is not opposed to our best interest."*

Have you ever said to yourself, "I've wanted to do something like this, but never quite had the courage?" Take a look at the urge within your being that may be prompting you to step forward. When the time comes to venture out and accept new challenges, remember that everyone has an innate ability not only to survive but to prosper. We are designed, by God, with the possibility to achieve high levels of success and to enjoy fulfillment and satisfaction in life. This means we do not have to settle for less than we're capable of, unless that is our choice.

The following quote taken from the *Association for Humanistic Psychology Newsletter* was written by an eighty-five-year-old woman. Take a moment and reflect on the wisdom shared through her observations:

"If I had my life to live over, I'd dare to make more mistakes next time. I'd relax. I'd limber up. I would be sillier than I've been this trip. I would take fewer things seriously. I would take more chances. I would take more trips. I would climb more mountains and swim more rivers. I would eat more ice cream and less beans. I would perhaps have more actual 'troubles,' but I'd have fewer imaginary ones!

"You see, I'm one of those people who live sensibly and sanely hour after hour, day after day. Oh, I've had my moments, and if I had it to do over again, I'd have more of them! In fact, I'd try to have nothing else!

"Isn't that delightful! Just moments, one after another, instead of living so many years ahead of each day.

"I've been one of those persons who never goes anywhere without a thermometer, a hot water bottle, a rain coat, and a parachute! If I had to do it again, I would travel lighter than I have.

"If I had my life to live over, I would start barefoot earlier in the

"Whatever course you have chosen for yourself, it will not be a chore but an adventure if you bring to it a sense of the glory of surviving—if your sights are set far above the merely secure and mediocre."
–David Sarnoff

"Courage is a special kind of knowledge: the knowledge of how to fear what ought to be feared and how not to fear what ought not to be feared."
–David Ben-Gurion

"God gives nothing to those who keep their arms crossed."
–Bam Bara (West African proverb)

spring and stay that way later in the fall. I would go to more dances. I would ride more merry-go-rounds. I would pick more daisies."

So often, we have within our grasp a whole new way of life and fail to explore it. Why? Could one reason be that we may not be secure enough in who and what we are to release the pioneering spirit? An interesting thing is that we do have our life to live over. Every day life comes for us to live a new experience. Over and over, around the calendar, twenty-four new hours present themselves to us. Perhaps we could ask ourselves, regardless of our age, "Have I really lived all my years, or has each year been one day lived over and over again?"

Within each of us are resources that can be realized only when we climb to the edge of the nest, slip off into the air—and fly!

Spotlights!

1. Giving freely, without guarantee of return, sets into motion an irresistible momentum of goodness.
2. When we give, everyone can be a winner!
3. How much of what you believe about yourself may come from what others believe about you?
4. Understanding the truth that God is within all his creations may bring the abundant living and the peace on earth for which many people yearn.
5. Beliefs are the simple convictions of one's life.
6. If you desire peace, the first place to look is within yourself.
7. One way to progress in consciousness is by going on to the next larger context of thought and realization.
8. A habit is a pattern of behavior we have acquired that has become so automatic it may be difficult to modify or eliminate.
9. Every day life comes for us to live a new experience.
10. Take a look at the urge within your being that may be prompting you to boldly step forward into new experiences.

Living the Law!

In his book *An Operator's Manual for Successful Living*, Nicholas R. M. Martin offers the following illustration of a "time line of experience." He states that human experience can be subdivided into component parts that follow an orderly and predictable sequence: we encounter events about which we think, then feel, then act; and our actions then lead to consequences for self, others, and the situations that confront us. The diagram below illustrates Martin's universal time line. Study the flow of events presented, then parallel this analogy with the flow of events in your life.

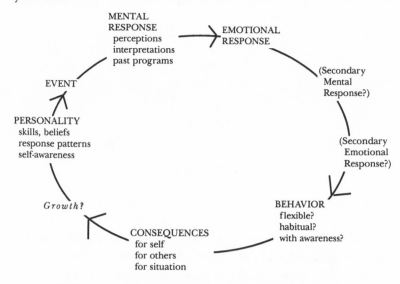

The importance of this illustration relates to the question of whether we learn from experience or simply continue through life responding in the same old habitual ways and receiving the same results. In other words, are our lives enhanced by the patterns of thought and behavior we enact and the consequences that follow, or have we become stuck in rigid and limiting response patterns that keep us from our goals and potentials?

Our emotions are, in a real sense, events about which we think and then feel. So, a person who feels hurt might start feeling sorry for himself and then feel inadequate. He may also believe that feeling inadequate is to become vulnerable, and so decide that showing his feelings is dangerous, and then he may end up getting angry instead. This could be done without conscious awareness and thus without conscious control. Do you see from this illustration how self-awareness can be a major key to success, and the willingness to look for growth may have impact on whether our time lines "leave room for growth"?

Week Eighteen

❖

LAW 1

No one's education is ever complete
–John M. Templeton

There is a children's story about a young man who went in search of the most stupid person he could find. As he walked down a country lane early one morning, the man heard strange noises coming from a small house near the road. There was a thump-thump-thumping, followed by a crash and the sounds of groaning. He stopped and listened for a few minutes. The sounds were repeated several times. Finally, the young man was unable to contain his curiosity. He walked up to the porch of the house and peered through the curtains. To his astonishment, he saw an older man in his underwear run across the room—thump-thump-thump—leap into the air, and crash into the back of a chair where a pair of trousers was hanging. The older fellow fell to the floor and lay there a moment, groaning from the pain. Then he pulled himself up, picked up the chair, hung the trousers on it, and backed across the room. Again came the thump-thump-thump. A leap into the air. Crash! Then, "Ooooohhh."

The young man rapped on the door. The older man answered the knock and let him in. "Tell me, sir," said the young man, "Why are you doing what you're doing?"

"This is how I put my trousers on. I hang them on the chair and run and jump into them," the man replied. "My daddy did it that way and his daddy before him did it that way, and what was good enough for them is good enough for me."

"Isn't that a slow and painful way to get dressed? Most men put their trousers on one leg at a time. It's much easier and faster." the young man said. "Here, sit on the chair and I'll show you."

It was the older man's turn to be astonished. "It was a lucky day for me when you came by. I guess you're never too old to learn."

Perhaps this seems like an illogical story, but the message is pertinent. Anyone who believes that he has learned everything he needs to know, or all there is to learn, makes a critical error. Albert Einstein, one of the great geniuses of our age, once said, *"A day without learning is a day wasted. There is so much to learn and so little time to learn it."* He followed his own precept by continuing to work and study diligently until his death. Many examples of great people who never stopped learning offer inspiration for us.

Grandma Moses, who painted in a primitive style, took up art late in life. We might not have the opportunity to enjoy her work if she had lacked the courage to continue her education and refused to stop growing in her creativeness. Colonel Sanders, of Kentucky Fried Chicken fame, learned about the fast food business and franchising in his sixties. Abigail Adams, American first lady, expressed the importance of learning and education in this way: *"Learning is not attained by chance. It must be sought for with ardor and attended to with diligence."*

"Live and learn" can be a wise motto to live by if you agree that no one's education is ever complete. It isn't by trying to squeeze the required thought out of our brain cells that we can get the knowledge we need. Rather, it is by opening up our mind, freeing, letting go, expanding, and broadening our thoughts with the implicit understanding that we may become more open to the great infinite mind of God in universal free form. Who knows what realms of knowledge and learning abide therein, waiting for us to be receptive! Wherever we are and whatever we are doing, it is possible to learn something that can enrich our lives and the lives of others. It may be necessary to release outmoded ways of thinking and acting in order to try something new. But when we do, we often find that life becomes more exciting and fulfilling than perhaps we dreamed possible.

Could this be what Jesus meant when he spoke of hiding our light under a bushel, or as translated by Moffatt, putting it "under a bowl"? We really cannot imprison light. If we took a glowing electric light bulb and turned a bowl upside down over it, some of the light would still spill out from under the bowl. Even if the burning light bulb was hermetically sealed inside the bowl, the light bulb could still communicate its existence by heating up the bowl and imparting some of its warmth to the surrounding air. Could this be saying to us that we can neither stifle nor suppress for very long the divine intelligence that is a part of our inherent nature?

"Learning is either a continuing thing or it is nothing."
—Frank Tyger

"Education is no longer thought of as a preparation for adult life, but as a continuing process of growth and development from birth until death."
—Stephen Mitchell

"A man should never stop learning, even on his last day."
—Maimonides

Sometimes, we try to place the bowl of human belief over the splendor that wants to shine. Is it possible that our frustrations and discouragements may be a little leakage from the great light wanting to shine? Perhaps we need to remove a bowl or two by denying the human belief that we might be too old, have too little education, or may not be smart enough to accomplish greater things. The good news is that, even though the light of creativity and knowledge may be suppressed and hidden under the innumerable bowls of belief we may place over it, it never loses its divinity or its immense and indefatigable energy. It will try to work through the subconscious facilities instead, and we may find ourselves having interesting dreams that make a deep impression upon us.

Edison said, *"If you are doing anything the way you did twenty years ago, there is a better way."* There can be great truth in this statement. Right now could be an excellent time to either expand or adopt the attitude that many wonderful things can be learned. Listen to your inner promptings. Since you are a functioning human being, you may have one or more fields in which you are strong. Accentuate these strong areas of your life, and humbly claim your degree of greatness by continuing to be eager to learn.

LAW 2

Accentuate the positive; eliminate the negative

—Johnny Mercer

"You gotta accentuate the positive; eliminate the negative; latch on to the affirmative; don't mess with Mr. In-Between!" so sang Johnny Mercer in the mid-1940s. This message is still a good one for us today.

When something seems to be going awry, it often becomes tempting to believe that everything in our lives is wrong. Unfortunately, this attitude can cause us to act in ways that seem to magnetize more negative influences, and we may overlook the positive aspects in our lives.

Have you ever gotten up late, only to find the shirt you planned to wear that day is dirty? or there's no cereal for breakfast? and your brother beat you to the bathroom? Whether or not the day goes downhill from this point depends on how you feel about what has already happened. Are you angry at yourself for forgetting to set the alarm or for not laundering the shirt the night before? How do you feel toward the person who failed to do the grocery shopping? And what about your brother who beat you to the bathroom—and seems to be taking his time?

We often tend to blame others for our misfortunes. But instead of wasting time and energy on anger and accusation, it is far more productive to focus on solutions and move away from the problem and into your day in a positive frame of mind. *"Accentuate the positive; eliminate the negative."* It can work for you!

Anger feeds on anger. If your brother is criticized or yelled at for staying too long in the bathroom, he may likely stay even longer, which won't get you out of the house on time. Refusing to argue with him and using the waiting time to prepare for your day not only keeps peace but maintains your schedule. If you discuss your needs and ask him to agree to a time limit, you both have the opportunity to "eliminate the negative."

Learning these lessons early on can stand you in good stead throughout life. There may continue to be times when you'll want to cry, "It's not fair!" But feeling sorry for yourself doesn't solve the problem. Better to think, "This is how it is. Now, what can I do about the situation?" Remember, anger is an emotion, and emotions seldom successfully solve problems. Instead, they may be more likely to create new ones.

As you practice thinking in positive ways, you may find that your life becomes smoother and exhibits less tension and anger. You can begin to manage your feelings, instead of allowing outer circumstances to be a controlling factor. You can begin at any time to shift your thinking and react positively, while still releasing negative thoughts.

Pleasant, more productive days can result from your new approach to positive thinking. Because your subconscious mind is the reservoir for your memories, you can get quick feedback on whatever situation may be occurring. Your subconscious mind remembers past events and records what your thinking and feeling responses were at that time. When a similar thing happens today, your mind sends a remembered message, which

"Personal deficiencies might be termed negative qualities and include unreliability, failure to co-operate, laziness, untidiness, trouble-making, interference, and dishonesty.

"Positive qualities would include willingness, cheerfulness, courtesy, honesty, neatness, reliability, and temperance.

"Many fail in their work because they are unable to overcome one personal deficiency. Check up on yourself. Don't be afraid to put yourself under a microscope.

"Eliminate your negative qualities. Develop your positive ones. You can't win with the check mark in the wrong place."
—M. Winette

could be a message of anger, resentment, or frustration. You have the ability to give your mind new messages as you choose to react emotionally or to meet the situation with poised and balanced thinking

Many respected teachers express the thought that *"when you control your mind and emotions, you control your life."* Outer circumstances may then have a less negative effect on you. Ralph Waldo Emerson reminded us that *"the ancestor to every action is a thought."* As a step toward an awakened awareness, consider how your thoughts may have contributed to a nonmiraculous, limiting approach to life. If you recognize areas of this kind of mental activity, then you know that you may produce the opposite of a joyous, abundant, and expansive life! Do you believe in this possibility?

Twenty years ago the idea of a remote control gadget that would allow you to switch from one television station to another, while seated in your chair, was an impossibility. Going to a nearby store and renting a movie was unthinkable. To microwave a meal in the comfort of your home wasn't a part of human consciousness. Did you know that the capacity to create these wonders *was available* at the time of Hannibal? The potential and possibility were present. The devices came along when various positive and possibility-thinking minds opened to the genius of spirit. *"Accentuate the positive, eliminate the negative,"* and be a person who is overflowing with gratitude for your talents and blessings!

LAW 3

Forgiving uplifts the forgiver
—John M. Templeton

A young woman named Sue had a puppy she frequently scooped up into her arms and showered with kisses. "Oh, I'm *so* thankful to have you in my life," she would coo. Yet, she rarely took the puppy for walks and often forgot to feed him. She may have felt she was thankful for the gift of the puppy's friendship, but true thanksgiving includes some way of expressing gratitude and love through positive action.

Love is more than a feeling. It is a way of setting a course through giving. It is a letting go of fear. True thanksgiving transcends fear and frees us to live in the present moment, where we can feel free to express our giving and forgiving natures. Most of us understand giving, but some of us may still be confused about the meaning of forgiveness. Some people may go through life in a groveling mode, mistakenly believing they have to receive forgiveness from others. Forgiveness offers more than a reprieve granted to us by another person. True forgiveness is a process of giving up the false for the true and allows us to rid our thinking of rigid ideas. We can develop the flexibility to change our mind and our behavior patterns to higher and greater expressions and find new avenues to freedom.

As a child, when caught doing something inappropriate, Sue would cry and beg to be forgiven, although she had no intention of changing her behavior. She was simply upset that she had been caught, and her pleas for forgiveness were a way to avoid the consequences of her behavior. A scenario of sincere forgiveness from Sue could have gone something like this. "Yes, I realize not caring properly for my puppy was inappropriate. I understand that being grounded for a week is a result of my behavior. This is a good lesson for me." Young children may not be able to accept and reason in this way, but as we mature, if our role models have been adequate, we can learn and grow from our mistakes rather than repeating them.

Forgiveness is about loving one's self enough to be honest, open-minded, and willing to move forward in life. It is about learning to be grateful, not only for our own mistakes but for all our experiences, even if they are painful. Forgiveness can be about knowing that although we experience pain, we don't have to suffer. The faith expressed through giving thanks for our challenges can help dissolve the appearance of negative circumstances as we look for the good in the situation. We learn not to resist the changes that truly come to bless us.

It may not be easy to let go of old ideas, even though we recognize they can be self-defeating. Sometimes we struggle to hold on to the familiar. Growth, however, is not intended to be a struggle but rather a surrender to higher good. When you forgive yourself, you cease doing the hurtful thing. You make a deep and conscious commitment to live in accordance with universal law. Your mind changes from a material to a spiritual base. When an error is discovered and there is a willingness to

"He who forgives ends the quarrel."
—African proverb

"Learning to forgive is much more useful than merely picking up a stone and throwing it at the object of one's anger; the more so when the provocation is extreme. For it is under the greatest adversity that there exists the greatest potential for doing good, both for yourself and others."
—Dalai Lama

*"Joy to forgive and joy to be forgiven,
Hang level in the glances of love."*
—Richard Garrnett

correct it, under the law of forgiveness, we can erase the mistake as easily as a child erases false figures in an arithmetic exercise. The moment we correct our error, we align ourself in harmony with the truth of being, and the law wipes out our transgressions. Self-forgiving is uplifting, but total forgiving is even more uplifting.

Through giving and forgiving, the old ego-structures that have been built up over a lifetime can start to crumble. When that wall comes down, we are free to build healthy structures in our minds. And when the mind is strong and healthy, then our world reflects strength and health. During this process, there may be the appearance of chaos, turmoil, and confusion from time to time. But let us remember that it's thanksgiving that sustains this wonderful, self-perpetuating, positive cycle not only in our lives but in the larger scheme of things. As we give thanks and forgive, we are uplifted.

*"Learn we the larger
life to live,
To comprehend is to
forgive."*
—Henrietta Huxley

LAW 4

*The light of understanding dissolves
the phantom of fear*
—Ellie Harold

*"Nothing in life is to
be feared. It is only to
be understood."*
—Marie Curie

Many of our fears are no more real than the eerie ghosts that haunt the houses of Elm Street on Friday the 13th! These phantoms of doubt, confusion, and pain are often fabrications of our minds. They may cause us to run away and hide or scream with fright, but when seen in the light of understanding, our fears can dissolve.

There once was a woman who became terribly upset when she returned home from a trip to find that her beloved cat was missing. She spent the day searching the neighborhood, calling her cat by name, and asking the neighbors if they had seen her beloved pet. Between heaving sobs, all she could repeatedly say was, "I know she's out there starving somewhere. Or else dogs have killed her. She can't protect herself, she's a house cat. She

*"Fear fades when facts
are faced."*
—Frank Tyger

has no front claws." In her mind, the woman visualized a variety of horrible things that could happen to her cat. Twilight finally drew her away from the search, and the grieving woman went into her house and began to unpack from the trip. As she walked to a closet to hang up a dress, deep from within the closet came the cry of her hiding cat. The poor woman nearly fainted with relief.

By allowing her thoughts to run wild and unchecked, the woman created a "worst-case" scenario. Job lamented, *"The thing that I fear has come upon me, what I dread befalls me"* (Job 3:25). When we let fear overwhelm us, the worst possibilities often flash before our minds. Perhaps it's an instant replay of some disaster from the evening news, personalized to involve our children, or our parents, or a nightmare childhood. Thoughts stained by fear cannot perceive reality accurately. It's like trying to study objects through a clouded lens. Little may be seen clearly for what it is. Vision can be reduced to diffused and shadowy images. Sometimes we may feel seemingly paralyzed by our fear. Other times we may react defensively because doom seems so imminent. Like the woman who thought her cat had been destroyed by dogs, only to find it safely hiding in her closet, we often put ourselves and others through a lot of anguish before we discover that the facts do not support our worst fears.

Cases are recorded of individuals whose hair actually grew out white on receiving tragic news about a loved one, only to learn later that the report was unfounded. In other difficult situations, people received horrible news and emerged, after great pain and despite their loss, with a strong sense of wholeness. The difference between the two groups lies in how they received bad news rather than in the nature of the news they received. The first group succumbed to imaginings that were ultimately proved incorrect, while the second group faced their fears and dealt with reality.

Fear is also F.E.A.R. (*False* Evidence Appearing *Real*)—a famous acronym that sheds the light of understanding on those phantoms of fear. There are at least two false premises regarding fear. First is the belief that things are as they appear to be. Increasingly, scientists are discovering evidence to the contrary. For example, what seems to be solid mater is, in fact, composed of patterns of subatomic units of energy. Second, the fearful individual assumes that he or she lacks the resources to handle a tragic situation. The truth is, courage belongs not only to heroes and heroines but can also be developed within you as you meet life's challenges. As Eleanor Roosevelt wrote, *"You gain*

"Only in quiet waters things mirror themselves undistorted. Only in the quiet mind is adequate perception of the world."
—Hans Margolius

"Be not afraid of life. Believe that life is worth living, and your belief will help create the fact."
—William James

"People who enjoy life and radiate their happiness fear nothing. Fear never has led, and never will lead, a man victoriously in any phase of life. . . . A cheerful frame of mind, reinforced by relaxation, which in itself banishes fatigue, is the medicine that puts all Ghosts of Fear on the run."
—George Matthew Adams

strength, courage and confidence by every experience in which you really stop to look fear in the face." When you look fear in the face, you may see right through it for, after all, it is often only a phantom!

LAW 5

Only one thing is more important than learning from experience, and that is not learning from experience
–John M. Templeton

Today can be a day filled with opportunities for you to express yourself, expand yourself, and experience the world around you. A lot of people talk about life. Some love it. Some disparage it. And a few realize that life can be what you make it because they have learned from past experiences. Lessons learned from these experiences have often contributed greatly toward seeing the possibilities in what some people call "the game of life." When we've "been there" and "done that," we can have as good of an idea of what we *don't* want as what we *do* want. Experience is certainly an excellent teacher!

A lot of emphasis is placed on winning in today's world. We've been taught that everyone loves a winner and, as the former baseball manager Leo Durocher put it, *"Nice guys finish last."* In professional sports, winning is everything. In business, often striving for the top rung of the ladder can be a constant goal. Nations compete with other nations to win control of markets. Companies spend millions of advertising dollars to help win over the consumer. The saying *"It's not whether you win or lose, it's how you play the game"* may seem to some to be a worn shibboleth, judged by current competitive standards. However, there is great wisdom in the Chinese proverb, *"Those who play the game do not see as clearly as those who watch."*

While the experience of winning can be a good thing, placing an inflated value on being first can be destructive. There is often a mistaken assumption that you can be a better and happier person if you often come in first. But the fact is, many who hold the top seat in their sphere of expertise prove to be unhappy and insecure on a personal level. What does coming in first

"Our destiny is not predetermined for us; we determine it for ourselves."
–Arnold Toynbee

"Everyone has fair turn to be as great as he pleases."
–Jeremy Collier

actually mean? It simply means you outperformed someone else on a given day. Your next performance could be completely different, as new and eager talented competitors zealously vie for your position. You can be certain that the position on the top rung seldom goes unchallenged. If your self esteem rides on your ability to outmaneuver, outwit, or outsmart someone else, you might have a great deal riding on a very shaky foundation. Approached in this way, competition can become a weapon used to destroy those who threaten to depose your vulnerable empire.

Now, the experience of competition can be a positive force in our lives. In fact, it can be a necessary part of the continuing progress, improvements, and vigor of our social and economic development. On a personal level, competing with another in sports or business can provide you with an opportunity to sharpen and expand your skills. In addition, it often brings into focus those areas that need further development. You can gather a tremendous amount of experience and useful information quickly either by engaging in competition or observing others competing.

The problem lies not in competition but in our attitude toward whatever we're doing. So often we tend to measure ourselves and our self-worth by how well we do against our opponents. If we lose the game, we may believe we're losers. If we come in second, we could feel we're second-rate. It's important to remember that productive competition with another can serve as a yardstick that measures our performance, not our value as a person.

Mao Zedong, chairman of the People's Republic of China, commented, *"If you want to know the taste of a pear, you must change the pear by eating it yourself. . . . If you want to know the theory and methods of revolution, you must take part in the revolution. All genuine knowledge originates in direct experience."* We can learn from the experiences in the game of life, and we can also learn from not learning from experiences when life gives us another opportunity!

If you sincerely work toward making each performance a little better than the last one—and if you find your sense of life steadily expanding and improving because you are building on your experiences—you can emerge as a winner in more ways than one.

"Seize the moment of excited curiosity on any subject to solve your doubts; for if you let it pass the desire may never return, and you may remain in ignorance."
—William Wirt

"There is no merit where there is no trail; and till the experience stamps the mark of strength, cowards may pass for heroes and faith for falsehood."
—Aaron Hill

Spotlights!

1. This moment may be an excellent time to expand, or adopt, the attitude that there are many wonderful things to be learned.

2. It may be necessary to release outmoded ways of thinking and acting in order to try something new.
3. Make a daily commitment to *"accentuate the positive and eliminate the negative"* in the various aspects of your life.
4. Blaming others is a waste of time and energy. It can be far more productive to focus on positive solutions to problems.
5. Emotions seldom successfully solve problems.
6. Self-forgiveness can be a process of giving up the false for the true. It allows us to restore inner harmony and be free from the bitterness or pain of the past.
7. Self-forgiveness is also about loving one's self enough to be honest, open-minded, and willing to move forward in life.
8. F.E.A.R. is an abbreviation for *False* Evidence Appearing *Real!*
9. *"Nothing in life is to be feared. It is only to be understood"* (Marie Curie).
10. Experience shows that productive competition with another can serve as a yardstick to measure our performance, not our value as a person.

Living the Law!

Self-esteem is an issue that receives a lot of attention in many areas. Perhaps that is because in today's world of communication, we know that reasonable self-esteem has much to do with one's overall happiness in life and that it is important for our achievement and success. Low self-esteem has been shown by various psychological studies to be a key factor in a wide range of emotional problems. So what *is* self-esteem? It includes the beliefs and attitudes we hold toward ourselves, in thought, feeling, words, and actions—both consciously and subconsciously—and the expressions in our life that those mental responses engender. Self-esteem plays this key role in our life because thought and faith are *creative*.

Because self-esteem is so very much a part of our mental attitude, the basics for strengthening this part of ourselves can begin with the awareness that we have the power to direct our mind as we choose. Let's look at some techniques we can work with that can help us strengthen our own self-esteem.

1. *Develop Your Spiritual Nature.* You can find your rightful place in the world when you give up the belief that it is hidden from you or that you are unworthy of success. Believe that the Spirit of God is within you and that the light of his presence reveals the way to you.

2. *Think Positively!* Decide to develop a positive sense of who and what you are by translating negative thoughts and feelings into more positive or neutral alternatives. Remember, you tend to become what you think.

3. *Value Your Emotional Nature* as you would a faithful friend and servant. Use your feelings to enhance growth, express love, facilitate communication, empower action, visualize your goals, and strengthen your capacity to live fully each day. Respect your feelings and be understanding and supportive and a good friend to *yourself as well as others.*

4. *Review and Release Negative Past Programming.* Confucius said, *"Settle one difficulty and you keep a hundred away."* Let go of feelings of guilt through the power of forgiving yourself and others. Be aware that habits are not something you *are* but something you *do.* Those that are less than positive can be released, if that is your desire. The decision to change a habit is conscious, and your ability to change a habit relates to your skill in mastering your own subconscious mind.

5. *Re-evaluate* where you presently are according to your own highest sense of what is true, helpful, and productive. Believe that peace exists within you and that you don't need to get caught up in the the turbulence of others or of outer circumstances. Build your faith with the following "bricks" of repeated belief:
   * you are filled with amazing life and health
   * you have plenty for all your real needs and desires
   * you are infolded in divine love
   * you are being awakened to infinite joy and usefulness, and the light of God within is your source of inspiration and guidance.

Now, rest for a while in contemplation of these things and write your thoughts, feelings, awarenesses, and experiences of inner promptings in your journal. God bless you.

Week Nineteen

❖

LAW 1

Make yourself necessary to the world and mankind will give you bread
—Ralph Waldo Emerson

Ralph Waldo Emerson, in many of his masterful essays, pondered this formula. He was expected to follow in the steps of his father and grandfather as a Unitarian minister. Although he did become an ordained minister, Emerson was not content to minister in the ways of his forefathers. He recognized his gift was different. On fire with enthusiasm to reveal his ideas on morality, self-reliance, and the soul, Emerson began to write. His ideas were new to many people, and his audience began to grow. Before long he met with success, and today Emerson's essays may be found in many bookstores and libraries. Emerson was true to his own formula, *"Make yourself necessary to the world and mankind will give you bread."* He bravely stepped forth and created a need for what he had to give the world by making his talent available.

A few years ago, a group of unemployed artists banded together to form a business called "The Starving Artists." Today, their paintings are sold throughout the United States. Another example of an entrepreneur is Wally Amos, the creator of Famous Amos Cookies. He began by baking a deliciously good chocolate-chip cookie. The word spread about how wonderful his cookies tasted, and his friends wanted more. From a small beginning, the business grew into national status. Wally found a need, or desire, and filled it!

These innovative people believed, along with Emerson, that if you find the special talent you have to offer and use that talent to produce something the world can use, the world can supply your needs. What activities bring you great joy? What activities do you perform well? What flows easily for you? If you could do whatever work you desired and had some assurance that you wouldn't fail, what would you do? What are your goals? You may wish to revisit them and think of a way people could benefit from what you have to offer . . . and then offer it! You might find, as did Emerson, Famous Amos, and the artists, that what it takes is a taste of something good—something you have to offer the world—and people will find themselves hungering for more.

With the sheer driving force of advancing technology, it becomes increasingly clear that opportunities are available in many areas for those who feel an inner pull to be of service. For example, the environment, the physical sciences, the economy, health and medicine, education, communications media, religion, charity, philanthropy, volunteerism are but some of the advancing technologies. The evolution of humanity and the universe seems to be vast in its conception, yet curiously experimental and tentative, a truly creative work in process. If you choose, you can be a conscious part of that creative process! You are necessary! We have come a long way from the cave shelters of the Ice Age, but it may well be, in God's great plan, that we have vastly further to travel. Science is beginning to reveal a creation of awesome magnitude, intricacy beauty, and order, and we sense that what lies beyond our instruments is vastly greater still.

Yes, my friend, there are abundant opportunities for the one who elects to make himself, or herself, necessary to the world. The rewards are not only the "bread" provided, but an inner awareness of your contribution to God's purpose and to the uplifting of the human race through loving service.

"If a man can write a better book, preach a better sermon, or make a better mouse-trap than his neighbor, though he builds his house in the woods, the world will make a beaten path to his door."
—Ralph Waldo Emerson, from the anthology *Borrowings*

"Taking delight in his own special kind of action, a man attains perfection"
—Bhagavat Gita

"I would rather choose to be a plumber or a peddler in the hope to find that modest degree of independence still available under present circumstances."
—Albert Einstein

LAW 2

Happiness comes from spiritual wealth, not material wealth
—John M. Templeton

Years ago, there was a television series in the United States called *The Millionaire.* Every week some deserving person would receive a cashier's check for a million dollars from an unknown benefactor. The recipient of the check could keep the money

"The gratification of
wealth is not found in
mere possession or in
lavish expenditure, but
in its wise applica-
tion."
—Miguel de
Cervantes

"Surplus wealth is a
sacred trust which its
possessor is bound to
administer in his life-
time for the good of the
community."
—Andrew Carnegie

and spend it in any way he wanted on the condition that he
never reveal the source. Each week the recipient faced many
challenges to his agreement with the benefactor. Quite a few
times the recipient had to return the money.

Hollywood has made many movies demonstrating that true
happiness does not come from material wealth. The movie
Money Grows on Trees concerned a family that suddenly became
rich when they discovered that one of the trees in their yard
grew money. In the course of the film, the family faced many
difficulties because of the money tree.

These are fictional examples of people who did not find happiness from the acquisition of great wealth. But what about real
life? There are accounts of people who have become instant mil-
lionaires by winning a large lottery or receiving an unexpected
inheritance. When asked how their lives changed since receiving
the money, some responded that life had become more complicated. A lot of money was at their disposal, but instead of finding happiness, new problems arose.

In many of these fictional and real situations, there seems to
be a missing link. If we have not developed a reservoir of spiritual wealth, no amount of money is likely to make us happy.
Spiritual wealth provides faith. It gives us love. It brings and
expands wisdom. Spiritual wealth leads to happiness because it
guides us into useful or loving relationships.

It is easy to determine our material wealth, but to determine
how wealthy we are spiritually, it is important to look at our
lives. What are our relationships like? Have we learned how to
love and accept others for who and what they are without reser-
vation? Have we learned how to forgive and forget perceived
wrongs done to us? Do we value all of life and the many forms
through which it expresses itself? Have we used our talents to
the utmost? The answers to these questions can offer us a fair
estimate of the extent and quality of our spiritual wealth.

We may think that happiness is a result of happy circumstances. A more mature view of happiness is that it is a by-product of sharing our good and serving others. It is a sense of
doing a job well, honest communication with another, visiting
someone who may be ill, or sharing a sense of humor.
Happiness is a spiritual principle that we can lay hold of and
use, regardless of outer conditions or circumstances.

It isn't necessary to wait for circumstances to bring happiness.
When we try to give it to others, it returns to us multiplied. We
can make our own joy, and let it act upon circumstances! One of

the great paradoxes of truth is that a happy heart draws to itself what it needs for happiness.

Spiritual wealth can be a pathway to true and lasting happiness because with it, we have a resource to provide for what may be needed. Material wealth may be dependent on many extraneous factors that can sometimes be outside our control. Spiritual wealth can be within our control because it is an "inside job." We are the ones who determine how much or how little we open our hearts and minds. If we take inventory and find ourselves lacking in spiritual wealth, we have the opportunity to replenish the supply. Within us can be found the necessary tools for building productive and happy lives. We can access the ability to be useful and, thereby, enjoy life, regardless of what may be taking place around us.

It's true, material comfort can be a positive force in our lives. With it we may eliminate any concern about being hungry, paying bills, or educating our children. When the economy is strong, material wealth can be a dependable security. What happens if the economic situation weakens? As we develop our spiritual wealth, our inner security is present to serve us. It is like a "blank check" that can be honored anytime. Should we lose our savings and financial resources, then our spiritual wealth can help us recover and recoup our losses. With spiritual wealth as the foundation and security for our lives, we gain a deep and abiding peace that can't be obtained with material wealth alone.

If we truly desire happiness in our lives, three important guidelines can be a powerful assistance to remember. (1) Happiness can be the *cause* as well as the *effect* of bringing more good into our lives. (2) Happiness increases for us through use, because when we think, speak, and act with joy, there is little room for anything less in our lives. (3) We can cultivate happiness through service to others.

The wise Aristotle said, *"If happiness is activity in accordance with excellence, it is reasonable that it should be in accordance with the highest excellence."*

"Wealth is the product of man's capacity to think."
—Ayn Rand

"The real duty of man is not to extend his power or multiply his wealth beyond his needs, but to enrich and enjoy his imperishable possession: his soul."
—Gilbert Highet

LAW 3

Thoughts held in mind produce after their kind
—Charles Fillmore

> *"Keep your thoughts right–for as you think, so are you. Thoughts are things; therefore, think only the things that will make the world better and you unashamed."*
> —Henry H. Buckley

Twenty years ago, comedian Flip Wilson made famous the phrase, *"What you see is what you get."* While this is a common belief, it would perhaps be more accurate to say, "What you *think* is what you get!"

Thoughts, like seeds, sprout and blossom according to their variety, and the thoughts you cultivate create your experiences of life. Just as a seed planted in fertile soil produces healthy fruit, your mind may be lightened or darkened depending on the type of thoughts planted in it. If apple seeds are planted and nurtured, you can harvest delicious, juicy apples. If you plant and nurture thistle seeds, you get prickly thistles. This analogy also holds true for the mind. Positive thoughts can produce positive results, whereas negative thoughts can lead to negative results. Understanding this cause and effect relationship can help you "think into being" the kind of life you wish to have.

The personality, ever in a state of change, creates itself anew based on ideas that move through the inlet and outlet of the thinking faculty. It is important to monitor the traffic because "thoughts held in mind do produce after their own kind." It may take practice, although no more energy, to direct the active, zealous, impulsive thinking faculty to retain thoughts that build one's world according to a wise pattern.

> *"All that we are is the result of what we have thought; it is founded on our thoughts and made up of our thoughts. If a man speak or act with an evil thought, suffering follows him as a wheel follows the hoof of the beast that draws the cart."*
> —Dhamapada

Each of us is born with the freedom to choose the thoughts we want to direct our lives. We can choose the path we desire to pursue; we may choose the pace at which we wish to travel, and also what we wish to carry along the way. Have you ever realized that you have the ability to *precondition* your mind to success? When you precondition your mind, you invest in the process of transforming your life. This is a basic principle of positive thinking. You can forecast whether you find future success or failure by your present type of thinking. How? Because what you consistently *think* is likely to happen, tends to happen! Let's take a further step and define the meaning of "success." In its deepest sense, success means to live graciously, humbly, orderly, lovingly, and compassionately as a person and to use fully your talents to help others, not merely to achieve things.

Napoleon Hill, the best-selling American author of *Think and Grow Rich*, was born and raised in a one-room log cabin in the mountains of southwest Virginia. Young Hill's home was so isolated that he was twelve years old before he saw his first railroad train. Adding to his impoverishment was the loss of his mother when he was only eight.

Dr. Hill, in his later years, remembered the day, a year after his mother's death, when his father brought home a new wife.

"My father introduced her to the relatives. When my turn came, I was standing in the corner with my arms folded and a scowl on my face. I was all set to show her how tough I could be.

"Father walked up to me and said, 'Martha, here is your son, Napoleon, the meanest boy in Wise County. I won't be surprised if he starts throwing rocks at you by tomorrow morning.'"

All the relatives roared with laughter.

"My stepmother walked up to me," Hill recalled, "put her hand under my chin, and lifted my head upward so she could look squarely into my sullen face. 'You are wrong about this boy,' she said. 'He is not the meanest boy in Wise County. He is a smart boy, who has not yet learned how to make the best use of his wisdom.'"

With his stepmother's encouragement, Napoleon Hill traded his rifle for a typewriter. She taught him to type, to research information, and to express his ideas in writing. When later he said, *"There is but one thing over which man has complete control. That is his own mental attitude,"* it was his own experience speaking. For when Napoleon Hill replaced the belief that he was mean with the seed-thought that he was wise and could do great things, he became the successful person he was meant to be. He went on to advise kings and presidents and to inspire millions through the power of the written word. His book *Think and Grow Rich* is still a best seller after some thirty years.

As you are reading this book, you presently reflect what your thoughts have created over a period of time. Defeatist thoughts, angry thoughts, dishonest thoughts, self-centered thoughts, and failure thoughts are destructive. Loving thoughts, honest thoughts, service thoughts, and success thoughts are creative.

Just as fruit generated from the best kind of seed is the most delicious and pleasing so, too, the life most worth living is cultivated from the best and most loving thoughts. Before you can utilize the positive power of your thoughts, it is necessary to become aware of your current pattern of thinking. You may not have a stepmother who was as helpful as Napoleon Hill's in

"The aphorism, 'As a man thinketh in his heart, so is he,' not only embraces the whole of man's being, but is so comprehensive as to reach out to every condition and circumstance of his life. A man is literally what he thinks, his character being the complete sum of all his thoughts.

And you . . . will realize the Vision (not the idle wish), of your heart, be it base or beautiful, or a mixture of both, for you will always gravitate towards that which you, secretly, most love. Into your hands will be placed the exact results of your thoughts; you will receive that which you earn; no more, no less. Whatever your present environment may be, you will fall, remain, or rise with your thoughts, your Vision, your Ideal. You will become as small as your controlling desire; as great as your dominant aspiration."
—James Allen, *As A Man Thinketh*

pointing out negative thought patterns. Nevertheless, in quiet times on your own, observe your habits of thought, and begin to weed out those that do not suit your higher purposes.

You can train your mind to nurture positive, loving, and unselfish thought patterns and, through them, develop a deeper, richer personality that may be the fulfillment and fruition of your greatest creative potential.

Try making friends with the most powerful and positive ideas that are available to you as a human being. Give them your attention and belief. Instead of filling your mind with aimless chatter or with fears and negativity, work at filling your mind with the presence and instruction of positive, constructive ideas. As you do, you are not only blessed but you can become a blessed representative in our world of the life-transforming "law of good ideas." You can grow from negativity and limitation to an abundance of usefulness and happiness.

LAW 4

Progress requires change
—John M. Templeton

"We should so live and labor in our time that when what came to us as seed may go to the next generation as blossom, and what came to us as a blossom, may go to them as fruit. This is what we mean by progress."
—Henry Ward Beecher

"And we all, with unveiled face, beholding the glory of the Lord, are being changed into his likeness" (2 Corinthians 3:18). If we look at life from one viewpoint, everything may seem unstable. Changes can take place so rapidly that it may seem nothing in the world could be looked upon as permanent. Friends may come and go. Possessions may be here today and gone tomorrow. The home of our childhood may have been razed for a new office building. The babe in arms grows into the young adult. Relationships begin and end. People die.

We may suffer from what is called "a broken heart" at one time or another during the course of a lifetime. This could result from the loss of a loved one, the diminishment of physical or mental health, or the loss of a job that provides much-needed income. Reaching out toward a goal that, for whatever reason, never materializes can cause upset and grief. Some of our cherished goals may go unrealized.

Looking at the universe from another viewpoint, everything is alive and growing. Everything is in joyous motion. New combinations appear. New beauties touch our souls. New opportunities spring up. Adventures may be ours for the adventuring!

When the billowing waves of change come rolling into our lives— and it has been said that "change is the one constant in life"—it may be upsetting to us if our heart is too attached to material things or we are too established in an erroneous concept of permanence. And if there is little or no understanding of how to handle change, it can seem heartbreaking. How do we deal with the pain of loss that seems to touch everyone's life at some point? If we are open and receptive to God's presence in every change, we ride safely on the crest of the wave.

When a seed falls or is planted in the darkness of the earth, the seed's outer shell must break so that new life can emerge. Jesus said, *"Unless a kernel of wheat falls to the ground and dies, it remains only a single seed. . . . But if it dies, it produces many seeds"* (John 12:24). When our outer shells break in pain, when our hearts seem broken, it is important to learn the lesson that Jesus set out to teach us. Whenever we lose something we may, in some way, gain something at the same time.

We can then come to understand and appreciate that life offers unexplainable experiences that may not always make rational sense. This understanding becomes a precious gift in and of itself. We might think that if we could just do everything "right" we could keep ourselves from pain. But life is often more complicated and mysterious.

A gift can be present in the midst of the loss. The very pain we experience may be the shell of our understanding, our wisdom, our maturity and compassion, breaking forth its gift, its new life. This understanding is not a drug to dull or deny the pain of the experience. Rather, it can be a means to open ourselves to pain's mystery, to what it has to offer, as well as what it takes away. Perhaps the prospect of making changes can be greeted more cordially by remembering that the journey of life is forward and progressive. And as you grow and progress, changes come.

Have you considered that to say, "This is not the time for change," could be the equivalent of saying, "this is not the time for new blessings to come into my life"? It is important to grow physically, mentally, and spiritually. The fact that changes come about in our life means that we should be prepared to handle them courageously and triumphantly. Have faith in your own soul capacity, realizing that there can be present within you the

"Limiting one's pursuits to one lone avenue without benefit of change or diversion can result in a form of vapidity which sometimes deadens imagination."
—Edward G. Uhl

"Action and reaction, ebb and flow, trial and error, change—this is the rhythm of our living. Out of our over-confidence, fear; out of our fear, clearer vision, fresh hope. And out of hope, progress."
—Bruce Barton

"The art of progress is to preserve order amid change and to preserve change amid order."
—Alfred North Whitehead

fullness of God's love, wisdom, and intelligence to draw upon. By making an inner preparation for change, you can gear yourself to the idea of change.

The next time you feel some shell breaking in your heart, feel it fully and deeply, and take comfort in knowing that living with and through pain can help you become a more understanding and compassionate person toward yourself and others. Adversity can be a rich and educational gift. Adversity can be a milestone in your mental and spiritual growth. Find it in your heart to welcome change and rejoice in the opportunities for soul growth and development.

From Pythagoras, the Greek philosopher, we learn, *"No man is free who cannot command himself."* Through the life experiences, often brought about by change, we may gain mastery of our emotions, our minds and bodies, our thoughts and feelings, and through this, we can become more productive and useful!

LAW 5

Fortune knocks at the door of those who are prepared
—Anonymous

"Nobody can really guarantee the future. The best we can do is size up the chances, calculate the risks involved, estimate our ability to deal with them and then make our plans with confidence."
—Henry Ford II

"In the field of observation chance only favors minds which are prepared."
—Louis Pasteur

By the time Dean began his second year of college, he was considering a career in education, so he scheduled a session with his counselor and the education department of his college to plan his course of study for the next three years. His advisors convinced him to work toward a master's degree and perhaps even a doctorate. Realizing, however, that many valuable lessons were not learned in the classroom, Dean considered the kinds of extracurricular activities and part-time work that would best prepare him for his chosen career. He became active in the Student Education Association and other campus activities geared for education majors, but he wondered how his part-time job as a salesman in a department store would fit with education.

Dean liked his job, and his employer was very supportive to his commitment to get an education. He worked out a schedule that allowed Dean to earn the money he needed and yet have the time he required for study. Another benefit of the job was his ability to buy shoes and clothing at a discount. Dean's salary was on a par with other jobs available on a part-time basis, and he decided the support of his employer was worth a great deal, even though his actual work seemed to have little to do with his life's goals.

Dean pondered what he could do at work to forward his career. He noticed that the new people hired had no idea how to utilize advantageously their time when not busy with customers. He knew from his own experience that although the owner attempted to train them well, he had many other priorities. New clerks were quickly left on their own. Dean created a checklist of items that would have been helpful when he was new to the job. He made notes of questions new employees asked and listened closely as they dealt with customers.

In a few short weeks, Dean accumulated pages of notes and recognized he had the bare bones of an employee training manual. He presented his boss with a rough draft of the manual, asking him to read it through and make suggestions and comments. Dean proposed that he write the book, which would then be printed and circulated to all new employees. His boss enthusiastically endorsed the plan and gave him a raise. Three years later, when Dean was applying for graduate school, his employer's sincere and strong recommendation became the deciding factor in Dean being granted a substantial scholarship to a university that was pre-eminent in the field of business education. Dean's good fortune was not a matter of luck or fate, as many of his classmates thought. It was a clear result of his applying his interest, skill, and energy in every part of his life. Dean had used all the resources available to him; consequently, he was given the chance to be successful.

Even in the little things, in the seemingly insignificant events of life, it is important to be prepared. Opportunities to learn new things can be readily available if we open our eyes to truly see. Almost every moment offers opportunities to grow, to expand in consciousness.

Spotlights!

1. Bravely step forth and make your talents available!
2. Revisit your goals and think of how people could benefit from what you have to offer . . . and then offer it!
3. A mature view of happiness can be that it is a by-product of sharing your good and serving others.

"He who every morning plans the transactions of the day and follows out the plan carries a thread that will guide him through the labyrinth of the most busy life. The orderly arrangement of his time is like a ray of life which darts itself through all his occupations. But where no plan is laid, where the disposal of time is surrendered merely to the chance of incident, chaos will soon reign."
—Victor Hugo

"Faith is the great motive power, and no man realizes his full possibilities unless he has the deep conviction that life is eternally important and that his work well done is part of an unending plan."
—Calvin Coolidge

4. Happiness is a spiritual principle you can cultivate and use, regardless of outer conditions or circumstances.
5. A happy heart tends to draw to itself that which it needs for happiness.
6. What you *think* is what you get! The thoughts you cultivate can create your experiences of life.
7. *"Thoughts held in mind produce after their kind."*–Charles Fillmore
8. It has been said that *"change is the one constant in life."*
9. Outer changes need not affect the unchanging spirit within you.
10. Opportunities to learn new things can be readily available to the one who is prepared to receive them.

Living the Law!

Everyone can improve himself regardless of his situation, place in life, or circumstances. Sometimes it becomes necessary to prove to yourself that by your own thoughts and actions you have the power to work toward your goal, regardless of whatever seeming obstacles may be present.

The following true story, taken from *Macro-Mind Power,* by Rebecca Clark, offers you an opportunity to review several of this week's key ideas presented in the essays. May your heart and mind catch a powerful glimpse of the face of courage and overcoming that is shared in this story.

Thomas Carlyle heaved a great sigh of relief as he finished writing his great work, *The French Revolution.* This massive manuscript represented two years of the hardest work he had done in his entire life. He had literally poured himself into his work, striving to capture on paper the thought images that rampaged through his brilliant mind. But at last the work was finished, and he bundled up the huge manuscript and took it to a close friend, John Stuart Mill, for Mr. Mill's personal evaluation.

Several days passed and one evening at tea, a rap came at the door. Thomas Carlyle walked to the door in great strides, eager to learn his friend's thoughts about his new work. As he opened the door, he came face to face with a John Stuart Mill whose face was chalky white and actually looking ill.

"What on earth happened?" Thomas Carlyle asked as he pulled his friend into the house. The words then tumbled out of his mouth like a flood as Mr. Mill told Mr. Carlyle that his maid had used the bundle of papers that was the manuscript to start a fire, not knowing what precious fuel she used!

Thomas Carlyle was disgruntled and distraught. For days he

paced the floor, back and forth, ranting and raving at the fate that would do such a dastardly thing to him. *Two years of his life had simply gone up in smoke!* What was he going to do? He had poured *everything* into this work, and now he was drained. There was nothing more left inside. He couldn't recapture the fire and the feeling and knowledge that had flowed into his original work. He shook his head in despair as he gave in to despondency.

Thomas Carlyle then began to spend long hours at an upstairs bedroom window, staring bleakly into the nothingness he felt. One morning, as he stood dejectedly gazing out the window across the rooftops, a flicker of movement caught his attention. He focused his eyes toward the movement and noticed a brick mason preparing to lay the bricks for a wall. Mr. Carlyle watched. Brick by brick, the mason worked, gently and lovingly spreading the mortar and laying each brick individually in place. As Mr. Carlyle watched throughout the day, he saw a beautiful decorative and serviceable brick wall taking shape as the brick mason patiently continued his work.

Suddenly, the idea struck Thomas Carlyle's mind like a flash of lightening—just as patience, persistence, and singleness of purpose could erect a brick wall, so would he reconstruct his work of *The French Revolution!*

Peace came at last to his mind, and ideas began to flow again. Thomas Carlyle pushed aside seeming defeat and began again on what has become the most colossal work of his lifetime. His own understanding had increased in leaps and bounds and was reflected in a new and greater version, giving the world a work that far surpassed the original.

Yes, brick by brick, word by word, thought by thought, dream by dream, we can build the substance from which the masterpieces of our lives are produced. Remember, though, that a brick mason puts together bricks that someone else has made, while one who is truly inspired is a creator, putting together something new, beautiful, and meaningful!

(Note: By the latter part of September of the same year [1837], Carlyle had rewritten the destroyed manuscript, though the second version was considerably different from the first.)

Week Twenty

LAW 1

A good reputation is more valuable than money
—Publilius Syrus

"Whatever you lend, let it be your money, and not your name. Money you may get again, and if not, you may contrive to do without it; name once lost you cannot get again."
—Edward Bulwer-Lytton

Your reputation is mostly the result of how others see you. A good reputation is slowly built on a firm foundation of humility, integrity, love, and charity. Building a good reputation can be similar to building a house. You begin with a basic firm foundation and build from that point. The finished house is a product of the choices you made during the construction—from plan to completion. If your house is carelessly constructed of thin walls, then the slightest wind may destroy it. If you have chosen your building materials with attention to strength, quality, and durability, your house can withstand the strong winds that may blow.

Reputation is the perception by others of what they feel is your character. Again, building character may be likened to building a house. As you respond to life's experiences, the choices you make become the building blocks that create and construct your character. *What you are at this point in your life is the product of those choices!* The responsibility of making right choices is yours. Advice from others may be helpful; learning from experiences can bring greater understanding and wisdom; and studying the laws of life can open new doors for consideration. But you are the one who decides how to use the knowledge you acquire. No one else can act for you.

Let's look at an example. By the time he was eighteen, John was saddled with a very poor reputation. He often lied. He would make promises to his friends and fail to keep them, no matter how important those promises were to the other person. He had even been arrested for shoplifting. Because John's father was very well off financially, John thought he had everything. He lived in a fine house, wore the latest fashions, had his own car, and plenty of spending money.

But John did not have everything. Far from it! He did not have a good reputation. One summer, between his high school graduation and the start of college in September, John tried for a summer job in the field of his planned future career. But he didn't get the job. His poor reputation cost him the position. Then, for the first time, he fell in love. But because of his well-known reputation, the girl refused to date him. Behavior often speaks as plainly as words, and sometimes even more plainly. Many of us listen to words, and many people listen to the sometimes more harsh language of behavior. If we do not pay attention to both, we can be blundering in our human relations. Alexander Pope commented, *"At every word a reputation dies."*

Fortunately, John came to realize that money is not so important in life if it's joined to a poor reputation. Your reputation, not your money, is the most valuable currency of all. John began to make changes in his life, but many years passed before people completely accepted the "new" John.

Again, what you do in everyday life affects your reputation. It is up to you, and you alone, to make appropriate decisions. Friends, parents, co-workers, clergy, and teachers can help you, advise you, stand by you, but they cannot act for you. If you take the time to think about what effects any action can have on your life and make your decisions based upon that awareness, you can earn a good reputation. It doesn't matter if you're rich or poor, a good reputation increases your chances of leading a life rich in meaning and happiness. This doesn't mean you may not make a mistake. Everyone makes mistakes. It is important, however, to admit your mistakes when you make them and take what steps you can to correct them. This can keep your reputation intact.

When you have a good reputation, you feel in integrity with yourself. And remember, every moment of your life is spent with yourself. If you don't like and respect who you are, it can be extremely difficult for you to like or respect others. Work to build that good reputation. Money cannot buy it, but hard work can earn it.

What would you like to be able to say about yourself and to have others say about you? Create a fantasy in your mind and imagine exactly how you would most like to be. Would you like to feel from within yourself that what you say is honest and true? Would you like for your friends and associates to know the integrity of your intents? What level of confidence would you like to exhibit as you interrelate with people in your everyday

"The most important thing for a young man is to establish a credit–a reputation, character."
—John D. Rockefeller

"Man does not live by bread alone. Many prefer self-respect to food."
—Mohandas K. Gandhi

"If I take care of my character, my reputation will take care of itself."
—Dwight Moody

world? Would you like to be more loving and gentle? Create in your mind a living picture of the kind of personality and attributes that would serve you best. For a moment, know that those inner imaginings can be translated into physical behavior. That is precisely what you have been doing all along, ever since you showed up in your present physical body. Your vision of the way you wish to be and what you wish to express in your life may require giving up old habits and ways of doing things, if those ways did not present the image of yourself you desire. Write down the attributes of a good reputation—as you desire it. Then, look at ways you can begin living the desire.

LAW 2

To err is human, to forgive is divine
—Alexander Pope

"To be able to forgive, we must come down from the citadel of pride, from the stronghold of hate and anger, from the high place where all emotions that issue from one's sense of being wronged shout only for vengeance and retaliation."
—John Hess

Imagine a majestic mountain, its granite peaks towering thousands of feet into the sky. Nothing would seem to be more invincible than this giant fortress of rock. Yet, in time, it is possible that certain forces can reduce this mountain to tiny pebbles. Ironically, the forces that wield such power are among the softest, most yielding elements of nature—water and air! The blowing of winds and the gentle flowing streams can ultimately conquer the mightiest of mountains. The power of the gentle approach can be illustrated by a statement from the *Tao Te Ching*, the sacred writings of the Chinese religion of Taoism: *"What is of all things most yielding can overcome that which is the most hard."* And is not the spiritual power of forgiveness a loving, gentle approach than can soften the hardest of situations?

When someone is unkind, critical, or spiteful—yes, you can suffer. But is the suffering not greater if we allow our thoughts and emotions to become hardened and resistant? If our mind is filled with resentment, anger, or a desire for revenge, these feelings within ourself can do far more harm than any outside influence can possibly do! Revenge is not a solution to anything. It merely starts a new cycle of negation.

Someone made the statement, *"If your life is not all you want it to be, it may be that you have some forgiving to do!"* The action of forgiveness may not necessarily come easily. Someone has also said, *"A person's ability to forgive is in proportion to the greatness of his soul."* When forgiveness is genuine and complete, it goes to the depths of the situation. Hatreds, resentments, even mild dislikes can be dissolved by the power of forgiveness.

Do you currently blame someone for a wrong you may believe has been done to you? Do you hold any resentments toward someone for your present situation? Is there a part of you that says, "If only so-and-so had not done such-and-such to me, I would be happier and more successful"? In one way or another, we often try to find a scapegoat for a lack we feel in our lives. Can you realize that what you hold on to, holds on to you? Have you heard yourself say, "I will never forget the way she or he treated me." And you didn't forget! Humanly, it may be difficult to keep such thoughts and feelings from recurring. But it can be done. Assistance is at hand when you truly begin to understand and know that God's law of love and justice adjusts all matters for those who trust it.

A story has been told down through the years about Leonardo da Vinci when he was painting the *Last Supper* on the walls of Santa Maria delle Grazie, a church in Milan. It seems a significant event occurred while da Vinci was working on the face of Jesus. The artist became so angry and upset at someone that, the story goes, a violent argument took place during which da Vinci threatened bodily harm to the man and chased him away. When da Vinci returned to work on the fresco, he was so filled with hatred and resentment that the flow of inspiration dried up. Try as he might, da Vinci couldn't paint the face of Jesus. Repeatedly he attempted to apply subtle brush strokes to the wet plaster, only to be unhappy with the results and become more frustrated and upset. Finally, on realizing that his anger and upset was depriving him of the peace of mind necessary for him to be creative, the great artist laid aside his brushes and went in search of the man with whom he had quarreled to apologize and ask for forgiveness. It took a while to find the man, but on doing so, and after much persuasion, da Vinci convinced the man of his pure intent, and the situation was resolved. With a peace-filled and loving heart, da Vinci was able to return to his work, and the magnificent face of the Christ that flowed from his brushes became a mystical moment captured by the great artist. It is said that even now, in spite of the pathetic con-

"When a deep injury is done to us, we never recover until we forgive."
—Alan Paton

"We forgive so long as we love."
—François La Rochefoucauld

"Benevolence is one of the distinguishing characters of man."
—Mencius Aggripa

dition of the walls of the ruined church, the *Last Supper* remains as one of the great art treasures of the world.

We need to be aware of the price we may have to pay for holding grudges and resentments. We need to understand that we are the ones who suffer from this unforgiveness. It takes a lot of energy, which could be much better spent, to hold onto a grudge. We may feel temporarily justified in our attitude, but in the long run what does it really matter? Why would we punish ourselves even further by dwelling on negative thoughts and emotions? A tremendous cost in sickness of mind and body affects those who cling to feelings of unforgiveness.

It has been rightly said, *"To err is human, to forgive is divine."* The highest and best qualities we possess urge us to get on with our lives and stop making excuses for our failures. We do ourselves a disservice when we blame our failures on someone else rather than choosing to learn and grow from our experiences.

Complete and total forgiveness can be a sure way to health and happiness and to new energy and enthusiasm. It is a sign that we are taking responsibility for our lives. Once we realize that we're in the driver's seat, we can move swiftly and surely to greater good.

"Victory comes through surrender," is another beautiful truth from the *Tao Te Ching.* Yielding. Surrendering. Forgiving. Are these not attitudes of mind wherein we recognize that our "battles" may be won not by personal strength but by allowing a higher power to work through us?

LAW 3

Never do anything that you'll have to punish yourself for
—Anonymous

A lot of us know people who appear to live on the "right" side of life. Everything works out well for them. They hold good jobs. They enjoy splendid health. Their relationships with people and the affairs and activities of their lives seem happy and harmonious. On the other hand, there are those who some-how manage to get on the "wrong" side of life. There may be times when nothing seems to work favorably. The good they are seeking appears to have gone on vacation. And it seems that the harder they try, the further away from health, happiness, and success they seem to be.

There's a story in the Bible, in John 21:1–6, that describes this situation somewhat. The disciples went fishing but failed to make a catch. They toiled throughout the night but caught noth-ing. With the coming of daylight, they headed their boat toward the shore—tired and discouraged and ready to quit. But Jesus was standing on the shore, and when the crestfallen disciples called to him and told him of their failure, he suggested they try just once more. His words to them were, *"Cast the net on the right side of the boat, and you will find some."* The disciples followed instructions and the story continues, ". . . and now they were not able to haul it (the net) in, for the quantity of fish." This story points to something of great importance. Namely, just as there was a "right side" to that fishing boat, so is there also a "right side" to life! What is this right side of life?

Have you ever noticed that when you cheat, or lie, or don't support a friend, and then realize what you've done, an inner alarm system goes off? It's a kind of moral wakeup call! What if your friends knew what you did? How would you feel if your parents found out? If your best friends found out? If the person you respected most in the world discovered you had let him down?

Hiding a cruel, selfish, uncaring, or unloving act deep down inside doesn't make it go away. Often it festers, and you begin to feel guilty and full of shame. Even if no one knows but you, those bad feelings come back to haunt you whenever you think about them.

Unfortunately these bad feelings about ourselves rarely go away without some kind of self-examination. And it's by experi-encing the emotions and accepting the ramifications of what you've done that you can begin to accept and change yourself. There are several ways you can come to terms with yourself.

First, you can admit the truth, even if it's only to yourself and one other person, perhaps a counselor or a minister. Talking about a painful situation with someone you trust can pull the situation out into the open and remove a weight from your mind and heart. You're being honest and have a chance to for-give yourself.

Second, if it's something that can be corrected by telling the

"Worry affects the cir-culation, the heart, the glands, the whole ner-vous system, and pro-foundly affects the health. I have never known a man who died from overwork, but many who died from doubt."
—Charles W. Mayo

"Good humor is a tonic for mind and body. It is the best anti-dote for anxiety and depression. It is a busi-ness asset. It attracts and keeps friends. It lightens human bur-dens. It is the direct route to serenity and contentment."
—Grenville Kleiser

"Ridicule may be the evidence of evil or bit-terness and may grat-ify a little mind, or an ungenerous temper, but it is no test of reason or truth."
—Tyron Edwards

*"A clean and sensitive
conscience, a steady
and scrupulous
integrity in small
things as well as large,
is the most valuable of
all possessions, to a
nation as to an indi-
vidual."*
—Henry Van Dyke

truth, then do so. The truth in any situation can clear the air.
Speaking the truth is an affirmation of light and can release the
emotions of shame and guilt. It takes a lot of courage to be honest, and many friendships have deepened because of honesty
between the people involved in a situation.

Lastly, you can choose to make a contract with yourself to do
only deeds you can be proud of in the future. This contract is a
commitment to live in your own integrity, regardless of whether
or not others around you choose to live in theirs. Remember
that ultimately you are the one who benefits by living in honor
and integrity. It is a powerful key to good health, good relationships, and self esteem.

How can you develop this right attitude of mind? Pause in
your efforts, if only for a moment, to adjust your thinking
process. In the Scripture story, the disciples cried, *"Master, we
toiled all night and took nothing!"* You, too, may have been working, struggling, striving to attain—and succumbed to temptation.
But you don't have to punish yourself. The short step from
"nowhere" to "now here" is the moment's pause you take to
become still and know the truth!

LAW 4

Reverse the word evil
and you have the word live
—Phinius P. Quimby

*"Never let a man
imagine that he can
pursue a good end by
evil means, without
sinning against his
soul. The evil effect on
himself is certain."*
—Robert Southey

Why do bad or evil things seem to happen to good people?
That question has perplexed artists, philosophers, and religious
thinkers throughout the ages. When accident, disease, financial
misfortune, or other personal tragedy happens to the morally
responsible, it piques our sense of justice, especially when those
with less than honorable behavior often seem to live
problem-free lives, at least on the surface. Wouldn't it be only
fair that those upstanding ones should be rewarded with an existence unmarked by tragedy? Instead, we hear repeatedly how
some innocents are victimized while some oppressors go free.
What flaw in the order of the universe, some people ask with

no small amount of bitterness, allows misfortune to plague the existence of good people?

A story is told about a young seeker who trekked over treacherous mountain trails to find a particular teacher who, he had been told, could answer any question he might present. After several days of walking, asking for directions from local villages, looking for clues, and depending on little more than intuition, the pilgrim found the one he sought.

"Master," the earnest young man immediately asked, "How can I know what is *Real*?"

The sage was silent for a few moments, but not because he needed to think. Then he spoke, "Young man, if you want to know what is Real, then you must realize what is the nature of the mind that you ordinarily use to look at your life."

The student was somewhat puzzled, "But how can this understanding show me what is Real?"

"Because," the teacher explained, "the mind is the slayer of the Real!"

What did the wise teacher mean? How can the mind slay that which is Real? Is not the Real impervious to any threat? And what is the mind anyway?

No, the mind cannot mar one iota of Truth. The Truth is eternal and unassailable. However, our perceptions of Truth are vulnerable and easily distorted by the web of ignorance, spun by the spider of the rational mind.

In the fullness of time, the pain of personal catastrophe can often give way to new understanding and inner growth. That which is called "evil" may be typically experienced by the victim as a destructive reversal of fortune that causes unnecessary suffering. For example, an honest, hard-working political candidate is undermined by her opponent's slanderous remarks to the media. A star football quarterback is made a paraplegic in an accident caused by a drunk driver. These two examples of gratuitously evil acts may invite the beginning of transformation for the victims. From these tragedies can emerge the possibility of a deeper, more meaningful life. "Evil," transformed and reversed, often can indeed spell "live." The passage of a good person through a painful experience can mobilize inner resources and open doorways into a new and more expanded and useful life.

In an Old Testament story, Joseph was cast into a pit by his jealous brothers and abandoned to die. He was saved by traders who sold him into Egyptian slavery, where again he incurred the wrath and jealousy of some people he met. He was jailed, once more an innocent victim; but instead of destroying Joseph, the

"Nobody has any right to find life uninteresting or unrewarding who sees within the sphere of his own activity a wrong he can help remedy, or within himself an evil he can hope to overcome."
—Charles W. Eliot

"In my humble opinion, non-cooperation with evil is as much a duty as is cooperation with good."
—Mohandas K. Gandhi

prison experience served as a new beginning. He learned to channel his dreams toward constructive ends, and eventually he was able to serve the Egyptian people. To his brothers who sought his forgiveness, Joseph granted it, telling them, *"You meant evil against me; but God meant it for good"* (Genesis 50:20).

Seeming evil can multiply and triumph when good people become resentful and bitter over misfortunes, but, just as surely, evil may be often overcome when they find it within themselves to transcend despair, forgive ignorance, heal betrayals, love everyone, and go on with a life of spiritual growth. In fact, as was true with Joseph, such transcendence may be the hard road good people can travel to become great people.

Great people refuse to be victimized by circumstance. Instead, they often use even the most traumatic event as a springboard for a creative and helpful response to life. From his wheelchair, the paralyzed quarterback mobilized his leadership skills to help handicapped children. The victimized politician spoke her simple truth, and thus gave an example in humility to millions. Those who grow in stature through adversity have learned to reverse the word EVIL to the word LIVE.

LAW 5

He who has a "why" for which to live, can bear with almost any "how"
—Friedrich Nietzsche

In his book *Man's Search for Meaning*, Austrian psychiatrist Viktor Frankl documents the profound power that a life purpose exerts over an individual under even the worst of circumstances. Frankl, who survived the Nazi concentration camps, described how prisoners who felt they had nothing to live for succumbed, while those who perceived themselves as having a mission to complete struggled to survive. Deprived of all external supports that might give life meaning, these survivors came to realize that, in Frankl's words, *"It did not really matter what we expected of life, but rather what life expected of us."* Their sense of an inner purpose pulled them through the most horrible physical and emotional experiences so that they might make their unique contribution to the world.

Everyone has a purpose in life beyond one's immediate interests and gratifications, though that purpose frequently goes undiscovered. Since God has given us everything potentially, we need to learn how to discover his gifts by making them spiritually active in our lives. Many people devote their entire lives to the pursuit of greater ease and pleasure. Those who have not found the "why" that gives meaning to existence may achieve material success, yet the real goodness of life eludes them. One true meaning of life lies in sharing our particular qualities of greatness with others.

There is a simple way you can discover your special purpose in life. Draw up a list of all the qualities you value in yourself and that other people admire in you. If you're a humorous person, you have the ability to uplift and entertain. If clear thinking is your strong suit and you're skilled at developing ideas, accept this as a gift that can benefit those around you in many ways. Since we sometime think poorly of ourselves, it is important to dig a little to unearth those skills and talents that may lie hidden.

Next, examine the ways in which you interact with other people and make a list of those ways that work the best. Does it excite you to teach someone a skill that will help him? Do you enjoy simply listening while someone shares a problem with you? Are you happiest when organizing a group for a project, or perhaps when encouraging someone who feels hopeless about himself?

Finally, imagine what your world would be like under the best of all possible circumstances. Would it be clean, peaceful, and productive? Form a mental picture of the world that you'd like you and your loved ones to live in, and write down that vision in as much specific detail as possible.

Your mission in life is to have a "why" to live for, to use your best qualities in the service of the kind of world in which you would like to live. That is your purpose. This is what life expects of you. And when you live according to your purpose, setting goals that support it, you may find the pieces of your life drawn together into a strong internal whole. Then, no matter how difficult life's experiences may prove to be, you can be able to endure and even prevail.

"No man is free who is not master of his soul and controller of his spirit."
—Thomas Crombie

"The survival of the fittest is the ageless law of nature, but the fittest are rarely the strong. The fittest are those endowed with the qualifications for adaption, the ability to accept the inevitable and conform to the unavoidable, to harmonize with existing or changing conditions."
—Dave E. Smalley

"I don't know how to fight. All I know is how to stay alive."
—Alice Walker

Spotlights!

1. Behavior often speaks plainly as words, and sometimes even more plainly.

2. Your reputation, not your money, is the most valuable currency of all.
3. Revenge is not a solution to anything. It merely starts a new cycle of negation.
4. Can you realize that what you hold on to holds on to you?
5. Make a contract with yourself to do only deeds that you can be proud of.
6. The short step from "nowhere" to "now here" is the moment's pause you take to become still and know the truth!
7. Great people refuse to be victimized by circumstances.
8. Those who grow in statue through adversity have learned to reverse the word "evil" to the word "live."
9. One true meaning of life possibly lies in sharing our particular qualities of greatness with others.
10. In order to know the Truth, we need to learn to recognize a source other than facts.

Living the Law!

Since communications are a key to successful relationships and effective living, it can be meaningful and helpful to know that conversational give and take is among the most enjoyable and rewarding of mental and social activities. Like study, it informs. Like travel, it broadens. Like friendship, it nourishes the soul. Good conversation calls for a willingness to alternate the role of speaker with that of listener, and occasional "digestive pauses" by both! As you review this week's essays, look for the many ways being a good listener, to yourself and others, can be effective in utilizing the ideas presented into your life and world. The following anonymous reflections on listening can offer a guideline or introspection for self-analysis in this area.

Listening

When I ask you to listen to me and you start giving me advice, you have not done what I asked.

When I ask you to listen to me and you begin to tell me why I shouldn't feel that way, you are trampling on my feelings.

When I ask you to listen to me and you feel you have to do something to solve my problems, you have failed me, strange as that may seem.

LISTEN! All I asked was that you listen, not talk or do . . . just hear me.

And I can do for myself. I'm not helpless. Maybe discouraged and faltering, but not helpless.

When you do something for me that I can and need to do for myself, you contribute to my fear and inadequacy.

But when you accept as a simple fact that I do feel what I feel, no matter how irrational, then I can quit trying to convince you and can get about this business of understanding what's behind this irrational feeling.

And when that's clear, the answers are obvious and I don't need advice. Irrational feelings make sense when we understand what's behind them.

Perhaps that's why prayer works, sometimes, for some people . . . because God is mute and doesn't give advice or try to fix things.

God just listens and lets you work it out for yourself.

So please listen and just hear me.

And if you want to talk, wait a minute for your turn . . . and I'll listen to you.

—Author Unknown

Week Twenty-One

❖

LAW 1

All that we are is the result of what we have thought
—Buddha

"The life each of us lives is the life within the limits of our own thinking. To have life more abundant, we must think in the limitless terms of abundance."
–Thomas Dreier

"There is always something beautiful to be found if you will look for it. Concentrate your thoughts on the good, beautiful, and true things of life rather than the reverse. This positive, loving attitude of mind towards life and people will help you to perceive the presence of God active in your life, helping you to wonderfully utilize your vital life force and put into operation the divine magic that opens all doors." Thus commented Rebecca Clark in her book *Breakthrough*.

Thought—the act or process of thinking—can be acknowledged as one of the greatest powers or abilities we possess, and, like most of these attributes, it may be used positively or negatively, as we choose. Many people haven't been taught the understanding and utilization of the positive power of thought, which is often philosophically referred to as "the master power of the mind." Could it be as essential to balanced living to know how to think correctly as it is to know how to speak or act correctly? Our thoughts provide the tools with which we carve our life story on the substance of the universe. Does it not make sense, as Imelda Shanklin says in her book *What Are You?*, that *"when you rule your mind you rule your world. When you choose your thoughts you choose results. The mind is kept active through thought."*

"You are today where your thoughts have brought you. You will be tomorrow where your thoughts take you."
–James Allen

How our attitudes can make a difference in one's life is shared by a friend in this wonderful story. "A friend and I were walking recently in the park. We stopped to sit and chat on a bench overlooking the children's swings and playground equipment. As we relaxed, enjoying the warm sunlight and the sounds of children's happy laughter, a man in his 'latter years' came walking sprily along, swinging an umbrella, wearing a baseball cap and a bright red cardigan over his khaki pants and red and white plaid shirt. He smiled a greeting at us and proceeded directly to a nearby swing set. Laying his umbrella on the

ground, he settled himself into one of the swings and vigorously, with great joy, exercised his inner and outer child! His
image and actions held me transfixed for a moment. Shortly,
the man stopped swinging, picked up his umbrella, and started
up the path toward where my friend and I sat. As he came
abreast of our bench, he paused, smiled, and said that he came
to the park every day, swung exactly fifty times in the swing,
and continued his walk. This man glowed with the fullness of
life. His eyes sparkled with the joy of living, and he had no
knowledge of the gift he gave to us that day. His simple, childlike exuberance and enthusiasm for life touched me deeply. I
have thought of him many times since that incident, and his joy
touches my soul. He must be quite a remarkable presence in this
world, bringing joy where he goes, and his age is clearly of no
concern to him. He has the joy of spirit!"

Many people find it hard to understand the tremendous
energy power manifested in ordinary thought. It is easier for
them to understand the power generated by steam or electricity.
They can see these forces at work and understand their functions, whereas thought power may seem more vague and not
quite as easy to understand.

Mental analysts often observe thought power as being present
in two avenues of operation: direct and indirect. The indirect
action of thought seems easy to understand for, obviously, a person must think on some level before he does anything. Thought
can be felt to be the motivating power behind an action, just as
electricity is known to be the motivating power behind lighting
our home. Everyone, rich and poor, young and old alike, holds
the power of thought in his mind. The important thing is to
learn to use this tremendous power beneficially.

Jesus called us to become as little children that we might
enter into the fullness of life which he called the kingdom of
Heaven. Yet, so often our self-imposed limitations of age, appro-
priateness of behavior, business of living, the shoulds and the
shouldn'ts, the cans and cannots, the images we hold of ourselves and what is possible for us may be robbing us of our
life-full-ness. The older gentleman in my friend's story didn't
seem to have limitations. He honored the fullness of life within,
and the joy of his livingness reflected the results of his
thoughts.

When did you last swing on a swing? When did you last do
something "outrageous" that pushed you beyond your present
boundaries and radiated to the world that you are fully alive?
When did the childlike spirit within you run free in joy and

*In 1848 when Marx
was denying that
people have immortal
souls, psychosomatic
medicine was consid-
ered superstition.
Today, it is widely
believed that health
can be restored to the
body not only by chemi-
cals, but by the mind
and spirit as well.
Recent studies around
the world reveal the
close interaction of
body and mind, the
mortal and the immor-
tal, in the healing
process. More and more
doctors are now talking
about "healing the
patient" in addition to
"curing the disease."
The latter may be
achieved by chemistry
and physical therapy.
The former, however,
requires psychic and
spiritual remedies not
always available to the
health care delivery
system. Total health is
not reducible to mater-
ial explanations alone.
—John M.
Templeton, The
Humble Approach*

"Man being made a reasonable and a thinking creature, there is nothing more worthy of his being, than the right direction and employment of his thoughts; since upon this depends both his usefulness to the public, and his own present and future benefit in all respects."
–William Penn

excitement? Age is no excuse; other people's opinion of you is no excuse; and your own limiting opinion of yourself is no excuse for not embracing the gift of life and living it to the fullest expression. The spirit within you can represent both the excited child and ageless wisdom. Do you *truly believe* that the spirit within you is unlimited? If so, what is stopping you from expressing abundance in your life? And we're talking about abundance on all levels—health, relationships, business, studies, financial, mental, and emotional!

In the *Tripitaka* there is a collection of proverbs, called "The Way of the Doctrine" (the *Dhamapada*), which covers the basic beliefs of Buddhism presented in a way that makes them easy to understand and remember. Among these proverbs we find the following that speak about the importance of our thoughts:

"All that we are is the result of what we have thought: it is founded on our thoughts and is made up of our thoughts.

"If a man speaks or acts with an evil thought, pain follows him, as the wheel follows the foot of the ox that draws the cart; if a man speaks or acts with a pure thought, happiness follows him, as the shadow that never leaves him.

"By thoughtfulness, by restraint and self-control, the wise man may make for himself an island which no flood can overwhelm.

"Though a man go out to battle a thousand times against a thousand men, if he conquers himself he is the greater conqueror.

"Good people shine from afar, like the peaks of the Himalayas."

LAW 2

Once a word has been spoken, it cannot be recalled
—Wentworth Roscommon

There are times when we say something in anger and later wish we could recall our words. Unfortunately, once spoken, words cannot be erased. Anger is an emotion that often leads to sadness, hurt, and possibly even violence. And anger is most often vented in two ways—*physically* and through *words*. A boy, angry over what should have been a simple difference of opinion, told a close friend, "I hate you." After calming down, he deeply regretted having told his good friend that he hated him. He realized that people have a right to different viewpoints. The trouble was, even though his friend accepted his apology, something was lost in their relationship. They were no longer completely relaxed and happy in each other's company. The element of total trust was no longer present.

What we say may sometimes be overheard or repeated. If your words are harsh, they can cause a great hurt, both to the person directly affected by what you said and to yourself. It might be something you consider minor. "Carol's new hairstyle looks terrible on her" may be an idle opinion, not meant to harm. But what if Carol is told what you said? She may feel hurt. She may worry that her friends and classmates think her new hairdo is unattractive. She may be so unhappy that she'll wear her hair in another style, even though she loved the one you disliked. You've made a friend miserable through your spoken word. If only you hadn't made that unkind comment! If only you could take it back! But you can't. It's too late. The damage is done.

You can avoid this type of situation by following a very simple rule: *Always think before you speak!* Think about the words that may be about to issue from your mouth. When a friend asks, "Do you like Carol's new hairdo?" take that important pause to think about your answer. If you don't really care for the style and you do not want to speak falsely, simply respond with something like, "Well, I'm not used to it yet. Ask me in two weeks." You haven't lied nor have you said a harmful thing.

"To make an apt answer is a joy to a man—and a word in season, how good it is!" is a Scripture from Proverbs 15:23 that may reflect the power of the spoken word. Prosperity principles tell us our words may determine whether we "have" or "have not," because our words are one of the instruments with which we build our world. Some metaphysical teachers believe that we literally shape our world with words. A statement spoken in spiritual consciousness may have great spiritual power. Sound (speaking the word) can change things as well as consciousness itself. Let's expand this idea a bit. Everything, from thoughts to rocks to tables and chairs, to you and me, is composed of units of energy in unique configurations of vibrations. Our scientists tell us that everything vibrates and everything has its own sounds which are its own peculiar vibrations. Sound vibrations affect physical matter.

In the book *Physics Without Mathematics*, the author tells of an experiment in which vibrations in metal or glass plates may pro-

"Words can destroy. What we call each other ultimately becomes what we think of each other, and it matters."
—Jeanne J. Kirkpatrick

"When you have spoken the word, it reigns over you. When it is unspoken, you reign over it."
—Arabian proverb

"What is lofty can be said in any language. What is mean should be said in none."
—Maimonides

duce wave patterns that can be seen with the eye. By sprinkling sand upon the plates and drawing the bow of a violin across the edge, geometrical figures are formed as the plate vibrates. In this simple experiment, we see how sound vibrations affect physical matter. Could this mean that the words we speak throughout the day indirectly take physical shape in our bodies and help form our life circumstances according to their nature? Think for a moment. What happens to your face and your body when you speak in joy? In concern? In anger? In excitement? In expectancy? How do you feel when someone speaks to you in joy, concern, anger, excitement, or expectancy? A woman who once described her feelings about the angry comments of a friend said, "The words were so intense that it felt like a physical slap in the face!" When we consider these facts, getting into the habit of watching our words may certainly be beneficial!

Eric Butterworth once commented on his radio program *Voice of Unity*, broadcast in New York, that *"No one is born with habits, good or not so good. They feed on repetition of an act or a thought. Even with the act, the thought comes first. You can master and overcome your habits, whatever they are. They were not inherited, nor were they laid upon you. They were acquired. If your subconscious mind can learn one habit of reaction, it can form others. You can change. You don't have to stay any one way."*

Ella Wheeler Wilcox wrote in her poem "Attainment" these words: *"Use all your hidden forces. Do not miss the purpose of this life, and do not wait for circumstances to mold or change your fate!"*

Get into the habit of thinking before you speak. You'll never regret it.

Speak positive affirmations during your prayer time to identify with spirit.

Aim for the highest relations with self and others.

Refrain from gossip. Speak only words of truth.

Learn to observe yourself with detachment. Be aware of your words.

LAW 3

*You have the most powerful weapons
on earth—love and prayer*
—John M. Templeton

You may be familiar with the inspirational writing called *The Desiderata*. Although the entire writing is exquisitely presented, one statement in particular can be quite beneficial. It states, *"Go placidly amid the noise and the haste."* This could be particularly relevant to life in a big city with all its hustle, rush, and sometimes confusion, and equally meaningful for smaller towns and areas when we seem to get caught up in the "busyness" of daily life. An important thing to remember is that whatever kind of confusion may be around you, what is within your own consciousness is what counts. And you have available two of the most powerful tools to use—love and prayer.

The Hebrew greeting *"Shalom,"* a beautiful and meaningful word, means "surrender." We may have often thought of surrender as connoting coming to the end of a struggle, such as a war or some major dispute or conflict. To say, "Oh, I give up," may seem to indicate futility and resignation. But the Oriental idea of surrender is quite different. It is that which comes first. It is a spiritual state that establishes harmony and brotherhood and oneness with other people and conditions. What more meaningful way can we bring this feeling of oneness about than through love and prayer!

In the New Testament, Jesus admonishes his followers to *"become as little children"* and to *"love your enemies."* Probably no two commands may be more difficult to follow in today's world, confronted as sometimes happens with our own negative thoughts, whether in business, within our family, or among our friends.

It may be easy to look at a negative example set by others and shrug off our responsibility to "love one another," even as God has loved us. We might use the excuse that if no one else follows these spiritual principles, why should we? And yet, throughout history, it seems almost impossible not to notice the success of those who have acted on the courage of their convictions to "love thy neighbor as thyself."

There are some in modern times who, if asked how to handle

*"Prayer is the little
    implement
Through which Men
    reach. . . ."*
—Emily Dickinson

*"Do not lie in a ditch
and say, God help me;
use the lawful tools he
hath lent thee."*
—George Chapman

a difficult relationship, may respond by saying, "Just tell them you love them." Mother Theresa, as she lives out these spiritual principles of love in her own life, declares that *"love for God is love in action."* She states, *"loving Him through words is not enough,"* and she has shown her love for God through a lifetime of dedicated work with the poor. But what really sets the Mother Theresas of the world apart is their ability to enjoy the "fruits of the Spirit," as described by St. Paul after his conversion to Christianity on the road to Damascus.

Most people now understand the term "the laws of nature," the multitude of principles discovered by scientists, primarily in the last four centuries, explaining or describing the physical universe. However, as mentioned in my book *The Humble Approach*, not everyone yet understands the phrase "the laws of the spirit." There is a difference between laws of the spirit and religious laws such as those formulated by Moses, Hammurabi, Muhammad, and other ancient lawgivers. More benefits may result in the domains of the spirit if each individual drew up his own personal list of the laws governing spiritual matters. It may be that when we understand and claim as our own some actual laws of the spirit—such as love and prayer—that we begin to build our own heaven.

As the anthropologist Margaret Mead states in her book *Twentieth Century Faith,* "Each man is indeed his brother's keeper and the need to love our enemies ought to be given new scientific meaning. If only we are able to love those who are our enemies, in the sense of cherish and protect, can we hope to protect the lives of men and the life of the world?

Once we understand how to express this love to others through our own lives, we may then be better able to direct our prayers to make God's priorities our own. As we learn to share and give and care, love increases. A person who knows how to love does not seem to feel lonely or alone. In this sense, the power of love can become a true weapon against harm. As a friend of mine is fond of saying, *"Love given is love received,"* and happiness is a by-product of that kind of love. This law of life, when put to use through loving expressions and prayer, can guide us in fulfilling our every aspiration, as well as enriching the lives of those around us.

LAW 4

Remember, no one can make you feel inferior without your consent
—Eleanor Roosevelt

A thermometer is a long, thin glass tube filled with mercury—a simple device designed to give a reading of the temperature of its surrounding environment. When the environment becomes warmed, the mercury rises. When it becomes cooler, the mercury descends. At a glance you can know how warm or cold the air is around the thermometer. Some thermometers can tell you whether your body is functioning at a normal temperature, and others indicate if your food has been properly cooked.

Unfortunately, many people operate like a thermometer. Instead of mercury, their self-esteem may rise and fall according to the "temperature" of other people's opinions of them. When others think highly of them, these people tend to feel good about themselves. When they are criticized, their opinion of themselves may drop to a low, cold level. Eleanor Roosevelt, former first lady in the United States, stated an important truth to remember. *"No one can make you feel inferior without your consent."* Think carefully about these words. You are under no obligation to let the world decide how you are going to feel about yourself. You have the right and the opportunity to discern the events in your life and judge yourself. Criticism may take on many forms, the majority of which seem petty and trivial. And criticism, whether directed toward us or coming from us, can be a deterrent to progress and may lead us into discord and trouble. By feeling confident and enhancing the positive qualities in others we may actually be revealing our own fine qualities.

Many of us may have been raised giving others a great deal of control over our feelings. But, as we grow, it's important to learn that how we feel about ourselves, in spite of the opinions of others, can be an essential ingredient of a happy life. If you allow people the power to set or adjust the thermostat of your self-esteem, you may find yourself at the mercy of their opinions. Your happiness could then seem to depend on many conditions over which you have no healthy inner control.

How you feel about yourself can determine, to a large extent, your experience of life. You cannot afford to surrender control

"Literature is strewn with the wreckage of men who have minded beyond reason the opinion of others."
—Virginia Woolf

"If you have no confidence in self, you are twice defeated in the race of life. With confidence, you have won even before you have started."
—Marcus Garvey

of your feelings to the whims of others. If you know persons who seem to be going through life constantly miserable, and for no apparent reason, it may be likely that they have relinquished power over their feelings. Like a thermometer, they simply reflect the world's opinions. They have handed over to others the power to judge themselves, and this state of powerlessness often creates a high level of tension and anxiety.

Unlike the thermometer, you can take your own "temperature." You can feel good about yourself and your life, despite what others think. No one knows you or your capabilities as well as you do. Therefore, it is important that you be in charge of how you feel about yourself.

Be open enough to learn from others, but make a commitment to stay in control of your feelings about yourself and your estimate of your worth. What works wonderfully well for a thermometer can prove to be disastrous for you. If you find that you have put someone else in charge of your self-esteem, begin making a simple statement like the following to set you free: *"Today, I feel good about myself despite what others say, think, or do. I am the master of my feelings and hold that authority in my life today!"* Self-knowledge may be difficult to obtain because the tendency to self-protection may seem so great. But it is in looking squarely at our own feelings and possible shortcomings that we may be able to see the work that needs to be done to bring about transformation in our lives. Once the decision is made about a "weak spot"—whether it be a "short-fuse" temper, feelings of unworthiness, feelings of being inferior, or whatever—we can engage ourself in thinking about the opposite quality. For instance, if you desire to curb feelings of inferiority, think about the desirability of a pleasant disposition and feeling confident of the spirit within you. You can give your thoughts and feelings a new direction.

When you live from the center of your own being, life can become much more productive and joyful at the circumference.

"Beware of allowing a tactless word, a rebuttal, a rejection to obliterate the whole sky."
—Anaïs Nin

"Whoever will be free must make himself free. Freedom is no fairy gift to fall into a man's lap. What is freedom? To have the will to be responsible for one's self."
—Max Stirner

Law 5

No person was ever honored for what he received. Honor has been the reward for what he gave
—Calvin Coolidge

In the Gospel according to Luke, Jesus said, *"Give, and it will be given to you; good measure, pressed down, shaken together, running over, will be put into your lap. For the measure you give will be the measure you get back"* (Luke 6:38). Jesus states a fundamental law of life that has been recognized by most great spiritual leaders as well as by many truly successful men and women.

If you love the work you do, you are going to put all of yourself into it, giving freely of energy and of your talents. When you give of yourself, when you work for the joy of achievement, when you share your bounty with others, the gift of appreciation, tangible or intangible, becomes a part of your daily life. Tangible appreciation could be a monetary return or a gift from someone for work accomplished. Intangible appreciation could be gratitude from others for what you have done and a good reputation. On the other hand, if you're working for the pay check, willing only to do what you believe you're getting paid to do and no more, chances are you'll grow to despise your job.

Bob was such a man. For eight hours a day, five days a week, year after year, he pulled down a salary while putting forth as little effort as possible. He always seemed to be tired and discontented, and he blamed his job for many of his problems.

One thing Bob loved to do, however, was watch his daughter play softball. When he was offered the chance to coach her Little League team, he eagerly accepted. Although coaching the girls took a great deal of time and commitment, Bob didn't mind. He said the hours he spent with the team were energizing. The girls ended up taking a first-place trophy, and Bob received an outpouring of praise from the parents who were amazed by his commitment.

Fortunately, the story doesn't end there. At the prompting of his concerned wife, Bob decided to seek spiritual counseling about the problem in his professional life. The counselor suggested he begin to embrace his job with the same enthusiasm

The more love we give away, the more we have left. The laws of love differ from the laws of arithmetic. Love hoarded dwindles, but love given grows. If we give all our love, we will have more left than he who saves some. Giving love, not receiving, is important; but when we give with no thought of receiving, we automatically, and inescapably receive abundantly. Heaven is a by-product of love. When we say, "I love you," we mean that "a little of God's love flows from me to you." Thereby, we do not love less, but more. For in flowing, the quantity is magnified.
—John M. Templeton, *Riches for Mind and Spirit*

"He who wishes to secure the good of others has already secured his own."
—Confucius

246

"We must not judge a man's merits by his great qualities, but by the use he makes of them."
–François La Rochefoucauld

"Everything comes to us that belongs to us if we create the capacity to receive it."
–Rabindranath Tagore

"There is no road too long to the man who advances deliberately and without undue haste; no honors too distant to the man who prepares himself for them with patience."
–Bruyere

"A man is already of consequence in the world when it is known that we can implicitly rely upon him. Often I have known a man to be preferred in stations of honor and profit because he had this reputation: when he said he knew a thing, he knew it, and when he said he would do a thing, he did it."
–Edward Bulwer-Lytton

that he was pouring into coaching the girl's softball team. He reluctantly agreed to give it a try.

To his surprise, Bob began noticing things at work he could do to make the day more interesting. He began to take an interest in the lives of his fellow employees. He challenged himself to improve the ways in which he was doing his job. He began to pretend he was actually the owner of the plant instead of just another cog in the machine. He began to make suggestions to his superiors on how things could be run more efficiently in his department. And, to his great surprise, he found himself thinking about ways to improve his work after hours! Each day now he awoke with a sense of enthusiasm instead of dull despair. Bob learned the valuable lesson of honestly and sincerely giving of yourself in whatever you do.

You don't often get competent at something you ignore. And it may not be easy to release inner turmoil until you, as a unique human being, develop a feeling of being active in your own life mission. When you honor the spirit within, you are able to give so much more to life. Giving can be similar to financial investing. If you invest carelessly and without any effort or research, you are likely to fail in the long run. On the other hand, when you wisely invest your energies, interests, and abilities, you are more likely to succeed.

Remember that merely putting your time into something doesn't mean you're giving yourself to it. There are various levels or degrees of giving. Dedicate your attention, your interest, your love, your imagination, your creativity to the task at hand, and you can transform an undesirable condition into something that gives back to you, in "good measure, pressed, shaken together, running over. For the measure you give will be the measure you get back." This is a law of life that can work for you in the same way it worked for Bob and for millions of other people who have discovered it. Think less about what you can get and more about what you can give, and your life will take on a luster you haven't yet dreamed possible.

Spotlights!

1. *"Concentrate your thoughts on the good, beautiful and true things of life rather than the reverse."* — Rebecca Clark
2. Thought—the act or process of thinking—is said to be one of the greatest powers we possess and may be used positively or negatively, as we choose.
3. Words once spoken cannot be erased.

4. Anger is an emotion that may lead to sadness, hurt, and even possible violence. Take charge of your emotions!
5. Regardless of what may be happening around you, what is within your own consciousness is what counts.
6. Love and prayer may be two of the most powerful weapons on earth!
7. When you live from the center of your being, life can become much more productive and joyful at the circumference.
8. Criticism, whether directed toward us or coming from us, can be a deterrent to progress and may lead to discord and trouble.
9. *"The measure you give will be the measure you get back."* –Jesus
10. Think less about what you can get and more about what you can give, and your life may take on a luster you haven't yet dreamed possible!

Living the Law!

Ralph Waldo Emerson once said, *"Within man is the soul of the whole; the wise silence, the universal beauty, to which every part and particle is equally related; the eternal One."* Many spiritual teachers have commented that human life is ultimately about a search for meaning, *a path*, if you will, to enlightenment—to discovering the true creative and transcendent nature of ourselves and of the universe in which we live. Therefore, it is important and meaningful to define and stand for organizing principles, for our lives—those spiritual truths that bring us meaning, direction, groundedness, and the potential for transcendence.

In his book *Centered Living: The Way of Centering Prayer*, M. Basil Pennington introduces his readers to a very old, but valuable method of spiritual meditation, which he calls "centering." The author draws quite a bit from the writings and personal letters of Thomas Merton. In a letter to a Sufi scholar, Aziz Ch. Abdul, Merton gives a clear description of his ordinary way of praying, which Pennington calls "centering prayer." This method is shared here for your contemplation.

"Now you ask about my method of meditation. Strictly speaking, I have a very simple way of prayer. It is centered entirely on attention to the presence of God and to His will and His love. That is to say that it is centered on faith by which alone we can know the presence of God. One might say this gives my meditation the character described by the Prophet as 'being before God as if

*you saw Him.' Yet it does not mean imagining anything or con-
ceiving a precise image of God, for to my mind this would be a
kind of idolatry. On the contrary, it is a matter of adoring Him
as invisible and infinitely beyond our comprehension, and realizing Him as all. . . . There is in my heart this great thirst to recognize totally the nothingness of all that is not God. My prayer is
then a kind of praise rising up out of the center of Nothingness
and Silence. If I am still present 'myself,' this I recognize as an
obstacle. If He wills He can make the Nothingness into a total
clarity. If He does not will, then the Nothingness actually seems to
itself to be an object and remains an obstacle. Such is my ordinary way of prayer, or meditation. It is not 'thinking about' anything, but a direct seeking of the Face of the Invisible. Which cannot be found unless we become lost in Him who is Invisible."*

The idea of God being at the center was brought home to
Merton early in his life, in an experiential, rather than concep-
tual, way—in a way that spoke to him daily, almost constantly, in
one of the most formative periods of his life.

Guideline for Centering Prayer

Sit comfortably in a chair that will give your back good support, and gently close your eyes.

1. Be in faith and love to God, who dwells in the center of
   your being.
2. Take up a love word (like love, peace, joy, etc.) and let it be
   gently present, supporting your being in God in faith-filled
   love.
3. Whenever you become *aware* of anything else, simply, gently
   return to God with the use of your prayer word.

Let the "Our Father" (or some other prayer) pray itself within
you.

Week Twenty-Two

LAW 1

Material progress needs entrepreneurs
—John M. Templeton

The pyramids of Egypt are considered to be among the Seven
Wonders of the Ancient World. It is said that the Great Pyramid
near Cairo can accommodate the equivalent of ten football
fields! When we think of the tools that may have been used during those ancient times, one wonders how the seemingly miraculous feats of pyramid construction were accomplished. How
could the ancient people build such massive structures without
the benefit of modern machinery? What kind of blueprints did
they have to guide them with construction? Whose idea spear-
headed the first construction? What natural resources were
available? By their insight and foresight, the builders must have
seized every opportunity—even those that may have appeared to
be obstacles—and added their faith and creativity to leave such
impressive gifts to the world.

*"Fortune favors the
audacious."*
—Desiderius
Erasmus

In one sense, we, too, can be a part of that building process.
In fact, each new day with its possible obstacles offers opportunities to create or build that which we desire. Our ancestors
from around the world may have encountered a river, and built
a bridge and a dam; they entered a forest, and built and
warmed their homes; they cleared a field, and planted and har-
vested their crops; they tunneled through mountains, and
endured possible extremes of heat and cold; but they moved
onward, forward.

*"The weakest among
us has a gift, however
seemingly trivial,
which is peculiar to
him and which wor-
thily used will be a
gift also to his race."*
—John Ruskin

We are blessed to live in a time when one who desires to organize a business and is willing to take the steps necessary for the
project to unfold can experience the freedom and opportunity
to be an entrepreneur. And world progress needs entrepreneurs. If there is a blueprint or guideline to follow, getting
started may not be difficult. The value of a definitive plan is

"If there is no dull and determined effort, there will be no brilliant achievement."
—Hsun-tze

"Behind every advance of the human race is a germ of creation growing in the mind of some lone individual. An individual whose dreams waken him in the night while others contentedly sleep."
—Crawford H. Greenewalt

"Some men give up their designs when they have almost reached the goal; while others on the contrary, obtain a victory by exerting at the last moment, more vigorous effort than before."
—Polybius

easy to understand for it can help one to avoid wasting precious moments. Dedication to the goal and earnest hard work are important values that can help manifest the dream. The advice of Harlow Herbert Curtice, an automobile manufacturer, was to *"do your job better each time. Do it better than anyone else can do it. Do it better than it needs to be done. Let no one or anything stand between you and the difficult task. I know this sounds old-fashioned. It is, but it has built the world."*

Psychiatrist W. Beran Wolfe put it this way: *"If you observe a really happy man, you will find him building a boat, writing a symphony, educating his son, growing double dahlias, or looking for dinosaur eggs in the Gobi Desert. He will not be searching for happiness as if it were a collar button that had rolled under the radiator, striving for it as the goal itself. He will have become aware that he is happy in the course of living life twenty-four crowded hours of each day."*

And isn't "living life" an important foundation for building our dreams? Within you, within the creative genius of your mind, lies the real land of opportunity. Within you lies the insight, the foresight, the strength, courage, faith, freedom, and ability to accept and express your opportunities. From the circumstances around you, from the situations in which you may find yourself, from the relationships in which you may be involved, you can be creative!

Choose carefully and through much thought and prayer that which you desire. Be sure your desire is worthy of your energy, your time, your creativity, and can bring a blessing of service to others. Know what you desire to accomplish; and plan, step by step, day by day, how you may achieve your goal. The pyramid builders built upon one stone at a time. They started at the base of the pyramid and worked their way up. Most projects involve the same process—one step at a time. We start at the beginning and work our way to the finish line. If we are open and receptive, the resources needed can be provided.

A journalist was complaining to the French novelist, essayist, and playwright Marcel Ayme that the modern world hinders the free development of the human being. "I don't agree," said Ayme mildly. "I consider myself perfectly free."

"But surely you feel some limits to your freedom," the journalist commented.

"Oh, yes," replied Ayme, "from time to time I find myself terribly limited by the dictionary!"

What is necessary to become an innovator? First, recognize that you have within you the power to be creative. Next, be willing to try new experiences, to discover new fields that may offer scope for developmental activities. Being open and receptive can teach us much about the world and help sincere and creative individuals become innovative entrepreneurs. Success-bound people find it important to believe in themselves, because the frontier exists inside of them. Jesus' teaching concerning this is found in Luke 17:21, where we are reminded that *"the kingdom of God is not coming with signs to be observed . . . for behold, the kingdom of God is in the midst of you."* This is the true frontier that we must explore: our own inner being, our own divinity.

LAW 2

As you are active in blessing others, they find their burdens easier to bear
—John M. Templeton

"This is my commandment, that you love one another as I have loved you." With these immortal words, St. John sublimates Jesus' recognition of the very depth of the love we would seek to achieve. Pure love, untainted by doubt, undisturbed by worldly consideration or thought of personal gain, represents a pinnacle of achievement. In the wide sense, it can be important to see others as our brothers and sisters, and as our friends. St. Philip Neri said, *"Cast yourself with confidence into the arms of God; and be very sure of this: that if He wants anything of you, He will fit you for your work and give you the strength to do it."* When we look with the eyes of Spirit, could not a part of our "work" be that of loving service to others?

"Great blessings come from Heaven; small blessings come from man."
–Chinese proverb

When we desire to be a blessing, we find that there are many ways in which we can bless others. We can give material goods to others, and we can also offer them the benefit of our experience. People who have faced and overcome challenges with alcohol and drugs often involve themselves in helping others who are experiencing similar difficulties. They understand the value of overcoming the problem. In every area of the human experience, we may find those precious ones who are able and willing to be a blessing to others.

"Wealth is not of necessity a curse, nor poverty a blessing. Wholesome and easy abundance is better than either extreme; better for our manhood that we have enough for daily comfort, enough for culture, for hospitality, for charity. More than this may or may not be a blessing. Certainly it can be a blessing only by being accepted as a trust."
–Roswell D. Hitchcock

"Whatever you have received more than others–in health, in talents, in ability, in success, in a pleasant childhood, in harmonious conditions of home life–all this you must not take to yourself as a matter of course. In gratitude for your good fortune, you must render in return some sacrifice of your own life for another life."
–Albert Schweitzer

The exquisite spiritual poetry of a fourteenth-century poet Kabir may stir our souls if we listen with the heart: *"Suppose you scrub your ethical skin until it shines, but inside there is no music, then what? Mohammed's son pores over words, and points out this and that, but if his chest is not soaked dark with love, then what? The Yogi comes along in his famous orange. But if inside he is colorless, then what?"* Does this not speak of the service of blessings? A well-known building contractor begins his day with a prayer like this: "Father, you are the Master Architect. Let me never 'hammer and saw' so loudly that You can't get through to discuss Your blueprints with me. My business is Your business. Work through me to build good houses and a good life. Help me be a blessing to all I meet." Many people find that they receive more benefit from *being* a blessing than from being blessed. Oftentimes, being a blessing requires nothing more than a word of encouragement and hope to someone who may be experiencing situations that bring discouragement and despair.

E. Stanley Jones tells of seeing a little frail flower growing in the vast ruins of ancient Babylon. He wondered how a little flower, so frail that he could crush it in his fingers, could have survived while a vast empire founded on military power had perished. As he contemplated the mystery before him, he realized it was because the flower followed the ways of nature's gentleness, but the nation perished by its militaristic doctrine. He concluded that love is the answer; light is a continuing need, and each one of us can serve as a channel of blessing.

The English poet Elizabeth Barrett Browning wrote, *"God's gifts put man's best dreams to shame."* Since God has given us great potential, it can be important to learn to discover more of his gifts by making them spiritually active in our life. One way to do this can be to pass along the service of our talents and abilities to others with our love and blessings. Divine ideas can become more real to us and active within us when we share them with our friends, neighbors, and family.

The air we breathe is necessary to keep us alive, but we must continually breathe it out so we can breathe fresh air back into our lungs. God gives us his love, which we can keep in action by breathing it out to others, thus making room in our hearts for a fresh supply of love. Muhammad, the Prophet of Islam, wrote as follows: *"No man is a true believer unless he desireth for his brother that which he desireth for himself."* We must share our gifts to provide opportunity for increase in our life. For example, when knowledge is shared, it increases for those concerned. When we share with others our substance and our blessings, they can increase for us and for others as the loaves and fishes increased for Jesus and the multitude. When we share garden seed with nature by sowing it in the ground, the unfolding harvest brings increase. When we speak kind words, kindness can be multiplied in our lives.

The law of blessedness may indicate that a real part of our life's work may be to help other's burdens become easier to bear. Have we not each experienced—at some time in our life—a problem situation, a personal challenge, or possibly confusion? And perhaps we were the recipient of caring and compassion from another. As we humble ourselves to the multitude of expressions of the Spirit that sing to us each moment, as we come to appreciate and love the inner richness of our lives, we may become the blessing that adds the "flavor" to our life. What a wonderful awareness to know that as we open ourselves to rich blessings, those blessings flow through the channel of our love to bless and help others. Let's pause and give thanks for being blessed and for the opportunity to be a blessing.

"No longer talk at all about the kind of man a good man ought to be, but be such."
–Marcus Aurelius

LAW 3

Expect the best and your positive outlook opens the door to opportunity
—John M. Templeton

It is a natural fact that winter storms can be dangerous. With freezing temperatures, snow, sleet, and wind, icy conditions on the roads pose a threatening challenge to even the most experienced driver. Sometimes car batteries freeze up, and it's hard to get the car started, or snow has fallen that must be plowed away before cars can pass. Schools are often closed to keep the students at home and safe from the hazardous roads. Yet, those same conditions that close the schools may offer most children delight at the prospect of an unexpected holiday in the middle of the week! The fun-loving person can find myriad ways to play in the fluffy white stuff whether they sled, slide, or ski; roll it into balls for throwing; or into boulders for building. To the

"A pessimist is one who make difficulties of his opportunities; an optimist is one who makes opportunities of his difficulties."
–Reginald B. Mansell

expectant student, who has followed the weather reports more faithfully than a meteorologist, a snowy day is no problem. An optimistic expectation converts the problem into an opportunity for enjoyment.

What is a problem? One dictionary defines a problem as *"a question proposed for a solution."* A problem that occurs in your life, then, may simply be a question that life asks you. It can look like a jigsaw puzzle that has just been taken from its box. There may be a thousand small pieces, each with the potential of joining together to complete a pattern or picture. The pieces mean nothing strewn about unconnected on the table. The fun of the jigsaw puzzle is in finding the relationship between the pieces and fitting them together. You may also find in various life situations that the search and discovery of various pieces of the puzzle can be more enjoyable than the finished image—because the process can be as important as the resolution of the problem the puzzle poses. An old Arabian proverb states, *"Everything is small at the beginning and then increases, except trouble, which is great at its beginning and then decreases."*

There are circumstances, however, in which a problem may cause difficulty. For example, solving a challenging engineering problem on a multi-million dollar building project can be more stressful than balancing your checkbook. There may be deadlines to meet, and you may feel pressure to perform well because your job, your future well-being, and the safety of many people depend on you. These stresses can make a problem seem like something larger than life and something you aren't sure you wish to tackle. You may question your ability to meet the challenge set before you. Doubt, uncertainty, and a sense of inadequacy can make a simple problem snowball into something more complex than it is. When an avalanche of negative emotions threatens, it becomes difficult to experience a ski slope as fun to traverse! A molehill may appear like an entire mountain and an obstacle rather than a challenge to your ability and skill. Because anxiety may occupy a large part of your thinking processes in intense situations, solutions might seem elusive, and your performance may falter.

Save the best for the best by experiencing the best! Your positive outlook can open doors to opportunity that fear might otherwise tightly lock. Your hopeful vision can assert potential in the face of limitation. Your trusting patience can persevere when doubt would have you quit. At his Viennese debut, Pablo Casals, the great Spanish cellist, conductor, and composer, suffered from nervousness. When he reached for his bow to play the first note, he found that his hand was too tense. To loosen it he tried a little twirl, but the bow flew from his fingers and landed in the middle of the orchestra. As it was carefully passed back to him along the rows of musicians, he remembered his mother's maxim about calmness and steadiness in the pursuit of one's purpose. By the time the bow was returned to him his hand was steady. The concert was one of his greatest triumphs!

Helen Keller may have had many problems, but she never allowed negative emotions to sink her into a pit of self-pity. Imagine the optimistic expectation and hope she must have expressed to break out of a dark and silent prison to become self-expressive. With her teacher, Anne Mansfield Sullivan, Helen lectured all over the United States, answering questions from the audience that were communicated to her by Miss Sullivan. A stock question was, "Do you close your eyes when you go to sleep?" Helen Keller's stock response was, "I never stayed awake to see." She kept a high, hopeful inner eye on a light that guided her to overcome incredible physical handicaps to design a life more creative than many people with full sight and hearing experience.

Look for the best of what can be possible in every situation, and you have the opportunity to turn any problem into a manifestation of greater good. Give thanks for the Spirit, which is working *for* you by working *through* you. Remember the words of the Persian poet Sa'ib of Tabriz: *"The march of good fortune has backward slips: to retreat one or two paces gives wings to the jumper."*

"God gave man an upright countenance to survey the heavens, and to look upward to the stars."
–Ovid

LAW 4

When anger reigns, negative consequences occur
—Charles D. Lelly

The high school students lifted their heads from their books when they heard Tracy in the hall yelling at Mr. Moorehead, the assistant principal. Tracy had been accused of stealing an expensive art book, and she was extremely upset over the false accusation. Ms. Taylor, the art teacher, believed Tracy had stolen the

*"The happiness of your
life depends upon the
quality of your
thought: therefore,
guard accordingly, and
take care that you
entertain no notions
unsuitable to virtue
and reasonable
nature."*
—Marcus Aurelius

*"A man without
self-restraint is like a
barrel without hoops,
and tumbles to pieces."*
–Henry Ward
Beecher

book because she was the last person seen reading it. Tracy, stung by the teacher's accusation, screamed at her that she'd put the book back on the shelf, but Ms. Taylor refused to believe her. The more Ms. Taylor refused to believe her, the more Tracy lost control. She began to swear at the older woman.

"I won't stand for this abuse," Ms. Taylor said, picking up the telephone to call Mr. Moorehead. "You'll stay for detention all this week after school."

Tracy had a record of getting into trouble at school. But this time, she had done nothing wrong.

"You're in deep trouble, young lady," Mr. Moorehead said quietly. "No one talks to me or any of the teachers this way and gets away with it."

The question to ask in this situation would be: How could Tracy have avoided needless trouble? Although anger may be a natural and immediate reaction when unfairly treated, it only makes matters worse to act out our anger. Remaining as calm as possible provides an avenue to examine the options that may be open to us. If Tracy had remained calm, she might have remembered that a very quiet, studious boy who was sitting in the back of the room could have been a witness. By talking calmly and rationally with Ms. Taylor and Mr. Moorehead, she may have had a better chance of convincing them of her innocence. Also, by maintaining her calm, Tracy could have heard Ms. Taylor's words more clearly. The art teacher told her she was very upset because so many art books were disappearing. Although it wasn't right for Ms. Taylor to accuse Tracy, a little understanding on Tracy's part might have helped ease the situation. Anger is a strong emotion that can have powerful detrimental effects on ourselves and others. When we can direct our angry feelings into positive actions that can help us find new ways to deal with intense situations, we're no longer needlessly wasting our energy. A calm Tracy could have checked at the library to see if the book was there, or she might have asked the studious boy or other art students if they had seen the book.

Angry words and actions cannot serve a useful purpose because they tend to set up a chain of negative reactions that often result in a communication breakdown. Not that it's easy to remain level-headed when we're falsely accused, or even when we may have made a mistake. But it makes an already bad situation worse when we don't. Once anger takes over, common sense and reasonableness often fly out the window. Hurt feelings often ensue, and seeds may be planted that sprout into negative consequences that are hard to turn around. Abu'l-Fath al-Busti, a Persian poet, said, *"If you yield to your anger, you only cease to be civil."* And the Chinese philosopher Chu Hsi gave the following good advice: *"When one is angry, if one can directly forget his anger and examine the right and wrong according to principle, then right and wrong will be clearly seen and desires will naturally be unable to persist."*

President Lincoln's secretary of war, Edwin Stanton, had some trouble with a major general who accused him, in abusive terms, of favoritism. Stanton complained to Lincoln, who suggested that he write the officer a sharp letter. Stanton did so, and showed the strongly worded missive to the president, who applauded its powerful language. "What are you going to do with it?" he asked. Surprised at the question, Stanton said, "Send it." Lincoln shook his head. "You don't want to send that letter," he said. "Put it in the stove. That's what I do when I have written a letter while I am angry. It's a good letter, and you had a good time writing it and feel better. Now, burn it, and write another."

Because anger is both an emotion and often a coping response, it falls into a special category, which Nicholas R. M. Martin, author of *An Operator's Manual for Successful Living,* calls "secondary emotions." He states that most of us have learned to feel more comfortable with anger than the underlying feelings it covers, and we are often more quick to express that anger than the "softer" feelings closer to the heart.

He mentions four standard feelings that *tend* to precede anger: fear, hurt, frustration, and injustice. Although the list of possible underlying feelings may be much longer, Martin feels these four are perhaps the most common and could be called the "four pillars that hold up the roof of anger."

Furthermore, because we tend to get back what we send out, the expression of anger usually invites a counterattack or defensiveness in return. Here is a partial list of the typical consequences of the choice to become angry:

1. Feelings of "distance" between you and others
2. Promotion of negative feelings in others that may be difficult to overcome
3. Covering up the true feelings and wishes of yourself and preventing others from being open and honest with you
4. Inviting retaliation and/or defensiveness
5. Establishing a roadblock that can hinder getting to the bottom of the situation and reaching a solution

"Clear therefore your head, and rally, and manage thy thoughts rightly, and thou wilt save time, and see and do thy business well; for thy judgment will be distinct, thy mind free, and the faculties strong and regular."
–William Penn

"Nature imitates herself. A grain thrown into good ground brings forth fruit; a principle thrown into a good mind brings forth fruit. Everything is created and conducted by the same master: the root, the branch, the fruits–the principles, the consequences."
–Blaise Pascal

6. Ending of friendships.

There is certainly a time to speak directly and honestly. But before you speak in anger, pause for a moment and ask yourself if another tool would serve the purpose just as well, or better. If there's a fly in your ointment, you can do the following: shoot it (*hostility*); hammer it into nothingness (*anger*); plead with it (*helplessness*); run away from it (*fear*); moan and groan (*hurt or self pity*); go forward indignantly (*injustice*); or carefully carry it outside (*kindness and love*). Any one of the above may get the job done, but with what consequences for yourself and any others who may be involved?

"If you are patient in one moment of anger, you will escape a hundred days of sorrow."
—Chinese proverb

LAW 5

The wise person looks within his heart and finds eternal peace
—Hindu proverb

Is it possible to find peace in our rapidly changing world, arrayed as it is with pleasures and pains, distractions and attractions? Can you be a part of the world, deal with its complexity, which impinges on you from every side, and still find peace in your heart? Is it only in removing yourself from the world to some remote mountaintop or desert that you can look upon your unperturbed heart and find peace? Is peace possible only in a place where you never have to deal with challenging people or situations? Or where there are no conflicts, no annoyances, misunderstandings, needs, pressures, or disappointments? Or does the wise person find peace even amidst the difficulties of life by simply not allowing his heart to be touched by them?

"Two things fill the mind with ever increasing wonder and awe . . . the starry heavens above me and the moral law within me."
—Immanuel Kant

Withdrawing from the world either physically or emotionally does not seem to be the wise person's path to eternal peace. We are placed in this world to deal with it, not escape it; to integrate ourselves with it, not separate into a fragment apart from it; and to find a way to be of benefit and service to the world, not to shun it or harden ourselves to it. However, if you are willing to be present in the world and involved with it, the impact your emotions may not always feel peaceful. We have both positive and negative feelings in our hearts, and our life experiences tend to stir up both. How, then, is it possible to find peace within your heart?

We tend to feel at peace when things are under control. And we do the best we can to control or manage our lives according to our ideas of order. But if inner peace depends on that control, your peace of mind could frequently be at risk. Can you control the economy or energy supplies? Another person's behavior or actions? The choices and destinies of loved ones or others on whom you depend? When you take a long, honest, and sincere look, there may be very little outside yourself that you can control. Therefore, real peace must be an inside job!

A person is truly wise who knows that the heart is the place where lasting peace may be found. The changeability from one day to the next of your personal world, or the world at large, may make outer things an unreliable source of peace. Try going away to that mountaintop, or to any place that seems serene and carefree to you, and you can still find yourself disturbed over something—a memory, a concern about a current situation, a fear about the future, or a mere gnat flying around—if you fail to realize that peace dwells at the center of your being.

This kind of peace has nothing to do with the fluctuation of life events that bring elation or grief with the passing of time. Rather, it has to do with the state of being that may be found within your heart of hearts, in the *"still point of the turning world,"* of which the poet T. S. Eliot wrote, where you are one with the very essence of life. *Webster's Dictionary* defines "essence" as the *"permanent as contrasted with the accidental element of being; the real, or ultimate nature of a thing, as opposed to its existence."* In the changing, often confusing fortunes of time when you know and act from what seems to be essential, it is possible to experience the peace of this unchanging state.

In Proverbs 14:30, Scripture states, *"A tranquil mind gives life to the flesh."* When your world goes topsy-turvy and turmoil threatens, try this exercise. Think about tranquility. Let the screen of your mind reflect whatever the word "tranquility" may bring. A gentle meadow in warm summer sunlight. A placid blue lake at dusk. A fragile butterfly lightly touching a flower. Cool green woods with sunlight filtering through the trees. A majestic snow-covered mountain peak. A fisherman leaning against a tree nonchalantly watching his float on a gently flowing river. It's your thought. Simply take a moment and become still. Speaking softly to yourself, affirm that deep within you is a place of com-

"Go placidly amid the noise and the haste, and remember what peace there may be in silence. As far as possible, without surrender, be on good terms with all persons. You are a child of the universe, no less than the trees and the stars."
—Adlai Stevenson

"The vision that you glorify in your mind, the ideal that you enthrone in your heart—this you will build your life by, this you will become."
—James Allen

"People are afraid to think, or they don't know how. They fail to realize that while emotions can't be suppressed, like minds can be strengthened. All over the world people are seeking peace of mind, but there can be no peace of mind without strength of mind."
–Eric B. Gutkind

plete tranquility. It is the secret place of the Most High, where peace and tranquility reign supreme. Nothing—no discord—can enter here without your consent. And you choose peace. You may turn often to this place within where you abide in the presence of God. *"I am poised, serene, and peaceful!"*

Eliot wrote, *"At the still point, there the dance is. . . . Except for the point, the still point, there would be no dance, and there is only the dance."* The dance of life continually shifts its tempo, rhythm, and form. As you move with it, you may find yourself facing unimagined situations. This is the flow the dance often uses to carry you beyond limited ideas of who you are and what you are capable of handling. Practice looking within your heart, not for emotion but to identify yourself with the still point of your essence and, regardless of "accidental elements" existing around you, peace can be found.

Spotlights!

1. Within you lies the insight, the possibility, the strength, courage, faith, freedom, and ability to accept and express your opportunities.
2. Choose carefully, and through much thought and prayer, that which you desire.
3. Although you may have challenges to face, the ability to overcome obstacles stirs within your soul.
4. The more deeply you come into your own spiritual kingdom, the more you may experience that which can only be seen from within.
5. One definition of the word "problem" is, *"A question proposed for a solution."* How would you define the word "problem"?
6. What seems to be a problem in your life may simply be a question that life asks you!
7. Angry words and actions cannot often serve a useful purpose because they tend to set up a chain of negative reactions that often results in the breakdown of communication.
8. Anger may be both an emotion or a coping response. Take an inner look at *why* you may feel angry. Four standard feelings that may precede anger are fear, hurt, frustration, and injustice.
9. When do you feel most at peace? What seems to enhance feelings of peace within you?
10. A person may be truly wise who knows that the heart is the place where lasting peace may be found.

Living the Law!

Difficulties can dissolve as you "let go and let God." Let's look at some of the possible meanings of "letting go" (author unknown) and how this activity can work for you.

* To "let go" does not mean to stop caring. It means I can't do it for someone else.
* To "let go" is not to cut yourself off. It's the realization that I can't control another.
* To "let go" is to admit powerlessness, which simply means the outcome is not in my hands.
* To "let go" is not to try to change or blame another. It's to make the most of myself.
* To "let go" is not to care for, but to care about.
* To "let go" is not to fix, but to be supportive.
* To "let go" is not to judge, but to allow another to be a human being.
* To "let go" is not to be in the middle, arranging all the outcomes, but to allow others to affect their own destinies.
* To "let go" is not to deny, but to accept.
* To "let go" is not to nag, scold, or argue, but instead to search out my own shortcomings and correct them.
* To "let go" is not to adjust everything to my desires, but to take each day as it comes and cherish myself in it.
* To "let go" is not to regret the past, but to grow and live for the present moment and the future.
* To "let go" is to fear less and to love more.

Week Twenty-Three

LAW 1

Preparedness is a step to success
—John M. Templeton

"Make no little plans, they have no magic to stir men's blood. Making big plans, aims high in hope. Work and let your watchword be order and your beacon, honesty."
–Daniel Burnham

It has been expressed that *"order is Heaven's first law."* Jesus acknowledged this when he said, *"The earth produces of itself, first the blade, then the ear, then the full grain in the ear"* (Mark 4:28). If we are to succeed in life, it becomes necessary to bring our methods of operation into an orderly process. And preparedness can often be considered the first step in the order of success. Another adage is that *"chance favors the prepared."* Opportunity knocks at the door many more times than people may realize. If the moment of opportunity is not seized, it may be because people don't recognize it or are unprepared to seize it.

Eleven-year-old Jeremy was ready and eager to seize the moment. In preparing for a fishing trip to Canada with his father and some of his father's friends, Jeremy insisted on buying a heavy-duty rod and reel so he could catch a big fish. Not wanting to dampen the boy's enthusiasm and knowing he could use the equipment for a deep-sea excursion he was planning, the father purchased the equipment.

When the other men saw Jeremy's new fishing equipment they joked with him. "You planning on catching a whale, Jeremy?" one of the men asked.

"I'm gonna get me a big pike," he responded confidently.

"Well, you could sure get a big pike with that rig," another said, laughing. Jeremy was undaunted by what seemed to be the men's lack of confidence in him.

Four days on the lake produced little for the men and the boy, and Jeremy's fishing rig became the butt of many a friendly joke. Then, suddenly one of the men shouted, "I have something!" His pole arched and strained. A moment later the pole quickly straightened and the line went limp. The line had broken! The disappointed man muttered that he should have come prepared with heavier equipment.

As the fishing party was about to return to the cabin after another day on the lake, Jeremy's line suddenly tightened. At first he thought he had hooked a log beneath the surface of the water. But then the line began to move with a force that almost frightened him. He had hooked his big fish!

Forty-five minutes later he hauled his pike in the boat—a thirty-two pounder! The men were flabbergasted, envious, and respectful, because Jeremy taught them that if you want to catch a big fish, then you had better come prepared!

Far too often many people do not prepare themselves for success. While they wish success would favor them, they may put just enough effort into life to get by, thinking that if by chance something big comes along, they'll grab it. But if you're not prepared for success, you may find it difficult to hold on to the opportunities that come your way. Success requires understanding, fortitude, and foresight to bring the "blade to the full grain in the ear."

As an exercise, ask yourself from time to time what you are doing to prepare yourself for success. Have you *established* and become *fully committed* to your goals? Are you willing not only to cultivate the soil and plant the seed but also to nurture and care for the tender blade and the young ear as it appears? Are you willing to go the extra mile, and give the energy and attention that the opportunity calls for? Are you willing to stand firm with your convictions, your principles? Are you prepared to stand alone if necessary? Have you trained yourself to recognize opportunity when it knocks?

And you never know when it may knock. Opportunity often presents itself in an unexpected form. It could seem to require of you more than you might presently be prepared to give. But if your desire is to catch a big fish, you must prepare yourself as Jeremy did to handle the fish when it strikes. Otherwise, it could be the big one that got away!

I appreciate the story of the young man who, a number of years ago, was seeking a job as a Morse-code operator. He found an ad in the paper and went to the office address that was listed. When he arrived, it was a large and busy office, and there was a certain amount of hustle, bustle, and noise, including the chatter of a telegraph key in the background. A sign on the wall instructed applicants to take a seat and wait until they were sum-

"If you don't have a plan of life, you'll never have order."
–Josemaria Escriva

"A life that hasn't a plan is likely to become driftwood."
–David Sarnoff

"Dreamers and doers–the world generally divides men into those two general classifications, but the world is often wrong. There are men who win the admiration and respect of their fellow man. They are the men worth while. Dreaming is just another name for thinking, planning, devising–another way of saying that a man exercises his soul. A steadfast soul, holding steadily to a dream ideal, plus a sturdy will determined to succeed in any venture, can make any dream come true. Use your mind and your will. They work together for you beautifully if you'll only give them a chance."
–B.N. Mills

moned to come into the inner office. More than a half-dozen applicants were waiting ahead of the man in our story. This could have been discouraging, but he figured he was prepared for the job and had nothing to lose, so he sat down along with the others to wait. After about two or three minutes, the young man stood up, walked over to the door where the sign was hanging and walked right on in. Naturally, the other applicants perked up and started looking at each other and muttering. Within about five minutes the young man came back out the door with the employer, who said, "You gentlemen may go now. The position has been filled."

At this, several of the applicants grumbled, and one spoke up and said, "I don't understand. He was the last person to come in, and we never even got a chance to have an interview, and, yet, he got the job. That's not fair!"

The employer said, "I'm sorry, gentlemen, but all the time you've been sitting here the telegraph key has been ticking out the message in Morse code, *'If you understand this message in Morse code, come right in. The job is yours.'* Apparently none of you heard it or understood the message. He did. The job is his."

In *The Templeton Plan*, I describe how strong spiritual values can help us as we search for financial success, personal success, and a happy and fulfilled life. If your basic values are rooted in spiritual principles, or laws of life, success is more likely to follow. By incorporating these laws of life into your code of behavior, you're on your way to becoming a fulfilled human being. You learn to give freely of yourself and to love without fear. Following the laws of life can give you a greater chance of succeeding at anything you attempt to do.

Continue to read, to learn, and experience new feelings and ideas. Show initiative at an early stage in a situation. Observe others. Listen carefully to others. Use whatever degree of intelligence you possess to the fullest. Remember that to help yourself is to help others. Ask yourself if you are using your talents and abilities in the most wise way. Do you live consciously the virtues of honesty, bravery, humility, gentleness, loyalty, and hope? Learn more about the virtues of life and what they mean in *your* life.

Look for the positive in what may seem to be a negative situation. Learn how to live in harmony with others in ways that may lead to productive change. These things are a part of "being prepared" and often lead to success.

LAW 2

You are on the road to success if you realize that failure is only a detour
—Corrie Ten Boom

If success were easy, then it would not necessarily be true success. Some of history's most successful people learned to cope with failure as a natural offshoot of the experimental and creative process and often learned more from their failures than their successes. By taking the attitude that failure is merely a detour on the way to our destination, hope can blossom into success.

How can we best define success? Does it simply mean that there was a task before us that we accomplished? If that is the case, then we could call walking down the driveway and retrieving the mail a success. Minor matters, regardless of how trivial, could be defined as successes so long as they were completed. Yet, success means so much more. Success comes when we face a challenge and struggle against odds to succeed. Historically, success often followed a series of failures.

For example, many of America's greatest heroes experienced their share of failures. Abraham Lincoln suffered a staggering defeat in the first election he ever entered, and was considered a poor and bumbling speaker. Yet, he became one of our greatest presidents, whose speeches are still regarded as masterpieces of political persuasion. William Faulkner experienced a number of rejections as a young writer by publishers who had no understanding of his innovative narrative style, but despite repeated failures and impoverishments, Faulkner went on to become one of the South's foremost novelists and to win the Nobel Prize for literature. Thomas Edison was another who struggled with failure. Nevertheless, through hard work and the understanding that *"failure is only a detour,"* he invented the electric light bulb, record players, and motion picture—to name only some of his inventions.

Because learning is a process that may result in a failure of one kind or another, failure can be essential to success. It is important to study our failures, to learn from them, and then to make a new attempt. Eventually this process can lead to success. However, if an individual gives up at the first failure, then noth-

"The best way is to forget doubts and set about the task in hand. . . . If you are doing your best, you will not have time to worry about failure."
–Robert Hillyer

"One who fears failure limits his activities. Failure is only the opportunity more intelligently to begin again."
–Henry Ford

"I'm proof against that word failure. I've seen behind it. The only failure a man ought to fear is failure in cleaving to the purpose he sees to be best."
–George Eliot

"The secret success of every man who has ever been successful lies in the fact that he formed the habit of doing those things that failures don't like to do."
–A. Jackson King

"The strong man, the positive man who has a program and is determined to carry it out, cuts his way to his goal regardless of difficulties. It is the discouraged man who turns aside and takes a crooked path."
–Orison Swett Marden

ing has been learned, and no skill has been gained that can improve our subsequent efforts. A person is seldom defeated by failure when he understands that failure can be considered as part of a natural process leading to a positive conclusion. He can then accept it as a mere detour and not a dead end.

Often success or failure, happiness or misery, in a situation may be a matter of perspective. In her book *The Hiding Place*, Corrie Ten Boom described a discussion with her mother about Tante Beb, the aunt who had lived with them for a number of years. Corrie observed how unhappy Beb was, always complaining and comparing their home to the "Wallers," where she had been "so happy" as their housekeeper. But mother knew better. "Corrie," she asked, "Do you know when she started praising the Wallers so highly? The day she left them! As long as she was there, she had nothing but complaints. The Wallers couldn't compare with the Van Hooks, where she had been before. But at the Van Hooks, she'd actually been miserable. Happiness isn't something that depends on our surroundings, Corrie. It's something we make inside ourselves."

If we want to succeed, we may consider blazing new trails rather than going down the worn-out paths of former or accepted success. Someone said that the difference between failure and success could be doing a thing "nearly" right or "exactly" right. George Horace Lorimer offered, *"Because a fellow has failed once or a dozen times, you don't set him down as a failure until he's dead or loses his courage–and that's the same thing."* And Elbert Hubbard commented, *"The line between failure and success is so fine that we are often on the line and do not know it!"* In *A Treasury,* W. R. Beattie presents the idea that real success can be enjoyed in the process of building—in the drafting of the plans, laying the foundation, selecting the materials, measuring the many parts, and then dove-tailing them together. He felt a person's greatest joys often came from the anticipation of each day's accomplishments and the satisfaction gained from a task well done.

For a moment, consider a most important room in your "house of living"—the room of your mind. What you are can be dependent upon what is in this room. You are—first and foremost—a spiritual being, so the plan for your inner room should be exquisite, comfortable, and satisfying. This place can represent a sanctuary of loveliness and peace. Its furniture consists of your thoughts. The walls must be sturdy in faith, with the colors showing forth the beauty of strength and courage, joy and peace, love and goodness, praise and thanksgiving, and positive, confident, success. Most importantly, the light of wisdom must fully illuminate this room, for it is in this inner room that you shape your world, and it is here that you may fashion the self that you give to the world.

As Alexander Crummell, American minister and writer, said, *"All real success springs from that inward might which we exert upon society."*

Law 3

Thanksgiving leads to giving and forgiving, and to spiritual growth
–John M. Templeton

Thanksgiving may often be called "the law of gratitude," with fear as its opposite. Gratitude enhances the open-hearted, genuine appreciation for what is wonderful in our life. Fear can be a contracting force that can take us out of our own power and make us the victim of lack. In the book *Lazy Man's Guide to Enlightenment*, Thaddeus Golas writes, *"We think fear is a signal to withdraw when it is really a sign that we are already withdrawing too much."*

A Course in Miracles, published by Foundation for Inner Peace, states there are two basic forces in the universe, love and fear. Another way of saying that may be thanksgiving and lack. If we recognize these forces when something is happening, we can ride out the negative current much more easily and find our way back to the positive one through the practice of gratitude. *A Course* also describes two ways of learning, the path of joy and the path of pain. We may listen to the inner voice of the spirit guiding us along the way and choose to follow that guidance, in which case our lessons may be learned free from burdening pain. We can feel the joy of spirit and give thanks. The other and often more frequently chosen alternative is that we learn through trial and error, through making mistakes until we are tired of the mistakes and don't want to go through them any more. Learning through pain doesn't always "stick," so we may keep learning our lessons over and over again.

"I count him as a great man who inhabits a higher sphere of thought, into which other men rise with labor and difficulty; he has but to open his eyes to see things in a true light and in large relations, whilst they must make painful corrections and keep a vigilant eye on many sources of error."
–Ralph Waldo Emerson, *Uses of Great Men, Representative Men*

"It is a grand mistake to think of being great without goodness; and I pronounce it as certain that there was never yet a truly great man that was not at the same time truly virtuous."
–Benjamin Franklin, "The Busy-Body Papers," *American Weekly Mercury*

When was the last time you felt grateful for the simple conveniences of your life? Think about it. There is so much in our lives to be grateful for that we often fail to recognize. Eighty years ago, most homes in the United States had "outhouses" instead of plumbing. Today almost every home in America has a working bathroom. Fifty years ago, it was not uncommon to have the central rooms of a house heated by a pot-bellied stove or a single fireplace, and to close off the other rooms until you went to bed. There was also a time when feather mattresses, so soft you would sink in the middle, were used against the cold. Forget the idea of a posture-pedic bed!

How about washing machines? In many Third-World countries, the idea of a local laundromat is a dream. A documentary on life in Russia in 1990 showed that the average family shared accommodations with two or three other families in an apartment the size of one of our normal houses. The women hand-washed clothes in a tub, and the waiting list to get one's own apartment averaged ten years!

We often take so many things for granted. It is important to learn the art of looking for and appreciating the real blessings of life, great and small. There is an old saying that "a donkey may carry a heavy load of sandlewood on its back without ever knowing its value; all the donkey knows is the weight of the load!" Often we, too, may go through life, feeling only the weight of circumstances, unable to know the precious nature of life, simply because we may have a chronically negative attitude. Cultivating the attitude of gratitude can lead to self-appreciation and a more positive mental perception of life.

Cicero once said, *"There is no quality I would rather have, or be thought to have, than gratitude. It is not only the greatest virtue; it is the mother of all the rest."* The word "gratitude" actually comes from the Latin *gratis,* which means "pleasing" or "thankful." And, "-itude" implies a quality or state of mind. So, literally, gratitude is an attitude of pleasure and joy and thanksgiving.

A newspaper article of a few years ago described the Japanese and their remarkable sense of appreciation. A grower of chrysanthemums awaited a visit from the emperor, who was coming to enjoy his blossoms, of which there were hundreds in bloom. The grower selected one magnificent specimen, then cut down all the others, leaving this one perfect flower. The emperor arrived and sat for several hours quietly gazing at this beautiful flower, letting its beauty have its way with him. Can you imagine being so caught up in appreciation of one flower that everything else fades into the background?

The law of gratitude and thanksgiving is considered an aspect of the universe that deals with the flow of energy. That is, as you give out energy it returns to you. This works in almost every department of life. As one gives love, love can be magnetized toward you. It may come back in a different form, but it can return when it is given without manipulation. This law of life is about combining the expectations of the mind with the power of the heart. You create a "mold" for something good in your life, and with the power of gratitude, good things continue to be drawn to you as to a magnet.

"Ask and it shall be given you," says Matthew 7:7, 8. As you work in this state of thanksgiving you may find that money follows the same law. Have you ever noticed that when we hoard our resources, be it friendship, help, or affection, the flow of the energy circuits often stops? But as we give in love and appreciation, abundance flows to us.

This can also be true with the law of forgiveness. The lack of self-forgiveness in any single area of life can fester like a poison within and may bring anger, pain, and illness. Psychologists and sociologists often infer that the damage from childhood experiences can set patterns into motion that may follow an adult through life, being projected outward, unless forgiveness is attained.

"Dwell not on the past," Eileen Caddy writes in *God Spoke to Me.* *"From this moment onward you can be an entirely different person, filled with love and understanding, ready with an outstretched hand, uplifted and positive in every thought and deed."*

Have you ever wondered what it might be like if we couldn't appreciate the good things of life, such as spirituality, music, art, drama, literature, friends, dance, sports, nature, and all that makes life worth living? Have you ever considered the possibility that gratitude, thanksgiving, and the power of forgiving could be as creative as other works achieved in the world? Every person may not be great according to the terms of the world, but we can be grateful! Perhaps true appreciation is a fantastic kind of creativity that can lead to spiritual growth. Let us choose our lives with love and gratitude. Let us use the laws of thanksgiving and forgiving to bless ourselves and others and make our lives more complete.

"The measure of a man is not determined by his show of outward strength or the volume of his voice, or the thunder of his action. It is to be seen rather in terms of the strength of his inner self, in terms of the nature and depth of his commitments, the sincerity of his purpose and his willingness to continue 'growing up.'"
–Grade E. Poulard

"Staggering amounts
of manpower and
money are devoted
each year to discover-
ing, understanding,
and harnessing the
forces of nature. Almost
everyone agrees, how-
ever, that one of the
greatest forces on
earth is love. Should
churches finance
research into this ele-
mental force? Should
schools offer courses for
credit, with homework,
examinations and
grades? The real
wealth of a nation does
not come from mineral
resources, but from
what lies in the minds
and hearts of its
people. . . . This love
force can be harnessed
if we listen to our
hearts and minds, and
follow its laws of life
that lead to a joyous
existence."
–John M. Templeton,
Riches for the Mind
and Spirit.

"Love means to love
that which is unlov-
able, or it is no virtue
at all."
–Gilbert Keith
Chesterton

LAW 4

There is no difficulty that enough love will not conquer
—Emmet Fox

On his seventh birthday, Simon Evans adopted Sam, an eighteen-month-old gray cat, from the animal pound. Sam had been very badly treated for most of his life. His former master was a drug addict, whose unpredictable and often cruel behavior had obvious effects on the cat. This became obvious once Simon got him home. Sam acted nervous and frightened, and spent most of his time hiding behind the dishwasher.

Simon was very wise for his age and persisted with his new friend, being very gentle and loving. Gradually, this uncondi-tional love began to pay dividends. Sam stayed out from behind the dishwasher for longer periods of time. He was still jumpy and nervous, and would eat only with Simon guarding his back. But as the weeks progressed, the boy's love turned the little feline into a more trusting and responsive creature.

Constant, unconditional love can communicate itself to even the most badly abused. Love is one power that can eventually cut through the obstacles. Students in a class taught by a friend-ly and warm teacher who is understanding and patient respond far more positively than those in a class taught by a tyrant. Grades are better, and there is laughter, joy, and a willingness to learn. The same constancy of love and caring can work in almost every area of human relationships—between a supervisor and worker, an executive and manager, a politician and con-stituents, or wherever there is a relationship.

A little pamphlet entitled *The Golden Key,* by Emmet Fox, emphasizes that when we are in the midst of working with diffi-culties, it is important to *"stop thinking about the difficulty, what-ever it is, and think about God instead."* This awareness could have been the guidance for Chiara Lubich, the fifth winner of the Templeton Foundation Prize for Progress in Religion. When Chiara was a young teacher, she read in the Bible that Jesus commands us to love all others, including the unlovable, with his degree of passion. She realized that she had not yet met the test.

She then assembled a group of young people, and they discussed how they could learn to love as Jesus loved. Their discussions were successful. Chiara and the others began to express a much deeper form of love. The movement she founded is called *Focolare*, from the Italian word meaning "fireplace." She chose this name because her followers radiate love just as a fireplace radiates heat. Their purpose is to promote the unity of all peoples and unity between generations. By their experience of living the gospel, and through songs, music, and dance, they launch the message of love with wonderfully beneficial results.

Those connected with the Focolare movement live ordinary lives as employees of companies or members of secular societies and organizations. In that sense, they are so low profile as to be nearly invisible to the casual observer. But to the people who are in contact with them every day, they are likely to be a breath of fresh air, or an energizing influence in an otherwise drab environment.

Loving, kind, nurturing behavior is considered our natural state. We were born with these innate and positive social and moral gifts, but over the years we may have assumed many defense mechanisms that block our true selves. Love, of the type offered by Simon to Sam, can be a great healer. The pure and unconditional love of which Emmet Fox speaks is the type employed by young Simon to Sam, his cat, and it is this love that Teilhard de Chardin had in mind when he wrote, *"Someday, after we have mastered the winds, the waves, the tides and gravity, we shall harness the energies of Love. Then, for the second time in history, man will have discovered fire!"*

"Peace comes only from loving, from mutual self-sacrifice and self-forgetfulness. Few today have humility or wisdom enough to know the world's deep need of love."
—Horace W. B. Donegan

"We anticipate a time when the love of truth shall have come up to our love of liberty, and men shall be cordially tolerant and earnest believers both at once."
—Phillips Brooks

"To infinite ever present Love, all is Love, and there is no error, no sin, sickness, nor death."
—Mary Baker Eddy

LAW 5

Self-control leads to success
—John M. Templeton

Sometimes you may be tempted to think that life seems to be one big muddle and doesn't make any sense at all. Well, there may be a good reason for thinking that way! Let's look at an analogy. We could be very much like one who goes to the

"For want of
self-restraint, many
men are engaged all
their lives in fighting
with difficulties of their
own making and ren-
dering success impos-
sible by their own
cross-grained ungentle-
ness."
–Samuel Smiles

"For want of
self-restraint, many
men are engaged all
their lives in fighting
with difficulties of their
own making and ren-
dering success impos-
sible by their own
cross-grained ungentle-
ness."
–Samuel Smiles

"Than self-restraint
there is none better."
–Lao Tzu

theater after the curtain has gone up and the play has been in progress for some time. The latecomer has no knowledge of the beginning of the story, nor any idea of what the ending may be. The script may not make sense, and the person may feel confused regarding the plot of the story.

Similarly, in the drama of life, we may not always know or understand the plot. Sometimes the script seems pointless. We may fail to grasp the grand scope of the universal dramas in which we may be participating. At that point, there could be an attempt to blame the "director," the "producer," perhaps even the playwright, for the situation. However, in the universal drama of life, there are no "bit players." And there is no one to blame! Life can seem less of a muddle if we read the script correctly and become aware that we have unique qualities and can bring gifts to the "show" that no one else can give.

Perhaps you've heard the expression, *"the buck stops here."* This saying is cousin to another one that is quite commonly used in the United States, *"passing the buck."* When a person is accused of passing the buck, he may be said to be avoiding responsibility and passing it on to someone else. When someone says, "The buck stops here," he infers that he will handle the matter himself and take full responsibility for the outcome. Which one of these expressions do you find yourself in the habit of using?

You may know of someone at this moment in your life who may be rebelling against unfairness of one sort or another. Perhaps you, yourself, may be choosing to be antagonistic? Many people throughout history have chosen to rebel against their government or their society in order to bring about a higher purpose. Some may have understood that the cost of their rebellion could be their very lives; yet, they consented to pay that price. These people have often assisted in making great changes for the benefit of the people.

If a student chooses to rebel against his parents, for example, and as a result finds himself without a place to live or without any money for college, he must be willing to accept this as the cost of his rebellion. Likewise, it makes no sense to complain if our employer cuts our pay when we have failed to do the work we agreed to do. In that situation, we have received what we have deserved, and we should learn to accept it without protest.

One time at a county fair, a farmer exhibited a pumpkin grown in the exact shape of a two-gallon jug. "When it was no bigger than my thumb," he said, "I stuck it in the jug and just let it grow. When it filled the jug, it quit growing." What the glass jug did for the pumpkin, our thoughts do for our life. We may grow as big, as mature, and become as creative as the things we think about and believe in. But we stop growing at the limit of our thoughts.

One of the first things we need to do is to banish the thoughts that say the control of our life is held by another. We have a built-in control tower called the faculty of free will, and nothing can move into our mind unless we are willing to place the "stamp of approval" on the delivery.

The law of responsibility applies in every area of our lives. For example, if we choose to abuse our bodies with drugs or alcohol, it becomes imperative that we know the cost of this decision. We must ask ourselves if the drugs and alcohol are worth the cost in sickness and wasted time.

One may ask the question, "How can I take control over my life when I am faced with such inner turmoil and confusion and my problems are so large?" One thing we can do at once is take the same thought energy we have expressed in "how can I take control?" and turn it around into the thought, "I am one with the wisdom of God; I know what to do, and I do it!" One of the best ways to exhibit the self-control that leads to success is to know that faith, not fear; love, not hate; joy, not sorrow; peace, not tension; freedom, not bondage is the role we choose to play.

Whatever we choose in terms of our behavior in this life, we will be much better off if we can truly say, *The buck stops here. I am willing to pay the price for my decision. I am willing to accept the consequences of my actions.*

"The most intelligent men, like the strongest, find their happiness where others would find only disaster: in the labyrinth, in being hard with themselves and with others, in effort; their delight is self-mastery; in them asceticism becomes second nature, a necessity, an instinct."
—Friedrich W. Nietzsche

Spotlights!

1. If you are to succeed in life, it may become necessary to bring your methods of operation into an orderly process.
2. Being prepared is often considered the first step in the order of success.
3. Historically, success has often followed a series of failures.
4. It is important to study your failures, learn from them, and then make a new attempt to achieve your goal.
5. Success or failure, happiness or misery, in a situation are often a matter of perspective.
6. Gratitude enhances the open-hearted, genuine appreciation for what is wonderful in your life.
7. Be overwhelmingly grateful for all your blessings.
8. Love is a power that can eventually cut through obstacles.
9. Banish any thoughts that say control over your life is held by another.

"To rule self and subdue our passions is the more praiseworthy because so few know how to do it."
—Francesco Guicciardini

10. Seek to face even the most difficult situations with equanimity and grace.

Living the Law!

We often learn by stories that make an impact on our consciousness by presenting a parable with a simple, yet beautiful, analogy. The following story, taken from *Guidepost Treasury of Faith*,
is presented as this week's opportunity to observe the laws of
life in action. Read it, think about the analogies, and then write
in your journal the laws of life you see represented.

Cecil B. DeMille, the famous motion-picture producer, was a
man of great talents and keen insights. He liked to go off by
himself at times to think out a problem. One such time, when
he was faced with some vexing personal problems, he went out
in a canoe on a lake in the state of Maine.

After a while, the canoe floated onshore to a place where the
water was only a few inches deep. Looking down, DeMille saw
that the bottom of the lake was crowded with beetlelike bugs.
As he watched, one of the water beetles came to the surface of
the water and slowly crawled up the side of the canoe. Finally,
reaching the top, it grasped fast to the wood and died.

DeMille soon forgot the beetle, and his thoughts went back to
his own problem. Several hours later, he happened to notice the
beetle again and saw that, in the hot sun, its shell had become
very dry and brittle. As he watched, the shell slowly split open,
and there emerged from it a new form, a dragonfly, which took
to the air, its scintillating colors flashing in the sunlight.

That winged insect flew farther in an instant than the water
beetle had crawled in days. Then it circled back and swooped
down to the surface of the water. DeMille noticed its shadow on
the water. The water beetles below might have seen the shadow,
too, but now their erstwhile companion was in a world beyond
their comprehension. They were still living in their limited
world while their winged cousin had gained for himself all the
freedom between earth and sky.

Later, when DeMille told of this experience, he concluded
with a very penetrating question. *"Would the great Creator of the
universe,"* he asked, *"do that for a water beetle and not for a human
being?"*

Week Twenty-Four

LAW 1

Your thoughts are like boomerangs
—Eileen Caddy

The continent of Australia has given us many unusual things. Cut off from the rest of the world by vast ocean waters for millions of years, even animal life there has developed into strange forms—for example, the kangaroo and the platypus, the goose-billed, furbearing animal that lays eggs and feeds on earthworms.

Its primitive people have their own peculiar customs and inventions. Of the latter, the boomerang is the most famous. It is a "stick that comes back." When thrown by a skilled handler, a boomerang, which comes in a variety of different shapes, may sail far away and still return to the thrower's hands. Some Australian natives are so skilled in its use that they can kill birds and other game for food with the boomerang, or it returns to the thrower—*the one who sent it out.*

Our conduct, the way we act, may be similar to the boomerang—especially loving acts of kindness. For kindness has a way of returning to those who express it to others. You may have heard of the old fable of the lion and the mouse. One day a hungry lion caught a tiny mouse who pleaded for its life, saying, "I am such a tiny mouthful for you, O great lion. Besides, if you release me, some day I may be able to do you a return favor." The lion laughed at the mouse and let it go.

Sometime later, the lion was caught in a rope net trap which had been set by hunters. And who do you think gnawed the ropes apart and saved the lion? The tiny mouse, of course.

For many people, television and movie actors often become role models. And because many of these actor-heroes sometimes portray a rough and tough character in their roles, some

"Thoughts are the pinions of the soul, And carry far when they're set free. And if they're good, great good they'll do And benefit both you and me; So we should gladly do our share Of wonderful work and thinking, too; And spread the thoughts of brotherhood— Think thoughts that none have cause to rue."
—Alonzo Newton Benn

"*The world is good-natured to people who are good-natured.*"
—William Makepeace Thackeray

"*It is a singular fact that many men of action incline to the theory of fatalism, while the greater part of men of thought believe in divine providence.*"
—Honoré de Balzac

may think it meaningful to imitate those "stars" and not appear too softhearted. Yet, this notion can be childish and silly.

It is the truly brave, the truly great, the truly unafraid who often exhibit the greatest kindness in their activities. They are often rewarded with kindness from others and positive things happening to and for them. When a job opening, or an opportunity for advancement becomes available, or a chance to accompany a friend on a trip or to a special event, often the friend who has acted kindly towards others may receive the special invitation first. One author commented, "*disease and unhappiness come from the violation of the law of love. Our boomerangs of hate, resentment, and criticism, come back laden with sickness and sorrow.*"

That which returns to us may often be decreed by what we send out. The good Samaritan in the Bible narrative could have walked by the injured man lying beside the road and sincerely prayed that the man would somehow be helped. Instead, he did the practical thing by stopping to assist a fellow traveler and proved to be a noble instrument for God, binding the man's wounds and helping him to shelter.

When we look at the great leaders of our world, those in present and past times, the men and women who acted with sincere intent for the good of all and with kindness toward others often come to mind first. And when we look a little more closely at their lives, we find they were often people of action. The world could not know the talent of an artist who prays for ideas but does not put brush and paints to canvas. A composer who may be open for a beautiful melody to come to his receptive mind may not bring out much of that beauty if he fails to write down the notes of the music of his inspiration.

God has given his children so many blessings. We may draw forth from the reservoir of spirit as much as we choose to receive and use. In her book *The Game of Life and How to Play It*, Florence Scovel Shinn says, "*Every man has within himself a gold nugget; it is his consciousness of gold, of opulence, which brings riches into his life. In making his demands, man begins at his journey's end, that is, he declares he has already received. 'Before ye call I shall answer.'*" When we begin to realize and appreciate spiritually the wonders of God's creation, we become like an explorer who visits a new country filled with abundant, amazing, and beautiful opportunities. As we abide in this consciousness of love and kindness, we begin to pass along to others our love and our blessings in many ways. This energy may then return to us, like a boomerang. It might take years to return, and the blessings may come from a different direction, but the law of life of giving and receiving can do its precious work in our life.

LAW 2

You make yourself and others suffer just as much when you take offense as when you give offense
—Ken Keyes

Have you ever walked into a room where everyone stopped talking and you were certain they were talking about you? Or perhaps you looked over at a group of people sitting together and they started whispering? You may have been convinced they were saying something about your clothes or your manners. Whether we choose to *react* or *respond* to these situations can bring either suffering to those involved or peace and understanding.

If we react in a thin-skinned manner, the slightest remark could bring pain to the core of our being. We might see offenses where none were intended and possibly become paranoid in our thinking. Our hurt feelings may cause us to feel we're justified in accusing our accusers. If our reaction to the situation is to become quiet and introspective, we might sulk alone and nurse our self-pity. If we allow ourselves to become immersed in miserable isolation, we may fail to see that we are not the only ones suffering.

"How can the other person be suffering when I'm the one injured?" you may reason. When you fail to rise above your own paranoia and self-pity, you often cut yourself off from others. Should you perceive insults where none were intended, you might falsely accuse others, and, after a while, friends may choose the company of someone else. If you carry this type of negative energy within, your emotions could be like a destructive storm waiting to happen, and desired friendships may fail to materialize.

"An insult is either sustained or destroyed, not by the disposition of those who insult, but by the disposition of those who hear it."
—St. John Chrysostom

"Examine what is said, not him who speaks."
—Arabian proverb

"The longer we dwell on our misfortunes, the greater is their power to harm us."
—Voltaire

"Few things are more bitter than to feel bitter. A man's venom poisons himself more than his victim."
—Charles Buxton

The person who knows his own worth makes an effort to respond to situations in ways that can bring harmony and peace to his relationships. He demonstrates the ability to accept criticism for what it may be worth. Instead of allowing himself to be overcome with negative feelings, he often pauses to review what may have been said and look for the seeds of truth. When he finds those seeds, he can then apply them to the situation at hand and choose his behavior to support the highest and best good, based on his perception, for those involved. Paranoia does not become a problem, because his self-image remains strong.

The development of effective communications may be one of the most pressing needs in our world today. Our methods of communicating, one with another, may bring about pain and suffering as well as happiness and exhilaration. One question we might ask ourselves is, "How am I communicating? What kind of image am I projecting when I talk with another person, when working with someone, whether in family, social, community, or business life?" The person who is aware of his internal worth and value often understands how to respond to the people and situations in his life. He treats people with dignity and respect. He is kind and considerate. When faced with someone's bad behavior, he may carefully weigh the situation to see what can be gained in a positive way to his response. Sometimes no response may be the best response. The person who has a solid knowledge of his internal worth generally finds the appropriate words to speak.

A woman shared a story that when her son called the family from Vietnam, the call had to be relayed through an amateur radio station in Hawaii. The operator asked if they had ever talked by radio before, and they told him "No." "Well," the operator said, "you have to say what you want to say, then say 'Over,' and then listen. You see, you can't both talk at the same time."

When we talk to God, we may come to a point where we need to say "Over," and then listen. By the same token, in communicating with others, it is important to learn to say "Over," and listen. As we keep our lines of communication open between ourself and God and between ourself and other people, we can communicate through our true self—the self that is loving, caring, understanding, helpful, progressive, and creative. On this great journey through life, our relationships can be rewarding, for we can choose how we wish to respond to any given situation.

LAW 3

Little things mean a lot
—Edith Linderman

One morning during rush hour in a large metropolitan area, a large moving van became stuck in an underpass. The driver's estimate of the height of the opening was off by a few inches, and the truck could neither go forward nor backward. Within minutes the police arrived on the scene, and a large crowd of spectators gathered. Engineers were called to advise on the best way to free the truck. In the midst of all the noise and excitement, a small boy made his way to the truck driver.

"I can tell you how to get out, Mister," he said.

"Okay! Okay! So everybody's an expert around here!" growled the driver impatiently.

"Just let some air out of the tires," said the boy.

Only minutes later, that became the conclusion arrived at by the engineers. Those few inches made a difference and the truck moved smoothly through the underpass. The solution to the problem was such a little thing—so simple that it had been overlooked.

Sometimes the solutions to our problems can be like that; just one small thing. One small candle lit in the darkness can make a difference. Take friendship, for example. It's natural to want to be liked, to be popular with our friends and co-workers. But often some little thing may hold us back. We may feel stuck in present circumstances and find it difficult to move forward to make friends. Perhaps if we made one small change in some aspect of ourselves, we might become more interesting and more pleasant, and forming friendships might be easier.

Maybe we appear conceited to others, and too full of ourselves. Certainly a "nose-in-the-air" attitude can be a block in making friends. Most people do not enjoy spending time with an "I-I-I" sort of person. Learn to drop the egotistic "I" from your vocabulary, and you may find it easier to move through the underpass to friendship.

Could it be that we have some habits that turn friends off, possibly a tendency to be overly critical of others, making catty remarks behind their backs, or saying things in front of others that may be embarrassing?

"A little that makes for concord is better than a great deal that makes for division."
—Al-Jahiz, Islamic philosopher

"Those who cannot feel the littleness of great things in themselves are apt to overlook the greatness of little things in others."
—Kakuzo Okakura

"Life is made up of little things. It is very rarely that an occasion is offered for doing a great deal at once. True greatness consists in being great in little things."
—Charles Simmons

"Do little things now; so shall big things come to thee by and by asking to be done."
—Persian proverb

"Sometimes when I consider what tremendous consequences come from little things–a chance word, a tap on the shoulder, or a penny dropped on a news stand–I am tempted to think . . . there are no little things."
—Bruce Barton

Could it be that we lack a genuine interest in others? Do we honestly like to see our friends win honors and recognitions? Are we wholeheartedly happy when good fortune comes their way? Do we let our friends know we're sincerely interested in them and happy for them?

We need to look honestly within ourselves and do a personal check to see if some quality might be holding us back and keeping us from making the friendships we desire. To have a friend, it is often necessary to be willing to *be* a friend. So, let's take a moment to look at ourselves in the mirror honestly and do whatever may be necessary to become the friend we want to be. Enjoying the blessings of life could depend on "just one little thing."

An old stonemason was laying a rock wall, which, because it looked natural, was a thing of great beauty. The owner of the estate, while walking in his fields, noticed that the stonemason took as much care in placing the small stones as he did in placing the larger ones. So the estate owner walked over to the worker and said, "My friend, wouldn't the wall go up much faster if you used more of the larger stones?"

"Aye, most certainly, Sir," the old man replied. "But you see, I'm building for lasting beauty and strength, not for speed."

He thought for a moment and added, "Sir, these stones are like men. Many small ones are needed to support the fewer big ones and hold them in place. If you leave out the small stones, the big ones will have no support, and they will fall!"

So it often seems to be with life. It may be that the cohesion of many small and beautiful thoughts and feelings, built one upon one, can create the ordered and well-balanced life.

LAW 4

To be upset over what you don't have is to waste what you do have
—Ken Keyes

Many media commercials encourage us to believe that if we buy a certain product, we can be physically appealing, or popular, or successful. According to the commercial message, it may be easy to make friends and influence people if we simply do what we're told to do. It would be wonderful if that were true, but unfortunately life does not seem to work that way. What is inside of us can be much more important and influential than what is outside.

Many people today think that money and the things it can buy are the measures of success. But, in truth, things we can buy are simply things we can buy—no more, no less. They do not remake the real person in any way. We can change the color of our hair, the style of our clothes, and the car we drive, but these things may not be accurate indicators of the kind of person we are inside.

We may fret and fuss about "the way we are" and wish we were different. We may wish we were taller, shorter, thinner, more muscular, or athletic. We can wish, but nothing usually happens until we become willing to do what we can to make a change.

Before making a change of any sort, think about who you are and what you have now. You may be fine just as you are, even though you may admire someone who is different from you. The difference may be in looks, in abilities, in work, or in family or love relationships, and the difference can be very attractive to you. You may think how much better it would be to be like them than to be like yourself. But is it?

Each of us has things we would like to change, problems we might prefer not to have. Consider that the challenging situations in your life may not be as intense as the problems in the life of the person you would like to emulate. Ken Keyes says, *"To be upset over what you don't have is to waste what you do have."*

How important is the thing you might like to change? If it is very important, give it your attention! Change what you can, being aware of what may right for you. You don't like brown hair? How about red? You want to be more muscular? Lift weights! But do not expect the change to make you into a different person. Underneath the red hair or the muscles, you continue to be the "real" you.

Before attempting a drastic change, it can be a good idea to take an inventory of your assets. You may not be an accomplished athlete or an attractive redhead with a witty tongue, but you can work at developing what is already present. Take stock of your strengths, knowing almost everyone has some talent that others can appreciate. Think about the people you really enjoy being with. Is it because of the size of their biceps or the color

"Hundreds would never have known want if they had not at first known waste."
—Charles H. Spurgeon

"Nobody's problem is ideal. Nobody has things just as he would like them. The thing to do is to make a success with what material I have. It is sheer waste of time and soul-power to imagine what I would do if things were different. They are not different."
—Frank Crane, D.D.

of their hair? Or is it because you recognize a true friend in them and may be inspired to be a friend in return.

Your mind can be a useful tool for you to use in creating your ideal life, and there may be many ways in which to use this tool. Belief in yourself—in what you are—is often the beginning of positive change. Another effective way of bringing about changes in your life may be through employing the *law of reversibility*. In physics an expression of force is reversible. Sounds on audio or video tape can be played back to reproduce sounds and images. In this same sense, experiences may tend to cause feelings, and if the feelings can be reproduced in the absence of the experience, it may tend to bring the experience back for review in fact and expression. As example, through the use of mental imagery, you can experience the feeling of being in the center of a sea of substance and abundant good, which can tend to open the way to its flow into your life.

If you are unemployed, you may feel depressed and "out of it." To turn this experience around, the idea may be to get out of the "being-out-of-it" consciousness and move into the "with-it" feeling. You may pray for work and get another job. However, unless you reverse the patterns of consciousness that could have lead to the employment instability, you have only temporarily solved the problem.

It is not too late to turn your life around or to break patterns of negativity that may have manifested themselves. You can bring about change by getting into the kind of attitude and feeling that you might have if you were experiencing the desired conditions.

❖❖
❖

LAW 5

Honesty is the best policy
—Miguel de Cervantes

In African legend, an old chief needed to test the wisdom of the young man he had chosen to be his successor as tribal head. He asked the boy to prepare two meals for him. The first meal was to contain the very best ingredients life had to offer; the second meal would contain the worst.

On the appointed day, the chief sat down to his first meal and was served a delicious plate of sliced cow tongue with vegetables. The chief was delighted with the food, and upon finishing, asked the boy why he had chosen tongue.

"The tongue is one of the finest parts of our being," the young man replied. "It can speak wonderful words of truth that can help our people grow and prosper. The right words can give our people courage and bolster their integrity. Tongues can speak of love and harmony and hold our village together."

The chief was quite impressed and waited for his second meal with eager anticipation. On the appointed day the chief sat down to eat his second meal and found it to be identical to the first. When he finished the meal, he asked the boy why he had prepared the same food twice.

The young man answered, "The tongue can be the best part of us, but it can also be the worst. The tongue can speak words of anger and discouragement that can tear people down and rob them of hope. It can weave deceit; it can speak untruths that may cause disharmony. The tongue, more than any other weapon, could destroy our village life." The old chief listened closely and slowly nodded his head. He knew he had chosen the next leader wisely.

There may be times when it seems that one little lie—what is called a "little white lie"—might make life easier. "After all, who would know?" can be a rationalization we may use when considering taking the easy way. But deceptions can become linked to further, and more damaging, deceptions, which may cause our thoughts and actions to become confused and impure. This sad state of affairs may be clearly expressed in the saying, *"Oh, what a tangled web we weave, when first we practice to deceive."* Deceit often takes a terrible toll on our sense of integrity and self-worth.

Even if our lies are only "little white lies," the tangled web of dishonesty can choke the joy and spontaneity from our lives. We may try to convince ourselves they weren't really lies at all, but at some level of awareness, truth whispers to us that the path of honesty can be a peaceful policy.

A story is told that Frederick II, king of Prussia, arranged an inspection tour of the prison in Berlin. The prisoners fell on their knees before him, all vigorously protesting their innocence. One man alone remained silent and aloof. Frederick called to him, "You there. Why are you here?"

"The most casual student of history knows that, as a matter of fact, truth does not necessarily vanquish. What is more, truth can never win unless it is promulgated. Truth does not carry within itself an anti-toxin to falsehood. The cause of truth must be championed, and it must be championed dynamically."
–William F. Buckley, Jr., *God and Man at Yale*

"It is astonishing what force, purity, and wisdom it requires for a human being to keep clear of falsehoods."
–Margaret Fuller

"With lies you may go ahead in the world—but you can never go back."
–Russian proverb

"We must make the truth as simple, as persuasive, as impelling, and as interesting as the lie often seems to be. The truth can never enslave, it can never mesmerize. The truth is always within us. We do not awaken to an eternal fact, but to an eternal birthright which is the innermost of realities. Let us, then, recapture our thinking by getting back to first principles. When once we see the meaning of God, and man's relationship to Him, nothing can ever enslave our thinking again."
–Erwin D. Canham

"Armed robbery, Your Majesty."

"And are you guilty?"

"Yes, indeed, Your Majesty. I entirely deserve my punishment."

Frederick summoned the warder. "Guard, release this guilty wretch at once. I will not have him kept in this prison where he will corrupt all the fine innocent people who occupy it!"

Jordanian King Hussein, during a conference of Arab chiefs of state, commented, *"We should face reality and our past mistakes in an honest adult way. Boasting of glory does not make glory, and singing in the dark does not dispel fear."* And Fanny Brice, American comedian and singer, promoted honesty by saying, *"Let the world know you as you are, not as you think you should be, because sooner or later, if you are posing, you will forget the pose, and then where are you?"*

The ability to choose lies or truth can, indeed, be a powerful weapon, as the old African chief understood well in naming his successor. The young man did not sugarcoat the truth. He refused to make a white lie out of it. What we may not realize is that by choosing deceit we often end up hurting ourselves. There may be times when we might be tempted to believe that a lie could protect us. But the best protection—that which can assure us of a happy and successful life—is the knowledge that in every circumstance, as Cervantes said, *"Honesty is the best policy."*

Spotlights!

1. Our conduct may be similar to the boomerang: what we send out, we get back!
2. The truly great, brave, and unafraid often exhibit the greatest kindness in their activities.
3. Whether we choose to *react* or *respond* to a situation can bring either pain and suffering, or peace and understanding to those involved.
4. The development of effective communication is one of the most pressing needs in our world today.
5. Sometimes, the solution to a problem may be one simple thing!
6. Discover your strengths, and then use them to the best advantage.
7. What is inside of you can be more important and influential than what is outside!
8. Explore your talents carefully; choose your career with care; and make certain you love what you do.

9. Belief in yourself is often the beginning of positive change.
10. *"Honesty is the best policy."*–Cervantes

Living the Law!

If you were to visit a diamond mine, you most likely would see only ordinary earth, because diamonds in the rough state bear little resemblance to the brilliant, valuable gems that sparkle in the windows of jewelry stores or adorn someone's person. The diamonds must be found and cut and polished before they become the precious gems of great beauty and value.

If you were to analyze the chemical properties that compose a diamond, these properties may be worth little individually, but the slow hand of God, working with these elements, produces a work that is magnificent to behold.

Thus it can be with you. Through the steady molding and changing by God's laws of life, you have become what you presently are. God has made you a *gem of life.* Now, you have the opportunity to take this diamond in the rough and fashion it into a thing of beauty and brilliance.

Each person is the diamond cutter of his own life. You, alone, determine what facets you choose to cut upon your stone. Each action and reaction can determine its brilliance, value, and beauty. As the perfection of the cutting determines the value of the diamond, the value of your life is determined by what you cut into it. There are many facets that you might cut. Are you cutting the facets of love, understanding, integrity, tolerance, faithfulness, beauty, honesty, awareness, charity, humility, grati-tude, and hope into your diamond? Or are you cutting the facets of hate, greed, intolerance, inharmony, distrust, fear, lust, avarice, anger, unfaithfulness, and misunderstanding? It is well to ask yourself what facets you are cutting as you go through each life experience *for the diamond will reflect each facet as it is cut!*

A diamond is smoothed and polished by rubbing one dia-mond against another. This is what is happening to you in your daily relationships with your fellows. You are constantly rubbing the diamond of your life against the diamonds of their lives, and a smoothing and polishing process is taking place. Greater beauty and luster comes forth from your life as you allow your rough edges to be smoothed off as you come into contact and understanding with others. This is life. This may be why you were placed upon earth with fellow human beings, that you might each be buffed and smoothed and beautified, that your spiritual brilliance might be brought forth.

When the diamond is perfected, it is placed in a setting so that its beauty might be further enhanced and displayed. Your "setting" is the brotherhood and sisterhood of humanity. There you will give forth beauty and light as you become the perfect reflector of Divine Love (adapted from Indiana P.T.A. State Committee on Mental Health).

After reading the above, what do you see as "facets" to your personality, to your talents and abilities? What is the setting that you envision enhancing those talents and abilities? How do you see your "radiance" reflecting out into your world?

Week Twenty-Five

LAW 1

Your prayers can be answered by "yes," but also by "no," and by "alternatives"
—Ruth Stafford Peale

For several years, the power of positive thinking has offered avenues for making wonderful progress. Many ministers, philosophers, psychologists, and psychiatrists teach that the power of the mind may be one of the great tools with which men and women can overcome challenges and live life meaningfully and successfully. As with anything else, we can become more skillful in using this tool the more we work with it.

However, with so much emphasis on positive thinking, some people may have held the erroneous idea that saying "no" can be a negative statement. The truth is that there may be times when "no" may be the right answer, and we could be expressing ourselves as positive thinkers when we say "no" at these times.

This idea may also be applicable to our prayers, for our prayers can be answered by "yes," or by "no," or by "alternatives." Let's look at this possibility from three perspectives. First, when we become very still and ask for guidance, we may be directed, clearly and unmistakably, with a "yes" or "no," and often in a way that may not require us to make a decision. Perhaps on an inner level, our decision may have already been made! Even though the immediate result appears to be a failure, or a "no" answer to our prayer, the successful outcome can eventually be revealed by life itself.

Second, when we have done our work, when we have prayed and then followed our inner leading, we can release the outpicturing to God. We can continue about our daily routines with the assurance that the manifestation of the desires of our heart may progress according to God's perfect plan. This awareness often brings a wonderful feeling of peace and serenity as we trust the flow of divine order in our life.

"Prayer begins where human capacity ends."
—Marian Anderson

"So many religions, so many paths to reach the one and the same goal."
—Ramakrishna, Hindu mystic

"The path is one for all; the means to reach the Goal must vary with the Pilgrims."
—Tibetan precept

"Proper praying is like a man who wanders through a field gathering flowers—one by one, until they make a beautiful bouquet. In the same manner, a man must gather each letter, each syllable, to form them into words of prayer."
—Rabbi Nachman of Bratslav

Third, a most significant lesson for us may be to realize that no matter how impossible a situation seems, no matter how desperate the circumstances may appear, there can be a blessing for us and for others concerned. And that blessing may come in a manner we have not thought about! These can be alternative possibilities in answer to our prayers.

Sometimes, when our prayers seem to be unanswered in the manner we think they should, we may feel that we are not in tune with the timeless, unlimited universal Creator called God. But nothing can be separate from God. Everything that touches you, everything that touches each individual in the universe, is a part of God. Scripture tells us that every hair on our head is numbered. We become more aware of God's infinite love as we tune into the silent place within, the realm of God's creation. The divine ideas we receive from God in the silence are like mamma from heaven. They pour forth through us ever new, ever alive, ever beautiful, ever more wonderful every day.

In Revelation 3:20, Scripture tells us, *"Behold, I stand at the door and knock; if any one hears my voice and opens the door, I will come in to him."* Today, we can realize God's presence with us in our life as love, wisdom, health, and happiness. We can observe God's presence in the events of our life as we move safely and easily through many trials. Trials can help us grow and may come into our life to offer a greater realization of God's presence and power. As we maintain our trust and peace, our problems are more likely to be solved, and sometimes in a mysterious manner, and sometimes even at the eleventh hour!

It is a good idea to monitor the thoughts, ideas, and impressions that enter our field of awareness for there might be wonderful opportunities to learn. Rufus Matthew Jones taught that those who worship God can be empowered by the Spirit . . . and can be lifted up to new heights of joy and philanthropic achievement. He felt that the divine spirit in which we live can enable us to change from within so that things may be seen in a new light and love, for such awareness may become the spontaneous expression of a Spirit-filled soul.

When we allow ourselves to be Spirit-filled, we move into an area of trust and confidence that helps our prayers to be answered in whatever manner God's great wisdom expresses. It matters not whether the answer is "yes," "no," or an "alternative," because we can go forward in confidence, if our actions are in tune with the Infinite.

LAW 2

Healthy minds tend to cause healthy bodies, and vice versa
–John M. Templeton

Take a look at any of today's news-stand magazines, and chances are one of the leading articles may be on the management of stress or fitness. Stress is one of the leading causes of illness in today's world, and more and more doctors and scientists are discovering vital links between body, mind, and spirit.

Emotional stress can weaken the immune system, making the body more susceptible to disease. Dr. Ronald Grossarth-Maticek, a Yugoslavian oncologist, published the results of three studies, which were begun in the 1960s, that stirred international excitement. On the basis of interviews and questionnaires given to a large group of men and women, he assigned people to one of four personality types. By following their medical histories for ten to thirteen years, he found evidence that certain aspects of mental and emotional behavior may be linked to cancer or heart disease.

Disease-prone people often exhibit emotional dependence, passivity, and dissatisfaction with their key relationships. They tend to be unduly influenced by the way others respond to them and may find difficulty in improving unsatisfying relationships. They also often seem unable to take the initiative in forming or maintaining close emotional ties with others.

"There is no single cause for cancer," says psychiatrist Hans Eysenck. *"It is always a combination of risk factors such as smoking, drinking, genetic factors, environmental factors, psychosocial factors. We find that all these reinforce each other. But personality is one of the most important."*

Louise Hay, author of *Heal Your Body and Heal Yourself,* says, *"I find that resentment, criticism, guilt, and fear cause the most problems in ourselves and our lives. Whatever is happening 'out there' is only a mirror of our own inner thinking."*

Tests have shown that people who develop heart disease often have problems handling anger, either by failing to control it or by overcontrolling it so that their feelings may not be adequately expressed. Frustration, fear, and helplessness are also emotions that may create disease in the body.

"It is a religious duty to maintain health. Eating and drinking, sleeping and waking, and exercise are not outside the province of religion. They are as much a part of it as prayer and worship and daily work. They vitally affect temper and temperament and the way people look at the world. A healthy body makes for a healthy soul. It is essential to the finest and fullest kind of life.
–Robert J. McCracken

"The mind by its very nature, persistently tries to live forever, resisting age and attempting to give itself a form. . . . When a person passes his prime and his life begins to lose true vigor and charm, his mind starts functioning as if it were another form of life; it imitates what life does, eventually doing what life cannot do."
—Yukio Mishima

So, where do we look for an answer? The fast pace of today's world makes it hard to avoid some stresses. We might get on the freeway, and the intensity of the traffic may cause our blood pressure to go up. We often work hard to make a living and achieve the life-style we want, but that may mean putting in fifty to sixty hours or more a week at our work. We might take an evening class to improve our minds, but then we may sacrifice needed rest.

Unfortunately, there are no easy answers. It could be important, however, to have some strong stress relievers at the top of our list. First, take some time to be out of doors. Nature may be a good medicine in the world for many of us. The beauty of the earth can stimulate joy, thanksgiving, and healthy thoughts.

There have been many stories in recent years of terminally ill patients who may have literally laughed themselves back to health. Those men and women had nothing to lose when they began a systematic program of watching funny television shows and reading humorous books. Without realizing it, they may have stimulated a stronger immune system and helped to conquer, or at least stabilize, their disease.

Meditation can be a proven method of achieving a more relaxed state of consciousness. Recent findings reported by Stanford University researcher Kenneth Eppley review the effects of transcendental meditation. He reports that *"TM has consistently beneficial effects on anxiety."* The health benefits of meditation are recognized today by many physicians; it can lower blood pressure, slow the aging process, and help keep the emotions in balance. It is said that one insurance company now gives a discount to those who practice transcendental meditation.

Another proven method for reducing stress can be owning a pet. Long-range studies with the elderly and the ill many times report that having a dog or cat to stroke and love can increase happiness and extend longevity. Mother Teresa of Calcutta often provides animals as therapy for insane children.

In order to be happy, healthy, and stress-free, it is important to believe in yourself and your individual right to happiness and health. Louise Hay writes, *"Our subconscious mind accepts whatever we choose to believe. Life is very simple. What we give out, we get back. I believe that all of us are responsible for every experience in our lives, the best and the worst. Every thought we think is creating our future. Each one of us creates our experiences by the thoughts we think and the words we speak. If you accept a limiting belief, then it will become a truth for you. The universal power never judges or criticizes us. It only accepts us at our own value."*

LAW 3

Outward beauty is transient, but inner beauty lasting
—Seyyed Hossein Nasr

Almost every day, in a magazine or on television, we can see a handsome man and a lovely woman, often hugging, always smiling and, without exception, selling something. The message: *you can be just like us if you buy this product!* But, of course, in real life it may not be true that you can be beautiful, happy, loved, and popular just by using the right product, driving the right car, or wearing a fancy brand name.

Do you know someone who may buy all the "right" things and still not be liked? The beautiful, happy, lovable part of you comes from within. It remains unaffected by clothes, cars, or other outer considerations. Beauty is more than skin deep. It begins at the center of your spiritual being and is reflected in face, posture, mannerisms, speech, and tone of voice—all the qualities that are recognizable as uniquely you.

Beauty often lies in your attitude toward other people, perhaps toward those who may not be popular or cannot afford the "right" clothes, expensive cars, or other possessions. Can you see beyond the clothes or cars to the deeper identity of the person? Do you make an effort to get to know the being within? Mohandas K. Gandhi, the great Indian spiritual leader, commented on beauty, *"All truths, not merely ideas, but truthful faces, truthful pictures, or songs, are highly beautiful."* And Hsi K'ang, another Chinese philosopher said, *"To have reached two noble goals, selflessness and flawlessness, is the highest beauty."*

Many of the most influential people in history progressed from humble beginnings, without the material goods and advantages others may enjoy. They called upon the richness of their minds, the depths of their creativity, their high respect for the

"Beauty is the mysterious quality that shouts loudly, 'Ah, this experience is right for me now!' It is an abstract term that is difficult to define because it has a slightly different meaning for each of us. But I think we will agree that when we accept or experience beauty, we intuitively know that life contains much more than we can comprehend. Beauty always suggests something beyond—something greater than ourself.

"The search for beauty is a journey into the meaning of the universe. The experience of something beautiful is a reward for our perseverance. Beauty goes beyond the hardships of life and can make it all worthwhile. When beauty finally suffuses our soul, nothing else will take precedence, because we will have discovered the essence of God."
—Charles D. Lelly,
The Beautiful Way of Life

*"Beauty is the outward
form of truth."*
—Grace Aquilar

*"Beauty is the virtue of
the body, as virtue is
the beauty of the soul."*
—Ralph Waldo
Emerson

*"As truths not merely
ideas, but truthful
faces, truthful pictures
or songs, are highly
beautiful."*
—Mohandas K.
Gandhi

*"To have reached two
noble goals, selflessness
and flawlessness, is the
highest beauty."*
—Hsi K'ang, Chinese
philosopher

*"The test of beauty is
whether it can survive
close knowledge."*
—Marjorie Kinnan
Rawlings

worth of others, and expressed their willingness to stand apart
from the crowd. St. Francis of Assisi, Mahatma Gandhi, and
many others, who on the inside were truly beautiful and rich in
spirit, chose to live in poverty.

Back in the 300s (B.C.E.), Kungfutse asked the Chinese
philosopher Mencius, "We are all human beings. Why is it that
some are great men and some are small men?"

Mencius replied, "Those who attend to their greater selves
become great men, and those who attend to their smaller selves
become small men. "But we are all human beings," Kungfutse
continued to inquire. "Why is it that some people attend to
their greater selves and some attend to their smaller selves?"

Mencius replied, "When our sense of sight and hearing are
distracted by the things outside, without the participation of
thought, then the material things act upon the material senses
and lead them astray. That is the explanation. The function of
the mind is thinking: when you think, you keep your mind, and
when you don't think, you lose your mind. This is what heaven
has given to us. One who cultivates his higher self will find that
his lower self follows in accord. That is how to become a great
man."

The contributions of truly great people to our lives can be
measured not by the size of their bank accounts but by the
depth of their victorious spirits. They may not have been leaders in the popularity polls or included in the Forbes "400"
wealthy list, but their contributions often changed lives and can
continue to do so as long as truth is valued.

Often the people and styles we choose for patterns in life may
be no more than trivia questions in five or ten years. It is important to learn how you want to live your life, and one way to start
is by answering these questions in preparation for the years
ahead. Is what you are doing now going to be appropriate and
beneficial in thirty years—in fifty years? While being grateful for
your present life, what are you doing now to prepare for that
future time? What are you doing to leave the world a better
place than you found it? Queen Christina of Sweden felt, *"It is
necessary to try to surpass one's self always. This occupation ought to
last as long as life."*

Love yourself by being the very best you can possibly be. Treat
yourself as a close friend, one for whom you want only the best
of everything—respect, honor, solid relationships, and the joy of
a life well-lived. These things will be yours by living honorably,
at the highest level of which you are capable.

LAW 4

*A happy person is not a person
in a certain set of circumstances,
but rather a person with
a certain set of attitudes*
—Anonymous

"What do you see, the donut or the hole?" "Is your glass half full or half empty?" Your responses to these often-asked questions can tell you whether you're an optimist or a pessimist, as the following scenario illustrates.

Two young women work in the same office and receive the same salary. Anne often complains that she is underpaid. She feels she is asked to handle too many things for someone on her salary level. She arrives, dreading the day ahead, and leaves tired and discouraged. Mary, on the other hand, is happy to have a secure job and enough money to pay her bills, with some left for extras and savings. She looks at each task as a challenge and does her best to accomplish whatever is required of her. She arrives, looking forward to the day, and leaves, happy to be heading home to her family, feeling good about what she has accomplished. Not surprisingly, after an employee review, positive Mary received both a promotion and a salary increase. Negative Anne was let go.

The simple things in life can bring much joy if you look at them with a positive attitude. Flying a kite with a child can be fun, or it can be time wasted if you wish you were doing something else. Receiving a compliment from your employer, your teacher, or a family member for something you did especially well can make you feel wonderful. Facing each task with the determination to do the job to the very best of your ability can bring something positive to the actual doing and a solid feeling of accomplishment after the job is completed. You can get out of bed in the morning, ready to make the day an adventure. Or, you can stay under the covers as long as possible and rush to work with mind and body already weary and your thoughts possibly scrambled from hurrying. Your attitudes can help create your life's circumstances. Attitudes may make you either a happy or an unhappy person. Of course, the inevitabilities of life can

"'A happy man or woman,' said Robert Louis Stevenson, 'is a better thing to find than a five-pound note. He or she is a radiating focus of good will and their entrance into a room is as though another candle has been lighted.' Learn to be cheerful and you will come near being happy. Life's race can best be run with a light heart and a buoyant countenance. Cheerfulness will open a door when other keys fail."
—B.C. Forbes

"The happiest people are those who are too busy to notice whether they are or not."
—William Feather

"I must accept life unconditionally. Most people ask for happiness on condition. Happiness can only be felt if you don't set any condition."
—Arthur Rubenstein

"The happiness of this life depends less on what befalls you than the way in which you take it."
—Elbert Hubbard

bring problems, troubles, and sadness to us all, but if your glass remains half full, your attitudes can help you triumph over those times.

A part of the makeup of our personality has to do with the things we reinforce mentally and emotionally. If we have anxiety, we may reinforce that anxiety and get caught in a circle of negativism. And other habitual thoughts or feelings may begin to affect, and even seem to control, our life if we continually reinforce them. The same can be true from the positive perspective.

If you read *Alice in Wonderland,* you may recall the event when Alice became involved with the Queen of Hearts, and during a jury trial the Queen says, *"Off with her head!"* Alice is about to succumb to a fit of terror when, all of a sudden, she makes a discovery, *"Why, you're nothing but a pack of cards,"* she said. And with that remark, they all flew away! How many times do you possibly become involved in a situation that seems to be made real by fear or worry and realize you can cause these emotions to "fly away" by knowing their "nothingness" to control your life?

A man once stopped in the train aisle before two fellow passengers who were playing chess. One of the contestants, a teenager, was about to concede defeat when the man in the aisle remarked that there was one more move. The youth invited the man to take his place at the chessboard. Taking over, the man made one deft move that changed the entire complexion of the game. Soon he won the game, although minutes before the youth would have given up. The man remarked that, in chess, there may not always be one more move, but in life, when our best efforts have seemed to fail to bring the happiness we desire, there is always one more move. This is the move where we turn to God for inspiration, the indwelling presence to whom all things may be made possible.

Several years later the young chess player was an infantryman cut off from his company and alone in a foxhole. Enemy patrols were closing in on him, and all seemed lost. Suddenly, he recalled the chess game and the remark about "one more move." He prayed, affirming the presence and activity of God, and consciously let go in faith. Then, he felt a surprising inspiration to call to his adversaries and demand that they surrender and save themselves. He did so, with an authority of voice that even surprised himself. Every one of them lay down their arms and became his prisoner. His one more move, letting God take over, saved several lives. His set of circumstances may not have been happy ones, but his set of attitudes saved the day!

LAW 5

Help yourself by helping others
—John M. Templeton

Select with care the area of your livelihood and make certain you love what you do. When you love your work and hold the attitude that what you do may be done on behalf of others, your life and your work can take on special meaning and deep significance. As one who gives joyously and thankfully; as one who is ever ready to assist another, you may be much more likely to be successful than the person who works simply to earn a living.

The more one works and plants, the more one can harvest. The more good one can do, the more success one can achieve. Lou Rawls, the actor and singer, talked about loving his work. He said, *"Singing has been my life, and I love to sing. Sure, I get paid for singing, and I wouldn't put that down. But when I put all that is in me into a song, and those who listen let me know we're together, that's really living. I would suggest to anyone that if you don't love what you're doing, find something you love to do and do it—especially if it makes you feel that you and other people are together. That's been my life, and I thank God for it."* Why is it that by giving ourself to others in loving service, we may bring a sense of integration into our life that nothing in all our knowledge and techniques for living ever seems to bring? Why do we find inner wholeness and well-being from acts of assistance and love? Good questions!

Service to others is a creative process that releases energy which can manifest itself in many ways and bring deeper meaning into your life. When we love deeply enough, coupled with the desire to be helpful to those around us and to our world, we often find fulfillment and true closeness with others that can satisfy our desire to reach the heart of them. On the other hand, when we do not love enough to enter into this wholesome, freeing union with others, we may try to solve our basic

"Tse-king asked, saying, 'Is there one word which may serve as a rule of practice for all one's life?' The Master said, 'Is not reciprocity such a word?'"
—Confucius

"My humanity is bound up in yours, for we can only be human together."
—Desmond Tutu

"We cannot be independent of the kindly give and take spirit of cooperation."
—Roderick Stevens

"The very core of peace and love is imagination. All altruism springs from putting yourself in the other person's place."
—Harry Emerson Fosdick

"If we could all agree that the world belongs to God, we would see the world as a cooperative fellowship. We of the human race are so bound together and so interdependent—that it behooves us all to live for the good of the whole."
—W. Earl Waldrop, D.D.

problem of separation by seeking power over others. We may tend to live by comparison, by being overly competitive, or by feeling better or more important than others. And these attitudes do not move us toward our goals of unity, love, and helpfulness.

When we "give ourself away" our life often has greater meaning, and we may find an expanding joy in what is accomplished. Certainly, the results of our efforts often seem to be more long lasting!

In Acts 3:6, the apostle Peter is speaking to a lame man. He said, *"I have no silver and gold, but I give you what I have. . . ."* Reflection on these words can teach us to be sensitive to the needs of the people around us. May we desire to give what is ours to give, trusting that whatever we give can be a real blessing.

I can give of my time.

I can give my love, support, and understanding.

I can give of patience and compassion.

I can share the gift of joy and laughter.

I can offer encouragement and companionship.

Perhaps, most importantly, I can give my prayers and see the Spirit of God supplying the needed comfort—uplifting, upholding, and sustaining.

We can give our assistance cheerfully, abundantly, and from a heart overflowing with God's love.

Perhaps reading the Parable of the Talents, found in Matthew 25:14-29, can help us become aware that God gives talents to each of us. And God may hand those talents out in uneven measure. But, although God may have given more talents to one person than another, everyone is expected to use those they have to the utmost, no matter how great or meager they might be, and to use them in the service of others. The point is simply this: God is responsible for what inborn talents you possess. From there on, the responsibility is yours. It is up to you to develop them as far and as deeply as they may go. And the people who use their talents completely—and most of all to help and love others less fortunate—will be rewarded and find success.

Success takes many forms; wealth and fame are only one kind of success. Perhaps you have a talent to help those who seem to have no talent. Every act of helping is a way of saying "Yes!" to life.

Spotlights!

1. Ask yourself, Am I doing or preparing for the things that I am best qualified to do? Do I love what I am doing?

2. Share your talents in ways that truly benefit others, particularly those less fortunate. (Suggested reading, Matthew 25:14–29).

3. Emotional stress and the seven deadly sins listed by St. Paul may weaken the immune system, making the body more susceptible to disease.

4. The health benefits of meditation or prayer are now recognized by many physicians.

5. The beautiful, happy, lovable part of you comes from within and can always be created by you.

6. Love yourself by being the best you can possibly be.

7. The simple things in life can bring much joy if you look at them with a positive attitude.

8. Use your material gains in ways that benefit others, and gain joy by giving away more than you spend on yourself.

9. Listen to people you admire and learn from them.

10. Use common sense plus your creative imagination.

Living the Law!

In his book *You'll See It When You Believe It*, Dr. Wayne Dyer offers some interesting and helpful suggestions for personal transformation. A synopsis of these suggestions is shared here for your reflection.

* Practice thinking about yourself and others in formless ways. Take a few moments each day to evaluate yourself . . . in terms of pure thought and feeling. Watch yourself acting and interacting. . . . Do not criticize or judge, simply note how your form is behaving and how it is feeling.

* Use the observer exercise (mentioned above) with other people. Notice how they may destroy their potential for happiness and success because they identify exclusively with their forms.

* Make an effort to go beyond your comfort zone on a regular basis. Listen to the real you inside who is encouraging you to transcend yourself.

* Make an effort to cease labeling yourself as a means of identifying who you are as a human being.

* Begin to view your mind, your nonform side, as new and miraculous. Know that your mind is capable of transcending your form and that your body is in a larger part controlled by your mind.

* Work each day to clear yourself of the two factors that do the most to inhibit your personal transformation: negativity and judgment.
* Examine how you treat the physical or visible you.
* Allow yourself time to meditate quietly by yourself. Meditation is a powerful tool, and it is as simple as breathing. You should choose your own style of meditation.
* Above all else, be kind and understanding of yourself. Be especially kind to yourself if you behave in a way you dislike. Talk kindly to yourself. Be patient with yourself when you find it difficult to be a "holy" person. . . . Forgive yourself.

Week Twenty-Six

L AW 1

You create your own reality
—Jane Roberts

Do you believe that "reality" may be something outside of your-self? We often hear reference made to the "real world out there." To be sure, there can be a world beyond our own personal reality—an outer world that may have an appearance and distinction of its own. However, another world, an inner one, may be much more real. This is the place where your beliefs, thoughts, and feelings reside. This inner world may be less tangible and less solid than the outer world, yet this is the true place of livingness. Your happiness, peace of mind, and enjoyment of work, friends, and loved ones often depends more on this inner world than on the outer one.

Some would say that the world within can be simply a reflection of the outer world—that the outer world presents the true reality, whereas personal perceptions, thoughts, and feelings can be the effect of outer conditions. (After all, when we're unhappy, don't we often try to change the external conditions of our lives first?) Yet, it may be possible that our inner world can quite capably reflect a strength that is independent of outer circumstances.

Two people could have similar *external* circumstances and have very different *internal* experiences. Suppose, for example, two men were given the task of speaking before a large audience. Mr. Smith may enjoy speaking in public, and the experience can be a most pleasant one for him. Mr. Jones, on the other hand, may be extremely fearful of public speaking and find the experience a harrowing test of willpower. Both men share a similar reality, but their internal realities may be far removed from each other. To cite another example, two youngsters may jump into a pool of deep water. While one enjoys a

*"Fetch me the fruit of
   the banyan tree.
Here is one, sir.
Break it. . . . What do
   you see?
Nothing, sir.
My son, what you do
   not perceive is the
   essence,
and in that essence the
   mighty banyan tree
   exists.
That is the true, that
   is the self,
And you are that self."
—Upanishads*

"*The grand difficulty is so to feel the reality of both worlds as to give each its due place in our thoughts and feelings–to keep our mind's eye, and our heart's eye ever fixed on the land of Promise without looking away from the road along which we are to travel toward it.*"
—Julius C. Hare

"*Circumstances are so complicated, thought is so deeply rooted, and the conditions of happiness vary so vastly with individuals that a man's entire soul-condition (although it may be known to himself) cannot be judged by another from the external aspect of his life alone.*"
—James Allen

wonderful swim, the other may be terrified of drowning. The pool of water is the same, but the experience of the two individuals may be vastly different.

A dozen people could carefully study a lovely panoramic view and then draw or paint a picture of it, and the result may reveal a dozen different pictures with striking differences of detail. Each person is seeing the scene that appears before him with eyes that may be basically the same in physical anatomical structure. However, each person can bring a preconditioning of consciousness that may be unique to him. An unhappy person may see things that tend to justify his unhappiness. The pessimist may see discouraging signs wherever he looks. The positive person usually seeks to find the good in a situation. And the honest person can find the truth in the situation at hand and create his own reality.

An interesting story comes out of the lore of the island of Java. A young man spied a beautiful girl on the highroad and followed her for a mile. Finally, she turned and demanded, "Why do you dog my footsteps?"

He declared feverishly, "Because you are the loveliest thing I have ever seen, and I have fallen madly in love with you at sight. Be mine!"

The girl replied, "But you have merely to look behind you to see my younger sister, who is ten times more beautiful that I am."

The gallant swain wheeled about, and his gaze fell on as homely a girl as could be found in Java. "What mockery is this?" he demanded of the girl. "You lied to me!" "So did you," she replied. "If you were so madly in love with me, why did you turn around?"

We may have lived many years believing that experiencing happiness and peace of mind can result from changing our outer world. Happiness is an inside job. Outer changes alone may not make us happy.

It may help to remember that we have far more control over our inner world than our outer world. Not to say that changing our inner world can be necessarily easy. We may have developed thinking and feeling patterns or belief systems that are deeply ingrained. Change may not always be easy, but it can be accomplished. Examining our beliefs and attitudes and observing our thoughts and feelings can be a place to begin. Change often starts to happen when we recognize false beliefs and make an effort to bring them in line with reality; when we recognize negative thoughts and choose not to listen to them; and when we recognize negative feelings and choose to give them no power over us. We have the power to create our own reality by choosing thoughts and beliefs that are positive and true. So, in truth, you do create your own reality, your inner reality, the only reality in which you truly live.

We are essentially spiritual beings. Our world is essentially a spiritual world, and the underlying controlling forces may be identified as spiritual laws. When we "fall in love" with this spiritual essence or establish our spiritual unity with it, when we begin to recognize that this is a good world and that the people in it have innate goodness within, then perhaps we may be seeing with the "eyes of spirit." We can see goodness in all people, and we can draw goodness from them.

"To be or not to be is not a question of compromise. Either you be, or you don't be."
—Golda Meir

LAW 2

A task takes as long as there is time to do it
—Parkinson's Law

Put your imagination to work for a moment. It is the week before school vacation. The thought of sunny days filled with time for vacation and relaxation is so sweet you can almost taste it. Another school year will soon be completed. It's been a long time coming, but summer is almost here. Only three more finals and a term paper in social studies and your work is done. Moving toward completion of what seems like endless study and writing papers in a small amount of time may bring some feelings of pressure. Yet this deadline (or targeted date), which may seem to threaten certain doom if not met, can have the power to save you from what is often called "the worst enemy you can have when it comes to accomplishing great things and seemingly impossible projects"—yourself!

A deadline has been said to "be to a task what a corral is to a herd of wild horses." It surrounds untamed impressions, thoughts, and feelings with a clear boundary that can allow your ideas to formulate as an attainable goal. Many people find it dif-

"All that I have accomplished, or expect or hope to accomplish, has been and will be by that plodding, patient, persevering process of accretion which builds the ant heap particle by particle, thought by thought, fact by fact."
—Elihu Burritt

"It is asked, how can the laboring man find time for self-culture? I answer, that an earnest purpose finds time, or makes it. It seizes on spare moments, and turns fragments to golden account. A man who follows his calling with industry and spirit, and uses his earnings economically, will always have some portion of the day at command. And it is astonishing how fruitful of improvement a short season becomes, when eagerly seized and faithfully used. It has often been observed that those who have the most time at their disposal profit by it the least. A single hour in the day, steadily given to the study of some interesting subject, brings unexpected accumulations of knowledge."
—William Ellery Channing

ficult to effectively begin a project until they can see an end to it, a point of fulfillment. A goal without some kind of deadline is a goal most likely not attained. A deadline may also serve as an inspiration to complete a project, as exampled in Publilius Syrus's statement, *"Do not turn back when you are just at the goal."* Objectives not accomplished can lead to frustration and a sense of failure. A deadline or target date can help you know when your goal may be attained.

Without a deadline, you could exhaust yourself, galloping around in an open, often bleak, desert of unspecific thoughts and nonproductive activity. A deadline, properly developed, can actually be a lifeline—like a lasso that can save you from wandering the plains of an endeavor that may seem without a beginning or an end. As a lifeline, a deadline draws you into alignment with your purpose and allows you to tame your time, talent, and resources, and apply them where they may be most useful.

A deadline concentrates time into an area of manageable interest. If you were asked to look in the flame of a candle for five minutes you could probably do this with little or no difficulty; but a request to look into a flame for an extended or unspecified length of time might seem so unreasonable you would not want to do it at all.

A deadline also invites you to concentrate your energies on those interests that have greater value to you. Just as a spoonful of honey can sweeten a cup of tea more readily than it would a lake, our efforts need to be concentrated in the direction of our priorities in order to be more effective. If you want to avoid summer school this year, it may be clear that research and writing need to take precedence in the next week, or other short period of time. To divert your attention to other interests could dilute your efforts and blur the sharp focus your purpose must have right now. However, in a week, your deadline will have passed, and you can have the satisfaction of having completed something extremely worthwhile and be free to enjoy the next project you undertake.

Time-management experts say the best deadlines are the ones you choose for yourself. Setting reasonable deadlines often results in a more effective use of your time. However, when other people impose deadlines on you, you may sometimes waste much valuable time in resisting and resenting them. When you are tempted to feel that others' deadlines are arbitrary or unfair, you can choose them for yourself anyway. As you meet the challenge of doing the best you can with what you have, your vigorous cooperation can reward you with a sense of great vitality and feeling of accomplishment. Auguste Comte remarked, *"Love our principle, order our foundation, progress our goal."*

What would you like to achieve in your lifetime? How do you visualize making a difference in this world? Whatever large or small ambition you may have, begin today to create goals that suit your purpose, and set deadlines or target dates for those goals. Remember, deadlines can be lifelines that define your success!

LAW 3

Often, a pat on the back works better than a kick in the pants
—William Juneau

In the early American days of the great cattle drives from the state of Texas to the railhead, the cook played one of the key roles on the drive. If things didn't go right and the cook couldn't do his job, everybody suffered! During the cattle drive, the cook usually supervised one or two well-stocked wagons that were pulled by mules. Some say mules are generally stronger than horses and require less food and water.

A story is told about an old cook who was teaching his new helper the tricks of the trade. He began with instructions on how to handle the mules. Calling the helper over to where the mules were tied, the cook picked up a piece of firewood and hit the mule a terrific blow between the eyes. The young helper was upset and incredulous. "Why did you do that?" he asked. The old cook answered, "The first thing you do is get their attention."

That's the way some people often go about dealing with their fellow humans, browbeating them into submission before they attempt to get them to accomplish something. It doesn't work with humans; and it really doesn't really work with mules either!

In the late 1960s and early 1970s, the Texas Education

"Criticism should not be querulous and wasting, all knife and root pulling; but guiding, instructive, inspiring."
—Ralph Waldo Emerson

"Consider carefully before you say a hard word to a man, but never let a chance to say a good one go by."
—George Horace Lorimer

"The praises of others may be of use in teaching us not what we are, but what we ought to be."
—Augustus Hare

"Praise is sometimes a good thing for the diffident and despondent. It teaches them properly to rely on the kindness of others."
—Letitia Landon

Agency in the United States began a program of hiring experienced people from industry to teach vocational education. The theory was that it would be easier and faster than teaching trades to certified teachers. This program became remarkably successful, and some of these industry people brought exciting and innovative teaching methods to the students.

One such person was an experienced home builder and cabinet maker who undertook to teach a class in construction trades. His supervisor told him that his class would be composed of underachievers and slow learners and that too much should not be expected of them. The supervisor also told him that he could not be friends with the students and still receive their respect; they would not bother to learn from someone who let them "get too close."

That was not this man's way of doing things. He could not be distant and formal with the students. He enforced discipline when needed, but his years of experience had taught him that people often respond to positive treatment in a positive way and to negative treatment in a negative way. He knew he could find something positive about every effort the students made; just making the effort itself was a positive action. He pointed out the things the students did right and suggested ways they could improve their skills. A lot more work was accomplished by being their friend.

The last year he taught the class, nine of the twenty-seven students in the class advanced to the state finals in skills competition, and four of those received first place blue ribbons. Most of those students found good jobs after graduation. Their self-confidence had been improved by their successes in the class, and they remembered the teacher as a friend who cared.

A Thessalian brought an exceptionally beautiful horse, named Bucephalus, to the Macedonian court, offering to sell it to King Philip. However, when the royal grooms tried to test its paces it proved wild and unmanageable. The young Alexander asked his father for permission to try his skill. Philip reluctantly agreed, saying that if the prince failed to ride Bucephalus he was to pay his father a forfeit equal to its price. Alexander walked quickly to the horse's head and turned it to face into the sun, for he had noticed that the horse's own shadow was upsetting it. He calmed the horse, then mounted it, and Bucephalus obediently showed off his paces.

The court, which had feared for the prince's safety, broke into loud applause. Philip was overjoyed. He kissed his son, saying,

"Seek another kingdom that may be worthy of your abilities, for Macedonia is too small for you."

In almost all cases, a pat on the back indeed accomplishes more than a kick in the pants.

LAW 4

Give credit and help to all who have helped you
—John M. Templeton

Edward is the president of a large corporation, and he worked hard to reach that position. He speaks as though he has reached a final destination and often refers to himself as "a success." It is unfortunate that he doesn't realize success is a journey, not a destination. There can still be many more steps to be taken in his life. His journey is not over. Even more unfortunate, Edward doesn't see that successful people work around him, many of whom contributed to his own success.

Millie had to leave school at age sixteen when her mother became seriously ill. But Millie attended night school when her father was home, and after earning a high school diploma continued on in night classes at a business school. After her mother died, Millie secured a position in a secretarial pool. She began taking some night classes again, with the hope of becoming a personal secretary. She became engaged to a nice young man and looked at the possibility of giving a few years to being a full-time wife and mother before she began a career in her chosen field. Millie is on the journey called success.

As a high school junior and senior, Bill worked after school as a stock boy in a men's shoe store. When he graduated, Bill went to work full time, at first as a stocker, then as a salesman. He later learned how to measure for made-to-order shoes, and now he's being groomed to become the manager of a second store. Bill, too, is on the path of success.

How we make a living, while most certainly an important part of our existence, does not represent the whole of what success

"A man can make what he wants of himself if he truly believes that he must be ready for hard work and many heartbreaks along the way."
—Thurgood Marshall

"As in the case in all branches of art, success depends in a very large measure upon individual initiative and exertion, and cannot be achieved except by dint of hard work."
—Anna Pavlova

truly is or who we may be. A successful life also involves our personal relationships, our family experiences, and our spiritual involvement. Happiness is a part of success, but the ability to handle the disappointments, the illnesses, or whatever problems life brings to us, and to handle them with dignity and fortitude, is also a part of success. Success can unfold as a lifelong journey. We do not come to a certain destination point marked "success" and then sit on it smugly, without concern for further events. People who live each day to the fullest, with the excitement and challenges those twenty-four hours can bring, become successful people. They don't need to have an important position or make a great deal of money or be famous. Success may be described as making the journey called life as deep and profound an experience as possible. It is a giving not a taking experience.

Each person's life can be infinitely complex. It is said that "within each of us is the life we have chosen and the lives we might have led." Our thoughts and dreams of what we might have been or might have done live within us. The little boy may wish one day to be a fireman. Another day, a policeman. For a few weeks, he may be certain he's going to be a doctor. As he matures, he begins to sort through his dreams and starts to make choices. He moves forward on his journey. And he is a success because he has learned to choose and meditate and search. He realizes that he might change his mind, that he might make mistakes, and that things may not always work out according to his plans and hopes. But this is all right because he can handle change and learn from it.

There may be many life possibilities for each one of us. Success is finding out which of these possibilities may be most meaningful. Through choices, we select our values, our work, the person we marry, how we raise our children, the church we attend, and the food we eat. Some choices can change or direct our future; others may be short lived. How we choose and what we do with our choices indicate the road signs of our journey and, if we follow the right road, success can be with us through good times and bad. Success is indeed a journey. It is not a destination, for a destination means the journey is over.

When others have played a meaningful role in our achievements, it is important to acknowledge their contribution. During the rehearsals for the movie *Jumbo*, Charles Lederer, an American playwright and director, watched comedian Jimmy Durante trying to spirit the elephant past the sheriff, who was trying to serve a writ of attachment. "You could have the sheriff say, 'Where are you going with that elephant?'" suggested Lederer, "and then you could have Jimmy say, 'What elephant?'" The suggestion was taken up and provided the biggest laugh in the show. Ben Hecht and Charles MacArthur, the writers, acknowledged their friend's contribution with the following note in the program: "Joke by Charles Lederer!"

Another beautiful expression of acknowledging the help we receive is this story. It was the late 1800s and an important member of the British Parliament was hurrying through the rain and fog of the bleak Scottish countryside to deliver a crucial speech. Still miles from his destination, his carriage was forced off the road, its wheels plunging axle deep in mud. Try as they might, the horse and driver could not move the carriage. So important was his speech that even the aristocratic Englishman, in his formal attire, gave a hand. But it was no use. The carriage would not budge.

A young Scottish farm boy happened to be driving a team of horses past the distraught parliamentarian and volunteered to help pull the carriage loose. After much effort and considerable exertion, the carriage was finally pulled free. When the boy steadfastly refused to take any money for his help or for his clothes, which were torn and dirty from the ordeal, the Englishman asked him what he wanted to be when he grew up.

"A doctor, sir. I want to be a doctor," was the reply. The gentleman was so impressed with the boy and so grateful for his kindness that he said, "Well, I want to help." And surely enough, he kept his word. Through his generosity, he made it possible for the young lad to attend the university.

More than fifty years later, Winston Churchill became dangerously ill with pneumonia while in Morocco. His life was saved by a new wonder drug called penicillin, which had been discovered a few years earlier by a Scottish-born physician, Sir Alexander Fleming.

Fleming was the farm boy who helped the member of Parliament on that dark and rainy night in Scotland half a century before. The member of Parliament? None other than Winston Churchill's father, Randolph!

"From success to failure is one step. From failure to success is a long road."
—Yiddish proverb

LAW 5

Thoughts can crystallize into habit, and habit solidifies into circumstance
—Anonymous

A gentleman we can call Mr. Smith was the richest man in the small town in Tennessee where he had lived all of his life. He was not rich in money. He and his wife lived comfortably but carefully on social security and a small pension check. The wealth Mr. Smith enjoyed was quite different from the financial kind.

The days did not seem long enough for him to do the many things he enjoyed. He began each day by filling the feeders and water container for the birds. A neighbor once asked him why he bought so much bird seed on a fixed income. He commented that he was well paid for the bird seed. The birds sat on the white picket fence, the porch rail, tree limbs and bushes, and they chirped, giving the Smiths a world filled with music. In this way, Mr. Smith received much more than he gave. His positive thoughts of loving life crystallized into the habit of enjoying each day's activities and solidified into the beauty and sound in his world.

Each weekday morning, Mr. Smith walked two blocks to the handsome old Victorian house that housed SARC—The Seaton Association for Retarded Citizens—where he worked with the children. They were unable to attend regular school, but the center assisted each child toward reaching his potential. Although Mr. Smith was not a trained teacher, there was much he could do. With endless patience he helped little ones learn to tie a shoe or eat with a fork and spoon. Friends tried to tell the retired man that with his talent for this work he could certainly find a part-time paying position. But Mr. Smith was paid a huge salary for his work with these youngsters—a tearful "thank you" from a mother and father, a bear hug from a tot overjoyed at successfully doing something on his very own, or a "God bless you" from one of the paid workers. Mr. Smith gave much to the children, but he received abundant personal blessings in return.

While Mr. Smith was at the center, Mrs. Smith worked in the chamber of commerce office, which helped the business and

"Explosions of temper, emotional cyclones, and needless fear and panic over disease or misfortune that seldom materialize, are simply bad habits. By proper ventilation and illumination of the mind it is possible to cultivate tolerance, praise and real courage."
—Elie Metchnikoff

professional people in town. Money was not plentiful, so the office had only two regular people, the director and the office manager/secretary. Mrs. Smith gladly helped with mailings, copying, telephoning, filling the counter rack with town maps and postcards and other free literature. She even watered the plants. Mrs. Smith loved the office, because she was right in the middle of what was going on. She gave a lot of herself in that office, but she received so much back that it literally filled her heart with joy.

The couple also gave time to their children and to their grandchildren, and the Smith's lifestyle was so inspirational it was reflected in their children. Their son was an accountant, who spent every Saturday morning at a senior center in his city helping seniors handle their money situations. No charge! His wife was a volunteer at the grade school their son attended. And the little boy was raising a puppy for the seeing-eye-dog group. Their daughter assisted five mornings a week at the town's small hospital. Her husband, an insurance executive, was a member of the finance board at his church and worked many hours in this role. Their children were members of a youth group that visited a nursing home on Saturday mornings, listening, writing letters, combing hair, taking someone for a ride outside in a wheelchair. They gave and they gave. And received and received!

Every thought we allow into our mind can affect the thoughts, feelings, and actions we express. If we hold negative thoughts, our actions are likely going to be negative. In turn, negative habits might develop, and negative results may be returned to us. On the other hand, positive thoughts aid in developing positive habits and positive results, and life can become a happy, motivating adventure in which we see ourselves and others in the true light of what we really are—a wonderful, magical, mysterious expression of life. As long as our thoughts remain positive and are grounded in accomplishing the goal in front of us, the progress we make on the path of life can be steady and rewarding. Thoughts can crystallize into habits, and habits can solidify into circumstances in our life.

Overcoming bad habits may not seem so difficult if we remember that we are not the habit, rather the operator making choices that often result from our mental patterns. It is important to remember that a habit is not something we *are*, but something we *do*. Or, as one writer expressed it: *"Habits are simply the behavioral extensions of well-established subconscious programs. . . . The decision to change a habit is conscious, and our ability*

"To speak well supposes a habit of attention which shows itself in thought; by language we learn to think and, above all, to develop thought."
—Carl Victor de Bonstetten

to change it directly relates to our skill in mastering our own subconscious mind"

Spotlights!

1. The inner world is the abiding place of our thoughts, feelings, and beliefs.
2. Individual perspectives may define individual "realities."
3. Change often happens when we recognize false beliefs and make an effort to bring them in line with reality.
4. A goal without some kind of deadline may be a goal most likely not attained.
5. Objectives not accomplished may lead to frustration and a sense of failure.
6. Successful people finish what they begin. Be sure to think carefully before you take on a task, but, once you start it, complete it with thoroughness, energy, and resolve.
7. Success may be described as making the journey of life as deep and beneficial for others.
8. There may be many life possibilities for each of us.
9. When others play a meaningful role in our achievements, it is important to our inner well-being to acknowledge their contribution.
10. Accept each assignment as a fresh challenge and a chance to grow in your profession as a person.

Living the Law!

If someone gave you a magnificent birthday present and you tucked it away in a closet or a drawer and never opened it, what good would it bring to you? If someone gave you a luxurious new car, with the stipulation you must pick up the keys at the factory, dust would likely billow from your heels as you hastened to claim your gift. You wouldn't think of neglecting to claim the car. Yet, this is exactly what many persons are doing with the greatest gift in the world–they are neglecting to claim it!

"The Creator's supreme gift to you is the ability to arrange your life into the happy, attuned existence it is created to be.

"Discover this marvelous gift buried within yourself. Use it to strengthen your dormant spiritual muscles. Put these muscles to work for you. Perhaps certain of your faculties may have been sleeping. These faculties can be awakened and developed to an even greater extent than is necessary in developing the muscles and nerve centers in your fingers and hands in order to demonstrate a physical skill.

The results of your application can be a "new you.". . .

Welcome each new day. It is another glorious opportunity for you. It can be a thrilling new experience and a happy adventure in soul growth. You can find the sky becoming brilliantly blue, the trees and grass an alive green, and every creation of nature radiating an effervescent glow. No, nothing has changed–except you. You are beginning to see the work of the Creator through the eyes of Spirit–and it is good. It is very good!" (from Rebecca Clark, *Breakthrough*)

Meditate on the above comments about awakening your inherent abilities, and write your thoughts in your journal.

Week Twenty-Seven

❖

LAW 1

You can build your own heaven or hell on earth
—John M. Templeton

Do you remember as a child asking the question, "Where do people go when they die?" It may have been an unsettling question, and perhaps you hoped to receive a reassuring answer. The response from adults may have been that "people go to heaven or hell." This statement could have been puzzling enough for you to ask the inevitable next question, "What is that and where is it?"

Many people believed that "heaven was a place up in the sky filled with harp-playing angels, where a white-bearded God sat on his throne and made judgments about who had been good and bad, and doled out rewards and punishments accordingly. Hell, may have been defined as a fiery pit, where the devil, a horrifying apparition with red skin, horns, a tail and a pitchfork, made life miserable for the bad people who got sent there. Heaven was where the good people would go to live in eternal bliss, while the bad people would burn in hell forever."

Because to a child hell may have seemed such a frightening alternative, it was important to be as good as possible so we could be assured of a place in heaven, where we would be happy and our needs would be met. However, as we grew and became more independent and were challenged by the complexities of adult life, we may have begun to doubt whether a reward for our behavior such as heaven, or a punishment like hell, existed.

After all, we watched astronauts travel into outer space; and while they brought back rocks from the moon, they did not bring back any evidence of a physical "heaven." And where deep drills penetrated the earth, the drillers found oil, not hell, in the depths. The definitive descriptions of the afterlife we received as children could possibly call for some improvement

"Living is the thing to do–now or never. Which do you?"
—Piet Hein

"No one can live my life for me. If I am wise, I shall begin today to build my own truer and better world from within."
—Horatio W. Dresser

in the light of scientific discoveries of the modern age and our increased sophistication of thought. With maturity, our concepts of heaven and hell may have improved.

A number of philosophers offer a variety of definitions and descriptions of heaven and hell. Charles Fillmore, cofounder of the Unity Movement, describes heaven as *"a state of consciousness in harmony with the thoughts of God. It is the orderly, lawful adjustment of God's kingdom in man's mind, body, and affairs."* His definition of hell states: *"It (hell) symbolizes that purifying fire which consumes the dross of man's character; a corrective state of mind. When error has reached its limit, the retroactive law asserts itself, and judgment, being part of that law, brings the penalty, called hell, upon the transgressor. This penalty is not punishment, but discipline."*

The *Bhagavat Gita* states the following: *"Hell has three gates: lust, anger, and greed."* Mencius, a Chinese philosopher, wrote, *"Heaven sees as the people see. Heaven hears as the people hear."* And Jorge Luis Borges commented, *"Let heaven exist, even though our estate be hell."*

At times, despite our best and most positive intentions, the experience of heaven may seem to elude us, and the experience of hell may seem to pursue us. This often happens if we compare what we have with what others have and feel either superior or inferior to them. In subtle ways, we may become like yo-yos, with our emotions yanked up or down by the state of someone else's fortune. We may become obsessed by the *form* rather than the *content* of life.

If we judge only the outer appearances of anything, we can create a private hell that could permeate the various areas of our life. To the extent that we look outside ourselves for heaven, we may possibly create a hell of discontent and dissatisfaction for ourselves. What we really want is not "out there," and we may exhaust ourselves in searching hither and yon. We may rail against the world or other people in frustration, but the very real place where we can experience heaven is within our own hearts.

There is an ancient legend about three men, each of whom carried two sacks that were tied around their necks, one in front and one in back. When the first man was asked what was in his sacks, he said, "All my friends' kind deeds are in the sack on my back where they're hidden from sight and soon forgotten. The sack in front carries all the unkind things that have happened to me; and as I walk along, I often stop, take those things out, and look at them from various angles. I concentrate on them and study them. I direct all my thoughts and feelings toward them."

"The true purpose of life, aside from resisting oppression from without, each individual carries within himself, the responsibility of living nobly or ignobly."
—David O. McKay

"Be such a man and live such a life, that if every man were such as you, and every life such as yours, this earth would be God's paradise."
—Phillip Brooks

"Earth's crammed with heaven,
And every common bush afire with God."
—Elizabeth Barrett Browning

Consequently, because the first man was frequently stopping to mull over unfortunate things that had happened to him in the past, he made little progress.

When the second man was asked what he was carrying in his two sacks, he replied, "In the front sack are all my good deeds. I keep those before me and continually take them out and flash them around for everyone to see. The sack in the rear holds all my mistakes. I carry them with me wherever I go. They're heavy and slow me down, but for some reason I just can't put them aside."

The third man, when asked about his two sacks, replied, "The front sack is full of wonderful thoughts about people, the kind deeds they've done, and all the good I've had in my life. It's a big sack and very full, but it isn't heavy. The weight is like the sails on a ship—far from being a burden, it helps move me onward. The sack on my back is empty because I have cut a big hole in the bottom of it. In that sack, I put all the evil I hear of others and all the bad thoughts I sometimes have about myself. Those things fall through the hole in the sack and are lost forever, so I have no weight to make my journey more difficult."

From time to time, as each of us journeys along the path of life, it is important to examine what we are carrying with us. Are we weighted down by negative thoughts about ourselves? Are we weighted down by lumps of fear that tell us we may not measure up to some artificial standard? Are we weighted down by protective shields and psychological armor that may prevent us from relating to others in a free and wholehearted manner? Do we carry with us those misdeeds of friends and family that may have caused us distress in the past? Do we carry with us false lessons that teach us to look for undesirable characteristics in others and then run the other way when we think we detect one of those characteristics? Are we making our life a heaven or a hell?

Each of us is born with the freedom to choose the thoughts that direct our lives. We may choose the path we want to walk and what we wish to carry along the way. With this awareness in mind, would it not be preferable to chose thoughts that can form positive attitudes and emphasize our unlimited potential? Negative thoughts and attitudes weigh us down and make our journey through life more difficult.

The sixteenth-century monk Fra Giovanni wrote these words one Christmas: *"There is nothing I can give you which you have not. But there is much which, while I cannot give, you can take. No heaven can come to us unless our hearts find rest in it today. Take heaven."*

Our innate goodness is an essential fact of our existence and cannot be taken from us. Neither can it be given to us by someone else. When we perceive this truth, we experience heaven on earth. When we experience heaven within, we naturally are inclined to share that heaven with others through a pure, generous motive and a loving, positive attitude.

LAW 2

A soft answer turns away wrath, but a harsh word stirs up anger
—Proverbs 15:1

In living our day-to-day life, we may have been involved in situations where tempers flared out of control. Although anger may be considered a natural, self-protective reaction in moments of great frustration, "meeting fire with fire" often seems to compound the problem. Usually a moderate approach is best, and water, not fire, extinguishes a fire. The writer of the book of Proverbs acknowledged this truth when he wrote, *"A soft answer turns away wrath, but a harsh word stirs up anger."* Learning the art of giving "a soft answer" can give you an advantage in moments of great tension, when emotions tend to take over.

Giving in to anger can rob you of good judgment and leave you regretting things said or done, once the intense emotions have subsided. A gentle and controlled approach to an angry situation can often provide an opportunity to choose your words and actions rationally and bring a more desirable conclusion to a potentially damaging situation. Taking charge of your emotions can allow you to assess a troubled and clouded area of misunderstanding with a clearer mind and then take the wisest course toward a resolution.

People sometimes assume, mistakenly, that they have no power over their emotions. In these instances, they may have given their power to others. "He made me so angry," someone might say. Or, "she really gets under my skin." The truth is that no one except yourself has the power to make you angry. If

"Restraint does not mean weakness. It does not mean giving in."
—Jawaharlal Nehru

"Discretion of speech is more than eloquence."
—Francis Bacon

"Remember not only to say the right thing, in the right place, but far more difficult still to leave unsaid the wrong thing at the tempting moment."
—Benjamin Franklin

someone else assumes that power over you, you have, in some way, granted them that right! You may have reacted in anger because you felt the other persons drove you to it, but the choice—to be angry or to try a more rational approach—is yours to make. Louise Nevelson, an American artist said, *"You must create your own world. I am responsible for my world."*

There can be two ways to approach a situation that has triggered heated, hard-to-control feelings. You can *react* to the words and actions of others, or you can *act* from attitudes of your own choosing. The word "react" is a composite of the prefix *re-*, which means "again," and the word *act*, which means "to perform an action." In other words, to react can be to *perform the actions of another.* And reacting to someone else's negativity can have the potential to raise the stakes to an explosive level. To act out of understanding, on the other hand, to give a "soft answer," allows you to remain poised and calm and may create the potential for a peaceful, happy solution.

A humorous story is told about British professor John Burdon Sanderson Haldane. A discussion between Haldane and a friend began to take a predictable turn. The friend said with a sigh, "It's no use going on. I know what you will say next, and I know what you will do next." The distinguished scientist promptly sat down on the floor, turned two back somersaults and returned to his seat. "There," he said with a smile. "That's to prove that you're not always right!"

The next time you are faced with an angry, escalating situation, make a decision to try the "soft-answer" approach. Bring your emotions under your control, and proceed from a calm and more peaceful state of mind. By doing so, you can remain in control of the most vital resource you possess—your mind. You can find, with practice, that the soft answer may be your best defense against harsh words.

Eleanor Roosevelt, American humanitarian and first lady, affirmed taking responsibility. She said, *"Somewhere along the line of development we discover what we really are, and then we make our real decision for which we are responsible. Make that decision primarily for yourself, because you can never really live anyone else's life, not even your own child's. The influence you exert is through your own life and what you become yourself."*

If you examine daisies, or sunrises and sunsets, or snowflakes, or people, you may observe that the great laws of life provide a wonderful uniqueness in the Creator's many expressions. For example, there is nothing secretive or magical in the instructions for starting a car. We follow the instructions so the power can be released into action to transport us to our destination. Where was that power before we turned the key in the ignition? It was present, ready and waiting, but it was inactive. It was power in potential, but we needed to activate it to get results. The power within us can also be ready and waiting. We activate it by turning the key of our consciousness—our mind power. However, it is important to operate this inner power with care for the best results. In many instances, the best results may be obtained by the soft answer that turns away wrath and fans the precious embers of love and compassion.

LAW 3

The pen is mightier than the sword
—E. G. Bulwer-Lytton

Some of the old sayings we often hear may not be true. For example, "Sticks and stones may break my bones, but words will never hurt me!" could be a hundred and eighty degrees off the mark. Sticks and stones *do* hurt; but so do unkind words, and the healing process can take much longer. Wounds to the body can be visible where they may be more easily treated. Wounds caused by harsh words are often hidden inside of us, and we may think or pretend they don't hurt. Words can be powerful because we believe them or fear that others believe them.

"A broken bone can heal, but the wound a word opens can fester forever."
—Jessamyn West

An emaciated beggar stopped Count Leo Tolstoy, who was out for an evening stroll. The great author, so the story goes, perceiving that the man was hungry, groped through his pockets for some money to give him but found not a single cent. Tolstoy was distraught at his inability to help the man. He took the beggar's worn and dirty hands in his, lamenting, "Forgive me, brother. I have nothing with me to give you." The pale, tired face of the beggar lit up. "Oh, but you have just given me a great gift," he smiled. "You called me brother!"

Never underestimate the power of words. In 1896 an obscure congressman from the state of Nebraska attended the Democratic National Convention as an alternate delegate. He was only thirty-six years old. Yet, he made a speech that was so powerful that the convention ended by nominating him as its candidate for president of the United States. The man's name was William Jennings Bryan, and his powerful words and delivery set him on the road to the White House!

Perhaps it would be helpful to consider the creative essence of speech, which, Scripture tells us, has its derivation in the creative power of sound. In Genesis, God "speaks" the universe into existence: *"Let there be light. . . . Let there be a firmament."* Each verse of the entire first chapter of Genesis begins with the notable exclamation, *"Let there be. . . ."* With a similar potency begins the Gospel of John: *"In the beginning was the word."*

Some theologians describe the "word" as God's creative essence ensouling, permeating, informing, and conveying creative energy through all living things, here and now. Could there be a correspondence between the "word of God" and our spoken words? Perhaps we may recall instances when someone spoke sharply to us and we felt the "sting" of harsh words. Fortunately, we can do something to change the hurt. Because the hurt is an inner response, we can turn within to find help.

A classmate may try to pressure you to do something that doesn't feel right. But would a true friend insist you do something that may go against your ethical and moral standards?

Remember, your spirit is powerful. It takes words and ideas, sorts them, and provides guidance on how to act and feel. If you remain poised and balanced, putting forth your best effort every day, speaking your most loving and caring words, and, under all circumstances, remaining compassionate, kind, and generous with those you meet on life's journey; if you continue doing your best work and thinking your best thoughts every day, you can meet life with an awareness that can help you take appropriate and successful action.

Keep your mind open to receive lots of positive messages and loving thoughts because they can be powerful fuel. Be aware of the words that go into your mind, both conscious and unconscious, because words and ideas can be great tools for your mind to use in coming to appropriate decisions. Remember that a statement spoken in spiritual consciousness can contain great spiritual power. Speaking powerful words of love changes things and outer circumstances as well as consciousness itself.

In his comment, *"Beneath the rule of men entirely great, the pen is mightier than the sword,"* E. G. Bulwer-Lytton, the British novelist and politician, may have been referring to the power of the word—written and spoken. And do you remember the power of the spoken word in the movie *Ben Hur,* when Judah Ben Hur said, "I heard him say, 'forgive them for they know not what they do,' and his voice took the sword right out of my hand"? If we desire to become instruments of a higher consciousness, the laws of life can offer some guidelines to help us attune our words to God's word. How? Let's look at some things we can do.

1. Speak words of prayer to identify ourself with God.
2. Aim for honest relations with ourself and others.
3. Refrain from gossip and speak only words of truth.
4. Become observant of yourself, of how you write and speak.
5. Speak of others as you would want others to speak of you.
6. Decide for yourself how you choose to respond to whatever judgments or criticisms may come your way. Your spirit and mind belong to you!

It can be so important to use the spirituality we presently know. A soap manufacturer and a minister were talking one day as they strolled along a street. The soap manufacturer raised the question of what various religions have accomplished for the world. He said, "People continue to hate, fight, cheat, and steal, and the world seems no better than if there were no religions."

The minister reflected on his companion's words and pointed to a small boy who was playing in the mud along the gutter, "Look at that little fellow," he commented. "He is covered with dirt. I don't see that soap has done him a bit of good. Look at all the dirty people in the world. Would the world be better off without soap?"

The soap manufacturer replied indignantly, "Well, of course not. Everybody knows that soap is good. You have to use it!"

The minister smiled, "And so it is with spiritual truth. You have to use it to receive the greatest benefits!"

LAW 4

Worry achieves nothing and wastes valuable time
—John M. Templeton

A talented young woman thought seriously of becoming a doctor. She considered how wonderful it would be to make people feel better. She would be given the opportunity to heal the sick and help save lives. She fantasized about the good income she could earn by following her deepest desire.

Then she began to worry. She worried about the length of time it would take to become a doctor. She worried about the cost of her studies. She even worried about worrying so much. Because of her vacillating between desire and doubt, the young woman never took the entrance exams for the school to which she applied. Her behavior led to failure to achieve her principle goal in life and dramatized the old adage, *"Worry is like a rocking chair that gives you something to do, but doesn't get you anywhere."*

Many of us know the enjoyment of the soothing activity of rocking in a rocking chair. A frightened child can be comforted by a gentle, rocking motion. A physically injured person may often rock back and forth to temper sensations of pain. Rocking not only soothes the body, it can also be as comforting to the spirit as watching the ocean rise and fall in the rhythm of the waves. However, rocking leaves us in the present place; it doesn't move us forward.

In some ways, worrying is the same as rocking. Worrying can become a familiar behavior and, in this sense, a comfortable one that might trick us into believing we may be doing something to solve a problem. Once worrying becomes a habit, we may no longer be conscious of choosing to do it. It can become automatic. Worry, like rocking, doesn't move us forward or achieve anything. It can waste valuable time that could be spent in finding ways to approach a challenge creatively. Worry can occupy a place better given to rest and relaxation; and rest and relaxation often allow us to approach a challenge with refreshed and revitalized energies. There can be numerous ways to meet life—to look at, experience, and overcome obstacles. One of the most destructive and self-defeating ways to meet a challenge can be worrying about it.

"Worry saps a man's strength."
—Talmud

"Worry is evidence of an ill-controlled brain; it is merely a stupid waste of time in unpleasantness. If men and women practiced mental calisthenics as they do physical calisthenics, they would purge their brains of this foolishness."
—Arnold Bennett

If we trace the history of a word in an unabridged dictionary, we can learn the original meaning of the word. Let's look at the word "worry" for example. *Webster's New World Dictionary* describes "worry" as to "strangle or choke, to annoy or bother." Think about this for a moment. When we worry, we can strangle the flow of ideas that could help us solve the problem. We can choke (or block) the life current and keep it from flowing freely through us. When we worry, we often come into a state of concern and, sometimes, anxiety. Anxiety is defined as *"worry or uneasiness about what may happen."* You have probably already agreed in your mind that worry is not a particularly attractive or successful way to meet life.

One of the quickest ways we can free ourselves from worry is to accept our self-responsibility, which is a marvelous option. In his book *Your Erroneous Zones*, Dr. Wayne Dyer writes, *"The tragedy of being guilty and worrying is that we immobilize ourselves in the present moment."* If we focus our attention on the present moment and take responsibility for our thoughts and feelings, we can refuse to allow worry to interfere with our success.

A husband and wife were having a discussion about a domestic situation. The husband spent long hours worrying about how they would meet the month's financial responsibilities. The wife, having listened to his discouraging remarks for a couple of days, called him to sit with her at the kitchen table. She laid the bills on the table, picked up a pencil and a piece of paper, and said, "Now you give me one good reason how worrying can help pay these bills, and I'll sit here and worry with you for the rest of the day! Otherwise, let's look at possible ways we can increase our income to meet our responsibilities!"

We can decide in the present moment to release ourself from worry and choose more positive life options, more creative and freeing attitudes, more enlightened states of mind and healthier beliefs. You are a growing and unfolding creation. You can accept your wonderful capacity for constructive actions. Most things people worry about tend not to happen. Worry can be one way to meet life, but self-responsibility can be the better way. Worry often stems from fear, but self-responsibility and self-respect move from an attitude of faith in God, faith in the goodness of life, faith in the universe, and faith in our own potential.

The ineffectiveness of worry can be humorously described in the following story. A man was complaining of insomnia caused by worrying over a situation. He said, "Even counting sheep is no good. I counted ten thousand, sheared them, combed the

"Worry is a thin stream of fear trickling through the mind. If encouraged, it cuts a channel into which all other thoughts drain."
—Arthur Somers Roche

"You'll break the worry habit the day you decide you can meet and master the worst that can happen to you."
—Arnold Glasgow

"Worry, whatever its
source, takes away
courage and shortens
life."
—John L. Spalding

wool, had it spun into cloth, made into suits, took them to town, sold them, and lost a thousand dollars on the deal! I haven't slept in a week!"

If the young woman who wanted to become a doctor had used the time she spent worrying to study for her entrance exams and concentrate on a positive attitude, she may have taken a positive action, no matter how minor. It can certainly be acceptable to rest for a while when necessary, then get up and move forward by placing one foot in front of the other, one step at a time.

LAW 5

The greatness is not in me;
I am in the greatness

—Anonymous

"Greatness, after all,
in spite of its name,
appears to be not so
much a certain size as
a certain quality in
human lives. It may be
present in lives whose
range is very small."
—Phillips Brooks

Sunlight travels ninety-three million miles in a little over eight minutes to reach Earth. It is tasteless, odorless, and, unless a rainbow occurs, invisible. Prismatic droplets of mist can make what was there all along suddenly visible. The rainbow can be a powerful symbol reminding us that the unseen world holds many treasures for those with eyes to see.

As we live each day, our senses are bombarded with stimuli. As a result of coming in constant contact with objects, we may attach special significance to them. We might begin to believe that a slice of cake, for instance, can cheer us faster than a good word. We may count on sweets to sweeten our disposition because our senses tell us the taste and sugar-high are reality.

In fact, many material goods may be designed to distract us from feeling sad when it could be important to our well-being to grieve a loss. Outer appearances may disguise our errors when greater good could come from admitting a mistake. Material condolences may stimulate carelessness when our health and environment warn us of disease. The moment our welfare seems threatened, many of us may rush to the nearest commodity center for a "fix," expecting money to buy for us what it cannot buy—spiritual happiness.

Eventually, though, stabilizing forces bring us back into balance—just as gravity acts on a pendulum's swing. These forces may come in the form of an economic recession, a job transfer, a change in our home life, or a health crisis. These setbacks can become important opportunities to grow spiritually.

Not that one cannot be materially wealthy and spiritually enriched at the same time. It is not gold or silver in themselves that may be dangerous; rather, our attachments to them. We need to ask ourselves, "With what consciousness and purpose do I utilize the things in my world? Am I a slave of materialism, or a good trustee, acting selflessly and ethically in the handling of my worldly assets?"

Apart from its ability to serve the legitimate trading needs of humanity, money can be meaningless. And spiritual belief, divorced from the tangible world, can be naïve. True happiness often comes from bringing a wonderfully creative idea from the world of spirit into the world of matter, enjoying the benefit it can bring others, and then reclaiming it through gratitude. Furthermore, spiritual affluence can operate under some of the same universal principles as material wealth. The physical objects in our everyday world can be merely the manifestations of their spiritual essence. The adage, *"as above, so below,"* affirms that ideas in the spiritual world can also have results in the physical plane. Creative imagination can correspond to finite action; spiritual wisdom to worldly knowledge; unconditional love to actual service; and the dreaming self to the conscious self. The flow between the spiritual and the material world needs to be honored if we are to live fully and with purpose.

"Nothing is more simple than greatness; indeed, to be simple is to be great."
—Ralph Waldo Emerson

Ultimately, money can be a convenience for organizing and harmonizing human enterprise. Material wealth can be directed for this higher purpose. In fact, much of our fretting over what is and isn't adequate can be released, if we remember, *"The greatness is not in me; I am in the greatness."* What a freeing notion this can be! We are not the *source* of generosity and fruitful acts. We can be the *vessels* through which these virtues may be poured upon humanity. We are the overseers, rather than the owners of earthly resources.

"We can do no great things—only small things with great love."
—Mother Teresa

When we begin to act out of this knowledge of the heart, the masks that conceal truth can fall away. Desiring a new car can often be an awareness that the old car no longer functions satisfactorily. When this is recognized, the "newness" of the car becomes secondary. Moving from a larger home to a smaller place may be a need for simplification. Far more than a setback, it can be a reordering of priorities.

If we happen to be spellbound by materialism, all may not be lost. Is not the breaking of a spell often the turning point of many great tales? We can think of the days that may have seemed enchanted as the world initiating us in lessons of abundance and the secrets of the rainbow.

Spotlights!

1. We can build our heaven or hell by the state of consciousness in which we live each day.
2. Our innate goodness can be an essential fact of our existence and cannot be taken from us. Neither can it be given to us by someone else. When we perceive this truth, we can experience heaven on earth.
3. Learning the art of giving "a soft answer" can give you an advantage in moments of tension, when emotions take over.
4. Giving in to anger can rob you of good judgment.
5. Words may seem powerful because you believe them, or fear that others believe them.
6. Words, in and of themselves, do not cause us pain. Pain can stem from our belief and acceptance of what the words say to us.
7. A statement spoken in spiritual consciousness can contain spiritual power.
8. Accepting self-responsibility can offer a workable and quick way to free yourself from worry.
9. True happiness comes from bringing a wonderfully creative idea from the world of spirit into the world of matter or form.
10. The flow between the spiritual and material world needs to be honored if we are to live fully and with purpose.

Living the Law!

The following guidelines may be helpful:

1. Be aware that you are created for success, not failure. Refuse to allow your mind to dwell on worry or the negative side of things. Go to an uplifting movie, or visit with a friend—take a positive action to change your thoughts.
2. Take the first step. Act affirmatively, and the resources of Spirit will be your support.
3. Train yourself to realize that nothing outside of yourself can control your life. You have the power to decide how you will

deal with your thoughts. Control your imagination and keep it focused on positive outcome.

4. Direct everything in your life toward service to God and service to others. You may own things, but let them not own you. Find the proper, workable balance between yourself and others.

5. Know that you are important to the world, and there is a niche in life for you to fill.

6. Examine two key principles of success—honesty and perseverance. By investing in these virtues, you will find that others are more likely to invest in you.

7. Look upon loving as an essential ingredient in your life. One way to be in touch with our common humanity can be through the kindness, love, and patience we bring to our relationships.

Week Twenty-Eight

❖

LAW 1

Laugh and the world laughs with you; weep, and you weep alone
—Ella Wheeler Wilcox

In talking about solitude, Ella Wheeler Wilcox commented, *"Laugh and the world laughs with you; Weep, and you weep alone."* You may have heard the adage that "a smile breeds a smile." Like a bonfire on a crisp autumn evening, a smile has a way of sparking a light that may joyously ignite into happiness. Those with excessively serious minds and heavy hearts may need to exercise caution around it; for a smile may consume that which seems somber in its gentle flame, leaving in its glowing embers a sense of warm well-being.

"In laughter there is always a kind of joyousness that is incompatible with contempt or indignation."
—Voltaire

While there are times when it may not be appropriate to giggle or laugh aloud, your genuine smile is never out of place. Can you think of a time or place when the world could use a little more light and love? Every person has the capacity to bring these vital qualities to life with a smile. While not all of us smile in the same situations or in the same way, we can bring a little more warmth into a sometimes cold world with a smile that brings forth the best part of us. The smile we bring to a difficult challenge in life may infuse it with the light of understanding and with love, which can attract harmonious solutions. It may also inspire those around us to respond in a similar manner. Our smile can make a difference wherever we are!

Studies have shown that it takes far fewer facial muscles to create a smile than it does to make a frown. The choice to smile in a trying time may be a decision to take life in a way that is lighter on you and loving to everyone around you. A smile is often the expression of a grateful person. A smile can show your willingness to relax, enjoy the moment, and share in a good feeling no matter what stressful circumstance may be testing you. And when you take life more easily, life may be easier on you, for the energy you might have spent on a frown is freed for more useful purposes.

The spirit to whistle when we may not feel like whistling, the heart to sing when we may not feel like a song, the faith to affirm the goodness of God when we may see few visible facts to justify our affirmation—from these often has greatness sprung, and with these attributes have many victories of life been won. A happy heart may not assure you that you have no difficulties to meet in life's journey or that the world will laugh with you. It does assure you of a happy heart with which to meet each experience that blesses your life. And a happy heart can bear time's strains.

Author Mary Katherine MacDougall tells a story about a group of students who had attended a lecture and were talking together afterward about their own experience in understanding what is truth. "I have a real problem," one man said, "and I've been working hard on it."

The man next to him nodded his head. "I know. Sometimes it seems the harder I work to know what is true about something, the longer it takes."

"That may be the answer," the third man said. "When we work hard we seem to set the problem in concrete. We may want to solve our difficulties so much that we get tense, and I believe what we are really doing is intensifying the negative parts of them."

"That always makes me think of my daughter. When she could walk, she wanted to help carry the groceries. My wife let her carry a loaf of bread because it wasn't either heavy or breakable, but Annette, in trying to do a good job of carrying the bread, squeezed it on the way to the car and all the way home. The center slices were unusable!"

"Sounds sensible," the first man said, "but how can you deal lightly with something that means a lot to you?"

"Perhaps by not being so tense," the first man replied. "Perhaps by realizing that *we* don't have to, in fact, *can't* do all the work. Perhaps by being aware that in trying so hard we are really insisting on our own way of solution."

"Maybe we have thought God is a little hard of hearing," the second man said, his eyes dancing. "You know, I sometimes feel a little silly, the way you do when you're yelling at someone you thought was in the next room and you find he's right behind you!"

"You're right," the third man said. "My teenager tells me every so often, 'Don't sweat it, Dad. Take it easy. Easy does it!'"

"The acceptance of the truth that joy and sorrow, laughter and tears are not confined to any particular time, place or people, but are universally distributed should make us more tolerant of, and more interested in, the lives of others."
—William M. Peck

*"If its nothing more
than a smile—give that
away and keep on
giving it."*
—Beth Brown

Taking it easy could be good advice when you are faced with a difficult situation. Others may not express a great deal of interest in what is happening in your world, and you may feel that you are totally on your own. Your eyes may fill with tears, and laughter and happy times may seem far away at the moment. Being on your own does not mean being deserted. It does not mean that you are without help. It does not mean that you are truly alone. Being on your own may be perceived as important to growth, important to maturity, and important to the expression of one's God-given powers and possibilities. Even when we are alone we have God's *power* within us; we have God's *Spirit* always with us. To know this can make the difference between feeling devastated by circumstances or being filled with an awareness of strength and confidence in our ability to carry on and rise above self-doubts. A smile of quiet confidence can return to our face.

LAW 2

If nothing is ventured, nothing is gained
—Sir John Heywood

*"You must do the thing
you think you cannot
do."*
—Eleanor Roosevelt

*"You can't cross the sea
merely by standing and
staring at the water."*
—Rabindranath
Tagore

Have you ever wondered what the world may have been like at the birth of the human race? The first people understood a very small portion of the earth's surface. To them, the rest of the world must have seemed like a vast and frightening place. Great creatures wandered the earth; there were volcanic eruptions, exposure to the natural elements, and a constant search for food and shelter. It would come as no surprise that the earth's earliest inhabitants found life fragile indeed. We can be grateful to those intrepid ancestors who had the courage to venture forth, risking their lives to explore the unknown. What would have happened if they had not gone forth to explore the world's awesome riches and possibilities? We might not be here at all! Fortunately, a strong urge to learn more impelled those early people to improve their circumstances by going beyond familiar bounds.

Today we think nothing of flipping a switch to heat our house or of turning a knob to light the flame under the teapot. When we barbecue, we often soak the charcoal with lighter fluid and strike a match to start the flame. The innovation of fire is something we often take for granted. Try to think back to prehistory when people encountered fire for the first time. It must have piqued their curiosity and, at the same time, perhaps terrified them. And like a small child who puts his hand on the flame and gets burned, fire may have revealed its more ominous side to our ancestors and discouraged them from further investigations. It took an adventurer, who risked getting burned, to discover the beneficent possibilities of fire and further risk to learn how to contain and use it.

The spirit of adventure is a deeply human trait and one that has helped us develop over thousands of years of recorded history. It is the potential you have within you "to leave the world a better place than you found it." Not that you have to; few are likely to notice if you do nothing with your life. You can be one of those who plays it safe, who ventures nothing. But, *"nothing ventured, nothing gained"* applies to you as well as everyone. However, when you choose to leave what seems safe and familiar and voyage into uncharted waters of intellect and creativity, you can become like that first person who set out to conquer fire—an adventurer who dares to go forward into the unknown, a pioneer. You become one who can make a difference.

The courage to venture forth in life paves the way for many a success. Alex Haley was raised from infancy by his grandmother because his mother had passed away and his father, a student in another state in the United States, was unable to care for him. As an adult, Haley served twenty years in the Coast Guard, then left to pursue a career as a free-lance writer in New York. The years after Haley left the Coast Guard were not easy, personally or financially. He endured overwhelming poverty. Yet, Haley had a burning desire to become a successful and self-supporting writer. He committed himself to writing the saga of his family's genealogy. Despite the hardship and lack of material resources, Haley spent twelve years writing *Roots*. Finally, seventeen years after he left the Coast Guard, *Roots* was published. The book was translated into thirty-seven languages and became the basis for two incredibly successful television miniseries.

The 1992 Summer Olympics featured two tremendously poignant moments. American sprinter Gail Devers, the clear leader in the 100-meter hurdles, tripped over the last barrier.

"Determine that the thing can and shall be done, and then we shall find a way."
—Abraham Lincoln

"He conquers who endures."
—Italian proverb

"God is with those who patiently persevere."
—Arabian proverb

She agonizingly pulled herself to her knees and crawled the last five meters, finishing fifth—but finishing.

Even more heart rending was the 400-meter semifinal in which British runner Derek Redmond tore a hamstring and fell to the track. He struggled to his feet and began to hobble, determined to complete the race. His father ran from the stands to help him off the track, but the athlete refused to quit. He leaned on his father, and the two limped to the finish line together, to thunderous applause.

We are as travelers continuing on a journey began so long ago by our ancestors, and we have arrived at today. To the brave of heart and the inquisitive of mind the journey can offer an infinite variety.

Today's frontiers may no longer be the uncharted earthly lands that challenged our ancestors; yet the territories of the human mind and heart and soul can be even more awesome in their mystery. The exploration of the power of love may be one of the next great challenges. Father Pierre Teilhard de Chardin, the priest-scientist, wrote that *"when we have learned how to harness the energies of love for mankind, we will have discovered fire for the second time in history."*

Will you be the one to help?

❖

LAW 3

Honesty is the first chapter in the book of wisdom
—Thomas Jefferson

"To be or not to be; that is the question." So speaks Hamlet in his famous soliloquy of self-doubt and reason. If you remember, he is trying to decide whether to follow his own conscience or to pretend that he does not know the truth of his father's murder. He is torn by the desire to be honest with himself and therefore, the world, or to turn his back on that which he believes. Sometimes in our own lives, we may find ourselves in variations of this peculiar predicament. Not quite as melodramatic as Hamlet's, yet just as real for us.

"Honesty is the first chapter in the book of wisdom," Thomas Jefferson wrote. This statement rings out a great truth for people everywhere in every period of the world's history. The fight to honor truth within and without may not be an easy one, but our efforts must be directed in the line of honesty and integrity if we aim to be truly successful.

"Know thyself" is the inscription of the Delphic Oracle of ancient Greece. *"Hold faithfulness and sincerity as first principles,"* Confucius wrote, *"When you know a thing, to hold that you know it; and when you do not, to allow that you do not know it—this is knowledge."* Lao Tzu wrote over 2,500 years ago, *"He who knows others is wise; he who knows himself is enlightened."*

These great philosophers and sages began with one truth—be honest and "all things will be added unto you." They understood that people share the same basic drives: a need for love, for freedom and respect, and the desire to feel as if their lives have meaning. By looking within, the keys to understanding human behavior can be revealed if you are courageous enough to search your innermost heart.

But how many of us know where that heart is? How many of us have fallen into the habit of being out of touch with what we intuitively know? Often this seems to be most true when we apply it to knowing our own feelings. The noisy hustle and bustle of the outer world can distract us so much that we have a hard time listening to that still, small voice that usually knows the truth of any situation.

In *Hamlet*, Shakespeare says, *"This above all: to thine own self be true, and it must follow, as the night the day, thou canst not then be false to any man."* Yet, not listening regularly to the intuitive voice within, we may fall out of practice. It can then become easier to be false to ourselves—and then to others without this being our intent.

Thomas Jefferson wrote as follows in a letter to one of his contemporaries: *"He who permits himself to tell a lie once, finds it much easier to do it a second and third time, til at length it becomes habitual. He tells lies without attending to it, and truths without the world's believing him. This falsehood of the tongue leads to that of the heart, and in time depraves all its good dispositions."*

Jefferson tried to be as far-sighted as possible so that a nation of honest men and women would endure. *"Sometimes it is said,"* he wrote, *"that a man cannot be trusted with the government of himself. Can he, then, be trusted with the government of others?"* A compelling thought when we extend it beyond our small personal world. But what is any nation made up of, except the entwining

"Do not veil the truth
with falsehood, nor
conceal the truth
knowingly."
—Qur'an

of many people's small worlds? How often have we read in the newspapers of injustices in our own cities and towns, and shrugged? What can we do? How can we make a difference? Truth isn't our jurisdiction. Or is it?

One important thing you can do is get into the practice of being honest with yourself and others at all times. When we disconnect from our feelings to avoid a scene or to appear "cool," we often silence the voice within. We may silence truth. After a while we may no longer hear its voice. This may be one reason why there seem to be so many busy psychologists and psychiatrists in today's world. We may be paying to learn how to reconnect to our own inner promptings.

Begin today. The following exercise can offer meaningful insights into yourself. Take a sheet of paper and divide it into two columns. On one side write down the things you *like* about human nature—the things you *honor*. You may write down qualities like tenderness, strength, humor, diplomacy, love, or hard work. Whatever comes to mind. Then, in the other column, write down those qualities that you may find *offensive*—the ones that may "push your buttons." In this column you may write down anger, laziness, deception, cowardice, brutality, or jealousy.

Then take a look at both columns. In total truth, claim them both. Name the aspects of honorable character as you see them in yourself. Find where they may resonate with you. And recognize which, if any, need to be strengthened and worked on. Take the undesirable column and address these items. Recognize that you have smidgings of these characteristics in some small measure, even if they may be hidden from the sight of most people. Acknowledge them for the times when they arise. Do not deny them utterly, or they could creep up on you as the disowned enemy in yourself—sometimes coming only in the guise of the people that you draw to you, because they are denied within.

Be honest. Be true. Love all parts of yourself. You are human, and, like the rest of us, the godhood within you—the goodness within you—is in a state of coming to magnificent expression. With honesty and free will you can claim those aspects of yourself that you choose to express in your world.

There is a part of you that can be larger than any littleness, stronger than any weakness, wiser than you may think, and more brave than any fear. There is a part of you that is of the earth—earthy, as there is also a part of you that is of the Spirit—spiritual. This is the important part of you. That which is the real of you can transform the unreal. Be honest with yourself and others. Learn to know your real self.

LAW 4

A man can fail many times, but he isn't a failure until he begins to blame others
—Ted Engstrom

Have you ever heard the statement, *"If you are going to learn anything, you will make mistakes"*? It is true. Sometimes people refuse to try new things because they are afraid of failing and, consequently, of being considered a failure.

There is a distinction between failing and being a failure. Few things are learned in life without failing at least once. Did you learn to roller skate without falling a few times? Did you learn to ride a bike without losing your balance? Chances are you didn't. You may have wanted to be able to do those things so intensely that you quickly put unsuccessful attempts behind you and kept trying. Soon you acquired the skill to do the thing you wanted. Even though in the process of learning you may have failed many times, you were not a failure. "Failing" simply became an open door to try again!

Do you remember that sometimes in your frustration with the process of learning you may have blamed your interim failure on the person trying to teach you? If it was bike riding, maybe someone was running along beside you, holding you up. Soon you wanted them to let go so you could ride on your own. If you then fell, perhaps you blamed them for letting go too early, or too late.

As you gained confidence and skill, you may have been riding along the sidewalk and someone was walking there. You may not have been sure you could guide the bike through the small space available, and going off the walk seemed too scary to try. If you fell, did you think or say something like, "You made me fall! If you hadn't been in my way, I would not have gone over!" The reality was that if you had more skill and practice, you could have easily handled the situation, as you surely did many times in your subsequent biking experience.

In life, it sometimes seems as if there may be someone or something that causes us to fail. It is not unusual to feel that another person or a circumstance may have prevented us from achieving our goals. Would it be more meaningful to analyze our own preparation and effort and perhaps admit we could

"Apparent failure may hold in its rough shell the germs of success."
—Frances Ellen Watkins Harper

"Our success or failure is the result of our mental condition—our thoughts about people and about ourselves—our attitudes toward people and toward ourselves."
—David Custer

"Always there will be, along the sidelines of life, inferior souls who throw mud at those whose attainments they do not quite understand. The man who really accomplishes doesn't pay attention to such detractors. If he did, he'd be on their level. He keeps an eye singled on the higher goal—and the mud never touches him."
—Jerome P. Fleishman

have done better? Ask yourself whether you did the best you possibly could have and be fearless in admitting mistakes and oversights. Simply resolve not to repeat the error, forgive yourself for the mistake, and move on. Remember as you learned to ride the bike, as you kept trying and persisted, you got better and better until bike riding became almost as natural as walking.

There is no one to blame, not even ourselves. The person who gets stuck in self-blame or in blaming others or circumstances often slows his or her own recovery and risks becoming a failure instead of simply having a temporary setback. Rather than feeling sorry for yourself or being angry at others ask, "What now? What else can I do to accomplish my goals?"

If we waste time and energy blaming others, we may not see what we need to learn about ourselves in order to grow and achieve better results from our efforts. We can fail many times, but it does not have to be final. Those who fail are not failures, unless they let blame and self-pity prevent them from reaching their goals.

Some seventeen publishers rejected the novel *Auntie Mame*, Patrick Dennis's novel about a free-spirited older woman, before Vanguard accepted it. An immediate hit, the book was soon made into a popular film starring Rosalind Russell. Ten years later a musical version of the play, now called *Mame*, started a long Broadway run. The film *Mame* was released in 1974. Total book sales have been around two million copies. Patrick Dennis did not give up after the first—or even several—rejection slips!

Winston Churchill did not become prime minister of England until he was age sixty-two, and then only after a lifetime of defeats and setbacks. Many of his greatest contributions came when he was a senior citizen. And in 1962, the Decca Recording Company turned down the opportunity to work with the Beatles. Their rationale? *"We don't like their sound. Groups of guitars are on their way out."* Of course, the Beatles turned that imminent failure into prominent success.

Remember this important statement: Regardless of what may seem to be happening, there are new opportunities. There is a way to inner peace and stability. There is a way to rise above seeming failures and become a success. There is a way to the right attainment of many good desires of your heart. There is a way.

LAW 5

A soul without a high aim is like a ship without a rudder
—Eileen Caddy

A ship with properly trimmed sails can travel in any direction in relation to the wind except directly into it. While the set of the sails determines the most efficient use of the available wind, the rudder enables the ship to travel in a specific heading. Without a rudder, the ship can do little more than blow aimlessly downwind.

What is true of the wind-powered boat is also true of people. There are many things you can do to contribute to your success. You can cultivate a charming personality, develop a dynamic appearance, and receive a fine education. Making these preparations are like setting your sails. However, without a rudder, a proper steering device, you still may fail to get anywhere in life. You need a goal, a purpose, an ideal that can steer you in the direction of your choice. *"A soul without a high aim,"* said Eileen Cady, cofounder of the Findhorn Community," *is like a ship without a rudder."*

Many people seem to work hard throughout their lives with a minimum of personal and professional satisfaction. But often the problem could be that they engage in aimless thought and useless activity rather than steering themselves in a charted direction. Like a rudderless ship, they blow helplessly on the winds of circumstance, wasting their precious mind energy, failing to build vast knowledge and expertise. Feeling ineffective, they often live in a chronic state of unhappiness. High aims and clear purposes, however, act as a rudder for the unlimited potential of your mind and helps you move in directions that can build your reputation and usefulness. As effectiveness and productivity increase, feelings of uselessness, of drifting, diminish.

Consider how Montgolfier invented the hot-air balloon. Looking into the fireplace one day, one of the brothers saw burnt paper scraps rise above the flames and up the chimney. That simple incident helped him realize heated air could make a balloon rise from the earth! Samuel Colt, inventor of the revolver that bears his name, got the idea for its revolving cylin-

"The man without a high purpose is like a ship without a rudder—a waif, a nothing, a no man."
—Thomas Carlyle

der as a sixteen-year-old seaman watching the helmsman turn the ship's wheel—each spoke aligning with a clutch that held it fast. And, while working on a better way to make glass, British inventor Alastair Pilkington noticed a film of fat floating in his wife's dishwasher. That idea hook inspired a process where molten glass is floated on a layer of melted metal to provide an otherwise unachievable smoothness! It pays to be observant while reaching for high vision!

If you choose carefully and navigate your course with care, you can move in positive directions. Chances are you might set your sights on many things before you find the directions you really want to pursue. That is perfectly natural. We often gradually evolve into the field that best suits our deepest interests and abilities. Each time you set and attain a specific goal, you can learn that much more about the dynamics involved in taking command of your life. Then, when you find the things you most want to do, you can be prepared to reach out and attain your goals. Success then becomes no longer a mystery that only comes to others. You can be well acquainted with it and ready to seize the moments of opportunity

Consider the sparkling truths in the poem *Within the Depths of Me*, by Kalar Walters, that can help you aim high:

"The heights I reach, the worlds I touch,
the wonders that I dream of,
Or all the things I ever wished
or ever could conceive of
Are things beyond, and things below,
and things that cannot be,
Except for those that live and grow
within the depths of me.
So very deep and hidden that,
save for times like these,
I can only dream of them
and wish that they could be
A thing apart, a thing alive,
a thing that I could see,
A thing to touch, a thing to hold,
a thing to comfort me.
But if I watch and if I wait,
and hold to all that's true,
There will come a time, and then a place,
and what I'll see is You.
For you are what I dream of,
the things that cannot be,

"By every part of our nature we clasp things above us, one after another, not for the sake of remaining where we take hold, but that we may go higher."
—Henry Ward Beecher

Except for those that live and grow
within the depths of me."

Spotlights!

1. *"Taking it easy"* could be good advice when you are faced with a difficult situation.
2. A smile has a way of sparking a light that may joyously ignite into happiness.
3. The courage to venture forth in life can pave the way for many a success.
4. Whether we find ourselves sojourning in a valley or climbing among mountains, let us make the most of where we may be.
5. *"Honesty is the first chapter in the book of wisdom."*—Thomas Jefferson
6. Get into the practice of being honest with yourself at all times.
7. Understand the distinction between "failing" and being a failure.
8. *"Half the failures in life arise from pulling in one's horse as he is leaping."*—Julius Hare
9. Plan carefully and navigate your course with care, and you can move in a positive direction.
10. *"Nothing contributes so much to tranquilize the mind as a steady purpose—a point on which the soul may fix its intellectual eye."* —Mary Shelley

Living the Law!

In a booklet entitled *Triumphant Living,* Dr. Donald Curtis presents "Five Steps to Spiritual Power." Take a look at excerpts from these five recommended steps, and see how they may parallel your own spiritual purposes:

There are five steps to spiritual power: *unity, vision, devotion, joy,* and *release.*

1. *UNITY. Become one with the source of all power.* There is only *One,* and you are one with it. In unity there is strength. Strength is the basis of power.

All thought, feeling, and action emanate from and return to the center of inner spiritual awareness. This center is the source of life—the source of power. Become aware of this magnificent potential within yourself. . . . Let spiritual power do it through you. Jesus said, *"The Father who dwells in me does his works."* (John 14:10).

2. *VISION. Learn to see the larger scope of things.* How far can you see? That is how far you can go! Each horizon is but the springboard for new goals—the taking-off place for new accomplishments. Develop unlimited vision. Probe into the meaning of things. Discern the causes back of all phenomena. Look past the error. See through to the Truth. Extend the range of your sight. Broaden your viewpoint. Get the larger picture. Contemplate the facts of life from the highest point of view. Remove the obstruction from your eye and you will see everyone and everything differently. Look into the distance. See as far as you can. New vistas are beckoning. *"If your eye is sound, your whole body will be full of light."* (Matt. 6:22).

3. *DEVOTION.* Love, praise, and worship the wonder of life. Spiritual power is the direct result of our worship. Worship is the process of loving, praising, and blessing the oneness which is God. Call it by any name, but devote your inner attention to it. Contact and unify with the higher self—the spirit within you. Fall in love with infinite goodness and give your entire self to it. Surrender completely. Give thanks to the source from which all things come. Praise the creative power that produces all things. Adore the very idea of life. Devote yourself to serving the good, the true, and the beautiful.

4. *JOY. Let the magnificence and beauty of life fill you to overflowing.* Sing your praises from the hilltops. Let joy be unrestrained. It is great to be alive! Exultantly proclaim the good news. Let the vital surge of divine energy fill you to overflowing. Have a good time with what you are doing. . . . Let your laughter ring out. Bubble! Sparkle! Scintillate! Overflow with good will. Get interested in everything and everyone. . . . Let your excitement, interest, and enthusiasm color everything you do. Infect others with your joyousness. Let your life be set to music. Love life and love to live it. Joyously greet each day. Joyously perform each task.

5. *RELEASE. Let the unobstructed flow of life fill you and work through you.* Effort, struggle, strain, and concern must go. Why should you wear yourself out when there is a better way? Get in tune with Spirit within you; unify with it. Know what you want to accomplish, then let the spiritual power produce it for you. Emerson said, *"It is only the finite that has wrought and suffered; the Infinite lies stretched in smiling repose."*

Develop these five steps and you can have spiritual power.

Week Twenty-Nine

❖

LAW 1

Joy provides assurance, envy brings loneliness
–John M. Templeton

Whether it be a day, a week, a month, a year, or a lifetime, joy lies within our power to express because no person, condition, circumstance, or outside influence can really separate us from joy or prevent us from sharing it with all whom we meet. Charles F. Lummis said, *"I am bigger than anything that can happen to me. All these things–sorrow, misfortune, and suffering are outside my door. I am in the house, and I have the key."* And we do have the key! We *can* live in the happy medium of being spiritually aware and fully present with life.

When those days come along where things may seem to go awry—perhaps your car was fussy and didn't want to start, an anticipated luncheon date fell through, or you forgot an appointment you really wanted to keep—you have the key to turn it around. Your attitude! Just like so many other things in our day-to-day living, the "bad-day" syndrome or "good-day" experience can be outgrowths of our general attitude toward life. We can get so involved in examining and dwelling on the unfortunate, minor irritations of living that we may miss or disregard the small delights that occur just as frequently and regularly.

Joy may be difficult to define, but we know it when we experience it; and we know it when we lose it! The desire for joy can be one thing that most people have in common. What can constitute a day in joy? Some people find great joy when they are involved in doing things that bring others happiness, when they knowingly live in harmony with the laws of life, when their thoughts, feelings, and actions are honest and honorable, and when they have a quiet and peaceful conscience.

On the other hand, there may be those who feel jealous or envious when they hear good news about others. Shakespeare

"Life is a place of service and in that service one has to suffer a great deal that is hard to bear, but more often to experience a great deal of joy. But that joy can be real only if people look upon their life as a service, and have a definite object in life outside themselves and their personal happiness."
—Leo Tolstoy

"It is the spirit of a person that hangs above him like a star in the sky. People identify him at once, and join with him until there is formed a paradise of men and women, thus inspired. No matter where you find this spirit working, whether in a person or an entire organization, you may know that Heaven has dropped a note of joy into the world!"
—George Matthew Adams

"Two thousand years ago, more time was devoted to spiritual education than to mental education. The same was true two hundred years ago. Most older universities were founded by ministers to train ministers. But in the last two centuries, we have increased mental education enormously, so that now twenty times as many hours are spent on mental as on spiritual improvement. No wonder the world is out-of-joint! Let us not work less for mental education, but could we not expect both children and adults to study at least seven hours a week for spiritual growth? The result might be rewarding.

"It is not surprising that our world has problems. Many churches are no longer 'relevant' because so little time is actually set aside for spiritual activities. If we tried to teach chemistry by such methods, there would be very few able

had a good understanding when he wrote, *"I am a true laborer. I earn that I eat, get that I wear, owe no man hate, envy no man's happiness."* In Matthew 30:22 we read, *"Gladness of the heart is the life of a man, and the joyfulness of a man prolongeth his days."* And in Matthew 30:24 Scripture states, *"Envy and wrath shorten the life, and carefulness bringeth age before the time."*

A writer and musician once said, *"People may envy and despise you, not because they dislike you, but because they are not like you!"* When we are benevolent and consistently live our life in accord with our highest sense of right, joy often provides assurance of our well-being. Our deeds are remembered.

When the Rev. Sabine Baring-Gould, author of the hymn *Onward Christian Soldiers*, was pastor of the North Devon Church in England, he used to delight in taking visitors around the church and churchyard and pointing out to them the things of special interest.

He never failed to show them the tomb of a predecessor of his, of many years before, which was set just inside the churchyard wall. The tombstone had been erected by grateful members of the parish, and it listed the ways in which the pastor had faithfully fulfilled his ministry of caring and loving service.

When Baring-Gould asked visitors if they noticed anything unusual about the stone, the more observant visitor would remark, "Why, yes! There is no name on it! Who was this person?"

"That's the point," said Baring-Gould. "Generations of school boys have sat on the bank above the stone, and their feet have gradually worn away the inscription of the name on the top line. So, we don't know who the person was, only what he did!"

People may not remember who we are, but if there is some piece of service, some word of encouragement, some deed of mercy that we have contributed to their lives, that is our true memorial. To be thought of as a happy, joyous, loving, caring, compassionate person could be one of our greatest compliments and most important accomplishments.

Benevolent people have a distinct advantage over the envious. People who get caught up in envy may be tormented, not only by various ills that may befall them, but by the good that happens to others. Those who are joyous *with* life and *in* life are better prepared to handle any situation because of the inner serenity they have acquired by watching for the beauty and abundance that is around them.

"Joy provides assurance; envy brings loneliness" can be a good guideline for checking out our personal feelings. Is not

envy based on discontent or ill will over what may seem to be another's advantages, or on a desire for something another has? But what is the bottom line here? Could the true discontent be a sense of lack within the person's consciousness? We may get so bound up in looking at one aspect of a situation or relationship that we may miss the other facets. A politician who loses an election can retreat into oblivion and envy—or he can examine the reasons for his loss, re-evaluate his position on the issues, and begin to plan his next campaign. A person who has his heart set on going to college, but finds that outer circumstances prevent his immediate entrance, can look to even greater intellectual growth through on-the-job-training rather than envying those who immediately become students.

If you have lost the ability to feel joy in living, try your best to regain it. It is vital to your well-being. Real joy is a deep and lasting quality that helps transcend difficulties and restores a zest for life and living no matter what happens. Remember that joy and strength can walk hand in hand to help us meet and overcome whatever challenges that may come our way.

chemists and few new discoveries in chemistry. Should not schools include in the curriculum courses in ethics, philanthropy, character-building, self-denial techniques, freedom from envy, joy of giving, thought control, philosophy of life, etc.? To say that religion should not be included in university studies because it cannot be seen or accurately measured seems as questionable as saying that love should not be studied for the same reason."
—John M. Templeton, *The Humble Approach*

LAW 2

All sunshine makes a desert
—Oriental proverb

A story is told about a group of children who were playing in the sand, writing their names and spreading shells in simple patterns. The gentle breeze coming in off the water tousled their damp hair, and the swish of the waves was pleasant background for the babble of young voices. Suddenly, one of the boys had an idea.

"Let's make a swimming pool right here," he exclaimed.

The other children agreed, and they promptly set to work with shells and shovels and soon had a hole about a foot deep and several feet across. They ran down to the water's edge with their buckets and brought water to fill the hole. But as fast as the children poured the water into the hole, it drained off into the sand.

"For the benefit of the flowers, we water the thorns, too!"
—Egyptian proverb

They surveyed the hole dolefully. Then, the boy who had the first idea had another. "I know, we'll line the hole with shells. That will keep the water in."

The children were busy for a time gathering and placing more shells. Then the bucket brigade started again. But no matter how fast the children worked, they still could not fill the hole with water.

One of the nearby parents had become fascinated with the children's activities and walked over to watch. A little girl saw her father standing nearby and ran over to him. "Daddy, what can we do?" she asked. "We're trying to make a swimming pool, and the water won't stay in the hole."

The father smiled. "Why, of all things, do you want to make a swimming pool?" he asked. "Look at the beautiful one already made for you. You haven't even been in it yet." And he waved his hand toward the expanse of water stretching out as far as the eye could see.

The little girl ran back to her friends, excitedly calling, "Come on. Here's a much better swimming pool than we can build," and she dashed down to the water with her friends.

How much like those children we may sometimes be! The great ocean of life may be before us, but we scurry about on the shore, writing our names in the sand, perhaps gathering shells, and trying to build our own private swimming pools. We forget to look about us and see the many-faceted blessings that may often be right before our eyes.

For example, what would life be like on earth if we had no clouds, no rain, nothing but sunshine? Sometimes we think we would like to have only sunshine, but without the rain we would be left with a dry, barren planet, incapable of supporting life as we know it.

Our lives seem filled with such variety—sunny days and stormy days, good times and frightening times, pleasure and pain, joy and sadness. Often we try to create only experiences of pleasure and happiness. However, by attempting too much control over our experiences, we set ourselves up for a fearful existence.

Have you ever known someone who lived in fear? There was once an escaped convict, a man who had run from the law enforcement officials of his country for many years. He was plagued by confusion and doubt and, over time, began to use drugs in an attempt to feel happier. His need to escape his doubts and confusion was so great that he did whatever was

"If we had no winter, the spring would not be so pleasant; if we did not sometimes taste of adversity, prosperity would not be so welcome."
—Anne Bradstreet

necessary to buy the drugs. The drugs numbed his inner pain and blurred his mind, blotting out the things that bothered him. This desperate attempt at control worked for a while, but soon he required even more drugs to push away the pain and fear. He began to steal from others to buy his drugs, and eventually he was caught and imprisoned. The man's desire to feel happier by avoiding pain ended in a long prison term and in an environment that he later said was designed to support the dying not the living.

We all need balance in our lives. Very few of us would survive an existence that is totally filled with fear, doubts, and negativity. Just as rain nurtures beautiful green grass and sunlight can kindle a sense of warmth and inner peace, so challenges can compel us to seek for a greater understanding—engendering new beliefs and ideas about life. Happy times can provide for pleasant memories to relive during the difficult experiences, and, like old friends, good memories can fill the void when we mistakenly feel like everything joyous has abandoned us.

As a youth, Sidney was raised in poverty on Cat Island in the Bahamas. At sixteen, with less than two years of education and three dollars in his pocket, he moved to New York City in search of a better life. When he arrived, the only place he could find to sleep was a rooftop, and his first job was that of a dishwasher.

Although he knew nothing about acting, Sidney responded to a want ad listed by the American Negro Theater. Because of his limited education, he could not read all the words in the script. The director interrupted his audition, shouting, "Stop wasting my time."

While that rejection would have stopped and maybe even destroyed the ambitions of most people, the young man walked away more determined than ever. Saving money from his meager dishwasher's salary, Sidney bought a radio. He used it as an educational tool, listening to people's voices for hours, trying to enunciate as clearly as they did. At the restaurant, he found a waiter who was willing to tutor him in reading.

Later Sidney returned to the American Negro Theater, persuading officials to let him take acting lessons. Privately, he resolved to become not only the best black actor but the *best actor*. Sidney Poitier is now one of the finest actors of his generation. The rain that fell in his life only served to water the seeds of desire and determination to bring a better life and greater balance into his world.

Remember the following Chinese proverb when the road

"Only in growth, reform, and change, paradoxically enough, is true security to be found."
—Anne Morrow Lindbergh

"We would never learn to be brave and patient if there were only joy in the world."
—Helen Keller

ahead looks rocky: *"All sunshine makes a desert."* Remember that a desert cannot support life without some rain. Look for the balance in your life. If it is not there, then it's time to create it!

❖

LAW 3

Whether you think you can or not, you are right!
—Henry Ford

"A man's mind is the man himself."
—Latin proverb

Would it surprise you to learn that everything in your life right now may be pretty much the way you made it? Have you thought recently that from hundreds of options, you choose your responses to whatever situations present themselves? Would you agree that you have exercised the capacity to choose what you have received? If so, doesn't it stand to reason that if you made the choice in the first place, you can change your mind and change a situation?

What a powerful notion! Whatever happens to you, you can say, "I am the master of my life." In order to meet life joyously and successfully, we need to cultivate a positive attitude toward life. This can give us a feeling of being in tune with our good and can help bring that good into manifestation. After all, our attitude in life plays a big part in bringing us joy in living.

"I am never so happy as when a new thought occurs to me and a new horizon gradually discovers itself before my eyes. When a fresh idea dawns upon me, I feel lifted up, apart from the world of men, into a strange atmosphere of the spirit. It is a new freedom."
—William Somerset Maugham

But just as good comes to you as a demonstration of your mastery, so can negative conditions reflect the other side of the coin. Consider how hopping fleas are trained. The fleas are put into a glass jar. As they try to jump in the jar, they bump their heads against the lid. Over time, they forget they can jump and, for fear of bumping their heads, never go beyond the limits of the jar, even though the lids may have been removed. Through continued failure, the fleas have become conditioned to confinement. So it might be with us if we allow negative or restrictive thoughts to live in our mind. Our self-made limitations can sometimes cause us to forget that we can fly with the freedom of thought. We often needlessly confine ourselves to "glass jars." Our invisible mental prisons remind us from time to time, "You can't do that. It isn't practical. You're not smart enough. It will cost too much. People will laugh at you. You're too young. You're too old. Your health won't allow it. Your parents won't allow it. It will take too long. You don't have the education," etc.

A humorous aspect of how our thoughts can back us into a corner was printed in the *Los Angeles Times Syndicate*. A woman moving into a strange town called a dentist who had been recommended by a friend. She saw the name on his certificate on the wall and remembered that a tall, handsome boy with the same name had been a member of her high school class some forty years before. A first glimpse of the dentist revealed a partly bald head, graying hair, and a deeply lined face, and she decided that he was much too old to have been in her class. She did ask him, though, if he had attended her school. An affirmative answer brought the question, "When did you graduate?"

"In 1940," he replied.

"Why, you were in my class!" she cried out.

The dentist looked at her closely with a blank expression and then asked slowly, "What subject did you teach?"

It sometimes seems true that many people have become accustomed to searching out, examining, and even magnifying signs of trouble in their lives and in their world. It can be easy to see unpleasantness around us if this is where we choose to place our focus. Anne Frank, who underwent great hardship during World War II, wrote in her diary that in spite of all she had been through, she still believed in the basic goodness of people. This is the kind of optimism that we can live with and that can help us to live. The world we live in has been in existence for a long time. There may be some facets of it that we cannot change, and, of course, they may have an effect upon us. Yet, each of us creates an important part of the world in which we live—our own inner world.

Suppose we made it a point to remember that we were made to achieve? What might happen? Suppose we really believed that we are children and heirs of this magnificent universe? Would we then still allow our "jars" to limit us to hopping just so far and no farther? Suppose we became aware that resentments, hurts, hates, grudges, illness, greed, and the like can be mental glass jars that have been, or can be, removed; that, indeed, we may be hampered by the illusion of our own self-imposed limitations? Are we willing to consider that we just might attract to ourselves whatever our minds are focused on? That if we think we can do something, we can; and if we think we cannot do something, often we can't?

Life is not all chance; life is mostly choice. We can be the

"By the mind one is bound, by the mind one is freed. . . . He who asserts with strong conviction: 'I am not bound, I am free,' becomes free."
—Ramakrishna, Indian mystic

"We live what we know. If we believe the universe and ourselves to be mechanical, we will live mechanically. On the other hand, if we know that we are part of an open universe, and that our minds are a matrix of reality, we will live more creatively and powerfully."
—Marilyn Ferguson

"builders of our life," with the freedom to choose our thoughts and thereby establish our habits and our attitudes. These attitudes then can determine the direction and quality of our life. We are thinking and feeling beings. Through the power of our mind, we become more able to experience and accomplish that on which we place our attention. There may be few subjects that we know and understand less about than the formative power of the mind. Many people know how difficult it can be to break a habit, but it can be accomplished. Whether we think we can or not, we are right!

LAW 4

The mind can make a heaven into a hell, or a hell into a heaven
—John Milton

An article in *Sunshine* magazine mentioned the way most people talk. It said that they use *D*s instead of *P*s. The string of *D*s that people vocalized every day included debt, doubt, disease, disaster, discouragement, depression, decay, deception, danger, defeat, difficulty, discord, deception, disappointment, distrust, disagreement, dread, dejection, destitution, and desolation!

"The mind is its own place, and in itself can make a heaven of Hell, a hell of Heaven."
—John Milton

The article then goes on to say we would be much better off talking about the *P*s: peace, prosperity, plenty, power, pluck, persistence, purpose, promotion, possession, proficiency, progress, perseverance, prayer, and possibilities.

Which of the two types—the *D*s or the *P*s—do you think lives in a more heavenly state of consciousness?

A story is told about a man who went to call at the place of business of one of his friends, a jeweler with a large clientele. The jeweler showed his friend a store filled with superb diamonds and other precious stones. Among them was a stone so lusterless that the friend said, "That one has no beauty at all."

"Hasn't it?" asked the jeweler, lifting the stone from the tray and closing his fist over it. In a few minutes, when he opened his hand, the stone glowed with all the splendor of the rainbow.

"Why, what have you done to it?" asked the friend.

The jeweler smiled. "That is an *opal*," he said. "It is what we call a *sympathetic* jewel. It needs only to be gripped with the human hand to bring out all its wonderful beauty!"

Living on the "right" side of life, or the "heavenly" side, can bring sparkle and beauty to the many facets of our individuality and the way our life unfolds. Maybe you know someone who lives in a "heavenly" state of consciousness, and things seem to work out well for them. They enjoy splendid health. The affairs of their life seem to be happy and harmonious, and the much-desired "good things of life" have a habit of coming their way.

However, there seem to be other people who somehow manage to get on the "wrong side of life," regardless of their desire for things to be otherwise. They experience times when nothing seems to work out in their favor. The harder they try, the farther away they seem to be from good health, happiness, success, or whatever good they may be seeking. What makes the difference between these two seemingly opposite ways of life?

The truth is that our attitude of mind can actually help the good things of life either to gravitate toward us or move away from us. Our mind and our thinking processes can make a heaven into a hell, or a hell into a heaven. How, then, can one cultivate and develop the right attitude of mind?

The first step can be to pause right where we are, stop the chattering noise of our thoughts, and allow our thinking to become rightly adjusted. To pause for a moment in your activities does not mean to give up, quit, or "lie down on the job." Far from it! Such a pause can help you regain the proper perspective of life and to get your thoughts going into a positive direction again.

A second step can be to reaffirm your faith, lift your consciousness—and your thoughts—to a higher level of expression. Let's look at an example. Suppose you are experiencing some difficulty. Daily living may seem to be hard going at the moment, and you may feel uncertain about what you need to do next. Instead of beginning to panic and put pressure on yourself, pause for a moment and affirm, *"Spirit goes before me, guiding and directing my efforts and my direction."* Lifting your thoughts to a higher level can renew and restore the peace and serenity of your awareness—and your life!

One further step is often necessary. This can be to go forward

"Wisdom and beauty are the twin arches of that invisible bridge which leads from the individual conscience—ever rebellious against its destiny—to man's collective conscience, ever in search of general progress."
—Jaime Torres Bodet

"A good mind is lord of a kingdom."
—Seneca

"You must live in the present, launch yourself on every wave, find your eternity in each moment."
—Henry David Thoreau

"Blessed is he who carries within himself a God, an ideal, and who obeys it."
—Louis Pasteur

with confidence and courage, trusting the inner guidance that you receive and know that the way may indeed be made clear.

A minister tells a story about a little boy who was supposed to be helping him straighten chairs and place hymnals in the sanctuary in preparation for the Sunday service. The two had been working side by side for about twenty minutes. The boy was working a little and whistling a lot, while the minister simply worked. Finally, the minister called the boy over and asked, "Whatcha doing?"

The boy paused, and answered, "Passing out hymnals and whistling." Another pause, and he continued, "but mostly whistling!"

After a moment of reflection, the minister decided the boy had a pretty good idea—to whistle in the midst of the work at hand. In fact, whistling may well be one of the most redemptive activities we can take part in. This capacity to whistle, to flow freely, and to enjoy what we're doing in the middle of a busy day could be an art that needs to be cultivated.

Many of us can take our activities pretty seriously most of the time because we are searching and trying to contribute creatively to life. But, how much whistling do we do in the midst of this? While life may be serious, it doesn't need to be somber. It does not have to be hellish; it can be a heavenly experience. It can be a great challenge or adventure; like mountain climbing, it is meant to be an exhilarating experience every step of the way.

Life involves both "passing out hymnals" and "whistling." And perhaps there are times when we need to be "mostly whistling"!

LAW 5

*No man is free
who is not master of himself*
—Epictetus

"No man is free who is not master of himself." The Greek philosopher and slave Epictetus declared this truth in the first century C.E. Of course, if you were a slave, then as now, freedom to control your own destiny would very likely be the foremost thought

in your mind. While it may be true that the owner, the slave master, stands between the slave and his freedom, Epictetus understood that true freedom results not merely from escaping the slave master but also from becoming master of yourself.

There are many paths—and a wide diversity of philosophies and practices—that lead to self-mastery, as countless books written on this subject can attest. Yet a common theme runs through each of them. In Christian teaching, it is stated this way: *"The kingdom of God is within you."* Freedom, happiness, peace of mind, all that we seek, and more, lies within us.

Self-mastery begins the moment you realize that you make your own prison and that you're the only person who can set you free. What is freedom? Is it the right to do what we want without restriction? Not really, for even in the freest of all societies, laws are needed to insure freedom for everyone. Perhaps true freedom is not the freedom to *do* but rather the freedom to *become* all that we can be.

How do you earn the right to play a musical instrument or to create a work of art? It isn't a right given to you by someone else, but only comes once you master the skills necessary to create music or art. How do you attain the freedom to live a happy, creative life? Can anyone else grant you that freedom? No, that freedom also results from mastering the attitudes and skills needed to create a happy life.

When you conquer those twin enemies—your own fear and ignorance—you can be on your way to true freedom. Fear and ignorance can be tough slave masters, and we remain enslaved as long as we give them living space in our hearts and minds. By overcoming thoughts of fear and by knowing the truth we can become truly free.

A good way to overcome fear is to face squarely whatever makes us fearful. Avoiding fear-provoking situations does not resolve them. Like the mouse that roared, often the things that cause us the greatest anxiety can be much less threatening than we imagined. Whenever life challenges you with something unknown and you find yourself afraid, face and analyze your fear and watch it diminish.

Jill Jackson, who wrote the words to that beautiful song sung around the world *Let There Be Peace on Earth and Let It Begin with Me*, has another idea that can spread in the same way her song keeps reaching more and more people. Millions of people are singing the "Peace Song." Many more are believing that each of us is "one" of four billion neighbors on earth, and that each one of us can make a difference. An inner prompting

"Many people have the ambition to succeed; they may even have special aptitude for their job. And yet they do not move ahead. Why? Perhaps they think that since they can master the job, there is no need to master themselves."
—John Stevenson

"The highest purpose of intellectual cultivation is to give a man a perfect knowledge and mastery of his own inner self."
—Novalis

"You may need only claim the events of your life to make yourself yours. When you truly possess all you have been and done, which may take some time, you are fierce with reality."
—Florida Scott Maxwell

seems to be urging more people to experience the inner freedom and take positive steps to help others.

Jill prayed for a way to help her life have real meaning for bringing peace, in thought, word, and deed and came up with the following masterful inspiration.

In a letter to a friend, she wrote, "I send out mail. I can write at an angle across each letter and postcard, saying a prayer as I write, 'Let There Be Peace On Earth and Let It Begin with Me.' I can tell others."

Promise yourself to do your part, and try to be so strong in self-mastery that almost nothing can disturb your peace of mind. Try to talk health, happiness, and prosperity to most every person you meet; to look at the sunny side of life and make your optimism come true. Try to think only the best, and to expect only the best; to be too large for worry, too noble for anger, too strong for fear, and too happy to permit the presence of troubling thoughts.

Freedom can be ours when we recognize that we create our own prisons and that we can set ourselves free at any time. By facing our fears, we can learn to relinquish them and begin to take full responsibility for the usefulness of our lives. That is true self-mastery and true freedom.

Spotlights!

1. No person, condition, circumstance, or outside influence can separate you from joy or prevent you from sharing it.
2. Joy is a deep and lasting quality that can help transcend difficulties and restore a zest for life and living.
3. When you awaken each morning, set your thought pattern for the day. Think of five things for which you are grateful, and keep them in mind throughout the day.
4. Think about this: A desert cannot support life without some rain!
5. You can change your mind (thinking processes) and change a situation for the better.
6. To meet life joyously and successfully, it is important to cultivate a positive attitude toward life.
7. Our attitudes of mind can cause the good things of life either to gravitate toward us or move away from us.
8. Our mind can make a heaven into a hell, or a hell into a heaven.
9. When you conquer the twin enemies of fear and ignorance, you can be on your way to true freedom.

10. Things that cause anxiety can be much less threatening than we imagined.

Living the Law!

Pause for a moment now. Think about the following intriguing bit of prose entitled "The Advancing Human Soul." How do your thoughts, feelings, and actions parallel the ideas expressed here?

As human souls grow and develop, they become increasingly interested in their fellow human beings who endure the joys and sorrows, successes and strifes, health and suffering brought about by the ever-active universal law of cause and effect.

Advancing human souls empathize with their fellow travelers and try to cheer and encourage those whom they meet. Every firm handclasp that is offered in assistance brings a greater humbleness in the joy of true and selfless service. These evolving children of God long for more and deeper illumination and wisdom. Hatred and vengeance begin to fade from their evolving consciousness, and they increasingly realize that true justice ultimately prevails.

Ascending spirituality sparks the understanding of the necessity of life on Earth—this earthly existence enables such souls to purify and evolve in direct proportion to their love and compassion and transmutation of any negatives that may remain in them. The advancing human soul uses regularly the keys of experience and discernment—of themselves and of their fellow travelers—to solve unknown mysteries.

Advancing human souls learn to recognize the masks covering the faces of their fellow travelers. In such persons, the expression of the eyes often fails to agree with the set of the mouths. They may use cosmetics—material and emotional—to hide the wrinkles that depict years of suffering, anxiety, struggle, hardship, and, yes, of joy and progression. A downturned mouth may attempt to smile, but the glow of inner happiness does not sparkle in eyes which are dull and lackluster.

What a vast amount of experience lies hidden behind the eyes of a human being! This is a secret known only to each one whom Spirit carries along the cosmos, moving the advancing souls ever nearer to the light of God.

Week Thirty

❖

LAW 1

It is by forgetting self that one finds self
—St. Francis

"Some people think supernatural events, such as miracles, are needed to prove God's existence. But natural processes and the laws of nature may be merely methods designed by God for His continuing creative purposes. When new laws are discovered by human scientists, do they not merely discover a little more of God?

"Each of us every day is swimming in an ocean of unseen miracles. For example, each living cell is a miracle; and the human body is a vast colony of over a hundred billion cells. The miracle of this body includes both our ability to recognize it as well as our inability ever to exhaust the true significance of it."
—John M. Templeton, *The Humble Approach*

There is an inspired painting by the German artist Rosenthal entitled *The Blessing of Work*. It depicts a young boy working on a life-size carving of the Virgin Mary. The almost-completed figure towers above the young artist, and while he works intently carving the details of the feet, Mary looks down on him with love and outstretched arms, blessing him. While he is giving himself in the creative flow, he is dynamically receiving immeasurably in return. The painting reveals much more: light is streaming through the open window, its rays bathing him with an aura of illumination. On a large plaque on the wall, a heavenly choir is singing paeans of praise directly toward him. By his side, there is what we assume is a picture of his mother, which he is using for a model, and with hands clasped in devotion, she is blessing him. Thus, the entire tone of the work suggests that the whole universe is rushing, streaming, pouring into the boy, while he quietly gives himself in creative effort. It is a beautiful visual testimony to Jesus' message in Scripture, "Give and it will be given to you" (Luke 6:38).

Much in life depends on the view we take of it. Is it a gently flowing river with trees growing along the bank, or is it people strolling on a sandy beach, or perhaps walking in the midst of a bustling city? The look of things changes as you take a close-up, or a distant, view. When our thoughts are directed toward giving in some manner to others, we expand the horizons of our perspectives.

Because we are part of life, we have experiences that are part of life. Some of these may be easy; some of them may seem more difficult. The easy experiences we can meet with rejoicing and the tough experiences we can meet triumphantly. For it is the nature of the human person—the dreamer and builder—that we need not accept things as they may appear, but we have the ability to change them into something better. When we forget self and let sincere caring and love flow from our heart to others, we have an opportunity to turn a wilderness into a garden, to make the desert bloom, to build dikes against the sea, to change poverty into abundance, sickness into health, war into peace, and remake ourself and our world closer to the heart's desire. We can live in the heart of love, whose infinite compassion encompasses all people, places, and things.

A unique example of putting others first is given by Charles E. Harvey, Jr., in a story in *Reader's Digest*. He told about driving for an important job interview and running about fifteen minutes late when he saw a middle-aged woman stranded by the side of the road with a flat tire. His conscience caused him to stop. He changed the tire and headed for the interview, thinking that he could probably forget about getting the job. Nevertheless, he filled out the job application and went into the personnel director's office. Imagine his surprise when the personnel director hired him on the spot. She was the woman whose tire he changed on the way to the interview!

Edward was fifty-two years old when he finally admitted that he was an alcoholic. Like many before him, he knew that Alcoholics Anonymous was his remaining option. It was a move he felt reluctant to make, however. Edward did not want to admit defeat, although he seemed thoroughly beaten, not only physically but also emotionally. He felt embarrassed that others might know he was an alcoholic, although, in fact, everyone who knew him well was aware of his condition.

After a few weeks of attending AA meetings, the fog began to clear from his mind. He kept hearing the strange phrase, "You've got to give it away to keep it." The "it" was sobriety, and AA told him that once he attained it, he would have to share it with others to maintain his own good. Unfortunately, Edward was a self-centered and selfish individual at that time. He thought to himself, "No way. Whatever it is, as soon as I get it I'm going to hold on to it and keep it for myself!"

When we hoard things instead of passing them on, they often become of less value. Greater satisfaction comes when we follow St. Francis's edict, *"It is by forgetting self that one finds."* When we choose to get beyond our personal self and act with a loving, generous spirit, then we receive what we're giving away. And more!

But how can we help someone become something they don't

"Material things which appear, appear only because God has given us five senses with which to perceive a few traits of a few of the myriad notes in the giant symphony of life which surrounds us. The unknown is found to extend vastly beyond the area of the known, even after scientists have multiplied the known a hundredfold as they have in this century alone."
—John M. Templeton, *The Humble Approach*

"There is no room for God in a person who is full of himself."
—Baal Shem Tov

"Humility is the most difficult of all virtues to achieve; nothing dies harder than the desire to think well of self."
—T. S. Eliot

"Real charity and a real ability never to condemn—the one real virtue—is so often the result of a waking experience that gives a glimpse of what lies beneath things."
—Ivy Compton-Burnett

want to be, or give them something they may not want to receive, even if they may ultimately benefit from it? Perhaps the best way is to lead by example. If we are willing to perform a service for another, others may be more likely to replicate our actions. And now a paradox comes into play. For example, someone who finds it difficult to receive love may not be able to give love. The first step in giving is to receive God's love in order to give it away, for we cannot give what we do not have. In order to be a true giver, our motives for giving must be pure. Give because you genuinely want to give. Give because you believe in life. Give willingly and joyfully, and peace and joy can be your reward.

Let us return to Edward, who truly changed through the gifts that others shared with him. He became an avid sharer of experience, strength, hope, time, and love. He learned to give to others that which was given to him with an open heart and hand. Sometimes what he gives may not be accepted, but the good he is trying to give away returns to him in some manner.

So the ripples of love and giving from the stone thrown in the pond move out, and those of us privileged to watch and experience this movement play a vital role in passing on the good we receive in order that others may benefit. And when others benefit, so do we.

LAW 2

Leave no stone unturned
—Euripides

"Diligence is the mother of good fortune, and idleness, its opposite, never brought a man to the goal of any of his best wishes."
— Miguel de Cervantes

Could this statement by the Greek playwright Euripides be intended to express the idea of going to whatever lengths of strength and effort may be necessary to achieve a worthwhile goal? Perhaps he was advocating the virtue of diligence. Cervantes spoke of diligence as *"the mother of good fortune, and idleness, its opposite, never led to good intention's goal."* Mother Teresa of India goes so far as to declare that *"diligence is the beginning of sanctity.*" And "sanctity" in simple terms is a closer walk with God in the path that higher power has lovingly designed for each person. In working with steady, trusting effort, a person can arrive at the place prepared by divine order, even though obstacles may be present. The person possessing diligence does not allow stones or other obstacles to remain in the way of his progress.

While turning over the stones along one's search for direction and movement toward one's goals, an important awareness may also be not to allow the process itself to cause us to lose sight of what we are striving for. Frantically wasting energy in trying to move enormous obstacles blocking our way can sometimes be an exercise in futility. Calmly allowing our inner guidance to suggest an alternate method of action often shows greater wisdom.

Many explorers, inventors, scientists, and artists have, at one time or another, transcended the limits of the known world in their journeys of discovery. Applying diligence, such individuals often found the strength to struggle onward toward elusive goals.

Leaving no stone unturned, Noah Webster spent twenty-five years compiling the first dictionary of the English language. Robert E. Peary tried for twenty-three years to reach the North Pole before succeeding in the early 1900s. Songwriter Irving Berlin received only thirty-three cents for his first song, yet remained undaunted until he ultimately received international recognition for his music.

Diligence can often produce startling success that, at first, may seem to stretch the imagination. Before he was able to set sail, Christopher Columbus left no stone unturned in acquiring financial backing for his expedition. He convinced Spanish monarchs Ferdinand and Isabella of the viability of his plan to sail westward to reach India and, after the initial voyage, made several further exploratory expeditions. His diligent pursuit of a new trade route to the Indies resulted in the discovery of entirely new lands—the Americas.

Madame Curie spent her entire adult life conducting scientific research. Her diligence in the laboratory resulted in the discovery of the elements radium and polonium and laid the groundwork for nuclear physics and theories of radioactivity. In her case, one stone overturned became a stepping stone to the next discovery. Madame Curie was the first person to be awarded the Nobel Prize twice.

Removing obstacles often requires stamina. When strength is

"Every individual should have a purpose in life which is worthy of intense effort—and constantly work toward the definite goal ahead."
—Roderick Stevens

"Diligence is to be particularly cultivated by use; it is to be constantly exerted; it is capable of effecting almost everything."
—Cicero

"He who destructs the security of chance takes more pains to effect the safety which results from labor. To find what you seek in the road of life, the best proverb of all is that which says, 'Leave no stone unturned.'"
—Edward Bulwer-Lytton

"To keep a lamp burning, we have to keep putting oil in it."
—Mother Teresa

severely tested, discouragement may result, at least temporarily. At such times, repeating the edict of Euripides and continuing to exert more energy may seem fruitless. In truth, the time right now is filled with opportunities for you to express and expand yourself. Expand your awareness and perspective. Expand yourself by doing more, giving more, being bigger in your thinking and feeling. Words found in the New Testament may help us to continue our efforts. *"God did not give us a spirit of timidity, but a spirit of power and love and self-control"* (2 Timothy 1:7). Renewed and refreshed, keeping in mind the power within, a person may have greater strength to follow the counsel of Euripides and continue to *"leave no stone unturned."*

LAW 3

What we focus on expands
—Arnold Patent

"Act with a determination not to be turned aside by thoughts of the past and fears of the future."
—Robert E. Lee

When we focus on a particular thought, our mind often immediately responds by calling up similar thoughts. Positive and loving thoughts and feelings spark a whole range of thoughts and feelings that can lift our spirits. If, on the other hand, we concentrate on negative thoughts and fearful emotions, we may conjure up an ever-greater negativity. Our success in performing a task often depends on whether we focus on positive or negative thoughts. Remember, if we become preoccupied with what we *don't* have (the negative side of our thinking), we may be unable to see clearly what we *do* have (the positive side).

Let's try an exercise. Pause for a moment and focus on the word "blue." Images probably come to mind of the sky or the ocean. We can observe a similar effect with words of a more intangible nature. Consider the word "happy." Focusing on this word might expand our image to such things as a wonderful vacation we enjoyed, a smiling child at play, or to an entertaining movie we once saw. Whatever we choose to focus on, our mind automatically expands that image for us.

Given this truth, wouldn't you rather focus on positive images than on negative ones? In a short scenario, suppose you are faced with a complicated task, and your mind focuses on the word "failure." Suddenly, an image might be evoked in which you fail at your task. This image could expand to the point where you may fail at other tasks and, possibly, to the point where people may ridicule you for your failure. Now, clear your mind, and visualize that you are faced with the same task, and decide to focus on the word "success." Let positive images of accomplishing the task fill your mind. You see images of others appreciating your success, shaking your hand, smiling with admiration. This success image snowballs, and you can see yourself succeeding at other, more difficult, tasks. End of scenario.

But can these thoughts affect your actual performance? Yes! When you focus on a particular image, you tend to talk about what's on your mind. Thus, if your mental focus is on positive images, you're more likely to mention these ideas and images in communication with others. A good listener, who focuses on what is being said, can absorb your positive words and actions, and many constructive images or ideas might come to him. Like the spark that ignites the flame, he may share these good ideas with others, and they, in turn, may share them with still others. Thoughts expand not only within our own minds but expand through others as well.

Doesn't it make sense that if you really *know* something, you can walk forward with greater confidence, greater assurance, and increased capacity to accomplish your desires? Focusing on positive thoughts often produces more positive thoughts, and these can help improve our success when performing tasks. What we focus on, we often talk about to our friends, family, and associates. Thus, our thoughts can expand to those around us. Make a commitment to keep in mind the law of life that states, *"What we focus on expands."* By developing a happy, positive acceptance of the good you have right now, you can ascertain that in the future you can learn how to enjoy the surprises that come your way. It takes practice to do anything well. Instead of dwelling on thoughts or feelings of dissatisfaction, focus on happy and positive expressions of ideas and watch them expand.

Many spiritual teachers know that the human mind is molded from an omnipresent element that takes form, shape, and intelligence, and becomes a part of our thought world. The knowledge and awareness that compose your world often come from what you have held in mind as your inner ideal. Be confident

"In this life we get only things for which we hunt, for which we strive, and for which we are willing to sacrifice. It is better to aim for something that you want–even though you miss it–than to get something that you didn't aim to get, and which you don't want! If we look long enough for what we want in life, we are almost sure to find it, no matter what the objective may be." "He who destructs the security of chance takes more pains to effect the safety which results from labor. To find what you seek in the road of life, the best proverb of all is that which says, 'Leave no stone unturned.'"
—George Matthew Adams

with your mental focus. Are you really alive, alert, awake, and enthusiastic about life? If so, the harvest of abundant living can fill your world with gladness.

❖

LAW 4

As you think, so you are
—Charles Fillmore

"When one's thoughts are neither frivolous nor flippant, when one's thoughts are neither stiff-necked nor stupid, but rather, are harmonious—they habitually render physical calm and deep insight."
—Hildegarde of Bingen

In the course of his spiritual instruction Jesus said, *"By their fruits you shall know them."* He went on to say, *"Are grapes gathered from thorns, or figs from thistles. So, every sound tree bears good fruit, but the bad tree bears evil fruit"* (Matthew 7:15-17). In this message, Jesus was warning the people of false prophets, who might lead them astray—people who were saying one thing while demonstrating something quite different. "Wolves in sheep's clothing," he called them. Beyond that, he was also revealing a very important law of life—a law that, when understood, can help you to demonstrate success in virtually every area of your life.

The unique conditions you may find in your life are like the fruit of which Jesus spoke. The condition of your health, your finances, your relationships, your livelihood; all of these reflect the fruit of certain attitudes. If you don't like the fruit you're harvesting—for example, poor health, financial struggle, difficulty in maintaining meaningful relationships, unhappiness with your work—it's essential that you harvest from another tree!

The writer of Proverbs said, *"As a man thinketh in his heart, so is he."* He understood that it's what we think in our heart that expresses itself in our lives. What you believe about yourself, what you believe about life, can work itself into and through everything you do. Successful living begins by believing yourself worthy of success.

A young woman named Marianne believed she was inferior and her life bore the fruit of that belief. She had grown up on the so-called wrong side of the tracks. Throughout her young life, well-meaning friends warned her not to expect too much because life was hard and it was unfair. For years her life bore the fruit of that belief. She became a prostitute and a drug addict. She was in and out of jail regularly. One day, while walking through a shopping mall, Marianne stole a wallet from another woman's purse. The wallet contained a few dollars, some credit cards, and, among other things, a small pamphlet. Intending to take only what was of immediate value and get rid of the rest, a sentence from the pamphlet caught her attention, *"As a child of God, you are worthy of the best life has to offer."*

In the moments that followed, something strange began to happen to Marianne. Her cold, bitter attitude toward life and people began to melt. Somehow those words struck a familiar note that had long been lost but not quite forgotten. She was further surprised when she found herself desperately feeling the need to return the wallet to the woman. Getting the phone number from a blank check in the wallet, Marianne phoned the woman that day. She explained what she had done and said that she wanted to bring the wallet over to her home immediately.

To Marianne's surprise, there was no bitterness in the woman's attitude. Instead, there was compassion and understanding. Marianne told the woman of her hard life, and her story was received with tender sympathy. The woman offered Marianne a job in one of the many dress shops she owned in the city. She went out of her way to help Marianne release the harsh training of her past and begin to believe in herself. In time, the young woman's life began to bear a whole different kind of fruit. She gradually gained confidence in herself and was able to begin to trust others and see the good in them.

And another person's faith in us can strengthen our own faith in ourself. The mother of a fifteen year old named Doug became increasingly worried when her son's temperature kept rising until it reached 105 degrees. Doug was taken to the hospital, where blood tests revealed leukemia. The doctors were frank, telling Doug that for the next three years he would have to undergo chemotherapy. He may go bald and gain weight. Learning this, Doug became discouraged; although he was told that there was a good chance of remission, he was smart enough to know that leukemia can be fatal.

On the day Doug was admitted, his first time in a hospital, he had opened his eyes, looked around the room, and said to his mother, "I thought you got flowers when you are in the hospital." Hearing this, an aunt called to order an arrangement. The

"Only by much searching and mining are gold and diamonds obtained, and man can find every truth connected with his being, if he will dig deep into the mind of his soul; and that he is the maker of his character, the molder of his life, and the builder of his destiny. He may unerringly prove, if he will watch, control, and alter his thoughts, tracing their effects upon himself, upon others, and upon his life and circumstances, linking cause and effect by patient practice and experience, even to the most trivial, everyday occurrence, as a means of obtaining that knowledge of himself which is Understanding, Wisdom, Power.
—James Allen, *As A Man Thinketh*

*"It is the mind that
makes the body rich."*
—William
Shakespeare

*"What you think
means more than any-
thing else in your life.
More than what you
earn, more than where
you live, more than
your social position,
and more than what
anyone else may think
about you."*
—George Matthew
Adams

voice of the sales clerk was high pitched, and she sounded young. The aunt imagined an inexperienced person who may be unaware of the arrangement's significance. So she said, "I want the planter especially attractive. It's for my teenage nephew who has leukemia."

"Oh," said the sales clerk, "Let's add some fresh-cut flowers to brighten it up."

When the arrangement arrived at the hospital, Doug was feeling strong enough to sit up. He opened the envelope and read the card from his aunt. Then he saw another card. His mother said it must have been meant for another flower arrangement, but Doug removed it; opened it, and began to read. The card said, "Doug, I took the order for your flowers. I work at the flower shop. I had leukemia when I was seven years old. I'm twenty-two years old now, and my life is good. Keep your chin up. You can do what you think you can do. My prayers go out to you. Sincerely, Laura Bradley." Doug's face lit up. For the first time since he entered the hospital, he felt inspired. He had spoken with many doctors and nurses, but this one card was the thing that caused him to believe he might beat the disease.

This story was reported in the *Chicago Tribune* newspaper by Bob Greene. "It's funny," wrote Mr. Greene, "Doug was in a hospital filled with millions of dollars of the most sophisticated medical equipment. He was being treated by expert doctors and nurses with medical training totaling hundreds of years. But it was a sales clerk in a flower shop who, by taking the time to care and by being willing to go with what her heart told her to do, inspired Doug with the hope and will and belief to carry on. The human spirit can be an amazing thing, and sometimes you encounter it at its very best when you aren't even looking!"

Pay close attention to what your heart tells you. If you are working toward prosperity and harmony in life, be certain you truly believe you are worthy of having them. This inner conviction, coupled with action, may produce the fruit in life you so deeply desire. Remember, as you think, so you are!"

LAW 5

You choose the path you want to walk down
−John M. Templeton

"As above, so below" has in recent years also been translated to *"As within, so without,"* and there are many variations on the theme, *"As you think, so you are."* Each of us has a choice about how we respond to any given situation and a choice of the pathway we decide to travel in our journey of life.

As spiritual beings, we were designed to be filled with love and trust. More people seem increasingly to be aware of their responsibility to each other as a member of the human family. Physicists and scientists are conducting experiments in an attempt to prove that we are united; that each living soul is interlinked with others; that we are indeed part of the whole; and that what each of us does affects others. In the last two decades there has been an enormous upsurge of people choosing to believe this and acting accordingly, and, as a result, our world seems to be changing for the better. More and more people are coming to believe that a power greater than themselves is in charge.

Sophie is a recent convert to a belief in spiritual progress. She experienced a dysfunctional childhood, and much of her thinking was very negative. As long as she continued to hold on to old ideas, her journey to spiritual maturity seemed difficult and slow. One day, she was moaning, as was her habit, about a headache. She was rehearsing the headache's progress, how it would probably develop into a migraine by the evening, and how she would miss work the next day—which she really couldn't afford to do. A friend overheard her and suggested that she just might be enjoying her misery. "Why don't you take an aspirin and a hot drink and lie down? Stop holding on to what you don't want. Start believing the headache can go away, and look forward to a wonderful day at work tomorrow—or do you *prefer* being miserable?"

The truth of her friend's words struck Sophie. She followed her friend's advice, and her headache was gone when she awakened from a nap. It was then that Sophie started doing some serious self-examination. She could comprehend how she often

"I have to be wrong a certain number of times in order to be right a certain number of times. However, in order to be either, I must first make a decision."
−Frank N. Giampietro

used sickness as a way of getting attention and vowed to begin reprogramming her thinking process.

Like Sophie, we, too, can begin to work to become masters of our world instead of its victims. Rather than allow ourselves to be consumed by our egos, we need to remember that each of us is a co-creator in life. When we abide in this truth, we can rise above doubts, fears, and negativity and allow the indwelling divinity in each of us to guide us to better solutions.

It is said, *"Hope springs eternal in the human breast,"* but this spark of hope may sometimes seem to be but a faint glimmer. Many persons cry out with Shakespeare's Juliet, *"Come, weep with me!"* These people feel trapped in situations and relationships that seem destructive and depleting, moving from resistance to resignation. Yet, they have a choice!

You may be living in trying times and faced with problems or situations over which you may feel you have no control. You may be confronted—as many people are—with taxes that seem a burden, rising costs of supplies that may make the challenge of financial management precarious. You may feel like an innocent bystander in a world of international conflicts, a society replete with injustices. You may even feel there can be little you can do to change any of this. Yet, you have a choice!

As the poet said, *"Every day that is born into the world comes like a burst of music, and rings the whole day through and you will make of it a dance, a dirge, or a life march, as you will!"* And Scripture tells us, *"Choose this day whom you will serve"* (Joshua 24:15). The winds of circumstance may blow—and not always in the direction you wish! You cannot regulate the winds, and there may really be little to be gained in complaining about them. But you do have a choice.

Ella Wheeler Wilcox sat by the East River in New York City years ago reflecting on the fact that people coming from the same home environment may turn out so differently. Inspired by some sailing vessels pulling up the river to their docks, she wrote the following poem:

> *One ship drives east, and the other drives west,*
> *With the self-same winds that blow.*
> *'Tis the set of the sails and not the gales,*
> *Which tells us which way to go."*

Let's take another quick look at Abraham Lincoln. The winds of circumstance could have blown him into the harbor of stalwart mediocrity, a small circle of farm, home, church, and community life. But he tacked into the teeth of the gale of circumstances, every tack bringing him an opportunity to more education and greater understanding about life, until his mind became a fitting vehicle for the responsibility of sailing the great ship of state as president of the United States.

You may say, "Oh, you're talking about attitudes!" Absolutely! For it can often be our attitude that colors our life. Perhaps you may not be able to change the *fact* of a condition in your life, but you do have a choice in how you think about it. Aldous Huxley said, *"Experience is not what happens to you; it is what you do with what happens to you."* We can choose how we handle anything that comes into our life. We can choose love or hate. We can worry about the situation, or we can pray about it. We can struggle, or we can meet the experience with nonresistance. We can accept the experience as a crushing blow of defeat, or we can lift our eyes and move toward victory. An old Oriental axiom says, *"You may not be able to keep the birds from flying over your head, but you can keep them from building nests in your hair!"*

A man who was crippled from birth hobbled painfully about on crutches. Yet, he was so highly motivated and productive in his field that he put many "whole" people to shame with his accomplishments. He was once asked, "Hasn't your physical handicap colored your thinking about life?" He replied, "Of course it has colored my thinking—but I've always chosen the colors!"

When we rule our minds in a positive way, we choose the path we want to walk down. We are no longer driven by egos. Instead, we become masters of our world and our destiny, and create a life that is happy, joyous, and free.

"There is nothing more to be esteemed than a manly firmness and decision of character. I like a person who knows his own mind and sticks to it; who sees at once what, in given circumstances, is to be done and does it."
—William Hazlitt

Spotlights!

1. The more one works and plants, the more one can harvest. The more good one can do, the more success one can achieve.
2. Much in life depends on the view we take of it.
3. A diligent person allows no stone or other obstacle to remain in his way.
4. One stone overturned can become a stepping stone to the next discovery.
5. Whatever we choose to focus on, our mind can expand.
6. It has been wisely said that things may happen around you; things may happen to you; but the things that really matter are the things that happen within and through you. Be positive and loving!

7. Pay close attention to the wisdom and guidance of your heart.
8. You cannot clear your own fields while you are counting the rocks on your neighbor's farm.
9. How you live your life can help paint your friend's picture of God.
10. Choose to do what you can, where you are, and with what you have!

Living the Law!

The following consciousness conditioners are offered for your contemplation. After reading and thinking about each idea, write your perspectives in your journal.

Symptoms of Inner Peace

1. A tendency to think and act spontaneously, rather than based on past experience
2. An unmistakable ability to enjoy each and every moment
3. A loss of interest in judging others
4. A loss of interest in judging self
5. A loss of interest in conflict
6. A loss of interest in interpreting the actions of others
7. A loss of the ability to worry
8. Frequent overwhelming episodes of appreciation
9. Contented feelings of connectedness with others and nature
10. Frequent attacks of smiling through the heart
11. Increasing susceptibility to love extended by others as well as the uncontrollable urge to extend it
12. An increasing tendency to let things happen, rather than to manipulate them and make them happen.

—author unknown

Week Thirty-One

LAW 1

Destructive language tends to produce destructive results
—John M. Templeton

When David's parents were divorced, the settlement provided that he would live with his mother. Because tightened financial circumstances forced them to move to another city, David had to attend a new school and make new friends. The changes were traumatic for him. He resented the children whose parents were still married, and he often got into fights, with little or no provocation. In his bitterness, he developed the habit of being overly critical of others. He rarely had a kind word to say about anyone.

One day a classmate, who was aware of David's situation, approached him. "My parents are divorced too," he said gently. "I know what you're going through. But you have to let go of your anger and bitterness. You're really hard on people, and it only hurts you. If you can't say something good, it's better not to say anything at all."

"What is lofty can be said in any language. What is mean should be said in none."
—Maimonides

In his pain, David found it difficult at first to appreciate the boy's advice. But since things only seemed to be getting worse, he became more cautious about what he said to others. He often refrained from speaking, whereas before he would have quickly said something sarcastic and cutting. He began to see how insensitively he responded to those around him. Understanding developed that he was not alone in his particular situation. Many of the other children had also experienced difficult family break-ups, and David began to find ways to encourage them and help them deal with their own pain and confusion. By the end of the school term, David made a complete turn-around in his attitude and gained the respect of many whom he had alienated in his earlier anger.

"There are three things that ought to be considered before some things are spoken: the manner, the place, and the time."
—Robert Southey

"A man is seldom better than his conversation."
—German proverb

Any one of us may experience stressful times at home, at school, or in our work. When things are not going well, it is often tempting to criticize others. We may think finding fault with someone else can help us feel better about ourselves or our condition. Or maybe it could be simply that misery loves company!

In those "down" moments that each of us has experienced, it may be best to remain silent if we cannot say things that are helpful and kind. Destructive language tends to produce destructive results. Besides causing unnecessary pain and suffering for those around us, our negative words frequently compound our own problems.

We may feel justified in using harsh and cutting words if we are having difficulty dealing with life's challenges. The young man whose parents were divorced was torn by many unresolved emotions and many feelings he did not understand. He eventually found, though, that belittling and hurting others was not the way to resolve his problems. Through kind and understanding words, or simply by listening with compassion, he learned to give support to others and, in turn, to receive support from those around him and to find it within himself.

In his book *When Bad Things Happen to Good People*, Rabbi Harold Kushner wrote about perspective. He said, *"God has created a world in which many more good things than bad things happen. We find life's disasters upsetting not only because they are painful, but because they are exceptional. Most people wake up on most days feeling good. Most illnesses are curable. Most airplanes take off and land safely. . . . The accident, the robbery, the inoperable tumor are life-shattering exceptions, but they are very rare exceptions. When you have been hurt by life, it may be hard to keep that in mind. When you are standing very close to a large object, all you can see is the object. Only by stepping back from it can you also see the rest of the setting around it. When we are stunned by some tragedy, we can only see and feel the tragedy. Only with time and distance can we see the tragedy in the context of a whole life and a whole world."*

If we could keep this perspective in mind when situations are disruptive or disturbing and learn to "hold our tongue" until the bigger picture becomes more clear, perhaps a lot of destructive language could be avoided. In various areas of life, people who are burdened with problems can cast a deadening influence on themselves and others. They stress the negative rather than the positive. It is important to learn that inventive thinking can result from a constant search for solutions.

The time-honored adage *"If you can't say something good, then don't say anything at all"* can be a benchmark for the words you speak throughout the day. If you feel discouraged about something, talk to a friend or a counselor if necessary. Everyone has dark moments. But be careful not to lash out and hurt others when you're not feeling good about yourself because they, too, may need words of understanding and support. Always be sensitive in what you say to others. Try to remember that the bad moments will pass, and, when they do, there may be no unnecessary wounds to heal!

"Gentle speech makes friends."
—Wisdom of Sirach

Law 2

Success feeds on itself and creates more success
—John M. Templeton

Sometimes, as we start out in adult life, we may not feel like much of a success. Our society frequently defines success as the material goods and lifestyle secured by large amounts of money earned over a long period of time. We tend to think success is something that occurs only later in life. However, this belief may impede us from achieving success even then. Success takes practice, and successful people start practicing when they are young!

Think about it for a moment. A musician must practice diligently to become a virtuoso. A medical doctor studies for many years and interns for an additional period of time prior to beginning a viable practice. An athlete trains long hours before becoming a star. Likewise, it takes practice to experience success in life. If you want to feel like a success, it is important for you to begin to acknowledge your successes right now.

Many times the things at which we're naturally gifted are the hardest for us to claim as a success. We may make statements like, "If I can do it so easily, why can't everyone else? If I can do it, it cannot be that hard!" It is important to listen to the acknowledgment we receive from parents, teachers, employers, and friends. Don't brush it off as if they're just being nice. They

"To follow, without halt, one aim: There's the secret of success."
—Anna Pavlova

"In achieving success, backbone is more important than wishbone."
—Frank Tyger

"Whoever perseveres
will be crowned."
—Johann Gottfried
von Herder

"He that succeeds
makes an important
thing of the immediate
task."
—William Feather

"Success consists of a
series of little daily
victories."
—Laddie F. Hutar

"The road to success is
not to be run upon by
seven-leagued boots.
Step by step, little by
little, bit by bit—that is
the way to wealth, that
is the way to wisdom,
that is the way to
glory."
—Charles Buxton

may be telling you, "You are a success right now!" Answer with a sincere "Thank you." There is no need to say anything else. Making disparaging remarks about yourself or your performance can be false modesty and negates the compliment that was given to you.

Occasionally, when a compliment is delivered with some criticism, you may be tempted to give up. You may feel that since nothing you do is good enough, why bother to try. Don't give in to those feelings. Many people, especially your family, may have a difficult time making it clear that they appreciate your talent and are supportively behind you. Although they may want you to develop your skill to the best of your ability, it might be difficult for them to express this feeling in words. And if they take time to point out your mistakes, they may be really saying, "I know you can do better that this. I care and I want to help you."

We are often our own harshest critics, and we have a tendency to hear only criticism from others and not their praise. It is important to practice hearing both compliments and constructive remarks from those who have good advice to offer. As you begin to recognize and build on the success you're experiencing now, you may discover that this is a feeling you can create again and again in various aspects of your living.

Whenever anyone says to you, "Good work!" think to yourself, "Yes, it *is* good work. I am successful with this." A swelled head is never helpful, of course, but to acknowledge your gifts is not necessarily self-indulgent, especially if you recognize you couldn't have achieved success without the support and guidance of others—like parents, teachers, friends, and co-workers. If they comment, "Okay, but you might do better," realize you may have more to give, and receive this advice with an open mind and heart. Determine to do your best. You are the one who will benefit.

A story is told about a little boy who called at a house selling picture postcards for a quarter each. The man who answered his knock asked the lad what he was going to do with the money he earned.

"Oh," he said, "I'm raising $100,000 for our new church building."

The startled customer responded, "Do you expect to raise it all by yourself?" The young man answered with a straight and serious face, "Oh, no, sir. There's another little boy helping me!" This young man had the spirit of success at an early age!

Knowing right now—feeling inside right now—that you're successful, whether you're a singer in the church choir, a waitress in a restaurant, the coach of the softball team, or the budding mechanic spending every spare moment in the garage rebuilding the engine of that antique car, can prepare you for greater and greater success. Success is not a one-time event. It can be an accumulated series of wins and other experiences that create a successful life.

LAW 3

Never put off until tomorrow
what you can do today
—Lord Chesterfield

Did you ever experience a problem so difficult and complex that you didn't know how to begin to solve it? Have you faced an examination that involved so much material you didn't know where to begin to study for it? Most people have found themselves in such situations and have often felt overwhelmed.

In the mid-1770s, Philip Dormer Stanhope, known to the world as Lord Chesterfield, decided to write his son a series of letters that would pass along sensible advice for living what he considered to be a positive life. His witty and elegant writings instructed the young man in all aspects of a gentleman's conduct and accomplishments. Among the counsel offered was the now famous statement: *"Never put off until tomorrow what you can do today."*

There can be many reasons why one should not delay action. Problems can grow more serious and complex when they're not addressed promptly, as they arise. Minor difficulties treated in a positive, active manner generally do not become major issues. For example, a minor cut properly treated can heal quickly. But if left untreated and exposed to additional adverse conditions, it can become infected and require serious medical attention. Thus, a minor inconvenience may become a major problem.

In the same way, loans of money that are not repaid on a timely basis can become major debts when interest on such loans accumulates. Doing what is possible today to make life

"People today distinguish between knowledge and action and pursue them separately, believing that one must know before he can act. . . . They say (they will wait) til they truly know before putting their knowledge into practice. Consequently, to the end of their lives, they will never act and also will never know."
—Wang Yang-ming,
Instructions for
Practical Living

"Concern should drive us into action and not into a depression."
—Karen Horney

"In the dim background of our mind, we know what we ought to be doing, but somehow we cannot start. Every moment, we expect the spell to break, but it continues, pulse after pulse, and we float with it."
—William James

"It is an undoubted truth that the less one has to do the less time one finds to do it in. One yawns, one procrastinates, one can do it when one will, and therefore, one seldom does it at all; whereas those who have a great deal of business must (to use a vulgar expression) buckle to it; and then they always find time enough to do it in."
—Lord Chesterfield

better can translate into a more orderly and productive tomorrow. The key can be careful assessment of what needs to be done immediately, and then how much of what needs to be done can be sensibly accomplished without damage to other areas of one's life.

If you are one of those persons who may feel overwhelmed by an approaching examination or job test, take heart. By steadily reviewing notes and asking questions about confusing material when confusion first surfaces, you can lessen your ordeal considerably. When studying is approached sensibly, there may be no need to lose sleep or to forgo healthy exercise and relaxation. Good study habits practiced today can prevent the need tomorrow for ineffective cramming because of panic.

Steady effort is more productive than sudden, frenzied activity. Orderly progression toward a goal prevents the tangle of problems that so often occurs when too many small areas needing attention suddenly come together. Doing the best you can do on a daily basis often frees more energy for further study progress in the future. Steady effort can move a person comfortably toward a goal, with energy left to handle unforeseen difficulties.

If a person were to ship a fragile vase in a carefully packed, sturdy box directly to a friend, most likely the vase would arrive in good condition. If, instead, the vase was poorly packed in a thin-walled box and delayed at many stations along the way, it would most likely arrive in a damaged condition. This analogy can also be true of problems or difficulties. The longer you ignore them and the more poorly they are handled, the bigger the problems can become.

Elizabeth Blackwell, the first woman doctor in the United States, started her practice in New York in 1851. Not only was she unable to find patients, no one would even rent her a room once she mentioned that she was a doctor. After weeks of trudging the streets, she finally rented rooms from a landlady who asked no questions about what Elizabeth planned to do with the rooms.

Quaker women, who had been receptive to the goal of equal rights, became Elizabeth's first patients. But no hospital would allow her on its staff. Finally, with financial help from her Quaker friends, Elizabeth opened her own clinic in one of New York's worst slums.

The clinic opened in March, 1853. Elizabeth hung out a sign announcing that all patients would be treated free. Yet, for the first few weeks, no one showed up. Then one day a woman in such agony that she didn't care who treated her staggered up the steps and collapsed in Elizabeth's arms.

When the woman was treated and recovered, she told all her friends about the wonderful woman doctor on Seventh Street. The dispensary was soon going well and eventually expanded into the New York Infirmary for Women and Children—now a large and thriving hospital on East Fifteenth Street.

Each of us moves toward major goals by steps in a process. Usually these steps are small ones. Whenever we put off taking the necessary steps, progress can come to a standstill or recede even farther into the future. By following Lord Chesterfield's advice and not putting off until tomorrow what can be done sensibly today, we can achieve an orderly, harmonious, steady movement toward whatever goal we have set for ourselves.

"Do not delay; the golden moments fly!"
—Henry Wadsworth Longfellow

LAW 4

Nothing is interesting if you are not interested
—John M. Templeton

Many people have heard the phrase, *"What you see is what you get."* This saying calls to mind a law of life that has nothing to do with *what* is being seen and everything to do with *who* is doing the seeing. Two people can wake up in the same neighborhood, on the same day, to the same conditions, and yet have a vastly different day depending on who is doing the seeing. One person may have a positive attitude and awaken with the thought, "Good morning, God!" The other may dwell in pessimistic shadows and greet the day with "Good God, morning!" Same words, but a vastly different emphasis. So, what *you* see is what you get and what *I* see is what I get! Perspective can be the key ingredient.

This same analogy holds true with how interestingly life unfolds for you. Nothing is interesting if you are not interested in life. The concept of choice can be of utmost importance

"The world is as large as the range of one's interests. A narrow-minded man has a narrow outlook. The walls of his world shut out the broader horizons of affairs."
—Joseph Jastrow

"Age is not a question of years. The years may wrinkle your skin but it is the lack of interest that wrinkles your soul."—General Douglas McArthur

"A person with a hundred interests is twice as alive as one with only fifty and four times as alive as the man who has only twenty-five. What are you interested in? Are your interests confined to your food, your home, your business, your clothes, your immediate family? If you would be free from nervous tension and live a healthier life, widen your interests, broaden yourself. There is a rich world around you in books, paintings, music, sports, and most important, people."
—Dr. Norman Vincent Peale

when we talk about perception. It is important to understand that we may be making a choice to see the proverbial glass half full or half empty.

Belief can be another important factor and concept to reflect upon as part of how we view life. What is your belief about life? Think about this for a moment. Perhaps even write down some concepts you may presently hold. Do you believe that life is moving forward? How do you view the variety of experiences that life brings you each day? Do you view life as a progression? Do you believe that the very nature of the universe is progressive? Do you believe that you are endowed with a wonderful potential for creating good in your life? Perhaps potential that may be limited only by your thoughts about yourself? If you answer "yes" to the above questions, you are living an interesting life because you are interested in the multifaceted aspects of living.

An Eastern legend tells of a fair maiden who was offered a rare gift by the king of the land. The king presented her with a bag of pearls and promised her she could keep the largest, most perfect pearl she could find in the bag. However, he set down these conditions: she must choose one pearl only; she must remove one pearl at a time from the bag and either accept it or reject it; and she could not take that pearl up again for another look once it was rejected.

So, joyously the maiden began taking the pearls, one at a time, from the bag. In the process, she saw and held many large and perfect pearls. But she was looking for the one gem that would be just a little larger and a little more perfect. So she passed up many special treasures.

As she delved more deeply into the bag, the pearls became smaller and of poorer quality. Occasionally, she found pebbles instead of pearls. Now, inasmuch as she could not go back to the pearls she had formerly discarded, she had to keep on looking. The pearls continued to become smaller and less valuable. Even the pebbles became more common. When the maiden reached the bottom of the bag, she sadly went away as empty handed as when she arrived at the place.

This legend can also portray us when we may sometimes rush through life seeking to get a better job, a bigger house, a better mate, a more glamorous social life, or whatever, and we miss the great pearls of abundance all around us every day. Where is our focus of interest?

We may be searching for the kingdom of heaven, which is right within us all the time, yet often we recognize it not. Then we sit down, dreading to go on because of our concern that things may get worse tomorrow. Either way—the rushing around or the sitting down and waiting—can produce the same results. Nothing much happens! This is why we often hear the phrase from philosophers and teachers, *"Now is the most important moment of your life."* We cannot go back even two seconds, nor can we leap forward two seconds. We live in the eternal moment of now, and our interest in life and its offerings exist in this moment. *NOW* is the time of choice and blessing.

It can take every moment that we live of life's days to think on the true, honest, just, pure, and lovely things of life. These are the things that guide us into experiencing the true happiness and excitement available for our lives. These become the pearls of great price.

The American philosopher Charles Fillmore said, *"When you experience any kind of inharmony, you can be certain that you are entertaining some kind of false illusion. We have the priceless pearl of truth right in front of us, but are we willing to sell all to obtain it. Are we ready to give up all false illusions and head straight for truth?"* Wow!

When you look at yourself in the mirror, the important thing is not your face, but your mind that looks back at you. Jesus taught that what you think in your mind is the source of what really counts. The Bible says, *"Out of the heart are the issues of life"* (Proverbs 4:23). If you are curious about your future condition, take a look at how you interact with life in the present moment. Are you excited about new adventures and experiences the day may bring? Do you eagerly anticipate the opportunities that may knock on your door? Are you expectantly looking for the good in every situation? Do you give thanks at the close of each day for the abundance of blessings you may have received?

Remember, the more sincere interest you express in life, the more joy and success life can bring into your world. A big difference between happiness and misery, success and failure, effectiveness and uselessness, competence and ineptitude, courage and fear, strength and weakness, cannot be blamed on circumstances or other people. Rather, the condition of your mind is the more causative factor. Nothing is interesting if you are not interested!

"People do not get tired out from working where work is intelligently handled. Work, if it is interesting, is a stimulant. It's worry and a lack of interest in what one does that tire and discourage. Every one of us should have our pet interest—as many as we can handle efficiently and happily. Our interest should never be allowed to lag or get cold so that all enthusiasm is spent. Each day can be one of triumph if you keep up to your interests—feeding them as they feed you!"
—George Matthew Adams

LAW 5

What is done is done
—William Shakespeare

Two Zen monks were on their way to the market one day when they came to a large mud puddle that prevented them from continuing on without getting dirty. By the puddle was a fair young maiden who wished to continue on but also didn't wish to get dirty. To solve the problem, one of the monks offered to carry her across the puddle, even though this kind gesture violated the vows he had taken never to speak to or have contact with a woman.

Once safely across the puddle, the woman thanked the monk and went on her way. The two monks continued on to the market but did not exchange a single word for the remainder of the day. That evening, when they returned to the monastery, the monk who had watched the other carry the woman across the puddle accused his friend of being unfaithful and sacrilegious. Over and over, he asked the other monk how he could have taken his vows so lightly. The angry tirade continued for well over an hour. Finally, the monk who had done the good deed turned to his fellow monk and said, "I'm the one who violated my vows by carrying her across the mud puddle, but whereas I set the woman down on the path many hours ago, you continue to carry her!"

In examining our own lives, we might be able to spot the heavy weight of yesterday's deeds that we persist in carrying with us. We might be carrying bitterness and resentment because we may have felt betrayed by a friend. We might be carrying anger and a feeling of injustice because we lost out on something we really wanted while someone else got it. We might be carrying hurt feelings because someone we liked criticized us. But continuing to carry harsh and negative feelings from the past can be like picking up a pebble in your shoe while you are out walking. You can stop and remove the pebble, or you can continue to walk and let the pebble irritate your foot and cause pain. The choice is yours. You can release your anger and hurt feelings, just as you can remove the pebble from your shoe.

Dr. Carl Simonton, among others, has said that the bodies

"I look back on my life like a good day's work; it was done and I am satisfied with it."
–Grandma Moses

that develop cancer have often been weakened by emotional or psychological factors as well as physical factors. He said, *"Our body responds to the way we live, particularly our emotional reactions to life. We don't know how many cancer cells we normally develop during a lifetime, but it is probably thousands, if not millions–or even billions–in a normal lifetime without developing the disease. So, our body normally has intact mechanisms for handling this very easily and automatically."* An important knowledge we can gain in staying healthy is that there is a natural healing mechanism in the human body. Could a part of that mechanism be releasing, letting go, and forgiving people or situations that may have caused us pain?

When you try to continue living a normal life while carrying harsh feelings about someone else, other things in your life become affected. A small, dark cloud seems to hang overhead that warns of foul weather. The next time you feel angry or hurt, give the situation time to settle down, then go directly to the source of your anger. Explore the situation; make peace with the circumstances; and release the angry thoughts and feelings. This may oftentimes mean swallowing your pride and forgetting about who is right or wrong so that you can continue along the path of life without the extra weight of negative feelings.

In his letter to the Romans, Paul wrote, *"If possible, so far as it depends upon you, live peaceably with all"* (Romans 12:18). This is sound advice. The great law of cause and effect is the avenger and is permanently active. You may not see the connection between cause and effect, but nevertheless the law of cause and effect is operative. How foolish it seems to send out vindictive, unforgiving thoughts toward a so-called enemy. We can make an effort to "live peaceably with all." We can forgive and forget injuries, hurts, and disappointments. We can have as our focus loving and harmonious thoughts toward ourself and toward others. As Shakespeare said, *"What is done is done!"* Nothing you or anyone else can do will erase the events of the past. Forgive, but also forget!

"The past is a bucket of ashes, so live not in your yesterdays, nor just for tomorrow, but in the here and now. Keep moving and forget the post-mortems."
–Carl Sandburg

"Look not sorrowfully into the past; it comes not back again. Wisely improve the present; it is thine. Go forth to meet the shadowy future without fear, and with a manly heart."
–Henry Wadsworth Longfellow

Spotlights!

1. Destructive language tends to produce destructive results.
2. Kind and understanding words, and compassionate listening, can provide support and, in turn, enable one to receive support.
3. Inventive thinking results from a constant search for solutions.

4. Making disparaging remarks about yourself or your performance can be false modesty and negate the compliment you received.

5. Success may not be a one-time event. It can be an accumulated series of wins that create a successful life.

6. Through the exercise of steadfast focus on your goals, you may come closer each day to becoming a more successful and happy person.

7. The concept of "choice" can be of utmost importance when we talk about "perception."

8. The more sincere interest you express in life, the more joy and success life can bring into your world.

9. Do you persist in carrying around yesterday's deeds, or do you live in the present moment?

10. Maintain loving and harmonious thoughts toward yourself and others.

Living the Law!

It has been said that the one thing that can limit the expression of your happiness and the fulfillment of your sincere desires is your own non-application of the laws of life and the power of infinite mind in your life. Priceless pearls of happiness are before you NOW to claim as yours. Let's take a look at ten of them from the book *Helping Yourself with Macrocosmic Mind* by Rebecca Clark.

1. KNOW WHO AND WHAT YOU ARE. FIND YOURSELF. Realize you are an important part of God's plan, a unique link in the human chain that extends from creation into the unknown future. Not again will an "aggregate of magnificent atoms" just like you stand on this earth. Know this. Be secure in your beingness as a child of God. See yourself as God sees you—Glorious! *"I and the Father are one."* (John 10:30).

2. COUNT YOUR BLESSINGS! When problems loom and confusion and troubles mount, we sometimes forget the good already expressing in our life. It has been said that every atom in the universe responds to praise and thanksgiving. You really cannot afford not to count your blessings! *"I will give you the keys of the kingdom of heaven."* (Matthew 16:19).

3. ACT MATURELY. *"When I was a child, I spoke as a child, I understood as a child; I thought as a child; but when I*

became a man, I put away childish things." (I Cor. 13:11). Grow up a little more each day. Learn from life, but wear the learning lightly, remembering that we must put away childish things. However, we need not lose the childlike simplicity of those who are the "children of God."

4. ELIMINATE FEAR. Life may be so often filled with fear—of ourself, of others, of unknown things, of what we regard as obstacles, of what we may feel as "being outside of God." (As if we ever could be!) Fear thwarts happiness. Fear is the most destructive of emotions, surpassing even jealousy in its corrosiveness. And it's totally unnecessary! *"Fear not, little flock, for it is your Father's good pleasure to give you the kingdom."* (Luke 12:32).

5. GIVE OF YOURSELF. No one can live happily solely unto himself. It is part of normal living to want to give of what we have—our love, service, devotion, help, praise, friendship, encouragement, or plain, ordinary kindness. The more quickly we seek to respond to this inner core of our nature, the more quickly we may achieve happiness. *"Give and it shall be given unto you."* (Luke 6:38).

6. VALUE SIMPLICITY. It is important to rediscover simplicity. Truth is simple. Simple pleasures of life are often counted among the greatest, and the simple truth qualities of love and goodness—although not always the most sophisticated or highly valued in our so-called advanced technological society, are still great sources of happiness. *"The law of the Lord is perfect, reviving the soul; the testimony of the Lord is sure, making wise the simple."* (Psalms 19:7).

7. WELCOME CHANGES. One of Nature's immutable law is that all things must either progress or perish. Perhaps you may have heard the phrase: *"Nature abhors a vacuum and allows not the static."* This being so, it becomes important to our happiness to learn to flow like a gentle river through the changes that enter our life. We can welcome changes with a knowing that it may be for the "better." Label no new idea as impossible. If life seems to hand you a lemon, then make lemonade! Without changes, we might still be wearing skins and living in caves! *"And we all, with unveiled face, beholding the glory of the Lord, are being changed into his likeness from one degree of glory to another."* (II Cor. 3:18).

8. EXERCISE THE LAW OF UNLIMITED SUPPLY. What goal would you set for yourself if you absolutely knew

you could not fail? What dream would you manifest if you knew you had unlimited resources? What exciting work would you choose if you absolutely knew you could acquire the skill necessary to perform this work? What projects would you launch if you knew you had the wisdom and the power to remove all obstacles and be totally successful? *"The Lord was with him; wherever he went forth, he prospered."* (II Kings 18:7).

9. PAUSE TO ENJOY LIFE! Serenity is never in a rush, never impatient, or short of time. Take the time to enjoy life to the fullest, to stand and stare at something beautiful. A painting. A tree. Hug a tree! Praise a glorious sunset, or sunrise. Appreciate your child, your mate. *"Your sorrow will turn into joy."* (John 16:20).

10. GOD FIRST! This is the best way! God and you form a majority of one. There is nothing that cannot be accomplished when you place your hand in God's care and keeping. Perhaps happiness cannot be "perfect" or "total" on this earth plane, but we can come mighty close to expressing our inner light and obtaining as much peaceful happiness as possible. Remember, a smile is the light in the window of your face that tells everyone that your heart is at home. *"God is my salvation."* (Isaiah 12:2).

Week Thirty-Two

❖

LAW 1

We can become bitter or better as a result of our experiences
—Eric Butterworth

Identical twins brothers attended their twentieth high school class reunion. One brother was a successful writer. The other failed miserably at everything he tried. The successful brother was asked what he perceived as the critical factor that helped him achieve success, and he quickly answered, "My parents."

This story illustrates how two people can come from the same background and yet interpret its effect on them in entirely different ways. The story doesn't tell us how the parents treated each of the brothers as they grew up. It may be possible they favored the successful one. They may have seen a potential in him and gave him advantages the other brother did not have. It is also possible they may have favored the one who failed! The parents may have absorbed the consequences of his mistakes instead of allowing him to learn from them. Whatever the case may have been, as a result of their childhood experiences, one brother was prepared to move ahead and explore his potential, while the other brother held back and wallowed in negativity—a truth expressed eloquently by minister Eric Butterworth, who said, *"We can become bitter or better as a result of our experiences."*

An article in *Abundant Living* magazine tells of an Irish uprising in 1848 in which the men were captured, tried, and convicted of treason against Her Majesty Queen Victoria. All were sentenced to death. Passionate protest from all over the world persuaded the queen to commute the death sentences. The men were banished to Australia—a place as remote and full of prisoners as Russian Siberia was later. Years passed. In 1874 Queen Victoria learned that a Sir Charles Duffy who had been elected prime minister of Australia was the same Charles Duffy who

"But there are roughly two sorts of informed people, aren't there? People who start off right by observing the pitfalls and mistakes and going around them, and the people who know they're there because of that. They both come to the same conclusions, but they don't have quite the same point of view."
—Margery Allingham

had been banished twenty-six years earlier. She asked what had become of the other eight convicts and learned that Patrick Donahue became a brigadier general in the United States Army; Morris Lyene became attorney general for Australia; Michael Ireland succeeded Lyene as attorney general; Thomas McGee became minister of agriculture for Canada; Terrence McManus became a brigadier general in the United States Army; Thomas Meagher was elected governor of Montana; John Mitchell became a prominent New York politician, and his son, John Purroy Mitchell, became a famous mayor of New York City; and Richard O'Gorman became governor of Newfoundland!

What happens to us on the journey of life is not nearly as important as *how we handle what happens*. Life sometimes takes unexpected twists and turns that can throw us off course for a time. We may have experienced an unhappy childhood in a broken home or with parents who were alcoholics. We may have been considered the "black sheep," the one who just never fit in with the others. Almost anyone can find reasons for not doing as well as he thinks he should have. The key to successful living, however, is to learn from our experiences, good and bad, and go on from there. If we choose, we can try to move forward and forge the kind of life we desire to live in spite of some of the falls we may have taken.

"Our patience will achieve more than our force," said Edmund Burke. The longer we live, the more opportunity life gives us to perfect ourselves if we but put purpose in living. If you want to know whether or not you are successfully walking the path of life, ask yourself this question: "Is my life like a brush pile or a tree?" In contrasting your life in this manner, remember that the brush pile is a heap of cut and broken branches. From a distance it may look like a tree, but its branches have no communion with a living stem, and they are in a process of decay. The tree, however, is still alive, and its branches are vitally related to one another. Thus, you can tell the difference!

Imagine for a moment that you have reached the end of your life and are reflecting on the many and varied scenarios that have comprised your world. Wouldn't you want to look back with pride, knowing you had made the best of each situation, regardless of how difficult it may have been? Isn't this better than looking back and sorrowfully wishing you had handled things differently? To guard against possible regrets, it is important to handle every experience to the best of your current ability. You may have to practice more patience; strive a little harder to accomplish your goal; reach inside yourself a little deeper to garner greater strength; and muster a little more faith in God and yourself. You may need to make a commitment to push yourself harder and farther than at any time in the past. After you have given everything you feel you have to give and still seem to come up short, there is nothing to be ashamed of because you have done your best. You can experience the inner peace of those who know they gave their all. You can be a success regardless of the outcome. You can be better, not bitter, from the experience because you know you really gave your best effort.

The commitment of giving your best at all times enables one to find value in—and lend value to—every experience in life. Take what is given to you to accomplish today, and make it a most wonderful expression of your gifts and talents. Utilizing your inner resources in this manner, you can look back over the events of your life with satisfaction and peace of mind, because there will likely be no regrets.

"The world is a looking glass and gives back to every man the reflection of his own face. Frown at it and it will in turn look sourly upon you; laugh at it and with it and it is a jolly kind of companion."
—William Makepeace Thackeray

LAW 2

Joy is not in things, but is in you
—John M. Templeton

How beautifully the great teacher Jesus trod the path of joy! He said, *"These things I have spoken to you, that my joy may be in you, and that your joy may be made full"* (John 15:11).

Jean Paul Richter once said, *"Joys are our wings; sorrows our spurs."* And Henry Ward Beecher commented, *"Joy is more divine than sorrow, for joy is bread and sorrow is medicine."* Joy is an experience almost everyone seeks, but the question becomes *Where do we find it?* The response can be, "Long-lasting and true joy is found in the spiritual dimension." *The seed idea of joy is hidden within you!* If you desire to walk the paths many master teachers trod, you can walk the path of joy. And this becomes easier to do when you sincerely love people!

In his book *Human Destiny*, LeCompte DuNouy pointed out that there are many levels of observation on the physical, men-

"When the power of imparting joy is equal to the will, the human soul requires no other heaven."
—Percy Bysshe Shelley

tal, and spiritual planes. Many scientists in certain fields of research agree that there are also many levels of human consciousness. We know we have a physical body, and we know that we have myriads of thoughts. However, it appears that not all people are aware of their spiritual levels.

Have you ever listened to your own voice on a tape recorder? Or saw yourself on videotape for the first time? Were you just a little shocked to learn how you actually sound or look to others? Often we think we sound or look differently from others' perspective of us. We may not be communicating to others what we really feel and what we really are. The love-light of Spirit needs to shine through us clearly and brightly if we are to bring the harmony and order of God into our family and friends.

For the positive qualities of our spiritual nature to be expressed fully, it needs to move through three phrases of expression. First must come acceptance of the fact that we have a spiritual nature. Next, the idea expands and develops into an attitude that we hold toward life. Most of all, the idea and attitude must shine forth through the avenues of communication we use with one another.

As an example, let's look at the quality of joy. To actually have joy and happiness present in us and in our lives in any real sense, it is important to first believe that we were meant (created) to live happy, fulfilling lives. This belief then progresses to become an attitude or a habitual way of looking at life and responding to it. This habitual way of looking at life can then allow us to recognize that persons, places, things, and situations can hold possibilities that may simply be awaiting our discovery. By making a full circle of joy—from an idea that we accept to the actual expression of that idea in our life—we can not only communicate this joy to others and bring the blessing of joy expressed, but we can also gain a wonderful feeling of confidence in knowing that others may receive happiness from the expressions we give to life!

When Jesus said, *"Let your light so shine before men that they may see your good works and glorify your Father who is in heaven"* (Matthew 5:16), he may have been talking about letting the joy of the spirit shine forth from us. Charles Fillmore held the idea that *"Life for every person should be a journey in jubilance!"* When we think of the pain and suffering, the poverty and hardship, the personal and worldwide conflicts that seem to abound, these words may seem to be the height of pure Pollyannaism. However, Fillmore's statement is a concept that touches the very heart of truth. Did Jesus not say, *"You will know the truth and the truth will make you free"* (John 8:32)? This freedom is not that which comes by *revolution* against the enslaving forces in the world but by *revelation* from within so that one can see things from the high perspective that evokes the consciousness of joy. Actually both of the above statements suggest an excellent test of consciousness. Ask yourself, Am I an incorrigibly happy person? Is the life I am living a "journey in jubilance"? If your answers are negative, then perhaps you may not be receiving the full benefits from your studies of spirituality. Or, your answer might indicate that the insights of love and joy may have been stimulating to the mind but not yet registering in the heart.

A rich parent can force wealth upon his children through a cunningly contrived will. The board of health can, and often does, force health upon those who otherwise refuse to keep themselves sanitary. But there is no way that one who is not happy and who makes no effort to achieve happiness has the blessed state of joy thrust upon him by an act of Congress, by God, or by any other agency! Why is this? Simply as Seneca once put it, *"A happy life is one which is in accordance with its own nature."* This is but another way of saying that joy comes not from outer things or experiences but from our inner consciousness.

Within each of us is an unborn possibility of abounding joy, and ours is the privilege of giving birth to it at any time. It is the little fire of spirit that one may smother but never quite extinguish.

"To complain that life has no joys while there is a single creature whom we can realize by our bounty, assist by our counsels, or enliven by our presence, is to lament the loss of that which we possess, and is just as rational as to die of thirst with the cup in our hands."
—Thomas Fitzborne

LAW 3

Misfortunes can be blessings
—John M. Templeton

An old story tells about missionary Robert Livingston, who lived among the natives in a small, primitive African tribe. He suffered from a rare blood disease that required him to drink fresh goat's milk daily. During a visit to the village, the tribal king became enchanted with Livingston's goat. Now, it was the local custom that everything belonging to the villagers was automatically considered to be the king's property if he so desired.

"Our real blessings often appear to us in the shape of pains, losses and disappointments; but let us have patience, and we soon shall see them in their proper figures."
—Joseph Addison

"The difficulties, hardships, and trials of life, the obstacles one encounters on the road to fortune, are positive blessings. They knit the muscles more firmly, and teach self-reliance. Peril is the element in which power is developed."
—William Matthews

"To believe that no misfortune will befall you is like not wishing to live; misfortunes are a necessary part of life."
—Solomon ibn Gabriel

Having no choice but to honor the village custom, the missionary offered his goat to the king, knowing that he had just given away the very thing his life depended on.

The king appreciated Dr. Livingston's gesture and, in return, handed him what appeared to be a long walking stick he had been carrying. As Livingston turned away to go home, he sadly lamented to his house servant that he was afraid he wouldn't be able to live without his daily supply of goat's milk. The servant quickly turned to Livingston and said with a gasp of surprise: "Master, don't you realize what the king has given you? That's his scepter, and anything you desire in the entire kingdom is yours!"

How many times have we faced a disappointment or misunderstanding in our relationship with a colleague, family member, or friend? Whatever the difficulty, it is important for us to realize that a positive outlook can make a difference, can turn a "stick" into a "scepter." A poor evaluation at work can actually lead to a promotion if you accept it as a positive challenge to do a better job.

Throughout history there are countless examples of famous scientists and explorers who set out to prove one thing and failed, but who went on to discover something more significant. For example, Christopher Columbus was trying to find a new trade route to China and Japan. Imagine his disappointment when, instead of landing in the Orient, he found himself thousands of miles away from his original destination on some strange, unknown land mass, later called America. This failure, however, would eventually earn him a permanent place in history as one of the world's greatest discoverers.

British Conservative statesman and prime minister Benjamin Disraeli was once asked to define the difference between a calamity and a misfortune. Taking the name of his great rival, Gladstone, as his example, Disraeli said in jest, *"If, for instance, Mr. Gladstone were to fall into the river, that would be a misfortune. But if anyone were to pull him out, that would be a calamity!"* In his journal of December 10, 1801, Stendhal (Henri Beyle) wrote words of wisdom, stating, *"Almost all our misfortunes in life come from the wrong notions we have about the things that happen to us. To know men thoroughly, to judge events sanely, is, therefore, a great step toward happiness."*

Challenges have a way of cropping up when we least expect them, and because they seem constantly to surprise us, we may not be prepared to handle them in an appropriate manner. Many people tend to "get their hackles up" before taking a moment to remember that *misfortunes can be blessings*. Regardless of the appearances of the situation, the truth is that God is there in the midst of the confusion, ready and willing to respond to our needs. Often when we feel unprepared, we may become alarmed, confused, frustrated, irritated, and perhaps even become frightened and angry. These emotions can be overcome when we "stand firm and see the salvation of the Lord."

Friedrich Von Hugel once said, *"How greatly we add to our crosses by being cross with them!"* Think for a moment, do you get cross with your crosses? Jesus said, *"Take up your cross and follow me"* (Matthew 16:24). This is a very clear instruction to follow the pathway of love in solving a problem, isn't it? It doesn't help to sit and complain about a situation. The experience may have come to you for a purpose, and when you follow the guidance of the spirit within, you may find that the purpose is a good one.

By turning our thoughts around, we can turn our own lives around. If we let negative ideas and fears invade our minds when our plans fail, our world may be filled with self-doubt and insecurity. Once we become aware of how often we limit ourselves through negative attitudes, we can begin to concentrate on positive thoughts. A consistent, positive attitude—making a stick into a scepter—can allow us to turn an impossible situation into a positive opportunity to find happiness and success.

"The sages do not consider that making no mistakes is a blessing. They believe, rather, that the great virtue of man lies in his ability to correct his mistakes and continually make a new man of himself."
—Wang Yang-ming

LAW 4

Happiness pursued, eludes; happiness given, returns
—John M. Templeton

There once was a man who determined to find happiness for himself. He created a business that brought great wealth, but he worked much too hard and found no happiness in that. He gathered other wealthy people around him who were quite interesting and led fascinating lives. Yet, something was missing, and their companionship did not bring him the happiness he sought. He then married a woman who he thought had all the qualities of wit and grace that would make any man happy. But she, too, was looking for someone to give her happiness, and neither of them could live up to the other's expectations. When a child was born, the man was convinced that, at last, this would give him happiness, but children require time, patience, and nurturing; and he was much too busy with his career and many friends to devote so much time to child care. So instead of happiness, he found that his children simply became another responsibility. One day he decided happiness might be found in having no responsibilities at all. He left his business, his friends, his wife and family and ran away where he could live an idyllic life of leisure.

There is no end to this story. It is doubtful that a life of leisure brought this man any happiness either. He is probably still looking. He might even try a new career, new friends, new family, thinking that it may have been these things in his earlier life that caused the problems. He may never realize that it is within himself that happiness can be found. In truth, he has always carried it within him. His own uniqueness as an individual is like a deep well of happiness. But it needs the pump "primed" so the good can flow forth, circulating to others and back into his own life. It is a choice that must be made. If only he had learned that "happiness adds and multiplies as it is divided with others."

If the man's work had been about sharing his special talents and giving and serving others instead of just accumulating money he might have found happiness in the joy of freely giving. If he had learned to give of himself to his friends and family, to consider their happiness instead of just his own, then the love he gave could have returned abundantly. This man can represent a possibility in each of us. We also may have believed that the outer things in life bring contentment. We may be outwardly in pursuit of happiness and find that it eludes us. But if happiness is already within us as a product of our own individuality, how can we recognize it, draw it forth, and give it away?

We can initiate the flow of good by first appreciating our own uniqueness. Then, it is important to feel secure enough in recognizing and knowing ourselves that we can look for and appreciate that same uniqueness and diversity in others.

Be aware of the power of your words. Sometimes loving and positive words may be the greatest gift we can give. Look with sincerity for the special talents of others, and tell them the good you see. Give encouragement when it is needed. Be a pleasant reminder of past accomplishments, joys, and triumphs. Be appreciative and accepting. Be willing to say, "I love you."

Forgive generously. And perhaps most important of all, learn to say, "I'm sorry," when it needs to be said. No matter who may be right or wrong, these sincere words can be a gift that reverberates happiness to everyone involved.

Be kind. Happiness can be a phone call to a friend who may be lonely or ill or facing a difficult time. It may be listening, without giving advice, to someone who needs to talk, helping with a chore, running an errand, or anticipating a need.

Can money and possessions be gifts from our own well of happiness? Yes, they can when they are given with a joyful heart. Sharing what we have with those who are in need can multiply our happiness if our motivation is appropriate. We should give with the idea of sharing or easing another's pain or hardship, and not to glorify a false sense of benevolence, or to get our name in the paper, or provide a good tax write-off.

When Ernest Hemingway won the Nobel Prize for the novel *The Old Man and the Sea*, he gave the money to the Shrine of the Virgin in eastern Cuba, where he lived. He said, *"You don't ever have a thing until you give it away."* True giving is done with no other motive than to share the happiness we find within ourselves. It is not manipulation of others. When we are blind to our reservoir of happiness and believe we are empty inside, we often give from our own sense of lack or unworthiness. We may try to fill the void by buying or earning happiness. This defeats our purpose. To sacrifice self and always put others' needs before our own can become as destructive as not giving at all. We can measure our giving by the barometer of our inner feelings of peace and well-being. If we have given in love from our store of happiness, it becomes like the ripples on a pond that move outward but also ripple inward to their source.

Like the man who hungered after happiness, it may be easy to mistake "getting" with "being." Adding anything to our lives in a material or outer sense only gives a very fleeting, and often false, sense of contentment. The paradox of achieving personal peace and happiness may be that what we are looking for is already within us, and in giving it away we experience it most powerfully for ourselves.

"Those who are not looking for happiness are the most likely to find it, because those who are searching forget that the surest way to be happy is to seek happiness for others."
—Martin Luther King, Jr.

"An effort made for the happiness of others lifts us above ourselves."
—Lydia M. Child

LAW 5

Thoughts of doubt and fear are pathways to failure
—Brian Adams

One summer evening a man sat alone in his backyard, which bordered upon a peaceful forest. His goal was to relax and enjoy the quiet pleasures of an evening close to nature. As darkness fell, the man began to notice the wind blowing stronger in the trees. Soon he began to wonder if the fine weather would last. Next, he became aware of the strange sounds stirring from the depths of the forest. He imagined menacing animals stalking close by. Before much time passed, the man's mind was completely taken up with negative thoughts, and he grew increasingly tense. The more the man allowed the thoughts of doubt and fear to enter his mind, the farther he moved from his goal of enjoying the peaceful summer evening. His experience illustrates the law of life expressed by Brian Adams that states, *"Thoughts of doubt and fear are pathways to failure."*

The twin monsters of doubt and fear frequently play a leading role when a goal is not achieved. When allowed to remain in mind, these two negative forces can multiply and overrun a person's ability to enjoy a situation or to see positive strategies that can help overcome temporary difficulties. *"Attempt the end, and never stand to doubt,"* said Robert Herrick, *"Nothing's so hard but search will find it out."* And we can affirm with Emily Brontë, *"No coward soul is mine, No trembler in the world's storm-troubled sphere; I see Heaven's glories shine, And faith shines equal, arming me from fear."*

For example, a student who is mentally or physically fatigued, poorly nourished, or emotionally upset may provide doubt and fear with a resting place. A student who seriously doubts his ability to perform on a test may, in fact, perform poorly. Tension created by a growing sense of insecurity can mentally erase the facts a person needs to remember.

"Thoughts of doubt and fear are pathways to failure" holds true in the animal kingdom as well. A horse about to take a hurdle sometimes balks short of the jump if it senses doubt or fear in its rider. The situation that the rider fears most— failure to complete the jump—can be the end result. Doubt and fear are like

"The thing we fear we bring to pass."
—Elbert Hubbard

"Doubts and jealousies often beget the fact they fear."
—Thomas Jefferson

thieves who rob the precious moment of its rightful dominion and joy. They bring about manifestations of disease, lack, and inharmonious relationships.

To avoid failure in a situation, thoughts need to be focused on positive directions. Successful athletes illustrate such positive thinking when they perform. Concentrating on successfully completing the play at hand leaves no room to consider any outcome other than success. A supportive audience can also aid the player's performance by concentrating on the action along with the athlete. In professional golf, the audience surrounding the player often joins him in deep, silent concentration. The audience collectively holds its breath until the golfer takes the shot. After the shot is completed, onlookers let out their emotions in the form of shouts, hand clapping, and cheers. Even the disappointed "ohs," should the shot fall short, indicate the audience believed the shot would be successfully completed.

In 1914, a doctor advised Selig Grossinger to take a vacation from the fast pace on the Lower East Side of New York City. After three weeks in the mountains, Grossinger returned to the city rested, strengthened, restored to clear thinking, and determined to buy a small farm in the Catskill Mountains for his family. The rock-strewn farm that the Grossingers purchased had no electricity or indoor plumbing and did not provide an income. So they decided to take in boarders who sought good food, fresh air, and quiet surroundings. The Grossingers were such good hosts that, in spite of the farm's primitiveness, they soon had more guests than they could handle. Within five years, the family was able to buy a larger, more modern place nearby, which became the world-famous resort hotel *Grossingers*. The family was so busy following the adventure of a dream, they allowed no possibility for doubt or fear to mar their vision.

Thoughts are pathways and positive thoughts are upward pathways. When clogged by doubt and fear, our thoughts are often of failure and defeat. When the pathways are well chosen and fortified with positive thoughts and expectations, the monsters are usually defeated. In a positive mind, doubt and fear are not allowed to be present to sabotage ultimate success.

"A person who doubts himself is like a man who would enlist in the ranks of his enemies and bear arms against himself. He makes his failure certain by himself being the first person to be convinced."
—Alexandre Dumas

"Valor grows by daring, fear by holding back."
—Publilius Syrus

Spotlights!

1. Reflect on the story of the brush pile and the tree to provide an analysis of present perspective in your life.
2. It is important to handle every experience to the best of your current ability.
3. Three phases of expression are (1) *accepting an idea,*

(2) *allowing the idea to become a positive attitude, and* (3) *communicating that idea and attitude through daily living.*

4. Within each of us is an unborn possibility of abounding joy, and we can give birth to it at any time.
5. By turning our thoughts around, we can turn our lives around.
6. Each experience may come to us for a purpose.
7. Be aware of the power of your words.
8. Give encouragement when it is needed.
9. Forgive generously and be kind.
10. Share your abundance with loving motivation.
11. Worry can create doubt, and doubt can draw fear as its companion.

Living the Law!

In the Unity booklet *Take the Wings of the Morning,* Rev. Eugene Sorensen wrote an effective formula for knowing that what you are expressing can be what you want to express to others. Simply stated it is PROJECT. REJECT. ACCEPT.

> *As soon as you get up each morning, consider the attitudes of mind and heart you wish to portray in your day's activities and to the people with whom you work or come into contact.*
>
> *PROJECT joy, love, peace, and assurance on the screen of your mind. Determine that this is the way you are going to live all day long.*
>
> *Now, walk over to a mirror and see if you can put these qualities into your facial expression, into your eyes, into your mouth, into your posture. Notice how you feel inside. Notice the way you look on the outside.*
>
> *The next step is simply to go through your day, and the moment you are aware that you are not looking on the outside the way you felt early that morning on the inside, REJECT the false picture you are portraying and immediately accept once again your original radiant expression. Do this right in the midst of the many activities of your day.*
>
> *You will probably be amazed at the response of people and conditions in your life. ACCEPT that your attitude will foster happy, satisfying relationships, and you will have a new sense of peace and calm that will promote harmony and order in all the things you do. Actually, you are praying in a very powerful way and making yourself an instrument through which your prayers can be answered. . . . PROJECT, REJECT, ACCEPT, and you will know the light of Truth shines through you!*

Week Thirty-Three

LAW 1

By their fruits you shall know them
—Matthew 7:18

We can realize how rich we are when we pause to count our blessings! The wonderful substance of God flows in and through us and extends from us in every direction. Truly, there is no place we can go where we are not bathed in the infinite sea of the substance of the universe. There may be a number of ways to open the channel for our good to flow *to* us, but have we looked recently at the many ways good can flow *from* us? And what are some of the areas of this abundance?

During his ministry, Jesus told those who were near, *"You will know them by their fruits"* (Matthew 7:16). Later, the apostle Paul tells us what those good fruits are: *"The fruit of the Spirit is love, joy, peace, patience, kindness, goodness, faithfulness, gentleness, self-control; against such there is no law."*

Why is there no law against such characteristics? If we look around us, we see that laws are needed only when these good fruits are lacking. The fruits of the Spirit are available for every person, all the time, and in every circumstance or situation. God has packed these good possibilities away in the divine ideal for every person just as God has hidden within every watermelon seed the possibility of a delicious, full-grown melon. The good fruits of Spirit have been given to every one of us, but it is our job to cultivate them and bring them into abundant harvest in our lives. How can we do this? Let's take a closer look at each of the "fruits."

So much has been written and spoken about *LOVE*. Love has been called our "human rose." Many flowers grow in many gardens, but none may be more beautiful than some roses. And in our soul-soil, flowers also grow, and none more beautiful than love! Love is more than affection. It is that magnetic, attractive

"Man is man because he is free to operate within the framework of his destiny. He is free to deliberate, to make decisions, and to choose between alternatives. He is distinguished from animals by his freedom to do evil or to do good and to walk the high road of beauty, or tread the low road of ugly degeneracy."
—Martin Luther King, Jr., *The Measure of Man*

force that binds families, friends, states, and countries together. Love has been called the "harmonizing glue of the universe." It is an inner quality that beholds good everywhere and in everyone. It has been called the "great healer," and *"Love, therefore is the fulfillment of the law"* (Romans 13:10).

JOY has been referred to as the happiness of God expressed through his perfect idea—humanity! We find that joy and gladness are strength giving, especially when our mind is fixed on being a channel for good. I often feel God isn't really solemn or else he wouldn't have blessed man with the incalculable gifts of joy and gladness.

All of us, on some level of our being, desire the gift of *PEACE* to manifest itself to a greater degree in our life. Peace is more than freedom from strife; it is a positive assurance that only the good is true. When we are peaceful within, external events rarely disturb that "calm peace of our soul." A modern-day teacher said, *"Steadfast affirmations of peace will harmonize the whole body structure and open the way to attainment of health conditions in mind and body."*

And how many of us have, at times, longed for more *PATIENCE!* This is that powerful attitude of mind that is often characterized by poise, serenity, inner calmness, and quiet endurance—especially in the face of trying or upsetting conditions. The gift of patience has its foundation in faith. *"The proving of your faith worketh patience"* (James 1:3).

KINDNESS is one of the gentle expressions of love. We grow in grace when we become aware that one of God's gifts to us can be that we may share our loving kindness with all of creation. People all over the world are seeking peace of mind, solutions to everyday problems, better relationships with other people, and a more meaningful way of life. Surely we are aware of the room for improvement within ourself and in our life. A healthy serving of loving kindness—both giving and receiving—could make a difference!

Lowell Fillmore said, *"GOODNESS is more than simply refraining from doing evil. It is a definite positive awareness of God's unfailing perfection."* Goodness can be as much a commission as it is a possession. We don't really "possess" it until we are committed to living it, when we carry it out into action in our own life. When we establish an enduring consciousness of good, we can see many problems disappear as darkness before light.

FAITHFULNESS is being always reliable. If you are faithful, you are dependable and always keep your promises. You are honest and inspire confidence in your neighbors.

GENTLENESS is a tremendous assist to anyone who seeks to develop understanding. The wise pray, as King Solomon so well knew, for an understanding heart. An understanding heart is filled with love and wisdom, compassion, vision, and the ability to bring vision into manifestation. An understanding heart is trusting and expectant of good. An understanding heart is undisturbed by the clamor, noise, and confusion that may reign around it, for it is kind and gentle! Gentleness brings calmness, quietness, and humility.

SELF-CONTROL is truly the starting point of all control. Have we not heard that all things begin on an inner level? Have you ever watched a marionette or puppet show where the characters appeared so lifelike that you forgot they had no will of their own; that they were controlled by the puppeteer? We are created to be the master of our life, not a puppet. When we begin to know of our self-control through prayer and thrift and forward planning in daily living, life begins to take on deeper meaning. We understand we have the ability to take charge of our life, and we begin with self-control.

How could we be truly happy working with any plan that failed to produce the harvest of the good fruits of the Spirit? Our nature is designed to produce and to live on the fruits of the Spirit; and when, by our choices, other fruit may be produced by us, we can have a crop failure! Scripture reminds us of the importance of the fruits of the Spirit in Matthew 4:4, *"Man shall not live by bread alone, but by every word that proceeds from the mouth of God."*

"I think one's feelings waste themselves in words, they ought all to be distilled into actions and into actions which bring results."
—Florence Nightingale

"The great things you intend to do some time must have a beginning if they are ever to be done, so begin to do something worthwhile today."
—Grenville Kleiser

LAW 2

Optimism has its roots in the abiding goodness
—Anonymous

It may be an oddity of human society that the people who are the most distrustful, who raise the most objections to what is happening or what might happen, who can point out the most faults in a system or proposed idea, and who can see other's

"The optimist may not understand, or if he understands he may not agree with prevailing ideas; but he believes, yes, knows, that in the long run and in due course there will prevail whatever is right and best."
—Thomas A. Buckner

"Goodness is always an asset. A man who is straight, friendly, and useful may never be famous, but he is respected and liked by all who know him. He has laid a sound foundation for success and he will have a worthwhile life."
—Herbert N. Casson

"Goodness consists not in the outward things we do, but in the inward thing we are. To be good is the great thing."
—Edwin H. Chapin

lowest possible motives, are often considered by some to be wise! These cynical views are actually considered insightful, realistic, and helpful to the common good because they see the areas and things that pose a threat.

Cynicism often brings unproductive consequences into a person's life, while optimism has its roots in the abiding reality of life's basic goodness. The optimist interprets life in the most favorable way possible and confidently trusts that whatever is best can happen. Have you noticed that things often work out well for the people who expect good things to happen? As Ralph Waldo Emerson wisely said, they know that their *"welfare is dear to the heart of being"* and that the universe is a hospitable place.

Optimism doesn't necessarily mean that nothing "bad" can ever happen to you and that you will receive everything you desire. Everyone faces challenges in life, but an optimistic attitude knows that any situation has the potential of being made better and, therefore, contains the potential for good. The intent of the optimist is to discover that good. When confronted by difficulty, the healthy optimist doesn't pretend there is no confusion, fear, or pain. He is honest about his feelings and still believes in a good outcome, even if he doesn't yet see how it may manifest itself.

Father Tom Walsh, a psychotherapist, has taught a popular course called "Humor, Hilarity, Healing, and Happy Hypothalmia" at the Franciscan Renewal Center and at various churches in Phoenix, Arizona. Walsh, who has counseled many depressed persons, observes, *"You cannot be depressed, or anxious, or angry when you're laughing. It can't be done."*

Emerson writes fervently and eloquently about optimism, and he did so in the years following the ill health and deaths of his first wife, two brothers, and his adored six-year-old son. Such tragedies could cause some people to become bitter and cynical. But though he experienced deep grief, Emerson's love of life's goodness would not allow any warping of that high belief.

You, too, can carry what Emerson called that *"infallible trust and . . . the vision to see that the best is the true. In that attitude, one may dismiss all uncertainties and fears, and trust that time will reveal the answers to any private puzzlement."*

LAW 3

*If you think you know it all,
you are less likely to learn more*
–John M. Templeton

As you go about your daily activities, perhaps you meet people whose lives seem tangled and for whom living seems a hard experience. Not in every case, but certainly in many instances, the trouble may be that the people are often caught up in the trap of personal ego; they feel that they know everything already and fail to listen. And it is a truth that if you think you know it all, you are less likely to learn more.

Bill Johnson, well known for his overinflated ego, was constantly reminding his employees, family, and friends of his many accomplishments in life. As president of a successful business, Bill was quick to seize any opportunity to tell his workers how he single-handedly took over a company on the brink of bankruptcy and turned it almost overnight into a profit-making machine. To his friends, Bill constantly boasted about having the most talented and attractive children in the neighborhood. At home, Bill always had the last word. In fact, Bill was so full of himself that he had a custom wall plaque made to hang over his fireplace that read, "Bill Johnson is God." After returning from the office one evening, Bill discovered a small note placed below the plaque. It read, "One small step for Bill Johnson; one giant step for atheism!"

Perhaps the idea of humility and of giving life the humble approach could work effectively in many instances. Those taking the humble approach acknowledge that their humility comes from the ultimate realization that the universe and all the creatures within it, both visible and invisible, may be manifestations of infinite creative power. The divine spirit may move in your life and make it over from within so that things are seen in a new light, and love can become the spontaneous expression of a Spirit-filled soul.

In *Sand and Form*, Kahlil Gibran wrote, *"I have learned silence from the talkative, tolerance from the intolerant, and kindness from the unkind; yet strange, I am ungrateful to those teachers."* Are there some important lessons to learn from reflecting on these words? Sometimes, if we listen to learn, the things that may

"To think of learning as a preparation for something beyond learning is a defeat of the process. The most important attitude that can be formed is that of desire to go on learning."
–Daniel Bell

"If a man has come to that point where he is so content that he says, 'I do not want to know any more, or do any more, or be any more,' he is in a state in which he ought to be changed into a mummy."
–Henry Ward Beecher

"He who comes up to his own idea of greatness must always have had a very low opinion of it in his mind."
–William Hazlitt

"By learning humility, we find that the purpose of life on earth is vastly deeper than any human mind can grasp. Diligently, each child of God should seek to find and obey God's purpose, but not be so egotistical as to think that he or she comprehends the infinite mind of God.

"The problem with pride is that it puts you in competition with everyone and everything and thus makes it difficult to seek the Truth. As C. S. Lewis said, 'Pride gets no pleasure out of having something, only out of having more of it than the next man.'

"Humility and pride–the former is in tune with God, whereas the latter is out of harmony with His teachings. Pride can learn this lesson of great value from humility–that no one is better or worse than anyone else."–John M. Templeton, *Riches of the Mind & Spirit*

make us uncomfortable can provide valuable insights. We can recognize what we don't want as well as what we do want in our life.

Lao Tzu also commented about listening in his writing,

> *We look at it (Tao) and do not see it;*
> *Its name is The Invisible.*
> *We listen to it and do not hear it;*
> *Its name is The Inaudible.*
> *We touch it and do not find it;*
> *Its name is The Subtle (formless).*

"Build thee more stately mansions, O my soul." How clearly the poet saw that one of the great laws of life is growth. No one is exempt from this law, and no one lacks the equipment or the ability to grow. The Bible tells us that man was created and given dominion and authority over the earth, and the requirement for us is to demonstrate that dominion. The real dominion we need to attain is not an outer one at all; it is within ourselves. Building more stately mansions is an inner project, and the spirit within helps us build these mansions. How can we hear the guidance of the whisperings of spirit if we are too busy talking about unessential things to listen?

The art of listening can be an humbling experience. When we open ourselves to another's point of view, we may discover many new and exciting ways to look at any subject. If we examine a single leaf that has fallen from a giant tree, we can literally discover a number of ways to observe the leaf. The artist or poet may see form, color, and beauty. The biologist may see evidence of the purpose of the leaf to the tree. The atomic physicist may see trillions of atoms amazingly organized. The groundskeeper may see the leaf as littering his garden path. The caterpillar may see food for metamorphosis into a glorious butterfly. The wonders of God's creation abound—even in a simple leaf!

Our thoughts can turn to the Old Testament prophets who seemed to have such a wonderful rapport and communication with God. Back in the time of Moses, according to the Scriptures, it seemed that God's voice was clearly audible. From the heights of a mountaintop, God spoke. From the fiery center of a burning bush, God spoke. Through significant dreams, God spoke—and the people listened.

We may not know whether or not God actually spoke to Moses in an audible voice or through an inner voice. In our present time, we do need to listen and hear God through the many ways in which he speaks to us. For instance, we may have heard God speaking through our quiet thoughts, through good books and expressive music, through conversations with other people, through children's activities, and through the beauty and wonder of nature. And in everything, it seems something worthwhile can be learned.

Often in our ignorance, or nonthinking, we hinder God and stop the current of divine messages. But when we are permeated with a lively faith and sincere desire to learn, messages of love and guidance flow to us and through us like a beautiful river that has found smooth passage through our life-stream.

LAW 4

We carry within us the wonders that we seek without us
—Eric Butterworth

When you were a baby, you may have been aware of your own needs and desires and nothing beyond them. If you needed food or a dry diaper, you didn't care whether your parents were asleep or needed time to finish their own meal; you simply demanded what you wanted. As you grew, confident that your survival needs would be met, you moved on to other aspects of the world around you. Have you ever watched a baby playing with its toes and fingers? There abides a fascinating exploration of a whole new world. You did that also as a child, and as you gained mastery over each little bit of your physical world, you continued your explorations.

During childhood years, you were perhaps mostly concerned with your parents' expectations. When you started school, you also became concerned with the various teachers' expectations. During adolescent years, you may have became preoccupied with what your peers thought about you. As an adult, you may have had many opportunities to experiment with creating a satisfying life. Each of these stages prepared you for the time when you could discover the deeper truth: what really makes the difference in the way you experience life is what you believe *about*

"He got the better of himself, and that's the best kind of victory one can wish for."
—Miguel de Cervantes

"Every man's work,
whether it be literature,
or music, or architec-
ture, or anything else,
is always a portrait of
himself."
—Samuel Butler

"I soon realized that
no journey carries one
far unless, as it extends
into the world around
us, it goes an equal
distance into the world
within."
—Lillian Smith

yourself and what you believe *is possible* for yourself.

The love and approval we first seek from our parents and family, then from other authorities, such as teachers, then finally from our friends, can be felt and experienced more easily if we love and approve of ourselves. Adam Smith, writing on this subject, stated, *"It is not from the benevolence of the butcher, the brewer, or the baker that we expect our dinner, but from their regard to their own interests. We address ourselves, not to their humanity, but to their self-love."*

Can you remember an incident from your childhood when you worked very hard to accomplish something? You felt proud, good about yourself; and if your parents or someone else told you how well you did, you knew they were right. You felt affirmed. Do you also remember a time when you thought you got away with something? Maybe someone talked about you when you had not accomplished your work or hadn't done the best you could. Can you recognize your feelings at the time as confusing, embarrassing, or deceitful?

Can you now see that in the first incident, what happened was that someone merely affirmed what was true about you? Your feeling of value did not come *from* them but was merely confirmed *by* them.

If you are fortunate, you have a teacher or a mentor whom you admire and from whom you want to learn. Sometimes you may feel you could never be like that admired person, but you can. The fact that you are attracted to that person can be proof you have the capacity to express some qualities you so admire in another. It works the other way as well. Sometimes we may feel repelled by or hateful toward another. Those feelings can be inner warnings that we, too, may be capable of behaving in that same unattractive manner. At such times, it becomes important to recognize that you can choose to express the loving, kind, caring qualities you possess.

One of the greatest gifts we have to give to humanity and the world can be our own growing consciousness of life. As we rejoice in the refreshing currents of life that flow through us mentally, emotionally, physically, and spiritually, we can bless our world and everyone in it. *"Work wonders from within"* are the words to a song that encourages us to reach deeper and higher. But we are not likely to rise any higher than we believe we can. And we have such a wide variety of beliefs to choose from that we may sometimes get confused. However, if we believe we are made in the image and likeness of God, a life-giving spirit and therefore master of life, we can seek to develop those wonders within!

Because, as children, our needs are basic and are met by others, it may be easy to believe others always have the answers for us. As we grow and our needs change, we can come to recognize that we have within us the things we need to create lives of joy, usefulness, wonder, and value.

LAW 5

The shadow of ignorance is fear
—J. Jelinek

Fear is one of the greatest challenges we face today, as individuals and as a society. Fear holds us back from the fullest expression of ourselves; it prevents us from loving ourselves and others. Unreasoning, irrational fear can lock us in an invisible prison. Yet, fear may also have uses that can serve us. Some fear may be necessary for self-preservation. An instinctive awareness of danger can alert us to potential harm and help us mobilize the resources we need to keep ourselves from injury. Without fear of consequences in risky situations, we might rush in "where angels fear to tread."

As advanced communication technology brings world events into many homes, we learn about other cultures, and the shadow of ignorance can be dissipated along with fear of the unknown. Thomas Henry Huxley spoke of this in *A Liberal Education*. He wrote, *"The chess board is the world, the pieces are the phenomena of the universe, the rules of the game are what we call the laws of Nature. The player on the other side is hidden from us. We know that his play is always fair, just, and patient. But also we know, to our cost, that he never overlooks a mistake, or makes the smallest allowance for ignorance."*

Many times we fear things that cannot hurt us. We may accelerate a natural anxiety we feel in an uncomfortable emotional situation into a state of fear and panic. When this happens, we become unable to live fully. We may cower in the face of possi-

"Fear is a question: What are you afraid of, and why? Just as the seed of health is in illness, because illness contains information, our fears are a treasure house of self-knowledge if we explore them."
—Marilyn Ferguson

"No power is strong enough to be lasting if it labors under the weight of fear."
—Cicero

*"And I will show you
something different
from either
Your shadow at morn-
ing striding behind
you
Or your shadow at
evening rising to
meet you;
I will show you fear
in a handful of
dust."*
—T. S. Eliot, *The
Waste Land*

ble humiliation and forgo making a creative contribution. Fear of rejection may prevent us from working for the things we really need. We may refuse to commit ourselves because of the risk of failure. Fearing nonconformity, we may relinquish our individuality. It is important to distinguish between fears that can assist us and those that may hurt or hinder us.

Perhaps you've heard the old saying, *"What you don't know won't hurt you."* That is far from the truth. Ignorance is not equivalent to bliss. Instead, it often produces fear and confusion. However, once you know the multitude of your blessings and how you may help others, the shadow of false fear should no longer have control over you.

Franklin Delano Roosevelt wrote, in his message to Congress on January 6, 1941, these immortal words: *"We look forward to a world founded upon four essential human freedoms. The first is freedom of speech and expression–everywhere in the world. The second is the freedom of every person to worship God in his own way–everywhere in the world. The third is freedom from want . . . everywhere in the world. The fourth is freedom from fear . . . anywhere in the world."*

Spotlights!

1. Review the "fruits-of-the-Spirit" essay. How well are you harvesting this crop in your daily life?
2. The fruits of the Spirit are available for you, all the time, and in every circumstance or situation.
3. An optimist interprets life in the most favorable way possible and trusts that the best can happen.
4. The pessimist fears misfortunes and, therefore, can attract them!
5. Be willing to realize there is always much to learn, regardless of how much you presently know.
6. Your feeling of value may be affirmed by others, but it has its birth within you.
7. Work wonders from within. You can do it!
8. We can come to see that most of our fears are phantoms.
9. Ignorance is not equivalent to bliss!

*"Present fears are less
than horrible imagin-
ings."*
—William
Shakespeare

Living the Law!

Life offers many opportunities for self-reflection. After reading the following prose, ask yourself these questions. If I portrayed the monk in the story, what would be the splendor of service I may have given? What elements of my character could benefit from greater development?

A story is told of a monk who earnestly prayed that a vision of Jesus Christ might be revealed to him. After praying for many hours, the monk heard a voice telling him the vision would appear the next morning at daybreak. Before the first rays of dawn appeared the following morning, the monk was on his knees at the altar.

A fierce storm was brewing, but the monk paid it no heed. He watched and prayed that the vision would appear. As the storm broke in great fury, a soft knock came at the door. Interrupted in his devotions, the monk turned away from the altar to open the door. He knew that some poor wayfarer was seeking shelter from the raging storm. As he turned, he caught a glimpse of the vision for which he prayed.

Torn between his desire to stay and see the vision—which he felt would last but for a moment—and his desire to help a brother in distress, he decided that duty must come first. Upon opening the door, he gazed into the bright blue eyes of a small child who had lost her way. She was tired, shivering from the cold, and hungry.

The monk gently reached out his hand and led her into the warm room. He placed a bowl of milk and some fresh bread before her, and did everything he could think of to make her comfortable.

Then with a heavy heart, he went back toward his altar, fearing that the vision had vanished. To his joy and surprise, it was there—clear and bright and shining with radiant glory! As the monk gazed rapturously upon the previous vision for a long time, he heard a gentle voice saying, "If thou hadst not attended to my little one, I could not have stayed."

It is often said that life is but a day. But let us reverse this statement and say with greater awareness that each day is a life! Each new day is a life, fresh and filled with reinstated power, enabling you to go forward on an untrod path of wonderful experience. You are born anew every time the sun rises and lights up the world. Each new day embodies the fullness of the past, the excitement of the present, and the promise of tomorrow. Each day is a new opportunity for service!

Week Thirty-Four

❖

LAW 1

You're either part of the problem, or part of the solution
—Eldridge Cleaver

"Bad times have a scientific value. There are occasions a good learner would not miss."
—Ralph Waldo Emerson, *Considera-tion by the Way, The Conduct of Life*

It has been said there are two kinds of people in the world: those who see a problem, define and describe the problem, complain about the problem, and finally become part of the problem; and those who look at a problem and immediately begin to search for a solution. For the person who focuses on the problem, life can seem like an uphill battle. However, if you are among the solution seekers, life can present you with many exciting opportunities for growth. The choice of how you respond to life's situations is up to you. The result? *"You're either part of the problem, or part of the solution."*

It can be easy to become part of the problem. Anyone focus-ing on a number of conflicting facts and possible scenarios may perceive a dozen different reasons why something cannot be accomplished. It may require more effort to discipline your mind to work on ways in which the problems can be solved. What might seem to be an insurmountable obstacle for "prob-lem" people can become an opportunity for growth for the solu-tion seekers.

"Adversity is the school of heroism, endurance the majesty of man and hope the torch of high aspiration."
—Albert A. Whitman

A story is told about two men who were walking along a forest path late one night. It was quite dark, and the men had difficulty in seeing the path. Suddenly, both men fell into a large pit, loosely covered with brush and leaves. Escape seemed impossible without outside help. Lamenting their terrible mis-fortune, one man sat down, buried his face in his hands, and did nothing. The other man immediately began to search for an escape. While groping in the dark, his hand touched a long tree root hanging from the side of the wall. He quickly pulled himself out of the pit and extended his hand to assist his complaining friend out as well.

The challenges you face may not be as extreme as falling into a pit, but the decisions you make about handling the situations can be crucial in terms of success or failure, now and in the future. You may be given the opportunity to engage in gossip. Perhaps you might join others in complaining about a co-worker. You may be tempted to disregard a company policy just because everyone else is doing it. In each case, you can be either a part of the problem or a part of the solution. Whichever role you choose can have an enormous impact on your future.

Make a conscious effort to be a solution seeker. Remember, it doesn't take courage, genius, or effort to be a problem person. Becoming a solution seeker helps you feel good about yourself and more confident about your capabilities. It can also evoke feelings of admiration and respect from those around you. They see that you are a person who knows how to get things done. Through your positive, goal-driven approach, you may even inspire them to greater levels of achievement.

Indian prime minister Jawaharlal Nehru commented, *"Crises and deadlocks, when they occur, have at least this advantage: that they force us to think."* And Mao Zedong of China had this to say about solving problems: *"You can't solve a problem? Well, get down and investigate the present facts and the problem's past history! When you have investigated the problem thoroughly, you will know how to solve it."* The words of these leaders can encourage us to become more observant and aware of the facts in a situation. Time taken to consider these facts can often restrain the urge to jump to incorrect conclusions.

A wise boss helped his colleagues to become problem solvers by keeping on his desk a sign saying, "What do you suggest?" When brainstorming new and better ways to accomplish a goal, he encouraged each assistant to begin with the words, "Would it be better if . . . ?" Do you see how this thought-provoking attitude can open doors to new possibilities?

"A thorn can only be extracted if you know where it is."
—Rabindranath Tagore

"All adverse and depressing influences can be overcome, not by fighting, but by rising above them."
—Charles Caleb Colton

LAW 2

A loving person lives in a loving world
—Ken Keyes

Two students, Bill and Mike, moved to new towns with their parents. Bill disliked his new community from the first day. He felt the new school was inferior to the one he had attended in his former hometown. His new classmates seemed boring and unfriendly. "I wish we hadn't moved here," Bill told his parents. "This is a cold, dull place, and I'll never fit in."

Mike was far more fortunate. He discovered his new school was not only excellent academically but provided many interesting activities and challenges. "I can't believe how many new friends I made today," he stated to his family at the dinner table after his first day at Miller High. "I feel as though some of the students have been my friends forever." Before you pity Bill for not moving to a town as warm and friendly as the one Mike moved to, you should know that they moved to the same town, the same neighborhood, and they attend the same school!

Why did two young people respond to a similar situation so differently? Bill tends to expect the worst in life, whereas Mike is outgoing and friendly. Mike went to the new school with a smile on his face and an open and positive outlook. Mike is a loving person who lives in a loving world.

The loving person creates a positive atmosphere. Jill, for example, was a loving person. She was the friend you could count on—always ready to listen, to help, and to comfort. When Jill's mother died of cancer while Jill was still in high school, she was surrounded by love, not only from her family but also from her many friends. Jill's giving of herself was being returned tenfold. Even in great sorrow, she lived in a loving world.

The loving person can feel hurt, can experience anger, can be put out at someone for some reason. These are human emotions. Life, after all, offers its share of disappointments, troubles, worries, and sorrows for each of us. We cannot expect continuously happy days. But the loving person refuses to allow negative emotions to become dominant. The loving person can forgive another who may have hurt him. The loving person goes for a long walk or becomes involved in an activity that takes his mind off the feelings of anger or frustration that may be threat-

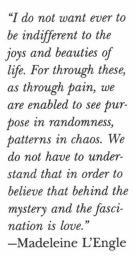

"I do not want ever to be indifferent to the joys and beauties of life. For through these, as through pain, we are enabled to see purpose in randomness, patterns in chaos. We do not have to understand that in order to believe that behind the mystery and the fascination is love."
—Madeleine L'Engle

"After we have recognized that we are all creatures who have received the love of God, who can but respond and show it in his own life."
—Edgar F. Romig

ening his peace of mind. The loving person clears the air by talking with the person with whom he may be angry, and then perhaps offers a hug or a handshake in reconciliation. Regardless of the degrees of stress or confusion he or she must undergo, that person's world continues to be a loving world.

Try a smile instead of a scowl. Expect the best and not the worst. Do your utmost to be understanding and to care for the people in your life. The "Bills" of this world often find things to complain about throughout their lives. The "Mikes," on the other hand, not only look for the best but help to create that best through their own attitudes and integrity. The loving person, from youth to old age, lives in a loving world and leads a full and happy life, finding the strength to face problems and tragedies because of the loving world they inhabit.

Dr. Glenn Mosley wrote the following in an article entitled "Love and Friendship": *"Love is more than sentiment; it is a need, a hunger, and a thirst that is perfectly natural. No one can live happily without giving and receiving love. It is the fulfilling of the law, and the fulfilling of life. We must understand Jesus' teachings on love. . . . 'God is love, and he who abides in love abides in God, and God abides in him.' In other words, to the extent that we let this divine activity hold sway in us we become a portion of the divine heart of God."*

It may sometimes seem difficult to be open to others who may seem cranky, ill-tempered, selfish, and hostile. Yet, a loving person realizes that understanding another's problems and frustrations can help open the way to compassion. A loving person, living in a loving world, knows that the miracle of love can find a way to pass the "impassable" human relations obstacle.

"We are all shaped and fashioned by what we love."
—Ralph Waldo Emerson

LAW 3

The borrower is a servant to the lender
—Proverbs 22:7

The person who borrows money often finds himself nervous or uneasy in the presence of the lender. There is a comfort and confidence in managing your finances so well that you are free

"Remember that time
is money. . . .
Remember that credit
is money. . . . *He that
is known to pay punc-
tually and exactly to
the time he promises,
may at any time, and
on any occasion, raise
all the money his
friends can spare.* . . .
*In short, the way to
wealth, if you desire it,
is as plain as the way
to market. It depends
chiefly on two words,*
industry *and* frugal-
ity; *that is, waste
neither time nor
money, but make the
best use of both."*
—Benjamin Franklin,
*Advice to a Young
Tradesman*

to choose how you spend your money. How can you enjoy
spending the money when it really belongs to someone else? In
their book *Owe No Man,* Ann Ree Colton and Jonathan Murro
write of Scriptural principles of good stewardship and divine
providence, *"Travel light: 'Owe no man' (Romans 13:8); hasten to
leave your offering, your spiritual promises on the Altar; go forth and
work diligently to pay off the debt carelessly made in time of blind
motive."* And the words of William Shakespeare invite us to
"Neither a borrower nor a lender be."

A borrower may find his joy diminished because he is worrying about how to repay the loan. Picture a person attending a
party who has borrowed money when in walks his lender.
Somehow, without a word being spoken between the two on the
subject of the loan, the borrower may begin to feel guilty. The
mere sight of the lender could cause the borrower to feel
uncomfortable and think perhaps that he should be spending
the borrowed money on things that may be more important.
Perhaps the borrower bought a new sports jacket to wear to the
party. Now, buying a new jacket to wear to a party is normally
no cause for concern. But if your lender thought the money was
needed to pay medical bills or finance the expansion of your
business, he may have doubts about trusting your judgment.

Another facet of the relationship between borrower and
lender often affects people who have fallen behind with loan
payments. In recent times it has become easy to obtain credit
cards, but this convenient access to money can also become a
burden. If the cardholder loses his job or faces a real emer-
gency, such as an accident or unexpected medical expenses, he
may suddenly find himself unable to repay his creditors.

Phone calls may start coming from the bank with greater frequency. Often these calls assume a condescending tone that can
cause the debtor to feel sorry he ever accepted the loan. Gone
may be the friendly tone that was contained in the letters inviting him to "buy now and pay later." After a few months of being
behind in his payments, the attitude can become "pay now or
face dire consequences."

Initially, when the cardholder finds himself in the position of
trying to pay the hospital or auto repair bill plus the credit card
issuer for all those nice clothes and meals in restaurants, he may
find himself facing choices he never thought he would have to
make. Of course, there can be a sense of urgency and responsibility to repay all of those lenders. But without enough money
to satisfy all of them, some may have to come first, and some
may have to come last.

Unfortunately, many people have arrived at a step even further down the ladder. When they don't want, or can't get, another loan and they see no clear avenue to repay their creditors, bankruptcy may seem to be the only solution left. For most people it is embarrassing and inconvenient to admit that they have difficulty in handling their finances. And the stigma of bad credit may take much time and effort to overcome.

Abraham Lincoln in his wisdom stated, *"You cannot keep out of trouble by spending more than you earn. You cannot establish security on borrowed money."* A debt can be like quicksand, pulling one downward into feelings of fear, insecurity, and indignity. An increasing number of small debts can act as patches of quicksand that demand more of one's time and thought. Large debts can gradually draw one emotionally downward until the quicksand of restriction is over his head. When this occurs, the person may find it difficult to think about important issues of daily living other than the demands of the indebtedness. Persons who continue to increase their debts in order to make many purchases are experiencing a sense of false prosperity and often confining themselves to a limited range of thoughts and actions. This can also happen with nations as well as individuals.

People don't like to be servants, but it's easy to forget that is what you become when you cast your lot with such modern conveniences as credit cards, home equity loans, revolving charge accounts, and time payments. No matter what they may be called, loans can make the person receiving them feel subservient to the person giving them.

While it may be a fact of life that for many people certain bills may seem necessary—for example, utility bills, mortgage payment, medical bills, or unexpected necessities that may arise—we can agree with R. Buckminster Fuller, *"I consider it essential to pay all my bills in the swiftest manner possible."*

"The surest way to establish your credit is to work yourself into the position of not needing any."
—Maurice Switzer

"Covetousness, by a greediness of getting more, deprives itself of the true end of getting; it loses the enjoyment of what it had got."
—Thomas Sprat

LAW 4

Whatever you have, you must use it or lose!
—Henry Ford

We can look at various physical gifts and see how this law works. The natural state of the human body is that of health, strength,

"The use we make of our fortune determines as to its sufficiency. A little is enough if used wisely, and too much if expended foolishly."
—Christian Bovee

"There is a vitality, a life-force, an energy, a quickening which is translated through you into action, and because there is only one of you in all time, this expression is unique."
—Martha Graham

"Each golden sunrise ushers in new opportunities for those who retain faith in themselves, and keep their chins up. No one has ever seen a cock crow with its head down. Courage to start and willingness to keep everlastingly at it are the requisites for success. Meet the sunrise with confidence. Fill every golden minute with right thinking and worthwhile endeavor. Do this and there will be joy for you in each golden sunset."
—Alonzo Newton Benn

"Putting off a hard thing makes it impossible."—George Horace Lorimer

and flexibility. But what if the various aspects of the body are not used? If we spend most of our time inactive, then muscular atrophy, stiffness, and weakness set in, along with the devitalization of our internal systems. This, in turn, can affect the mind and can lead to lethargy and depression. Our natural state of health can be lost. Time is often lost in the same way. Twenty-four hours a day are available to everyone, but, if they are not utilized for constructive purpose, they may be irretrievably gone. Likewise, unused talents can become rusty.

In the United States, in 1956, Harland Sanders was an out-of-work sixty-six year old. Colonel Sanders's principle asset was his method of frying chicken. Loading up his automobile with a fifty-pound can of seasoning and his beloved pressure cooker, he took to the road. As he visited various restaurateurs he requested, "Let me cook chicken for you and your staff. If you like the way it tastes, I'll sell you my seasoning, teach you how to cook the chicken, and you pay me a four-cent royalty on every chicken you sell." He was so successful with his marketing idea that in his promotional travels, which averaged 250,000 miles annually, he wore out eight suits a year! Colonel Sanders acted upon an idea that provided a useful service.

The gifts of the inner being are just as clearly seen to be used or lost. Confidence is a good example. Think of the confidence you feel when an idea comes to you that holds real potential for success, usefulness, and satisfaction. Develop the idea and act on it! A fruition of some sort can be realized, whether or not it may be exactly what you had in mind in the beginning. Allow fear, doubt, and hesitation to hold you back, and everything can be lost as the possibilities the idea held disappear and your confidence dissolves.

The human endowment of love can provide the most fundamental illustration of this law, since love is proclaimed to be the basis of other forms of good that we experience. Loving life, self, and others generates confidence, empowerment, joy, wholesome relationships, generosity, service, good-will, humor, and health. These attributes can be used, shared, and expressed in their myriad possible forms. However, love that is withheld, stifled, suppressed, and guarded appears to wither out of sight. Having no outlet or no expressed use, it develops no ongoing life to sustain it and can therefore be lost.

LAW 5

It's nice to be important,
but it's more important to be nice
—John M. Templeton

American television's J. R. Ewing, the character in *Dallas*, is the epitome of someone who places great value on being important and absolutely no value on being nice. In the game of life, getting what he wants becomes the all-important rule. No act seems too devious or mean. He'll lie, cheat, or steal to achieve his goals. J. R. is a firm believer in the theory that "nice guys finish last." Because he is "important" in his social circle, he often gets what he wants. J. R. Ewing represents the classic "playground bully." Everyone does things his way because they're afraid to challenge him. In the process of gaining importance, however, he also gains many enemies. They're always lurking around applauding when someone gets even with him.

Our lives are woven from the patterns of our thoughts and beliefs. If we believe that "nice guys finish last," we might live according to that belief. If we believe we have to lie, cheat, and steal to get ahead, we may accumulate as many enemies as J. R. Ewing. If we place more value on being important than on being nice, no act might be too devious for us. Like J. R., we may claw and scratch to get what we want. The fabric of our lives is then woven with flimsy thread that can break when we least expect it.

If we are successful in becoming the "playground bully," others may concede to our wishes, not because they believe in us or in our cause but because they may be afraid to challenge us. A life lived this way is certainly built on shaky ground. There can always be someone ready and eager for us to make a mistake. Playground bullies last only until other, bigger bullies come along to take their place, or until they learn that by being nice they can achieve more of what they want in life.

What a different story *Dallas* would be if the writers of the show had created a kind, generous, and loving J. R., who learned at an early age how important it was to be nice. What a difference it can make in *our* lives when we learn the importance of being nice to others. Not the "pretend" nice that every-

"Fools of poor understanding have themselves for their greatest enemies, for they do evil deeds which bear bitter fruits."
—Dhamapada

"The greater you are, the more you must practice humility."
—Ben Sira

one can see through but genuine niceness that comes from the heart. This kind of person acts on the golden rule. He has taken the theory, "Do it to them before they do it to you," and changed it to, "Do unto others what you would have done unto you, only do it first." This person believes in the value of being kind, considerate, loving, honest, and open to others without regard to return. To lie, cheat, or steal to gain importance would be foreign to him. This person knows the code of life is that *"what you sow you also reap."* He knows that making an effort to be kind to others brings importance and happiness for you also.

It's nice to be important, but it's more important to be nice. When the pattern of our life is woven from this philosophy, we set in motion a circular effect that can create for us the fulfillment of our sincere desires. What we do for others certainly comes back to us. If we are kind, generous, loving, honest, and open, others will often react the same way toward us. Our importance to others depends not on our bullying tactics but on showing through our actions that we sincerely care about them. As we weave our life with the golden thread of caring for others, the by-product can produce for us a life that is truly important.

Have you had the experience of looking at someone and seeing incredible potential in that person, a possibility or a capacity he may not have known he had? When you call this to his attention, you are calling forth something lovely and beautiful, a talent or characteristic that had to exist first in you. Have you ever thought about that? Some psychologist call this "a point of identification."

With my experience over more than half a century of studying corporations, it seems clear to me that the higher up the corporate executive ladder you interview, the greater proportion of executives are nice. I also have noted that they are more active in religious work. Maybe this is partly why they were promoted to their high posts and why they learned to be more effective executives. Perhaps they, too, realize that it's nice to be important, but it's more important to be nice!

Spotlights!

1. The choice of how you respond to the situations in life remains up to you.
2. A personal reflection for greater awareness: When situations occur, ask yourself, "Am I part of the problem or part of the solution?"

3. A loving person refuses to allow negative emotions to become dominant.
4. Help create a loving world through your own positive attitudes and personal integrity.
5. The stigma of bad credit may take much time and effort to overcome.
6. A debt can be like quicksand, pulling one downward into feelings of fear, insecurity, and indignity.
7. Use wisely what you presently have to expand greater possibilities in your life.
8. Life's true gifts are limitless in nature, and their free and constructive use can be self-generating and open new doors for increase.
9. Our lives are woven from the patterns of our thoughts and beliefs.
10. Making an effort to be kind to others is also making an effort to be kind to yourself!

Living the Law!

For this week's exercise, read the following thoughts on "wisdom" from Dr. Robert H. Schuller. Take each segment into your consciousness of introspection. What thoughts come to your mind as you read each statement? How do you feel about the action commitment following each statement? Could these "seed ideas" grow in the fertile soil of your mind? What can you do *right now* to implement this wisdom into your daily activities? Write in your journal your responses to the above questions. Revisit your journal in a week, and make any further notes you may desire.

Wisdom

People are unreasonable, illogical, and self-centered.
Love them anyway!

If you do good, people will accuse you of
selfish, ulterior motives.
Do good anyway!

If you are successful, you will win false friends
and true enemies.
Succeed anyway!

Honesty and frankness make you vulnerable.
Be honest and frank anyway!

The good you do today will be forgotten tomorrow.
Do good anyway!

The biggest people with the biggest ideas can be
shot down by the smallest people with the smallest minds.
Think big anyway!

People favor underdogs, but always follow top-dogs.
Fight for some underdogs anyway!

What you spend years building may be
destroyed overnight.
Build anyway!

Give the world the best you've got and you'll get
kicked in the teeth.
Give the world the best you've got anyway!

The point of this piece of philosophy is that you should find
joy and light in doing God's will, regardless of how people will
interpret it or accept it!

Week Thirty-Five

LAW 1

Those who seldom make mistakes seldom make discoveries
—John M. Templeton

In the Gospel of Matthew 25:14–30, Jesus tells the story of a man who left money with three servants before setting out on a journey. To one servant he gave five talents (approximately five thousand dollars today); to another he gave two talents; and to the third servant, he gave only one talent. Upon returning from his journey, he called in each of the three for an accounting of how they had used their portion of the money. The servant who received five talents had doubled that amount through investments, as had the man who had been given two talents. But the servant who had been given one talent, afraid of making a poor investment, had buried his portion in the ground. The two servants who doubled the man's money were rewarded handsomely, while the third servant was condemned and penalized.

How many times have you missed out on an opportunity because, like the fearful servant, you were afraid of making a mistake? How many times have you limited yourself because you were afraid you might appear foolish in the eyes of your peers? Self-imposed limitations based on fear can be very difficult to break. The sooner you learn to cope constructively with such fears, the better off you'll be, for *"those who seldom make mistakes, seldom make discoveries."*

Life can be as interesting and stimulating as the discoveries we allow ourselves to make. Staying within known parameters of thought and action may prevent mistakes, but they can also prevent your life from becoming rich and exciting. Exploring frontiers of thought, feeling, and action means you have to put yourself in places you may never have been before. In such places it

"The march of good fortune has backward slips: to retreat one or two paces gives wings to the jumper."
—Sa'ib of Tabriz

"If you shut your door to all errors, truth will be shut out."
—Rabindranath Tagore

"Progress is made by correcting the mistakes resulting from the making of progress."
—Claude Gibb

414

*"He who never makes
mistakes never makes
anything."*
—English proverb

*"Our mistakes won't
irreparably damage
our lives unless we let
them. It is said that in
making Persian rugs
the artist stands before
the rug while a group
of boys stand behind to
pull the thread after
the artist starts it. If
one of the boys makes a
mistake, the artist
adjusts the pattern
accordingly so that
when the rug is fin-
ished, no one can tell
where the mistake was
made. The same kind
of adjustment will take
place in our lives if we
will but let go of the
mental thread of each
mistake and let God
weave it into a success-
ful, orderly pattern."*
—James E. Sweaney

might be easy to make mistakes. But mistakes are negative only when they inhibit further growth. If you become fearful of testing out a new thought or trying a new approach to a stubborn problem because you're afraid of making a mistake, you may be making the biggest mistake of all. While it may be foolish to plunge into situations with no forethought, it may be equally foolish and futile to be afraid to venture into unknown territory. If you're committed to growth, you can learn that each new situation finds you better able to cope. Your guidance may come either intuitively or through someone else, but it will come.

While mistakes can cause stress and pain, they may also provide you with an excellent resource for learning what not to do next time. Often you learn more from your mistakes than from formal instruction on the correct way to proceed. Trial and error, which allows you to measure the impact of your misguided actions, is often a great teacher.

Tim Hansel talks about the importance of overcoming circumstances and seeing mistakes in his book *You Gotta Keep Dancing*. He describes how John Bunyan wrote *Pilgrim's Progress* from jail. Florence Nightingale, too ill to move from her bed, reorganized the hospitals of England. Semiparalyzed and under the constant menace of apoplexy, Louis Pasteur was tireless in his attack on disease. During the greater part of his life, American historian Francis Parkman suffered so acutely he could not work for more than five minutes at a time. His eyesight was so wretched that he could scrawl only a few gigantic words on a manuscript, yet he contrived to write twenty magnificent volumes of history. These people were dauntless in their efforts to do the most with what they had. E. Stanley Jones spoke of the strength of his faith in these words: *"I see that I am inwardly fashioned for faith and not for fear. Fear is not my native land; faith is. I am so made that worry and anxiety are sand in the machinery of life; faith is the oil. I live better by faith and confidence than by fear and doubt and anxiety. . . . To live by worry is to live against Reality."*

Whether you fully realize it or not, you are like the men in the parable. You have been given many "talents" that can take you as far as you want to go in life. Don't make the mistake of burying them for fear of making a mistake. You don't want to look back over your life one day with regret that you did not pursue an opportunity because you were afraid of making a blunder. Instead, develop your talents wisely, confidently, to the best of your understanding and with self-trust, and you are likely to enjoy a profitable and exciting life!

Life is truly an experience in growth and unfolding for each of us. It can be a wonderful and exciting experience. Along the road of life we have our challenges and problems; we may make mistakes and experience feelings of defeat. We may know reasons for these times, or we may not. Knowing the reasons may not be as important as knowing that we can do something about the needs, problems, and challenges. Should you experience a time of concern over what may be a perceived as a mistake, take courage from a quote from *Guideposts* magazine, *"Sorrow looks back, worry looks around, faith looks up."*

LAW 2

The measure of a man's real character is what he would do if he would never be found out
—Thomas Macaulay

Thomas Macaulay says that *"the measure of a man's real character is what he would do if he would never be found out."* Would he be totally honest and above-board with others? Would he cheat or steal? If what is done in secret stays a secret what would *you* do? How would *you* live? If you found a wallet stuffed with money, would you return it to the owner? Our conscience can often be our friend and our guide. It nudges us when we contemplate doing something wrong. It warns us of the danger that could be done to us or to others. It is important to listen to that inner voice. The person who learns or chooses to ignore his conscience often forsakes his best friend and lifetime guide.

"Real human progress depends not so much on inventive ingenuity, as on conscience."
—Albert Einstein

If the measure of a person's real character is determined by what he would do if he weren't found out, the only person capable of judging his actions is the person himself and God. If he can look at himself in the mirror each day and know he is living as honestly as he can, that honest and positive assurance will be reflected in his eyes. The essence of his character is written on his face, and he can read the lines. As John Lyly said in the 1500s, *"A clear conscience is a sure card."*

"The most infectiously joyous men and women are those who forget themselves in thinking about others and serving others. Happiness comes not by deliberately courting and wooing it but by giving oneself in self-effacing surrender to great values."
—Robert J. McCracken

"No virtue is more universally accepted as a test of good character than trustworthiness."
—Harry Emerson Fosdick

"To be worth anything, character must be capable of standing firm upon its feet in the world of daily work, temptation, and trial."
—Samuel Smiles

"Conscience is God's presence in man."
—Emanuel Swedenborg

We've been building our character since we were children, and part of the building process can be learning to listen to our conscience and following its guidance. We know there may be times when we can do something wrong and not be found out. We also know that if we get away with doing something wrong, *we* will know what we did, and we have to live with ourselves twenty-four hours a day. Every time we put a chink in our character, we become diminished, and our pride and self-esteem suffer. The importance of this inner guide was noted by Karl Barth when he said, *"Conscience is the perfect interpreter of life."*

Our real character can be measured by us. If we do a self-inventory and find we may be lacking in desired personal attributes, we can make the conscious choice to grow in areas of integrity, honesty, humility, sincerity, or other positive traits we desire. We can determine to live honestly with ourselves and others. We can determine to be as honest in secret as we are when others are present. We can determine that our character will be of value to *us*.

Life situations can sometimes seem to push us to violate the moral and ethical standards by which we seek to live. Desperation may tempt us to abandon our highest standards for the sake of short-term gain or a quick solution. When we succumb to such pressures, we walk a path that may lead to further deception, pain, and the erosion of self-respect. William James wrote, *"The greatest use of life is to spend it for something that will outlast it."* A good reputation, built on honesty and integrity, can continue its good works long after the physical person may have gone on.

You alone live with your motives and secret actions, and only you can set the standard of your personal integrity. Eventually the temptation to abandon your high standards can arise. It may be encouraged through unexpected circumstances, a friend, a co-worker, a mate, or even an employer. It can come unexpectedly, and it may even seem the logical thing to do. Certainly it may appear to be the easiest answer to a complicated situation. At such times you would do well to ask yourself if you will be able to look back later, satisfied that you did your best. Will you be able to review your conduct and feel successful deep within? Perhaps no one may ever find out how you performed—whether you cut corners or, instead, went the "extra mile" to do the appropriate thing. But *you* know. Will you be inwardly proud of your performance or have the gnawing feeling that you could have been more honest?

Your life can openly display what you do in secret. If you

always remain true to your ethical principles, your personal integrity can become an attractive beacon for success on every level. What is the focal point of your life? How do you focus on living? What can you accomplish in this life that can make your world better? How can you make your life more meaningful?

Each person is here for a purpose. Each person has a place to fulfill and a job to do that can improve the overall situation just because he is living. Can you feel this inner longing? The accomplishment doesn't have to be a big, spectacular job, but it can be important for you to feel that you are doing something to make the world a little better than it was before. Listen carefully to the inner promptings of conscience. As the writer of Proverbs states, *"Only a fool rejects wisdom and good advice"* (Proverbs 1:7).

LAW 3

Change your mind to change your life
—John M. Templeton

What does your mind have to do with your life? Everything! To illustrate: If you believe you're unworthy of love and happiness, you may attract to yourself situations that disappoint, frustrate, and hurt. Conversely, healthy self-esteem can build positive results. Our mind is considered to be the starting point of every act and thought and feeling. Charles Fillmore said, *"The mind is the seat of perception of the things we see, hear, and feel. It is through the mind that we see the beauties of the earth and sky, or music, of art, in fact, of everything. That silent shuttle of thought working in and out through cell and nerve weaves into one harmonious whole the myriad moods of mind, and we call it life."*

Thinking is a creative force that is constantly at work in humanity and in creation. That magnetic atmosphere of thought travels with you and is a part of you. To cultivate a positive attitude toward life, it is important to put your faith in strong and positive ideas, rather than allowing circumstances and conditions to rule and create unhappy and resistant attitudes toward things that happen.

"The ability to choose puts human beings in control of their actions. Implied in choice is that the action taken is best, and that all other options are over-ruled. We cannot knowingly choose what is not good for us. The ability to pursue a course, whether it is a popular one or not, is measured in courage. The greater the courage, the greater the possibility we will act for change."
—Mildred Pitts Walter

"As a human being, you have no choice about the fact that you need a philosophy. Your only choice is whether you define your philosophy by a conscious, rational, disciplined process of thought and scrupulously logical deliberation—or let your subconscious accumulate a junk heap of unwarranted conclusions, false generalizations, undefined contradictions, undigested slogans, unidentified wishes, doubts and fears, thrown together by chance, but integrated by your subconscious into a kind of mongrel philosophy and fused into a single, solid weight: self-doubt, like a ball and chain in the place where your mind's wings should have grown."
—Ayn Rand,
Philosophy, Who Needs It?

It's up to you! Your mind is the projector; your attitudes are the film; and your experience is the movie projected on the screen. If you see a pattern of sincere good feelings and satisfying relationships, it demonstrates that you have a healthy respect for yourself and others. Frequent hurt and frustration can be caused by negative thinking and a belief inside you that says you don't deserve better.

Listen to this negative thinker: "I know I'm kind of pessimistic, and lots of things frighten me. I'm told I'm hard to get along with and too negative about things, but it's no wonder! It seems there are always people out to get you and take advantage of you. It's not safe to trust anybody. Besides, I know I'm unattractive, so why should anybody really care about me?"

You can guess the nature of this person's experiences. Her relationships are often difficult or fleeting. She can walk into a restaurant with her negative energy and, sure enough, people may treat her rudely, or eye her disapprovingly. The prices are too high; the food's no good. Everything seems to work against this person while others get the breaks. Does she think the way she does because of the bad things that happen to her, or do bad things happen because of the way she thinks?

Both perspectives can be true, and it's hard to get to the source of the problem without knowing the person's entire history. But even if you can point to unfortunate circumstances and say, "There's the origin, that's why she thinks the way she does," what good does it do? Can blaming the past do anything to lessen its negative influence? And if we say a person can't be expected to think well of herself or others because of something that happened in childhood, is she burdened that way for the rest of her life?

Not at all. It's within anyone's power, regardless of the circumstances, to change a thinking process. Thought by thought, moment by moment, it can be done. Indeed, it's important to move from negative to positive thinking if a person wants the quality of life to improve. You can think in a new way and begin finding the good that exists in you and in others by making a decision to change. You only need to be willing to try. Your mind can be powerfully creative. It is capable of continually higher levels of thinking. Exercise your mental muscles! You are the one who controls the attitudes your mind will hold, express, and project. It's your projector and your film. You have the freedom and authority to create the best life and attitude you can possibly envision.

Making the change does require being continually alert and

aware of your thoughts so the negatives don't slip in. Changing your thinking can require the courage of facing your negative thoughts with mindful, compassionate honesty. It also requires a firm belief in the equal value of yourself and others. Inferiority and superiority can work equally well to hold life's goodness away from you. If you tell yourself, "Life is good and people are good," but you don't really believe this, then the good in life and people can elude you. If you regard yourself highly but hold critical thoughts about others, it may be difficult for people to please you. A judgmental attitude can keep you from appreciating others' good qualities.

In the book *Macro-Mind Power,* author Rebecca Clark emphasizes, *"Begin now to school your impulses and feelings into desired areas. Your dreams and ideals are the parents of your impulses and feelings. What you think concerning people, places, situations, and things can take shape in your life. Refuse to entertain a thought about someone else which you would not have objectified in yourself. You are the assemblage of your thoughts!"*

If you desire to change your life to a more positive living experience, examine your thinking processes. Change your mind, and you can find life's unlimited good in every situation, awaiting your recognition and acceptance.

"A closed mind is a dying mind."
—Edna Ferber

"The strongest principle of growth lies in human choice."
—George Eliot

LAW 4

Progress and growth are impossible if you always do things the way you've always done things
—Wayne Dyer

In 1633, the English colonists established a settlement on a peninsula between the James and York rivers in Virginia in the United States. They called it Middle Plantation because it lay in the middle of the peninsula. In 1699, they renamed their settlement Williamsburg in honor of King William of England, and it became the capital of the Virginia colonies. At one time the most important city in the Virginia colony, Williamsburg began to decline after the Revolutionary War. In 1926, John D.

"At first people refuse to believe that a strange new thing can be done, then they begin to hope it can be done, then it is done and the world wonders why it was not done centuries ago."
—Frances Hodgson Burnett

"Innovation is more than a new method. It is a new view of the universe, as one of risk rather than of chance or certainty. It is a new view of man's role in the universe; he creates order by taking risks. And this means that innovation, rather than being an assertion of human power, is an acceptance of human responsibility."
—Peter Drucker

Rockefeller, Jr., became interested in restoring and preserving Williamsburg, and today it attracts more than a million visitors a year.

Visiting historic Williamsburg is a wonderful experience because one gets to see how life was lived in the past. It can also offer a way to be thankful for the progress that's been made up to the present time. But progress would not have come if the settlers and those who came after them had continued to do things the same way. If they had continued to bake food in an open fire, there would have been no progression to the microwave oven. If the military had continued to use muskets, America's defense system would be totally inadequate.

Change is both good and necessary. Our evolution as a people and a planet depends on change. It is important to find new and better ways of doing things in our individual lives as well. Just because we've always done things a certain way doesn't mean that way is the only way. We can experience change in our lives by beginning with little things. We can take a new route to work, or order a different item on the menu. As we consciously choose to see life in a different light, as we expand our minds to learn new things, growth can certainly come. In order for us to see life with fresh eyes, we must keep our minds open to new and different experiences.

Each individual human being has the capacity to grow and become both useful and happy. For this growth to take place, it is important to allow the natural process of change to occur. There is a saying that *"life is change, and change is life."* In other words, change is all about us. It is when we resist change that progress and growth are often stunted. By forging ahead and looking for new and better ways of living and perhaps discovering unseen resources, we can bring about progress and growth for ourself and for others. Just as the Pilgrims in early American history experimented and learned new ways of living in order to survive, we, too, can experiment and not only survive but thrive in the process.

W. G. Montgomery writes in *Your Hidden Treasure* about two brothers who landed in New York in the year 1845. The older brother had learned the trade of making sauerkraut back in his native Germany. Hearing of possible fortunes to be made in America, he set off for California, where land was cheap. His goal was to grow cabbage, make the cabbage into sauerkraut, and begin a business. His venture was successful, and eventually he bought additional land, planted more cabbage, made more money, and was content.

The younger brother, meanwhile, remained in New York, working during the day and attending school at night. Taking a course in geology and metallurgy, he learned about the rocks and soils with which various minerals are associated. A few years passed and one day, he set out for California by stagecoach to visit his brother. Along the way he kept his eyes open to see what others had not seen.

Upon his arrival, the older brother took him into his cabbage patch to show what good crops he grew. But the younger brother wasn't interested in cabbage; he was staring at something else. He began picking up handfuls of the sandy soil, pressing it through his fingers, throwing it down, and picking up more.

Walking over to a nearby shallow stream, the young man stooped over and grabbed a handful of quartz and sand from the bottom of the stream and pointed to a dull, yellow piece. "Do you know what this is?" he asked his brother. The cabbage king shook his head, "No."

"That's a gold nugget," said the younger brother with excitement in his voice. "You've been growing your cabbage on a gold mine!" And so he had. One of the richest gold mines in California was found in that cabbage patch. While growing cabbage is a worthwhile enterprise, the cabbage can become quite costly when grown on a gold mine.

Our human mind can be just as rich in unseen resources as that cabbage patch was rich in the unseen gold in the ground where the cabbage grew. Again, it is important to be open to new possibilities, to better ways of doing things, to change. Like the butterfly going through its metamorphosis we may find we can no longer stay behind self-made walls of protection. Something within us struggles to be free, to break the bonds of stagnation and soar into a new dimension. Perhaps you desire to find out who you really are in this new day. You may be feeling greater development in your spiritual awareness. Your consciousness can be moving and stretching and recreating itself anew. You may feel you are entering a realm of new and increased good in and for your life. This change can be a continual process that happens daily.

Let the process of change bring about a wondrous time in your life. Think about the wisdom in Dr. Dyer's words, *"Progress and growth are impossible if you always do things the way you've always done them."* When the mind of a person is lifted high, he or she refuses to give up or allow defeat to thwart righteous ambitions. Dare to step out in faith. Refuse to be content to be a caterpillar!

"Whenever an individual or a business decides that success has been attained, progress stops."
—Thomas J. Watson

"The moment a man ceases to progress, to grow higher, wider and deeper, then his life becomes stagnant."
—Orison Swett Marden

LAW 5

It is more blessed to give than to receive
—Acts 20:35

"I feel that the greatest reward for doing is the opportunity to do more."
—Jonas Salk

"He is the wisest and happiest who, by constant attention of thought discovers the greatest opportunity of doing good, and breaks through every opposition that he may improve these opportunities."
—Philip Doddrige

"If you want to get more out of life, you have to give more to life." Sounds like a contradiction, doesn't it? The chances are good that you may have reached the opposite conclusion. You may believe that if you want more out of life, you have to go get it—and quickly—before the other fellow beats you to it. Getting ahead in the world seems to have become an obsession for many people who believe that a satisfying life comes from acquiring and holding on to great wealth.

Yet many of the world's most successful and influential people have proven otherwise. These people often seek and experience a greater reward in the giving of their wealth than in getting it. They understand the law of life that giving leads to more giving and greater personal rewards. Many a successful person can tell you that he first thought out his moves in his inner consciousness because he understands that the door to success opens from within. As Robert Dedman, a lawyer who has contributed $40 million to charity and who vows to give away at least one-third of his estimated $500 million before he dies, remarked in a 1986 interview in *Town & Country* magazine, *"The more you give, the more you live."*

There is certainly nothing wrong with getting ahead or being in a position where you can be a positive influence on those around you. But it is through giving, not getting, that you can exert a truly positive force for good.

"It is more blessed to give than to receive," Scripture tells us in Acts 20:35. If you only receive, that's all you end up having. If you give, you can also have the pleasure of knowing that you have helped others, plus the rewards your giving brings back to you. *If you want to be happy, strive to make someone else happy.* Give happiness. If you want to have more love in your life, strive to be a more loving person. Give love. *If you want to be successful, help others to succeed.* It's not difficult to see how much better and richer your life can be when you become a source of encouragement, inspiration, and friendship to others. Giving can make you a magnet for success, because good attracts good.

In nature, each species has to exist in a natural state of giving and receiving. Otherwise, imbalance is created in its environment, even to the point of its own extinction. A South American species of parasitic vine illustrates this point. The vine sustains itself by becoming attached to a certain kind of fig tree. The fig tree's nourishing elements are gradually diverted to the vine. The result is that the vine literally strangles the life out of its host, because it takes but gives nothing in return. And, once the fig tree dies, the parasitic vine must die.

Noel Vietmeyer shared this interesting story in *Reader's Digest* magazine about an unusual giving and receiving. *"If you had been in the rice fields of China last fall, you might have seen a strange sight: farmers building little teepees out of straw. But even though the conical huts–about waist high and scattered across thousands of acres–looked bizarre, they had a serious purpose: to house migrating spiders! Normally, winter kills most spiders, and it takes months for the population to recover. But this spring occupants of the spider motels awakened from hibernation healthy and ravenous. They scuttled into the fields in hordes, ready to attack the insects attempting to suck the life out of the young rice and cotton plants. By protecting the spiders and giving them an early start, the Chinese increased their crop yields and avoided having to use chemical insecticides."*

Almost everyone prefers the company of givers over takers. Takers leave you feeling depleted. You may be reluctant to become their friend. Givers, on the other hand, are a pleasure to be with because they help to establish an environment that blesses and enriches relationships. A taker often becomes someone to avoid, but a giver is always welcomed.

It is important to remember that the Creator is our true source, and there are many channels through which God's good can flow. We can easily forget where our ideas come from, and, when we do, we are likely to experience lack of some kind. Instead of habitually asking what you can get from the various people and situations in your life, ask what you can give to them. *The more you give to life, the more you get back.* This is a universal law that can go a long way toward creating for you an inner life that is well balanced, prosperous, happy, and fulfilled. Dr. Harry Koch said, "If you are giving while you are living, you are knowing where it's going."

In his book *Your Life–Understanding the Universal Laws,* author Bruce McArthur tells a story of Increase. He states, *"My wife has a greenhouse and a green thumb. She plants several tiny seeds. In a few months we are eating huge, delicious, fresh ripe tomatoes. She sowed only several tiny seeds. She was patient. She gave love, care, consideration, food, water. She reaps not just a few seeds, but wonderful,*

"In nothing do men approach so nearly to the gods as doing good to men."
—Cicero

"There is a singing ecstasy in good works."
—Channing Pollock

"Be grateful for the joy of life. Be glad for the privilege of work. Be thankful for the opportunity to give and serve. Good works is the great character-builder, the sweetener of life, the maker of destiny."
—Grenville Kleiser

nourishing, beautiful fruit and hundreds of new seeds. The miracle in this law is one of abundance and joy and beauty, wherein you reap not only what you sow, but far, far more–multiplied many times–when the right kind of seed is nurtured with the spirit of love and cooperation. The harvest is abundance! We reap abundantly in our gardens and in our lives according to the seeds we sow."

Giving is sowing seeds of caring and love. The more you give, the more you receive. As one minister friend so aptly remarked, "There is no way we can out-give God and the universe!"

Spotlights!

1. Life can be as interesting and stimulating as the discoveries we allow ourselves to make.
2. *"Sorrow looks back, worry looks around, faith looks up."* *—Guideposts*
3. Our conscience can often be our friend and our inner guide.
4. Only you can set the standards of your personal integrity.
5. Your mind is considered to be the starting point of every thought, feeling, and action.
6. It can be within anyone's power to change a thinking process.
7. Change is both good and necessary to growth.
8. Be open to new possibilities, to new ways of doing things, to change.
9 Giving leads to more giving and greater personal rewards.
10. Prosperity comes through the law of increase.

Living the Law!

In 1916, The Rev. William J. H. Botecker wrote the "Ten Cannots," which were later erroneously attributed to the writings of Abraham Lincoln in the Congressional Record in 1949. Later, in 1991, columnist Ann Landers printed these statements in her column as "worthy of repeating." They are shared here for your contemplation.

1. You cannot bring about prosperity by discouraging thrift.
2. You cannot help small men by tearing down big men.
3. You cannot strengthen the weak by weakening the strong.
4. You cannot lift the wage earner by pulling down the wage payer.

5. You cannot help the poor man by destroying the rich.
6. You cannot keep out of trouble by spending more than your income.
7. You cannot further the brotherhood of man by inciting class hatred.
8. You cannot establish security on borrowed money.
9. You cannot build character and courage by taking away men's initiative and independence.
10. You cannot help men permanently by doing for them what they could and should do for themselves.

Week Thirty-Six

LAW 1

Holding onto grievances is a decision to suffer
—Gerald Jampolsky

"So much that was beautiful and so much that was hard to bear. Yet whenever I showed myself ready to bear it, the hard was directly transformed into the beautiful."
—Etty Hillesum

For many years an old farmer plowed around a rock in one of his fields. As a result he grew actually morbid over it, for he had broken a cultivator and two plows, as well as lost a lot of valuable land in the rock's vicinity. One day, he made up his mind that he would dig it out and be done with it. When he put his crowbar under the rock, he found it was less than a foot thick and that he could loosen it with a trifling effort and carry it away in his wagon. He smiled to think how all through the years the rock had haunted him. As he mulled over the experience with the rock, he began to see other areas in his life where he was holding on to old thoughts and feelings that were like rocks in the middle of the field of his mind. One by one, he began to take these past experiences, reflect on them, and follow through with whatever appropriate action was necessary to remove them—in other words, to "loose them and let them go!" With each releasing and forgiving of old grievances, he felt his spirit lighten, his mind become more clear, and his heart fill with joy and delight in each new day.

Some of us may choose to hold onto old and painful thoughts as though they were treasures. We may sometimes seem to cherish memories of imagined or real mistreatment or slights, and forget the good and helpful things people have done for us, the good health with which we may be blessed, and the many successes we have enjoyed along the way.

I know a man who still lives with negative thoughts of events that happened to him more than forty years ago. Some of those things that he remembers as being so terrible are really the result of his poor perception of what actually happened. He has allowed those negative thoughts to alienate him from his family and refuses every attempt they make at reconciliation. Instead, he chooses to be alone, cut off from all of those who could love and understand him.

Although we may have experienced some difficult times and painful situations, it is unnecessary to remain locked in negative thoughts, nor is it beneficial to our peace of mind to react in a negative way to daily events. *The way in which we choose to interpret what happens to us has a great deal to do with how the important moments in our lives may be stored in our memory through the unfolding years.* We alone have control of our thoughts, although many of us may have forgotten how to exercise that control.

Try to hold this simple truth in mind: Yesterday is gone. No matter what happened in the past, it's over. We cannot go back. Tomorrow may never come, so the present is the moment we have. Let us strive to make the best, most positive use of every precious moment, each special day. The ill feelings and negative thoughts we may have had in the past were of no value to us then and have not increased in worth since. The choice is ours; we can hold on to negative thoughts, or we can put some "altitude in our attitude!" The Dalai Lama spoke of the power of forgiveness in his book *Freedom in Exile: The Autobiography of the Dalai Lama* with these words: *"Learning to forgive is much more useful than merely picking up a stone and throwing it at the object of one's anger, the more so when the provocation is extreme. For it is under the greatest adversity that there exists the greatest potential for doing good, both for oneself and others."*

A mind that is occupied by positive thoughts blossoms like a beautiful garden, free of the weeds of negativity. Whether your mind portrays a beautiful garden or a weed patch is up to you. You can choose to overlook and forgive the shortcomings of others, or you can keep a mental ledger listing all the unkind things people may have said or done to you.

A mind full of love, laughter, forgiveness, and thanksgiving refuses to dwell on past hurts. One man recites Abbott and Costello's "Who's on First" comedy routine whenever negative thoughts trouble him at bedtime. He laughs; his heart becomes light; and the old grievances begin to fade. A thankful prayer or the words to a joyous song or special poem may work equally well for you.

After all, you are the one who suffers most by holding on to grievances. If you can't overlook and forgive the faults of others, how can you forgive your own? A minister friend has defined holding on to old grievances as "useless and unnecessary suffer-

"Surely there is something in the unruffled calm of nature that overawes our little anxieties and doubts; the sight of the deep-blue sky, and the clustering stars above, seem to impart a quiet to the mind."
—Jonathan Edwards

"The greatest man is he who chooses right with the most invincible resolution; who resists the sorest temptation from within and without; who bears the heaviest burdens cheerfully; who is calmest in storms, and most fearless under menaces and frowns; whose reliance on truth, on virtue, and on god is most unfaltering."
—Seneca

ing." Yes, you can learn from suffering, but you can also learn the same, or similar, lessons through the process of joy and celebration. Any hardship—actual or imagined— can be undone, transformed, and healed to reveal a shining star of awareness where once there may have loomed a dark night of despair. One of the most powerful ways to accomplish this transformation into light is through the activity of forgiveness. There is a bumper sticker that proclaims, *Misery is optional*. And so it is. It doesn't matter what you have chosen in the past; your present choices are the ones that matter. *"Hatred stirs up trouble; love overlooks the wrongs that others do"* (Proverbs 10:12).

LAW 2

The seven deadly sins are pride, lust, sloth, envy, anger, covetousness, and gluttony
—St. Gregory

Although theologians differ in their definition of sin, most would agree that the nature of sin seems to distort the gift of life as it has been given to us to live. When someone "misses the mark" with an error in thinking or behavior, the individual's relationship to life often changes. A sin can, therefore, be deadly because it often diminishes the sinner's potential of living a life full of peace, joy, happiness, and usefulness.

A person out of step with life's truest and highest aims may fail to see life's infinite potential for good. He or she can become deadened to life's possibilities for fulfillment and may attempt to find a sense of fulfillment through further distortions of life's reality. The "seven deadly sins" are seven common ways many people continue to deaden themselves to life's goodness. They often use pride, lust, laziness, envy, anger, covetousness, and excess in an effort to gain satisfaction and fulfillment in areas where it can never be found.

To have *pride* in yourself, or high self-esteem, can be important to success in every area of life, and most of us spend a lifetime in building a stronger sense of self-worth. And that is not a sin. However, if you set yourself up as special and more important that others, you may have fallen into the sin of arrogance. *"Pride goeth before destruction, and an haughty spirit before a fall,"* Proverb 16:18 says, which in turn recalls the adage, *"What goes up, must come down."* An inflated sense of importance can be like a hot-air balloon that is bound to cool down sooner or later. If we don't feel good about ourselves as we are, we may try to find ways to make ourselves look better than someone else. We may try to make others seem wrong in an attempt to appear more righteous. But when we begin to understand that we are all equal as human beings, that there is no basis in reality for either extreme shame or pride, the balloon of our vanity can deflate. In order to keep our world from crashing down around us, we need to come to rest in a balanced and realistic view of ourselves as the equal of others. We can then hope to find true contentment in expressing the unique and valuable qualities we do possess.

If we were to judge from television and other contemporary media, we might come to believe that *lust* rather than love makes the world go around. Some of us may wonder how lust found its way onto the list of deadly sins. We might reason that perhaps St. Gregory was simply a prude. On the other hand, we might look more closely at some of the present-day consequences of indulging our lustful passions. The AIDS epidemic, unwanted teenage pregnancy, and drug addiction all suggest that there can be much to be gained from the delay of such gratifications. Your sexuality is a wonderful part of who you are, and how you choose to express that sexuality says a great deal about your integrity as a person. If you express it as part of friendship, caring, devotion, and commitment, then the people involved benefit. Lust seems to have more to do with selfishness than with love. Truly intimate, healthy relationships, and a deeper experience of our own emotional reality may result if we can set aside our craving for excitement and enjoy the blessings life brings to us from self-control.

Although the term *sloth* is no longer in current usage, you are probably familiar with its synonymous cousin, laziness. Everyone needs a time to slow down and relax from the business of the day—which is different from indolence or habitual laziness. Psychiatrist M. Scott Peck observed in *The Road Less Traveled,* *"In the struggle to help my patients grow, I found that my chief enemy was invariably their laziness."* He noted the universal reluctance of all humankind to *"extend to new areas of thought, responsibility, and maturation."* Laziness, which as Peck suggests, may be fear in disguise, can limit life by giving full license to inertia. Many times

"Be ye transformed by the renewal of your mind."
—Romans 12:2

"The real nature of man is originally good, but it becomes clouded by contact with earthly things and, therefore, needs purification before it can shine forth in its native clarity."
—I Ching

we may feel a task is just too much trouble to complete. Even when it's in our own best interests to persevere, our laziness may prevent us from doing the job. Meeting our fears and overcoming our lazy resistance can be an enlivening experience. The sin of sloth often lies in a wasted life.

When we feel *envy* or covet another's possessions, it may be a sure sign that life is inviting us to grow into new forms of self-expression. Envy literally means to "look at with malice." The fact that we see a quality of personality in someone else we would like to embody is not a deadly sin. Most people feel this way sometimes, but the sin lies in letting this emotion so fill our life with discontent and resentment that we cannot enjoy the other aspects of life all around us. When we see someone with a good quality we want and believe we can't unfold that quality from within, we may be distorting the truth about our own potential. When we make ourselves miserable comparing ourselves to what others are or have, we're wasting time and energy that could be better spent mobilizing our own inner resources. Let any feelings of envy that may arise be a signal that a change may need to take place in our own attitude. Real life can be found in using the unique gifts we've been given. And the more of ourselves we give to life, the more life gives back to us.

Everyone may be tempted by *anger* from time to time and feel it is justified. When things don't go according to plan, when we're hurt by someone we love or frustrated in some way, it's likely we may feel at least a spark of anger, if not an explosion. The temptation itself is not a deadly sin. It's what we do with it. Anger can be used to mobilize energy to bring about change. But anger often seems to be an immobilizing reaction to not getting one's own way. Anger can cripple communication, break apart loving relationships, and close the door on happiness and good feelings. The sin of anger is that it often leads to destructive behavior. Many times we project judgment and blame onto the person whose behavior triggered our reaction rather than take responsibility for our own anger. When we project blame in this way, we may feel the need to punish the perpetrator by denying them our friendships. We miss the mark when we fail to see both sides of a dispute and realize others may also be trying to do the best they can with what they have in life. Instead of denying anger, we can identify its source and let that energy be transformed into some constructive action that can improve the quality of our life.

Covetousness or avarice means *greed*. Greed can be deadly in its opposition to the natural, abundant flow of life. The greedy person is the one who tries to dam the stream and keep all the water for himself. He doesn't realize that it's not the water in the river that's really important; it's the love and activity the flow of the water brings into our experience. As old King Midas learned the hard way, a self-centered life based on greed is really no kind of life at all. Desperately afraid, the greedy person builds guarantees for his material well-being, which, in fact, cut him off from the true prosperity of sharing, giving, and loving.

Gluttony refers to anything we do in life to excess. Frequently it has to do with physical addictions. When a person concentrates most of his energy on one thing—such as drinking, eating, drugs, or sex—addictions can occur. Just like greed, these addictions can become so self-absorbing that other things in life—such as learning, working, friends, and family—may often be ignored. The sin of gluttony reflects in the damage it does to your physical body, your spiritual awareness, your relationships, and your life. An antidote to gluttony can be to seek to live a balanced life by doing things in moderation.

The person caught up in the energy of any of these "sins" can be like one who tries to dam the flow of the river of life. The river, however, can find its way around obstacles, including the ones that would try to prevent its flow. Whether engaged in one or the other of St. Gregory's seven deadly sins, the sinner, over time, becomes frustrated and discouraged at the waste of his own life energy spent uselessly blocking the inevitable flow of the river. At some point it is hoped he will accept the forgiveness that is always available, and simply let go and enter the flow of life.

LAW 3

Appearances are often deceiving
—Aesop

One of the better-known statements from Aesop's fables could be the one that describes persons, places, situations, or things as being different from what they may seem: *"Appearances are often deceiving."* And perhaps we may have experienced some sit-

"One of the chief objects of education should be to widen the windows through which we view the world."
—Arnold Glasgow

uation in our life where we felt disappointment, discouragement, or disillusioned because a situation or experience didn't unfold according to its appearance, or our interpretation of how things seemed to be. Epictetus wrote, *"Appearances to the mind are of four kinds. Things are either what they appear to be; or they neither are, nor appear to be; or they are, and do not appear to be; or they are not, and yet appear to be. Rightly to aim in all these cases is the wise man's task."* The Gospel according to John gives a much more simple counsel regarding being aware of appearances: *"Judge not according to appearance"* (John 7:24).

The essence in this law of life is that we need to look more deeply into any manifestation—whether it be physical, mental, or spiritual. The benefit of looking at everything more closely can be that the world opens itself to wonders we may have heretofore thought impossible.

One example of reality being deeper than appearances can be found in a story told about St. Thomas Aquinas. As a pupil of the scholastic teacher Albertus Magnus in Paris, Aquinas made a poor impression on his fellow students, who nicknamed him "the dumb ox." One day, Albertus summoned Thomas to a private interview at which they discussed all the subjects in the university curriculum. At the next lecture the master announced to the students, *"You call your brother Thomas a dumb ox; let me tell you that one day the whole world will listen to his bellowings."* Of course, Thomas went on to become a renowned theologian and scholastic philosopher, who aimed to reconcile human reason and Christian faith. His arguments for the existence of God have exercised theologians and philosophers for many centuries. This was quite a contrast from the quiet and seemingly withdrawn student.

There may be occasions in life that could be unsettling when various situations seem to approach from all sides, awaiting your attention. You might mentally review several times some area of work that needs to be done, when actually you may need to think about the project only once! It can be important to train yourself to be able to look beyond appearances and perceive what is before you with clarity and openness. Begin now to use the attributes you already have, whether they are special talents or abilities, material possessions, or special opportunities for service to yourself and to others. Do the most you know how to do with your present awareness and abilities! Let the guidance come from *within* rather than from outer appearances. Take one step at a time and begin with the step immediately ahead of you. Use what you already have to good advantage. Clear the way in your mental and emotional consciousness and in the activities in your life for the abundant good you earnestly desire. Give things the "light" touch with a gentle sense of humor and air of positive expectancy.

Clarence Seward Darrow, a lawyer renowned for his conduct of labor litigation and murder cases, would often look at the lighter side of life. This attitude often provided a balance with the intensity of his work efforts. Reporters would on occasion tease Darrow about his disheveled appearance. Darrow, in good humor retorted, "I go to a better tailor than any of you and pay more for my clothes. The only difference is that you probably don't sleep in yours!"

We often admire a person who seems calm and collected, poised and self-controlled, a person who is not given to fits of temper and outbursts of anger when something disturbing occurs. A very competent teacher once said that habits and inclinations are as teachable as Latin and Greek and much more essential to happiness. Some people think they have no control over their emotions, no power over the way they react to certain situations or conditions in their lives. But we do have this power. The calm person we so admire may be working just as diligently as ourself to overcome a situation. Appearances do not always speak the truth of a situation. Once, when someone commented on his amazing achievements, Sir Isaac Newton remarked, *"I do not know what I may appear to the world; but to myself I seem to have been only like a boy, playing on the seashore and diverting myself and now and then finding a smoother pebble or a prettier seashell than ordinary, while the great ocean of truth lay all undiscovered before me."*

Cecil Beaton was showing the Queen Mother a selection of photographs of herself from a sitting she had recently given him. After she had chosen one, Beaton suggested that he could have the picture discreetly retouched to conceal a few wrinkles. The Queen Mother rejected the proposal. "I would not want it to be thought that I had lived for all these years without having anything to show for it," she explained.

Rather than place our focus on outer appearances or illusions, we can step forward with inner assurance to make the most of every day. We can make the commitment to be honest, steadfast, and true to the laws of life with our own development and growth, knowing that positive results must then manifest themselves in other areas of our life. With a peaceful mind and a song of joy in our heart, we can step forth each morning with a smile on our lips and wings on our feet to greet the world and all with whom we come in contact. In this manner we go forth to meet our good. With a strong faith, we place our family,

"Though we travel the world over to find the beautiful, we must carry it with us or we find it not."
—Ralph Waldo Emerson

"No man looks at the world with pristine eyes. He sees it edited by a definite set of customs and institutions and ways of thinking."
—Ruth Benedict

friends, loved ones, and acquaintances in God's care, knowing they, too, are enfolded in abundant love. Should unexpected situations occur, we can remember that at any time in our life, at any place in our experience, or wherever we may be, we can begin anew with an increased awareness as we allow the wisdom of spirit to flow through our mind.

Think about the power of God active throughout the entire universe, which, through dedicated faith, can dissolve every appearance of error, help to adjust whatever situation may be happening, and bring strength and power to clear vision and so enable you to make positive and wiser decisions. Yes, *"appearances are often deceiving,"* whereas loving thoughts, peaceful thoughts, optimistic thoughts are like a strong shield from which destructive appearances can glance off like wisps of straw.

LAW 4

Zeal is the inward fire of the soul that urges you onward toward your goal
—Charles Fillmore

Each time an opportunity comes your way that allows you to express your talent, welcome that opportunity with open arms! Feel the stirrings of zeal and enthusiasm move within you, providing the impetus to transform that opportunity into a full realization of good. Zeal can often be described as that part of us which generates spiritual motivation, resulting in forward or progressive unfoldment. When Charles Fillmore was 94 he remarked, *"I fairly sizzle with zeal and enthusiasm and spring forth to do that which should be done by me."* What a tremendous attitude! Zeal can be the inner fire that stirs us into action. It offers the ability to gain distinction through concentrated effort directed toward our goals. Zeal has been called the "impulse to go forward" and "the urge behind all things."

In his book *Helping Heaven Happen*, Dr. Donald Curtis writes about when he was a child going about his daily tasks; there was a little chant that gave him encouragement and enthusiasm to get the job done:

"Man is so made that when anything fires his soul impossibilities vanish."
—Jean de la Fontaine

Good, better, best,
Never let it rest,
'Til the good is better,
And the better best.

"We would keep this up for several minutes," he said, *"going faster and faster until we fell in a heap, laughing. And you know something, often the task at hand was completed with much less difficulty, and we were all eager to direct our energy to the next one."* There can be a tremendous energy in doing well what is before you to accomplish. Then you can move forward to the next opportunity that may be beckoning. Just as a tuning fork vibrates to the note that is struck on the piano, so each of us vibrates to the notes that sound around us and within us. This principle has been referred to as "the mirror principle" or the "law of reflection."

There is no need to drag yourself through life bored, tired, or dull. It is unnecessary to allow yourself to be the victim of erroneous belief, limited thinking, superstitions, ignorance, or fear. You can grow new wings of awareness. Let me share a story with you. The Rockefeller Institute conducted an enlightening series of tests involving parasites (organisms living in or on another living organism). The tests demonstrated to the institute that even the so-called lowly creatures have the power to call upon nature's intelligence for the resources to meet any need. The institute brought potted rosebushes into a room and placed them in front of a closed window. They found that if the plants were allowed to dry out, the parasites, which had previously been wingless, grew wings! After this metamorphosis, the parasites left the dead plants that could no longer provide them with food and drink. The only way the insects could survive was to grow wings and fly, which they did. When their source of supply was shut off, they had to find a means of migrating or they would perish. There is a great line in *A Sleep of Prisoners*, a play by Christopher Fry. It says, *"Oh those fabulous wings unused fold in my heart."* Those fabulous wings are within each of us as mental and spiritual forces, powers, and potentials. Could not the uplifting power of zeal be the invisible wings of spirit that can move us wondrously toward the achievement of our sincere heart desires? The poet Philip Doddridge seems to share this thought, *"Awake my soul! Stretch every nerve, And press with vigor on; A heavenly race demands thy zeal, And an immortal crown."*

Scripture tells us, *"For God did not give us a spirit of timidity, but a spirit of power"* (2 Timothy 1:7). We have within our being a source of power with which to accomplish whatever it may be that is desirable. Doctors can confirm that every cell and organ

"I fairly sizzle with zeal and enthusiasm and spring forth with a mighty faith to do the things that ought to be done by me."
—written by Charles Fillmore in his ninety-fourth year!

"Fires can't be made with dead embers, nor can enthusism be stirred by spiritless men. Enthusiasm in our daily work lightens effort and turns even labor into pleasant tasks."
—Stanley Baldwin

of our being is literally crammed with vital energy. Can zeal be a part of this vital force, this tremendous energy, with which to create a wonderful new world? Are you willing to put zeal to the test in your life?

Exploring beyond the boundaries of the personal mind, keep asking yourself, "What if?" "What would happen if I injected zeal and enthusiasm to a greater degree in my work?" "In communication with others?" "In family and personal relationships?" Look at everyday situations with a new perspective of that propelling forward force of zeal. Think of possibilities in various situations, and let your imagination soar. Then engineer these ideas into workable possibilities. A lot of human progress has come from those who keep asking, "What if?" and then add the life-giving ingredient of zeal!

LAW 5

Minds are like parachutes— they only function when they are open
—Dick Sutphen

At one time people were certain that the earth was the center of the cosmos, and those who thought otherwise were ridiculed and scorned. People once laughed at the Wright brothers for building a machine they believed could fly through the air. These are obvious examples of closed minds on a global scale, but a closed mind can also affect our everyday life in subtle ways.

For example, Alice believed her classmate Amy was rich because her father owned a factory that made small metal springs. When Alice and her mother saw Amy and her mother shopping for groceries, Alice asked, "Why are they comparing prices and selecting the least expensive items when they can buy whatever they want?"

Two weeks later, the factory was placed in bankruptcy! Many kinds of electronic equipment that had once used the springs that Amy's father had manufactured now operated with batteries and microchips. The lack of demand for his product caused the business to fail. But Alice had already made up her mind about Amy's circumstances. Even though some of the other students at Alice's school talked about the problems Amy's family were facing, Alice had not heard them. She tailored her convictions to fit her own sense of reality. She believed that owning a business meant financial security, and her mind was closed to other possible interpretations.

A closed mind can have an important effect on your future. Two high school seniors, Bill and John, were invited to an open house at a college they both were interested in attending. They joined a group of students who were discussing physics. Bill broke in, talking confidently as though he had a good grasp of the subject, although he had never studied physics and his knowledge was superficial. John was as ignorant of physics as Bill, but he listened carefully to the discussion, which had to do with atomic structure and the origin of the universe. Before long he realized the ideas he held concerning the subject were different from those being discussed by the college students—different and not very informed.

Bill, who had acted as if he knew it all and whose ignorance was exposed, went home and told his parents he didn't want to attend "that stupid college." John, on the other hand, pulled out his encyclopedia and read as much as he could on the subject of physics. Even though physics was not his major subject of interest, he realized he didn't fully understand the principles involved, so he made the effort to learn. He followed this up by reading a book recommended by his high school librarian. He ended up attending the college and graduating in the top quarter of his class.

While you should not turn away from values and ideas you have good reason to believe are true, it is important to continue learning and growing mentally. A narrow mind can be the straightest avenue to a narrow life. Listen to others more informed than you are, and don't be afraid to ask questions. Reading can increase your knowledge and open doors of learning and understanding. Remember that our *minds are like parachutes—they only function when they are open.*

Let's look at the parachute analogy. A parachute used when jumping out of an airplane is constructed with a small pilot chute that is released first to activate the larger chute, which is tightly packed within its protective cover. A handle is attached to a rip cord that must be forcefully pulled to release the pilot chute, which then fills with air and provides the initial power to pull the tightly packed main chute from its container.

"There is only one thing that will really train the human mind and that is the voluntary use of the mind by the man himself. You may aid him, you may guide him, you may suggest to him and, above all else, you may inspire him. But the only thing worth having is that which he gets by his own exertions, and what he gets is in direct proportion to what he puts into it."
—Albert Lowell

"The lightening spark of thought, generated or, say rather, heaven-kindled, in the solitary mind, awakes its express likeness in another mind, in a thousand other minds, and all blaze up together in combined fire."
—Thomas Carlyle

Your mind is like the parachute—unless you open it, it remains tightly packed and inactive. It does take courage to open the parachute of your mind to the mysterious unknown, but once accomplished, life unfolds wondrously before you.

A closed mind is a sad waste of possibilities when a person chooses inaction over progress. One of the important purposes of this book is to encourage you, the reader, to open yourself to the joys and wonders of your existence. It is with sincere hope that you will accept the challenge to continue a life-long pursuit of progress toward awareness of the spirit within you.

If we look at some of the great minds that have gifted humanity with wonderful discoveries and inventions, in many instances we become aware of an open and questing mind. In 1865, German chemist Friedrich Kekule fell asleep puzzling over the structure of the benzene molecule. Kekule dreamed of thousands of atoms dancing before his eyes, some forming patterns and twisting like snakes. Suddenly one snake grabbed its own tail. In a flash, Kekule awakened with the idea of a closed-chain structure of benzene. His mind opened to the idea, and further work gave the world a brilliant scientific discovery.

Ross Bagdasarian, creator of the singing Alvin and the Chipmunks, first conceived of the chipmunks after nearly running over one on a country road. He named them Alvin, Simon, and Theodore, after a trio of record executives!

It was in 1950 that Frank McNamara ate a fancy meal in a classy New York restaurant and realized along about dessert time that he had no available cash. Embarrassed, he phoned his wife to come pay the check. Shortly thereafter, he borrowed $10,000 and founded Diner's Club—the first credit card accepted by restaurants.

J. M. Haggar, founder of the Haggar Company, became inspired by Henry Ford's idea of the production line and mass production. If automobiles could be mass produced, why couldn't men's trousers be mass produced and sold at popular prices? Those in the clothing industry said he would never make it. However, using the ends of suit fabrics instead of denim, Haggar made a new kind of dress pants he called "slacks," and in the process, J. M. Haggar revolutionized the clothing industry.

The thinking faculty in humanity can make us free agents. Our minds are our creative center, and when we are open and receptive to thoughts and ideas, our accomplishments can be tremendous.

"Just as the soil that has lain fallow produces a richer harvest, so it is with human beings—the bare and silent moments are those when the busy mind finds light and air. The thoughts that arise in these brief intervals, when one takes time to look up, are growing thoughts."
—Mariska Karasz

Spotlights!

1. We, alone, have control over our thoughts.
2. Strive to make the best and most positive use of every precious moment of every day.
3. A mind that is occupied with positive thoughts blossoms like a beautiful garden, free of the weeds of negativity.
4. An error (sin) in thinking or behavior can be deadly because it often diminishes one's potential of living a peaceful, happy life.
5. Believe that you can, and you may find that you can!
6. Train yourself to look beyond appearances with clarity and openness.
7. Do the most you know how to do with what you have to do with!
8. *"If we did all the things we are capable of doing, we would literally astonish ourselves."*—Thomas Edison
9. Welcome every opportunity with open arms, open mind, and enthusiasm.
10. Zeal can be the inner fire that stirs us into action.

Living the Law!

This week's opportunity to work with the laws of life comes with the invitation to ponder the thoughts from Rebecca Clark's beautiful writing "The Voice in the Wilderness," excerpted from her book *Breakthrough.* Then spend some time thinking about how you interact with the energies of life through the realm of nature. After quiet reflection along this line, write your thoughts in your journal.

The Voice in the Wilderness

When I climb to the summits of majestic mountains covered with stately trees towering above daisy-speckled meadows, I find around me breathless beauty. When in awe I behold vast quiet reaches of desert—golden sands flowing to meet sky-blue waters, I am touched with the majesty of creation. When I stand on a rocky cliff by the ocean and watch the tide come and go, I feel the presence of God and recognize my oneness with Him.

Our beautiful earth is a place where birds sing, animals and children play, the sun shines, and rain falls. It is a special place. It is our home.

Is it a better place because you were born?

Different countries have their own stories and legends, and there is an old American Indian myth which goes like this. When a tribe member made the journey through the doorway to another life called "death," before he could go forward in the new life, he had to face the Great Hunter and answer one question affirmatively: Was the earth a better place because you were born?

As a child, I remember my parents saying to me, "Wherever you are, whatever you do, make earth better because you passed through."

As the present is heir to the past, so will the future be the child of the present. The present is where you are *right now*. You can fearfully anticipate the future or you can make a conscious effort to build a better future, which means that you work today with a positive attitude and begin shaping your world right now in the manner you desire for tomorrow.

A skeptic may object by saying, "But with our recent history of wars and hostility and in view of the present world situation, is there any reason to believe in civilization and to be optimistic about the future?"

Absolutely!

Remember that you are living in an age in which men have walked on the moon. You are living in an age when research in consciousness is rapidly gaining momentum. You are living in an age when more people are being born than ever before. You are living in an age of communication between planets. You are living in an age when people are seeking and finding the presence of God in their personal lives, even amid the tension of our present society. Man's divine spirit is getting tired of residing in turmoil and confusion. Humanity is ready for enlightenment.

You do not live in a time of decline, but in a time of transition. Think about this: not a time of decline but a time of transition. The world often may seem at odds and appearances may seem hopeless. Not so!

Even the darkest night must relent before the approaching dawn—the coming of the new day, and *we are living at the beginning of a new day . . . a new age . . . an age that some call "golden."*

The shocks and upheavals of our time are but the storms of a forthcoming spring which sweep away what is decayed to make room for the newer, the better. These are but the growth pains of a new era, an era that gives birth to a race of men and women who are strong and supreme because they are united in one cause—mankind's evolution.

Week Thirty-Seven

LAW 1

You are more defined by what comes out of your mouth than by what goes in
—Anonymous

A middle-aged man attended a male therapy support group one evening when he felt he was at his lowest ebb. His wife was leaving him. His business was teetering near bankruptcy. He had gained weight over the last few years, and his self-esteem wasn't very high. Even his hair was thinning!

The moderator explained the group purpose for that evening. They would go around in a circle and each man would take a few minutes to explain what wasn't working in his life. On the second round, the participants would discuss what they were going to do to change these situations.

The middle-aged man listened patiently as each of the other group members spoke. When it was his turn to unburden himself, he believed that his was one of the saddest stories in the room. A secret part of him felt almost proud to be so pathetic. As the sharing continued around the circle, the man found himself trying to second guess why the other group members had come. As he looked around the circle, he noticed that the last person was a handsome young man about twenty years old.

Why, he thought, would such a young man be here? The youngster's face looked sympathetic as he nodded at each person's story. When the time came for him to speak, he was smiling.

"My friends," he said almost wistfully, "I have been diagnosed with terminal cancer." The gasp was audible in the room. "My doctors have given me three to six months to live. I have struggled with this awareness for a month now and have finally made a decision." His voice gained self-confidence as it grew. "I am going to take flying lessons!"

"Language exerts hidden power, like the moon on the tides."
—Rita Mae Brown

"Wisdom does not show itself so much in precept as in life–in firmness of mind and mastery of appetite. It teaches us to do as well as to talk; and to make our words and action all of a color."
—Seneca

"Words have their genealogy, their history, their economy, their literature, their art and music, as too they have their weddings and divorces, their successes and defeats, their fevers, their undiagnosable ailments, their sudden deaths. They also have their moral and social distinctions."
—Virginia Peterson

The words hung in the air. Flying lessons?

"I have chosen to live!"

Flying lessons! The middle-aged man drew in his breath. His mind flew over all the imaginary reasons he had created for this young man to have spoken, realizing each of them had been trite and pretentious next to the reality of his plight. Then his thoughts rested, for the first time without self-pity, on his own small problems. He felt almost ashamed.

This young man was dying. He would not have a chance to live a long life. "I've lived more than twice the boy's number of years," the man thought to himself. "And what have I really done with my life?"

Yet, here was a young man, facing a critical situation, with almost a look of triumph, a look of . . . could he say it . . . joy! And what had the young man said? He chose to live! Those were the words that came from his mouth.

When the man left the meeting that night, he and the other members of the circle had once again taken up their torch of believing in their own lives. They had seen light in another and had heard words of truth spoken. They were reminded that they had a choice about how they might carry their burdens.

Each of us carries who and what we are within and with us. Sometimes this can be quite visible on the faces of those we pass on the street. At other times, it may be more subdued and hidden from even the most discerning eyes. We cannot know what has happened to another person unless we have truly walked in that person's shoes. But how we perceive a person may often be determined by what that person says. How many times have you seen people who may be lovely in appearance yet speak with language that would curl a sailor's toes?

The Bible says, *"Hear and understand: not what goes into the mouth defiles a man, but what comes out of the mouth, this defiles a man"* (Matthew 15:10, 11). The sacred Hindu *Kaushitaki Upanishads* express the wisdom of looking beyond the spoken words in the statement, *"Speech is not what one should desire to understand. One should know the speaker."* Again, in Psalms, we are made aware of the importance of our words: *"Let the words of my mouth, and the meditation of my heart be acceptable in thy sight, O Lord, my strength, and my redeemer"* (Psalm 16:13).

We are living in a marvelous time when humanity appears to be awakening to a greater awareness of our spirituality. Paralleling this inner awakening often come discoveries in various areas of human endeavor—psychology, physics, science, religion. We are learning that our words can be instruments with which we build and shape our world. In this context, doesn't it seem possible that a statement spoken in spiritual consciousness can have great spiritual power? When we speak affirmations in a time of prayer, we can identify ourself more closely with God.

The spoken word can be like an arrow shot from a bow. It cannot be recalled. There may be words that we have spoken which we regretted, either at the time we made the comment or later. *"My words declare the uprightness of my heart, and what my lips know they speak sincerely,"* proclaims the writer of Job 33:3. Right now can be a good time to begin to exercise utmost care in the selection and formation of our thoughts and, particularly, our words and speech. We can avoid using words that are negative, ugly, and harmful. We can make it a point to express ourself in a harmonious, cheerful, tactful, and caring manner. We can avoid gossip, falsehood, and careless and unnecessary talk. We can refrain from trying to force our viewpoint on others through too much talking. Being aware of our words is one way we can add to life only that which may bless and uplift. Remember what an impact the young man's words, "I have chosen to live," made on the therapy group? Who knows how many lives may have been affected, directly or indirectly, by that one simple statement! Who knows the effect your words may have on another? Choose them well!

"The instruments of both life and death are contained within the power of the tongue."
—Proverbs 18:21

LAW 2

The journey of a thousand miles begins with one step
—Lao Tzu

Perhaps one of the most important and meaningful journeys we make is that of finding our place in the world. Think of the condition that might be set up if we become indolent, restless, or rebellious toward our surroundings—or if we think the world owes us a living. Many persons look at some place or position

"The first step . . . which we make in this world, is the one on which depends the rest of our days."
—Voltaire

444

"If you have a great ambition, take as big a step as possible in the direction of fulfilling it, but if the step is only a tiny one, don't worry if it is the largest one now possible."
—Mildred MacAfee

"Seize this very moment! What you can do or think you can do, begin it."
—J. W. von Goethe

that they would like to have but don't take the time or the steps necessary to attain their desire. Discouragement or despair can be the enemy of progress; so it becomes important to be happy, peaceful, joyous, and interested in where you are in order to move forward and upward.

Our position in the great universal scheme may often be something that must be attained through development. There are many steps along the way, and some of them may appear to be difficult at times. But every journey begins with the first step, and that first step can be the most difficult because of the law of inertia. The science of physics proves that it takes more energy to get a stationary mass moving than it does to keep it moving. For example, it takes a great deal more energy to start a train from a standing position than it does to keep it moving down the tracks.

As a child, Ralph Waldo Emerson once watched a sawyer cutting up some wood. The task was beyond young Emerson's strength, but finally he saw a way to be useful. "May I," he asked, "do the grunting for you?" Small as he was, "the grunting" could have been Emerson's first step in wanting to be of assistance to his friend. First steps can be very simple!

On a visit to Sir Jacob Epstein's studio, George Bernard Shaw noticed a huge block of stone standing in one corner and asked what it was for. "I don't know yet," said the sculptor. "I'm still making plans." Shaw was astounded. "You mean you plan your work? Why, I change my mind several times a day!" he exclaimed. "That's all very well with a four-ounce manuscript," replied Epstein, "but not with a four-ton block." From this story, we can perceive that planning played an important first step in the journey of Epstein's bringing forth his art.

Each new day can be the first step into a brand-new lease on life. This morning you awakened to a day of many possibilities, a day of new experience, and a day that may be capable of bringing great joy into your life. The dawning of a new day can be like a vestibule to a new world. You can have an eminent appreciation of each day and feel better equipped to meet its activities if your first step is to give thanks for the day, and know within your heart that something of immense value can be in store for you.

The first step into a well-rounded life could be your outlook on life or your plan for living life. Do you feel an urge to increase the circumference of your life? To expand your world? To adventure farther than you may have gone before? Then the first step can be to broaden the scope of your mind and to develop mentally, physically, and spiritually. Allow no limiting belief to restrict your outlook on life. Begin to live without self-imposed bonds and fetters. Let the wings of your soul lift you from narrow surroundings and above material beliefs in limitations.

Are you among those who stand before open doors, at the threshold of opportunities and success, filled with the high vision of the journey, and ready to take the first step through that door?

"No matter how small and unimportant what we are doing may seem, if we do it well, it may soon become the step that will lead us to better things."
—Channing Pollock

LAW 3

The dark of night is not the end of the world
—Anonymous

Many ancient people thought that the earth was flat, and, if one ventured too close to the edge, he would fall off. The phrase "the end of the world" became representative of a place where there was no solid ground for support. It was as if the earth ended at a particular point, and only emptiness lay beyond.

Many of us have times when there seems to be no solid support on which we can walk, stand, or even rest. Our world may seem to be crumbling under our feet, and we might wish we were anywhere but our present place. The situation may be one where we are certain our family doesn't understand how we feel. It may be difficult to convince those close to us of the seriousness of our thoughts and feelings. And there may seem to be no outside avenue of assistance in making major decisions. We may feel completely alone in the midst of a difficult situation.

The mystic St. John of the Cross called this type of crisis *"the dark night of the soul."* And "dark night" is a pretty-descriptive analogy. If you have been wakeful during the predawn hours while the world is still sleeping, you may know how lonely it can feel. There is no one to talk to, and the feeling can be almost as if you are the only person alive in the world. The night can

"Part of our time is snatched from us, part is gently subtracted, and part slides insensibly away."
—Seneca

seem endless, and, in those moments, you might believe that morning may never come.

In his book *Make Your Life Worth While*, Emmet Fox parallels the "up" and "down" times in our life with the tide flowing in and out. He said, *"We do not make our spiritual unfoldment in a steady straight line. Human nature does not work in that way. No one moves upward in a path of unbroken progress to the attainment of perfection. What happens is that–if we are working rightly–we move upward steadily for a while, and then we have a little setback. Then we move forward again, and presently we have another little setback. Those setbacks are not important as long as the general movement of our lives is upward. . . . The tide flows in and out. . . . This mode of progression seems to be general throughout nature."* An awareness of this natural cycling can help immensely in maintaining a sense of calm and balance during the times of intense events.

Some of the crises that come into our life may seem to be endless and without hope of a positive outcome. At such times, we might be tempted to believe that life may not seem to be worth living. Perhaps we think the world (including our family, school, job, and relationships) would be better off without us. However, this is not true! You have a reason for living. Each person in the world has a reason for living. You have a part to play in this life, as does every other person in the universe. You *do* matter.

What we often see as "no reason for living" can be, in truth, a situation in which we may have an opportunity to learn a valuable lesson for becoming a whole person. The most stressful event can be a gift in the form of a powerful learning experience that can help us to grow in wisdom and understanding of life's true and deeper meaning.

When involved in a situation that feels like the end of the world, picture yourself standing at the beginning of a stairway. If there is no light, you do not know there are steps that can support your weight. If you ask for light, you can be shown that there is indeed a stair, with each step leading you from the problem to the solution. Empty your mind of unhealthy thoughts, and replace them with wholesome, creative concepts. Take charge of your thoughts instead of allowing them to control you. Refrain from making emotional judgments. Pause and think objectively and dispassionately. Be aware that nothing can replace gloom as completely as the practice of caring and goodwill. Theodore Roethke had an understanding of the possible benefits of these dark times when he said, *"In a dark time, the eye begins to see."* It's true. As we move into the new dawn after one of these "dark nights of the soul," we may often have a clearer perspective of the situation and a greater awareness of the blessing it has brought. One man meets these challenging experiences with the following statement: "This comes to bless me!" And he looks for—and finds—the blessing!

There is a part of you that knows the right action for any problem that might arise. Remember, even if you have tried various things that haven't worked, there may still be many different ways to attempt a solution. There are few insoluble problems, only those we haven't yet learned how to solve. Not knowing how to solve a problem doesn't make you a worthless person. You are simply being given an opportunity for growth. You are a valuable and a valued being.

After the darkest night, the sun always rises. What you are experiencing may be only a cloud hiding the face of the sun. Let the power and warmth of the sun within you burn away the cloud that may attempt to dim your inner light. Let the sun of belief in life energize you as you climb to the pinnacle of overcoming.

"Every man is two men; one is awake in the darkness, the other asleep in the light."
—Kahlil Gibran

LAW 4

Love conquers all things
—Virgil

Many fables and fairy tales depict stories of a mythical monster called a dragon. This large, winged, reptilian-like creature is often described as guarding a mysterious castle or lair, spewing his fiery breath and attempting to destroy white knights, fair maidens, and complete villages. It always seems to be in a roaring rage. The main character in these fables and stories is often a brave knight in shining armor who may make many complicated attempts to overcome or eliminate the dragon. In reading these adventures, have you ever wondered why no one seemed to make an effort to tame the dragon with love, understanding, and compassion?

Whether or not we like to admit it, we, too, may have our inner dragons. When intense anger "rears its head" in our life; when we are overcome by sadness and grief over a major loss;

"Many waters cannot quench love, neither can floods drown it."
—Song of Solomon 8:7

when our world seems to drop from beneath our feet, we face our personal dragons. Few of us travel the road of life and escape occasional feelings of anger, sadness, and grief. The big question is, What do we do with these "beasts" when they attack us? Sometimes we have to wrestle with a paper tiger, or a dragon, for a while before we realize that it is a fraud.

Upon reflection, can you remember times when you may have felt angry and either lashed out at someone, or tried to "kill" your angry feelings? Have there been times in your life when you could feel understanding and compassion for yourself, although you may have felt angry and upset? Even though you may not have been very happy with your actions, could you still feel loving toward the spirit within you?

Being compassionate might mean taking your anger out on a pillow instead of your best friend, or going for a run in the park instead of letting your feelings smolder and fester inside. Being understanding can mean knowing you have a right to *all* of your feelings—even the negative ones—and that you're not a bad person for feeling the way you do. Being loving can indicate a willingness to forgive yourself for unacceptable actions and continuing on with your life.

As Virgil recognized, *"Love conquers all things."* And Teilhard de Chardin elevated love thus: *"The day will come when, after harnessing space, the winds, the tides and gravitation, we shall harness for God the energies of love. And on that day, for the second time in the history of the world, we shall have discovered fire."*

You can be a conscious (and unconscious!) *loving* influence in the lives of others as you simply move throughout your day. You may feel that others do not pay a lot of attention to what you say or do, or you may feel other people do not necessarily think of you except when they are with you. But the loving things you think, say, and do can have a real effect on others. Someone may be comforted by the memory of your loving words. A friend may meet a difficult experience with greater faith and fortitude because he or she may have seen you stand strong in your faith in a similar situation. Someone you know may perse-vere toward a special goal because you were observed following through on some course of action you set for yourself. A family member, co-worker, or fellow student may express greater poten-tial because you lovingly recognized and commented on the possibilities you saw in him or her.

Love is a powerful creative force that can dissolve misunder-standings and help adjust inharmonious situations. Mother Teresa said, *"Spread love everywhere you go: first of all in your own house. Give love to your children, to your wife or husband, to a next door neighbor. . . . Let no one ever come to you without leaving better and happier. Be the living expression of God's kindness; kindness in your face, kindness in your eyes, kindness in your smile, kindness in your warm greeting."*

The poet Shelley speaks of the importance of love: *"The great secret of morals is love; or a going out of our own nature, and an identification of ourselves, with the beautiful which exists in thought, action, or person. . . ."* The power and effectiveness of love in a person's life is described thus by William Wordsworth: *"That best portion of a good man's life, his little, nameless, unremembered acts of kindness and of love."*

So the next time you feel a dragon breathing down your neck, pause and think about the following possibilities:

1. What is the dragon trying to say to me?

2. Observe and acknowledge the presence of your feelings.

3. Take the dragon (anger, fear, grief, or whatever) to a place where it can't hurt you or anyone else, and let it blow off steam.

You may want to talk about your feelings with a trusted friend or a counselor. Sometimes a "listening ear" may be sufficient for you to find a new perspective. These emotional feelings could be delivering a message you need to hear. They could be saying, for example, "I don't want to do this any more." Or, "I don't like the way this feels." Once the dragon learns it can trust you to love it, you may not need to fear it again.

There is an old saying that *"he who lives with acceptance, friendship, and love will find those very qualities everywhere he looks."* Lovingly search and find!

"Oh, if at every moment of our lives we could know the consequences of some of our utterings, thoughts and deeds that seem so trivial and unimportant at the time! And should we not conclude from such examples that there is no such thing in life as unimportant moments devoid of meaning for the future?"
—Isabelle Eberhardt

"The conquest of oneself is better than the conquest of all others."
—Dhamapada

LAW 5

Count your blessings every day and they will grow and multiply like well-tended plants
—William Juneau

In his book *The Positive Principle Today*, Dr. Norman Vincent Peale talks about the power of words, or of word combinations,

"Blessings we enjoy
daily; and for the most
of them, because they
be so common, most
men forget to pay their
praise."
—Izaak Walton

"As bread is the staff of
life, the simple suste-
nance of the body, so
appreciation is the food
of the soul."
—Priscilla Wayne

to affect persons and situations. He describes a seven-word combination that has affected many people he has known. This
statement demonstrates power to erase failure, increase
strength, eliminate fear, and overcome self-doubt. He says these
seven words can help any individual become a more successful
human being in the best meaning of that term. That seven-word
formula is this: *I can do all things through God.* These words indicate an awareness that the creative power of God can be the
motivating energy behind our endeavors.

Thank You, God, for all my good is another seven-word statement that can propel us forward in wonderful ways. One secret
of a grateful heart can be that thanksgiving lifts one into a
higher consciousness where we know that life is good. Ask yourself: "Do I take sufficient time to be grateful, to pour out my
thanks for all the blessings in my life?" And where do you begin
to count your blessings?

The gifts of life and health—what precious gifts!

Family and friends—how bare and perhaps dreary life would
be without these!

Food, shelter, clothing, and daily needs—things we so often
take for granted, but what would our life be like without them?

Daily work—whatever that work may be, it can provide an
avenue of creative expression for you at this time.

Depressed moments—possibly, but moments only! They pass,
and faith can break through like the sun breaking through the
clouds.

Wisdom and understanding—the joy of learning and growing
in awareness. Life, in order to move us forward, often confronts
us with situations that we can answer or resolve by growing a
little wiser.

Peace of mind—and the opportunity to radiate joy, encouragement, good cheer.

Healing—of mind, body, and spirit. Nearly everyone needs
some kind of healing at some point in life. When we believe
healing is possible and we become open and receptive to the
stream of healing life, healing may occur.

The Psalmist says, *"Know that the Lord is God! It is he that made
us, and we are his people, and the sheep of his pasture. Enter into his
gates with thanksgiving, and his courts with praise! Give thanks to
him, bless his name!"* (Psalm 100:3, 4). If we take this Scripture
into our heart and wait expectantly for our heart and mind to
take up the activity the words describe, we may suddenly realize
that praise and thanksgiving can become almost wordless

actions of heart and mind! Although, for some of us, the words can be a necessary start!

If the circumstances of your life reflect joy and happiness, then praise and thanksgiving can open the door to even greater joy and happiness. If the circumstances in your life seem to reflect the other side of the coin, praise and thanksgiving can help you become aware of a new and exciting current of energy flowing within you which can become a living flame that can consume old negative ways of thinking and believing. The product of continual praise and thanksgiving can be a happy, peaceful, joyous, successful new you! Times of seeming struggle, uncertainty, or problems can simply be the growing pains of that new you emerging. And, what is incredible, you can praise and give thanks for the growing pains!

For many people, when we speak of "living life more abundantly," it probably means having a greater abundance of things, which include health and strength, work and play, love and friendship, wisdom for today and security for tomorrow. Have you ever considered that abundant living can include another dimension? A dimension that cannot be engendered by the acquisition of things nor eliminated by their absence? This is the dimension of faith, appreciation, and giving thanks.

When we plant a garden, we often mulch and fertilize the soil. We carefully place the tender plants in the ground and continue to care for them regularly until the mature plant provides the harvest—whether of fruits, vegetables, or flowers. When we count our blessings—expressing our appreciation for life, its lessons, and its gifts—they can also grow and multiply like those well-tended plants.

A story is told of a businessman who wanted to give his customers a unique gift. So he printed the words "Thank You" a million times in book form and titled the book, *A Million Thanks to You.* He sent a copy to the Library of Congress, requesting a copyright. The library refused, noting that single words are not able to be copyrighted. When the businessman received the library's letter, he chuckled, "Go ahead, everyone, use 'Thanks' as much as you like. It is not copyrighted!"

When we consciously focus on the good in our lives—such as making a list of things for which we are thankful—we unite our mind with the power of appreciation and make ourselves available to receive even more blessings.

"For all that has been, Thanks. For all that will be, Yes."
—Dag Hammarskjöld

"When you put on your clothes, remember the weaver's labor; when you take your daily food, remember the husbandman's work."
—Chinese proverb

Spotlights!

1. Each of us carries "who" and "what" we are within us.
2. *"Let your speech always be gracious, seasoned with salt, so that you may know how you ought to answer everyone"* (Colossians 4:6).
3. Every journey we take involves the first step, the beginning of how we proceed.
4. Planning can be an important first step in any endeavor.
5. Allow no limiting belief to restrict your outlook on life.
6. There are few insolvable problems, only those we haven't yet learned how to solve.
7. Believe that you are bigger than your difficulties for, indeed, you are!
8. Can you recall times when "dragons" of fear, anger, or grief appeared in your life—and how the dragon became your friend?
9. You can be a conscious (and unconscious) loving influence in the life of others as you move through your day.
10. Practice turning your thoughts toward appreciation and thanksgiving.

Living the Law!

The following insights can offer some deep spiritual truths taken from everyday events. Think on these things!

Your belief about your destiny is your belief about yourself!

Don't be afraid to be "different"! Believe in your divine origin.

Allow for delays. You will enjoy life's journey more!

God can heal a broken heart, but he needs all the pieces!

Don't get so busy adding up your troubles that you forget to count your blessings!

Take time to enjoy the abundance of nature.

Pinpoint your primary goal in life.

Learn how to accept defeat—temporarily!

Be flexible! God has many doors!

Believe that the power of your thoughts can change your life.

"Humble yourself therefore under the mighty hand of God, that he may exalt you in due time."—1 Peter 5:6

Don't cry over spilled milk!

When you can't solve a problem—manage it!

The power of God is at work in you and through you.

Week Thirty-Eight

L AW 1

You never really lose until you stop trying
—Mike Ditka, Football Coach

Have you ever invested your enthusiasm and your sincerity—to say nothing of hard work—in an activity or a relationship, only to have the fruits of your labors seem to slip right through your fingers? Perhaps just when it looked as if success and fulfillment were about to appear, something happened! Something changed unexpectedly . . . and your good seemed to be blocked.

Surely there are times when each of us feels that we need more strength and courage to get things done. We feel inadequate to meet some new challenge that appears in our life, or we feel tired of coping with the old ones.

An Olympic swimmer strains every muscle to push himself over the finish line a fraction of an inch in front of his competitors. A computer technician may work far into the night puzzling out the final solution to a complex problem. An artist may painstakingly make changes in the detail of a flower in a painting. As different as their goals may appear, something within seems to beckon to the individual to strive for the vision of excellence until the goal is achieved.

John Hockenberry, American Broadcasting Company newsman, has been paralyzed from the waist down since he was nineteen, but he has covered news stories all over the world in his wheelchair. Ernest Hemingway rewrote the ending of his book *A Farewell to Arms* no less than thirty-nine times before he was finally satisfied with it! When we begin to feel discouraged, perhaps that is the time to take a deep breath and a long look at where we may be placing our faith. If we are willing to keep our eye on our goals, continue to see ourself achieving them, and do the necessary work along that line, we can ultimately claim our good.

Many years ago there was a gentleman taking a trip by stagecoach. Along the route was a narrow stretch of road made tun-

"If there is no struggle, there is no progress. Those who prefer to favor freedom, and yet deprecate agitation, are men who want crops without plowing the ground. They want rain without thunder and lightening. . . . Men may not get all they pay for in this world; but they must certainly pay for all they get."
—Frederick Douglass

"'I can't do it' never yet accomplished anything; 'I will try' has performed wonders."
—George P. Burnham

"Until you try, you don't know what you can't do."
—Henry James

"No mistake or failure is as bad as to stop and not try again."
—John Wanamaker

"Life is a process of becoming, a combination of states we go through. Where people fail is that they wish to elect a state and remain in it. This is a kind of death."
—Anaïs Nin

nel-like and somewhat dark by a thick covering of overhanging tree branches. As the coach approached this bit of road, the driver cracked his whip over the heads of the horses several times. The gentleman who was riding topside asked, "Why did you do that? The horses were proceeding at a nice steady pace."

The driver replied, "Well, the horses often shy when we reach this section of road, so I give them something else to think about, and they forget the darkness from the overhanging trees!"

There may be some good logic in this simple old story. If our attention is taken up by something else, we often forget what has been worrying us. We may sometimes become locked in old patterns of thinking and keep re-creating the same challenges for ourself. We may even be working to make corrections and not seem to be getting results. Could the manner in which we are working be energizing the situation rather than improving it? We may be holding a situation too closely to us and fail to see the winning possibilities just beyond our current view. Perhaps a change of focus is needed, a new direction, to take our mind completely off the situation. Refocusing often helps to release pent-up anxiety and allows us to redirect energy into new avenues.

It is hard to solve a problem from the same level of consciousness that created it. We should lift our awareness higher. In many instances, we have learned to look outside ourself for an authoritarian guide to give us direction. And there are times this is appropriate. Instead of thinking about "giving up" or "losing" when times seem difficult, we need to reconsider the motive behind our desires or goals and redirect our attention to the indwelling ability and "keep on keeping on!"

LAW 2

Everyone should keep in reserve an alternate plan for livelihood
—John M. Templeton

Just when we might think we have settled into a comfortable niche and everything seems to be going smoothly, we may find our lives turned completely upside down! We might be facing dramatic changes that require we "sing a new song." In some instances, our comfortable routine of daily living may be interrupted to the point that a different theme may unfold. When times like these occur, we have a choice. We can feel sad and sorry for ourself and complain that we are a victim of circumstance, or we can accept the challenge of the moment and choose another direction!

As the poet once asked, *"Can you see the flowers when no flowers are there? When the sky is empty and the fields are bare, can you see the beauty."* Those moments when our world seems to do an about-face could be an invitation from life to walk in another direction, to move toward a new frontier, or pioneer a heart-held dream!

One pioneering woman is Chiara Lubich. Her *Focolare,* or "Fireside," movement, begun in Italy in 1943 has become a successful international means of providing lay communities structured as families and imbued with the loving ethos of family life. She has taken seriously the challenge to become a co-creator with God through a perpetually advancing mind. Charles Kettering, a scientist whose research included the invention of automotive starting and ignition systems said, *"There will always be a frontier where there is an open mind and a willing hand."*

Our willingness to try new experiences can teach us much about the world and assist us on the way to success. Lewis Browne was an American rabbi and author, born in England. Having been a rabbi for six years, he decided to become a writer. Once at a literary dinner, Browne was questioned by another rabbi about his early career. "You were a rabbi, eh," the rabbi remarked. "Were you unfrocked?" Browne replied, "No, just unsuited."

Jean Louis Rodolphe Agassiz, the Swiss naturalist, made many major contributions to paleontology. He also became professor of zoology at Harvard in 1848, deeply influencing the teaching of natural history in the United States. And one of the many jobs William Faulkner took before he established himself as a writer was as postmaster at the University of Mississippi post office.

If you look at the people you know in everyday life, you may find several who have, for various reasons, moved into an alternate plan of livelihood. One such young lady, whom we shall call Marion, married early in life. After four short but happy years together, her husband was killed in an automobile accident, leaving Marion with two small children. She immediately

"It is much better to know something about everything than to know everything about one thing."
—Blaise Pascal

"The more you learn what to do with yourself, and the more you do for others, the more you will learn to enjoy the abundant life."
—William J. H. Botecker

*"My contemplation of
life and human nature
in that secluded place*
(cell 54 of Cairo
Central Prison)
*taught me that he who
cannot change the very
fabric of his thought
will never, therefore,
make any progress."*
—Anwar Sadat

found a secretarial job, which provided a small income.
Realizing that in order to better provide for her family she
needed additional education, Marion also began attending
evening classes at a nearby college. She was fortunate in having
a wonderful neighbor who helped care for the children.

Several years passed, during which time Marion took care of
her family, studied intently, and held a variety of part-time jobs
to supplement her secretarial income. Then one day, the door
of opportunity opened, and Marion could choose from several
possible positions. She was well known and respected in the
community for her commitment to the raising of her children
and her dedication to excellence in her work. Her efforts had
provided her a well-rounded education, and Marion knew she
could always have an alternate plan of livelihood.

Major changes often occur when we least expect them and
can result in conditions beyond our conscious imagination. As
in Marion's story, after the initial shock of an unexpected
change begins to lessen and some objectivity is gained, we can
look around for alternatives. Start by clearing your mind of
doubts and fears about your ability to bring into being the
desires of your heart. A well-known Boy Scout motto is "Be prepared!" Explore various avenues of interest. Get involved with a
hobby. A number of receptive thinkers have turned these interests into lucrative livelihoods when life circumstances necessi-
tated change. Think creatively.

In the book *Jonathan Livingston Seagull*, by Richard Bach,
Jonathan's teacher Chiang tells him, *"The trick is to stop seeing
yourself as trapped inside a limited body with a 42-inch wingspan. . . .
The trick is to know that your true nature lives, as perfect as an
unwritten number, everywhere at once across space and time."* The
Chinese patriarch Chuang-Tsu taught the same principle thousands of years ago. He said, *"In a dream I saw myself as a great
butterfly with wings that spanned the entire universe. Now I am not
quite sure if I am Chuang-Tsu dreaming I am a butterfly, or perhaps I
am a butterfly dreaming I am Chuang-Tsu!"*

It takes courage to face the challenges of life. When we keep
in reserve an alternate plan for our livelihood, we can have the
strength to do whatever we need to do. Find your source. Live
from it. And keep your heart open.

LAW 3

If you are facing in the right direction, all you need to do is keep walking
—Buddhist proverb

A long time ago, a young girl loved to walk in the deep woods surrounding the village in which she lived. She would chat happily to the birds, chipmunks, and squirrels of the forest in her morning stroll, and rest on the cool moss-covered rocks in the afternoon. One day, the girl walked deeper into the woods than usual. Soon the sky began to turn dark, and she realized she was lost. All she could see were giant pines and the tip of the highest steeple in her village.

Frightened, she began to cry as she looked around. The giant pines hovered close to comfort her. Finally, one of the taller trees whispered to her. "Walk toward the steeple," it said. "Don't take your eyes off the steeple, and soon you'll be home."

So the girl gathered her cape around her, lifted the basket of mushrooms she had picked for dinner, and continued on her way. She watched the tip of the steeple with urgency, knowing if she walked toward it, she would soon be safely home.

Before long, she heard footsteps behind her. Taking her eyes from the steeple for a moment, she turned her head to see who was behind her. Lo and behold, a red fox was so close on her heels she could almost feel its warm breath. "Little girl," said the fox, "there is a beautiful field of wild violets just over the ridge. If you'll follow me, you can take a bouquet home to your mother."

Knowing how much her mother loved wild violets, the girl forgot her fear and ran after the fox, who had visions of juicy mushrooms dancing in his head. Suddenly, the sun went behind a cloud. The forest darkened, and the girl remembered the comment of the pine tree to watch the tip of the steeple. When she looked up from her new path, it was nowhere to be seen.

Again fearful, the child began to run. Without realizing she had been running in a circle, the girl found herself once more among the giant pines. Recognizing them, she looked up and caught a glimpse of the tip of the steeple. Concentrating as hard as she could, she fixed her gaze on the steeple and didn't look away again until she was safely home.

"I might have been born in a hovel, but I determined to travel with the wind and the stars."
—Jacqueline Cochran

"If one concentrates on one thing and does not get away from it . . . he will possess strong, moving power."
—Cheng Yi

"However small in proportion the benefit which follows individual attempts to do good, a great deal may be accomplished by perseverance, even in the midst of discouragement and disappointments."
—George Crabbe

"That which we persist in doing becomes easier for us to do. Not that the nature of the thing has changed, but that our power to do is increased."
—Hever J. Grant

Have you ever had a cherished goal that appeared to be just out of reach? Maybe it seemed years away from fulfillment and the direction to travel unclear. For some of us, our present direction might lead to a new vocation, or to money for a child's education. Whatever waits for you at the end of your path, however, the only way to get there is to keep your eyes on your goal. Something exotic may entice you to choose a diversion or an easier path, but the surest path—although perhaps not the easiest—is the one that leads directly to your goal with the fewest distractions and false starts.

If you plan to go from point *A* to point *B* in the woods and you prepare yourself for the journey by studying the trail and bringing along a compass, you can keep from getting lost. Like the Buddhist proverb says, *"If you are facing in the right direction, all you need to do is keep on walking!"*

Conditions today are vastly different from those of even fifty years ago. Thus, the needs of the individual and the human family are different from those of ages past. We live in a time of tremendous change. We think and feel in progressive capacities as we have evolved from the ox cart, through the horse and buggy, the automobile, the airplane, supersonic jets, and into the age of space travel. We've come a long way from a pale tallow candle to lamps, gas, electricity, and quantum advances into the age of electronics. The children of today live with, understand, and use items that even the greatest minds of the past knew nothing about! Best-selling author and Harvard Business School professor Rosabeth Moss Kanter likens the constant changes happening today to the croquet game in *Alice in Wonderland*—a game in which *"nothing remains stable for very long, because everything is alive and changing."* The reality of life is that one cannot live in the past or in the future. You can only live in the present moment, and the direction in which you are facing is vitally important.

Oliver Wendell Holmes indicated this when he said, *"I find the great thing in this world is not so much where we stand, as in what direction we are moving. To reach the port of heaven, we must sail sometimes with the wind and sometimes against it—but we must sail, and not drift, nor lie at anchor."* This speaks of taking action, and of forward movement. You cannot control anything in your world as long as you are controlled by it. And sometimes, when we become caught up in past events, we may be mental prisoners of old attitudes. As a friend once said, "It's all right to look back, but don't stare!"

Open your mind to light and truth. There never need be a

time when you are at a loss for ideas, inspiration, or guidance. Believe in yourself. Believe in your ability to cope with difficulties. Look at how you have grown through the experiences of your life. Think of the insight and understanding each situation brought. Exercise your ability to rejoice in the positive events that have happened. Continue to walk in the direction of greater illumination. Let joy be your compass!

LAW 4

The unknown is not unknowable and is vastly greater than the known
—John M. Templeton

An old proverb states, "We learn what we look for." If we take an open look around us, we can see signals of transcendence and pointers to the infinite that are coming to us not, only from mystics but through many recent findings of science. The evolution of human knowledge is accelerating quickly, and we are reaping the fruits of generations of scientific thought. Many fields of exploration are finding "what is looked for" and more!

In the book *The God Who Would Be Known*, a number of examples are given which suggest that the unknown is not unknowable and is vastly greater than the known. The authors comment, *"We can see an exciting world in dynamic flux, an unexpected universe whose mechanisms are ever more baffling and staggering in their beauty and complexity, where predictability is uncertain instead of deterministic, where matter and energy are interchangeable, and where evolutionary change occurs by leaps and bounds that defy mechanistically simple explanation. And ourselves; what has become of us? The physicists tell us that we are peculiarly situated midway between the immense parameters of the cosmos and the infinitude of the smallest particles of matter and energy. Our arrival on this planet seems remarkable, whether looked at in terms of the requirement for a special relationship among the forces controlling elementary particles, or in terms of the mechanisms of biological evolution. What is becoming increasingly obvious is that the evolutionary process that has resulted in humankind is a unique and undirectional one. And the*

"Gaining knowledge is like working a quarry. As we chip out bits of information, the mining face gets larger and larger. The more knowledge we gain the more we can see the extent of the unknown. As we grow in knowledge, we grow in humility. This may be just as true in studying the soul as in the investigations pursued by natural sciences."
—John M. Templeton, *The Humble Approach*

steps peculiar to Homo sapiens are remarkable in both their timing and their developmental aspects. We are a once-for-all happening, and, most wonderful of all, our journey has just begun!"

Could this be an invitation to "draft your dream"? Both on an individual and international level? To bring forth your special purpose; to direct your talents to action in a chosen area? Whatever your dream may be, does it subtly nag at your consciousness, urging you to do something about it? No matter what circumstances may appear in your life or what obstacles seem to stand in your way, once you draft that dream and take the first step on its journey of development, the way can be magically cleared. When you take the first step, the universe responds. God works with you when you make that beginning in faith.

The quantity of knowledge that has become known within the last century is said to be greater than all of that discovered since the beginning of humanity. A great deal of this recorded knowledge occurred in the physical sciences, and these discoveries continue to accelerate exponentially. The science of physics now reveals a vast variety of previously unknown particles, and particles within particles. Chemistry has revealed the presence of hundreds of processes going on within matter that were previously never dreamed of. The science of biology has evolved from merely naming and classifying living matter to how a seed germinates and to the genetic code of a living plant. And yet, there is still so much we don't know!

In some instances it seems that the creative spirit of the universe may be spreading and energizing new dimensions of research and information for present and future humankind. In the majestic language of the New Testament we read, *"In the beginning was the Word and the Word was with God and the Word was God. All things were made through Him, and without Him was not anything made that was made. In Him was life, and the life was the light of men"* (John 1:1, 3–4). "Word" in Greek is *logos*, which means "a thought" or a "concept." *Logos* has also been referred to as "the divine archetype idea that contains all ideas." With this understanding and based on the language of modern science, the above Scripture might be translated to mean, "God is the foundation and the Creator of the universe and all therein—and much more. Creation proceeds from idea, to word, to material manifestation." Thus, we get a vague idea of the concept of co-creation.

What would happen if research foundations and religious institutions around the world would begin to devote additional resources and increased energy to scientific studies into the spiritual realm? Could this bring an unprecedented opportunity for greater progress in spiritual information through science?

One of the visions I hope for is the establishment of a new branch of hard science: The Science of Spiritual Research. Slight though it may seem in some areas, the various world media appear to be opening more to spiritual subjects such as prayer and love. Could this be the threshold of growing information in spiritual areas?

In the book *The Wonder of Being Human*, by Sir John Eccles and Daniel N. Robinson, Sir John writes, "*We have the strong belief that we have to be open to the future in the adventure of human personhood. This whole cosmos is not just running on and running down for no meaning. In the context of natural theology, we come to the belief that we are creatures with some supernatural meaning that is as yet ill defined. We cannot think more than that we are all part of some great design. Each of us can have the belief of acting in some unimaginable supernatural drama.*"

What movement these words stir within the soul! Can you feel the call to expand your boundaries of thoughts, feelings, and actions? Research in the hard sciences for new spiritual information can help the unknown become the known!

"Both the man of science and the man of art live always on the edge of mystery surrounded by it. Both, as the measure of their creation, have always had to do with the harmonization of what is new and what is familiar, with the balance between novelty and synthesis, with the struggle to make partial order in total chaos."
—J. Robert Oppenheimer

❖

LAW 5

Forgiveness benefits both the giver and the receiver
—John M. Templeton

Who has not at one time or another held a grudge? Perhaps we may have felt hurt by something someone said. We may have felt taken advantage of by another person. Our ego may have been wounded because we felt taken for granted—in our work or in a relationship. Whatever the cause may have been, we possibly worked with feelings of frustration or anger because we felt wronged. Old fears, grudges, and feelings of injustice can make your present world seem almost unbearable.

"The fragrance always remains in the hand that gave the rose."
—Heda Bejar

When these situations occur, do you sometimes wish you could wipe out the personal world in which you live and move into a clean, fresh, new world? It is possible mentally to erase a negative experience like erasing a blackboard and drawing a new life for yourself. How? Through the power of forgiveness!

Have you heard Mark Twain's story of the jumping frog of Calaveras County? That frog could jump higher and farther than any frog around until some stranger, just before a contest, opened the frog's mouth on the sly and filled it with quail shot! When the time for action came, the frog heaved and hunched, but he was so weighted down that he couldn't budge and, thus, lost to the stranger's untrained frog! What's the lesson here for us? In any athletic race run by human beings, the athletes are careful to carry no more weight than absolutely necessary. In running to win the race of life, it is equally important for us not to weigh ourselves down by clinging to the mistakes we may have made in the past, or by grudges or any negative thoughts. We can release these burdens and let go. As Anne Swetchine says, *"The heart has always the pardoning power."* And an African proverb states, *"He who forgives ends the quarrel."*

Let's look for a moment at the meaning of forgiveness and some of its benefits. Forgiveness means *for giving. For*, "in favor of"; *giving*, "to give." In favor of giving! Forgiveness is a process of giving up that which is false for that which is true. It can be giving positive energies for something that may have been less than positive. For example, giving love for less than loving actions. When we forgive, we release unproductive thoughts and attitudes from our mind so we can partake more fully of the ever-renewing life and vitality God has prepared for us.

After you have forgiven the transgression and released any judgment of the situation or the person, then forget it! The value of forgetting is, again, in the word—to be in favor of getting, of receiving. The thing that seems to hurt most about past hurts is our memory. When we remember the pain and suffering of what happened, we simply hurt again. Replacing a negative memory with a positive one can bring about a healing. Let the old image fade. Take whatever steps you may be able to take to heal the situation. A tightly clenched fist cannot receive. When you release the fist, you have an open hand and are then able to receive.

Charles R. Loss wrote, *"To forgive is the quickest way to end trouble and to have peace and unity. For a forgiving spirit is, by its very nature, a unifying force. It can remove the barriers of separation between peoples and nations and weld them together in peace and goodwill, something that legislation with the help of armies can never accomplish. To hate is to die physically and spiritually, but to forgive is to live."* Hatred, bitterness, and resentment—these feelings do not belong in a healthy mind and heart. The ability to forgive may not come quickly or easily, and it may be necessary to forgive "seventy times seven."

Forgiveness plays such a vital role in our life. It may take varying lengths of time for us to realize that the spiral of holding more tightly to hurts we may have sustained only brings grief to all parties. The person who was perceived as causing the problem may feel ostracized and verbally abused. The person holding on to the injustice often plays the martyr and perpetuates the problem. George Herbert said, *"He who cannot forgive breaks the bridge over which he himself must pass."* The wisdom hidden in this statement is that forgiveness benefits both the giver and the receiver. When true forgiveness takes place, no scars are left, no hurts, no thoughts of revenge; only healing. Forgiveness is a healing power. And forgiveness can bring out the greatness in you!

"We are rich only through what we give, and poor only through what we refuse." —Anne-Sophie Swetchine

Spotlights!

1. When we begin to feel discouraged, perhaps that is the time to take a deep breath and a long look at where we may be placing our faith!
2. Maintain a clear vision of your chosen objectives, and rejoice in working toward them.
3. Be open to alternative means of livelihood.
4. Expand your consciousness in both directions—the great within and the inexhaustible without!
5. Open your mind to light and truth. There need never be a time when you are at a loss for ideas, inspiration, or guidance.
6. It's all right to look back—but don't stare!
7. Evolution of human knowledge is accelerating quickly, and we are reaping the fruits of generations of scientific thought.
8. *"Our life is at all times and before anything else the consciousness of what we can do."*—José Ortega y Gasset
9. Forgiveness can release unproductive thoughts and attitudes from your mind.
10. Forgiveness can bring out the greatness in you!

Living the Law!

A few years ago the following article appeared in several newspapers. The author is unknown, but the wisdom contained in the article deserves becoming well-known! It speaks of the meaningfulness of cooperation. As you read these words, look at the various areas in your life where they may apply. Discuss these ideas with your friends; then write your thoughts in your journal.

A Sense of a Goose

The next time you see geese heading south for the winter, flying along in 'V' formation, you might consider what science has discovered as to why they fly that way. As each bird flaps its wings, it creates an uplift for the bird immediately following. By flying in 'V' formation the whole flock adds at least 71 percent greater flying range than if each bird flew on its own.

People who share a common direction and sense of community can get where they are going more quickly and easily, because they are traveling on the thrust of one another.

When a goose falls out of formation, it suddenly feels the drag and resistance of trying to go it alone—and quickly gets back into formation to take advantage of the lifting power of the bird in front.

If we have as much sense as a goose, we will stay in formation with those people who are headed the same way we are.

When the head goose gets tired, it rotates back in the wing and another goose flies point.

It is sensible to take turns doing demanding jobs, whether with people or with geese flying south.

Geese honk from behind to encourage those up front to keep up their speed.

What message do we give when we honk from behind?

Finally, and this is important—when a goose gets sick or is wounded by gunshot, and falls out of formation, two other geese fall out with that goose and follow it down to lend help and protection. They stay with the fallen goose until it is able to fly or until it dies; and then only do they launch out on their own, or with another formation to catch up with their group.

If we have the sense of a goose, we will stand by each other like that!

Week Thirty-Nine

LAW 1

Humility opens the door to progress
—John M. Templeton

Humility is a gateway to greater understanding. As thanksgiving opens the door to spiritual growth, so does humility open the door to progress in knowledge and open-mindedness. It is difficult for a person to learn anything more if he is certain he knows everything already. When we begin to comprehend how little we know, then we begin to seek and to learn. Unless we realize our ignorance, why should we broaden our horizon and investigate?

To be successful, it would seem that each of us must build our own soul in imitation of the Creator. This means it is important to appreciate, honor, and respect other people. Endeavoring to express our faith in all situations, whether at home, at work, or with friends, can often lead to greater growth. Even with our vast technologies, how little we know and how eager we need to be to learn!

"Wisdom engenders humility."
—Abraham ibn Ezra

Are we as egotistical as the two-dimensional people of the comic strip, "Flatland," who denied evidence of a third dimension? Do we think humans are the end-product of creation? And that other planets can not have life forms as far beyond us as we are beyond the prehistoric amoeba? If information doubled each millennium at the time of Buddha, and now seems to be doubling every three years, would we dare to think that progress would stop with present human knowledge? Does not even logic depict that further acceleration of progress could be part of God's plan?

An ocean-wave analogy can be helpful in approaching God with more humility. A wave is part of the ocean, having no existence apart from the larger body of water. The wave is temporary, whereas oceans are relatively permanent. Each wave is different from every other wave. In a sense, the wave is created by the ocean and is a child of the ocean. When it dies, it returns to and continues to be a part of the surging oceans creating new breakers on the beach. The wave moves naturally with the "isness" of its being—without inhibiting ego!

Egotism is a stumbling block that inhibits future progress. The broad-minded person expands beyond the limiting self and sees truth in a variety of expressions: in theosophy, in science, in philosophy. And to those in whom love dwells, the whole world is but one family in various manifestations. The humble person is ready and willing to admit and welcome these various manifestations.

What are the practical applications of a sense of humility and an appreciation of God's infinite powers? There are many, including love of God, love of your work, love of others, self-appreciation, patience, steadfastness, and the ability to see more clearly. This is important for things are not always as they seem. Sometimes phenomena that may appear "real" to us are actually hoaxes perpetrated by our lack of knowledge and limited senses.

For example, until about five hundred years ago it was assumed that lying in bed was a relatively motionless experience. However Copernicus's discovery that the Earth and the planets move around the Sun implied that the Earth rotates, and a person sleeping in bed moves eastward at one thousand miles an hour! The sleeper also flies one thousand and eighty miles a minute in another direction because of the Earth's revolution around the Sun! In humility we should be able to admit that many things may be unknown to us presently. By becoming humble, we can learn more and make greater progress.

A quiet, inner joy often seems to be a banner of the humble person. On the other hand, you may have witnessed the person who shouted his attributes to the world, only to face humiliation at his own hand. As the Bible tells us, *"For every one who exalts himself will be humbled, and he who humbles himself will be exalted"* (Luke 14:11).

Bishop Gerald Kennedy commented, *"The greater a man is, the more humble he is as he remembers the faith, the dream, the hope, that made his life possible. If any man is tempted to pride because of his accomplishments, let him remember what he has received from all those people of the past. It was their faith that set the direction of his life, and the best he can strive for is to become the fulfillment of their father."* And Proverbs 11:2 states, *"Too much pride can put you to shame. It's wiser to be humble.*" Humility, however, can open the door to progress and make you a benefactor.

Each passing day, scientists discover increasing wonders of the universe—both in the microcosm and the macrocosm. Many of them stand in *awe* of the complexity, the diversity, and the exquisite organization of the universe. Often a sense of humility is experienced by them as well, as they contemplate such ineffability. Many of these scientists are also aware that their humility toward research can open new doors to progress, and surprisingly in areas seemingly unrelated to their particular area of science.

LAW 2

Your dreams can come true when you activate them
—John M. Templeton

There are dreams . . . and there are dreams!

Elias Howe, American inventor of the sewing machine, was experiencing a major problem in determining the appropriate location for the eye of the needle in his new invention. He was rapidly running out of money and ideas when, one night, he had a peculiar dream. He was being led to his execution for failing to design a sewing machine for the king of a strange country. He was surrounded by guards, all of whom carried spears that were pierced near the head. Realizing instantly that this was a solution to his problem, Howe awakened and rushed straight to his workshop. By nine o'clock that morning, the design of the first sewing machine was well on the way to completion!

Sir William Johnson, the British soldier who became an administrator of American Indian affairs, had an interesting experience with dreams. He ordered some suits of rich clothing from England, and when they arrived and were unpacked, the Mohawk chief Hendrick admired them greatly. Shortly afterward, the chief told Sir William that he had dreamed that Sir William gave him one of the suits. Sir William took the hint and presented Hendrick with one of the most handsome outfits. Not

"One can never consent to creep when one feels an impulse to soar."
—Helen Keller

"There will always be a frontier where there is an open mind and a willing hand."
—Charles F. Kettering

"The will is the strong blind man who carries on his shoulder the lame man who can see."
—Arthur Schopenhauer

long after that, when Sir William said that he, too, had a dream, Hendrick asked him what it was. Sir William explained that he had dreamed that Hendrick had presented him with a certain tract of land on the Mohawk River, comprising five thousand acres of the most fertile terrain. Immediately Hendrick presented the land to Sir William, remarking as he did so that he would dream no more with him. "You dream too hard for me, Sir William," he observed.

Dreams, or magnificent ideas, have often played a major part in discovery, and discoveries have fulfilled many dreams. Jonas E. Salk, the American virologist who developed the first effective antipolio vaccine, worked hard to publicize his discovery, but he received no money from the sale of it. Someone once asked him who owned the patent. He replied, "The people—could you patent the sun?"

The structural formula for benzene eluded Kekule von Stradonitz, the German chemist, for a long time. He claimed that the initial insight came to him in 1858 while he was dozing on a London bus traveling to Clapham Road. He saw atoms dancing before his eyes and then things like snakes, which contorted and took their tails in their mouths, thus creating rings. The ancient alchemical symbol of the snake biting its tail suggested that the two ends of the benzene chain were joined, and the Kekule formula for benzene was thus established.

The foregoing examples of dreams, visions, ideas—whatever you may wish to call them—exhibit an important factor. In each instance, the person *took some kind of action* to bring the dream into manifestation! This can be an encouragement to each of us that *your dreams can come true when you activate them!*

"Act while you can— while you have the chance, the means, and the strength."
—Simeon ben Eliezar

From Rebecca Clark's book *Breakthrough* comes a stirring description of a dreamer. Does it call to the vision within you? *"Who are the dreamers? They are the souls who are the architects of the world's greatness. Their futuristic vision lies seeded within the rich soil of their adventurous souls. The dreamers never see the limiting mirages of so-called fact. Their vision can peer beyond the veils and mists of doubt and uncertainty and pierce the walls of time.*

"Makers of empires have fought for bigger things than crowns and higher seats than thrones. They are the 'Argonauts,' the seekers of the priceless fleece—the Truth. Through all the ages they have heard the voice of destiny call to them from the unknown vasts. Their brains have wrought all human miracles. In lace of stone, their spires stab the old world's skies and with their golden crosses they kiss the sun.

"They are the blazers of the way—who refuse to wear doubt's bandage on their eyes, who may starve and chill and hurt, but who hold to

courage and hope because they know there is always proof of Truth for those who try. They know that only cowardice and lack of faith can keep the seeker from his chosen goal; but if his heart be strong and if he dreams enough in sincerity, he can attain the goal, no matter that men may have failed before."

❖

LAW 3

Work is love made visible
—Kahlil Gibran

When a person begins learning how to swim, he often splashes, struggles, and resists, even in peaceful waters. He takes short strokes, works hard, becomes exhausted, and accomplishes little. Then he learns that by being calm and turning his face toward God's sky, he can float. Slight movement of his arms can propel him across the water. In this little scenario, the person has made conscious connection with fundamental reality through learning the principles involved in the art of swimming.

The transition from adolescence to adulthood may sometimes be filled with stress and fueled with anger and confusion. Suddenly, it seems you become more independent, and, while the freedom can feel great, there can come with it a certain responsibility you may not feel quite ready to shoulder. The realization grows that the time may be near when you move from the childhood years into the adult world.

And with this movement into the adult world often comes—work! "Work" can be defined in so many ways: employment, occupation, task, labor, toil, etc. To some people, the ideal occupation seems to be the one that doesn't keep them too occupied! But what if we take a closer look at this activity that may consume a considerable amount of our time. J. H. Patterson said, *"It is only those who do not know how to work that do not love it."* Henry Ward Beecher wrote, *"Why do birds sing? Because the song is in them, and if they did not let it forth, they would split; it must come out. It is the spontaneity and the urgency of this feeling in them that impels their utterance. Why should men work?*

"Everyone has a vocation by which he earns his living, but he also has a vocation in an older sense of the word—the vocation to use his powers and live his life well."
—Richard W. Livingstone

*Because their hearts want some outlet to give expression to the feeling
of earnest sympathy that is in them. Where a man has a strong and
large benevolence, he will always be busy, and pleasantly busy."*

Did these writers tap into some great mysterious understanding? Perhaps they simply learned the principle of "swimming
with the tide" of possibilities. A minister friend once said that
we are here to work out our soul's destiny, and the work we do
can simply be an avenue through which this may be accomplished. If we keep poised and balanced, doing our best every
day, realizing that under all circumstances it is important to be
compassionate, kind, and generous with those we meet on life's
journey; if we continue doing our best work and thinking our
best thoughts every day, we can gradually wear away concerns
over problems, as the swimmer wears away concerns over the
water. We learn how to meet new situations, and this awareness
helps us take successful, correct action.

There seems to be a simplicity in what we seek to do when we
dedicate ourself to the doing. When we choose to accept into
our consciousness only what uplifts, but do not reject that which
we may not understand, we do those things that are to be done
by us in a more loving state of mind. And that which we do in a
loving state of mind can become love made visible through our
work.

An artist can become so enmeshed in the design of a painting
and the flow of the palette of colors that hours may go by without notice of time. A surgeon can become so focused in his
work that the healing energy of the universe flows through his
intelligence, his love for the great calling, and his hands. An
assembly-line operator in an automobile manufacturing plant
can feel satisfaction in knowing that his work contributes to a
safe vehicle for those who will drive the cars he helps build. A
worker in a furniture manufacturing company can feel an inner
joy in knowing the effects of his craftsmanship may grace a
home for many years.

Thomas Edison often ate and slept in his laboratory and
worked there for eighteen hours a day. But it wasn't toil to him.
"I never did a day's work in my life," he exclaimed. *"It was all fun!"*
A humorous story is told about former U. S. President Lyndon
Baines Johnson and his love for his work. The Senate worked
hard and late when Johnson was majority leader. One weary
senator complained to a colleague, "What's all the hurry? Rome
wasn't built in a day." "No," the colleague replied," but Johnson
wasn't foreman on that job!"

One mother gave tremendous advice to her children when

she told them, *"Do what you love and love what you do!"* On one level, a career can be described as a job that sustains your interest while you make enough money to support yourself in a comfortable life-style. But a career can be much more than that; it can be a vocation. The word "vocation" comes from the Latin root "to call." Your vocation then is a calling, and in a very deep sense, finding your vocation can be finding yourself. When you have found your calling, you can give love through your work. In fact, love may be the key to success in mastering your vocation. It directs you to those special talents you can give to the world and shows you how to share them with others.

Kahlil Gibran wrote in *The Prophet* that *"work is love made visible."* Inventions and works of art may begin with love. The Wright brothers loved the idea of flight. Their vocation produced the first airplane. Your own careful choice of a career can be a contribution to others as well as to your own sense of fulfillment. It can be an expression of love. It can be a life's work with rewards far greater than the accumulation of wealth.

Don't expect to find your life's work—your true vocation—in a college catalogue, nor should you expect that the company you join will have a ready-made position waiting for you. A vocation cannot be given out by order of a personnel department. It grows, as an original idea, not a copy, within each one of us. A vocation is more than putting in hours to earn a pay check. Rather, it can be your most valuable asset and the greatest gift of yourself and your talent that you can offer the world. Every useful work can be a ministry of service in your chosen field.

"He was in love with his work, and he felt the enthusiasm for it which nothing but the work we can do well inspires in us."
—William Dean Howells

Law 4

For every effect, there is a cause
—Hermetic principle

Have you ever paused to think that a reason may exist for whatever may have happened to you in your life? If you became ill, had an accident, broke an arm, got married, got divorced, stayed together, had a wonderful day, made a new friend—some-

"THE ALL IS SPIR-IT! But what is spirit? This question cannot be answered, for the reason that its definition is practically that THE ALL, which cannot be explained or defined. Spirit is simply a name that men give to the highest conception of Infinite Living Mind–it means "the Real Essence"–it means Living Mind, as much superior to Life and Mind as we know them, as the latter are superior to mechanical Energy and Matter. Spirit transcends our understanding, and we use the term merely that we may think to speak of THE ALL."
—The Kybalion, A Hermetic Philosophy

"Nothing escapes the Principle of Cause and Effect, but there are many planes of Causation, and one may use the laws of higher to overcome the laws of the lower."
—The Kybalion, A Hermetic Philosophy

where, on some level, there may have been a reason, a cause, behind each of these experiences. For example, let's look at the following simple law of nature: "As you sow, so shall you reap." If you sow grains of corn, or any other kind of seed, you set the law in motion, and your action of sowing the seeds is the cause. Nature responds and will bring into your life the effect, which is the harvest from the seeds.

Cause and effect has often been called "the law of sequence, the balance wheel of the universe." Several sacred Scriptures refer to this activity.

In the Bible we read, *"Whatsoever a man soweth, that shall he also reap"* (Galatians 6:7). Sound familiar?

In the *Bhagavat Gita* we find, *"Find the reward of doing right, in right."* Also from the *Gita* comes the statement, *"No man shall escape from acting by shunning action; and none shall come by mere renunciation to perfection."*

One of the proverbs in the Buddhist *Tripitaka* reads, *"The deed of which a man must repent, and the results of which he receives with tears, is not well done; the deed which a man does not repent, and the results of which he receives with joy, is well done."*

From the sayings of Jainism we find, *"As imprisoned birds do not get out of their cage, so those ignorant of right or wrong do not get out of their misery."*

Confucianism: Confucius was asked, "Is there one word that sums up the basis of all good conduct?" And he replied, *"Is not 'reciprocity' that word? What you yourself do not desire do not put before others."*

From the Hebrew Scriptures we read, *"As he thinks in his heart, so is he."* Also, *"Cast your bread upon the waters; for you shall find it after many days."*

The Qur'an tells us, *"Wrong not and you will not be wronged."* And *"If you do good, you do good for your own souls; if you do evil, you do it to yourselves."*

The Kybalion, a study of Hermetic teachings of ancient Egypt and Greece, includes in its seven basic principles of truth the following profound statement about cause and effect: *"Every cause has its effect; every effect has its cause; everything happens according to law; chance is but a name for a law not recognized; there are many planes of causation, but nothing escapes the law."*

In the book *The Psyche and Psychism*, Torkom Saraydarian writes, *"The Inner Presence and the presence in nature may be called the Law of Cause and Effect. This law is an energy field extending throughout the Cosmic planes, and any action upon this energy field creates a corresponding reaction relative to the level and intensity of the action. Thus a wish, a desire, an aspiration, a thought can be an act of prayer, a form of action which creates the corresponding reaction from the energy field, from the Law of Cause and Effect.*

These expansive and universal awarenesses of cause and effect indicate a very important understanding: we are usually responsible for the things that happen to us! We may not be fully comfortable with this fact because a lot of people really do not want to take full responsibility for their lives. It is often easier to blame our parents, our neighbors, friends, spouse, the government, or some other organization or condition.

But think about this for a minute. If you and I are responsible for what happens to us, can this not also mean that we have vast and unlimited opportunity to create, or cause, our lives to be that which we desire? This idea can be exciting! Whatever situation may be present in our life, we can create a positive experience from the set of circumstances before us. How? Through the power of choice.

But what about this thing called "chance"? A lot of people grow up with the belief that chance, or luck, or even accidental happenings contribute, for better or worse, to our life. One woman was in an automobile accident and refused to accept any responsibility for the collision, even though she failed to stop at the traffic sign and received a citation! Another woman was stopped at a traffic signal when she was rammed from behind by a speeding car. Being familiar with the laws of life and how they operate, she proceeded to move calmly through the circumstances by communicating with the other driver, filing the police report, and getting her car repaired. The other driver's insurance paid all related bills, and her life continued on. She did wonder what this little interlude was all about but had the wisdom to realize that "it's not *what* happens to you that is most important but *how* you handle the situation." Physiologist Daniel H. Osmond declared in an article entitled "A Physiologist Looks at Purpose and Meaning in Life": *"Belief in chance says more about the ignorance of the one who believes than about how we got here."*

Can we bring a new scientific perspective to the age-old question of purpose? In the last twenty or thirty years, the number of scientists raising philosophical and religious questions as a result of recent scientific discoveries has multiplied. Albert Einstein openly and movingly spoke of the religious attitude as essential to good science, and Sir James Jeans said that *"the universe was beginning to look not like a great machine but rather like a great thought."*

If there is such order and purpose in the cycling of the plan-

"Every duty brings its peculiar delight, every denial its appropriate compensation, every thought its recompense, every cross its crown; pay goes with performance as effect with cause."
—Charles Mildmay

"Not merely what we do, but what we try to do and why, are the true interpreters of what we are."
—C. H. Woodward

"Cause and effect, means and ends, seeds and fruit cannot be severed; for the effect already blooms in the cause, the end pre-exists in the means, and the fruit in the seed."
—Ralph Waldo Emerson

ets of our solar system around our Sun (which we don't fully understand), can there not also be a potency and purpose to our individual lives that we may not presently understand? Dr. John Polkinghorne, president of Queens' College, Cambridge, wrote, *"The most obvious sign of purpose is an artifact, a contrivance constructed to fulfill a particular role."* Could the events in our life be the "contrivance" (effect) constructed to prod us to move beyond our present boundaries of thinking to seek greater understanding of the principle of "for every effect, there is a cause"?

LAW 5

Those who do good do well
—John M. Templeton

Mary Kay Ash, the founder of Mary Kay Cosmetics in Dallas, Texas, is as well known for her charitable giving to worthy causes as she is for her fabulous business success. She gives out two golden shovels, fastened together; the small one symbolizes the way we give, and the larger one symbolizes how God gives. Her observation is, *"You can't outgive God."* The result of this thinking is that even though we cannot outgive God, we can certainly outgive ourself. We can go beyond the level of our previous giving, regardless of how much we have given.

Scripture says, *"Freely ye have received, freely give"* (Matthew 10:8). Over and over we hear that giving makes it more possible to receive. The purpose for which we give is vital. To give with secret hope of reward is in direct opposition to the law of love. When we give from a heart of love that simply must give because it loves, we are expressing unconditional love. True giving, with no strings attached, manifests love. Through true giving we express our love to others, and when we give in this manner we gain in understanding. Those who do good do well.

In the Holy Land, there are two seas—the Sea of Galilee and the Dead Sea. The Sea of Galilee has both an inlet and an outlet. The water that circulates through it is fresh and sweet, and marine life, both flora and fauna, abound in its depths. The Sea of Galilee is fertile and productive; and by giving of the fruits of its being, it supports the entire surrounding land and the multitudes who rely upon it for nourishment and refreshment. The water of life circulates through the Sea of Galilee and flows on into the Dead Sea, which portrays a direct contrast to the Sea of Galilee.

The water of the Dead Sea is brackish and dead. It is stagnant because, even though it has an inlet that receives the fresh water of the River Jordan, which flows through the Sea of Galilee, the Dead Sea has no outlet. It only receives; it does not give. Therefore, it cannot flourish. The surrounding desert area is also sterile and lifeless. The business man who seeks to give most to his customers will gain more customers and do well in his profession and in prosperity.

The activity of giving is part of the law of cause and effect. Giving (the cause) prompts circulation (the effect). It is the returning energy of circulation that brings our increased abundance. In helping others, we help ourself, for whatever mood we send out completes the circle and returns to us.

"Every good act is charity," says Mohammed Mahomet. *"Your smiling in your brother's face is charity; an exhortation of your fellow-man to virtuous deeds is equal to alms-giving; your putting a wanderer in the right road is charity; your assisting the blind is charity; your removing stones, and thorns, and other obstructions from the road is charity; your giving water to the thirsty is charity. A man's true wealth hereafter is the good he does in this world to his fellow-man. When he dies, people will say, 'What property has he left behind him?' but the angels will ask, 'What good deeds has he sent before him?'"*

Giving and receiving has to do with every area of life, not just money and other tangible or material goods. In a much larger sense, giving has to do with our health, happiness, and overall well-being. Does your being not sing when you give from the love within your mind and heart? Is there not a spring in your step and a light in your eyes when you have helped another—just from the sheer pleasure of helping? And perhaps especially if you did your good deed anonymously!

From the Talmud we are told, *"There are ten strong things. Iron is strong, but fire melts it. Fire is strong, but water quenches it. Water is strong, but the clouds evaporate it. Clouds are strong, but wind drives them away. Man is strong, but fears cast him down. Fear is strong, but wine allays it. Wine is strong, but sleep overcomes it. Sleep is strong, but death is stronger, but loving kindness survives death."*

Ruth Stafford Peale defines giving in this manner: *"Giving is*

"Kindness works simply and perseveringly; it produces no strained relations which prejudice its working; strained relations which already exist, it relaxes. Mistrust and misunderstanding it puts to flight, and it strengthens itself by calling forth answering kindness. Hence it is the furthest-reaching and the most effective of all forces."
—Albert Schweitzer

"After years of living with the coldest realities, I still believe that one reaps what one sows and that to sow kindness is the heart of all investments."
–Joseph E. Martin, Jr.

using what you have, both time and resources, for the benefit of others, without regard to the consequences to yourself. This giving is uniquely human and, most certainly, spiritually motivated." Mrs. Peale identifies three areas of giving: charity, philanthropy, and volunteerism. Charity is giving away a portion of what you have for the benefit of others. Philanthropy involves the giving of private or corporate wealth to projects or individuals. And volunteerism is the giving of time to charitable causes and involves working with essential tasks such as teaching illiterate adults to read, mentoring a juvenile offender, assisting in relief agencies, or nursing AIDS babies.

Right now is a wonderful time to be alive, and an especially exciting time to be involved in giving. The opportunities for giving opening before us on a personal, as well as global, scale are unprecedented. Look around you and find an emerging core need of someone and reach out to help. Think about this principle taught by Jesus when his disciples asked him, *"Lord, when did we see you hungry and feed you, or thirsty and give you drink? When did we see you a stranger and take you in or naked and clothe you?" . . .The King will answer and say to them, "assuredly, I say to you, inasmuch as you did it to one of the least of these my brethren, you did it to me"* (Matthew 25:37–40).

Spotlights!

1. Handle all of your relationships—business and personal—as a sacred trust.
2. Accept the challenges and changes in your life and be transformed!
3. Your dreams can come true when you activate them!
4. Inspired ideas can quickly bloom into manifestation when placed in the rich soil of a spirit-filled mind.
5. We are on the planet to advance our soul's destiny, and the work we do can be an avenue through which this may be accomplished.
6. That which we do in a loving state of mind can become love made visible through our work.
7. Every useful purpose can be a ministry of service in your chosen field.
8. We are responsible for the things that happen to us.
9. True giving with no strings attached can manifest love.
10. You cannot outgive God!
11. Giving and receiving has to do with every area of life, not just money and other tangible or material goods.

Living the Law!

We have within us the power and ability to bring forth new life. We have within us the power and ability to be stronger than things that distress, grieve, or try to limit us. But it is necessary to recognize and affirm this recognition through courageous action. Right now is a good time to ask yourself, "What do I really believe?"

This week's exercise is an invitation to write your own credo. A credo is a statement of belief. How long has it been since you took the time to come away from the business of the world around you and focus on what you truly believe. Our beliefs can change as we move through the various experiences of life, so it can be quite meaningful to do a checklist on our beliefs from time to time. Following is a brief example of a credo to get you started. Read it, find a quiet place for contemplation, and let your beliefs flow into your journal.

I BELIEVE that there is a divine expression for my life. It is etched within the folds of my being, even as the rose is wrapped in the bud.

I BELIEVE in God. I believe the foundation from which we draw all our good is the omnipotent, omnipresent, and omniscient source of everything. My soul grows greater day by day. (What are some examples of your increasing spirit?)

I BELIEVE in the power of thought. (Expand.)

I BELIEVE in the powerful element of God that holds every atom of the universe in its proper place—LOVE! I look around me and see love manifested in many ways. (List some of the ways.)

I BELIEVE in the law of growth, for the law of growth is the law of expansion. It is a law of life, giving expression to the inherent, dynamic urge for fulfillment throughout creation.

I BELIEVE in the power of prayer.

Let this time of quiet begin the cultivation of the precious seeds of your eternal soul so your life can unfold in its greatest expression.

Week Forty

LAW 1

Focus on where you want to go instead of where you have been
—John M. Templeton

In his book *Helping Heaven Happen*, Dr. Donald Curtis presents a short dialogue that could well describe the situation in which many people find themselves. It goes like this:

"How is everything going?"

"Well, I've got bad news and I've got good news. I'll give you the bad news first. We're lost."

"We're *lost*? And what's the good news?"

"We're making very good time!"

From this conversation, these people do not seem to know where they are going. Instead of formulating a plan and following it, they run around in circles, gaining speed and momentum, but going nowhere. They are like a rudderless ship.

And with no focus or definite direction, how can their goals be achieved? An old axiom from the Qur'an says, *"If you don't know where you're going, any road will get you there."* When you want to achieve a goal, first have a mental picture or vision of it. Be sure your goal is genuine. Do not let yourself get caught up in spurious appearances or illusions of the outer world. Keep on track. Doing something about your goal comes next if you are to translate your vision into reality in your world.

"To focus," says *Webster's New World Dictionary*, "is an adjustment to make a clear image." Also, "to concentrate as in *focusing* one's attention." Therefore, our aim in life is similar to focusing a camera lens for good pictures.

Keeping your eye on the vision becomes necessary throughout the process. Focus on where you want to go, instead of where you have been. So much valuable time can be wasted in getting bogged down in past experiences or mistakes that have

"The difference between transformation by accident and transformation by a system is like the difference between lightening and a lamp. Both give illumination, but one is dangerous and unreliable, while the other is directed, available."
—Marilyn Ferguson

no relevancy to the present goal. It is good to learn from past experiences and then continue forward. As you set your priorities, your objectives, and your direction in life, think positively and optimistically. And be aware of others who may come behind you.

A story comes to us from long ago of a king who organized a great race within his kingdom. All the young men of the kingdom participated. A bag of gold was to be given to the winner, and the finish line was within the courtyard of the king's palace. The race was run, and the runners were surprised to find a great pile of rocks and stones in the middle of the road leading to the palace. However, they managed to scramble over it, or run around it, and eventually to come into the courtyard.

Finally, all of the runners had crossed the finish line except one. Still the king did not call the race off. Everyone waited. After a while one lone runner came through the gate. He lifted a bleeding hand and said, "Oh, King, I am sorry to be so late. But you see, I found a large pile of rocks and stones in the road, and it took me a while to remove them. I wounded myself in the process." Then the runner lifted the other hand in which he held a bag. "But Great King, I found this bag of gold beneath the pile of rocks and stones!"

The king responded, "My son, you have won the race, for that one runs best who makes the way safer for those who follow."

We have a choice. We can live in the past and be miserable and unhappy, or we can pick ourselves up and move ahead in life. When we choose to focus forward, we can find the energy and ability to remove any "rocks" that may appear to be hindering our smooth progression. If you take stock of yourself and find you may be spending time frequently reliving unhappy experiences of the past, make the decision to rid yourself of the ties that bind you to a former way of life.

Where would we be as a human race—scientifically, technically, economically, medically, culturally, or environmentally—if those fine minds who made many unprecedented discoveries had looked backward and dwelled in the past instead of visioning growth and new horizons and setting goals to reach them? In preparing material for the book *Looking Forward: The Next Forty Years*, some amazing statistics came to my attention. For example, The evolution of human knowledge is accelerating enormously. More than half of the scientists who ever lived are alive today. More than half of the discoveries in the natural sciences have been made in this century. More than half of the goods produced in the history of the earth have been produced

"In the long run, you hit only what you aim at. Therefore, though you should fail, immediately you had better aim at something high."
—Henry David Thoreau

"It is happily and kindly provided that in every life there are certain pauses, and interruptions which force consideration upon the careless, and seriousness upon the light; points of time where one course of action ends and another begins."
—Samuel Johnson

"Concentration is my motto–first honesty, then industry, then concentration."
—Andrew Carnegie

since 1800. More than half the books ever written were written in the last fifty years. More new books are published each month than were written in the entire historical period before the birth of Columbus. And there's still more!

What does this say to us now? Choose this day to move ahead into life. Focus on where you want to go. Look forward to new horizons. As we read in Maya Angelou's work *All God's Children Need Traveling Shoes*, the future is "plump with promise." Open your visioning to new possibilities. Let the value of your present wisdom ascend. Experience the peace that passes understanding and the joy of abundant living!

LAW 2

You get back what you give out
—John M. Templeton

"The way you prepare the bed, so shall you sleep."
—Yiddish proverb

"The generous who is always just, and the just who is always generous, may unannounced, approach the throne of heaven."
—Johann Lavater

When she was seventy-one, Golda Meir became prime minister of Israel and governed for five years, including the period of the Arab-Israeli War. With a dedicated heart, she worked assiduously for peace, meeting with world figures such as Egyptian president Anwar Sadat and Pope Paul VI. Known affectionately in Israel as "Golda Lox," she was much loved and respected by her people.

Golda Meir's story is a good example of receiving back what we give out. Her sincerity, integrity, loyalty, and strong desire for peace flowed from her like a mighty magnet to draw these attributes from others. During the negotiations with the Arabs, Mrs. Meir insisted on meeting her opponents face to face. A journalist suggested that this was not necessary. "Even divorces are arranged without personal confrontation," he argued. To which Mrs. Meir retorted, "I'm not interested in a divorce, I'm interested in a marriage."

You are present in your life on earth at this moment for the purposes of living, loving, learning, and growing. Be assured that life can reliably provide a wide variety of adventures, experiences, and situations that may require you to draw from the depths of your being. Your level of self awareness and manner of expression can determine the quality of living you experience. Why? Because you get back what you give out.

It is wise to embark on a personal program of self-development, greater understanding of the laws of life, and self-discipline. Science of Mind founder Ernest Holmes said once in a class lecture, *"What you are looking for, you are looking at, and you are looking with."* And an anonymous quote states, *"Projection often makes perception. The world you see is what you give it. It can be the witness to your state of mind, the outside picture of an inward condition. Therefore, seek not to change the world, but choose to change your mind about the world."*

Within you is the power to meet life and all that lies before you with unshakable assurance. If you truly believe this, you can radiate a confidence that draws greater good into your life. To repair a watch requires the use of delicate instruments. Adjusting the affairs of life by the use of spiritual principles also requires the use of delicate instruments. The person who tries to get things done in a hurry in the ordinary manner is like a man trying to repair a watch with a hammer. Employment of the laws of life can bring peace, harmony, abundance, and well-being into your world.

Many people seem needlessly to make their lives difficult by failing to realize the importance of the attitudes they send out. We may mistakenly think we live in the world—in our physical environment. In reality, we live in our minds. We move through a world of physical facts, but we do our real living in our mind. For some, it may be a perfectly miserable afternoon with people pushing, cars cutting in on them, and traffic directors favoring every line of cars except the one they are in. For others, the afternoon can be sparkling with adventure and happiness with people acting courteously and friendly, and everything flowing smoothly.

Have you ever gotten up on "the wrong side of the bed," perhaps in a grumpy mood, only to find other people seeming to be in that same discordant mood. Then, perhaps you made a conscious effort to become more positive and appreciative and found others responding in a like manner. You could have simply been "getting back what you were giving out."

Begin cleaning out those things in your mind that you know make for more problems, such as resentment, self-pity, blaming others, anger. We pay a high price for this kind of self-indulgence. It may not be bothering the other person, but it can sure

"Talk about the joys of the unexpected, can they compare with the joys of the expected, of finding everything delightfully and completely what you knew it was going to be?"
—Elizabeth Bibesco

"I have faith that the time will eventually come when employees and employers, as well as all mankind, will recognize that they serve themselves best when they serve others most."
—B. C. Forbes

"In a world of checks and balances, the most successful man is the one who stores up 'credits' for the future rather than the one who insists on a daily quota of praise, reward, and compensation for all he gives or does."
—Edgar Paul Hermann

raise havoc with our hearts and stomachs and who knows what else. Become more aware of the kind of emotions you may be sending out. The Roman philosopher Seneca perhaps said it best, *"Live among men as if God beheld you; speak to God as if men were listening."* Then you can know that what you are giving out is your best!

LAW 3

Thanksgiving opens the door to spiritual growth
—John M. Templeton

Samuel Johnson hit the nail squarely on the head when he said that *"Gratitude is a fruit of great cultivation; you do not find it among gross people."* Many of the good things in life need cultivating and refining. We may not be born with a taste for good music, but it can be acquired. Great art often needs to be researched and studied before a person may fully appreciate it. One's personality may be somewhat abrupt, but tactfulness and consideration can be developed.

In the magazine *The Clergy Journal* (October, 1986), C. Thomas Hilton tells the story of Ben Weir. Ben Weir was a Presbyterian minister who had recently been released from five hundred days in captivity in Lebanon. He was held hostage by terrorists in solitary confinement for fourteen months. At first he had nothing to read, no conversation with his captors, and he was thrown back upon his own inner resources. Ben described how he began to remember certain passages of Scriptures that were significant to him. He recalled favorite hymns. He described how he used the chain that bound him to the room's radiator as a Protestant rosary, whose links he would use at the day's end, or anytime, to count off and remember all the things for which he was thankful. Yes, he really did say thankful! He described his day by saying, "When I awakened in the morning I usually could hear the birds twittering, or dogs

"A desire to kneel down sometimes pulses through my body, or rather, it is as if my body had been meant and made for the art of kneeling. Sometimes, in moments of deep gratitude, kneeling down becomes an overwhelming urge."
—Etty Hillesum

barking, or other sounds of life going on, and I would respond in a spirit of thanksgiving that God had given me another day with health and strength." There can be no doubt that in Ben's situation, thanksgiving truly did open the door to greater spiritual growth.

Is thankfulness a passive attitude? No, it is active. *Give* thanks! As we've mentioned earlier, the law of giving and receiving is *"Give and it shall be given unto you." The law is* give *and then* receive, not receive *and then give!* The giving is the first activity—the giving of our thanks for the good that is already in our world. Can you imagine what could happen if we prefaced our prayers with "Thank You, God for . . ."? It is possible our entire approach to prayer could be changed, as well as our outlook on life. Gone could be the beseeching prayers, the supplications, and perhaps many tears. Our focus could be transferred from perceptions of lack to appreciation of the abundance in our life.

"Gratitude, where it is hardly manifest in a gesture or smile, is thus something like a secret restitution, a restoration—a spiritual present given in return."
—Gabriel Marcel

An article appeared in a newspaper about a missionary to India who was traveling through a city and stopped to speak to a man beside the road. He talked with the man for a time about spiritual virtues, then having to travel on, he gave the man a few pages of the Bible in the man's language. The Indian read the pages and was thrilled with what he read.

To show his gratitude, the man measured the footprints left by the missionary and made a pair of moccasins. He then traveled two hundred miles to give them to the missionary as an expression of thanks.

"Be thankful for the smallest thing, and you will be worthy to receive something greater."
—Thomas à Kempis

The missionary's life was enriched by the gift, but the Indian man was much more enriched because he had expressed his thanks. Have you ever tried to give two hundred miles of appreciation? Or five hundred days of thanks? How about beginning with one day devoted to giving thanks for your life and its blessings, and watch what happens!

If your spirit of thanksgiving seems to be sagging because of anxieties or concerns or a variety of worries, try releasing these limiting and restricting attitudes and begin to affirm the right and perfect outcome for whatever the situation may be.

Carl Holmes wrote, *"A habit for all of us to develop would be to look for something to appreciate in everyone we meet. We can all be generous with appreciation. Everyone is grateful for it. It improves every human relationship, it brings new courage to people facing difficulties, and it brings out the best in everyone. So, give appreciation generously whenever you can. You will never regret it."* And is not appreciation an aspect of thanksgiving?

"Gratitude is not something monetary; it is sustained, it is enduring. At its foundation it is 'remembering' and not a mere conservation: it must be regarded as a 'wakefulness, as a watchfulness of the soul.'"
—Gabriel Marcel

*"Gratitude originates
in spiritual vitality
and is its expression."*
—Ferdinand Ebner

There is something quite powerful and life-giving in the act of giving thanks. It is a lot like recharging a battery. As you open your mind and let your heart sing for joy, you can receive a recharging of spiritual energy in your mind, body, spirit, and activities of your daily life. There is no greater tonic and perhaps no more potent tonic for our spirit than gratitude. When we are grateful for the blessings we already have, our very attitude of gratitude attracts extra good to us. Thanksgiving is like a powerful magnet that can draw to us friends, love, peace, joy, health, and material good.

Yes, it can be easy to give thanks when we are richly showered with good health, a comfortable living, and many wonderful gifts and experiences. But what about being grateful when the days may seem dark and it might be difficult to see our way? Those are the times when it becomes especially important to give thanks! During the "dark and difficult" times, one woman would pause during her day, sit down, and write three things for which she was thankful. They were (1) being alive, (2) having a good mind, and (3) having the wisdom to say "Thank You, God!"

LAW 4

*The more love we give,
the more love we have left*
—John M. Templeton

A woman told a story about the time when her daughter announced that she no longer believed in Santa Claus and flatly refused to leave milk and cookies out for this nocturnal visitor on Christmas Eve. Upset at losing a four-year tradition, the child's father tried bribing and cajoling her. Nothing worked. As the evening transformed into night, imagine the mother's surprise when the daughter walked into the living room carrying a bowl of oatmeal. Her father helped her put the bowl under the tree, next to eight others just like it. "What on earth are you doing?" the mother asked. "I thought you didn't believe in Santa."

"She doesn't," the father replied beaming. "But the reindeer—they're a different story!"

A humorous little story, but one that tells of a child's love for animals. The little girl was giving from an inexhaustible heart of love, and such is the way of love. The more love we give the more love we have left. Would it not seem meaningful then to let love pour forth from us in all our thoughts, words, and actions? To let love be the bond between ourself and each person who touches our life daily? To let love be the forgiving force where forgiveness may be needed? To ask love to purify our consciousness of every vestige of selfishness, bitterness, revengefulness, and unhappiness? To allow the harmonizing power of love to restore our body, renew our mind, and lift us to ever-higher levels of understanding and compassion? Oh, what love can do when we give it the opportunity!

From the Midrash comes this story of love in action that has been given an opportunity! Rabbi Joshua ben Ilem dreamed that his neighbor in paradise would be Nanas, the butcher. He visited this Nanas to inquire what good deeds he was performing to deserve such a high place in paradise. The butcher replied, "I know not, but I have an aged father and mother who are helpless, and I give them food and drink, and wash and dress them daily."

The rabbi then said: "I will be happy to have thee as my neighbor in paradise."

To allow a full and free flow of love from the heart into life can be a secret of rich and satisfying living. It is true that sincere love can overcome every obstacle, from the smallest irritation to the largest problem we may meet. Perhaps one reason is because as we grow in the consciousness of love, we come to realize that love takes no account of the seeming shortcomings of others. Too often we react to the moods of others, letting their words and actions influence our own. When others may snap at us or are irritable, love can help us see beyond appearances, and to understand their mood may be the result of a dissatisfaction within themselves. It is not necessary to react to their mood, nor do we need to adopt that kind of energy into our own actions. Whenever we feel out of sorts with the world around us, we may need only to look within for love to pour out. Giving forth all the love we feel capable of giving at the time may help set a disorder aright. And we find we still have plenty of love left!

Giving more love can be a turning point for the soul. Turning points are the blessed moments when the hardships of life's

"I have found the paradox that if I love until it hurts, then there is no hurt, but only more love."
—Mother Teresa

"Love is like a reservoir of kindness and pleasure."
—Yehuda Amichai

"Love is the vital essence that pervades and permeates from the center to the circumference, the graduating circles of all thought and action. Love is the talisman of human weal and woe—the open sesame to every soul."
—Elizabeth Cady Stanton

adversity give way to awakening to the presence of God. It can be the dark hour of crisis that bears the golden dawning of the richness of Spirit. Sometimes we may need to discipline ourself with "tough love" to break a habit that may be working against our highest interests. But letting go of these blockages can open wide the doorway to greater giving of our love.

A spiritual teacher once asked a class, "What did you come to earth for?"

One student, feeling he had the right answer, rose and said, "Love!"

"Oh, really!" responded the teacher in the tone of voice that indicated the student was about to be taught a lesson. "Is there anyone you love more than anyone else."

The student thought for a moment and responded, "Yes."

To which the teacher answered, "Then you haven't lived up to your potential yet, for your work is not complete until you experience the joy of loving all as you love the one you love most!"

What food for thought this simple message by a spiritual teacher brings to each of us. Perhaps long-held beliefs about a personal understanding of love may be challenged. Beliefs about romance, about family, about special relationships, about life. This all-encompassing ideal of love can compel a person to look more deeply to the inner self to attempt to discover what love really is, and what it means truly to love someone in an unconditional manner. How many times have you spoken the words, "I love you," and really feel the reverence those sacred words deserve? How wide is the path of love you tread? Can it encompass all those around you? How aware are you of the love returning from others that may be prompted by the love you are giving? Pour out love in thought, in word, and in action. Try to think love, speak love, feel love, and become immersed in it, until all else in your life and world is absorbed and melted into giving love.

LAW 5

Every useful life is a ministry
—John M. Templeton

Albert Einstein said, "*A human being is a part of the whole, called by us "Universe," a part limited in time and space. He experiences himself, his thoughts and feelings as something separated from the rest—a kind of optical delusion of his consciousness. This delusion is a kind of prism for us, restricting us to our personal desires and to affection for a few persons nearest to us. Our task must be to free ourselves from this prison by widening our circle of compassion to embrace all living creatures and the whole nature in its beauty.*"

God's universe operates in rhythm and harmony and beauty. It is like a musical theme of a symphony in which the composer is the life and essence. It may be difficult to imagine the vastness and the orderliness of the stars, planets, and solar systems. It is so much more accurate than any human mechanism and has been maintaining its schedule for untold thousands of years, bringing the seasons and changing length of days according to a great plan. This perfect order and system can be found in even the smallest things.

Humanity is included in that universal plan. This infinite wisdom and harmony that flow through the universe also flow through the mind and affairs of humankind. As we choose to live our lives in a useful manner and in harmony with the laws of life, that which we do can become a meaningful ministry of service to others.

Oftentimes, when people hear the word "ministry," they think of a church or a government office. In truth, however, everything productive that you can accomplish in life is a ministry. By loving your work—whatever that work may be—and holding the attitude that it may be accomplished from the perspective of doing a good job for others, you are fulfilling a ministry of service. And the world needs many more ministers of service who are willing to dedicate their energies to the job at hand!

A favorite story is one about a priest named Bourne. An unhappy man had come for counseling. The man claimed to have no talents, and the priest disputed him. He said, "As long as you are able to speak to me, you are not one of those people. Anyone who can carry on a conversation has been given a tal-

"Be useful where thou livest."
—George Herbert

"We are a spectacular, splendid manifestation of life. We have language. . . . We have affection. We have genes for usefulness, and usefulness is about as close to a 'common goal' of nature as I can guess at. And finally, perhaps best of all, we have music."
—Lewis Thomas

ent. Suppose your talent is to keep a street clean. Suppose that's your chief qualification in life. Go ahead and clean up that street. Clean it with love and care to make others happy as they walk on it. Then, as your talent for cleaning that street grows, it could become a famous street." Remember, we've stated earlier that "love is a magnet"? If this man loved his talent for cleaning the street so much that the street "sparkled" with his care, he could have tourists coming from many miles around to marvel at his beautifully maintained street! Such can be the power of loving what you do.

Every effort contributed to helping another is a way of saying yes to life. And saying yes is a profound form of successful behavior, which can bring an increase in happiness. To the one who faces the light, the path is bright. It is the person who faces the other way, the way of selfishness, who may ultimately walk in his own shadow as it falls upon the path before him.

It takes courage to rise above the status quo, a bravery that each of us must learn in our own way. Thomas Huxley said, *"We live in a world which is full of misery and ignorance, and the plain duty of each and all of us is to try to make the little corner he can influence somewhat less ignorant than it was before he entered it."* Life is made up not necessarily of great sacrifices or high-level duties but of little things. The smiles, the kindnesses, the commitments and obligations and responsibilities that are given habitually and lovingly are the blessings that win and preserve the heart and bring comfort to one's self as well to others. This is the ministry of service performed by every useful life.

In an article entitled "Your Own Octillion Atoms," Winifred Wilkinson Hausmann wrote that scientists say that there are approximately one octillion atoms in the trillions of cells that make up the average human body. Just to get an idea of how many atoms that is, try writing out the number one (1) and following it with twenty-seven zeros! That is an octillion of atoms, or the number you have available to work for you in the present moment! Can you imagine the amount of service you can give with this kind of atomic power?

As you come to the end of this book on the laws of life, it may be helpful to review these laws from time to time and pay particular attention to those that seem to be more difficult to apply in your life. These may be the ideas you need to grasp more thoroughly because they could have a deeper meaning than you may have previously realized.

The way you think about the physical mechanism through

which you express your being determines the way in which it can work for you. Wouldn't you like to improve yourself? How would it feel to know you were making a real contribution to your world? Would you like to feel that because of you and your work someone's life was blessed? Just think, an octillion atoms, ready and waiting for your direction! Are you willing to grow to meet your good, and in the growing, give and receive?

Spotlights!

1. Learn from past experiences, and then continue forward.
2. Open your visioning to new possibilities.
3. You are present in your life at this moment for the purpose of living, loving, giving, learning, and growing.
4. You move through a world of physical facts, but you do your real living in your mind.
5. Thanksgiving is an *active* attitude!
6. Look for something to appreciate in everyone you meet.
7. Promote the free circulation of good will in your life by filling your mind with love.
8. Infinite spiritual resources are available to enhance your life and your world.
9. When you are at peace with everyone in your life, your relationships can be happy and loving.
10. Loving service is one of the greatest of ministries.

Living the Law!

In the book *The Rainbow Connection,* the author extended an invitation to move beyond present perimeters of consciousness and *"dare to witness the activity of divine love"* expressing in life. How do her words speak to you? Reflect on their message; then write in your journal a list of ways that come immediately to mind in which you can increase your outflow of love and service.

In a moment of deep inner silence, I heard a gentle voice whisper: "Beloved, dare to make the break out of the lonely crowd. There is a wonderful plan for your life. A magnificent purpose resounds through your unfoldment. Release and let go of your outdated and outworn self! Dare to be reborn in the brilliance of the freedom of Spirit, filled and motivated with universal energy flowing direct from the heart of God.

Fascinated, I listened: "Beloved, dare to lose old patterns of expression, old habits of weakness and death, old memories of destruction. Dare to witness the activity of divine love expressing through you as perfect life as it restores, rejuvenates, and regenerates every cell of your being! Live in the wholeness of spirit, and direct your light essence for the healing and uplifting of the world!"

Wow! I wondered, do I dare? The voice continued: "Beloved, go beyond your present understanding. Exceed your now consciousness of Truth. Be fully immersed in your divine blueprint through all good . . . on earth as it is in heaven. You carry within the keys to the kingdom. Use them to open all doors of joyous expression and to direct the wonder and effectiveness of the spiritual gifts you possess into your working knowledge."

In expectation, I remained silent, listening.

"Beloved, dedicate yourself to love. Watch as love dissolves undesirable situations, unwanted circumstances, and all thoughts and feelings of a negative nature. Dare to be magnificent! Dare to be a self-renewing temple of the living God! Dare to be beauty, harmony, light, and music as I created you to be! Remember, I have loved you with an everlasting love!"

Joy filled my heart as I asked: "Who are you? Who is saying this to me?"

And from infinity within came the answer, "I am!"

Bibliography

Adams, Brian. *How to Succeed.* New York: Taplinger, 1969.

Allen, James. *As A Man Thinketh.* Marina del Ray, CA: DeVorss, 1983.

Alexander, Denis. *Beyond Science.* Philadelphia and New York: A. J. Hoffman, 1973.

Asimov, Isaac. *Asimov's Biographical Encyclopedia of Science & Technology.* 2d rev. ed. Garden City, NY: Doubleday, 1982.

Bachelder, Louise, ed. *The Little Flowers of St. Francis of Assisi.* Mount Vernon, NY: Peter Pauper Press, 1964.

Barnet, Lincoln. *The Universe and Dr. Einstein,* New York: Athenaeum, 1948.

Braden, Charles Samuel, ed. *The Scriptures of Mankind.* New York: Macmillan, 1952.

Bucke, Richard Maurice, M.D. *Cosmic Consciousness.* 1st ed. New York: Causeway Books, 1900.

Burtt, E. A., ed. *The Teachings of the Compassionate Buddha.* New York: New American Library, 1955.

Burtt, Edwin A. *The Metaphysical Foundations of Modern Science.* New York: Harcourt Brace, 1925.

Canfield, Jack, and Mark Victor Hansen. *Chicken Soup for the Soul.* Deerfield Beach, FL: Health Communications, 1993.

Capra, Fritjof. *The Tao of Physics: An Exploration of the Parallels between Modern Physics and Eastern Mysticism.* Berkeley, CA: Shambhala, 1975.

Charon, Jean. *Man in Search of Himself.* London: George Allen & Unwin, 1967.

Chatterji, Mohini M. *The Bhagavad Gita.* New York: Julian Press, 1960.

Clark, Rebecca. *Breakthrough.* Unity Village, MO: Unity Books, 1977.

——. *Macro-Mind Power.* West Nyack, NY: Parker, 1978.

——. *The Rainbow Connection.* Unity Village, MO: Unity Books, 1983.

Cohen, Alan. *The Dragon Doesn't Live Here Anymore.* South Kortright, NY: Eden, 1981.

——. *Joy Is My Compass.* Somerset, NJ: Alan Cohen, 1990.

Colton, Ann Ree, and Jonathan Murro. *Owe No Man.* Glendale, CA: Ann Ree Colton Foundation, 1986.

Covell, Ralph R. *Confucius, the Buddha, and Christ*. Maryknoll, NY: Orbis Books, 1986

Curtis, Dr. Donald. *Helping Heaven Happen*. York Beach, ME: Samuel Weiser, 1992.

Dalai Lama. *Worlds in Harmony: Dialogues on Compassionate Action*. Berkeley, CA: Parallax Press, 1992.

dePurucker, G. *Wind of the Spirit*. Pasadena, CA: Theosophical University Press, 1984.

Dolphin, Lambert. *Lord of Time and Space*. Westchester, IL: Good News, 1974.

Dyer, Dr. Wayne W. *The Sky's the Limit*. New York: Pocket Books, Simon & Schuster, 1980.

——. *You'll See It When You Believe It*. New York: Avon Books, 1989.

Eliade, Mircea. *A History of Religious Ideas, II*. Chicago: University of Chicago Press, 1982.

Esterer, Arnulf K. *Towards a Unified Faith*. New York: Philosophical Library, 1963.

Fadiman, Clifton, gen. ed. *Little, Brown Book of Anecdotes*. Boston: Little, Brown, 1985.

Feldman, Christina, and Jack Kornfield, ed. *Stories of the Spirit, Stories of the Heart: Parables of the Spiritual Path from Around the World*. San Francisco: Harper, 1991.

Fillmore, Charles. *The Revealing Word*. Unity Village, MO: Unity Books, 1959.

Foster, Michael B. *Mystery and Philosophy*. London: SCM Press, 1957.

Fox, Emmet. *Make Your Life Worthwhile*. New York: Harper & Row, 1942.

Gaer, Joseph. *What the Great Religions Believe*. New York: Dodd, Mead, 1963.

Gibran, Kahlil. *The Prophet*. New York: Alfred A. Knopf, 1923.

——. *A Second Treasury of Kahlil Gibran*. New York: Citadel Press, 1962.

Goldsmith, Joel S. *Practicing the Presence*. New York: Harper & Row, 1958.

Greenberg, Rabbi Sidney, ed. *A Treasury of the Art of Living*. Hartford, CT: Hartmore House, 1963.

Greenlees, Duncan. *The Gospel of Zarathustra*. India: Vasanta Press, 1951.

Hart, Michael H. *The 100: A Ranking of the Most Influential Persons in History*. New York: Hart, 1978.

Heider, John. *The Tao of Leadership*. New York: Bantam Paperbacks, 1983.

Kaplan, Juston, ed. *Bartlett's Familiar Quotations*. 16th ed. New York: Little, Brown, 1992.

Keyes, Ken, Jr. *Handbook to Higher Consciousness*. Berkleley, CA: Living Love Center, 1975.

Lelly, Charles D. *The Beautiful Way of Life*. Unity Village, MO: Unity Books, 1980.

Martin, Nicholas R. M. *Operator's Manual for Successful Living*. Marina del Ray, CA: DeVorss, 1988.

McWilliams, John-Roger, and Peter McWilliams. *Life 101: Everything We Wish We Had Learned About Life in School–But Didn't*. Los Angeles: Prelude Press, 1991.

Mitchell, Stephen, ed. *The Enlightened Heart: An Anthology of Sacred Poetry*. New York: Harper & Row, 1989.

The Oxford Dictionary of Quotations. 3rd ed. New York: Oxford University Press, 1979.

Peale, Dr. Norman Vincent. *A Guide to Confident Living*. 1948.

——. *The Amazing Results of Positive Thinking*. New York: Prentice-Hall, 1959.

——. *The Positive Principle Today*. Carmel, NY: Guideposts, 1976.

——. *My Favorite Quotations*. New York: Harper-Collins, 1990.

Pennington, M. Basil, O.C.S.O. *Centered Living: The Way of Centering Prayer*. Garden City, NY: Doubleday, 1986.

Petras, Kathryn, and Ross Petras, comp. and ed. *The Whole World Book of Quotations: Wisdom from Women and Men Around the Globe Throughout the Centuries*. New York: Addison-Wesley, 1994

Price, John Randolph. *The Planetary Commission*. Austin, TX: Quartus Foundation for Spiritual Research, 1984.

Ramacharaka, Yogi. *The Kybalion: A Study of the Hermetic Philosophy of Ancient Egypt and Greece*. Des Plaines, IL: Yoga Publication Society, 1940.

Reader's Digest Association. *Great Lives, Great Deeds*. Pleasantville, NY: Reader's Digest, 1964.

Russell, Lao. *LOVE*. Waynesboro, VA: University of Science & Philosophy, Swannanoa, 1966.

Russell, Peter. *The Global Brain*. Los Angeles: J. P. Tarcher, 1983.

Schweitzer, Albert. *Reverence for Life*. New York: Harper & Row, 1969.

Shah, Idries. *The Way of the Sufi*. New York: E. P. Dutton, 1969.

——. *Tales of the Dervishes*. New York: E. P. Dutton, 1969.

Shanklin, Imelda. *What Are You?* Unity Village, MO: Unity Books, 1929.

Shinn, Florence Scovel. *The Game of Life & How to Play It*. 1941

Smith, Huston. *The Religions of Man*. New York: Harper & Row, 1958.

Strong, James. *Strong's Exhaustive Concordance of the Bible*, New York: Abingdon Press, 1890.

Templeton, John Marks. *The Humble Approach*. New York: Seabury Press, 1981.

——, with James Ellison. *The Templeton Plan*. New York: Harper Paperbacks, 1987.

——, with Robert L. Herrmann. *The God Who Would Be Known*. San Francisco: Harper & Row, 1989.

——, as told to Norman Berryessa and Eric Kirzner. *Global Investing: The Templeton Way*. Homewood: Dow Jones-Irwin, 1988.

——, ed. *Riches for the Mind and Spirit*. New York: Harper Collins, 1990.

——, ed. *Looking Forward*. New York: Harper Collins, 1993.

——, with Robert L. Herrmann. *Is God the Only Reality?*. New York: Continuum, 1994.

——. *Discovering the Laws of Life*. New York: Continuum, 1994.

——, ed. *Evidence of Purpose*. New York: Continuum, 1994.

Torrance, Thomas Forsyth. *Space, Time and Incarnation*. London: Oxford University Press, 1969.

Trine, Ralph Waldo. *In Tune With the Infinite*. New York: Bobbs-Merrill Co., 1957.

Webster's New World Dictionary. New York: Warner Books, 1979.

White, John. *The Meeting of Science and Spirit: Guidelines for a New Age*. New York: Paragon House, 1990.

Wolf, Fred Alan. *Taking the Quantum Leap: The New Physics for Non-scientists*. New York: Harper & Row, 1989.

Yogananda, Paramahansa. *The Divine Romance*. Los Angeles: Self-Realization Fellowship, 1986.

Yutang, Lin. *The Wisdom of Confucius*. New York: Modern Library, 1938.

Zukav, Gary. *The Seat of the Soul*. New York: A Fireside Book, Simon & Schuster, 1989.

Index